The Editors

KIRSTEN FERMAGLICH is the author of *American Dreams and Nazi Nightmares: Early Holocaust Consciousness and Liberal America, 1957–1965*, as well as articles about Betty Friedan and about American Jewish history. She is an associate professor of history and Jewish Studies at Michigan State University, where she teaches courses on American Jewish history and culture, the history of the family, the 1960s, and twentieth-century United States history.

LISA M. FINE is the author of *The Souls of the Skyscraper: Female Clerical Workers in Chicago, 1870–1930*; *The Story of Reo Joe: Work, Kin, and Community in Autotown USA*; and the co-editor, with Mary Anderson, Kathleen Geissler, and Joyce Ladenson, of *Doing Feminism: Teaching and Research in the Academy*. She is a professor of history and the Co-Director of the Center for Gender in Global Context at Michigan State University, where she teaches courses on United States women's history and United States labor and working-class history.

A NORTON CRITICAL EDITION

Betty Friedan

THE FEMININE MYSTIQUE

ANNOTATED TEXT

CONTEXTS

SCHOLARSHIP

Edited by

KIRSTEN FERMAGLICH
MICHIGAN STATE UNIVERSITY

and

LISA M. FINE
MICHIGAN STATE UNIVERSITY

W·W·NORTON & COMPANY · *New York* · *London*

W. W. Norton & Company has been independent since its founding in 1923, when William Warder Norton and Mary D. Herter Norton first published lectures delivered at the People's Institute, the adult education division of New York City's Cooper Union. The Nortons soon expanded their program beyond the Institute, publishing books by celebrated academics from America and abroad. By mid-century, the two major pillars of Norton's publishing program—trade books and college texts—were firmly established. In the 1950s, the Norton family transferred control of the company to its employees, and today—with a staff of four hundred and a comparable number of trade, college, and professional titles published each year—W. W. Norton & Company stands as the largest and oldest publishing house owned wholly by its employees.

Composition by Westchester
Manufacturing by Courier
Production Manager: Sean Mintus

Library of Congress Cataloging-in-Publication Data

Friedan, Betty.
    The feminine mystique : contexts, the scholarship on the Feminine mystique / Betty Friedan; edited by Kirsten Fermaglich and Lisa M. Fine. — A Norton critical ed.
        p. cm.
    Includes bibliographical references.
    ISBN 978-0-393-93465-6 (pbk.)
    1. Friedan, Betty. Feminine mystique.   2. Feminism—United States.
3. Women—United States—Social conditions.   4. Women—Psychology.
I. Fermaglich, Kirsten Lise.   II. Fine, Lisa M.   III. Title.
    HQ1426.F844 2013
    305.420973—dc23

                                                                2012018760

W. W. Norton & Company, Inc., 500 Fifth Avenue, New York, NY 10110
wwnorton.com
W. W. Norton & Company Ltd., Castle House, 75/76 Wells Street, London
W1T 3QT

1   2   3   4   5   6   7   8   9   0

To our children—Raphael Benjamin Fermaglich Gold, Dalia Gene Gold Fermaglich, Zoe Ruth Berg Fine, and Dana Hester Fine Berg

Contents

THE SCHOLARSHIP ON *THE FEMININE MYSTIQUE*

ORIGINS AND INFLUENCES

Introduction

On February 19, 1963, W. W. Norton published Betty Friedan's *The Feminine Mystique*, a powerful critique of women's roles in contemporary American society. Relying on recent scholarship in the social sciences, Friedan attacked a host of institutions, including women's magazines, women's colleges, and advertisers, for promoting images of women deliriously happy with—and limited to—the domestic life of a housewife. These images comprised a feminine mystique: a belief that "fulfillment as a woman had only one definition for American women after 1949—the housewife-mother" (Friedan, 33). This mystique, Friedan argued, exerted enormous control over women's perceived options, and the consequences were dire for women. With their horizons so narrowly focused on home and family, Friedan argued, women had lost any identity of their own.

Excerpted in two major women's magazines, sold to the Book Find Club, and publicized by the author on a nationwide tour, *The Feminine Mystique* became a national bestseller. By April, the hardback was in its fifth printing, and by 1964, riding on a "paperback revolution" that was bringing intellectual treatises to a more general reading audience, it had become the number-one bestselling nonfiction paperback of the year, with over one million copies sold.[1]

Even more impressive than its sales record, however, was its cultural significance. *The Feminine Mystique* became a phenomenon. Women bought copies for their daughters, their mothers, their friends; they bought copies so that they could loan them out to others. Newspaper articles reported that cocktail parties turned into shouting matches about *The Feminine Mystique*; religious leaders gave sermons about it; and critics—both enthusiastic and

---

1. For information on the publication and promotion of *The Feminine Mystique*, see Stephanie Coontz, *A Strange Stirring: The Feminine Mystique and American Women at the Dawn of the 1960s* (New York: Basic Books, 2011), 145–49; Susan Bradley, *Mass Media and the Shaping of American Feminism, 1963–1975* (Jackson: University of Mississippi, 2003), 3–28; and Judith Hennessee, *Betty Friedan: Her Life* (New York: Random House, 1999), 75–78.

appalled—penned responses in newspapers all over the country.[2] Perhaps most amazing were the hundreds of women who wrote to Friedan in language that made clear she had touched them personally. "I've this moment finished reading your book and find I need not introduce myself. You know me, my sister, my friends. My entire case history appears on your pages," wrote one reader from Minneapolis.[3] To be sure, some felt threatened and angry, not warm and admiring: "I am a housewife and a woman of great ability. The greatest peril that I face today [is] other women with the same opinion as Betty Friedan."[4] With *The Feminine Mystique*, Betty Friedan had clearly hit a nerve.

The immediate and overwhelming response to *The Feminine Mystique* gives us insight into the moment that the book was published. The late 1950s and early 1960s—an era we call "the turn of the 1960s"—was a unique moment of political and intellectual ferment. A host of "phenomenon" books joined *The Feminine Mystique* on the bookshelves during this era, including Vance Packard's *The Hidden Persuaders* (1957); John Kenneth Galbraith's *The Affluent Society* (1958); Jane Jacobs's *The Death and Life of Great American Cities* (1961); Michael Harrington's *The Other America* (1962); Rachel Carson's *Silent Spring* (1962); Hannah Arendt's *Eichmann in Jerusalem* (1963); and Ralph Nader's *Unsafe at Any Speed* (1965). These books were all written as exposés that shed light on contemporary society, and they all sparked controversy and gave life to political, social, or cultural movements.

At a moment when some Americans were mounting challenges to the most repressive practices of the Cold War and to Jim Crow segregation in the South, these books took advantage of a growing openness in political discourse. Unlike television and radio, which were hampered by self-censorship, these books were free to criticize the status quo, to expose hypocrisy, and to suggest possibilities of change in a host of arenas, from urban planning, to the environment, to consumer rights, to women's equality. Even if people did not read these books in their entirety, texts like *The Feminine Mys-*

---

2. For more on media responses to *The Feminine Mystique*, see Hennessee, *Betty Friedan*, 84–85; and Kirsten Fermaglich, *American Dreams and Nazi Nightmares: Early Holocaust Consciousness and Liberal America, 1957–1965* (Hanover, NH: Brandeis University Press, 2006), 74–80.

3. Letter to Betty Friedan, Minneapolis, MN, 5 October 1963, in Series III, Box 19, Folder 688, Betty Friedan papers, M-62, Schlesinger Library, Radcliffe Institute, Harvard University, Cambridge, MA.

4. Letter to Editors of *McCall's*, Glenview, IL, 1 March 1963, in Series III, Box 21, Folder 745, Betty Friedan papers, M-62, Schlesinger Library, Radcliffe Institute, Harvard University, Cambridge, MA.

tique became symbols of change in an era experiencing significant political and cultural upheaval.[5]

The Feminine Mystique was a book of its time, but it was also a product of Betty Friedan's intellectual journey of the three previous decades. Born in 1921, Friedan became a radical while taking economics and psychology classes at Smith College from 1938 to 1942 and while studying in the summer of 1941 at the Highlander Folk School, a radical school outside Monteagle, Tennessee for labor and civil rights organizers. In 1943, Friedan went on to work as a labor journalist; she would work for the next nine years for the Federated Press and the *UE (United Electric) News*, two progressive media institutions. With the perspective of a Jewish, committed leftist, and with a readership of radical union members, Friedan reported on some of the key events of the 1940s and 1950s, including the Holocaust, the atomic bomb, and corporations' attacks on industrial unionism after World War II.[6]

Friedan's experiences during these three decades placed her squarely in the midst of the Popular Front, a movement that united left-wing individuals around issues such as anti-fascism, anti-racism, and support for progressive unions. Many women in the Popular Front were vocal in criticizing the sexism embedded in American capitalism, as well as the sexism that they found on the American left. In the 1950s, Friedan herself wrote several significant pieces on women's work during this era, including two influential UE pamphlets, *UE Fights for Women's Workers* and *Women Fight for a Better Life!*

Although Friedan wrote *The Feminine Mystique* primarily about—and for—white middle-class women, and although she did not address her leftist politics in the book, her early experiences with the Popular Front are crucial to understanding the book's feminism. In her criticisms of advertisers who used unrealistic images of women to sell household goods (see chapter 9, "The Sexual Sell"), for example, Friedan echoed Popular Front feminists, who had described the ways that corporations relied on women's roles as consumers to maintain the capitalist system. Friedan's descriptions of the isolation and frustrations of housework similarly echoed Popular Front feminists' descriptions of the alienation of female labor in the home.

5. For this analysis of books as symbolic phenomena of change in the early 1960s, see Louis Menand, "Books as Bombs," *The New Yorker*, January 24, 2011, at www.newyorker.com/arts/critics/books/2011/01/24/110124crbo_books_menand?currentPage=all. Accessed July 25, 2011.

6. See, for these important connections between Friedan's radical past and *The Feminine Mystique*, the pathbreaking work of Daniel Horowitz, *Betty Friedan and the Making of The Feminine Mystique: The American Left, the Cold War, and Modern Feminism* (Amherst: University of Massachusetts Press, 1998).

Reading *The Feminine Mystique* closely, with an understanding of Friedan's history, thus allows us an important window into the expressions of feminism of the 1930s, 1940s, and 1950s and the connections between that feminism and other social movements, including the women's movement, of the 1960s and 1970s.[7]

Although historians can trace these connections now, it is important to note that Friedan did not volunteer her radical past in her book. Her decision not to include her leftist politics reflects equally important aspects of American life in the 1950s and the 1960s. Friedan's silence was probably, at least in part, a response to McCarthyism, a movement in the 1950s targeting and discriminating against communists and other leftist individuals associated with the Popular Front.[8] In this environment, many individuals chose not to foreground their political connections to Popular Front activities.

Friedan, joining in one of the major trends of postwar intellectual thought, turned to psychological explanations for human behavior in *The Feminine Mystique*. Friedan's own successful experience with psychotherapy in the 1950s, as well as her academic background in psychology, provided an important framework for understanding women's oppression. Even though she rejected Freudian orthodoxy in her book, Friedan nonetheless operated within the prevalent psychological discourse that blamed bad mothers for passivity and gender confusion in their children ("Momism"). She also embraced the existential and humanistic psychology of Abraham Maslow and Carl Rogers, a psychology that emphasized an optimistic approach to claiming one's identity and autonomy, as an answer to women's oppression. Other radicals of the 1960s, like Abbie Hoffman, were similarly impressed by the transformative potential that the concepts of identity and autonomy held for oppressed groups, and Friedan's work thus gives us insight into these changing psychological currents of the era.[9]

---

7. For more on Popular Front feminism, see Kate Weigand, *Red Feminism: American Communism and the Making of Women's Liberation* (Baltimore: Johns Hopkins University Press, 2001)); Dorothy Sue Cobble, *The Other Women's Movement: Workplace Justice and Social Rights in Modern America* (Princeton: Princeton University Press, 2004).

8. For a definition of McCarthyism broader than simply the work of Wisconsin Senator Joseph McCarthy, see Kate Weigand, *Red Feminism: American Communism and the Making of Women's Liberation* (Baltimore: Johns Hopkins University Press, 2001), 159, fn. 5; and Ellen Schrecker, *Many are the Crimes: McCarthyism in America* (Princeton, NJ: Princeton University Press, 1998).

9. See, for Friedan's reliance on Momism, Rebecca Jo Plant, *Mom: The Transformation of Motherhood in Modern America* (Chicago: University of Chicago Press, 2010), 146–77; for more on Friedan's (and other radicals') use of Abraham Maslow, see Ellen Herman, *The Romance of American Psychology: Political Culture in the Age of Experts* (Berkeley: University of California Press, 1995); and Herman, "Being and Doing: Humanistic Psychology and the Spirit of the 1960s," in Barbara Tischler, ed., *Sights on the Sixties* (New Brunswick: Rutgers University Press, 1992), 87–101.

The Feminine Mystique also reflected the preoccupations with technological horror and mass destruction that dominated the post-World War II era. Friedan's decision to subtitle chapter 12 "The Comfortable Concentration Camp" was not simply an exaggeration to goad her readers: Friedan was part of a larger group of American Jewish intellectuals who made comparisons between American life and Nazi destruction at the turn of the 1960s. These intellectuals had been existentially shaken by the horrors of the Holocaust, and they believed that those horrors might help Americans to understand the dangers of mass society in their own lives.[1] While American Jews may have been particularly aware of Nazi camps as symbols of technological destruction, all Americans during the Cold War were acutely aware of the threat of nuclear warfare, particularly in the wake of the Cuban Missile Crisis of 1962. Antinuclear activists mounted a powerful critique of the arms race during the late 1950s and early 1960s, and some of the most influential activists were, in fact, women who used their roles as mothers to express their concerns about nuclear danger.[2] While the powerful domesticity of postwar culture called for women to remain in their homes to provide comfort for their families in these dangerous times, *The Feminine Mystique* offered an alternative vision: women needed to engage the world to help their families survive the nuclear threat.

Friedan's book was the product of her early life as an activist, student, and intellectual, but it also reflected her contemporary experiences as a wife and mother. Married to Carl Friedan in 1947, Friedan had three children between 1948 and 1956, and moved during that time from Manhattan to a series of suburban homes in the New York metropolitan area. After losing her job at *UE News* in 1952, Friedan stayed home for a period of time to take care of her children. Although she soon went back to work as a freelance writer, Friedan's experience as a suburban housewife made her acutely aware of the power, and the danger, of the prescriptive image of women that emerged in the 1950s: "I suffered, for a time, the reactions of terror—no future—feelings I had no personality that I have heard described by so many other women," she wrote in one unpublished note.[3] Even when she went back to work as a writer, she encountered the dissonance of her own desires for self-expression with the powerful cultural messages urging women to revel in domestic bliss. Like many feminists before her, she searched for

1. See Fermaglich, *American Dreams and Nazi Nightmares.*
2. Amy Swerdlow, *Women Strike for Peace: Traditional Motherhood and Radical Politics in the 1960s* (Chicago: University of Chicago Press, 1993); Dee Garrison, "Our Skirts Gave Them Courage: The Civil Defense Protest Movement in New York City, 1955–1961," in Joanne Meyerowitz, ed., *Not June Cleaver: Women and Gender in Postwar America, 1945–1960* (Philadelphia: Temple University Press, 1994), 201–26.
3. Cited in Fermaglich, *American Dreams and Nazi Nightmares,* 68.

answers and role models when few were available. Many of Friedan's solutions undoubtedly suggested themselves from the ferment of her own personal struggles.

The impact of *The Feminine Mystique* is both immeasurable and difficult to trace. Hundreds of women wrote letters to Friedan testifying that her book had changed their lives; one recent historian has conducted interviews with scores of additional women, many of whom made the same claim.[4] Scholars frequently credit *The Feminine Mystique* with sparking the women's movement of the 1960s and 1970s. The fact that Betty Friedan herself helped to create, and served as the first president of, the National Organization for Women (NOW) in 1966 has cemented the book's reputation as one of the few works that has launched a major social movement in American history, along with Harriet Beecher Stowe's *Uncle Tom's Cabin*, Upton Sinclair's *The Jungle*, and a handful of others.

Many participants in the women's movement of the 1960s and 1970s, however, rejected the notion that the movement began with Betty Friedan. Some older women had been working quietly for decades on women's issues in liberal and labor organizations and government agencies, such as the Women's Bureau of the U.S. Department of Labor. Although many, such as Catherine East, Kay Clarenbach, and Pauli Murray, worked with Friedan to establish NOW, *The Feminine Mystique* itself was not their reference point; instead, they looked to the first wave of feminism, or to women's networks of activism in liberal, labor, and civil rights organizations.

Other younger and more radical women had been more influenced by French philosopher Simone de Beauvoir's powerful *The Second Sex*, which was published in English in the United States in 1953. De Beauvoir's analysis struck deeper at the roots of women's oppression in the industrialized West, and her socialist solution to women's problems went far beyond Friedan's "New Life Plan for Women" (see chapter 14).[5] This radical analysis appealed more to younger women, such as Mary King and Casey Hayden, who were involved in the civil rights and student movements of the 1960s.[6] Perhaps even more crucial than either de Beauvoir or Friedan, however, were these young women's experiences in the movements: theories about participatory democracy, nonviolent resistance, colonialism, and opposition to the military-industrial complex shaped these women's perspectives on feminism, as did their personal experiences with sexism from fellow activists on the left.

---

4. Coontz, *A Strange Stirring*.
5. See Sandra Dijkstra, "Simone de Beauvoir and Betty Friedan: The Politics of Omission," *Feminist Studies* 6 (Summer 1980): 290–303.
6. For the impact of *The Second Sex* on King and Hayden, see Ruth Rosen, *The World Split Open* (New York: Penguin Books, 2001), 56–58.

Finally, and most importantly, there were millions of women to whom *The Feminine Mystique* literally did not speak. Women of color—African American, Latina, Asian American and Native American women—were completely absent from Friedan's vision, as were white working-class and poor women. Most of these women did not have the economic luxury of identifying themselves as housewives, and dominant cultural images of femininity at the time almost categorically excluded women who were not white and middle class. As the women's movement grew, women of color, working-class women, women on welfare, and lesbians all identified very different origins for their feminism, and they noted that their lives were not represented in Friedan's text. Moreover, lesbians were not only excluded from *The Feminine Mystique*, but Friedan's text actually reflected and contributed to the homophobia of the era. Uncomfortable with the label "lesbian," which had been used to delegitimize the women's movement throughout the twentieth century, Friedan resisted NOW's efforts to support lesbians' rights until 1977; the conflict helped shape her lasting reputation as a homophobe and marginalized her within the movement.[7]

Noting that the women's movement had multiple origins, as well as conflict surrounding issues of identity, however, should not distract us from the substantial impact that *The Feminine Mystique* did indeed have on women's lives. Friedan's powerful language aimed at white American middle-class women won large numbers of supporters to the feminist cause. Her emphasis on women's need for identity and autonomy became a part of NOW's statement of purpose: "NOW is dedicated to the proposition that women first and foremost are human beings, who . . . must have the chance to develop their fullest human potential."[8] Friedan's celebrity after *The Feminine Mystique*, moreover, drew attention to NOW and its battles for equality for women in education and the workforce. By 1973, NOW had achieved significant success in reshaping American gender roles, liberating women from the expectation that their lives would be limited to marriage and children. To be sure, *The Feminine Mystique* was not responsible for this change on its own, but Friedan (aided by the readers who had become her political supporters and by the celebrity that her book afforded her) played an important role in this turbulent political movement, and in the sea-change of attitudes toward women's roles that emerged in the 1970s.

---

7. See, for example, Benita Roth, *Separate Roads to Feminism: Black, Chicana and White Feminist Movements in America's Second Wave* (Cambridge and New York: Cambridge University Press, 2004); Rosen, *World Split Open*, 164–75, 263–94; Stephanie Gilmore and Elizabeth Kaminski, "A Part and Apart: Lesbian and Straight Feminist Activists Negotiate Identity in a Second-Wave Organization," *Journal of History of Sexuality* 16 (2007): 95–113.
8. See, for this point and this citation, Herman, *Romance of American Psychology*, 292.

Crucially, however, Friedan's celebrity also played a role in the backlash against feminism that emerged in tandem with the movement. Visible even in the earliest letters to Friedan were voices of anger, hostility, and wounded pride. Women who valued their roles as mothers and housewives interpreted Friedan's message as one that threatened their stability, devalued their labor, and disrespected their intelligence. Some of Friedan's early detractors, moreover, associated her message with communism; if the comfortable domestic space of a homemaker was to preserve the nation from the dangers of the Cold War, then voices that championed women's lives outside the home seemed designed to corrupt, infiltrate, and destroy American democracy. As a growing grassroots conservative movement in the 1960s mobilized women first against communism, and then against sex education, gay liberation, and legalized abortion, Friedan was not a specific target, but she had established herself as a prominent voice of liberal feminism, an easily identifiable threat to traditional values.[9]

By 1972, author and activist Phyllis Schlafly took direct aim at Friedan's feminism with a manifesto entitled "What's Wrong with 'Equal Rights' for Women?" and mobilized the growing network of conservative women into organized opposition to the Equal Rights Amendment (ERA). Although the Equal Rights Amendment would simply have prohibited discrimination based on sex, Schlafly won tens of thousands of supporters with her endorsement of traditional gender roles, and her insistence that the ERA would eliminate women's privileges. Women who felt attacked by feminists' rejection of the housewife's role responded eagerly to a political movement that vindicated and celebrated their lives.[1] Friedan, as the celebrity writer strongly identified with the ERA and with *The Feminine Mystique's* attack on the role of housewife, debated Schlafly publicly several times, but in the end, Friedan lost the battle. The Equal Rights Amendment passed the House and Senate easily in 1972, but it lost momentum after Schlafly's attack; in 1982, the ERA failed in its final bid to be ratified by the states. In the face of this political retrenchment, Friedan believed that the feminist movement's rhetoric had been too radical. Her third book, *The Second Stage* (1981), which called for feminists to pay attention to the needs of the family, rather than the needs of women alone, was seen by many in the

---

9. Lisa McGirr, *Suburban Warriors: The Origins of the New American Right* (Princeton, NJ: Princeton University Press, 2001), 227–37; Michelle Nickerson, "Moral Mothers and Goldwater Girls," in *The Conservative Sixties*, ed. David Farber and Jeff Roche (New York: Peter Lang, 2003), 51–62; and Mary C. Brennan, *Wives, Mothers and the Red Menace: Conservative Women and the Crusade Against Communism* (Boulder: University Press of Colorado, 2008), 115–27.

1. See Donald Critchlow, *Phyllis Schlafly and Grassroots Conservatism* (Princeton, NJ: Princeton University Press, 2005), 217–27.

women's movement as a conservative retreat from *The Feminine Mystique*, and a contribution to a broader cultural backlash against feminism in the 1980s.[2] Once again, Betty Friedan and *The Feminine Mystique* offer us a window (albeit a complicated one) into the major political movements of the twentieth century—this time, the growth of a vibrant conservative movement beginning in the 1960s and gaining power in the 1980s.

By the 1990s, Friedan's legacy had been reclaimed by a younger generation of feminists calling themselves a third wave, who recognized *The Feminine Mystique* as a founding document. And in the first decade of the twenty-first century, philosopher Linda Hirshman created fresh waves of public controversy as she invoked Friedan's *Feminine Mystique* to criticize the growing numbers of educated women who chose to stay home with their children rather than working.[3]

After Friedan died in 2006, many obituaries highlighted her significance as a "feminist icon" and a "feminist crusader," the woman who "almost single-handedly revived" the feminist movement, a leader of one of the most influential and successful social movements of the twentieth century.[4] These plaudits are mostly true, and they are crucial to understanding Friedan's historical significance. We believe that there are other, crucial, less-noticed ways of understanding the historical significance of Friedan's life and her text, *The Feminine Mystique*. Friedan was one of the major public intellectuals of the twentieth century, someone who took the complicated and jargon-laden ideas of psychologists, economists, and political theorists, and translated them in *The Feminine Mystique* into powerful, readable, relatable prose that touched millions of people and convinced them to think and act differently.

As a public intellectual whose lifetime spanned much of the twentieth century, moreover, Friedan offers an important window into

2. See, for responses to *The Second Stage*, Susan Faludi, *Backlash: The Undeclared War Against American Women* (New York: Crown, 1991); and Hennessee, *Betty Friedan*, 239–42.

3. See, for example, Linda Hirshman, "Homeward Bound," *The American Prospect* 16. 12 (December 2005): 20–26; Hirshman, *Get to Work: A Manifesto for Women of the World* (New York: Viking, 2006); Patricia Cohen, "Today Some Feminists Hate the Word 'Choice,'" *New York Times,* January 15, 2006, D3; Emily Bazelon, "Understanding Betty Friedan: Why Linda Hirshman Doesn't," *Slate*, June 26, 2006 at www.slate.com/articles/life/family/2006/06/understanding_betty_friedan.html (accessed January 10, 2012); and Rebecca Traister, "Your Guide to the Linda Hirshman Media Blitz!" *Salon*, June 15, 2006, at www.salon.com/2006/06/15/hirshman_2/ (accessed January 10, 2012).

4. See Sheila Rowbowtham, "Betty Friedan: Feminist icon of the 1960s, renowned for her bestseller, The Feminine Mystique," *The Guardian* 6 February 2006, at www.guardian.co.uk/news/2006/feb/06/guardianobituaries.gender (accessed August 1, 2011); Margalit Fox, "Betty Friedan, who ignited cause in Feminine Mystique, dies at 85," *New York Times*, at www.nytimes.com/2006/02/05/national/05friedan.html?emc=eta1 (accessed August 1, 2011); and Patricia Sullivan, "Voice of Feminism's 'Second Wave,'" *Washington Post* 5 February 2006, at www.washingtonpost.com/wp-dyn/content/article/2006/02/04/AR2006020401385.html?referrer=emailarticle (accessed August 1, 2011).

the history of that century. Her work indicates for us the ways that feminism was interconnected with the struggles of working-class men and women, with black and Jewish battles against racism and anti-Semitism, with the efforts of the peace movement to oppose war and eradicate nuclear weapons, and finally even with the fears and anxieties of the conservative movement as ideas about traditional female roles changed. *The Feminine Mystique* also shows us that those social movements all had a long and continuous history throughout the twentieth century. Friedan may have revitalized the women's movement, but she did not create it anew. If timing is everything, Betty Friedan had it all. *The Feminine Mystique* appeared at just the right moment to take advantage of the ideological work of the 1930s, 1940s, and 1950s from first wave feminists, unionists, socialists and communists, psychologists, and Jewish and black political activists while riding the first swell of the second wave of the feminist movement. As a result, *The Feminine Mystique* had substantial impact on a wide range of political activists, thinkers, and ordinary individuals. Betty Friedan thus continues to leave us all a legacy of political thought and activism for generations to come.

Acknowledgments

We have collective and individual thanks. We thank W. W. Norton for giving us the opportunity to work on this exciting project and we would like to acknowledge the speed and skill of the editorial staff, particularly Carol Bemis, Rivka Genesen, and Hannah Blaisdell. We had two excellent research assistants, Kristine Cooney and Rebecca Koerselman, who worked quickly and thoroughly on the background research for our annotations. Kristine Cooney received a Provost University Research Initiative (PURI) Grant from the Provost's office at Michigan State University and we are very grateful for the support from MSU for this project. The MSU Department of History funded Rebecca Koerselman's research, as well as funding the reproduction of images and permissions. Ilana Rosenbloom offered an undergraduate perspective on *The Feminine Mystique* to help us identify terms for annotation. Our colleague Leslie Moch also provided emotional support and made sure we were aware of every contemporary reference to Betty Friedan out there. Anna Pegler-Gordon originated the term "the turn of the 1960s" and we thank her for her brilliant way with words. Our work is indebted to the activists in second wave feminism and all those touched by this social movement, as well as the scholars who have taken on this topic, many of whose works are included here. We owe a huge intellectual debt to Daniel Horowitz, whose own work on Betty Friedan was crucial to our approach.

Fermaglich's acknowledgments

This book would never have made it to press if it were not for the careful, thoughtful, inspired work of Lisa Fine. Since I met Lisa my first year at Michigan State University, she has spurred me on to do my finest work. She has been a mentor, a colleague, and a friend. Working with her on this volume has been a true pleasure. My greatest challenge has been striving to live up to Lisa's example: she is a tireless worker, relentlessly organized and boundlessly enthusiastic about the material. She is also a great cook.

I have a number of other professional debts. Daniel Horowitz has been a staunch supporter of my work, as well as a mentor and colleague. His careful scholarship is a model for my own, and he offered important early help with this project. A conversation with Anne Pollock long before I began working on this book stuck with me and helped to shape some of the material here. I also had valuable conversations about Friedan with participants at the Projects in Progress Symposium on Feminist Work at Michigan State University and at the Jewish Feminine Mystique conference at New York University, both in 2007. And my friends, Jane Rothstein and Elizabeth Hatcher, pushed me long ago in graduate school to research Betty Friedan: their suggestion truly changed my life, and I will be forever grateful.

Finally, I would like to thank the people who helped me, in a variety of ways, to get this project done. The first people who must be thanked are the amazing women who have taken care of my children, Raphael and Dalia, as though they were their own: Hiromi Potter and Sarah Cook. Others, too, have helped me care for my children as I worked on this book: the thoughtful staff at Eastminster Day Care Center; the excellent teachers at Marble Elementary School; my wonderful parents, Lois and Danny Fermaglich; and my loving in-laws Linda and Jay Gold. Rafe and Dalia are too young now to understand this book, but their lives have been intertwined with it; their beauty and hilarity has made the work all worth the effort. Most of all, I need to thank my best friend, my husband, Jonathan Gold, who has supported me in everything I've ever wanted to do—except email at 2 A.M., and he was probably right about that.

Fine's acknowledgments

My most heartfelt thanks go to Kirsten, who got me this gig. Working on this volume has been the most fun I have had as a historian to date. Collaborating is often a hard task for historians who tend to research and write alone, but that has not been the case with this project. Because of her intelligence, honesty, and sense of humor, working with Kirsten has been a pleasure. During the early days as we were planning the volume, we would sit at Kirsten's dining room table with papers and books strewn here and there, drinking tea, and passing Dalia, Kirsten's infant daughter, back and forth. It was wonderful. We imagined that Betty Friedan herself would have approved.

Two colleagues in the Department of History at Michigan State University, David Bailey and Michael Stamm, were graciously available for very helpful chats on the twentieth century intellectual and cultural history of the United States. Many members of my family were supportive of this project and often helped. My husband Peter Berg, as the Head of Special Collections in the MSU Libraries, helped me find documents and he and his staff helped locate information to secure permissions. He was always a great fan of this project and I am very grateful. My dad, Al Fine, retrieved materials at the Smith College library and my niece, Isabel Reich, did the same at the Columbia University archives. My mom, Shirley Haas Fine, told me stories of what it was like to work as a secretary in New York City in the 1940s and the 1950s. And my daughters, Zoe Fine and Dana Berg, remind me every day why Betty Friedan's work is still so important.

The Text of
THE FEMININE MYSTIQUE

Contents

Preface and Acknowledgments

Gradually, without seeing it clearly for quite a while, I came to realize that something is very wrong with the way American women are trying to live their lives today. I sensed it first as a question mark in my own life, as a wife and mother of three small children, half-guiltily, and therefore half-heartedly, almost in spite of myself, using my abilities and education in work that took me away from home. It was this personal question mark that led me, in 1957, to spend a great deal of time doing an intensive questionnaire of my college classmates, fifteen years after our graduation from Smith. The answers given by 200 women to those intimate open-ended questions made me realize that what was wrong could not be related to education in the way it was then believed to be. The problems and satisfaction of their lives, and mine, and the way our education had contributed to them, simply did not fit the image of the modern American woman as she was written about in women's magazines, studied and analyzed in classrooms and clinics, praised and damned in a ceaseless barrage of words ever since the end of World War II. There was a strange discrepancy between the reality of our lives as women and the image to which we were trying to conform, the image that I came to call the feminine mystique. I wondered if other women faced this schizophrenic split, and what it meant.

And so I began to hunt down the origins of the feminine mystique, and its effect on women who lived by it, or grew up under it. My methods were simply those of a reporter on the trail of a story, except I soon discovered that this was no ordinary story. For the startling pattern that began to emerge, as one clue led me to another in far-flung fields of modern thought and life, defied not only the conventional image but basic psychological assumptions about women. I found a few pieces of the puzzle in previous studies of women; but not many, for women in the past have been studied in terms of the feminine mystique. The Mellon study of Vassar women was provocative, Simone de Beauvoir's insights into French women, the work of Mirra Komarovsky, A. H. Maslow, Alva Myrdal. I found even more provocative the growing body of new psychological thought on the question of man's identity, whose implications for

5

women seem not to have been realized. I found further evidence by questioning those who treat women's ills and problems. And I traced the growth of the mystique by talking to editors of women's magazines, advertising motivational researchers, and theoretical experts on women in the fields of psychology, psychoanalysis, anthropology, sociology, and family-life education. But the puzzle did not begin to fit together until I interviewed at some depth, from two hours to two days each, eighty women at certain crucial points in their life cycle—high school and college girls facing or evading the question of who they were; young housewives and mothers for whom, if the mystique were right, there should be no such question and who thus had no name for the problem troubling them; and women who faced a jumping-off point at forty. These women, some tortured, some serene, gave me the final clues, and the most damning indictment of the feminine mystique.

I could not, however, have written this book without the assistance of many experts, both eminent theoreticians and practical workers in the field, and, indeed, without the cooperation of many who themselves believe and have helped perpetrate the feminine mystique. I was helped by many present and former editors of women's magazines, including Peggy Bell, John English, Bruce Gould, Mary Ann Guitar, James Skardon, Nancy Lynch, Geraldine Rhoads, Robert Stein, Neal Stuart and Polly Weaver; by Ernest Dichter and the staff of the Institute for Motivational Research; and by Marion Skedgell, former editor of the Viking Press, who gave me her data from an unfinished study of fiction heroines. Among behavioral scientists, theoreticians and therapists in the field, I owe a great debt to William Menaker and John Landgraf of New York University, A. H. Maslow of Brandeis, John Dollard of Yale, William J. Goode of Columbia; to Margaret Mead; to Paul Vahanian of Teachers College, Elsa Siipola Israel and Eli Chinoy of Smith. And to Dr. Andras Angyal, psychoanalyst of Boston, Dr. Nathan Ackerman of New York, Dr. Louis English and Dr. Margaret Lawrence of the Rockland County Mental Health Center; to many mental health workers in Westchester County, including Mrs. Emily Gould, Dr. Gerald Fountain, Dr. Henrietta Glatzer and Marjorie Ilgenfritz of the Guidance Center of New Rochelle and the Rev. Edgar Jackson; Dr. Richard Gordon and Katherine Gordon of Bergen County, New Jersey; the late Dr. Abraham Stone, Dr. Lena Levine and Fred Jaffe of the Planned Parenthood Association, the staff of the James Jackson Putnam Center in Boston, Dr. Doris Menzer and Dr. Somers Sturges of the Peter Bent Brigham Hospital, Alice King of the Alumnae Advisory Center and Dr. Lester Evans of the Commonwealth Fund. I am also grateful to those educators valiantly fighting the feminine mystique, who gave me helpful insights: Laura Bornholdt of Wellesley, Mary Bunting of Radcliffe, Marjorie Nicolson of Columbia, Esther Lloyd-Jones of Teachers College, Millicent McIntosh of Barnard, Esther Raushenbush of Sarah Lawrence, Thomas Mendenhall of Smith, Daniel Aaron and many other members of the Smith faculty. I am above all grateful to the women who shared their problems and feelings with me, beginning with the 200 women of Smith, 1942, and Marion Ingersoll Howell and Anne Mather Montero, who worked with me on the alumnae questionnaire that started my search.

Without that superb institution, the Frederick Lewis Allen Room of the New York Public Library and its provision to a writer of quiet work space and continuous access to research sources, this particular mother of three might never have started a book, much less finished it. The same might be said of the sensitive support of my publisher, George P. Brockway, my editor, Burton Beals, and my agent, Martha Winston. In a larger sense, this book might never have been written if I had not had a most unusual education in psychology, from Kurt Koffka, Harold Israel, Elsa Siipola and James Gibson at Smith; from Kurt Lewin, Tamara Dembo, and the others of their group then at Iowa; and from E. C. Tolman, Jean Macfarlane, Nevitt Sanford and Erik Erikson at Berkeley—a liberal education, in the best sense, which was meant to be used, though I have not used it as I originally planned.

The insights, interpretations both of theory and fact, and the implicit values of this book are inevitably my own. But whether or not the answers I present here are final—and there are many questions which social scientists must probe further—the dilemma of the American woman is real. At the present time, many experts, finally forced to recognize this problem, are redoubling their efforts to adjust women to it in terms of the feminine mystique. My answers may disturb the experts and women alike, for they imply social change. But there would be no sense in my writing this book at all if I did not believe that women can affect society, as well as be affected by it; that, in the end, a woman, as a man, has the power to choose, and to make her own heaven or hell.

Grandview, New York
June 1957–July 1962

The Feminine Mystique

1
The Problem That Has No Name

The problem lay buried, unspoken, for many years in the minds of American women. It was a strange stirring, a sense of dissatisfaction, a yearning that women suffered in the middle of the twentieth century in the United States. Each suburban wife struggled with it alone. As she made the beds, shopped for groceries, matched slipcover material, ate peanut butter sandwiches with her children, chauffeured Cub Scouts and Brownies, lay beside her husband at night—she was afraid to ask even of herself the silent question—"Is this all?"

For over fifteen years there was no word of this yearning in the millions of words written about women, for women, in all the columns, books and articles by experts telling women their role was to seek fulfillment as wives and mothers. Over and over women heard in voices of tradition and of Freudian sophistication that they could desire no greater destiny than to glory in their own femininity. Experts told them how to catch a man and keep him, how to breast-feed children and handle their toilet training, how to cope with sibling rivalry and adolescent rebellion; how to buy a dishwasher, bake bread, cook gourmet snails, and build a swimming pool with their own hands; how to dress, look, and act more feminine and make marriage more exciting; how to keep their husbands from dying young and their sons from growing into delinquents. They were taught to pity the neurotic, unfeminine, unhappy women who wanted to be poets or physicists or presidents. They learned that truly feminine women do not want careers, higher education, political rights—the independence and the opportunities that the old-fashioned feminists fought for. Some women, in their forties and fifties, still remembered painfully giving up those dreams, but most of the younger women no longer even thought about them. A thousand expert voices applauded their femininity, their adjustment, their new maturity. All they had to do was devote their lives from earliest girlhood to finding a husband and bearing children.

By the end of the nineteen-fifties, the average marriage age of women in America dropped to 20, and was still dropping, into the teens. Fourteen million girls were engaged by 17. The proportion of women attending college in comparison with men dropped from 47 per cent in 1920 to 35 per cent in 1958. A century earlier, women had fought for higher education; now girls went to college to get a husband. By the mid-fifties, 60 per cent dropped out of college to marry, or because they were afraid too much education would be a marriage bar. Colleges built dormitories for "married students," but the students were almost always the husbands. A new degree was instituted for the wives—"Ph.T." (Putting Husband Through).

Then American girls began getting married in high school. And the women's magazines, deploring the unhappy statistics about these young marriages, urged that courses on marriage, and marriage counselors, be installed in the high schools. Girls started going steady at twelve and thirteen, in junior high. Manufacturers put out brassieres with false bosoms of foam rubber for little girls of ten. And an advertisement for a child's dress, sizes 3–6x, in the *New York Times* in the fall of 1960, said: "She Too Can Join the Man-Trap Set."

By the end of the fifties, the United States birthrate was overtaking India's.* The birth-control movement, renamed Planned Parenthood,† was asked to find a method whereby women who had been advised that a third or fourth baby would be born dead or defective might have it anyhow. Statisticians were especially astounded at the fantastic increase in the number of babies among college women. Where once they had two children, now they had four, five, six. Women who had once wanted careers were now making careers out of having babies. So rejoiced *Life* magazine in a 1956 paean to the movement of American women back to the home.

In a New York hospital, a woman had a nervous breakdown when she found she could not breastfeed her baby. In other hospitals, women dying of cancer refused a drug which research had proved might save their lives: its side effects were said to be unfeminine. "If I have only one life, let me live it as a blonde," a larger-than-life-sized picture of a pretty, vacuous woman proclaimed from newspa-

---

*   This large increase in the birthrate that took place between 1946 and 1964 is called the "baby boom," and those born during this time period are referred to as "baby boomers." Many factors contributed to this spike in fertility, including security and prosperity in the 1950s after decades of depression and war; lower ages of first marriage; and a pervasive domestic ideology that Friedan's book describes.

†   Planned Parenthood Federation of America, a private voluntary agency, was founded in 1942 by Margaret Sanger and other activists and was dedicated to providing reproductive healthcare to all American women. This organization replaced Sanger's American Birth Control League, originally founded in 1921. Its new name reflected the shift from providing birth control to individual women or mothers, to "family planning," a family-oriented service.

per, magazine, and drugstore ads. And across America, three out of every ten women dyed their hair blonde. They ate a chalk called Metrecal, instead of food, to shrink to the size of the thin young models. Department-store buyers reported that American women, since 1939, had become three and four sizes smaller. "Women are out to fit the clothes, instead of vice-versa," one buyer said.

Interior decorators were designing kitchens with mosaic murals and original paintings, for kitchens were once again the center of women's lives. Home sewing became a million-dollar industry. Many women no longer left their homes, except to shop, chauffeur their children, or attend a social engagement with their husbands. Girls were growing up in America without ever having jobs outside the home. In the late fifties, a sociological phenomenon was suddenly remarked: a third of American women now worked, but most were no longer young and very few were pursuing careers. They were married women who held part-time jobs, selling or secretarial, to put their husbands through school, their sons through college, or to help pay the mortgage. Or they were widows supporting families. Fewer and fewer women were entering professional work. The shortages in the nursing, social work, and teaching professions caused crises in almost every American city. Concerned over the Soviet Union's lead in the space race,* scientists noted that America's greatest source of unused brainpower was women. But girls would not study physics: it was "unfeminine." A girl refused a science fellowship at Johns Hopkins to take a job in a real-estate office. All she wanted, she said, was what every other American girl wanted—to get married, have four children and live in a nice house in a nice suburb.

The suburban housewife—she was the dream image of the young American woman and the envy, it was said, of women all over the world. The American housewife—freed by science and labor-saving appliances from the drudgery, the dangers of childbirth and the illnesses of her grandmother. She was healthy, beautiful, educated, concerned only about her husband, her children, her home. She had found true feminine fulfillment. As a housewife and mother, she was respected as a full and equal partner to man in his world.

---

* After World War II, the United States and the Soviet Union engaged in an intense economic, political, and military competition called the Cold War, which shaped intellectual and political life throughout the postwar era. The rivalry was ideological, opposing the United States' liberal democracy to the Soviet Union's communism, a political and economic system that called for collective ownership and control of property. Much of the competition revolved around the amassing of nuclear weapons; after the devastating dropping of atomic bombs on Hiroshima and Nagasaki in World War II, both the United States and the Soviet Union began to test a hydrogen bomb, colloquially called the H-bomb. The Cold War became a space race in 1957, after the Soviet Union successfully launched a satellite called Sputnik around the earth. Having believed that they had been technologically advanced in comparison to the Soviets, Americans reacted with shock and fear to the Sputnik launch, and they responded with increased attention to and funding of scientific education, research, and development.

She was free to choose automobiles, clothes, appliances, supermarkets; she had everything that women ever dreamed of.

In the fifteen years after World War II, this mystique of feminine fulfillment became the cherished and self-perpetuating core of contemporary American culture. Millions of women lived their lives in the image of those pretty pictures of the American suburban housewife, kissing their husbands goodbye in front of the picture window, depositing their stationwagonsful of children at school, and smiling as they ran the new electric waxer over the spotless kitchen floor. They baked their own bread, sewed their own and their children's clothes, kept their new washing machines and dryers running all day. They changed the sheets on the beds twice a week instead of once, took the rug-hooking class in adult education, and pitied their poor frustrated mothers, who had dreamed of having a career. Their only dream was to be perfect wives and mothers; their highest ambition to have five children and a beautiful house, their only fight to get and keep their husbands. They had no thought for the unfeminine problems of the world outside the home; they wanted the men to make the major decisions. They gloried in their role as women, and wrote proudly on the census blank: "Occupation: housewife."

For over fifteen years, the words written for women, and the words women used when they talked to each other, while their husbands sat on the other side of the room and talked shop or politics or septic tanks, were about problems with their children, or how to keep their husbands happy, or improve their children's school, or cook chicken or make slipcovers. Nobody argued whether women were inferior or superior to men; they were simply different. Words like "emancipation" and "career" sounded strange and embarrassing; no one had used them for years. When a Frenchwoman named Simone de Beauvoir wrote a book called *The Second Sex*,* an American critic commented that she obviously "didn't know what life was all about," and besides, she was talking about French women. The "woman problem" in America no longer existed.

If a woman had a problem in the 1950's and 1960's, she knew that something must be wrong with her marriage, or with herself. Other women were satisfied with their lives, she thought. What kind of a woman was she if she did not feel this mysterious fulfill-

---

* Simone de Beauvoir (1908–1986), French existentialist feminist, and author of one of the most important theoretical works of feminism of the twentieth century, *The Second Sex* (1953). See pp. 355–57 for description of and selection from this work and pp. 443–46 for a comparison with *The Feminine Mystique*. Friedan read and was influenced by de Beauvoir's ideas but by the 1970s the two were moving in different intellectual directions. Friedan interviewed de Beauvoir in the 1970s and wrote of this anticipated interchange, "To my horror, I discovered that Simone de Beauvoir and I disagreed on virtually everything." *Life So Far* (New York: Simon and Schuster, 2000), 281.

ment waxing the kitchen floor? She was so ashamed to admit her dissatisfaction that she never knew how many other women shared it. If she tried to tell her husband, he didn't understand what she was talking about. She did not really understand it herself. For over fifteen years women in America found it harder to talk about this problem than about sex. Even the psychoanalysts had no name for it. When a woman went to a psychiatrist for help, as many women did, she would say, "I'm so ashamed," or "I must be hopelessly neurotic." "I don't know what's wrong with women today," a suburban psychiatrist said uneasily. "I only know something is wrong because most of my patients happen to be women. And their problem isn't sexual." Most women with this problem did not go to see a psychoanalyst, however. "There's nothing wrong really," they kept telling themselves. "There isn't any problem."

But on an April morning in 1959, I heard a mother of four, having coffee with four other mothers in a suburban development fifteen miles from New York, say in a tone of quiet desperation, "the problem." And the others knew, without words, that she was not talking about a problem with her husband, or her children, or her home. Suddenly they realized they all shared the same problem, the problem that has no name. They began, hesitantly, to talk about it. Later, after they had picked up their children at nursery school and taken them home to nap, two of the women cried, in sheer relief, just to know they were not alone.

Gradually I came to realize that the problem that has no name was shared by countless women in America. As a magazine writer I often interviewed women about problems with their children, or their marriages, or their houses, or their communities. But after a while I began to recognize the telltale signs of this other problem. I saw the same signs in suburban ranch houses and split-levels on Long Island and in New Jersey and Westchester County; in colonial houses in a small Massachusetts town; on patios in Memphis; in suburban and city apartments; in living rooms in the Midwest. Sometimes I sensed the problem, not as a reporter, but as a suburban housewife, for during this time I was also bringing up my own three children in Rockland County, New York. I heard echoes of the problem in college dormitories and semiprivate maternity wards, at PTA meetings and luncheons of the League of Women Voters, at suburban cocktail parties, in station wagons waiting for trains, and in snatches of conversation overheard at Schrafft's. The groping words I heard from other women, on quiet afternoons when children were at school or on quiet evenings when husbands worked late, I think I understood first as a woman long before I understood their larger social and psychological implications.

Just what was this problem that has no name? What were the words women used when they tried to express it? Sometimes a woman would say "I feel empty somehow . . . incomplete." Or she would say, "I feel as if I don't exist." Sometimes she blotted out the feeling with a tranquilizer.* Sometimes she thought the problem was with her husband, or her children, or that what she really needed was to redecorate her house, or move to a better neighborhood, or have an affair, or another baby. Sometimes, she went to a doctor with symptoms she could hardly describe: "A tired feeling . . . I get so angry with the children it scares me . . . I feel like crying without any reason." (A Cleveland doctor called it "the housewife's syndrome.") A number of women told me about great bleeding blisters that break out on their hands and arms. "I call it the housewife's blight," said a family doctor in Pennsylvania. "I see it so often lately in these young women with four, five and six children who bury themselves in their dishpans. But it isn't caused by detergent and it isn't cured by cortisone."

Sometimes a woman would tell me that the feeling gets so strong she runs out of the house and walks through the streets. Or she stays inside her house and cries. Or her children tell her a joke, and she doesn't laugh because she doesn't hear it. I talked to women who had spent years on the analyst's couch, working out their "adjustment to the feminine role," their blocks to "fulfillment as a wife and mother." But the desperate tone in these women's voices, and the look in their eyes, was the same as the tone and the look of other women, who were sure they had no problem, even though they did have a strange feeling of desperation.

A mother of four who left college at nineteen to get married told me:

> I've tried everything women are supposed to do—hobbies, gardening, pickling, canning, being very social with my neighbors, joining committees, running PTA teas. I can do it all, and I like it, but it doesn't leave you anything to think about—any feeling of who you are. I never had any career ambitions. All I wanted was to get married and have four children. I love the kids and Bob and my home. There's no problem you can even put a name to. But I'm desperate. I begin to feel I have no personality. I'm a server of food and a putter-on of pants and a bedmaker, somebody who can be called on when you want something. But who am I?

---

*   A group of medications that began to become available by prescription in the 1950s to help reduce stress, tension, and anxiety as well as a variety of ailments such as insomnia, forms of neurosis and psychosis, and alcoholism.

A twenty-three-year-old mother in blue jeans said:

> I ask myself why I'm so dissatisfied. I've got my health, fine children, a lovely new home, enough money. My husband has a real future as an electronics engineer. He doesn't have any of these feelings. He says maybe I need a vacation, let's go to New York for a weekend. But that isn't it. I always had this idea we should do everything together. I can't sit down and read a book alone. If the children are napping and I have one hour to myself I just walk through the house waiting for them to wake up. I don't make a move until I know where the rest of the crowd is going. It's as if ever since you were a little girl, there's always been somebody or something that will take care of your life: your parents, or college, or falling in love, or having a child, or moving to a new house. Then you wake up one morning and there's nothing to look forward to.

A young wife in a Long Island development said:

> I seem to sleep so much. I don't know why I should be so tired. This house isn't nearly so hard to clean as the cold-water flat we had when I was working. The children are at school all day. It's not the work. I just don't feel alive.

In 1960, the problem that has no name burst like a boil through the image of the happy American housewife. In the television commercials the pretty housewives still beamed over their foaming dishpans and *Time*'s cover story on "The Suburban Wife, an American Phenomenon" protested: "Having too good a time . . . to believe that they should be unhappy." But the actual unhappiness of the American housewife was suddenly being reported—from the *New York Times* and *Newsweek* to *Good Housekeeping* and CBS Television ("The Trapped Housewife"), although almost everybody who talked about it found some superficial reason to dismiss it. It was attributed to incompetent appliance repairmen (*New York Times*), or the distances children must be chauffeured in the suburbs (*Time*), or too much PTA (*Redbook*). Some said it was the old problem—education: more and more women had education, which naturally made them unhappy in their role as housewives. "The road from Freud to Frigidaire, from Sophocles to Spock, has turned out to be a bumpy one," reported the *New York Times* (June 28, 1960). "Many young women—certainly not all—whose education plunged them into a world of ideas feel stifled in their homes. They find their routine lives out of joint with their training. Like shut-ins, they feel left out. In the last year, the problem of the educated housewife has provided the meat of dozens of speeches made by troubled presidents of women's colleges who maintain, in the face of complaints, that six-teen years of academic training is realistic preparation for wife-hood and motherhood."

There was much sympathy for the educated housewife. ("Like a two-headed schizophrenic . . . once she wrote a paper on the Grave-yard poets; now she writes notes to the milkman. Once she deter-mined the boiling point of sulphuric acid; now she determines her boiling point with the overdue repairman. . . . The housewife often is reduced to screams and tears. . . . No one, it seems, is apprecia-tive, least of all herself, of the kind of person she becomes in the process of turning from poetess into shrew.")

Home economists suggested more realistic preparation for housewives, such as high-school workshops in home appliances. College educators suggested more discussion groups on home management and the family, to prepare women for the adjustment to domestic life. A spate of articles appeared in the mass maga-zines offering "Fifty-eight Ways to Make Your Marriage More Exciting." No month went by without a new book by a psychiatrist or sexologist offering technical advice on finding greater fulfill-ment through sex.

A male humorist joked in *Harper's Bazaar** (July, 1960) that the problem could be solved by taking away woman's right to vote. ("In the pre-19th Amendment era, the American woman was placid, sheltered and sure of her role in American society. She left all the political decisions to her husband and he, in turn, left all the family decisions to her. Today a woman has to make both the family *and* the political decisions, and it's too much for her.")

A number of educators suggested seriously that women no longer be admitted to the four-year colleges and universities: in the grow-ing college crisis, the education which girls could not use as housewives was more urgently needed than ever by boys to do the work of the atomic age.

The problem was also dismissed with drastic solutions no one could take seriously. (A woman writer proposed in *Harper's* that women be drafted for compulsory service as nurses' aides and baby-sitters.) And it was smoothed over with the age-old panaceas: "love is their answer," "the only answer is inner help," "the secret of completeness—children," "a private means of intellectual fulfill-ment," "to cure this toothache of the spirit—the simple formula of handing one's self and one's will over to God."[1]

---

* *Harper's Bazaar, Newsweek, Life,* and *Look* and many others mentioned in *The Femi-nine Mystique* are mass market magazines. Starting in the late nineteenth century and continuing into the twentieth, mass-produced magazines, oriented to market niches related to race, class, and gender, were not only items of consumption but were also disseminators of information about consumption to millions of Americans before radio, TV, and the internet came on the scene.

The problem was dismissed by telling the housewife she doesn't realize how lucky she is—her own boss, no time clock, no junior executive gunning for her job. What if she isn't happy—does she think men are happy in this world? Does she really, secretly, still want to be a man? Doesn't she know yet how lucky she is to be a woman?

The problem was also, and finally, dismissed by shrugging that there are no solutions: this is what being a woman means, and what is wrong with American women that they can't accept their role gracefully? As *Newsweek* put it (March 7, 1960):

> She is dissatisfied with a lot that women of other lands can only dream of. Her discontent is deep, pervasive, and impervious to the superficial remedies which are offered at every hand. . . . An army of professional explorers have already charted the major sources of trouble. . . . From the beginning of time, the female cycle has defined and confined woman's role. As Freud was credited with saying: "Anatomy is destiny." Though no group of women has ever pushed these natural restrictions as far as the American wife, it seems that she still cannot accept them with good grace. . . . A young mother with a beautiful family, charm, talent and brains is apt to dismiss her role apologetically. "What do I do?" you hear her say. "Why nothing. I'm just a housewife." A good education, it seems, has given this paragon among women an understanding of the value of everything except her own worth . . .

And so she must accept the fact that "American women's unhappiness is merely the most recently won of women's rights," and adjust and say with the happy housewife found by *Newsweek*: "We ought to salute the wonderful freedom we all have and be proud of our lives today. I have had college and I've worked, but being a housewife is the most rewarding and satisfying role. . . . My mother was never included in my father's business affairs . . . she couldn't get out of the house and away from us children. But I am an equal to my husband; I can go along with him on business trips and to social business affairs."

The alternative offered was a choice that few women would contemplate. In the sympathetic words of the *New York Times*: "All admit to being deeply frustrated at times by the lack of privacy, the physical burden, the routine of family life, the confinement of it. However, none would give up her home and family if she had the choice to make again." *Redbook* commented: "Few women would want to thumb their noses at husbands, children and community and go off on their own. Those who do may be talented individuals, but they rarely are successful women."

The year American women's discontent boiled over, it was also reported (*Look*) that the more than 21,000,000 American women who are single, widowed, or divorced do not cease even after fifty their frenzied, desperate search for a man. And the search begins early—for seventy per cent of all American women now marry before they are twenty-four. A pretty twenty-five-year-old secretary took thirty-five different jobs in six months in the futile hope of finding a husband. Women were moving from one political club to another, taking evening courses in accounting or sailing, learning to play golf or ski, joining a number of churches in succession, going to bars alone, in their ceaseless search for a man.

Of the growing thousands of women currently getting private psychiatric help in the United States, the married ones were reported dissatisfied with their marriages, the unmarried ones suffering from anxiety and, finally, depression. Strangely, a number of psychiatrists stated that, in their experience, unmarried women patients were happier than married ones. So the door of all those pretty suburban houses opened a crack to permit a glimpse of uncounted thousands of American housewives who suffered alone from a problem that suddenly everyone was talking about, and beginning to take for granted, as one of those unreal problems in American life that can never be solved—like the hydrogen bomb. By 1962 the plight of the trapped American housewife had become a national parlor game. Whole issues of magazines, newspaper columns, books learned and frivolous, educational conferences and television panels were devoted to the problem.

Even so, most men, and some women, still did not know that this problem was real. But those who had faced it honestly knew that all the superficial remedies, the sympathetic advice, the scolding words and the cheering words were somehow drowning the problem in unreality. A bitter laugh was beginning to be heard from American women. They were admired, envied, pitied, theorized over until they were sick of it, offered drastic solutions or silly choices that no one could take seriously. They got all kinds of advice from the growing armies of marriage and child-guidance counselors, psychotherapists, and armchair psychologists, on how to adjust to their role as housewives. No other road to fulfillment was offered to American women in the middle of the twentieth century. Most adjusted to their role and suffered or ignored the problem that has no name. It can be less painful, for a woman, not to hear the strange, dissatisfied voice stirring within her.

It is no longer possible to ignore that voice, to dismiss the desperation of so many American women. This is not what being a woman means, no matter what the experts say. For human suffering there is a reason; perhaps the reason has not been found because the right questions have not been asked, or pressed far enough. I do not accept the answer that there is no problem because American women have luxuries that women in other times and lands never dreamed of; part of the strange newness of the problem is that it cannot be understood in terms of the age-old material problems of man: poverty, sickness, hunger, cold. The women who suffer this problem have a hunger that food cannot fill. It persists in women whose husbands are struggling interns and law clerks, or prosperous doctors and lawyers; in wives of workers and executives who make $5,000 a year or $50,000. It is not caused by lack of material advantages; it may not even be felt by women preoccupied with desperate problems of hunger, poverty, or illness. And women who think it will be solved by more money, a bigger house, a second car, moving to a better suburb, often discover it gets worse.

It is no longer possible today to blame the problem on loss of femininity: to say that education and independence and equality with men have made American women unfeminine. I have heard so many women try to deny this dissatisfied voice within themselves because it does not fit the pretty picture of femininity the experts have given them. I think, in fact, that this is the first clue to the mystery: the problem cannot be understood in the generally accepted terms by which scientists have studied women, doctors have treated them, counselors have advised them, and writers have written about them. Women who suffer this problem, in whom this voice is stirring, have lived their whole lives in the pursuit of feminine fulfillment. They are not career women (although career women may have other problems); they are women whose greatest ambition has been marriage and children. For the oldest of these women, these daughters of the American middle class, no other dream was possible. The ones in their forties and fifties who once had other dreams gave them up and threw themselves joyously into life as housewives. For the youngest, the new wives and mothers, this was the only dream. They are the ones who quit high school and college to marry, or marked time in some job in which they had no real interest until they married. These women are very "feminine" in the usual sense, and yet they still suffer the problem.

Are the women who finished college, the women who once had dreams beyond housewifery, the ones who suffer the most? According to the experts they are, but listen to these four women:

> My days are all busy, and dull, too. All I ever do is mess around. I get up at eight—I make breakfast, so I do the dishes, have lunch, do some more dishes and some laundry

and cleaning in the afternoon. Then it's supper dishes and I get to sit down a few minutes before the children have to be sent to bed. . . . That's all there is to my day. It's just like any other wife's day. Humdrum. The biggest time, I am chasing kids.

Ye Gods, what do I do with my time? Well, I get up at six. I get my son dressed and then give him breakfast. After that I wash dishes and bathe and feed the baby. Then I get lunch and while the children nap, I sew or mend or iron and do all the other things I can't get done before noon. Then I cook supper for the family and my husband watches TV while I do the dishes. After I get the children to bed, I set my hair and then I go to bed.

The problem is always being the children's mommy, or the minister's wife and never being myself.

A film made of any typical morning in my house would look like an old Marx Brothers' comedy. I wash the dishes, rush the older children off to school, dash out in the yard to cultivate the chrysanthemums, run back in to make a phone call about a committee meeting, help the youngest child build a block-house, spend fifteen minutes skimming the newspapers so I can be well-informed, then scamper down to the washing machines where my thrice-weekly laundry includes enough clothes to keep a primitive village going for an entire year. By noon I'm ready for a padded cell. Very little of what I've done has been really necessary or important. Outside pressures lash me through the day. Yet I look upon myself as one of the more relaxed housewives in the neighborhood. Many of my friends are even more frantic. In the past sixty years we have come full circle and the American housewife is once again trapped in a squirrel cage. If the cage is now a modern plate-glass-and-broadloom ranch house or a convenient modern apartment, the situation is no less painful than when her grandmother sat over an embroidery hoop in her gilt-and-plush parlor and muttered angrily about women's rights.

The first two women never went to college. They live in developments in Levittown, New Jersey, and Tacoma, Washington, and were interviewed by a team of sociologists studying workingmen's wives.[2] The third, a minister's wife, wrote on the fifteenth reunion questionnaire of her college that she never had any career ambitions, but wishes now she had.[3] The fourth, who has a Ph.D. in anthropology, is today a Nebraska housewife with three children.[4] Their words seem to indicate that housewives of all educational levels suffer the same feeling of desperation.

The fact is that no one today is muttering angrily about "women's rights," even though more and more women have gone to college. In a recent study of all the classes that have graduated from Barnard College,[5*] a significant minority of earlier graduates blamed their education for making them want "rights," later classes blamed their education for giving them career dreams, but recent graduates blamed the college for making them feel it was not enough simply to be a housewife and mother; they did not want to feel guilty if they did not read books or take part in community activities. But if education is not the cause of the problem, the fact that education somehow festers in these women may be a clue.

If the secret of feminine fulfillment is having children, never have so many women, with the freedom to choose, had so many children, in so few years, so willingly. If the answer is love, never have women searched for love with such determination. And yet there is a growing suspicion that the problem may not be sexual, though it must somehow be related to sex. I have heard from many doctors evidence of new sexual problems between man and wife—sexual hunger in wives so great their husbands cannot satisfy it. "We have made woman a sex creature," said a psychiatrist at the Margaret Sanger[†] marriage counseling clinic. "She has no identity except as a wife and mother. She does not know who she is herself. She waits all day for her husband to come home at night to make her feel alive. And now it is the husband who is not interested. It is terrible for the women, to lie there, night after night, waiting for her husband to make her feel alive." Why is there such a market for books and articles offering sexual advice? The kind of sexual orgasm which Kinsey[‡] found in statistical plenitude in the recent generations of American women does not seem to make this problem go away.

---

[*]   Part of a consortium of colleges referred to as the "The Seven Sisters" that also includes Bryn Mawr, Mount Holyoke, Smith, Radcliffe, Vassar, and Wellesley. The Seven Sister schools, founded in the nineteenth century, were designed to provide an Ivy League education for women who were not admitted into some Ivy League schools until the 1960s. Barnard was the sister school for Columbia College, which did not become coed until 1983.

[†]   Margaret Sanger (1879–1966), the founder of Planned Parenthood (see entry above, p. 10) and its predecessor, the American Birth Control League, was the most important activist on behalf of reproductive rights for women in the twentieth century. She started her efforts during the Progressive era, opening one of the first birth control clinics for immigrant and working-class women in the Lower East Side of New York City. She battled censorship and prison as she tried to provide women with information about contraception and services for reproductive health.

[‡]   Alfred Kinsey (1894–1956), a biologist at Indiana University, published two best-selling and controversial works, *Sexual Behavior in the Human Male* (1948) and *Sexual Behavior in the Human Female* (1953) after interviewing thousands of research subjects in the United States about their sexual practices. Both books were notable for their attention to the varieties of sexual experience, including masturbation, oral sex, extramarital sex, and homosexuality. In contrast with contemporary beliefs about female frigidity, Kinsey reported that 90 percent of women had achieved orgasms by the time they were 35.

On the contrary, new neuroses are being seen among women—
and problems as yet unnamed as neuroses—which Freud and his
followers did not predict, with physical symptoms, anxieties, and
defense mechanisms equal to those caused by sexual repression.
And strange new problems are being reported in the growing generations of children whose mothers were always there, driving them
around, helping them with their homework—an inability to endure
pain or discipline or pursue any self-sustained goal of any sort, a
devastating boredom with life. Educators are increasingly uneasy
about the dependence, the lack of self-reliance, of the boys and
girls who are entering college today. "We fight a continual battle to
make our students assume manhood," said a Columbia dean.

A White House conference was held on the physical and muscular
deterioration of American children: were they being over-nurtured?
Sociologists noted the astounding organization of suburban children's lives: the lessons, parties, entertainments, play and study
groups organized for them. A suburban housewife in Portland, Oregon, wondered why the children "need" Brownies and Boy Scouts
out here. "This is not the slums. The kids out here have the great
outdoors. I think people are so bored, they organize the children,
and then try to hook everyone else on it. And the poor kids have no
time left just to lie on their beds and daydream."

Can the problem that has no name be somehow related to the
domestic routine of the housewife? When a woman tries to put
the problem into words, she often merely describes the daily life
she leads. What is there in this recital of comfortable domestic detail
that could possibly cause such a feeling of desperation? Is she trapped
simply by the enormous demands of her role as modern housewife:
wife, mistress, mother, nurse, consumer, cook, chauffeur; expert on
interior decoration, child care, appliance repair, furniture refinish-
ing, nutrition, and education? Her day is fragmented as she rushes
from dishwasher to washing machine to telephone to dryer to station
wagon to supermarket, and delivers Johnny to the Little League field,
takes Janey to dancing class, gets the lawnmower fixed and meets the
6:45. She can never spend more than 15 minutes on any one thing;
she has no time to read books, only magazines; even if she had time,
she has lost the power to concentrate. At the end of the day, she is
so terribly tired that sometimes her husband has to take over and put
the children to bed.

This terrible tiredness took so many women to doctors in the
1950's that one decided to investigate it. He found, surprisingly, that
his patients suffering from "housewife's fatigue" slept more than an
adult needed to sleep—as much as ten hours a day—and that the
actual energy they expended on housework did not tax their capacity.
The real problem must be something else, he decided—perhaps

boredom. Some doctors told their women patients they must get out of the house for a day, treat themselves to a movie in town. Others prescribed tranquilizers. Many suburban housewives were taking tranquilizers like cough drops. "You wake up in the morning, and you feel as if there's no point in going on another day like this. So you take a tranquilizer because it makes you not care so much that it's pointless."

It is easy to see the concrete details that trap the suburban housewife, the continual demands on her time. But the chains that bind her in her trap are chains in her own mind and spirit. They are chains made up of mistaken ideas and misinterpreted facts, of incomplete truths and unreal choices. They are not easily seen and not easily shaken off.

How can any woman see the whole truth within the bounds of her own life? How can she believe that voice inside herself, when it denies the conventional, accepted truths by which she has been living? And yet the women I have talked to, who are finally listening to that inner voice, seem in some incredible way to be groping through to a truth that has defied the experts.

I think the experts in a great many fields have been holding pieces of that truth under their microscopes for a long time without realizing it. I found pieces of it in certain new research and theoretical developments in psychological, social and biological science whose implications for women seem never to have been examined. I found many clues by talking to suburban doctors, gynecologists, obstetricians, child-guidance clinicians, pediatricians, high-school guidance counselors, college professors, marriage counselors, psychiatrists and ministers—questioning them not on their theories, but on their actual experience in treating American women. I became aware of a growing body of evidence, much of which has not been reported publicly because it does not fit current modes of thought about women—evidence which throws into question the standards of feminine normality, feminine adjustment, feminine fulfillment, and feminine maturity by which most women are still trying to live.

I began to see in a strange new light the American return to early marriage and the large families that are causing the population explosion; the recent movement to natural childbirth and breastfeeding; suburban conformity, and the new neuroses, character pathologies and sexual problems being reported by the doctors. I began to see new dimensions to old problems that have long been taken for granted among women: menstrual difficulties, sexual frigidity, promiscuity, pregnancy fears, childbirth depression, the high incidence of emotional breakdown and suicide among women in their twenties and thirties, the menopause crises, the so-called passivity and immaturity of American men, the discrepancy between women's tested intellectual abilities in childhood and their adult achievement, the changing incidence of adult sexual orgasm in American women, and persistent problems in psychotherapy and in women's education.

If I am right, the problem that has no name stirring in the minds of so many American women today is not a matter of loss of femininity or too much education, or the demands of domesticity. It is far more important than anyone recognizes. It is the key to these other new and old problems which have been torturing women and their husbands and children, and puzzling their doctors and educators for years. It may well be the key to our future as a nation and a culture. We can no longer ignore that voice within women that says: "I want something more than my husband and my children and my home."

2

The Happy Housewife Heroine

Why have so many American wives suffered this nameless aching dissatisfaction for so many years, each one thinking she was alone? "I've got tears in my eyes with sheer relief that my own inner turmoil is shared with other women," a young Connecticut mother wrote me when I first began to put this problem into words.[1] A woman from a town in Ohio wrote: "The times when I felt that the only answer was to consult a psychiatrist, times of anger, bitterness and general frustration too numerous to even mention, I had no idea that hundreds of other women were feeling the same way. I felt so completely alone." A Houston, Texas, housewife wrote: "It has been the feeling of being almost alone with my problem that has made it so hard. I thank God for my family, home and the chance to care for them, but my life couldn't stop there. It is an awakening to know that I'm not an oddity and can stop being ashamed of wanting something more."

That painful guilty silence, and that tremendous relief when a feeling is finally out in the open, are familiar psychological signs. What need, what part of themselves, could so many women today be repressing? In this age after Freud, sex is immediately suspect. But this new stirring in women does not seem to be sex; it is, in fact, much harder for women to talk about than sex. Could there be another need, a part of themselves they have buried as deeply as the Victorian women* buried sex?

---

* Victorian womanhood, or the Cult of True Womanhood, was a prescription or idealized image of womanhood that emerged during the mid-nineteenth century, coinciding with and abetted by the reign of Queen Victoria in Great Britain. According to historian Barbara Welter, the true woman was pious, pure, submissive, and domestic. The appearance of this white, middle-class, and urban idealized version of womanhood also coincided with urbanization, industrialization, and immigration in the United States. This had serious consequences for those who could not or would not conform.

If there is, a woman might not know what it was, any more than the Victorian woman knew she had sexual needs. The image of a good woman by which Victorian ladies lived simply left out sex. Does the image by which modern American women live also leave something out, the proud and public image of the high-school girl going steady, the college girl in love, the suburban housewife with an up-and-coming husband and a station wagon full of children? This image—created by the women's magazines, by advertisements, television, movies, novels, columns and books by experts on marriage and the family, child psychology, sexual adjustment and by the popularizers of sociology and psychoanalysis—shapes women's lives today and mirrors their dreams. It may give a clue to the problem that has no name, as a dream gives a clue to a wish unnamed by the dreamer. In the mind's ear, a geiger counter clicks when the image shows too sharp a discrepancy from reality. A geiger counter clicked in my own inner ear when I could not fit the quiet desperation of so many women into the picture of the modern American housewife that I myself was helping to create, writing for the women's magazines. What is missing from the image which shapes the American woman's pursuit of fulfillment as a wife and mother? What is missing from the image that mirrors and creates the identity of women in America today?

In the early 1960's *McCall's* has been the fastest growing of the women's magazines. Its contents are a fairly accurate representation of the image of the American woman presented, and in part created, by the large-circulation magazines. Here are the complete editorial contents of a typical issue of *McCall's* (July, 1960):

1. A lead article on "increasing baldness in women," caused by too much brushing and dyeing.
2. A long poem in primer-size type about a child, called "A Boy Is A Boy."
3. A short story about how a teenager who doesn't go to college gets a man away from a bright college girl.
4. A short story about the minute sensations of a baby throwing his bottle out of the crib.
5. The first of a two-part intimate "up-to-date" account by the Duke of Windsor on "How the Duchess and I now live and spend our time. The influence of clothes on me and vice versa."
6. A short story about a nineteen-year-old girl sent to a charm school to learn how to bat her eyelashes and lose at tennis. ("You're nineteen, and by normal American standards, I now am entitled to have you taken off my hands, legally and

financially, by some beardless youth who will spirit you away to a one-and-a-half-room apartment in the Village while he learns the chicanery of selling bonds. And no beardless youth is going to do that as long as you volley to his backhand.")

7. The story of a honeymoon couple commuting between separate bedrooms after an argument over gambling at Las Vegas.

8. An article on "how to overcome an inferiority complex."

9. A story called "Wedding Day."

10. The story of a teenager's mother who learns how to dance rock-and-roll.

11. Six pages of glamorous pictures of models in maternity clothes.

12. Four glamorous pages on "reduce the way the models do."

13. An article on airline delays.

14. Patterns for home sewing.

15. Patterns with which to make "Folding Screens—Bewitching Magic."

16. An article called "An Encyclopedic Approach to Finding a Second Husband."

17. A "barbecue bonanza," dedicated "to the Great American Mister who stands, chef's cap on head, fork in hand, on terrace or back porch, in patio or backyard anywhere in the land, watching his roast turning on the spit. And to his wife, without whom (sometimes) the barbecue could never be the smashing summer success it undoubtedly is . . ."

There were also the regular front-of-the-book "service" columns on new drug and medicine developments, child-care facts, columns by Clare Luce and by Eleanor Roosevelt,* and "Pats and Pans," a column of readers' letters.

The image of woman that emerges from this big, pretty magazine is young and frivolous, almost childlike; fluffy and feminine; pas-

---

* Eleanor Roosevelt (1884–1962), wife of President Franklin Delano Roosevelt and First Lady of the United States between 1933 and 1945. She had her own active political agenda, however, working for reform measures to aid children, women, unemployed workers, minority groups, and poor people. After Franklin Roosevelt's death in 1945, Eleanor Roosevelt remained a visible liberal activist. She was appointed one of the first delegates to the United Nations and helped draft the UN Declaration of Human Rights; she also remained active in politics in the Democratic Party. Between 1935 and 1962, she wrote a newspaper column, "My Day," and published several books. See pp. 364–65 for her description of her participation in the Commission on the Status of Women. Clare Boothe Luce (1903–1987), journalist and playwright who worked with her husband, Henry Luce, to develop Life magazine, which became one of the most popular and influential mass-market magazines in the world. In 1940, Luce became involved in Republican politics, and she was elected to U.S. Congress from 1942 to 1946. From 1952 to 1957, she served as U.S. ambassador to Italy, the first woman to represent the United States in a major foreign embassy.

sive; gaily content in a world of bedroom and kitchen, sex, babies, and home. The magazine surely does not leave out sex; the only passion, the only pursuit, the only goal a woman is permitted is the pursuit of a man. It is crammed full of food, clothing, cosmetics, furniture, and the physical bodies of young women, but where is the world of thought and ideas, the life of the mind and spirit? In the magazine image, women do no work except housework and work to keep their bodies beautiful and to get and keep a man.

This was the image of the American woman in the year Castro led a revolution in Cuba and men were trained to travel into outer space; the year that the African continent brought forth new nations, and a plane whose speed is greater than the speed of sound broke up a Summit Conference; the year artists picketed a great museum in protest against the hegemony of abstract art; physicists explored the concept of anti-matter; astronomers, because of new radio telescopes, had to alter their concepts of the expanding universe; biologists made a breakthrough in the fundamental chemistry of life; and Negro youth in Southern schools forced the United States, for the first time since the Civil War, to face a moment of democratic truth. But this magazine, published for over 5,000,000 American women, almost all of whom have been through high school and nearly half to college, contained almost no mention of the world beyond the home. In the second half of the twentieth century in America, woman's world was confined to her own body and beauty, the charming of man, the bearing of babies, and the physical care and serving of husband, children, and home. And this was no anomaly of a single issue of a single women's magazine.

I sat one night at a meeting of magazine writers, mostly men, who work for all kinds of magazines, including women's magazines. The main speaker was a leader of the desegregation battle. Before he spoke, another man outlined the needs of the large women's magazine he edited:

> Our readers are housewives, full time. They're not interested in the broad public issues of the day. They are not interested in national or international affairs. They are only interested in the family and the home. They aren't interested in politics, unless it's related to an immediate need in the home, like the price of coffee. Humor? Has to be gentle, they don't get satire. Travel? We have almost completely dropped it. Education? That's a problem. Their own education level is going up. They've generally all had a high-school education and many, college. They're tremendously interested in education for their children—fourth-grade arithmetic. You just can't write about ideas or broad issues of the day for women. That's why we're publishing 90 per cent service now and 10 per cent general interest.

Another editor agreed, adding plaintively: "Can't you give us something else besides 'there's death in your medicine cabinet'? Can't any of you dream up a new crisis for women? We're always interested in sex, of course."

At this point, the writers and editors spent an hour listening to Thurgood Marshall* on the inside story of the desegregation battle, and its possible effect on the presidential election. "Too bad I can't run that story," one editor said. "But you just can't link it to woman's world."

As I listened to them, a German phrase echoed in my mind— "*Kinder, Kuche, Kirche*,"† the slogan by which the Nazis decreed that women must once again be confined to their biological role. But this was not Nazi Germany. This was America. The whole world lies open to American women. Why, then, does the image deny the world? Why does it limit women to "one passion, one role, one occupation?" Not long ago, women dreamed and fought for equality, their own place in the world. What happened to their dreams; when did women decide to give up the world and go back home?

A geologist brings up a core of mud from the bottom of the ocean and sees layers of sediment as sharp as a razor blade deposited over the years—clues to changes in the geological evolution of the earth so vast that they would go unnoticed during the lifespan of a single man. I sat for many days in the New York Public Library, going back through bound volumes of American women's magazines for the last twenty years. I found a change in the image of the American woman, and in the boundaries of the woman's world, as sharp and puzzling as the changes revealed in cores of ocean sediment.

In 1939, the heroines of women's magazine stories were not always young, but in a certain sense they were younger than their fictional counterparts today. They were young in the same way that the American hero has always been young: they were New Women, creating with a gay determined spirit a new identity for women—a life of their own. There was an aura about them of becoming, of moving into a future that was going to be different from the past. The majority of heroines in the four major women's magazines (then *Ladies' Home Journal, McCall's, Good Housekeeping, Woman's Home Companion*) were career women—happily, proudly, adventurously,

---

* Thurgood Marshall (1908–1993), the first African American to sit on the United States Supreme Court, and civil rights lawyer who worked for the National Association for the Advancement of Colored People (NAACP). He won numerous cases against segregation, the most famous and significant of which was *Brown v. Board of Education of Topeka* (1954).
† "Children, kitchen, and church" (German).

attractively career women—who loved and were loved by men. And the spirit, courage, independence, determination—the strength of character they showed in their work as nurses, teachers, artists, actresses, copywriters, saleswomen—were part of their charm. There was a definite aura that their individuality was something to be admired, not unattractive to men, that men were drawn to them as much for their spirit and character as for their looks.

These were the mass women's magazines—in their heyday. The stories were conventional: girl-meets-boy or girl-gets-boy. But very often this was not the major theme of the story. These heroines were usually marching toward some goal or vision of their own, struggling with some problem of work or the world, when they found their man. And this New Woman, less fluffily feminine, so independent and determined to find a new life of her own, was the heroine of a different kind of love story. She was less aggressive in pursuit of a man. Her passionate involvement with the world, her own sense of herself as an individual, her self-reliance, gave a different flavor to her relationship with the man.

The heroine and hero of one of these stories meet and fall in love at an ad agency where they both work. "I don't want to put you in a garden behind a wall," the hero says. "I want you to walk with me hand in hand, and together we could accomplish whatever we wanted to" ("A Dream to Share," *Redbook*, January, 1939).

These New Women were almost never housewives; in fact, the stories usually ended before they had children. They were young because the future was open. But they seemed, in another sense, much older, more mature than the childlike, kittenish young housewife heroines today. One, for example, is a nurse ("Mother-in-Law," *Ladies' Home Journal*, June, 1939). "She was, he thought, very lovely. She hadn't an ounce of picture book prettiness, but there was strength in her hands, pride in her carriage and nobility in the lift of her chin, in her blue eyes. She had been on her own ever since she left training, nine years ago. She had earned her way, she need consider nothing but her heart."

One heroine runs away from home when her mother insists she must make her debut instead of going on an expedition as a geologist. Her passionate determination to live her own life does not keep this New Woman from loving a man, but it makes her rebel from her parents; just as the young hero often must leave home to grow up. "You've got more courage than any girl I ever saw. You have what it takes," says the boy who helps her get away ("Have a Good Time, Dear," *Ladies' Home Journal*, May, 1939).

Often, there was a conflict between some commitment to her work and the man. But the moral, in 1939, was that if she kept her commitment to herself, she did not lose the man, if he was the right man. A young widow ("Between the Dark and the Daylight," *Ladies' Home Journal*, February, 1939) sits in her office, debating whether to stay and correct the important mistake she has made on the job, or keep her date with a man. She thinks back on her marriage, her baby, her husband's death . . . "the time afterward which held the struggle for clear judgment, not being afraid of new and better jobs, of having confidence in one's decisions." How can the boss expect her to give up her date! But she stays on the job. "They'd put their life's blood into this campaign. She couldn't let him down." She finds her man, too—the boss!

These stories may not have been great literature. But the identity of their heroines seemed to say something about the housewives who, then as now, read the women's magazines. These magazines were not written for career women. The New Woman heroines were the ideal of yesterday's housewives; they reflected the dreams, mirrored the yearning for identity and the sense of possibility that existed for women then. And if women could not have these dreams for themselves, they wanted their daughters to have them. They wanted their daughters to be more than housewives, to go out in the world that had been denied them.

It is like remembering a long-forgotten dream, to recapture the memory of what a career meant to women before "career woman" became a dirty word in America. Jobs meant money, of course, at the end of the depression. But the readers of these magazines were not the women who got the jobs; career meant more than job. It seemed to mean doing something, being somebody yourself, not just existing in and through others.

I found the last clear note of the passionate search for individual identity that a career seems to have symbolized in the pre-1950 decades in a story called "Sarah and the Seaplane" (*Ladies' Home Journal*, February, 1949). Sarah, who for nineteen years has played the part of docile daughter, is secretly learning to fly. She misses her flying lesson to accompany her mother on a round of social calls. An elderly doctor houseguest says: "My dear Sarah, every day, all the time, you are committing suicide. It's a greater crime than not pleasing others, not doing justice to yourself." Sensing some secret, he asks if she is in love. "She found it difficult to answer. In love? In love with the good-natured, the beautiful Henry [the flying teacher]? In love with the flashing water and the lift of wings at the instant of freedom, and the vision of the smiling, limitless world? 'Yes,' she answered, 'I think I am.'"

The next morning, Sarah solos. Henry "stepped away, slamming the cabin door shut, and swung the ship about for her. She was alone. There was a heady moment when everything she had learned left her, when she had to adjust herself to be alone, entirely alone in the familiar cabin. Then she drew a deep breath and suddenly a wonderful sense of competence made her sit erect and smiling. She was alone! She was answerable to herself alone, and she was sufficient.

"'I can do it!' she told herself aloud. . . . The wind flew back from the floats in glittering streaks, and then effortlessly the ship lifted itself free and soared." Even her mother can't stop her now from getting her flying license. She is not "afraid of discovering my own way of life." In bed that night she smiles sleepily, remembering how Henry had said, "You're my girl."

"Henry's girl! She smiled. No, she was not Henry's girl. She was Sarah. And that was sufficient. And with such a late start it would be some time before she got to know herself. Half in a dream now, she wondered if at the end of that time she would need someone else and who it would be."

And then suddenly the image blurs. The New Woman, soaring free, hesitates in midflight, shivers in all that blue sunlight and rushes back to the cozy walls of home. In the same year that Sarah soloed, the *Ladies' Home Journal* printed the prototype of the innumerable paeans to "Occupation: housewife" that started to appear in the women's magazines, paeans that resounded throughout the fifties. They usually begin with a woman complaining that when she has to write "housewife" on the census blank, she gets an inferiority complex. ("When I write it I realize that here I am, a middle-aged woman, with a university education, and I've never made anything out of my life. I'm just a housewife.") Then the author of the paean, who somehow never is a housewife (in this case, Dorothy Thompson,* newspaper woman, foreign correspondent, famous columnist, in *Ladies' Home Journal*, March, 1949), roars with laughter. The trouble with you, she scolds, is you don't realize you are expert in a dozen careers, simultaneously. "You might write: business manager, cook, nurse, chauffeur, dressmaker, interior decorator, accountant, caterer, teacher, private secretary—or just put down philanthropist. . . . All your life you have been giving away your energies, your skills, your talents, your services, for love." But still, the housewife complains, I'm nearly fifty and I've never done what I hoped to do in my youth—music—I've wasted my college education.

* Dorothy Thompson (1893–1961), one of the first female political columnists. After attending college and working as a suffrage activist in New York, Thompson lived in Europe during the 1920s and 1940s, where she reported on the most important international news of the day. She was an outspoken and respected columnist who alerted Americans to social injustice around the world.

Ho-ho, laughs Miss Thompson, aren't your children musical because of you, and all those struggling years while your husband was finishing his great work, didn't you keep a charming home on $3,000 a year, and make all your children's clothes and your own, and paper the living room yourself, and watch the markets like a hawk for bargains? And in time off, didn't you type and proofread your husband's manuscripts, plan festivals to make up the church deficit, play piano duets with the children to make practicing more fun, read their books in high school to follow their study? "But all this vicarious living—through others," the housewife sighs. "As vicarious as Napoleon Bonaparte," Miss Thompson scoffs, "or a Queen. I simply refuse to share your self-pity. You are one of the most successful women I know."

As for not earning any money, the argument goes, let the housewife compute the cost of her services. Women can save more money by their managerial talents inside the home than they can bring into it by outside work. As for woman's spirit being broken by the boredom of household tasks, maybe the genius of some women has been thwarted, but "a world full of feminine genius, but poor in children, would come rapidly to an end. . . . Great men have great mothers."

And the American housewife is reminded that Catholic countries in the Middle Ages "elevated the gentle and inconspicuous Mary into the Queen of Heaven, and built their loveliest cathedrals to 'Notre Dame—Our Lady.' . . . The homemaker, the nurturer, the creator of children's environment is the constant recreator of culture, civilization, and virtue. Assuming that she is doing well that great managerial task and creative activity, let her write her occupation proudly: 'housewife.'"

In 1949, the *Ladies' Home Journal* also ran Margaret Mead's* *Male and Female.* All the magazines were echoing Farnham and Lundberg's *Modern Woman: The Lost Sex,*† which came out in 1942, with its warning that careers and higher education were leading to the "masculinization of women with enormously dangerous

---

*   Margaret Mead (1901–1978), a cultural anthropologist, made important contributions to understanding adolescence, gender, and sexuality in comparative perspective in her *Coming of Age in Samoa* (1928). By the 1950s, Mead was a public intellectual commenting on a variety of issues to a mass audience while she served as a curator at the American Museum of Natural History in New York City. See Mead's article appearing in *Life* magazine in 1956 on pp. 345–46.

†   Dr. Marynia F. Farnham, a psychiatrist, collaborated with Ferdinand Lundberg to create *Modern Woman: The Lost Sex*, one of the most powerful expressions of the feminine mystique. Originally published in 1942 and republished throughout the 1940s and 1950s, this book's central thesis is that "contemporary women in very large numbers are psychologically disordered and that their disorder is having terrible social and personal effects involving men in all departments of their lives as well as women." Women were sick because they were abandoning their natural roles as women. See excerpts from this book on pp. 346–50 and Joanne Meyerowitz's article on pp. 474–80 where she addresses the impact that *Modern Woman* had during the 1950s.

consequences to the home, the children dependent on it and to the ability of the woman, as well as her husband, to obtain sexual gratification."

And so the feminine mystique began to spread through the land, grafted onto old prejudices and comfortable conventions which so easily give the past a stranglehold on the future. Behind the new mystique were concepts and theories deceptive in their sophistication and their assumption of accepted truth. These theories were supposedly so complex that they were inaccessible to all but a few initiates, and therefore irrefutable. It will be necessary to break through this wall of mystery and look more closely at these complex concepts, these accepted truths, to understand fully what has happened to American women.

The feminine mystique says that the highest value and the only commitment for women is the fulfillment of their own femininity. It says that the great mistake of Western culture, through most of its history, has been the undervaluation of this femininity. It says this femininity is so mysterious and intuitive and close to the creation and origin of life that man-made science may never be able to understand it. But however special and different, it is in no way inferior to the nature of man; it may even in certain respects be superior. The mistake, says the mystique, the root of women's troubles in the past is that women envied men, women tried to be like men, instead of accepting their own nature, which can find fulfillment only in sexual passivity, male domination, and nurturing maternal love.

But the new image this mystique gives to American women is the old image: "Occupation: housewife." The new mystique makes the housewife-mothers, who never had a chance to be anything else, the model for all women; it presupposes that history has reached a final and glorious end in the here and now, as far as women are concerned. Beneath the sophisticated trappings, it simply makes certain concrete, finite, domestic aspects of feminine existence—as it was lived by women whose lives were confined, by necessity, to cooking, cleaning, washing, bearing children—into a religion, a pattern by which all women must now live or deny their femininity.

Fulfillment as a woman had only one definition for American women after 1949—the housewife-mother. As swiftly as in a dream, the image of the American woman as a changing, growing individual in a changing world was shattered. Her solo flight to find her own identity was forgotten in the rush for the security of togetherness. Her limitless world shrunk to the cozy walls of home.

The transformation, reflected in the pages of the women's magazines, was sharply visible in 1949 and progressive through the fifties. "Femininity Begins at Home," "It's a Man's World Maybe," "Have

Babies While You're Young," "How to Snare a Male," "Should I Stop Work When We Marry?" "Are You Training Your Daughter to Be a Wife?" "Careers at Home," "Do Women Have to Talk So Much?" "Why GI's Prefer Those German Girls," "What Women Can Learn from Mother Eve," "Really a Man's World, Politics," "How to Hold On to a Happy Marriage," "Don't Be Afraid to Marry Young," "The Doctor Talks about Breast-Feeding," "Our Baby was Born at Home," "Cooking to Me Is Poetry," "The Business of Running a Home."

By the end of 1949, only one out of three heroines in the women's magazines was a career woman—and she was shown in the act of renouncing her career and discovering that what she really wanted to be was a housewife. In 1958, and again in 1959, I went through issue after issue of the three major women's magazines (the fourth, *Woman's Home Companion*, had died) without finding a single heroine who had a career, a commitment to any work, art, profession, or mission in the world, other than "Occupation: housewife." Only one in a hundred heroines had a job; even the young unmarried heroines no longer worked except at snaring a husband.[2]

These new happy housewife heroines seem strangely younger than the spirited career girls of the thirties and forties. They seem to get younger all the time—in looks, and a childlike kind of dependence. They have no vision of the future, except to have a baby. The only active growing figure in their world is the child. The housewife heroines are forever young, because their own image *ends* in childbirth. Like Peter Pan, they must remain young while their children grow up with the world. They must keep on having babies, because the feminine mystique says there is no other way for a woman to be a heroine. Here is a typical specimen from a story called "The Sandwich Maker" (*Ladies' Home Journal*, April, 1959). She took home economics in college, learned how to cook, never held a job, and still plays the child bride, though she now has three children of her own. Her problem is money. "Oh, nothing boring, like taxes or reciprocal trade agreements, or foreign aid programs. I leave all that economic jazz to my constitutionally elected representative in Washington, heaven help him."

The problem is her $42.10 allowance. She hates having to ask her husband for money every time she needs a pair of shoes, but he won't trust her with a charge account. "Oh, how I yearned for a little money of my own! Not much, really. A few hundred a year would have done it. Just enough to meet a friend for lunch occasionally, to indulge in extravagantly colored stockings, a few small items, without having to appeal to Charley. But, alas, Charley was right. I had never earned a dollar in my life, and had no idea of how money was made. So all I did for a long time was brood, as I continued with my cooking, cleaning, cooking, washing, ironing, cooking."

At last the solution comes—she will take orders for sandwiches from other men at her husband's plant. She earns $52.50 a week, except that she forgets to count costs, and she doesn't remember what a gross is so she has to hide 8,640 sandwich bags behind the furnace. Charley says she's making the sandwiches too fancy. She explains: "If it's only ham on rye, then I'm just a sandwich maker, and I'm not interested. But the extras, the special touches—well, they make it sort of creative." So she chops, wraps, peels, seals, spreads bread, starting at dawn and never finished, for $9.00 net, until she is disgusted by the smell of food, and finally staggers downstairs after a sleepless night to slice a salami for the eight gaping lunch boxes. "It was too much. Charley came down just then, and after one quick look at me, ran for a glass of water." She realizes that she is going to have another baby.

"Charley's first coherent words were 'I'll cancel your lunch orders. You're a mother. That's your job. You don't have to earn money, too.' It was all so beautifully simple! 'Yes, boss,' I murmured obediently, frankly relieved." That night he brings her home a checkbook; he will trust her with a joint account. So she decides just to keep quiet about the 8,640 sandwich bags. Anyhow, she'll have used them up, making sandwiches for four children to take to school, by the time the youngest is ready for college.

The road from Sarah and the seaplane to the sandwich maker was traveled in only ten years. In those ten years, the image of American woman seems to have suffered a schizophrenic split. And the split in the image goes much further than the savage obliteration of career from women's dreams.

In an earlier time, the image of woman was also split in two—the good, pure woman on the pedestal, and the whore of the desires of the flesh. The split in the new image opens a different fissure—the feminine woman, whose goodness includes the desires of the flesh, and the career woman, whose evil includes every desire of the separate self. The new feminine morality story is the exorcising of the forbidden career dream, the heroine's victory over Mephistopheles: the devil, first in the form of a career woman, who threatens to take away the heroine's husband or child, and finally, the devil inside the heroine herself, the dream of independence, the discontent of spirit, and even the feeling of a separate identity that must be exorcised to win or keep the love of husband and child.

In a story in *Redbook* ("A Man Who Acted Like a Husband," November, 1957) the child-bride heroine, "a little freckle-faced brunette" whose nickname is "Junior," is visited by her old college roommate. The roommate Kay is "a man's girl, really, with a good head for business . . . she wore her polished mahogany hair in a high chignon, speared with two chopstick affairs." Kay is not only divorced, but she has also left her child with his grandmother while she works in television. This career-woman-devil tempts Junior with the lure of a job to keep her from breast-feeding her baby. She even restrains the young mother from going to her baby when he cries at 2 A.M. But she gets her comeuppance when George, the husband, discovers the crying baby uncovered, in a freezing wind from an open window, with blood running down its cheek. Kay, reformed and repentant, plays hookey from her job to go get her own child and start life anew. And Junior, gloating at the 2 A.M. feeding—"I'm glad, glad, glad I'm just a housewife"— starts to dream about the baby, growing up to be a housewife, too.

With the career woman out of the way, the housewife with interests in the community becomes the devil to be exorcised. Even PTA takes on a suspect connotation, not to mention interest in some international cause (see "Almost a Love Affair," *McCall's*, November, 1955). The housewife who simply has a mind of her own is the next to go. The heroine of "I Didn't Want to Tell You" (*McCall's*, January, 1958) is shown balancing the checkbook by herself and arguing with her husband about a small domestic detail. It develops that she is losing her husband to a "helpless little widow" whose main appeal is that she can't "think straight" about an insurance policy or mortgage. The betrayed wife says: "She must have sex appeal and what weapon has a wife against that?" But her best friend tells her: "You're making this too simple. You're forgetting how helpless Tania can be, and how grateful to the man who helps her . . ."

"I couldn't be a clinging vine if I tried," the wife says. "I had a better than average job after I left college and I was always a pretty independent person. I'm not a helpless little woman and I can't pretend to be." But she learns, that night. She hears a noise that might be a burglar; even though she knows it's only a mouse, she calls helplessly to her husband, and wins him back. As he comforts her pretended panic, she murmurs that, of course, he was right in their argument that morning. "She lay still in the soft bed, smiling in sweet, secret satisfaction, scarcely touched with guilt."

The end of the road, in an almost literal sense, is the disappearance of the heroine altogether, as a separate self and the subject of her own story. The end of the road is togetherness, where the woman has no independent self to hide even in guilt; she exists only for and through her husband and children.

Coined by the publishers of *McCall's* in 1954, the concept "togetherness" was seized upon avidly as a movement of spiritual significance by advertisers, ministers, newspaper editors. For a time, it was elevated into virtually a national purpose. But very quickly there was sharp social criticism, and bitter jokes about "togetherness" as a substitute for larger human goals—for men. Women were taken to task for making their husbands do housework, instead of letting them pioneer in the nation and the world. Why, it was asked, should men with the capacities of statesmen, anthropologists, physicists, poets, have to wash dishes and diaper babies on weekday evenings or Saturday mornings when they might use those extra hours to fulfill larger commitments to their society?

Significantly, critics resented only that men were being asked to share "woman's world." Few questioned the boundaries of this world for women. No one seemed to remember that women were once thought to have the capacity and vision of statesmen, poets, and physicists. Few saw the big lie of togetherness for women.

Consider the Easter 1954 issue of *McCall's* which announced the new era of togetherness, sounding the requiem for the days when women fought for and won political equality, and the women's magazines "helped you to carve out large areas of living formerly forbidden to your sex." The new way of life in which "men and women in ever-increasing numbers are marrying at an earlier age, having children at an earlier age, rearing larger families and gaining their deepest satisfaction" from their own homes, is one which "men, women and children are achieving together . . . not as women alone, or men alone, isolated from one another, but as a family, sharing a common experience."

The picture essay detailing that way of life is called "a man's place is in the home." It describes, as the new image and ideal, a New Jersey couple with three children in a gray-shingle split-level house. Ed and Carol have "centered their lives almost completely around their children and their home." They are shown shopping at the supermarket, carpentering, dressing the children, making breakfast together. "Then Ed joins the members of his car pool and heads for the office."

Ed, the husband, chooses the color scheme for the house and makes the major decorating decisions. The chores Ed likes are listed: putter around the house, make things, paint, select furniture, rugs and draperies, dry dishes, read to the children and put them to bed, work in the garden, feed and dress and bathe the children, attend PTA meetings, cook, buy clothes for his wife, buy groceries.

Ed doesn't like these chores: dusting, vacuuming, finishing jobs he's started, hanging draperies, washing pots and pans and dishes, picking up after the children, shoveling snow or mowing the lawn, changing diapers, taking the baby-sitter home, doing the laundry, ironing. Ed, of course, does not do these chores.

For the sake of every member of the family, the family needs a head. This means Father, not Mother. . . . Children of both sexes need to learn, recognize and respect the abilities and functions of each sex. . . . He is not just a substitute mother, even though he's ready and willing to do his share of bathing, feeding, comforting, playing. He is a link with the outside world he works in. If in that world he is interested, courageous, tolerant, constructive, he will pass on these values to his children.

There were many agonized editorial sessions, in those days at *McCall's.* "Suddenly, everybody was looking for this spiritual significance in togetherness, expecting us to make some mysterious religious movement out of the life everyone had been leading for the last five years—crawling into the home, turning their backs on the world—but we never could find a way of showing it that wasn't a monstrosity of dullness," a former *McCall's* editor reminisces. "It always boiled down to, goody, goody, goody, Daddy is out there in the garden barbecuing. We put men in the fashion pictures and the food pictures, and even the perfume pictures. But we were stifled by it editorially.

"We had articles by psychiatrists that we couldn't use because they would have blown it wide open: all those couples propping their whole weight on their kids. But what else could you do with togetherness but child care? We were pathetically grateful to find anything else where we could show father photographed with mother. Sometimes, we used to wonder what would happen to women, with men taking over the decorating, child care, cooking, all the things that used to be hers alone. But we couldn't show women getting out of the home and having a career. The irony is, what we meant to do was to stop editing for women as women, and edit for the men and women together. We wanted to edit for people, not women."

But forbidden to join man in the world, can women be people? Forbidden independence, they finally are swallowed in an image of such passive dependence that they want men to make the decisions, even in the home. The frantic illusion that togetherness can impart a spiritual content to the dullness of domestic routine, the need for a religious movement to make up for the lack of identity, betrays the measure of women's loss and the emptiness of the image. Could making men share the housework compensate women for their loss of the world? Could vacuuming the living-room floor together give the housewife some mysterious new purpose in life?

In 1956, at the peak of togetherness, the bored editors of *McCall's* ran a little article called "The Mother Who Ran Away." To their amazement, it brought the highest readership of any article they had ever run. "It was our moment of truth," said a former editor. "We suddenly realized that all those women at home with their three and a half children were miserably unhappy."

But by then the new image of American woman, "Occupation: housewife," had hardened into a mystique, unquestioned and permitting no questions, shaping the very reality it distorted.

By the time I started writing for women's magazines, in the fifties, it was simply taken for granted by editors, and accepted as an immutable fact of life by writers, that women were not interested in politics, life outside the United States, national issues, art, science, ideas, adventure, education, or even their own communities, except where they could be sold through their emotions as wives and mothers.

Politics, for women, became Mamie's clothes and the Nixons'* home life. Out of conscience, a sense of duty, the *Ladies' Home Journal* might run a series like "Political Pilgrim's Progress," showing women trying to improve their children's schools and playgrounds. But even approaching politics through mother love did not really interest women, it was thought in the trade. Everyone knew those readership percentages. An editor of *Redbook* ingeniously tried to bring the bomb down to the feminine level by showing the emotions of a wife whose husband sailed into a contaminated area.

"Women can't take an idea, an issue, pure," men who edited the mass women's magazines agreed. "It has to be translated in terms they can understand as women." This was so well understood by those who wrote for women's magazines that a natural childbirth expert submitted an article to a leading woman's magazine called "How to Have a Baby in an Atom Bomb Shelter." "The article was not well written," an editor told me, "or we might have bought it." According to the mystique, women, in their mysterious femininity, might be interested in the concrete biological details of having a baby in a bomb shelter, but never in the abstract idea of the bomb's power to destroy the human race.

Such a belief, of course, becomes a self-fulfilling prophecy. In 1960, a perceptive social psychologist showed me some sad statistics which seemed to prove unmistakably that American women under thirty-five are not interested in politics. "They may have the vote, but they don't dream about running for office," he told me. "If you write a political piece, they won't read it. You have to translate it into issues they can understand—romance, pregnancy, nursing, home furnishings, clothes. Run an article on the economy, or the race

* Richard Milhous Nixon (1913–1994), Dwight D. Eisenhower's vice president between 1952 and 1960. He later went on to win the presidency himself in 1968 and 1972, although he resigned in 1974 because of the Watergate scandal. Patricia Nixon (1912–1993) promoted volunteerism as First Lady. *Mamie's*: Mamie Doud Eisenhower (1896–1979), wife of Dwight D. Eisenhower, Republican president of the United States between 1952 and 1960, exemplified the proper American housewife and hostess.

question, civil rights, and you'd think that women had never heard of them."

Maybe they hadn't heard of them. Ideas are not like instincts of the blood that spring into the mind intact. They are communicated by education, by the printed word. The new young housewives, who leave high school or college to marry, do not read books, the psychological surveys say. They only read magazines. Magazines today assume women are not interested in ideas. But going back to the bound volumes in the library, I found in the thirties and forties that the mass-circulation magazines like *Ladies' Home Journal* carried hundreds of articles about the world outside the home. "The first inside story of American diplomatic relations preceding declared war"; "Can the U. S. Have Peace After This War?" by Walter Lippman; "Stalin at Midnight," by Harold Stassen; "General Stilwell Reports on China"; articles about the last days of Czechoslovakia by Vincent Sheean; the persecution of Jews in Germany; the New Deal; Carl Sandburg's account of Lincoln's assassination; Faulkner's stories of Mississippi, and Margaret Sanger's battle for birth control.

In the 1950's they printed virtually no articles except those that serviced women as housewives, or described women as housewives, or permitted a purely feminine identification like the Duchess of Windsor or Princess Margaret. "If we get an article about a woman who does anything adventurous, out of the way, something by herself, you know, we figure she must be terribly aggressive, neurotic," a *Ladies' Home Journal* editor told me. Margaret Sanger would never get in today.

In 1960, I saw statistics that showed that women under thirty-five could not identify with a spirited heroine of a story who worked in an ad agency and persuaded the boy to stay and fight for his principles in the big city instead of running home to the security of a family business. Nor could these new young housewives identify with a young minister, acting on his belief in defiance of convention. But they had no trouble at all identifying with a young man paralyzed at eighteen. ("I regained consciousness to discover that I could not move or even speak. I could wiggle only one finger of one hand." With help from faith and a psychiatrist, "I am now finding reasons to live as fully as possible.")

Does it say something about the new housewife readers that, as any editor can testify, they can identify completely with the victims of blindness, deafness, physical maiming, cerebral palsy, paralysis, cancer, or approaching death? Such articles about people who cannot see or speak or move have been an enduring staple of the women's magazines in the era of "Occupation: housewife." They are told with infinitely realistic detail over and over again, replacing the articles about the nation, the world, ideas, issues, art and science; replacing the stories about adventurous spirited women. And whether the victim is man, woman or child, whether the living death is incurable cancer or creeping paralysis, the housewife reader can identify.

Writing for these magazines, I was continually reminded by editors "that women *have* to identify." Once I wanted to write an article about an artist. So I wrote about her cooking and marketing and falling in love with her husband, and painting a crib for her baby. I had to leave out the hours she spent painting pictures, her serious work—and the way she felt about it. You could sometimes get away with writing about a woman who was not really a housewife, if you made her *sound* like a housewife, if you left out her commitment to the world outside the home, or the private vision of mind or spirit that she pursued. In February, 1949, the *Ladies' Home Journal* ran a feature, "Poet's Kitchen," showing Edna St. Vincent Millay* cooking. "Now I expect to hear no more about housework's being beneath anyone, for if one of the greatest poets of our day, and any day, can find beauty in simple household tasks, this is the end of the old controversy."

The one "career woman" who was always welcome in the pages of the women's magazines was the actress. But her image also underwent a remarkable change: from a complex individual of fiery temper, inner depth, and a mysterious blend of spirit and sexuality, to a sexual object, a babyface bride, or a housewife. Think of Greta Garbo, for instance, and Marlene Dietrich, Bette Davis, Rosalind Russell, Katharine Hepburn.[†] Then think of Marilyn Monroe, Debbie Reynolds, Brigitte Bardot,[‡] and "I Love Lucy."

When you wrote about an actress for a women's magazine, you wrote about her as a housewife. You never showed her doing or enjoying her work as an actress, unless she eventually paid for it by losing her husband or her child, or otherwise admitting failure as a

---

[*] Edna St. Vincent Millay (1892–1950), writer, feminist, and champion of sexual freedom for women. She is associated with the sexual liberation of the "New Woman" of the Roaring Twenties. Millay attended Vassar and was the first woman to receive the Pulitzer Prize for poetry.

[†] Although they all had different personae, these movie stars of the 1930s and 1940s were all known for their independence, intelligence, strength, and ability to hold their own with men onscreen. Greta Garbo (1905–1990) and Marlene Dietrich (1901–1992) were both famous for their sexual ambiguity on- and off-screen, for example, while Bette Davis (1908–1989), celebrated for her dramatic roles, played strong-willed characters. Rosalind Russell (1911–1976) and Katharine Hepburn (1907–2003) sparred as equals with male counterparts in romantic comedies like *Adam's Rib* and *The Front Page*.

[‡] Brigitte Bardot (b. 1934), French actress of the 1950s and 1960s. She became a sex symbol in the film *Et Dieu Crea la Femme* (1956; *And God Created Woman*) with a persona that juxtaposed her voluptuous figure with a girlish voice and demeanor, as well as innocent pleasure in her own body. *Debbie Reynolds* (b. 1932), movie star of the 1950s and 1960s. Her persona in Hollywood films like *Singin' in the Rain* (1952) and *The Tender Trap* (1955) was that of the "girl next door," sweet, pretty, perky, and nonthreatening.

woman. A *Redbook* profile of Judy Holliday* (June, 1957) described how "a brilliant woman begins to find in her work the joy she never found in life." On the screen, we are told, she plays "with warmth and conviction the part of a mature, intelligent wife and expectant mother, a role unlike anything she had previously attempted." She must find fulfillment in her career because she is divorced from her husband, has "strong feelings of inadequacy as a woman. . . . It is a frustrating irony of Judy's life, that as an actress she has succeeded almost without trying, although, as a woman, she has failed . . ."

Strangely enough, as the feminine mystique spread, denying women careers or any commitment outside the home, the proportion of American women working outside the home increased to one out of three. True, two out of three were still housewives, but why, at the moment when the doors of the world were finally open to all women, should the mystique deny the very dreams that had stirred women for a century?

I found a clue one morning, sitting in the office of a women's magazine editor—a woman who, older than I, remembers the days when the old image was being created, and who had watched it being displaced. The old image of the spirited career girl was largely created by writers and editors who were women, she told me. The new image of woman as housewife-mother has been largely created by writers and editors who are men.

"Most of the material used to come from women writers," she said, almost nostalgically. "As the young men returned from the war, a great many women writers dropped out of the field. The young women started having a lot of children, and stopped writing. The new writers were all men, back from the war, who had been dreaming about home, and a cozy domestic life." One by one, the creators of the gay "career girl" heroines of the thirties began to retire. By the end of the forties, the writers who couldn't get the knack of writing in the new housewife image had left the women's magazine field. The new magazine pros were men, and a few women who could write comfortably according to the housewife formula. Other people began to assemble backstage at the women's magazines: there was a new kind of woman writer who lived in the housewife image, or pretended to; and there was a new kind of woman's editor or publisher, less interested in ideas to reach women's minds and hearts, than in selling them the things that interest advertisers—appliances, detergents, lipstick. Today, the deciding voice on most of these magazines is cast by men. Women often carry out the formulas,

---

* Judy Holliday (1921–1965), Broadway and film actress who specialized in playing "dumb blondes" in the 1950s. She won an Academy Award for her performance in the film *Born Yesterday* (1950), and a Tony Award for her work in the musical *Bells Are Ringing* (1957).

women edit the housewife "service" departments, but the formulas themselves, which have dictated the new housewife image, are the product of men's minds.

Also during the forties and fifties, serious fiction writers of either sex disappeared from the mass-circulation women's magazines. In fact, fiction of any quality was almost completely replaced by a different kind of article. No longer the old article about issues or ideas, but the new "service" feature. Sometimes these articles lavished the artistry of a poet and the honesty of a crusading reporter on baking chiffon pies, or buying washing machines, or the miracles paint can do for a living room, or diets, drugs, clothes, and cosmetics to make the body into a vision of physical beauty. Sometimes they dealt with very sophisticated ideas: new developments in psychiatry, child psychology, sex and marriage, medicine. It was assumed that women readers could take these ideas, which appealed to their needs as wives and mothers, but only if they were boiled down to concrete physical details, spelled out in terms of the daily life of an average housewife with concrete do's and don'ts. How to keep your husband happy; how to solve your child's bed-wetting; how to keep death out of your medicine cabinet . . .

But here is a curious thing. Within their narrow range, these women's magazine articles, whether straight service to the housewife or a documentary report about the housewife, were almost always superior in quality to women's magazine fiction. They were better written, more honest, more sophisticated. This observation was made over and over again by intelligent readers and puzzled editors, and by writers themselves. "The serious fiction writers have become too internal. They're inaccessible to our readers, so we're left with the formula writers," an editor of *Redbook* said. And yet, in the old days, serious writers like Nancy Hale, even William Faulkner,* wrote for the women's magazines and were not considered inaccessible. Perhaps the new image of woman did not permit the internal honesty, the depth of perception, and the human truth essential to good fiction.

At the very least, fiction requires a hero or, understandably for women's magazines, a heroine, who is an "I" in pursuit of some human goal or dream. There is a limit to the number of stories that can be written about a girl in pursuit of a boy, or a housewife in pursuit of a ball of dust under the sofa. Thus the service article takes over, replacing the internal honesty and truth needed in fiction with

---

* William Faulkner (1897–1962), considered one of the United States' greatest novelists. He won the Nobel Prize in Literature in 1949 for a body of work including *The Sound and the Fury* (1929), *Light in August* (1932), and *Absalom, Absalom!* (1936). *Nancy Hale* (1908–1988), successful, self-supporting writer born into an upper-class New England family. She received many awards throughout her lifetime for a variety of types of writing: journalism, nonfiction, biography, short stories, and novels. Her work often engaged the conflicts of modern womanhood.

a richness of honest, objective, concrete, realistic domestic detail—the color of walls or lipstick, the exact temperature of the oven.

Judging from the women's magazines today, it would seem that the concrete details of women's lives are more interesting than their thoughts, their ideas, their dreams. Or does the richness and realism of the detail, the careful description of small events, mask the lack of dreams, the vacuum of ideas, the terrible boredom that has settled over the American housewife?

I sat in the office of another old-timer, one of the few women editors left in the women's magazine world, now so largely dominated by men. She explained her share in creating the feminine mystique. "Many of us were psychoanalyzed," she recalled. "And we began to feel embarrassed about being career women ourselves. There was this terrible fear that we were losing our femininity. We kept looking for ways to help women accept their feminine role."

If the real women editors were not, somehow, able to give up their own careers, all the more reason to "help" other women fulfill themselves as wives and mothers. The few women who still sit in editorial conferences do not bow to the feminine mystique in their own lives. But such is the power of the image they have helped create that many of them feel guilty. And if they have missed out somewhere on love or children, they wonder if their careers were to blame.

Behind her cluttered desk, a *Mademoiselle* editor said uneasily, "The girls we bring in now as college guest editors seem almost to pity us. Because we are career women, I suppose. At a luncheon session with the last bunch, we asked them to go round the table, telling us their own career plans. Not one of the twenty raised her hand. When I remember how I worked to learn this job and loved it—were we all crazy then?"

Coupled with the women editors who sold themselves their own bill of goods, a new breed of women writers began to write about themselves as if they were "just housewives," reveling in a comic world of children's pranks and eccentric washing machines and Parents' Night at the PTA. "After making the bed of a twelve-year-old boy week after week, climbing Mount Everest would seem a laughable anticlimax," writes Shirley Jackson* (*McCall's*, April, 1956). When Shirley Jackson, who all her adult life has been an extremely capable writer, pursuing a craft far more demanding

---

* Shirley Jackson (1916–1965), novelist and essayist known for her macabre sensibility. Her most famous story, "The Lottery," created a sensation when it was first published in *The New Yorker* in 1948 because of its chillingly violent surprise ending. Jackson published several classic horror novels, including *We Have Always Lived in the Castle* (1957) and *The Haunting of Hill House* (1959), as well as comic pieces about her family's domestic life, collected into the books *Life Among the Savages* (1953) and *Raising Demons* (1957).

than bedmaking, and Jean Kerr, who is a playwright, and Phyllis McGinley,* who is a poet, picture themselves as housewives, they may or may not overlook the housekeeper or maid who really makes the beds. But they implicitly deny the vision, and the satisfying hard work involved in their stories, poems, and plays. They deny the lives they lead, not as housewives, but as individuals.

They are good craftsmen, the best of these Housewife Writers. And some of their work is funny. The things that happen with children, a twelve-year-old boy's first cigarette, the Little League and the kindergarten rhythm band are often funny; they happen in real life to women who are writers as well as women who are just housewives. But there is something about Housewife Writers that isn't funny—like Uncle Tom, or Amos and Andy.† "Laugh," the Housewife Writers tell the real housewife, "if you are feeling desperate, empty, bored, trapped in the bedmaking, chauffeuring and dishwashing details. Isn't it funny? We're all in the same trap." Do real housewives then dissipate in laughter their dreams and their sense of desperation? Do they think their frustrated abilities and their limited lives are a joke? Shirley Jackson makes the beds, loves and laughs at her son—and writes another book. Jean Kerr's plays are produced on Broadway. The joke is not on *them.*

Some of the new Housewife Writers *live* the image; *Redbook* tells us that the author of an article on "Breast-Feeding," a woman

---

* Phyllis McGinley (1905–1978), essayist, poet and children's author who specialized in both celebrating and gently satirizing suburban life. She won the Pulitzer Prize in 1960 for her collection of light verse, *Times Three*. After the publication of *The Feminine Mystique*, McGinley's publisher encouraged her to publish a new book, *Sixpence in her Shoe* (1965), as a rebuttal to Friedan. After that book became a bestseller, McGinley was profiled in a 1965 *Time* magazine cover story in which she extolled the role of a housewife and mother: "we who belong to the profession of housewife hold the fate of the world in our hands." Jean Kerr (1922–2003), playwright and author in the middle of the twentieth century. Among her successful plays—written with her husband, the drama critic Walter Kerr—were *Tough and Go* (1949), *King of Hearts* (1954), and *Mary, Mary* (1961). She also published several collections of humorous essays about domestic life, including the bestselling *Please Don't Eat the Daisies* (1957), which was made into a movie in 1960, and then a television situation comedy from 1965 to 1967.

† *Amos and Andy* began in 1926 as a radio show about two black men who had migrated from Alabama to Chicago. The show became a huge success almost immediately, and it ran on radio until 1950; it also inspired two films in the 1930s, and a television program from 1951 to 1953. Although some African American audiences appreciated the show's portrait of black life, many attacked it. *Amos and Andy* was created by white men from Southern backgrounds, and the radio program starred white men pretending to be black. The actors spoke in broad, caricatured dialect, and the characters reflected stereotypes of African American laziness, dishonesty, and stupidity. *Uncle Tom*: the hero of Harriet Beecher Stowe's influential abolitionist novel, *Uncle Tom's Cabin* (1852). In the novel, Uncle Tom is a virtuous enslaved man who endures great suffering, and yet is spiritually and morally superior to those who enslave him because he forgives them. In popular culture, the phrase "Uncle Tom," has come to signify a black person who is docile, loyal, and content in oppression, or an ambitious black person who is willing to submit to subordinate treatment by whites (and to betray other black people) in order to advance.

named Betty Ann Countrywoman, "had planned to be a doctor. But just before her graduation from Radcliffe *cum laude*, she shrank from the thought that such a dedication might shut her off from what she really wanted, which was to marry and have a large family. She enrolled in the Yale University School of Nursing and then became engaged to a young psychiatrist on their first date. Now they have six children, ranging in age from 2 to 13, and Mrs. Countrywoman is instructor in breast-feeding at the Maternity League of Indianapolis" (*Redbook*, June, 1960). She says:

> For the mother, breast-feeding becomes a complement to the act of creation. It gives her a heightened sense of fulfillment and allows her to participate in a relationship as close to perfection as any that a woman can hope to achieve. . . . The simple fact of giving birth, however, does not of itself fulfill this need and longing. . . . Motherliness is a way of life. It enables a woman to express her total self with the tender feelings, the protective attitudes, the encompassing love of the motherly woman.

When motherhood, a fulfillment held sacred down the ages, is defined as a total way of life, must women themselves deny the world and the future open to them? Or does the denial of that world *force* them to make motherhood a total way of life? The line between mystique and reality dissolves; real women embody the split in the image. In the spectacular Christmas 1956 issue of *Life*, devoted in full to the "new" American woman, we see, not as women's-magazine villain, but as documentary fact, the typical "career woman—that fatal error that feminism propagated"—seeking "help" from a psychiatrist. She is bright, well-educated, ambitious, attractive; she makes about the same money as her husband; but she is pictured here as "frustrated," so "masculinized" by her career that her castrated, impotent, passive husband is indifferent to her sexually. He refuses to take responsibility and drowns his destroyed masculinity in alcoholism.

Then there is the discontented suburban wife who raises hell at the PTA; morbidly depressed, she destroys her children and dominates her husband whom she envies for going out into the business world. "The wife, having worked before marriage, or at least having been educated for some kind of intellectual work, finds herself in the lamentable position of being 'just a housewife.' . . . In her disgruntlement she can work as much damage on the lives of her husband and children (and her own life) as if she were a career woman, and indeed, sometimes more."

And finally, in bright and smiling contrast, are the new housewife-mothers, who cherish their "differentness," their "unique femininity," the "receptivity and passivity implicit in their sexual nature." Devoted to their own beauty and their ability to bear and nurture children, they are "feminine women, with truly feminine attitudes, admired by men for their miraculous, God-given, sensationally unique ability to wear skirts, with all the implications of that fact." Rejoicing in "the reappearance of the old-fashioned three-to-five-child family in an astonishing quarter, the upper- and upper-middle class suburbs," *Life* says:

> Here, among women who might be best qualified for "careers," there is an increasing emphasis on the nurturing and home-making values. One might guess . . . that because these women are better informed and more mature than the average, they have been the first to comprehend the penalties of "feminism" and to react against them. . . . Styles in ideas as well as in dress and decoration tend to seep down from such places to the broader population, . . . This is the countertrend which may eventually demolish the dominant and disruptive trend and make marriage what it should be: a true partnership in which . . . men are men, women are women, and both are quietly, pleasantly, securely confident of which they are—and absolutely delighted to find themselves married to someone of the opposite sex.

Look glowed at about the same time (October 16, 1956):

> The American woman is winning the battle of the sexes. Like a teenager, she is growing up and confounding her critics. . . . No longer a psychological immigrant to man's world, she works, rather casually, as a third of the U. S. labor force, less towards a "big career" than as a way of filling a hope chest or buying a new home freezer. She gracefully concedes the top jobs to men. This wondrous creature also marries younger than ever, bears more babies and looks and acts far more feminine than the "emancipated" girl of the 1920's or even '30's. Steelworker's wife and Junior Leaguer alike do their own housework. . . . Today, if she makes an old-fashioned choice and lovingly tends a garden and a bumper crop of children, she rates louder hosannas than ever before.

In the new America, fact is more important than fiction. The documentary *Life* and *Look* images of real women who devote their lives to children and home are played back as the ideal, the way women should be: this is powerful stuff, not to be shrugged off like the heroines of women's magazine fiction. When a mystique is strong, it makes its own fiction of fact. It feeds on the very facts which might contradict it, and seeps into every corner of the culture, bemusing even the social critics.

Adlai Stevenson,* in a commencement address at Smith College in 1955, reprinted in *Woman's Home Companion* (September, 1955), dismissed the desire of educated women to play their own political part in "the crises of the age." Modern woman's participation in politics is through her role as wife and mother, said the spokesman of democratic liberalism: "Women, especially educated women, have a unique opportunity to influence us, man and boy." The only problem is woman's failure to appreciate that her true part in the political crisis is as wife and mother.

> Once immersed in the very pressing and particular problems of domesticity, many women feel frustrated and far apart from the great issues and stirring debate for which their education has given them understanding and relish. Once they wrote poetry. Now it's the laundry list. Once they discussed art and philosophy until late in the night. Now they are so tired they fall asleep as soon as the dishes are finished. There is, often, a sense of contraction, of closing horizons and lost opportunities. They had hoped to play their part in the crises of the age. But what they do is wash the diapers.
>
> The point is that whether we talk of Africa, Islam or Asia, women "never had it so good" as you. In short, far from the vocation of marriage and motherhood leading you away from the great issues of our day, it brings you back to their very center and places upon you an infinitely deeper and more intimate responsibility than that borne by the majority of those who hit the headlines and make the news and live in such a turmoil of great issues that they end by being totally unable to distinguish which issues are really great.

Woman's political job is to "inspire in her home a vision of the meaning of life and freedom . . . to help her husband find values that will give purpose to his specialized daily chores . . . to teach her children the uniqueness of each individual human being."

> This assignment for you, as wives and mothers, you can do in the living room with a baby in your lap or in the kitchen with a can opener in your hand. If you're clever, maybe you can even practice your saving arts on that unsuspecting man while he's watching television. I think there is much you can do about our crisis in the humble role of housewife. I could wish you no better vocation than that.

---

* Adlai Stevenson (1900–1965), liberal Democratic governor of Illinois who unsuccessfully ran for president against Eisenhower in 1952 and 1956. President John F. Kennedy appointed him U.S. ambassador to the United Nations.

Thus the logic of the feminine mystique redefined the very nature of woman's problem. When woman was seen as a human being of limitless human potential, equal to man, anything that kept her from realizing her full potential was a problem to be solved: barriers to higher education and political participation, discrimination or prejudice in law or morality. But now that woman is seen only in terms of her sexual role, the barriers to the realization of her full potential, the prejudices which deny her full participation in the world, are no longer problems. The only problems now are those that might disturb her adjustment as a housewife. So career is a problem, education is a problem, political interest, even the very admission of women's intelligence and individuality is a problem. And finally there is the problem that has no name, a vague undefined wish for "something more" than washing dishes, ironing, punishing and praising the children. In the women's magazines, it is solved either by dyeing one's hair blonde or by having another baby. "Remember, when we were all children, how we all planned to 'be something'?" says a young housewife in the *Ladies' Home Journal* (February, 1960). Boasting that she has worn out six copies of Dr. Spock's baby-care book* in seven years, she cries, "I'm lucky! Lucky! I'M SO GLAD TO BE A WOMAN!"

In one of these stories ("Holiday," *Mademoiselle*, August, 1949) a desperate young wife is ordered by her doctor to get out of the house one day a week. She goes shopping, tries on dresses, looks in the mirror wondering which one her husband, Sam, will like.

> Always Sam, like a Greek chorus in the back of her head. As if she herself hadn't a definiteness of her own, a clarity that was indisputably hers. . . . Suddenly she couldn't make the difference between pleated and gored skirts of sufficient importance to fix her decision. She looked at herself in the full-length glass, tall, getting thicker around the hips, the lines of her face beginning to slip. She was twenty-nine, but she felt middle-aged, as if a great many years had passed and there wasn't very much yet to come . . . which was ridiculous, for Ellen was only three. There was her whole future to plan for, and perhaps another child. It was not a thing to be put off too long.

---

* In 1946, Dr. Benjamin Spock (1903–1998) published the most influential how-to book on infant- and child-care in the twentieth century, *Common Sense Book of Baby and Child Care*, later retitled, *Baby and Child Care*. This book, which went through many printings, became the standard text for raising baby boom children. What distinguished this work from previous child-care manuals was its combination of practical/scientific information with advice to parents (mostly mothers) to trust their own judgment about what is best for their child, often taking the lead from the child him/herself. This alleged "permissiveness" and Dr. Spock's later political activity, particularly against the Vietnam War, provoked some to blame the widespread application of his childrearing practices for the social unrest among the young in the 1960s.

When the young housewife in "The Man Next to Me" (*Redbook*, November, 1948) discovers that her elaborate dinner party didn't help her husband get a raise after all, she is in despair. ("You should say I helped. You should say I'm good for something . . . Life was like a puzzle with a piece missing, and the piece was me, and I couldn't figure my place in it at all.") So she dyes her hair blonde, and when her husband reacts satisfactorily in bed to the new "blonde me," she "felt a new sense of peace, as if I'd answered the question within myself."

Over and over again, stories in women's magazines insist that woman can know fulfillment only at the moment of giving birth to a child. They deny the years when she can no longer look forward to giving birth, even if she repeats that act over and over again. In the feminine mystique, there is no other way for a woman to dream of creation or of the future. There is no way she can even dream about herself, except as her children's mother, her husband's wife. And the documentary articles play back new young housewives, grown up under the mystique, who do not have even that "question within myself." Says one, described in "How America Lives" (*Ladies' Home Journal*, June, 1959): "If he doesn't want me to wear a certain color or a certain kind of dress, then I truly don't want to, either. The thing is, whatever he has wanted is what I also want. . . . I don't believe in fifty-fifty marriages." Giving up college and job to marry at eighteen, with no regrets, she "never tried to enter into the discussion when the men were talking. She never disputed her husband in anything. . . . She spent a great deal of time looking out the window at the snow, the rain, and the gradual emergence of the first crocuses. One great time-passer and consolation was . . . embroidery: tiny stitches in gold-metal or silken thread which require infinite concentration."

There is no problem, in the logic of the feminine mystique, for such a woman who has no wishes of her own, who defines herself only as wife and mother. The problem, if there is one, can only be her children's, or her husband's. It is the husband who complains to the marriage counselor (*Redbook*, June, 1955): "The way I see it, marriage takes two people, each living his own life and then putting them together. Mary seems to think we both ought to live one life: mine." Mary insists on going with him to buy shirts and socks, tells the clerk his size and color. When he comes home at night, she asks with whom he ate lunch, where, what did he talk about? When he protests, she says, "But darling, I want to share your life, be part of all you do, that's all. . . . I want us to be one, the way it says in the marriage service . . ." It doesn't seem reasonable to the husband that "two people can ever be one the way Mary means it. It's just plain ridiculous on the face of it. Besides, I wouldn't like it. I don't want to be so bound to another person that I can't have a thought or an action that's strictly my own."

The answer to "Pete's problem," says Dr. Emily Mudd,* the famous marriage counsellor, is to make Mary *feel* she is living his life: invite her to town to lunch with the people in his office once in a while, order his favorite veal dish for her and maybe find her some "healthy physical activity," like swimming, to drain off her excess energy. It is not Mary's problem that she has no life of her own.

The ultimate, in housewife happiness, is finally achieved by the Texas housewife, described in "How America Lives" (*Ladies' Home Journal*, October, 1960), who "sits on a pale aqua satin sofa gazing out her picture window at the street. Even at this hour of the morning (it is barely nine-o'clock), she is wearing rouge, powder and lipstick, and her cotton dress is immaculately fresh." She says proudly: "By 8:30 A.M., when my youngest goes to school, my whole house is clean and neat and I am dressed for the day. I am free to play bridge, attend club meetings, or stay home and read, listen to Beethoven, and just plain loaf.

"Sometimes, she washes and dries her hair before sitting down at a bridge table at 1:30. Mornings she is having bridge at her house are the busiest, for then she must get out the tables, cards, tallies, prepare fresh coffee and organize lunch. . . . During the winter months, she may play as often as four days a week from 9:30 to 3 P.M. . . . Janice is careful to be home, before her sons return from school at 4 P.M."

She is not frustrated, this new young housewife. An honor student at high school, married at eighteen, remarried and pregnant at twenty, she has the house she spent seven years dreaming and planning in detail. She is proud of her efficiency as a housewife, getting it all done by 8:30. She does the major housecleaning on Saturday, when her husband fishes and her sons are busy with Boy Scouts. ("There's nothing else to do. No bridge games. It's a long day for me.")

"'I love my home,' she says. . . . The pale gray paint in her L-shaped living and dining room is five years old, but still in perfect condition. . . . The pale peach and yellow and aqua damask upholstery looks spotless after eight years' wear. 'Sometimes, I feel I'm

---

* Dr. Emily Mudd (1898–1998) attended Vassar and went on to earn a Ph.D. later in life in social work from the University of Pennsylvania. She was an early activist on behalf of reproductive rights and engaged in research in human sexuality. A professor of family study in psychiatry at the University of Pennsylvania, she assisted Alfred Kinsey in editing his *Sexual Behavior in the Human Female*. She also served as a consultant to the Masters and Johnson clinic in St. Louis, MO (see entry on Alfred Kinsey, p. 21). She is best known as a pioneer in the field of professional marriage and family counseling.

too passive, too content,' remarks Janice, fondly, regarding the wristband of large family diamonds she wears even when the watch itself is being repaired. . . . Her favorite possession is her four-poster spool bed with a pink taffeta canopy. 'I feel just like Queen Elizabeth sleeping in that bed,' she says happily. (Her husband sleeps in another room, since he snores.)

"'I'm so grateful for my blessings,' she says. 'Wonderful husband, handsome sons with dispositions to match, big comfortable house. . . . I'm thankful for my good health and faith in God and such material possessions as two cars, two TV's and two fireplaces.'"

Staring uneasily at this image, I wonder if a few problems are not somehow better than this smiling empty passivity. If they are happy, these young women who live the feminine mystique, then is this the end of the road? Or are the seeds of something worse than frustration inherent in this image? Is there a growing divergence between this image of woman and human reality?

Consider, as a symptom, the increasing emphasis on glamour in the women's magazines: the housewife wearing eye makeup as she vacuums the floor—"The Honor of Being a Woman." Why does "Occupation: housewife" require such insistent glamorizing year after year? The strained glamour is in itself a question mark: the lady doth protest too much.

The image of woman in another era required increasing prudishness to keep denying sex. This new image seems to require increasing mindlessness, increasing emphasis on things: two cars, two TV's, two fireplaces. Whole pages of women's magazines are filled with gargantuan vegetables: beets, cucumbers, green peppers, potatoes, described like a love affair. The very size of their print is raised until it looks like a first-grade primer. The new *McCall's* frankly assumes women are brainless, fluffy kittens, the *Ladies' Home Journal*, feverishly competing, procures rock-and-roller Pat Boone* as a counselor to teenagers; *Redbook* and the others enlarge their own type size. Does the size of the print mean that the new young women, whom all the magazines are courting, have only first-grade minds? Or does it try to hide the triviality of the content? Within the confines of what is now accepted as woman's world, an editor may no longer be able to think of anything big to do except blow up a baked potato, or describe a kitchen as if it were the Hall of Mirrors; he is, after all, forbidden by the mystique to deal with a big idea. But does it not occur to any of the men who run the women's magazines that

---

* During the 1950s, Pat Boone (b. 1934) provided the audiences for the new rock and roll music a wholesome, Christian alternative to singers like Elvis Presley.

their troubles may stem from the smallness of the image with which they are truncating women's minds?

They are all in trouble today, the mass-circulation magazines, vying fiercely with each other and television to deliver more and more millions of women who will buy the things their advertisers sell. Does this frantic race force the men who make the images to see women only as thing-buyers? Does it force them to compete finally in emptying women's minds of human thought? The fact is, the troubles of the image-makers seem to be increasing in direct proportion to the increasing mindlessness of their image. During the years in which that image has narrowed woman's world down to the home, cut her role back to housewife, five of the mass-circulation magazines geared to women have ceased publication; others are on the brink.

The growing boredom of women with the empty, narrow image of the women's magazines may be the most hopeful sign of the image's divorce from reality. But there are more violent symptoms on the part of women who are committed to that image. In 1960, the editors of a magazine specifically geared to the happy young housewife—or rather to the new young couples (the wives are not considered separate from their husbands and children)—ran an article asking, "Why Young Mothers Feel Trapped" (*Redbook*, September, 1960). As a promotion stunt, they invited young mothers with such a problem to write in the details, for $500. The editors were shocked to receive 24,000 replies. Can an image of woman be cut down to the point where it becomes itself a trap?

At one of the major women's magazines, a woman editor, sensing that American housewives might be desperately in need of something to enlarge their world, tried for some months to convince her male colleagues to introduce a few ideas outside the home into the magazine. "We decided against it," the man who makes the final decisions said. "Women are so completely divorced from the world of ideas in their lives now, they couldn't take it." Perhaps it is irrelevant to ask, who divorced them? Perhaps these Frankensteins no longer have the power to stop the feminine monster they have created.

I helped create this image. I have watched American women for fifteen years try to conform to it. But I can no longer deny my own knowledge of its terrible implications. It is not a harmless image. There may be no psychological terms for the harm it is doing. But what happens when women try to live according to an image that makes them deny their minds? What happens when women grow up in an image that makes them deny the reality of the changing world?

The material details of life, the daily burden of cooking and cleaning, of taking care of the physical needs of husband and children— these did indeed define a woman's world a century ago when

Americans were pioneers, and the American frontier lay in conquering the land. But the women who went west with the wagon trains also shared the pioneering purpose. Now the American frontiers are of the mind, and of the spirit. Love and children and home are good, but they are not the whole world, even if most of the words now written for women pretend they are. Why should women accept this picture of a half-life, instead of a share in the whole of human destiny? Why should women try to make housework "something more," instead of moving on the frontiers of their own time, as American women moved beside their husbands on the old frontiers?

A baked potato is not as big as the world, and vacuuming the living room floor—with or without makeup—is not work that takes enough thought or energy to challenge any woman's full capacity. Women are human beings, not stuffed dolls, not animals. Down through the ages man has known that he was set apart from other animals by his mind's power to have an idea, a vision, and shape the future to it. He shares a need for food and sex with other animals, but when he loves, he loves as a man, and when he discovers and creates and shapes a future different from his past, he is a man, a human being.

This is the real mystery: why did so many American women, with the ability and education to discover and create, go back home again, to look for "something more" in housework and rearing children? For, paradoxically, in the same fifteen years in which the spirited New Woman was replaced by the Happy Housewife, the boundaries of the human world have widened, the pace of world change has quickened, and the very nature of human reality has become increasingly free from biological and material necessity. Does the mystique keep American woman from growing with the world? Does it force her to deny reality, as a woman in a mental hospital must deny reality to believe she is a queen? Does it doom women to be displaced persons, if not virtual schizophrenics, in our complex, changing world?

It is more than a strange paradox that as all professions are finally open to women in America, "career woman" has become a dirty word; that as higher education becomes available to any woman with the capacity for it, education for women has become so suspect that more and more drop out of high school and college to marry and have babies; that as so many roles in modern society become theirs for the taking, women so insistently confine themselves to one role. Why, with the removal of all the legal, political, economic, and educational barriers that once kept woman from being man's equal, a person in her own right, an individual free to develop her own potential, should she accept this new image which insists she is not a person but a "woman," by definition barred from the freedom of human existence and a voice in human destiny?

The feminine mystique is so powerful that women grow up no longer knowing that they have the desires and capacities the mystique forbids. But such a mystique does not fasten itself on a whole nation in a few short years, reversing the trends of a century, without cause. What gives the mystique its power? Why did women go home again?

3

The Crisis in Woman's Identity

I discovered a strange thing, interviewing women of my own generation over the past ten years. When we were growing up, many of us could not see ourselves beyond the age of twenty-one. We had no image of our own future, of ourselves as women.

I remember the stillness of a spring afternoon on the Smith campus in 1942, when I came to a frightening dead end in my own vision of the future. A few days earlier, I had received a notice that I had won a graduate fellowship. During the congratulations, underneath my excitement, I felt a strange uneasiness; there was a question that I did not want to think about.

"Is this really what I want to be?" The question shut me off, cold and alone, from the girls talking and studying on the sunny hillside behind the college house. I thought I was going to be a psychologist. But if I wasn't sure, what did I want to be? I felt the future closing in—and I could not see myself in it at all. I had no image of myself, stretching beyond college. I had come at seventeen from a Midwestern town, an unsure girl; the wide horizons of the world and the life of the mind had been opened to me. I had begun to know who I was and what I wanted to do. I could not go back now. I could not go home again, to the life of my mother and the women of our town, bound to home, bridge, shopping, children, husband, charity, clothes. But now that the time had come to make my own future, to take the deciding step, I suddenly did not know what I wanted to be.

I took the fellowship, but the next spring, under the alien California sun of another campus, the question came again, and I could not put it out of my mind. I had won another fellowship that would have committed me to research for my doctorate, to a career as professional psychologist. "Is this really what I want to be?" The decision now truly terrified me. I lived in a terror of indecision for days, unable to think of anything else.

The question was not important, I told myself. No question was important to me that year but love. We walked in the Berkeley hills and a boy said: "Nothing can come of this, between us. I'll never win a fellowship like yours." Did I think I would be choosing, irrevocably, the cold loneliness of that afternoon if I went on? I gave up the fellowship, in relief. But for years afterward, I could not read a word of the science that once I had thought of as my future life's work; the reminder of its loss was too painful.

I never could explain, hardly knew myself, why I gave up this career. I lived in the present, working on newspapers with no particular plan. I married, had children, lived according to the feminine mystique as a suburban housewife. But still the question haunted me. I could sense no purpose in my life, I could find no peace, until I finally faced it and worked out my own answer.

I discovered, talking to Smith seniors in 1959, that the question is no less terrifying to girls today. Only they answer it now in a way that my generation found, after half a lifetime, not to be an answer at all. These girls, mostly seniors, were sitting in the living room of the college house, having coffee. It was not too different from such an evening when I was a senior, except that many more of the girls wore rings on their left hands. I asked the ones around me what they planned to be. The engaged ones spoke of weddings, apartments, getting a job as a secretary while husband finished school. The others, after a hostile silence, gave vague answers about this job or that, graduate study, but no one had any real plans. A blonde with a ponytail asked me the next day if I had believed the things they had said. "None of it was true," she told me. "We don't like to be asked what we want to do. None of us know. None of us even like to think about it. The ones who are going to be married right away are the lucky ones. They don't have to think about it."

But I noticed that night that many of the engaged girls, sitting silently around the fire while I asked the others about jobs, had also seemed angry about something. "They don't want to think about not going on," my ponytailed informant said. "They know they're not going to use their education. They'll be wives and mothers. You can say you're going to keep on reading and be interested in the community. But that's not the same. You won't really go on. It's a disappointment to know you're going to stop now, and not go on and use it."

In counterpoint, I heard the words of a woman, fifteen years after she left college, a doctor's wife, mother of three, who said over coffee in her New England kitchen:

> The tragedy was, nobody ever looked us in the eye and said you have to decide what you want to do with your life, besides being your husband's wife and children's mother. I never thought it through until I was thirty-six, and my husband was so busy with his practice that he couldn't entertain me every

night. The three boys were in school all day. I kept on trying to have babies despite an Rh discrepancy. After two miscarriages, they said I must stop. I thought that my own growth and evolution were over. I always knew as a child that I was going to grow up and go to college, and then get married, and that's as far as a girl has to think. After that, your husband determines and fills your life. It wasn't until I got so lonely as the doctor's wife and kept screaming at the kids because they didn't fill my life that I realized I had to make my own life. I still had to decide what I wanted to be. I hadn't finished evolving at all. But it took me ten years to think it through.

The feminine mystique permits, even encourages, women to ignore the question of their identity. The mystique says they can answer the question "Who am I?" by saying "Tom's wife . . . Mary's mother." But I don't think the mystique would have such power over American women if they did not fear to face this terrifying blank which makes them unable to see themselves after twenty-one. The truth is—and how long it has been true, I'm not sure, but it was true in my generation and it is true of girls growing up today—an American woman no longer has a private image to tell her who she is, or can be, or wants to be.

The public image, in the magazines and television commercials, is designed to sell washing machines, cake mixes, deodorants, detergents, rejuvenating face creams, hair tints. But the power of that image, on which companies spend millions of dollars for television time and ad space, comes from this: American women no longer know who they are. They are sorely in need of a new image to help them find their identity. As the motivational researchers keep telling the advertisers, American women are so unsure of who they should be that they look to this glossy public image to decide every detail of their lives. They look for the image they will no longer take from their mothers.

In my generation, many of us knew that we did not want to be like our mothers, even when we loved them. We could not help but see their disappointment. Did we understand, or only resent, the sadness, the emptiness, that made them hold too fast to us, try to live our lives, run our fathers' lives, spend their days shopping or yearning for things that never seemed to satisfy them, no matter how much money they cost? Strangely, many mothers who loved their daughters—and mine was one—did not want their daughters to grow up like them either. They knew we needed something more.

But even if they urged, insisted, fought to help us educate ourselves, even if they talked with yearning of careers that were not open to them, they could not give us an image of what we could be.

They could only tell us that their lives were too empty, tied to home; that children, cooking, clothes, bridge, and charities were not enough. A mother might tell her daughter, spell it out, "Don't be just a housewife like me." But that daughter, sensing that her mother was too frustrated to savor the love of her husband and children, might feel: "I will succeed where my mother failed, I will fulfill myself as a woman," and never read the lesson of her mother's life.

Recently, interviewing high-school girls who had started out full of promise and talent, but suddenly stopped their education, I began to see new dimensions to the problem of feminine conformity. These girls, it seemed at first, were merely following the typical curve of feminine adjustment. Earlier interested in geology or poetry, they now were interested only in being popular; to get boys to like them, they had concluded, it was better to be like all the other girls. On closer examination, I found that these girls were so terrified of becoming like their mothers that they could not see themselves at all. They were afraid to grow up. They had to copy in identical detail the composite image of the popular girl— denying what was best in themselves out of fear of femininity as they saw it in their mothers. One of these girls, seventeen years old, told me:

> I want so badly to feel like the other girls. I never get over this feeling of being a neophyte, not initiated. When I get up and have to cross a room, it's like I'm a beginner, or have some terrible affliction, and I'll never learn. I go to the local hangout after school and sit there for hours talking about clothes and hairdos and the twist, and I'm not that interested, so it's an effort. But I found out I could make them like me—just do what they do, dress like them, talk like them, not do things that are different. I guess I even started to make myself not different inside.
>
> I used to write poetry. The guidance office says I have this creative ability and I should be at the top of the class and have a great future. But things like that aren't what you need to be popular. The important thing for a girl is to be popular.
>
> Now I go out with boy after boy, and it's such an effort because I'm not myself with them. It makes you feel even more alone. And besides, I'm afraid of where it's going to lead. Pretty soon, all my differences will be smoothed out, and I'll be the kind of girl that could be a housewife.
>
> I don't want to think of growing up. If I had children, I'd want them to stay the same age. If I had to watch them grow up, I'd see myself growing older, and I wouldn't want to. My mother says she can't sleep at night, she's sick with worry over

what I might do. When I was little, she wouldn't let me cross the street alone, long after the other kids did.

I can't see myself as being married and having children. It's as if I wouldn't have any personality myself. My mother's like a rock that's been smoothed by the waves, like a void. She's put so much into her family that there's nothing left, and she resents us because she doesn't get enough in return. But sometimes it seems like there's nothing there. My mother doesn't serve any purpose except cleaning the house. She isn't happy, and she doesn't make my father happy. If she didn't care about us children at all, it would have the same effect as caring too much. It makes you want to do the opposite. I don't think it's really love. When I was little and I ran in all excited to tell her I'd learned how to stand on my head, she was never listening.

Lately, I look into the mirror, and I'm so afraid I'm going to look like my mother. It frightens me, to catch myself being like her in gestures or speech or anything. I'm not like her in so many ways, but if I'm like her in this one way, perhaps I'll turn out like my mother after all. And that terrifies me.

And so the seventeen-year-old was so afraid of being a woman like her mother that she turned her back on all the things in herself and all the opportunities that would have made her a different woman, to copy from the outside the "popular" girls. And finally, in panic at losing herself, she turned her back on her own popularity and defied the conventional good behavior that would have won her a college scholarship. For lack of an image that would help her grow up as a woman true to herself, she retreated into the beatnik* vacuum.

Another girl, a college junior from South Carolina told me:

I don't want to be interested in a career I'll have to give up. My mother wanted to be a newspaper reporter from the time she was twelve, and I've seen her frustration for twenty years. I don't want to be interested in world affairs. I don't want to be interested in anything beside my home and being a wonderful wife and mother. Maybe education is a liability. Even the brightest boys at home want just a sweet, pretty girl. Only sometimes I wonder how it would feel to be able to stretch and

---

* A pejorative term referring to a young person affiliated with the Beat movement of the 1950s. The Beat movement was comprised of writers who rejected middle-class values and embraced nonconformity, experimenting with both drugs and Eastern religions. It included famous writers like Jack Kerouac, Allen Ginsberg, and William Burroughs, but it also embraced a broader subculture of young people who admired the Beats' challenge to the system, and it laid a foundation for the cultural upheavals of the 1960s. Friedan's use of the pejorative "beatnik" suggests the generation gap that lay between herself and younger radicals of the 1960s, but it also reflects the negative image that mainstream popular culture promulgated of the Beat movement.

stretch and stretch, and learn all you want, and not have to hold yourself back.

Her mother, almost all our mothers, were housewives, though many had started or yearned for or regretted giving up careers. Whatever they told us, we, having eyes and ears and mind and heart, knew that their lives were somehow empty. We did not want to be like them, and yet what other model did we have?

The only other kind of women I knew, growing up, were the old-maid high-school teachers; the librarian; the one woman doctor in our town, who cut her hair like a man; and a few of my college professors. None of these women lived in the warm center of life as I had known it at home. Many had not married or had children. I dreaded being like them, even the ones who taught me truly to respect my own mind and use it, to feel that I had a part in the world. I never knew a woman, when I was growing up, who used her mind, played her own part in the world, and also loved, and had children.

I think that this has been the unknown heart of woman's problem in America for a long time, this lack of a private image. Public images that defy reason and have very little to do with women themselves have had the power to shape too much of their lives. These images would not have such power, if women were not suffering a crisis of identity.

The strange, terrifying jumping-off point that American women reach—at eighteen, twenty-one, twenty-five, forty-one—has been noticed for many years by sociologists, psychologists, analysts, educators. But I think it has not been understood for what it is. It has been called a "discontinuity" in cultural conditioning; it has been called woman's "role crisis." It has been blamed on the education which made American girls grow up feeling free and equal to boys—playing baseball, riding bicycles, conquering geometry and college boards, going away to college, going out in the world to get a job, living alone in an apartment in New York or Chicago or San Francisco, testing and discovering their own powers in the world. All this gave girls the feeling they could be and do whatever they wanted to, with the same freedom as boys, the critics said. It did not prepare them for their role as women. The crisis comes when they are forced to adjust to this role. Today's high rate of emotional distress and breakdown among women in their twenties and thirties is usually attributed to this "role crisis." If girls were educated for their role as women, they would not suffer this crisis, the adjusters say.

But I think they have seen only half the truth.

What if the terror a girl faces at twenty-one, when she must decide who she will be, is simply the terror of growing up—growing up, as women were not permitted to grow before? What if the terror a girl faces at twenty-one is the terror of freedom to decide her own life, with no one to order which path she will take, the freedom and the necessity to take paths women before were not able to take? What if those who choose the path of "feminine adjustment"— evading this terror by marrying at eighteen, losing themselves in having babies and the details of housekeeping—are simply refusing to grow up, to face the question of their own identity?

Mine was the first college generation to run head-on into the new mystique of feminine fulfillment. Before then, while most women did indeed end up as housewives and mothers, the point of education was to discover the life of the mind, to pursue truth and to take a place in the world. There was a sense, already dulling when I went to college, that we would be New Women. Our world would be much larger than home. Forty per cent of my college class at Smith had career plans. But I remember how, even then, some of the seniors, suffering the pangs of that bleak fear of the future, envied the few who escaped it by getting married right away.

The ones we envied then are suffering that terror now at forty. "Never have decided what kind of woman I am. Too much personal life in college. Wish I'd studied more science, history, government, gone deeper into philosophy," one wrote on an alumnae questionnaire, fifteen years later. "Still trying to find the rock to build on. Wish I had finished college. I got married instead." "Wish I'd developed a deeper and more creative life of my own and that I hadn't become engaged and married at nineteen. Having expected the ideal in marriage, including a hundred-per-cent devoted husband, it was a shock to find this isn't the way it is," wrote a mother of six.

Many of the younger generation of wives who marry early have never suffered this lonely terror. They thought they did not have to choose, to look into the future and plan what they wanted to do with their lives. They had only to wait to be chosen, marking time passively until the husband, the babies, the new house decided what the rest of their lives would be. They slid easily into their sexual role as women before they knew who they were themselves. It is these women who suffer most the problem that has no name.

It is my thesis that the core of the problem for women today is not sexual but a problem of identity—a stunting or evasion of growth that is perpetuated by the feminine mystique. It is my thesis that as the Victorian culture did not permit women to accept or gratify their basic sexual needs, our culture does not permit women to accept or gratify their basic need to grow and fulfill their potentialities as human beings, a need which is not solely defined by their sexual role.

Biologists have recently discovered a "youth serum" which, if fed to young caterpillars in the larva state, will keep them from ever maturing into moths; they will live out their lives as caterpillars. The expectations of feminine fulfillment that are fed to women by magazines, television, movies, and books that popularize psychological half-truths, and by parents, teachers and counselors who accept the feminine mystique, operate as a kind of youth serum, keeping most women in the state of sexual larvae, preventing them from achieving the maturity of which they are capable. And there is increasing evidence that woman's failure to grow to complete identity has hampered rather than enriched her sexual fulfillment, virtually doomed her to be castrative to her husband and sons, and caused neuroses, or problems as yet unnamed as neuroses, equal to those caused by sexual repression.

There have been identity crises for man at all the crucial turning points in human history, though those who lived through them did not give them that name. It is only in recent years that the theorists of psychology, sociology and theology have isolated this problem, and given it a name. But it is considered a man's problem. It is defined, for man, as the crisis of growing up, of choosing his identity, "the decision as to what one is and is going to be," in the words of the brilliant psychoanalyst Erik H. Erikson:*

> I have called the major crisis of adolescence the identity crisis; it occurs in that period of the life cycle when each youth must forge for himself some central perspective and direction, some working unity, out of the effective remnants of his childhood and the hopes of his anticipated adulthood; he must detect some meaningful resemblance between what he has come to see in himself and what his sharpened awareness tells him others judge and expect him to be. . . . In some people, in some classes, at some periods in history, the crisis will be minimal; in other people, classes and periods, the crisis will be clearly marked off as a critical period, a kind of "second birth," apt to be aggravated either by widespread neuroticisms or by pervasive ideological unrest.[1]

In this sense, the identity crisis of one man's life may reflect, or set off, a rebirth, or new stage, in the growing up of mankind. "In some

---

* Erik Homberger Erikson (1902–1994), pioneering psychoanalyst who developed the concept of identity. Expanding upon the psychological theory of Sigmund Freud (see entry on Sigmund Freud, p. 85), Erikson argued in *Childhood and Society* (1950) that normal development of personality throughout any individual's life occurred in eight stages from infancy through old age: as an individual mastered conflict in each stage, he or she would achieve a virtue. According to Erikson, the fifth stage, adolescence, was a struggle with identity, and it was that struggle that animated Erikson's writing in later books, such as *Young Man Luther* (1958) and *Identity: Youth and Crisis* (1968).

periods of his history, and in some phases of his life cycle, man needs a new ideological orientation as surely and sorely as he must have air and food," said Erikson, focusing new light on the crisis of the young Martin Luther, who left a Catholic monastery at the end of the Middle Ages to forge a new identity for himself and Western man.

The search for identity is not new, however, in American thought—though in every generation, each man who writes about it discovers it anew. In America, from the beginning, it has somehow been understood that men must thrust into the future; the pace has always been too rapid for man's identity to stand still. In every generation, many men have suffered misery, unhappiness, and uncertainty because they could not take the image of the man they wanted to be from their fathers. The search for identity of the young man who can't go home again has always been a major theme of American writers. And it has always been considered right in America, good, for men to suffer these agonies of growth, to search for and find their own identities. The farm boy went to the city, the garment-maker's son became a doctor, Abraham Lincoln taught himself to read—these were more than rags-to-riches stories. They were an integral part of the American dream. The problem for many was money, race, color, class, which barred them from choice— not what they would be if they were free to choose.

Even today a young man learns soon enough that he must decide who he wants to be. If he does not decide in junior high, in high school, in college, he must somehow come to terms with it by twenty-five or thirty, or he is lost. But this search for identity is seen as a greater problem now because more and more boys cannot find images in our culture—from their fathers or other men—to help them in their search. The old frontiers have been conquered, and the boundaries of the new are not so clearly marked. More and more young men in America today suffer an identity crisis for want of any image of man worth pursuing, for want of a purpose that truly realizes their human abilities.

But why have theorists not recognized this same identity crisis in women? In terms of the old conventions and the new feminine mystique women are not expected to grow up to find out who they are, to choose their human identity. Anatomy is woman's destiny, say the theorists of femininity; the identity of woman is determined by her biology.

But is it? More and more women are asking themselves this question. As if they were waking from a coma, they ask, "Where am I . . . what am I doing here?" For the first time in their history, women are becoming aware of an identity crisis in their own lives, a crisis which began many generations ago, has grown worse with each succeeding generation, and will not end until they, or their daughters, turn an unknown corner and make of themselves and their lives the new image that so many women now so desperately need.

In a sense that goes beyond any one woman's life, I think this is the crisis of women growing up—a turning point from an immaturity that has been called femininity to full human identity. I think women had to suffer this crisis of identity, which began a hundred years ago, and have to suffer it still today, simply to become fully human.

4

The Passionate Journey

It was the need for a new identity that started women, a century ago, on that passionate journey, that vilified, misinterpreted journey away from home.

It has been popular in recent years to laugh at feminism as one of history's dirty jokes: to pity, sniggering, those old-fashioned feminists who fought for women's rights to higher education, careers, the vote. They were neurotic victims of penis envy who wanted to be men, it is said now. In battling for women's freedom to participate in the major work and decisions of society as the equals of men, they denied their very nature as women, which fulfills itself only through sexual passivity, acceptance of male domination, and nurturing motherhood.

But if I am not mistaken, it is this first journey which holds the clue to much that has happened to women since. It is one of the strange blind spots of contemporary psychology not to recognize the reality of the passion that moved these women to leave home in search of new identity, or, staying home, to yearn bitterly for something more. Theirs was an act of rebellion, a violent denial of the identity of women as it was then defined. It was the need for a new identity that led those passionate feminists to forge new trails for women. Some of those trails were unexpectedly rough, some were dead ends, and some may have been false, but the need for women to find new trails was real.

The problem of identity was new for women then, truly new. The feminists were pioneering on the front edge of woman's evolution. They had to prove that women were human. They had to shatter, violently if necessary, the decorative Dresden figurine that represented the ideal woman of the last century. They had to prove that woman was not a passive, empty mirror, not a frilly, useless decoration, not a mindless animal, not a thing to be disposed of by others, incapable of a voice in her own existence, before they could even begin to fight for the rights women needed to become the human equals of men.

Changeless woman, childish woman, a woman's place is in the home, they were told. But man was changing; his place was in the world and his world was widening. Woman was being left behind. Anatomy was her destiny; she might die giving birth to one baby, or live to be thirty-five, giving birth to twelve, while man controlled his destiny with that part of his anatomy which no other animal had: his mind.

Women also had minds. They also had the human need to grow. But the work that fed life and moved it forward was no longer done at home, and women were not trained to understand and work in the world. Confined to the home, a child among her children, passive, no part of her existence under her own control, a woman could only exist by pleasing man. She was wholly dependent on his protection in a world that she had no share in making: man's world. She could never grow up to ask the simple human question, "Who am I? What do I want?"

Even if man loved her as a child, a doll, a decoration; even if he gave her rubies, satin, velvets; even if she was warm in her house, safe with her children, would she not yearn for something more? She was, at that time, so completely defined as object by man, never herself as subject, "I," that she was not even expected to enjoy or participate in the act of sex. "He took his pleasure with her . . . he had his way with her," as the sayings went. Is it so hard to understand that emancipation, the right to full humanity, was important enough to generations of women, still alive or only recently dead, that some fought with their fists, and went to jail and even died for it? And for the right to human growth, some women denied their own sex, the desire to love and be loved by a man, and to bear children.

It is a strangely unquestioned perversion of history that the passion and fire of the feminist movement* came from man-hating, embittered, sex-starved spinsters, from castrating, unsexed nonwomen who burned with such envy for the male organ that they wanted to take it away from all men, or destroy them, demanding rights only because they lacked the power to love as women. Mary Wollstonecraft, Angelina Grimké, Ernestine Rose, Margaret Fuller,

---

* Friedan is referring to what most historians call the nineteenth-century woman's rights movement. "Feminism," as a word, an ideology, and a movement did not appear until the late nineteenth century in Europe and the early twentieth century in the United States. When Friedan was writing *The Feminine Mystique*, the first stirrings of what would be called second wave feminism were appearing.

Elizabeth Cady Stanton, Julia Ward Howe,* Margaret Sanger all loved, were loved, and married; many seem to have been as passionate in their relations with lover and husband, in an age when passion in woman was as forbidden as intelligence, as they were in their battle for woman's chance to grow to full human stature. But if they, and those like Susan Anthony,† whom fortune or bitter experience turned away from marriage, fought for a chance for woman to fulfill herself, not in relation to man, but as an individual, it was from a need as real and burning as the need for love.

---

* Julia Ward Howe (1819–1910), prosperous middle-class Boston housewife who wrote moderately successful poetry critiquing domesticity. In 1862, during one of the darkest moments of the Civil War, she wrote the song "Battle Hymn of the Republic," which catapulted her onto the national stage. She used this notoriety to work for women's rights and continue her writing for the rest of her life. *Mary Wollstonecraft* (1759–1798), English intellectual and Enlightenment writer who commented on the political, artistic, and moral issues of the revolutionary moment in which she lived. Her most famous work was A *Vindication of the Rights of Woman with Strictures on Political and Moral Subject* (1792), in which she argues that women need to be educated equally to men and to be fully equal citizens and workers in society. It is considered one of the earliest expressions of women's rights. In addition to holding unconventional views, Wollstonecraft led an unconventional life, remaining single, having love affairs, and bearing a child while unmarried. She did eventually marry William Godwin, however, and they had a daughter, Mary Godwin, later Mary Shelley, the author of *Frankenstein*, but Wollstonecraft died shortly after her birth. *Angelina Grimké* (1805–1879) and her older sister Sarah (1792–1873) were born in South Carolina and grew up in a wealthy slave-holding family. They detested slavery, left South Carolina for Philadelphia, and became Quakers, promoting equality for enslaved people and women. As speakers on behalf of abolitionism, they were censured for their views and their public speaking at a time when it was considered indecent for women to speak before audiences that included men. *Ernestine Rose* (1810–1892) was born Ernestine Potowski in Poland, the daughter of a Jewish rabbi. She rejected her traditional upbringing and traveled through Europe to the United States, involving herself in a variety of progressive causes: abolitionism and rights for working-class people and women. She participated in the U.S. women's movement during these years, particularly for women's property rights and suffrage. *Margaret Fuller* (1810–1850) was educated like a boy by her politically prominent father. Because she was female, though, she could not attend Harvard as other socially elite intelligent boys in Massachusetts would have. Instead, she worked as a teacher and wrote. Her commentary was so good that she became an important participant in the transcendentalist movement, the only female in this intellectual brotherhood. She worked as a journalist, wrote travel literature, and in 1845 published *Woman in the Nineteenth Century*, the most important work to consider the position of women in U.S. society in the nineteenth century. She believed women should be educated equally to men and free to pursue any profession. *Elizabeth Cady Stanton* (1815–1902), the most important leader of the nineteenth century woman's movement. After witnessing the discriminatory treatment of women in the abolitionist movement, Stanton, with Lucretia Mott, organized the famous 1848 Woman's Rights Convention at Seneca Falls, New York. The document produced, "Declarations of Sentiments and Resolutions," articulated the goals of the women's movement for the rest of the century, including suffrage for women. Stanton worked in partnership with Susan B. Anthony, founding, after the Civil War, the National Woman's Suffrage Association. She was married to Henry Stanton and they had seven children.

† Susan B. Anthony (1820–1906) was born into an equalitarian Quaker family and became involved in many reform activities, such as temperance and abolitionism, as a young woman. After unequal treatment in these groups, she turned to women's rights and in the 1850s met Elizabeth Cady Stanton at a woman's rights convention. They formed a partnership and became the most important women's rights activists of the nineteenth century (see Stanton above). Anthony was convinced that suffrage was a crucial goal of the woman's movement and she worked tirelessly throughout her life as a public speaker to achieve this goal.

("What woman needs," said Margaret Fuller, "is not as a woman to act or rule, but as a nature to grow, as an intellect to discern, as a soul to live freely, and unimpeded to unfold such powers as were given her.")

The feminists had only one model, one image, one vision, of a full and free human being: man. For until very recently, only men (though not all men) had the freedom and the education necessary to realize their full abilities, to pioneer and create and discover, and map new trails for future generations. Only men had the vote: the freedom to shape the major decisions of society. Only men had the freedom to love, and enjoy love, and decide for themselves in the eyes of their God the problems of right and wrong. Did women want these freedoms because they wanted to be men? Or did they want them because they also were human?

That this is what feminism was all about was seen symbolically by Henrik Ibsen.* When he said in the play "A Doll's House," in 1879, that a woman was simply a human being, he struck a new note in literature. Thousands of women in middle-class Europe and America, in that Victorian time, saw themselves in Nora. And in 1960, almost a century later, millions of American housewives, who watched the play on television, also saw themselves as they heard Nora say:

> You have always been so kind to me. But our home has been nothing but a playroom. I have been your doll wife, just as at home I was Papa's doll child; and here the children have been my dolls. I thought it great fun when you played with me, just as they thought it fun when I played with them. That is what our marriage has been, Torvald . . .
>
> How am I fitted to bring up the children? . . . There is another task I must undertake first. I must try and educate myself—you are not the man to help me in that. I must do that for myself. And that is why I am going to leave you now . . . I must stand quite alone if I am to understand myself and every-thing about me. It is for that reason that I cannot remain with you any longer . . .

Her shocked husband reminds Nora that woman's "most sacred duties" are her duties to her husband and children. "Before all else, you are a wife and mother," he says. And Nora answers:

---

*   Henrik Ibsen (1828–1906), Norwegian playwright. He wrote plays that offered searing social commentary on European middle-class life, including A Doll's House (1879), which portrays the claustrophobic and stifled life of Nora Helmer, wife to Torvald Helmer. In the course of the play, she realizes that she has not been living a full authentic life and leaves her husband, home, and children to find out who she is. Scandalous when it first appeared, A Doll's House experienced new popularity during the 1960s and 1970s.

I believe that before all else I am a reasonable human being, just as you are—or, at all events, that I must try and become one. I know quite well, Torvald, that most people would think you right, and that views of that kind are to be found in books; but I can no longer content myself with what most people say or with what is found in books. I must think over things for myself and get to understand them . . .

It is a cliché of our own time that women spent half a century fighting for "rights," and the next half wondering whether they wanted them after all. "Rights" have a dull sound to people who have grown up after they have been won. But like Nora, the feminists had to win those rights before they could begin to live and love as human beings. Not very many women then, or even now, dared to leave the only security they knew—dared to turn their backs on their homes and husbands to begin Nora's search. But a great many, then as now, must have found their existence as housewives so empty that they could no longer savor the love of husband and children.

Some of them—and even a few men who realized that half the human race was denied the right to become fully human—set out to change the conditions that held women in bondage. Those conditions were summed up by the first Woman's Rights Convention in Seneca Falls, New York, in 1848,* as woman's grievances against man:

He has compelled her to submit to laws in the formation of which she has no voice. . . . He has made her, if married, in the eyes of the law, civilly dead. He has taken from her all right to property, even to the wages she earns . . . In the covenant of marriage, she is compelled to promise obedience to her husband, he becoming to all intents and purposes her master—the law giving him power to deprive her of her liberty, and to administer chastisement. . . . He closes against her all the avenues of wealth and distinction which he considers most honorable to himself. As a teacher of theology, medicine or law, she is not known. He has denied her the facilities for obtaining a thorough education, all colleges being closed against her. . . . He has created a false public sentiment by giving to the world a different code of morals for men and women by which moral delinquencies which exclude women from society are not only tolerated, but deemed of little account to man. He has usurped the prerogative of Jehovah himself; claiming it as his right to

* This convention, organized by Elizabeth Cady Stanton and Lucretia Mott, launched the first woman's movement in the United States and created a document, the "Declaration of Sentiments and Resolutions," that articulated the goals of the movement (see also entry on Elizabeth Cady Stanton, p. 66).

assign for her a sphere of action, when that belongs to her conscience and to her God. He has endeavored in every way that he could to destroy her confidence in her own powers, to lessen her self-respect, and to make her willing to lead a dependent and abject life.

It was these conditions, which the feminists set out to abolish a century ago, that made women what they were—"feminine," as it was then, and is still, defined.

It is hardly a coincidence that the struggle to free woman began in America on the heels of the Revolutionary War, and grew strong with the movement to free the slaves.[1] Thomas Paine, the spokesman for the Revolution, was among the first to condemn in 1775 the position of women "even in countries where they may be esteemed the most happy, constrained in their desires in the disposal of their goods, robbed of freedom and will by the laws, the slaves of opinion . . ." During the Revolution, some ten years before Mary Wollstonecraft spearheaded the feminist movement in England, an American woman, Judith Sargent Murray,[*] said woman needed knowledge to envision new goals and grow by reaching for them. In 1837, the year Mount Holyoke opened its doors to give women their first chance at education equal to man's, American women were also holding their first national anti-slavery convention in New York. The women who formally launched the women's rights movement at Seneca Falls met each other when they were refused seats at an anti-slavery convention in London. Shut off behind a curtain in the gallery, Elizabeth Stanton, on her honeymoon, and Lucretia Mott,[†] demure mother of five, decided that it was not only the slaves who needed to be liberated.

Whenever, wherever in the world there has been an upsurge of human freedom, women have won a share of it for themselves. Sex did not fight the French Revolution, free the slaves in America, overthrow the Russian Czar, drive the British out of India; but when the idea of human freedom moves the minds of men, it also moves the minds of women. The cadences of the Seneca Falls Declaration came straight from the Declaration of Independence:

---

[*] Judith Sargent Murray (1751–1820), writer born and raised in Massachusetts. Inspired by the revolutionary rhetoric and Enlightenment ideas of her era, she penned "On the equality of the sexes" in 1790. Throughout her life she wrote in support of women's intellectual equality and the need to educate girls equally to boys. She was one of the first advocates for women's rights in the United States.

[†] Lucretia Mott (1793–1880), wife, mother, and Quaker minister, participated in many social reform movements of the day, including abolitionism and women's rights (see entries on Elizabeth Cady Stanton, p. 66, and First Woman's Rights Convention at Seneca Falls, p. 68).

> When, in the course of human events, it becomes necessary
> for one portion of the family of man to assume among the
> people of the earth a position different from that they have
> hitherto occupied. . . . We hold these truths to be self-evident:
> that all men and women are created equal.

Feminism was not a dirty joke. The feminist revolution had to be
fought because women quite simply were stopped at a stage of evolution far short of their human capacity. "The domestic function of
woman does not exhaust her powers," the Rev. Theodore Parker
preached in Boston in 1853. "To make one half the human race
consume its energies in the functions of housekeeper, wife and
mother is a monstrous waste of the most precious material God
ever made." And running like a bright and sometimes dangerous
thread through the history of the feminist movement was also the
idea that equality for woman was necessary to free both man and
woman for true sexual fulfillment.[2] For the degradation of woman
also degraded marriage, love, all relations between man and woman.
After the sexual revolution, said Robert Dale Owen,* "then will
the monopoly of sex perish with other unjust monopolies; and
women will not be restricted to one virtue, and one passion, and
one occupation."[3]

The women and men who started that revolution anticipated "no
small amount of misconception, misrepresentation and ridicule."
And they got it. The first to speak out in public for women's rights
in America—Fanny Wright,† daughter of a Scotch nobleman, and
Ernestine Rose, daughter of a rabbi—were called respectively, "red
harlot of infidelity" and "woman a thousand times below a prostitute." The declaration at Seneca Falls brought such an outcry of
"Revolution," "Insurrection Among Women," "The Reign of Petticoats," "Blasphemy," from newspapers and clergymen that the
faint-hearted withdrew their signatures. Lurid reports of "free love"
and "legalized adultery" competed with phantasies of court sessions, church sermons and surgical operations interrupted while a
lady lawyer or minister or doctor hastily presented her husband
with a baby.

At every step of the way, the feminists had to fight the conception
that they were violating the God-given nature of woman. Clergy-

---

* Robert Dale Owen (1801–1877) founded with his father, Robert Owen, the utopian
community of New Harmony, Indiana. A "freethinker," he was a prolific writer and
social activist working for abolitionism, equal rights for women, education reform, and
the rights of the working class. He worked with Fanny Wright on many of these causes.
† Fanny Wright (1795–1852), independently wealthy, Scottish-born "freethinker." She
was one of the first women to speak to mixed audiences on controversial topics such as
abolitionism, sexual equality, free public education, and workers' rights. Because she
and Robert Dale Owen endorsed sexual education and birth control for women, they
were considered radical in their day.

men interrupted women's-rights conventions, waving Bibles and quoting from the Scriptures: "Saint Paul said . . . and the head of every woman is man" . . . "Let your women be silent in the churches, for it is not permitted unto them to speak" . . . "And if they will learn anything, let them ask their husbands at home; for it is a shame for women to speak in the church" . . . "But I suffer not a woman to teach, nor to usurp authority over the man, but to be in silence; for Adam was first formed, then Eve" . . . "Saint Peter said: likewise, ye wives, be in subjection to your own husbands" . . .

To give women equal rights would destroy that "milder gentler nature, which not only makes them shrink from, but disqualifies them for the turmoil and battle of public life," a Senator from New Jersey intoned piously in 1866. "They have a higher and a holier mission. It is in retiracy to make the character of coming men. Their mission is at home, by their blandishments, and their love, to assuage the passions of men as they come in from the battle of life, and not themselves by joining in the contest to add fuel to the very flames."

"They do not appear to be satisfied with having unsexed themselves, but they desire to unsex every female in the land," said a New York assemblyman who opposed one of the first petitions for a married woman's right to property and earnings. Since "God created man as the representative of the race," then "took from his side the material for woman's creation" and returned her to his side in matrimony as "one flesh, one being," the assembly smugly denied the petition: "A higher power than that from which emanates legislative enactments has given forth the mandate that man and woman shall not be equal."[4]

The myth that these women were "unnatural monsters" was based on the belief that to destroy the God-given subservience of women would destroy the home and make slaves of men. Such myths arise in every kind of revolution that advances a new portion of the family of man to equality. The image of the feminists as inhuman, fiery man-eaters, whether expressed as an offense against God or in the modern terms of sexual perversion, is not unlike the stereotype of the Negro as a primitive animal or the union member as an anarchist. What the sexual terminology hides is the fact that the feminist movement was a revolution. There were excesses, of course, as in any revolution, but the excesses of the feminists were in themselves a demonstration of the revolution's necessity. They stemmed from, and were a passionate repudiation of, the degrading realities of woman's life, the helpless subservience behind the gentle decorum that made women objects of such thinly veiled contempt to men that they even felt contempt for themselves. Evidently, that contempt and self-contempt were harder to get rid of than the conditions which caused them.

Of course they envied man. Some of the early feminists cut their hair short and wore bloomers, and tried to be like men. From the lives they saw their mothers lead, from their own experience, those passionate women had good reason to reject the conventional image of woman. Some even rejected marriage and motherhood for themselves. But in turning their backs on the old feminine image, in fighting to free themselves and all women, some of them became a different kind of woman. They became complete human beings.

The name of Lucy Stone today brings to mind a man-eating fury, wearing pants, brandishing an umbrella. It took a long time for the man who loved her to persuade her to marry him, and though she loved him and kept his love throughout her long life, she never took his name. When she was born, her gentle mother cried: "Oh, dear! I am sorry it is a girl. A woman's life is so hard." A few hours before the baby came, this mother, on a farm in western Massachusetts in 1818, milked eight cows because a sudden thunderstorm had called all hands into the field: it was more important to save the hay crop than to safeguard a mother on the verge of childbirth. Though this gentle, tired mother carried the endless work of farmhouse and bore nine children, Lucy Stone grew up with the knowledge that "There was only one will in our house, and that was my father's."

She rebelled at being born a girl if that meant being as lowly as the Bible said, as her mother said. She rebelled when she raised her hand at church meetings and, time and again, it was not counted. At a church sewing circle, where she was making a shirt to help a young man through theological seminary, she heard Mary Lyon* talk of education for women. She left the shirt unfinished, and at sixteen started teaching school for $1 a week, saving her earnings for nine years, until she had enough to go to college herself. She wanted to train herself "to plead not only for the slave, but for suffering humanity everywhere. Especially do I mean to labor for the elevation of my own sex." But at Oberlin,† where she was one of the first women to graduate from the "regular course," she had to practice public speaking secretly in the woods. Even at Oberlin, the girls were forbidden to speak in public.

---

* Mary Lyon (1797–1849), New England woman of modest means who, through her own intelligence and will, became educated and a teacher during a time when young women had very few opportunities to receive college training. Lyon, by appealing to wealthy patrons, financed the first permanent institution of higher learning exclusively for women: Mount Holyoke College in South Hadley, Massachusetts, founded in 1837. This was the first of the "Seven Sisters" (see entry on Seven Sisters, p. 21).

† Oberlin College (Oberlin, Ohio) was founded in 1833 to train Christian leaders and missionaries in the west. It was the first college to admit women and African Americans as students along with white males. Many leaders of the women's and abolitionist movements were educated at Oberlin.

Washing the men's clothes, caring for their rooms, serving them at table, listening to their orations, but themselves remaining respectfully silent in public assemblages, the Oberlin "coeds" were being prepared for intelligent motherhood and a properly subservient wifehood.[5]

In appearance, Lucy Stone was a little woman, with a gentle, silvery voice which could quiet a violent mob. She lectured on abolition Saturdays and Sundays, as an agent for the Anti-Slavery Society, and for women's rights the rest of the week on her own—facing down and winning over men who threatened her with clubs, threw prayer books and eggs at her head, and once in mid-winter shoved a hose through a window and turned icy water on her.

In one town, the usual report was circulated that a big, masculine woman, wearing boots, smoking a cigar, swearing like a trooper, had arrived to lecture. The ladies who came to hear this freak expressed their amazement to find Lucy Stone, small and dainty, dressed in a black satin gown with a white lace frill at the neck, "a prototype of womanly grace . . . fresh and fair as the morning."[6]

Her voice so rankled pro-slavery forces that the *Boston Post* published a rude poem promising "fame's loud trumpet shall be blown" for the man who "with a wedding kiss shuts up the mouth of Lucy Stone." Lucy Stone felt that "marriage is to a woman a state of slavery." Even after Henry Blackwell had pursued her from Cincinnati to Massachusetts ("She was born locomotive," he complained), and vowed to "repudiate the supremacy of either woman or man in marriage," and wrote her: "I met you at Niagara and sat at your feet by the whirlpool looking down into the dark waters with a passionate and unshared and unsatisfied yearning in my heart that you will never know, nor understand," and made a public speech in favor of women's rights; even after she admitted that she loved him, and wrote "You can scarcely tell me anything I do not know about the emptiness of a single life," she suffered blinding migraine headaches over the decision to marry him.

At their wedding, the minister Thomas Higginson reported that "the heroic Lucy cried like any village bride." The minister also said: "I never perform the marriage ceremony without a renewed sense of the iniquity of a system by which man and wife are one, and that one is the husband." And he sent to the newspapers, for other couples to copy, the pact which Lucy Stone and Henry Blackwell* joined hands to make, before their wedding vows:

---

* Henry Brown Blackwell (1825–1909), a British immigrant who became involved in abolitionist activity and then the women's movement, in part because of his sister Elizabeth Blackwell's efforts to become a physician. He married Lucy Stone (an Oberlin graduate) in a ceremony declaring their equality in marriage and helped her found the American Woman Suffrage Association.

> While we acknowledge our mutual affection by publicly assum-
> ing the relationship of husband and wife . . . we deem it a duty
> to declare that this act on our part implies no sanction of, nor
> promise of voluntary obedience to such of the present laws of
> marriage as refuse to recognize the wife as an independent,
> rational being, while they confer upon the husband an injuri-
> ous and unnatural superiority.[7]

Lucy Stone, her friend, the pretty Reverend Antoinette Brown
(who later married Henry's brother), Margaret Fuller, Angelina
Grimké, Abby Kelley Foster*—all resisted early marriage, and did
not, in fact, marry until in their battle against slavery and for
women's rights they had begun to find an identity as women
unknown to their mothers. Some, like Susan Anthony and Elizabeth Blackwell,[†] never married; Lucy Stone kept her own name in
more than symbolic fear that to become a wife was to die as a person. The concept known as "femme couverte" (covered woman),[‡]
written into the law, suspended the "very being or legal existence of
a woman" upon marriage. "To a married woman, her new self is her
superior, her companion, her master."

If it is true that the feminists were "disappointed women," as
their enemies said even then, it was because almost all women living under such conditions had reason to be disappointed. In one of
the most moving speeches of her life, Lucy Stone said in 1855:

> From the first years to which my memory stretches, I have been
> a disappointed woman. When, with my brothers, I reached
> forth after sources of knowledge, I was reproved with "It isn't

---

* Abby Kelley Foster (1810–1887), born a Quaker, was involved in abolitionism and
women's rights, attending some of the earliest woman's rights conventions. She was an
active anti-slavery speaker and she and her husband, Stephen Foster, opened their
Massachusetts house to enslaved people escaping North on the Underground Railroad. After the Civil War, she worked for equal rights for women. *Antoinette Brown
Blackwell* (1825–1921) attended Oberlin College and became the first ordained woman
minister in the United States in 1853. She married Samuel Blackwell, Henry Blackwell's brother, and was good friends with Lucy Stone. She was an active speaker on
behalf of abolitionism and women's rights, accompanying Susan B. Anthony and Julia
Ward Howe on suffrage tours.

† Elizabeth Blackwell (1821–1910), the first female to graduate from medical school in
the United States in 1849. She was the sister of Henry Blackwell and sister-in-law to
Lucy Stone and Antoinette Brown Blackwell. She and her sister Emily established the
New York Infirmary for Women and Children in 1857 and its school of medicine for
women in 1868. She did not work directly with the women's movement but championed women's participation in and provided an important role model for women in
medicine.

‡ Legal principle dating back to British Common Law that describes a married woman
as legally covered by her husband. This is sometimes referred to as unity in person—
the husband serves as the legal representative for the family, or as legal death—the
wife legally dies when she marries, her legal identity subsumed by her husband. When
married, women could not engage in any legal activity on their own. This is why
women could not vote, could not serve on juries, could not convey property on their
own, could not retain custody of their children after divorce, and were restricted in
many other public activities.

fit for you; it doesn't belong to women" . . . In education, in marriage, in religion, in everything, disappointment is the lot of woman. It shall be the business of my life to deepen this disappointment in every woman's heart until she bows down to it no longer.[8]

In her own lifetime, Lucy Stone saw the laws of almost every state radically changed in regard to women, high schools opened to them and two-thirds of the colleges in the United States. Her husband and her daughter, Alice Stone Blackwell, devoted their lives, after her death in 1893, to the unfinished battle for woman's vote. By the end of her passionate journey, she could say she was glad to have been born a woman. She wrote her daughter the day before her seventieth birthday:

I trust my Mother sees and knows how glad I am to have been born, and at a time when there was so much that needed help at which I could lend a hand. Dear Old Mother! She had a hard life, and was sorry she had another girl to share and bear the hard life of a woman. . . . But I am wholly glad that I came.[9]

In certain men, at certain times in history, the passion for freedom has been as strong or stronger than the familiar passions of sexual love. That this was so, for many of those women who fought to free women, seems to be a fact, no matter how the strength of that other passion is explained. Despite the frowns and jeers of most of their husbands and fathers, despite the hostility if not outright abuse they got for their "unwomanly" behavior, the feminists continued their crusade. They themselves were tortured by soul-searching doubts every step of the way. It was unladylike, friends wrote Mary Lyon, to travel all over New England with a green velvet bag, collecting money to start her college for women. "What do I do that is wrong?" she asked. "I ride in the stage-coach or cars without an escort. . . . My heart is sick, my soul is pained with this empty gentility, this genteel nothingness. I am doing a great work, I cannot come down."

The lovely Angelina Grimké felt as if she would faint, when she accepted what was meant as a joke and appeared to speak before the Massachusetts legislature on the anti-slavery petitions, the first woman ever to appear before a legislative body. A pastoral letter denounced her unwomanly behavior:

We invite your attention to the dangers which at present seem to threaten the female character with widespread and permanent injury. . . . The power of woman is her dependence, flowing from the consciousness of that weakness which God has given her for her protection. . . . But when she assumes the place and tone of man as a public reformer . . . her character becomes unnatural. If the vine, whose strength and beauty is to lean on the trellis-work and half conceal its cluster, thinks to assume the independence and overshadowing nature of the elm, it will not only cease to bear fruit, but fall in shame and dishonor in the dust.[10]

More than restlessness and frustration made her refuse to be "shamed into silence," and made New England housewives walk two, four, six, and eight miles on winter evenings to hear her.

The emotional identification of American women with the battle to free the slaves may or may not testify to the unconscious foment of their own rebellion. But it is an undeniable fact that, in organizing, petitioning, and speaking out to free the slaves, American women learned how to free themselves. In the South, where slavery kept women at home, and where they did not get a taste of education or pioneering work or the schooling battles of society, the old image of femininity reigned intact, and there were few feminists. In the North, women who took part in the Underground Railroad, or otherwise worked to free the slaves, never were the same again. Feminism also went west with the wagon trains, where the frontier made women almost equal from the beginning. (Wyoming was the first state to give women the vote.) Individually, the feminists seem to have had no more nor less reason than all women of their time to envy or hate man. But what they did have was self-respect, courage, strength. Whether they loved or hated man, escaped or suffered humiliation from men in their own lives, they identified with women. Women who accepted the conditions which degraded them felt contempt for themselves and all women. The feminists who fought those conditions freed themselves of that contempt and had less reason to envy man.

The call to that first Woman's Rights Convention came about because an educated woman, who had already participated in shaping society as an abolitionist, came face to face with the realities of a housewife's drudgery and isolation in a small town. Like the college graduate with six children in the suburb of today, Elizabeth Cady Stanton, moved by her husband to the small town of Seneca Falls, was restless in a life of baking, cooking, sewing, washing and caring for each baby. Her husband, an abolitionist leader, was often away on business. She wrote:

> I now understood the practical difficulties most women had to contend with in the isolated household and the impossibility of woman's best development if in contact the chief part of her life with servants and children. . . . The general discontent I felt with woman's portion . . . and the wearied, anxious look of

the majority of women, impressed me with the strong feeling that some active measures should be taken. . . . I could not see what to do or where to begin—my only thought was a public meeting for protest and discussion.[11]

She put only one notice in the newspapers, and housewives and daughters who had never known any other kind of life came in wagons from a radius of fifty miles to hear her speak.

However dissimilar their social or psychological roots, all who led the battle for women's rights, early and late, also shared more than common intelligence, fed by more than common education for their time. Otherwise, whatever their emotions, they would not have been able to see through the prejudices which had justified woman's degradation, and to put their dissenting voice into words. Mary Wollstonecraft educated herself and was then educated by that company of English philosophers then preaching the rights of man. Margaret Fuller was taught by her father to read the classics of six languages, and was caught up in the transcendentalist group around Emerson. Elizabeth Cady Stanton's father, a judge, got his daughter the best education then available, and supplemented it by letting her listen to his law cases. Ernestine Rose, the rabbi's daughter who rebelled against her religion's doctrine that decreed woman's inferiority to man, got her education in "free thinking" from the great utopian philosopher Robert Owen. She also defied orthodox religious custom to marry a man she loved. She always insisted, in the bitterest days of the fight for women's rights, that woman's enemy was not man. "We do not fight with man himself, but only with bad principles."

These women were not man-eaters. Julia Ward Howe, brilliant and beautiful daughter of the New York "400" who studied intensively every field that interested her, wrote the "Battle Hymn of the Republic" anonymously, because her husband believed her life should be devoted to him and their six children. She took no part in the suffrage movement until 1868, when she met Lucy Stone, who "had long been the object of one of my imaginary dislikes. As I looked into her sweet, womanly face and heard her earnest voice, I felt that the object of my distaste had been a mere phantom, conjured up by silly and senseless misrepresentations. . . . I could only say, 'I am with you.'"[12]

The irony of that man-eating myth is that the so-called excesses of the feminists arose from their helplessness. When women are considered to have no rights nor to deserve any, what can they do for themselves? At first, it seemed there was nothing they could do but talk. They held women's rights conventions every year after 1848, in small towns and large, national and state conventions, over and over again—in Ohio, Pennsylvania, Indiana, Massachusetts. They could

talk till doomsday about the rights they did not have. But how do
women get legislators to let them keep their own earnings, or their
own children after divorce, when they do not even have a vote? How
can they finance or organize a campaign to get the vote when they
have no money of their own, nor even the right to own property?

The very sensitivity to opinion which such complete dependence
breeds in women made every step out of their genteel prison a painful one. Even when they tried to change conditions that were within
their power to change, they met ridicule. The fantastically uncomfortable dress "ladies" wore then was a symbol of their bondage:
stays so tightly laced they could hardly breathe, half a dozen skirts
and petticoats, weighing ten to twelve pounds, so long they swept
up refuse from the street. The specter of the feminists taking the
pants off men came partly from the "Bloomer" dress—a tunic,
knee-length skirt, ankle length pantaloons. Elizabeth Stanton wore
it, eagerly at first, to do her housework in comfort, as a young
woman today might wear shorts or slacks. But when the feminists
wore the Bloomer dress in public, as a symbol of their emancipation, the rude jokes, from newspaper editors, street corner loafers,
and small boys, were unbearable to their feminine sensitivities.
"We put the dress on for greater freedom, but what is physical freedom compared to mental bondage," said Elizabeth Stanton and
discarded her "Bloomer" dress. Most, like Lucy Stone, stopped
wearing it for a feminine reason: it was not very becoming, except
to the extremely tiny, pretty Mrs. Bloomer herself.

Still, that helpless gentility had to be overcome, in the minds of
men, in the minds of other women, in their own minds. When they
decided to petition for married women's rights to own property,
half the time even the women slammed doors in their faces with
the smug remark that they had husbands, they needed no laws to
protect them. When Susan Anthony and her women captains collected 6,000 signatures in ten weeks, the New York State Assembly
received them with roars of laughter. In mockery, the Assembly
recommended that since ladies always get the "choicest tidbits" at
the table, the best seat in the carriage, and their choice of which
side of the bed to lie on, "if there is any inequity or oppression the
gentlemen are the sufferers." However, they would waive "redress"
except where both husband and wife had signed the petition. "In
such case, they would recommend the parties to apply for a law
authorizing them to change dresses, that the husband may wear the
petticoats and the wife the breeches."

The wonder is that the feminists were able to win anything at
all—that they were not embittered shrews but increasingly zestful
women who knew they were making history. There is more spirit
than bitterness in Elizabeth Stanton, having babies into her forties,

writing Susan Anthony that this one truly will be her last, and the fun is just beginning—"Courage, Susan, we will not reach our prime until we're fifty." Painfully insecure and self-conscious about her looks—not because of treatment by men (she had suitors) but because of a beautiful older sister and mother who treated a crossed eye as a tragedy—Susan Anthony, of all the nineteenth-century feminist leaders, was the only one resembling the myth. She felt betrayed when the others started to marry and have babies. But despite the chip on her shoulder, she was no bitter spinster with a cat. Traveling alone from town to town, hammering up her meeting notices, using her abilities to the fullest as organizer and lobbyist and lecturer, she made her own way in a larger and larger world.

In their own lifetime, such women changed the feminine image that had justified woman's degradation. At a meeting while men jeered at trusting the vote to women so helpless that they had to be lifted over mud puddles and handed into carriages, a proud feminist named Sojourner Truth* raised her black arm:

> Look at my arm! I have ploughed and planted and gathered into barns . . . and ain't I a woman? I could work as much and eat as much as a man—when I could get it—and bear the lash as well . . . I have borne thirteen children and seen most of 'em sold into slavery, and when I cried out with my mother's grief, none but Jesus helped me—and ain't I a woman?

That image of empty gentility was also undermined by the growing thousands of women who worked in the red brick factories: the Lowell mill girls† who fought the terrible working conditions which, partly as a result of women's supposed inferiority, were even worse for them than for men. But those women, who after a twelve- or thirteen-hour day in the factory still had household duties, could not take the lead in the passionate journey. Most of the leading feminists were women of the middle class, driven by a complex of motives to educate themselves and smash that empty image.

---

* Sojourner Truth (c. 1797–1883), African American evangelist who became an activist for abolition, African American rights, and women's rights in the nineteenth century. Born a slave in New York, Truth became a popular abolitionist speaker after New York abolished slavery. She dictated her memoir, *The Narrative of Sojourner Truth*, to abolitionist author Harriet Beecher Stowe (see entry on Uncle Tom, p. 45). Truth delivered her most famous speech, "Ain't I a Woman?" to a woman's rights conference in 1851; the speech was transcribed and published thirty years later, and became a classic work of American feminism.

† Some of the earliest textile factories in Lowell, Massachusetts, employed young Yankee farm daughters to work in the mills. Employers created boarding houses for them and while conditions were hard, in the early years many of the girls used the experience to save money for education, family support, and a dowry. In the 1830s, when economic conditions worsened and their pay and support were cut, many "turned out" in some of the first strikes by female workers in the United States.

What drove them on? "Must let out my pent-up energy in some new way," wrote Louisa May Alcott* in her journal when she decided to volunteer as a nurse in the Civil War. "A most interesting journey, into a new world, full of stirring sights and sounds, new adventures, and an ever-growing sense of the great task I had undertaken. I said my prayers as I went rushing through the country, white with tents, all alive with patriotism, and already red with blood. A solemn time, but I'm glad to live in it."

What drove them on? Lonely and racked with self-doubt, Elizabeth Blackwell, in that unheard-of, monstrous determination to be a woman doctor, ignored sniggers—and tentative passes—to do her anatomical dissections. She battled for the right to witness the dissection of the reproductive organs, but decided against walking in the commencement procession because it would be unladylike. Shunned even by her fellow physicians, she wrote:

> I am woman as well as physician . . . I understand now why this life has never been lived before. It is hard, with no support but a high purpose, to live against every species of social opposition . . . I should like a little fun now and then. Life is altogether too sober.[13]

In the course of a century of struggle, reality gave the lie to the myth that woman would use her rights for vengeful domination of man. As they won the right to equal education, the right to speak out in public and own property, and the right to work at a job or profession and control their own earnings, the feminists felt less reason to be bitter against man. But there was one more battle to be fought. As M. Carey Thomas,† the brilliant first president of Bryn Mawr, said in 1908:

> Women are one-half the world, but until a century ago . . . women lived a twilight life, a half life apart, and looked out and saw men as shadows walking. It was a man's world. The laws were men's laws, the government a man's government, the country a man's country. Now women have won the right to higher education and economic independence. The right to become citizens of the state is the next and inevitable conse-

---

* Louisa May Alcott (1832–1888), author of *Little Women*, a classic nineteenth-century novel that is still widely read and adored. She grew up in poverty, the daughter of the transcendentalist Bronson Alcott, and after taking many jobs traditionally held by women, began to support herself and her family by writing. She supported many progressive causes including women's rights.

† M. Carey Thomas (1857–1935), child of Quaker parents and a graduate of Cornell University. Just as she finished her doctorate in linguistics from the University of Zurich, a major bequest for a Quaker college for women became available, and she became a dean and professor at the new Bryn Mawr College. She became the college president in 1892 and promoted female education and feminist causes throughout her life.

quence of education and work outside the home. We have gone so far; we must go farther. We cannot go back.[14]

The trouble was, the women's rights movement had become almost too respectable; yet without the right to vote, women could not get any political party to take them seriously. When Elizabeth Stanton's daughter, Harriet Blatch, came home in 1907, the widow of an Englishman, she found the movement in which her mother had raised her in a sterile rut of tea and cookies. She had seen the tactics women used in England to dramatize the issue in a similar stalemate: heckling speakers at public meetings, deliberate provocation of the police, hunger strikes in jail—the kind of dramatic nonviolent resistance Gandhi used in India, or that the Freedom Riders* now use in the United States when legal tactics leave segregation intact. The American feminists never had to resort to the extremes of their longer-sinned-against English counterparts. But they did dramatize the vote issue until they aroused an opposition far more powerful than the sexual one.

As the battle to free women was fired by the battle to free the slaves in the nineteenth century, it was fired in the twentieth by the battles of social reform, of Jane Addams and Hull House,† the use of the union movement, and the great strikes against intolerable working conditions in the factories. For the Triangle Shirtwaist girls,‡ working for as little as $6 a week, as late as 10 o'clock at night, fined for talking, laughing, or singing, equality was a question of more than education or the vote. They held out on picket lines through bitter cold and hungry months; dozens were clubbed by

---

*   To illustrate the brutality of Southern segregation, white and black protesters traveled in 1961 on buses throughout the South, ignoring designations for "black" and "white" facilities; these actions were called "Freedom Rides." Freedom Riders were beaten severely by mobs in Anniston, Birmingham, and Montgomery, Alabama; one bus was firebombed. The international publicity received by the Freedom Rides led the Interstate Commerce Commission to integrate interstate bus terminals.

†   Born to a prominent Illinois politician, Jane Addams (1860–1935) attended the female-only Rockford Seminary. With few prospects for employment and failing health, she toured Europe and became aware of settlement work that served poor and immigrant communities. When she returned to the United States, she and her college friend Ellen Gates Starr founded the first American settlement house, Hull House, in a Chicago slum. Addams was a progressive reformer involved in many causes. Her work in the peace movement made her the first woman to win the Nobel Peace Prize, in 1931.

‡   The Triangle Shirtwaist Company was the largest maker of shirtwaists (blouses worn by women) in New York City in the early 1900s. The vast majority of the company's workers were Jewish and Italian immigrant women who worked thirteen hours a day in dirty, airless factory rooms that were locked to prevent them from stealing. In November 1909, Triangle workers struck for better conditions, and the strike spread to other companies, becoming known as "the uprising of the 10,000." Although employers used mass arrests and violence to try to break the strike, ultimately strikers won the public's sympathy, and they received a settlement that gave them a wage increase and better conditions. Employers never actually improved conditions, however, and two years later, the Triangle Shirtwaist Company went up in flames, killing 146 trapped people in less than fifteen minutes.

police and dragged off in Black Marias.* The new feminists raised money for the strikers' bail and food, as their mothers had helped the Underground Railroad.

Behind the cries of "save femininity," "save the home," could now be glimpsed the influence of political machines, quailing at the very thought of what those reforming women would do if they got the vote. Women, after all, were trying to shut down the saloons. Brewers as well as other business interests, especially those that depended on underpaid labor of children and women, openly lobbied against the woman's suffrage amendment in Washington. "Machine men were plainly uncertain of their ability to control an addition to the electorate which seemed to them relatively unsusceptible to bribery, more militant and bent on disturbing reforms ranging from sewage control to the abolition of child labor and worst of all, 'cleaning up' politics."[15] And Southern congressmen pointed out that suffrage for women also meant Negro women.

The final battle for the vote was fought in the twentieth century by the growing numbers of college-trained women, led by Carrie Chapman Catt,† daughter of the Iowa prairie, educated at Iowa State, a teacher and a newspaperwoman, whose husband, a successful engineer, firmly supported her battles. One group that later called itself the Woman's Party‡ made continual headlines with picket lines around the White House. After the outbreak of World War I, there was much hysteria about women who chained themselves to the White House fence. Maltreated by police and courts, they went on hunger strikes in jail and were finally martyred by forced feeding. Many of these women were Quakers and pacifists; but the majority of the feminists supported the war even as they continued their campaign for women's rights. They are hardly accountable for the myth of the man-eating feminist which is prevalent today, a myth that has cropped up continuously from the days of Lucy Stone to the present, whenever anyone has reason to oppose women's move out of the home.

In this final battle, American women over a period of fifty years conducted 56 campaigns of referenda to male voters; 480 campaigns to get legislatures to submit suffrage amendments to voters; 277 campaigns to get state party conventions to include woman's suffrage

---

*   Slang for large police vans or paddy wagons used to transport prisoners.
†   Carrie Chapman Catt (1859–1947) assumed the leadership of the National American Woman Suffrage Association after Susan B. Anthony. A skillful, shrewd politician, she led a divided women's suffrage movement to secure a suffrage victory for American women in 1920.
‡   After women won the right to vote in 1920, radical suffragists formed the National Woman's Party in 1921 to continue the struggle for women's rights. Its leader, Alice Paul, drafted the Equal Rights Amendment (ERA) in 1923, framing one of the goals of the feminist movement throughout the twentieth century. The National Woman's Party provided a link between suffrage-era women's rights activism and the women's movements of the 1960s and 1970s.

planks; 30 campaigns to get presidential party conventions to adopt woman's suffrage planks, and 19 campaigns with 19 successive Congresses.[16] Someone had to organize all those parades, speeches, petitions, meetings, lobbying of legislators and congressmen. The new feminists were no longer a handful of devoted women; thousands, millions of American women with husbands, children, and homes gave as much time as they could spare to the cause. The unpleasant image of the feminists today resembles less the feminists themselves than the image fostered by the interests who so bitterly opposed the vote for women in state after state, lobbying, threatening legislators with business or political ruin, buying votes, even stealing them, until, and even after, 36 states had ratified the amendment.

The ones who fought that battle won more than empty paper rights. They cast off the shadow of contempt and self-contempt that had degraded women for centuries. The joy, the sense of excitement and the personal rewards of that battle are described beautifully by Ida Alexa Ross Wylie, an English feminist:

> To my astonishment, I found that women, in spite of knock-knees and the fact that for centuries a respectable woman's leg had not even been mentionable, could at a pinch outrun the average London bobby. Their aim with a little practice became good enough to land ripe vegetables in ministerial eyes, their wits sharp enough to keep Scotland Yard running around in circles and looking very silly. Their capacity for impromptu organization, for secrecy and loyalty, their iconoclastic disregard for class and established order were a revelation to all concerned, but especially themselves. . . .
>
> The day that, with a straight left to the jaw, I sent a fair-sized CID officer into the orchestra pit of the theatre where we were holding one of our belligerent meetings, was the day of my own coming of age. . . . Since I was no genius, the episode could not make me one, but it set me free to be whatever I was to the top of my bent. . . .
>
> For two years of wild and sometimes dangerous adventure, I worked and fought alongside vigorous, happy, well-adjusted women who laughed instead of tittering, who walked freely instead of teetering, who could outfast Gandhi and come out with a grin and a jest. I slept on hard floors between elderly duchesses, stout cooks, and young shop-girls. We were often tired, hurt and frightened. But we were content as we had never been. We shared a joy of life that we had never known. Most of my fellow-fighters were wives and mothers. And strange things happened to their domestic life. Husbands came home at night with a new eagerness. . . . As for children, their attitude changed rapidly from one of affectionate toleration for poor,

darling mother to one of wide-eyed wonder. Released from the smother of mother love, for she was too busy to be more than casually concerned with them, they discovered that they liked her. She was a great sport. She had guts. . . . Those women who stood outside the fight—I regret to say the vast majority—and who were being more than usually Little Women, hated the fighters with the venomous rage of envy . . . [17]

Did women really go home again as a reaction to feminism? The fact is that to women born after 1920, feminism was dead history. It ended as a vital movement in America with the winning of that final right: the vote. In the 1930's and 40's, the sort of woman who fought for woman's rights was still concerned with human rights and freedom—for Negroes, for oppressed workers, for victims of Franco's Spain and Hitler's Germany. But no one was much concerned with rights for women: they had all been won. And yet the man-eating myth prevailed. Women who displayed any independence or initiative were called "Lucy Stoners." "Feminist," like "career woman," became a dirty word. The feminists had destroyed the old image of woman, but they could not erase the hostility, the prejudice, the discrimination that still remained. Nor could they paint the new image of what women might become when they grew up under conditions that no longer made them inferior to men, dependent, passive, incapable of thought or decision.

Most of the girls who grew up during the years when the feminists were eliminating the causes of that denigrating "genteel nothingness" got their image of woman from mothers still trapped in it. These mothers were probably the real model for the man-eating myth. The shadow of the contempt and self-contempt which could turn a gentle housewife into a domineering shrew also turned some of their daughters into angry copies of man. The first women in business and the professions were thought to be freaks. Insecure in their new freedom, some perhaps feared to be soft or gentle, love, have children, lest they lose their prized independence, lest they be trapped again as their mothers were. They reinforced the myth.

But the daughters who grew up with the rights the feminists had won could not go back to that old image of genteel nothingness, nor did they have their aunts' or mothers' reasons to be angry copies of man, or fear to love them. They had come unknowing to the turning-point in woman's identity. They had truly outgrown the old image; they were finally free to be what they chose to be. But what choice were they offered? In that corner, the fiery, man-eating feminist, the career woman—loveless, alone. In this corner, the gentle wife and mother—loved and protected by her husband, surrounded by her adoring children. Though many daughters continued on the passionate journey their grandmothers had begun, thousands of others fell out—victims of a mistaken choice.

The reasons for their choice were, of course, more complex than the feminist myth. How did Chinese women, after having their feet bound for many generations, finally discover they could run? The first women whose feet were unbound must have felt such pain that some were afraid to stand, let alone to walk or run. The more they walked, the less their feet hurt. But what would have happened if, before a single generation of Chinese girls had grown up with unbound feet, doctors, hoping to save them pain and distress, told them to bind their feet again? And teachers told them that walking with bound feet was feminine, the only way a woman could walk if she wanted a man to love her? And scholars told them that they would be better mothers if they could not walk too far away from their children? And peddlers, discovering that women who could not walk bought more trinkets, spread fables of the dangers of running and the bliss of being bound? Would many little Chinese girls, then, grow up wanting to have their feet securely bound, never tempted to walk or run?

The real joke that history played on American women is not the one that makes people snigger, with cheap Freudian sophistication, at the dead feminists. It is the joke that Freudian thought played on living women, twisting the memory of the feminists into the man-eating phantom of the feminine mystique, shriveling the very wish to be more than just a wife and mother. Encouraged by the mystique to evade their identity crisis, permitted to escape identity altogether in the name of sexual fulfillment, women once again are living with their feet bound in the old image of glorified femininity. And it is the same old image, despite its shiny new clothes, that trapped women for centuries and made the feminists rebel.

5

The Sexual Solipsism of Sigmund Freud

It would be half-wrong to say it started with Sigmund Freud.* It did not really start, in America, until the 1940's. And then again, it was less a start than the prevention of an end. The old

---

* Sigmund Freud (1856–1939), Austrian psychiatrist and the founder of psychoanalysis, a therapeutic method that calls for individuals to talk about their dreams, free associations, or childhood experiences. Freud believed that people are governed by their unconscious—feelings that they repress from conscious thought when they are young. Freud's ideas spread to the United States in the 1910s, and had filtered into popular American culture by the 1920s. In the 1960s, feminists like Friedan began to criticize Freud, arguing that his concepts of "penis envy" and the "Oedipus complex" (see entries on penis envy, p. 87, and Oedipus complex, p. 89) equated sexuality with masculinity, and that his claim that "anatomy is destiny" limited women's abilities to the sexual and reproductive spheres.

prejudices—women are animals, less than human, unable to think like men, born merely to breed and serve men—were not so easily dispelled by the crusading feminists, by science and education, and by the democratic spirit after all. They merely reappeared in the forties, in Freudian disguise. The feminine mystique derived its power from Freudian thought; for it was an idea born of Freud, which led women, and those who studied them, to misinterpret their mothers' frustrations, and their fathers' and brothers' and husbands' resentments and inadequacies, and their own emotions and possible choices in life. It is a Freudian idea, hardened into apparent fact, that has trapped so many American women today.

The new mystique is much more difficult for the modern woman to question than the old prejudices, partly because the mystique is broadcast by the very agents of education and social science that are supposed to be the chief enemies of prejudice, partly because the very nature of Freudian thought makes it virtually invulnerable to question. How can an educated American woman, who is not herself an analyst, presume to question a Freudian truth? She knows that Freud's discovery of the unconscious workings of the mind was one of the great breakthroughs in man's pursuit of knowledge. She knows that the science built on that discovery has helped many suffering men and women. She has been taught that only after years of analytic training is one capable of understanding the meaning of Freudian truth. She may even know how the human mind unconsciously resists that truth. How can she presume to tread the sacred ground where only analysts are allowed?

No one can question the basic genius of Freud's discoveries, nor the contribution he has made to our culture. Nor do I question the effectiveness of psychoanalysis as it is practiced today by Freudian or anti-Freudian. But I do question, from my own experience as a woman, and my reporter's knowledge of other women, the application of the Freudian theory of femininity to women today. I question its use, not in therapy, but as it has filtered into the lives of American women through the popular magazines and the opinions and interpretations of so-called experts. I think much of the Freudian theory about women is obsolescent, an obstacle to truth for women in America today, and a major cause of the pervasive problem that has no name.

There are many paradoxes here. Freud's concept of the superego* helped to free man of the tyranny of the "shoulds," the tyranny of

---

* According to Freud, the mind is divided into three parts. The id seeks satisfaction of unconscious, instinctual needs (particularly, though not exclusively, sexual needs). The superego represents the internalized ethical demands of parents and society. And the ego is the individual's voice of reason and rationality: it navigates among the demands of the id, the superego, and the outside world, (see entry on Sigmund Freud, p. 85).

the past, which prevents the child from becoming an adult. Yet Freudian thought helped create a new superego that paralyzes educated modern American women—a new tyranny of the "shoulds," which chains women to an old image, prohibits choice and growth, and denies them individual identity.

Freudian psychology, with its emphasis on freedom from a repressive morality to achieve sexual fulfillment, was part of the ideology of women's emancipation. The lasting American image of the "emancipated woman" is the flapper of the twenties: burdensome hair shingled off, knees bared, flaunting her new freedom to live in a studio in Greenwich Village or Chicago's near North Side, and drive a car, and drink, and smoke and enjoy sexual adventures—or talk about them. And yet today, for reasons far removed from the life of Freud himself, Freudian thought has become the ideological bulwark of the sexual counter-revolution in America. Without Freud's definition of the sexual nature of woman to give the conventional image of femininity new authority, I do not think several generations of educated, spirited American women would have been so easily diverted from the dawning realization of who they were and what they could be.

The concept "penis envy,"* which Freud coined to describe a phenomenon he observed in women—that is, in the middle-class women who were his patients in Vienna in the Victorian era—was seized in this country in the 1940's as the literal explanation of all that was wrong with American women. Many who preached the doctrine of endangered femininity, reversing the movement of American women toward independence and identity, never knew its Freudian origin. Many who seized on it—not the few psychoanalysts, but the many popularizers, sociologists, educators, ad-agency manipulators, magazine writers, child experts, marriage counselors, ministers, cocktail-party authorities—could not have known what Freud himself meant by penis envy. One needs only to know what Freud *was* describing, in those Victorian women, to see the fallacy in literally applying his theory of femininity to women today. And one needs only to know *why* he described it in that way to understand that much of it is obsolescent, contradicted by knowledge that is part of every social scientist's thinking today, but was not yet known in Freud's time.

Freud, it is generally agreed, was a most perceptive and accurate observer of important problems of the human personality. But in describing and interpreting those problems, he was a prisoner of his

---

* Freud believed that a girl's lack of a penis leads her to see herself as castrated and inferior. Women who cannot accept their lack of a penis and accept the passive feminine role suffer from penis envy, he believed. Female Freudian psychologists, such as Karen Horney (1885–1982), as well as feminists in the 1960s and 1970s like Friedan, rejected the concept of penis envy (see entry on Sigmund Freud, p. 85).

own culture. As he was creating a new framework for our culture, he could not escape the framework of his own. Even his genius could not give him, then, the knowledge of cultural processes which men who are not geniuses grow up with today.

The physicist's relativity, which in recent years has changed our whole approach to scientific knowledge, is harder, and therefore easier to understand than the social scientist's relativity. It is not a slogan, but a fundamental statement about truth to say that no social scientist can completely free himself from the prison of his own culture; he can only interpret what he observes in the scientific framework of his own time. This is true even of the great innovators. They cannot help but translate their revolutionary observations into language and rubrics that have been determined by the progress of science up until their time. Even those discoveries that create new rubrics are relative to the vantage point of their creator.

The knowledge of other cultures, the understanding of cultural relativity, which is part of the framework of social scientists in our own time, was unknown to Freud. Much of what Freud believed to be biological, instinctual, and changeless has been shown by modern research to be a result of specific cultural causes.[1] Much of what Freud described as characteristic of universal human nature was merely characteristic of certain middle-class European men and women at the end of the nineteenth century.

For instance, Freud's theory of the sexual origin of neurosis stems from the fact that many of the patients he first observed suffered from hysteria*—and in those cases, he found sexual repression to be the cause. Orthodox Freudians still profess to believe in the sexual origin of all neurosis,† and since they look for unconscious sexual memories in their patients, and translate what they hear into sexual symbols, they still manage to find what they are looking for.

But the fact is, cases of hysteria as observed by Freud are much more rare today. In Freud's time, evidently, cultural hypocrisy forced the repression of sex. (Some social theorists even suspect that the very absence of other concerns, in that dying Austrian empire, caused the sexual preoccupation of Freud's patients.[2]) Certainly the fact that his culture denied sex focused Freud's interest on it. He then developed his theory by describing all the stages of growth as sexual, fitting all the phenomena he observed into sexual rubrics.

---

* Psychological condition characterized by emotional instability and dramatic and attention-seeking behavior. Originally derived from the term "wandering uterus," the condition was traditionally found in women, rather than men. It was considered a major health problem during the Victorian era, but it is uncommon today.
† Long-term emotional or mental disorder, such as anxiety, that does not interfere with the sufferer's relationship to reality (as compared to a psychosis), and that the sufferer recognizes as abnormal.

His attempt to translate all psychological phenomena into sexual terms, and to see all problems of adult personality as the effect of childhood sexual fixations also stemmed, in part, from his own background in medicine, and from the approach to causation implicit in the scientific thought of his time. He had the same diffidence about dealing with psychological phenomena in their own terms which often plagues scientists of human behavior. Something that could be described in physiological terms, linked to an organ of anatomy, seemed more comfortable, solid, real, scientific, as he moved into the unexplored country of the unconscious mind. As his biographer, Ernest Jones, put it, he made a "desperate effort to cling to the safety of cerebral anatomy."[3] Actually, he had the ability to see and describe psychological phenomena so vividly that whether his concepts were given names borrowed from physiology, philosophy or literature—penis envy, ego, Oedipus complex*—they seemed to have a concrete physical reality. Psychological facts, as Jones said, were "as real and concrete to him as metals are to a metallurgist."[4] This ability became a source of great confusion as his concepts were passed down by lesser thinkers.

The whole superstructure of Freudian theory rests on the strict determinism that characterized the scientific thinking of the Victorian era. Determinism has been replaced today by a more complex view of cause and effect, in terms of physical processes and phenomena as well as psychological. In the new view, behavioral scientists do not need to borrow language from physiology to explain psychological events, or give them pseudo-reality. Sexual phenomena are no more nor less real than, for instance, the phenomenon of Shakespeare's writing *Hamlet*, which cannot exactly be "explained" by reducing it to sexual terms. Even Freud himself cannot be explained by his own deterministic, physiological blueprint, though his biographer traces his genius, his "divine passion for knowledge" to an insatiable sexual curiosity, before the age of three, as to what went on between his mother and father in the bedroom.[5]

Today biologists, social scientists, and increasing numbers of psychoanalysts see the need or impulse to human growth as a primary human need, as basic as sex. The "oral" and "anal" stages which Freud described in terms of sexual development—the child gets his sexual pleasure first by mouth, from mother's breast, then from his

---

* According to Freud, men are governed by an Oedipus complex in which they unconsciously desire their mothers and seek to supplant their fathers, from whom they fear retaliation in the form of castration. Initially, Freud claimed that women suffer from the Oedipus complex as well. They unconsciously seek to possess their mothers sexually, he argued, but cannot do so, nor can they identify with their fathers sexually: they therefore suffer until they can accept their roles as passive recipients of male desire. By 1931, however, Freud argued that only boys experience the Oedipus complex (see entries on Sigmund Freud, p. 85, and ego, p. 86).

bowel movements—are now seen as stages of human growth, influenced by cultural circumstances and parental attitudes as well as by sex. When the teeth grow, the mouth can bite as well as suck. Muscle and brain also grow; the child becomes capable of control, mastery, understanding; and his need to grow and learn, at five, twenty-five, or fifty, can be satisfied, denied, repressed, atrophied, evoked or discouraged by his culture as can his sexual needs.

Child specialists today confirm Freud's observation that problems between mother and child in the earliest stages are often played out in terms of eating; later in toilet training. And yet in America in recent years there has been a noticeable decline in children's "eating problems." Has the child's instinctual development changed? Impossible, if by definition, the oral stage is instinctual. Or has the culture removed eating as a focus for early childhood problems—by the American emphasis on permissiveness in child care, or simply by the fact that in our affluent society food has become less a cause for anxiety in mothers? Because of Freud's own influence on our culture, educated parents are usually careful not to put conflict-producing pressures on toilet training. Such conflicts are more likely to occur today as the child learns to talk or read.[6]

In the 1940's, American social scientists and psychoanalysts had already begun to reinterpret Freudian concepts in the light of their growing cultural awareness. But, curiously, this did not prevent their literal application of Freud's theory of femininity to American women.

The fact is that to Freud, even more than to the magazine editor on Madison Avenue today, women were a strange, inferior, less-than-human species. He saw them as childlike dolls, who existed in terms only of man's love, to love man and serve his needs. It was the same kind of unconscious solipsism that made man for many centuries see the sun only as a bright object that revolved around the earth. Freud grew up with this attitude built in by his culture—not only the culture of Victorian Europe, but that Jewish culture in which men said the daily prayer: "I thank Thee, Lord, that Thou hast not created me a woman," and women prayed in submission: "I thank Thee, Lord, that Thou has created me according to Thy will."

Freud's mother was the pretty, docile bride of a man twice her age; his father ruled the family with an autocratic authority traditional in Jewish families during those centuries of persecution when the fathers were seldom able to establish authority in the outside world. His mother adored the young Sigmund, her first son, and thought him mystically destined for greatness; she seemed to exist only to gratify his every wish. His own memories of the sexual jealousy he felt for his father, whose wishes she also gratified, were the basis of his theory of the Oedipus complex. With his wife, as with his mother and sisters, his needs, his desires, his wishes, were the sun around which the household revolved. When the noise of his sisters' practicing the piano interrupted his studies, "the piano disappeared," Anna Freud recalled years later, "and with it all opportunities for his sisters to become musicians."

Freud did not see this attitude as a problem, or cause for any problem, in women. It was woman's nature to be ruled by man, and her sickness to envy him. Freud's letters to Martha, his future wife, written during the four years of their engagement (1882–1886) have the fond, patronizing sound of Torvald in *A Doll's House*, scolding Nora for her pretenses at being human. Freud was beginning to probe the secrets of the human brain in the laboratory at Vienna; Martha was to wait, his "sweet child," in her mother's custody for four years, until he could come and fetch her. From these letters one can see that to him her identity was defined as child-housewife, even when she was no longer a child and not yet a housewife.

> Tables and chairs, beds, mirrors, a clock to remind the happy couple of the passage of time, an armchair for an hour's pleasant daydreaming, carpets to help the housewife keep the floors clean, linen tied with pretty ribbons in the cupboard and dresses of the latest fashion and hats with artificial flowers, pictures on the wall, glasses for everyday and others for wine and festive occasions, plates and dishes . . . and the sewing table and the cozy lamp, and everything must be kept in good order or else the housewife who has divided her heart into little bits, one for each piece of furniture, will begin to fret. And this object must bear witness to the serious work that holds the household together, and that object, to a feeling for beauty, to dear friends one likes to remember, to cities one has visited, to hours one wants to recall. . . . Are we to hang our hearts on such little things? Yes, and without hesitation. . . .
>
> I know, after all, how sweet you are, how you can turn a house into a paradise, how you will share in my interests, how gay yet painstaking you will be. I will let you rule the house as much as you wish, and you will reward me with your sweet love and by rising above all those weaknesses for which women are so often despised. As far as my activities allow, we shall read together what we want to learn, and I will initiate you into things which could not interest a girl as long as she is unfamiliar with her future companion and his occupation . . . [7]

On July 5, 1885, he scolds her for continuing to visit Elise, a friend who evidently is less than demure in her regard for men:

> What is the good of your feeling that you are now so mature that this relationship can't do you any harm? . . . You are far too

soft, and this is something I have got to correct, for what one of us does will also be charged to the other's account. You are my precious little woman and even if you make a mistake, you are none the less so. . . . But you know all this, my sweet child . . . [8]

The Victorian mixture of chivalry and condescension which is found in Freud's scientific theories about women is explicit in a letter he wrote on November 5, 1883, deriding John Stuart Mill's* views on "female emancipation and the woman's question altogether."

In his whole presentation, it never emerges that women are different beings—we will not say lesser, rather the opposite— from men. He finds the suppression of women an analogy to that of Negroes. Any girl, even without a suffrage or legal competence, whose hand a man kisses and for whose love he is prepared to dare all, could have set him right. It is really a stillborn thought to send women into the struggle for existence exactly as man. If, for instance, I imagined my gentle sweet girl as a competitor, it would only end in my telling her, as I did seventeen months ago, that I am fond of her and that I implore her to withdraw from the strife into the calm, uncompetitive activity of my home. It is possible that changes in upbringing may suppress all a woman's tender attributes, needful of protection and yet so victorious, and that she can then earn a livelihood like men. It is also possible that in such an event one would not be justified in mourning the passing away of the most delightful thing the world can offer us—our ideal of womanhood. I believe that all reforming action in law and education would break down in front of the fact that, long before the age at which a man can earn a position in society, Nature has determined woman's destiny through beauty, charm, and sweetness. Law and custom have much to give women that has been withheld from them, but the position of women will surely be what it is: in youth an adored darling and in mature years a loved wife.[9]

Since all of Freud's theories rested, admittedly, on his own penetrating, unending psychoanalysis of himself, and since sexuality was the focus of all his theories, certain paradoxes about his own sexuality seem pertinent. His writings, as many scholars have noted, give much more attention to infantile sexuality than to its mature expression. His chief biographer, Jones, pointed out that he was, even for those times, exceptionally chaste, puritanical and moral-

---

* John Stuart Mill (1806–1873), English politician and political philosopher who wrote *On Liberty* (1859) and *The Subjection of Women* (1869). A wide-ranging progressive thinker, Mill believed that one way to improve society was to allow each woman to fulfill her greatest potential.

istic. In his own life, he was relatively uninterested in sex. There were only the adoring mother of his youth, at sixteen a romance that existed purely in fantasy with a girl named Gisele, and his engagement to Martha at twenty-six. The nine months when they both lived in Vienna were not too happy because she was, evidently, uneasy and afraid of him; but separated by a comfortable distance for four years, there was a "grande passion" of 900 love letters. After their marriage, the passion seems to have quickly disappeared, though his biographers note that he was too rigid a moralist to seek sexual satisfaction outside of marriage. The only woman on whom, as an adult, he ever focused the violent passions of love and hate of which he was capable was Martha, during the early years of their engagement. After that, such emotions were focused on men. As Jones, his respectful biographer, said: "Freud's deviation from the average in this respect, as well as his pronounced mental bisexuality, may well have influenced his theoretical views to some extent."[10]

Less reverent biographers, and even Jones himself, point out that when one considers Freud's theories in terms of his own life, one is reminded of the puritanical old maid who sees sex everywhere.[11] It is interesting to note that his main complaint about his docile hausfrau* was that she was not "docile" enough—and yet, in interesting ambivalence, that she was not "at her ease" with him, that she was not able to be a "comrade-in-arms."

> But, as Freud was painfully to discover, she was not at heart docile and she had a firmness of character that did not readily lend itself to being molded. Her personality was fully developed and well integrated: it would well deserve the psychoanalyst's highest compliment of being "normal."[12]

One gets a glimpse of Freud's "intention, never to be fulfilled, to mold her to his perfect image," when he wrote her that she must "become quite young, a sweetheart, only a week old, who will quickly lose every trace of tartness." But he then reproaches himself:

> The loved one is not to become a toy doll, but a good comrade who still has a sensible word left when the strict master has come to the end of his wisdom. And I have been trying to smash her frankness so that she should reserve opinion until she is sure of mine.[13]

As Jones pointed out, Freud was pained when she did not meet his chief test—"complete identification with himself, his opinions, his feelings, and his intentions. She was not really his unless he could perceive his 'stamp' on her." Freud "even admitted that it was boring

---

* Housewife (German).

if one could find nothing in the other person to put right." And he stresses again that Freud's love "could be set free and displayed only under very favorable conditions. . . . Martha was probably afraid of her masterful lover and she would commonly take refuge in silence."[14]

So, he eventually wrote her, "I renounce what I demanded. I do not need a comrade-in-arms, such as I hoped to make you into. I am strong enough to fight alone. . . . You remain for me a precious sweet, loved one."[15] Thus evidently ended "the only time in his life when such emotions [love and hate] centered on a woman."[16]

The marriage was conventional, but without that passion. As Jones described it:

> There can have been few more successful marriages. Martha certainly made an excellent wife and mother. She was an admirable manager—the rare kind of woman who could keep servants indefinitely—but she was never the kind of Hausfrau who put things before people. Her husband's comfort and convenience always ranked first. . . . It was not to be expected that she should follow the roaming flights of his imagination any more than most of the world could.[17]

She was as devoted to his physical needs as the most doting Jewish mother, organizing each meal on a rigid schedule to fit the convenience of "der Papa." But she never dreamed of sharing his life as an equal. Nor did Freud consider her a fit guardian for their children, especially of their education, in case of his death. He himself recalls a dream in which he forgets to call for her at the theater. His associations "imply that forgetting may be permissible in unimportant matters."[18]

That limitless subservience of woman taken for granted by Freud's culture, the very lack of opportunity for independent action or personal identity, seems often to have generated that uneasiness and inhibition in the wife, and that irritation in the husband, which characterized Freud's marriage. As Jones summed it up, Freud's attitude toward women "could probably be called rather old-fashioned, and it would be easy to ascribe this to his social environment and the period in which he grew up rather than to any personal factors."

> Whatever his intellectual opinions may have been in the matter, there are many indications in his writing and correspondence of his emotional attitude. It would certainly be going too far to say that he regarded the male sex as the lords of creation, for there was no tinge of arrogance or superiority in his nature, but it might perhaps be fair to describe his view of the female sex as having as their main function to be ministering angels to the needs and comforts of men. His letters and his love

choice make it plain that he had only one type of sexual object in his mind, a gentle feminine one. . . .

There is little doubt that Freud found the psychology of women more enigmatic than that of men. He said once to Marie Bonaparte: "The great question that has never been answered and which I have not yet been able to answer, despite my thirty years of research into the feminine soul, is, what does a woman want?"[19]

Jones also remarked:

Freud was also interested in another type of woman, of a more intellectual and perhaps masculine cast. Such women several times played a part in his life, accessory to his men friends though of a finer caliber, but they had no erotic attraction for him.[20]

These women included his sister-in-law, Minna Bernays, much more intelligent and independent than Martha, and later women analysts or adherents of the psychoanalytic movement: Marie Bonaparte, Joan Riviere, Lou Andreas-Salomé. There is no suspicion, however, from either idolators or hostile biographers that he ever sought sexual satisfaction outside his marriage. Thus it would seem that sex was completely divorced from his human passions, which he expressed throughout the productive later years of his long life in his thought and, to a lesser extent, in friendships with men and those women he considered his equals, and thus "masculine." He once said: "I always find it uncanny when I can't understand someone in terms of myself."[21]

Despite the importance of sex in Freud's theory, one gets from his words the impression that the sex act appeared degrading to him; if women themselves were so degraded, in the eyes of man, how could sex appear in any other light? That was not his theory, of course. To Freud, it was the idea of incest with mother or sister that makes man "regard the sex act as something degrading, which soils and contaminates not only the body."[22] In any event, the degradation of women was taken for granted by Freud—and is the key to his theory of femininity. The motive force of woman's personality, in Freud's theory, was her envy of the penis, which causes her to feel as much depreciated in her own eyes "as in the eyes of the boy, and later perhaps of the man," and leads, in normal femininity, to the wish for the penis of her husband, a wish that is never really fulfilled until she possesses a penis through giving birth to a son. In short, she is merely an "homme manqué," a man with something missing. As the eminent psychoanalyst Clara Thompson put it: "Freud never became free from the Victorian attitude toward women. He accepted as an inevitable part of the fate of being a woman the limitation of outlook and life of the Victorian era. . . . The castration complex* and penis envy concepts, two of the most basic ideas in his whole thinking, are postulated on the assumption that women are biologically inferior to men."[23]

What did Freud mean by the concept of penis envy? For even those who realize that Freud could not escape his culture do not question that he reported truly what he observed within it. Freud found the phenomenon he called penis envy so unanimous, in middle-class women in Vienna, in that Victorian time, that he based his whole theory of femininity on it. He said, in a lecture on "The Psychology of Women":

> In the boy the castration-complex is formed after he has learned from the sight of the female genitals that the sexual organ which he prizes so highly is not a necessary part of every woman's body . . . and thenceforward he comes under the influence of castration-anxiety, which supplies the strongest motive force for his further development. The castration-complex in the girl, as well, is started by the sight of the genital organs of the other sex. She immediately notices the difference and, it must be admitted, its significance. She feels herself at a great disadvantage, and often declares that she would like to have something like that too and falls a victim to penis envy, which leaves ineradicable traces on her development and character-formation, and even in the most favorable instances, is not overcome without a great expenditure of mental energy. That the girl recognizes the fact that she lacks a penis does not mean that she accepts its absence lightly. On the contrary, she clings for a long time to the desire to get something like it, and believes in that possibility for an extraordinary number of years; and even at a time when her knowledge of reality has long since led her to abandon the fulfillment of this desire as being quite unattainable, analysis proves that it still persists in the unconscious, and retains a considerable charge of energy. The desire after all to obtain the penis for which she so much longs may even contribute to the motives that impel a grown-up woman to come to analysis, and what she quite reasonably expects to get from analysis, such as the capacity to pursue an intellectual career, can often be recognized as a sublimated modification of this repressed wish.[24]

---

* In Freudian theory, the castration complex is a boy's unconscious anxiety that his desire for his mother will lead his father to castrate him. In girls, the castration complex is a compulsion to demonstrate that they have the symbolic equivalent to the penis (see entries on Oedipus complex, p. 89, and penis envy, p. 87).

"The discovery of her castration is a turning-point in the life of the girl," Freud went on to say. "She is wounded in her self-love by the unfavorable comparison with the boy, who is so much better equipped." Her mother, and all women, are depreciated in her own eyes, as they are depreciated for the same reason in the eyes of man. This either leads to complete sexual inhibition and neurosis, or to a "masculinity complex" in which she refuses to give up "phallic" activity (that is, "activity such as is usually characteristic of the male") or to "normal femininity," in which the girl's own impulses to activity are repressed, and she turns to her father in her wish for the penis. "The feminine situation is, however, only established when the wish for the penis is replaced by the wish for a child—the child taking the place of the penis." When she played with dolls, this "was not really an expression of her femininity," since this was activity, not passivity. The "strongest feminine wish," the desire for a penis, finds real fulfillment only "if the child is a little boy, who brings the longed-for penis with him. . . . The mother can transfer to her son all the ambition she has had to suppress in herself, and she can hope to get from him the satisfaction of all that has remained to her of her masculinity complex."[25]

But her inherent deficiency, and the resultant penis envy, is so hard to overcome that the woman's superego—her conscience, ideals—are never as completely formed as a man's: "women have but little sense of justice, and this is no doubt connected with the preponderance of envy in their mental life." For the same reason, women's interests in society are weaker than those of men, and "their capacity for the sublimation of their instincts is less." Finally, Freud cannot refrain from mentioning "an impression which one receives over and over again in analytical work"—that not even psychoanalysis can do much for women, because of the inherent deficiency of femininity.

> A man of about thirty seems a youthful, and, in a sense, an incompletely developed individual, of whom we expect that he will be able to make good use of the possibilities of development, which analysis lays open to him. But a woman of about the same age, frequently staggers us by her psychological rigidity and unchangeability. . . . There are no paths open to her for further development; it is as though the whole process had been gone through and remained unaccessible to influence for the future; as though, in fact, the difficult development which leads to femininity had exhausted all the possibilities of the individual . . . even when we are successful in removing the sufferings by solving her neurotic conflict.[26]

What was he really reporting? If one interprets "penis envy" as other Freudian concepts have been reinterpreted, in the light of our new knowledge that what Freud believed to be biological was often a cultural reaction, one sees simply that Victorian culture gave women many reasons to envy men: the same conditions, in fact, that the feminists fought against. If a woman who was denied the freedom, the status and the pleasures that men enjoyed wished secretly that she could have these things, in the shorthand of the dream, she might wish herself a man and see herself with that one thing which made men unequivocally different—the penis. She would, of course, have to learn to keep her envy, her anger, hidden: to play the child, the doll, the toy, for her destiny depended on charming man. But underneath, it might still fester, sickening her for love. If she secretly despised herself, and envied man for all she was not, she might go through the motions of love, or even feel a slavish adoration, but would she be capable of free and joyous love? You cannot explain away woman's envy of man, or her contempt for herself, as mere refusal to accept her sexual deformity, unless you think that a woman, by nature, is a being inferior to man. Then, of course, her wish to be equal is neurotic.

It is recognized now that Freud never gave proper attention, even in man, to growth of the ego or self: "the impulse to master, control or come to self-fulfilling terms with the environment."[27] Analysts who have freed themselves from Freud's bias and joined other behavioral scientists in studying the human need to grow, are beginning to believe that this is the basic human need, and that interference with it, in any dimension, is the source of psychic trouble. The sexual is only one dimension of the human potential. Freud, it must be remembered, thought all neuroses were sexual in origin; he saw women only in terms of their sexual relationship with men. But in all those women in whom he saw sexual problems, there must have been very severe problems of blocked growth, growth short of full human identity—an immature, incomplete self. Society as it was then, by explicit denial of education and independence, prevented women from realizing their full potential, or from attaining those interests and ideals that might have stimulated their growth. Freud reported these deficiencies, but could only explain them as the toll of "penis envy." He saw women's envy of man *only* as sexual sickness. He saw that women who secretly hungered to be man's equal would not enjoy being his object; and in this, he seemed to be describing a fact. But when he dismissed woman's yearning for equality as "penis envy," was he not merely stating his own view that women could never really be man's equal, any more than she could wear his penis?

Freud was not concerned with changing society, but in helping man, and woman, adjust to it. Thus he tells of a case of a middle-aged spinster whom he succeeded in freeing from a symptom-complex that prevented her from taking any part in life for fifteen years. Freed of these symptoms she "plunged into a whirl of activity in order to develop her talents, which were by no means small, and derive a little appreciation, enjoyment, and success from life before it was too late." But all her attempts ended when she saw that there was no place for her. Since she could no longer relapse into her neurotic symptoms, she began to have accidents; she sprained her ankle, her foot, her hand. When this also was analyzed, "instead of accidents, she contracted on the same occasions slight illnesses, such as catarrh, sore throat, influenzal conditions or rheumatic swellings, until at last, when she made up her mind to resign herself to inactivity, the whole business came to an end."[28]

Even if Freud and his contemporaries considered women inferior by God-given, irrevocable nature, science does not justify such a view today. That inferiority, we now know, was caused by their lack of education, their confinement to the home. Today, when women's equal intelligence has been proved by science, when their equal capacity in every sphere except sheer muscular strength has been demonstrated, a theory explicitly based on woman's natural inferiority would seem as ridiculous as it is hypocritical. But that remains the basis of Freud's theory of women, despite the mask of timeless sexual truth which disguises its elaborations today.

Because Freud's followers could only see woman in the image defined by Freud—inferior, childish, helpless, with no possibility of happiness unless she adjusted to being man's passive object—they wanted to help women get rid of their suppressed envy, their neurotic desire to be equal. They wanted to help women find sexual fulfillment as women, by affirming their natural inferiority.

But society, which defined that inferiority, had changed drastically by the time Freud's followers transposed bodily to twentieth-century America the causes as well as the cures of the condition Freud called penis envy. In the light of our new knowledge of cultural processes and of human growth, one would assume that women who grew up with the rights and freedom and education that Victorian women were denied would be different from the women Freud tried to cure. One would assume that they would have much less reason to envy man. But Freud was interpreted to American woman in such curiously literal terms that the concept of penis envy acquired a mystical life of its own, as if it existed quite independent of the women in whom it had been observed. It was as if Freud's Victorian image of woman became more real than the twentieth-century women to whom it was applied. Freud's theory of femininity was seized in America with such literalness that women today were considered no different than Victorian women. The real injustices life held for women a century ago, compared to men, were dismissed as mere rationalizations of penis envy. And the real opportunities life offered to women now, compared to women then, were forbidden in the name of penis envy.

The literal application of Freudian theory can be seen in these passages from *Modern Woman: The Lost Sex*, by the psychoanalyst Marynia Farnham and the sociologist Ferdinand Lundberg, which was paraphrased ad nauseam in the magazines and in marriage courses, until most of its statements became a part of the conventional, accepted truth of our time. Equating feminism with penis envy, they stated categorically:

> Feminism, despite the external validity of its political program and most (not all) of its social program, was at its core a deep illness. . . . The dominant direction of feminine training and development today . . . discourages just those traits necessary to the attainment of sexual pleasure: receptivity and passiveness, a willingness to accept dependence without fear or resentment, with a deep inwardness and readiness for the final goal of sexual life—impregnation. . . .
>
> It is not in the capacity of the female organism to attain feelings of well-being by the route of male achievement. . . . It was the error of the feminists that they attempted to put women on the essentially male road of exploit, off the female road of nurture. . . .
>
> The psychosocial rule that begins to take form, then, is this: the more educated the woman is, the greater chance there is of sexual disorder, more or less severe. The greater the disordered sexuality in a given group of women, the fewer children do they have. . . . Fate has granted them the boon importuned by Lady Macbeth; they have been unsexed, not only in the matter of giving birth, but in their feelings of pleasure.[29]

Thus Freud's popularizers embedded his core of unrecognized traditional prejudice against women ever deeper in pseudoscientific cement. Freud was well aware of his own tendency to build an enormous body of deductions from a single fact—a fertile and creative method, but a two-edged sword, if the significance of that single fact was misinterpreted. Freud wrote Jung* in 1909:

---

* Carl Jung (1875–1961), psychoanalyst and early supporter of Sigmund Freud. After several years, however, Jung's ideas about the unconscious deviated significantly from those of Freud, and the two men severed contact. Jung developed many concepts that became commonplace in American culture, including the midlife crisis and the personality traits of extroversion and introversion (see entry on Sigmund Freud, p. 85).

Your surmise that after my departure my errors might be adored as holy relics amused me enormously, but I don't believe it. On the contrary, I think that my followers will hasten to demolish as swiftly as possible everything that is not safe and sound in what I leave behind.[30]

But on the subject of women, Freud's followers not only compounded his errors, but in their tortuous attempt to fit their observations of real women into his theoretical framework, closed questions that he himself had left open. Thus, for instance, Helene Deutsch,* whose definitive two-volume *The Psychology of Woman—A Psychoanalytical Interpretation* appeared in 1944, is not able to trace all women's troubles to penis envy as such. So she does what even Freud found unwise, and equates "femininity" with "passivity," and "masculinity" with "activity," not only in the sexual sphere, but in all spheres of life.

> While fully recognizing that woman's position is subjected to external influence, I venture to say that the fundamental identities "feminine-passive" and "masculine-active" assert themselves in all known cultures and races, in various forms and various quantitative proportions.
> Very often a woman resists this characteristic given her by nature and in spite of certain advantages she derives from it, displays many modes of behavior that suggest that she is not entirely content with her own constitution . . . the expression of this dissatisfaction, combined with attempts to remedy it, result in woman's "masculinity complex."[31]

The "masculinity complex," as Dr. Deutsch refines it, stems directly from the "female castration complex." Thus, anatomy is still destiny, woman is still an "homme manqué." Of course, Dr. Deutsch mentions in passing that "With regard to the girl, however, the environment exerts an inhibiting influence as regards both her aggressions and her activity." So, penis envy, deficient female anatomy, and society "all seem to work together to produce femininity."[32]

"Normal" femininity is achieved, however, only insofar as the woman finally renounces all active goals of her own, all her own "originality," to identify and fulfill herself through the activities and goals of husband, or son. This process can be sublimated in nonsexual ways—as, for instance, the woman who does the basic research

---

*   Helene Deutsch (1884–1982), psychoanalyst and psychiatrist. She went through training analysis with Freud in Vienna and became one of the leading figures of psychoanalysis. She was famous for her two-volume work, *The Psychology of Woman*, published in the United States in 1944, and for many years seen as the definitive work on women's psychology. Her espousal of Freud's theories on women made her a target of feminists like Friedan in the 1960s and 1970s (see entry on Sigmund Freud, p. 85).

for her male superior's discoveries. The daughter who devotes her life
to her father is also making a satisfactory feminine "sublimation."
Only activity of her own or originality, on a basis of equality, deserves
the opprobrium of "masculinity complex." This brilliant feminine fol-
lower of Freud states categorically that the women who by 1944 in
America had achieved eminence by activity of their own in various
fields had done so at the expense of their feminine fulfillment. She
will mention no names, but they all suffer from the "masculinity
complex."

How could a girl or woman who was not a psychoanalyst discount
such ominous pronouncements, which, in the forties, suddenly
began to pour out from all the oracles of sophisticated thought?

It would be ridiculous to suggest that the way Freudian theories
were used to brainwash two generations of educated American
women was part of a psychoanalytic conspiracy. It was done by
well-meaning popularizers and inadvertent distorters; by orthodox
converts and bandwagon faddists; by those who suffered and those
who cured and those who turned suffering to profit; and, above
all, by a congruence of forces and needs peculiar to the American
people at that particular time. In fact, the literal acceptance in the
American culture of Freud's theory of feminine fulfillment was in
tragicomic contrast to the personal struggle of many American psychoanalysts to reconcile what they saw in their women patients with
Freudian theory. The theory said women should be able to fulfill
themselves as wives and mothers if only they could be analyzed out
of their "masculine strivings," their "penis envy." But it wasn't as
easy as that. "I don't know why American women are so dissatisfied,"
a Westchester analyst insisted. "Penis envy seems so difficult to
eradicate in American women, somehow."

A New York analyst, one of the last trained at Freud's own Psychoanalytic Institute in Vienna, told me:

> For twenty years now in analyzing American women, I have
> found myself again and again in the position of having to
> superimpose Freud's theory of femininity on the psychic life of
> my patients in a way that I was not willing to do. I have come
> to the conclusion that penis envy simply does not exist. I have
> seen women who are completely expressive, sexually, vaginally,
> and yet who are not mature, integrated, fulfilled. I had a
> woman patient on the couch for nearly two years before I could
> face her real problem—that it was not enough for her to be just
> a housewife and mother. One day she had a dream that she
> was teaching a class. I could not dismiss the powerful yearning
> of this housewife's dream as penis envy. It was the expression
> of her own need for mature self-fulfillment. I told her: "I can't
> analyze this dream away. You must do something about it."

This same man teaches the young analysts in his postgraduate clinicum at a leading Eastern university: "If the patient doesn't fit the book, throw away the book, and listen to the patient."

But many analysts threw the book *at* their patients and Freudian theories became accepted fact even among women who never lay down on an analyst's couch, but only knew what they read or heard. To this day, it has not penetrated to the popular culture that the pervasive growing frustration of American women may not be a matter of feminine sexuality. Some analysts, it is true, modified the theories drastically to fit their patients, or even discarded them altogether—but these facts never permeated the public awareness. Freud was accepted so quickly and completely at the end of the forties that for over a decade no one even questioned the race of the educated American woman back to the home. When questions finally had to be asked because something was obviously going wrong, they were asked so completely within the Freudian framework that only one answer was possible: education, freedom, rights are wrong for women.

The uncritical acceptance of Freudian doctrine in America was caused, at least in part, by the very relief it provided from uncomfortable questions about objective realities. After the depression, after the war, Freudian psychology became much more than a science of human behavior, a therapy for the suffering. It became an all-embracing American ideology, a new religion. It filled the vacuum of thought and purpose that existed for many for whom God, or flag, or bank account were no longer sufficient—and yet who were tired of feeling responsible for lynchings and concentration camps and the starving children of India and Africa. It provided a convenient escape from the atom bomb, McCarthy,* all the disconcerting problems that might spoil the taste of steaks, and cars and color television and backyard swimming pools. It gave us permission to suppress the troubling questions of the larger world and pursue our own personal pleasures. And if the new psychological religion—which made a virtue of sex, removed all sin from private vice, and cast suspicion on high aspirations of the mind and spirit—had a

---

* Senator Joseph R. McCarthy (1908–1957), a Republican from Wisconsin, held office from 1946 through 1957. He came to prominence in 1950, claiming that he had a list of known communists in the U.S. State Department. Although he never produced that list, he used innuendo and bullying tactics to accuse individuals of being spies and traitors. He ruined reputations and inspired fear among political opponents. By tapping into the anxieties of the Cold War, McCarthy was able to rise to power in the U.S. Senate and to gain political clout in the Republican Party (see entry on the Cold War, p. 11). Ultimately, by 1954, McCarthy's tactics were exposed on national television; his popularity plummeted and he was censured by the Senate. The term McCarthyism has since become synonymous not only with anticommunism during the Cold War, but also with tactics that imply guilt by association. For more on the impact of the Cold War and McCarthyism on Betty Friedan's work, see the article by Daniel Horowitz on pp. 454–65.

more devastating personal effect on women than men, nobody planned it that way.

Psychology, long preoccupied with its own scientific inferiority complex, long obsessed with neat little laboratory experiments that gave the illusion of reducing human complexity to the simple measurable behavior of rats in a maze, was transformed into a life-giving crusade that swept across the barren fields of American thought. Freud was the spiritual leader, his theories were the bible. And how exciting and real and important it all was. Its mysterious complexity was part of its charm to bored Americans. And if some of it remained impenetrably mystifying, who would admit that he could not understand it? America became the center of the psycho-analytic movement, as Freudian, Jungian and Adlerian* analysts fled from Vienna and Berlin and new schools flourished on the multiplying neuroses, and dollars, of Americans.

But the practice of psychoanalysis as a therapy was not primarily responsible for the feminine mystique. It was the creation of writers and editors in the mass media, ad-agency motivation researchers, and behind them the popularizers and translators of Freudian thought in the colleges and universities. Freudian and pseudo-Freudian theories settled everywhere, like fine volcanic ash. Sociology, anthropology, education, even the study of history and literature became permeated and transfigured by Freudian thought. The most zealous missionaries of the feminine mystique were the functionalists, who seized hasty gulps of predigested Freud to start their new departments of "Marriage and Family Life Education." The functional courses in marriage taught American college girls how to "play the role" of woman—the old role became a new science. Related movements outside the colleges—parent education, child-study groups, prenatal maternity study groups and mental-health education—spread the new psychological superego throughout the land, replacing bridge and canasta as an entertainment for educated young wives. And this Freudian superego worked for growing numbers of young and impressionable American women as Freud said the superego works—to perpetuate the past.

> Mankind never lives completely in the present; the ideologies of the superego perpetuate the past, the traditions of the race and the people, which yield but slowly to the influence of the present and to new developments, and, so long as they work

---

*   Alfred Adler (1870–1937), Austrian psychiatrist who founded the discipline of individual psychology. He was a colleague of Sigmund Freud, but ultimately developed divergent ideas on psychology (see entry on Sigmund Freud, p. 85). Adler's system of psychotherapy emphasized an individual's striving to overcome feelings of inferiority, to establish positive self-esteem, and to achieve a goal of success.

through the superego, play an important part in man's life, quite independently of economic conditions.[33]

The feminine mystique, elevated by Freudian theory into a scientific religion, sounded a single, overprotective, life-restricting, future-denying note for women. Girls who grew up playing baseball, baby-sitting, mastering geometry—almost independent enough, almost resourceful enough, to meet the problems of the fission-fusion era—were told by the most advanced thinkers of our time to go back and live their lives as if they were Noras, restricted to the doll's house by Victorian prejudice. And their own respect and awe for the authority of science—anthropology, sociology, psychology share that authority now—kept them from questioning the feminine mystique.

6

The Functional Freeze, the Feminine Protest, and Margaret Mead

Instead of destroying the old prejudices that restricted women's lives, social science in America merely gave them new authority. By a curious circular process, the insights of psychology and anthropology and sociology, which should have been powerful weapons to free women, somehow canceled each other out, trapping women in dead center.

During the last twenty years, under the catalytic impact of Freudian thought, psychoanalysts, anthropologists, sociologists, social psychologists, and other workers in the behavioral sciences have met in professional seminars and foundation-financed conferences in many university centers. Cross-fertilization seemed to make them all bloom, but some strange hybrids were produced. As psychoanalysts began to reinterpret Freudian concepts like "oral" and "anal" personality in the light of an awareness, borrowed from anthropology, that cultural processes must have been at work in Freud's Vienna, anthropologists set out for the South Sea islands to chart tribal personality according to literal "oral" and "anal" tables. Armed with "psychological hints for ethnological field workers," the anthropologists often found what they were looking for. Instead of translating, sifting, the cultural bias *out* of Freudian theories, Margaret Mead, and the others who pioneered in the fields of culture and personality, compounded the error by fitting their own anthropological observations into Freudian rubric. But none of this might have had the same freezing effect on women if it had not been for a simultaneous aberration of American social scientists called functionalism.*

Centering primarily on cultural anthropology and sociology and reaching its extremes in the applied field of family-life education, functionalism began as an attempt to make social science more "scientific" by borrowing from biology the idea of studying institutions as if they were muscles or bones, in terms of their "structure" and "function" in the social body. By studying an institution only in terms of its function within its own society, the social scientists intended to avert unscientific value judgments. In practice, functionalism was less a scientific movement than a scientific word-game. "The function is" was often translated "the function should be"; the social scientists did not recognize their own prejudices in functional disguise any more than the analysts recognized theirs in Freudian disguise. By giving an absolute meaning and a sanctimonious value to the generic term "woman's role," functionalism put American women into a kind of deep freeze—like Sleeping Beauties, waiting for a Prince Charming to waken them, while all around the magic circle the world moved on.

The social scientists, male and female, who, in the name of functionalism, drew this torturously tight circle around American women, also seemed to share a certain attitude which I will call "the feminine protest." If there is such a thing as a masculine protest— the psychoanalytic concept taken over by the functionalists to describe women who envied men and wanted to be men and therefore denied that they were women and became more manly than any man—its counterpart can be seen today in a feminine protest, made by men and women alike, who deny what women really are and make more of "being a woman" than it could ever be. The feminine protest, at its most straightforward, is simply a means of protecting women from the dangers inherent in assuming true equality with men. But why should any social scientist, with godlike manipulative superiority, take it upon himself—or herself—to protect women from the pains of growing up?

Protectiveness has often muffled the sound of doors closing against women; it has often cloaked a very real prejudice, even when it is offered in the name of science. If an old-fashioned grandfather frowned at Nora, who is studying calculus because she wants to be a physicist, and muttered, "Woman's place is in the home," Nora would laugh impatiently, "Grandpa, this is 1963." But she

---

* Sociological school of thought that argues that cultural practices and social structures endure because they perform a useful function: they help society to maintain and reproduce itself. Functionalism rose in popularity in the United States after World War II with the work of sociologist Talcott Parsons (see entry on Talcott Parsons, p. 109). In the 1960s, however, functionalism attracted critics like Friedan, who argued that the theory did not account or allow for political or social change.

does not laugh at the urbane pipe-smoking professor of sociology, or the book by Margaret Mead, or the definitive two-volume reference on female sexuality, when they tell her the same thing. The complex, mysterious language of functionalism, Freudian psychology, and cultural anthropology hides from her the fact that they say this with not much more basis than grandpa.

So our Nora would smile at Queen Victoria's letter, written in 1870: "The Queen is most anxious to enlist everyone who can speak or write to join in checking this mad, wicked folly of 'Woman's Rights' with all its attendant horrors, on which her poor feeble sex is bent, forgetting every sense of womanly feeling and propriety. . . . It is a subject which makes the Queen so furious that she cannot contain herself. God created men and women different— then let them remain each in their own position."

But she does not smile when she reads in *Marriage for Moderns*:

> The sexes are complementary. It is the works of my watch that move the hands and enable me to tell time. Are the works, therefore, more important than the case? . . . Neither is superior, neither inferior. Each must be judged in terms of its own functions. Together they form a functioning unit. So it is with men and women—together they form a functioning unit. Either alone is in a sense incomplete. They are complementary. . . . When men and women engage in the same occupations or perform common functions, the complementary relationship may break down.[1]

This book was published in 1942. Girls have studied it as a college text for the past twenty years. Under the guise of sociology, or "Marriage and Family Life," or "Life Adjustment," they are offered advice of this sort:

> The fact remains, however, that we live in a world of reality, a world of the present and the immediate future, on which there rests the heavy hand of the past, a world in which tradition still holds sway and the mores exert a stronger influence than does the theorist . . . a world in which most men and women do marry and in which most married women are homemakers. To talk about what might be done if tradition and the mores were radically changed or what may come about by the year 2000 may be interesting mental gymnastics, but it does not help the young people of today to adjust to the inevitables of life or raise their marriages to a higher plane of satisfaction.[2]

Of course, this "adjustment to the inevitables of life" denies the speed with which the conditions of life are now changing—and the fact that many girls who so adjust at twenty will still be alive in the year 2000. This functionalist specifically warns against any and all approaches to the "differences between men and women" except "adjustment" to those differences as they now stand. And if, like our Nora, a woman is contemplating a career, he shakes a warning finger.

> For the first time in history, American young women in great numbers are being faced with these questions: Shall I voluntarily prepare myself for a lifelong, celibate career? Or shall I prepare for a temporary vocation, which I shall give up when I marry and assume the responsibilities of homemaking and motherhood? Or should I attempt to combine homemaking and a career? . . . The great majority of married women are homemakers. . . .
>
> If a woman can find adequate self-expression through a career rather than through marriage, well and good. Many young women, however, overlook the fact that there are numerous careers that do not furnish any medium or offer any opportunity for self-expression. Besides they do not realize that only the minority of women, as the minority of men, have anything particularly worthwhile to express.[3]

And so Nora is left with the cheerful impression that if she chooses a career, she is also choosing celibacy. If she has any illusions about combining marriage and career, the functionalist admonishes her:

> How many individuals . . . can successfully pursue two careers simultaneously? Not many. The exceptional person can do it, but the ordinary person cannot. The problem of combining marriage and homemaking with another career is especially difficult, since it is likely that the two pursuits will demand qualities of different types. The former, to be successful, requires self-negation; the latter, self-enhancement. The former demands cooperation; the latter competition. . . . There is greater opportunity for happiness if husband and wife supplement each other than there is when there is duplication of function . . . [4]

And just in case Nora has any doubts about giving up her career ambitions, she is offered this comforting rationalization:

> A woman who is an effective homemaker must know something about teaching, interior decoration, cooking, dietetics, consumption, psychology, physiology, social relations, community resources, clothing, household equipment, housing, hygiene and a host of other things. . . . She is a general practitioner rather than a specialist. . . .
>
> The young woman who decides upon homemaking as her career need have no feeling of inferiority. . . . One may say, as some do, "Men can have careers because women make homes." One may say that women are released from the necessity for

wage earning and are free to devote their time to the extremely important matter of homemaking because men specialize in breadwinning. Or one may say that together the breadwinner and the homemaker form a complementary combination second to none.[5]

This marriage textbook is not the most subtle of its school. It is almost too easy to see that its functional argument is based on no real chain of scientific fact. (It is hardly scientific to say "this is what is, therefore this is what should be.") But this is the essence of functionalism as it came to pervade all of American sociology in this period, whether or not the sociologist called himself a "functionalist." In colleges which would never stoop to the "role-playing lessons" of the so-called functional family course, young women were assigned Talcott Parsons'* authoritative "analysis of sex-roles in the social structure of the United States," which contemplates no alternative for a woman other than the role of "housewife," patterned with varying emphasis on "domesticity," "glamour," and "good companionship."

It is perhaps not too much to say that only in very exceptional cases can an adult man be genuinely self-respecting and enjoy a respected status in the eyes of others if he does not "earn a living" in an approved occupational role. . . . In the case of the feminine role the situation is radically different. . . . The woman's fundamental status is that of her husband's wife, the mother of his children . . . [6]

Parsons, a highly respected sociologist and the leading functional theoretician, describes with insight and accuracy the sources of strain in this "segregation of sex roles." He points out that the "domestic" aspect of the housewife role "has declined in importance to the point where it scarcely approaches a full-time occupation for a vigorous person": that the "glamour pattern" is "inevitably associated with a rather early age level" and thus "serious strains result from the problem of adaptation to increasing age," that the "good companion" pattern—which includes "humanistic" cultivation of the arts and community welfare—"suffers from a lack of fully institutionalized status. . . . It is only those with the strongest initiative and intelligence who achieve fully satisfying adaptations

---

*   Talcott Parsons (1902–1979), the preeminent American sociologist in the post–World War II era. His school of thought, called functionalism, was the dominant paradigm in American sociology during these years. Taking issue with theories that emphasized conflict as the fundamental condition of society, Parsons focused on the consensus of shared norms and values necessary to operate and reproduce the social order. Although Parsons himself was left-leaning, leftist critics in the 1960s viewed his work as inherently conservative and his work fell out of favor in the 1970s and 1980s (see entry on functionalism, p. 106).

in this direction." He states that "it is quite clear that in the adult feminine role there is quite sufficient strain and insecurity so that widespread manifestations are to be expected in the form of neurotic behavior." But Parsons warns:

> It is, of course, possible for the adult woman to follow the masculine pattern and seek a career in fields of occupational achievement in direct competition with men of her own class. It is, however, notable that in spite of the very great progress of the emancipation of women from the traditional domestic pattern only a very small fraction have gone very far in this direction. It is also clear that its generalization would only be possible with profound alterations in the structure of the family.

True equality between men and women would not be "functional"; the status quo can be maintained only if the wife and mother is exclusively a homemaker or, at most, has a "job" rather than a "career" which might give her status equal to that of her husband. Thus Parsons finds sexual segregation "functional" in terms of keeping the social structure as it is, which seems to be the functionalist's primary concern.

> Absolute equality of opportunity is clearly incompatible with any positive solidarity of the family. . . . Where married women are employed outside the home, it is, for the great majority, in occupations which are not in direct competition for status with those of men of their own class. Women's interests, and the standard of judgment applied to them, run, in our society, far more in the direction of personal adornment. . . . It is suggested that this difference is functionally related to maintaining family solidarity in our class structure.[7]

Even the eminent woman sociologist Mirra Komarovsky, whose functional analysis of how girls learn to "play the role of woman" in our society is brilliant indeed, cannot quite escape the rigid mold functionalism imposes: adjustment to the status quo. For to limit one's field of inquiry to the function of an institution in a given social system, with no alternatives considered, provides an infinite number of rationalizations for all the inequalities and inequities of that system. It is not surprising that social scientists began to mistake their own function as one of helping the individual "adjust" to his "role," in that system.

> A social order can function only because the vast majority have somehow adjusted themselves to their place in society and perform the functions expected of them. . . . The differences in the upbringing of the sexes . . . are obviously related to their respective roles in adult life. The future homemaker trains for

her role within the home, but the boy prepares for his by being given more independence outside the home, by his taking a "paper route" or a summer job. A provider will profit by independence, dominance, aggressiveness, competitiveness.[8]

The risk of the "traditional upbringing" of girls, as this sociologist sees it, is its possible "failure to develop in the girl the independence, inner resources, and that degree of self-assertion which life will demand of her"—in her role as wife. The functional warning follows:

> Even if a parent correctly [sic] considers certain conventional attributes of the feminine role to be worthless, he creates risks for the girl in forcing her to stray too far from the accepted mores of her time. . . . The steps which parents must take to prepare their daughters to meet economic exigencies and familial responsibilities of modern life—these very steps may awaken aspirations and develop habits which conflict with certain features of their feminine roles, as these are defined today. The very education which is to make the college housewife a cultural leaven of her family and her community may develop in her interests which are frustrated by other phases of housewifery. . . . We run the risk of awakening interests and abilities which, again, run counter to the present definition of femininity.[9]

She goes on to cite the recent case of a girl who wanted to be a sociologist. She was engaged to a GI who didn't want his wife to work. The girl herself hoped she wouldn't find a good job in sociology.

> An unsatisfactory job would, she felt, make it easier for her to comply eventually with her future husband's wishes. The needs of the country for trained workers, the uncertainty of her own future, her current interests notwithstanding, she took a routine job. Only the future will tell whether her decision was prudent. If her fiance returns from the front, if the marriage takes place, if he is able to provide for the family without her assistance, if her frustrated wishes do not boomerang, then she will not regret her decision. . . .
>
> At the present historical moment, the best adjusted girl is probably one who is intelligent enough to do well in school but not so brilliant as to get all A's . . . capable but not in areas relatively new to women; able to stand on her own two feet and to earn a living, but not so good a living as to compete with men; capable of doing some job well (in case she doesn't marry, or otherwise has to work) but not so identified with a profession as to need it for her happiness.[10]

So, in the name of adjustment to the cultural definition of femininity—in which this brilliant sociologist obviously does not herself believe (that word "correctly" betrays her)—she ends up virtually endorsing the continued *infantilizing* of American woman, except insofar as it has the unintended consequence of making "the transition from the role of daughter to that of the spouse more difficult for her than for the son."

> Essentially, it is assumed that to the extent that the woman remains more "infantile," less able to make her own decisions, more dependent upon one or both parents for initiating and channeling behavior and attitudes, more closely attached to them so as to find it difficult to part from them or to face their disapproval . . . or shows any other indices of lack of emotional emancipation—to that extent she may find it more difficult than the man to conform to the cultural norm of primary loyalty to the family she establishes later. It is possible, of course, that the only effect of the greater sheltering is to create in women a generalized dependency which will then be transferred to the husband and which will enable her all the more readily to accept the role of wife in a family which still has many patriarchal features.[11]

She finds evidence in a number of studies that college girls, in fact, are more infantile, dependent and tied to parents than boys, and do not mature, as boys do, by learning to stand alone. But she can find no evidence—in twenty psychiatric texts—that there are, accordingly, more in-law problems with the wife's parents than the husband's. Evidently, only with such evidence could a functionalist comfortably question the deliberate infantilization of American girls!

Functionalism was an easy out for American sociologists. There can be no doubt that they were describing things "as they were," but in so doing, they were relieved of the responsibility of building theory from facts, of probing for deeper truth. They were also relieved of the need to formulate questions and answers that would be inevitably controversial (at a time in academic circles, as in America as a whole, when controversy was not welcome). They assumed an endless present, and based their reasoning on denying the possibility of a future different from the past. Of course, their reasoning would hold up only as long as the future did not change. As C. P. Show* has pointed

---

*   Sir Charles Percy Snow (1905–1980), English scientist, fiction writer, and governmental advisor, best known for his intellectual work warning of the importance of moral and philosophical judgment in the work of science. He delivered a series of lectures at Cambridge University, published as *The Two Cultures and the Scientific Revolution* in 1960.

out, science and scientists are future-minded. Social scientists under the functional banner were so rigidly present-minded that they denied the future; their theories enforced the prejudices of the past, and actually prevented change.

Sociologists themselves have recently come to the conclusion that functionalism was rather "embarrassing" because it really said nothing at all. As Kingsley Davis pointed out in his presidential address on "The Myth of Functional Analysis as a Special Method in Sociology and Anthropology" at the American Sociological Association in 1959:

> For more than thirty years now "functional analysis" has been debated among sociologists and anthropologists. . . . However strategic it may have been in the past, it has now become an impediment rather than a prop to scientific progress. . . . The claim that functionalism cannot handle social change because it posits an integrated static society is true by definition. . . . [12]

Unfortunately, the female objects of functional analysis were profoundly affected by it. At a time of great change for women, at a time when education, science, and social science should have helped women bridge the change, functionalism transformed "what is" for women, or "what was," to "what should be." Those who perpetrated the feminine protest, and made more of being a woman than it can ever be, in the name of functionalism or for whatever complex of personal or intellectual reasons, closed the door of the future on women. In all the concern for adjustment, one truth was forgotten: women were being adjusted to a state inferior to their full capabilities. The functionalists did not wholly accept the Freudian argument that "anatomy is destiny," but they accepted whole-heartedly an equally restrictive definition of woman: woman is what society says she is. And most of the functional anthropologists studied societies in which woman's destiny was defined by anatomy.

The most powerful influence on modern women, in terms both of functionalism and the feminine protest, was Margaret Mead. Her work on culture and personality—book after book, study after study—has had a profound effect on the women in my generation, the one before it, and the generation now growing up. She was, and still is, the symbol of the woman thinker in America. She has written millions of words in the thirty-odd years between *Coming of Age in Samoa* in 1928 and her latest article on American women in the *New York Times Magazine* or *Redbook*. She is studied in college classrooms by girls taking courses in anthropology, sociology, psychology, education, and marriage and family life; in graduate schools by those who will one day teach girls and counsel women; in medical schools by future pediatricians and psychiatrists; even in theological schools by progressive young ministers. And she is read in the women's magazines and the Sunday supplements, where she publishes as readily as in the learned journals, by girls and women of all ages. Margaret Mead is her own best popularizer—and her influence has been felt in almost every layer of American thought.

But her influence, for women, has been a paradox. A mystique takes what it needs from any thinker of the time. The feminine mystique might have taken from Margaret Mead her vision of the infinite variety of sexual patterns and the enormous plasticity of human nature, a vision based on the differences of sex and temperament she found in three primitive societies: the Arapesh, where both men and women were "feminine" and "maternal" in personality and passively sexual, because both were trained to be cooperative, unaggressive, responsive to the needs and demands of others; the Mundugumor, where both husband and wife were violent, aggressive, positively sexed, "masculine"; and the Tchambuli, where the woman was the dominant, impersonal managing partner, and the man the less responsible and emotionally dependent person.

> If those temperamental attitudes which we have traditionally regarded as feminine—such as passivity, responsiveness, and a willingness to cherish children—can so easily be set up as the masculine pattern in one tribe, and in another be outlawed for the majority of women as well as for the majority of men, we no longer have any basis for regarding such aspects of behavior as sex-linked. . . . The material suggests that we may say that many, if not all, of the personality traits which we have called masculine or feminine are as lightly linked to sex, as are the clothing, the manners, and the form of head-dress that a society at a given period assigns to either sex.[13]

From such anthropological observations, she might have passed on to the popular culture a truly revolutionary vision of women finally free to realize their full capabilities in a society which replaced arbitrary sexual definitions with a recognition of genuine individual gifts as they occur in either sex. She had such a vision, more than once:

> Where writing is accepted as a profession that may be pursued by either sex with perfect suitability, individuals who have the ability to write need not be debarred from it by their sex, nor need they, if they do write, doubt their essential masculinity or femininity . . . and it is here that we can find a ground-plan for building a society that would substitute real differences for arbitrary ones. We must recognize that beneath the superficial classifications of sex and race the same potentialities exist,

recurring generation after generation, only to perish because society has no place for them.

Just as society now permits the practice of an art to members of either sex, so it might also permit the development of many contrasting temperamental gifts in each sex. It would abandon its various attempts to make boys fight and to make girls remain passive, or to make all children fight. . . . No child would be relentlessly shaped to one pattern of behavior, but instead there should be many patterns, in a world that had learned to allow to each individual the pattern which was most congenial to his gifts.[14]

But this is not the vision the mystique took from Margaret Mead; nor is it the vision that she continues to offer. Increasingly, in her own pages, her interpretation blurs, is subtly transformed, into a glorification of women in the female role—as defined by their sexual biological function. At times she seems to lose her own anthropological awareness of the malleability of human personality, and to look at anthropological data from the Freudian point of view— sexual biology determines all, anatomy is destiny. At times she seems to be arguing in functional terms, that while woman's potential is as great and various as the unlimited human potential, it is better to preserve the sexual biological limitations established by a culture. At times she says both things in the same page, and even sounds a note of caution, warning of the dangers a woman faces in trying to realize a human potential which her society has defined as masculine.

> The difference between the two sexes is one of the important conditions upon which we have built the many varieties of human culture that give human beings dignity and stature. . . . Sometimes one quality has been assigned to one sex, sometimes to the other. Now it is boys who are thought of as infinitely vulnerable and in need of special cherishing care, now it is girls. . . . Some people think of women as too weak to work out of doors, others regard women as the appropriate bearers of heavy burdens "because their heads are stronger than men's." . . . Some religions, including our European traditional religions, have assigned women an inferior role in the religious hierarchy, others have built their whole symbolic relationship with the supernatural world upon male imitations of the natural functions of women. . . . Whether we deal with small matters or with large, with the frivolities of ornament and cosmetics or the sanctities of man's place in the universe, we find this great variety of ways, often flatly contradictory one to the other, in which the roles of the two sexes have been patterned.

But we always find the patterning. We know of no culture that has said, articulately, that there is no difference between men and women except in the way they contribute to the creation of the next generation; that otherwise in all respects they are simply human beings with varying gifts, no one of which can be exclusively assigned to either sex.

Are we dealing with a must that we dare not flout because it is rooted so deep in our biological mammalian nature that to flout it means individual and social disease? Or with a must that, although not so deeply rooted, still is so very socially convenient and so well tried that it would be uneconomical to flout it—a must which says, for example, that it is easier to get children born and bred if we stylize the behavior of the sexes very differently, teaching them to walk and dress and act in contrasting ways and to specialize in different kinds of work?[15]

We must also ask: What are the potentialities of sex differences? . . . If little boys have to meet and assimilate the early shock of knowing that they can never create a baby with the sureness and incontrovertibility that is a woman's birthright, how does this make them more creatively ambitious, as well as more dependent upon achievement? If little girls have a rhythm of growth which means that their own sex appears to them as initially less sure than their brothers, and so gives them a little false flick towards compensatory achievement that almost always dies down before the certainty of maternity, this probably does mean a limitation on their sense of ambition? But what positive potentialities are there also?[16]

In these passages from *Male and Female*, a book which became the cornerstone of the feminine mystique, Margaret Mead betrays her Freudian orientation, even though she cautiously prefaces each statement of apparent scientific fact with the small word "if." But it is a very significant "if." For when sexual differences become the basis of your approach to culture and personality, and when you assume that sexuality is the driving force of human personality (an assumption that you took from Freud), and when, moreover, as an anthropologist, you know that there are no true-for-every-culture sexual differences except those involved in the act of procreation, you will inevitably give that one biological difference, the difference in reproductive role, increasing importance in the determination of woman's personality.

Margaret Mead did not conceal the fact that, after 1931, Freudian rubrics, based on the zones of the body, were part of the equipment she took with her on anthropological field trips.[17] Thus she began to equate "those assertive, creative, productive aspects of life on which the superstructure of a civilization depends" with the penis, and to define feminine creativity in terms of the "passive receptivity" of the uterus.

> In discussing men and women, I shall be concerned with the primary differences between them, the difference in their reproductive roles. Out of the bodies fashioned for complementary roles in perpetuating the race, what differences in functioning, in capacities, in sensitivities, in vulnerabilities arise? How is what men can do related to the fact that their reproductive role is over in a single act, what women can do related to the fact that their reproductive role takes nine months of gestation, and until recently many months of breast feeding? What is the contribution of each sex, seen as itself, not as a mere imperfect version of the other?
>
> Living in the modern world, clothed and muffled, forced to convey our sense of our bodies in terms of remote symbols like walking sticks and umbrellas and handbags, it is easy to lose sight of the immediacy of the human body plan. But when one lives among primitive peoples, where women wear only a pair of little grass aprons, and may discard even these to insult each other or to bathe in a group, and men wear only a very lightly fastened G-string of beaten bark . . . and small babies wear nothing at all, the basic communications . . . that are conducted between bodies become very real. In our own society, we have now invented a therapeutic method that can laboriously deduce from the recollections of the neurotic, or the untrammelled phantasies of the psychotic, how the human body, its entrances and exits, originally shaped the growing individual's view of the world.[18]

As a matter of fact, the lens of "anatomy is destiny" seemed to be peculiarly right for viewing the cultures and personalities of Samoa, Manus, Arapesh, Mundugumor, Tchambuli, Iatmul and Bali; right as perhaps it never was right, in that formulation, for Vienna at the end of the nineteenth century or America in the twentieth.

In the primitive civilizations of the South Sea islands, anatomy was still destiny when Margaret Mead first visited them. Freud's theory that the primitive instincts of the body determined adult personality could find convincing demonstration. The complex goals of more advanced civilizations, in which instinct and environment are increasingly controlled and transformed by the human mind, did not then form the irreversible matrix of every human life. It must have been much easier to see biological differences between men and women as the basic force in life in those unclothed primitive peoples. But only if you go to such an island with the Freudian lens in your eye, accepting before you start what certain irreverent anthropologists call the toilet-paper theory of history, will you draw from observations in primitive civilizations of the role of the unclothed body, male or female, a lesson for modern women which assumes that the unclothed body can determine in the same way the course of human life and personality in a complex modern civilization.

Anthropologists today are less inclined to see in primitive civilization a laboratory for the observation of our own civilization, a scale model with all the irrelevancies blotted out; civilization is just not that irrelevant.

Because the human body is the same in primitive South Sea tribes and modern cities, an anthropologist, who starts with a psychological theory that reduces human personality and civilization to bodily analogies, can end up advising modern women to live through their bodies in the same way as the women of the South Seas. The trouble is that Margaret Mead could not re-create a South Sea world for us to live in: a world where having a baby is the pinnacle of human achievement. (If reproduction were the chief and only fact of human life, would all men today suffer from "uterus envy"?)

> In Bali, little girls between two and three walk much of the time with purposely thrust-out little bellies, and the older women tap them playfully as they pass. "Pregnant," they tease. So the little girl learns that although the signs of her membership in her own sex are slight, her breasts mere tiny buttons no bigger than her brother's, her genitals a simple inconspicuous fold, some day she will be pregnant, some day she will have a baby, and having a baby is, on the whole, one of the most exciting and conspicuous achievements that can be presented to the eyes of small children in these simple worlds, in some of which the largest buildings are only fifteen feet high, the largest boat some twenty feet long. Furthermore, the little girl learns that she will have a baby not because she is strong or energetic or initiating, not because she works and struggles and tries, and in the end succeeds, but simply because she is a girl and not a boy, and girls turn into women, and in the end—if they protect their femininity—have babies.[19]

To an American woman in the twentieth century competing in a field which demands initiative and energy and work and in which men resent her success, to a woman with less will and ability to compete than Margaret Mead, how tempting is her vision of that South Sea world where a woman succeeds and is envied by man just by being a woman.

> In our Occidental view of life, woman, fashioned from man's rib, can at the most strive unsuccessfully to imitate man's supe-

rior powers and higher vocations. The basic theme of the initia-
tory cult, however, is that women, by virtue of their ability to
make children, hold the secret of life. Man's role is uncertain,
undefined, and perhaps unnecessary. By a great effort man has
hit upon a method of compensating himself for his basic inferiority. Equipped with various mysterious noise-making instru-
ments, whose potency rests upon their actual forms being
unknown to those who hear the sounds—that is, the women
and children must never know that they are really bamboo
flutes, or hollow logs . . . they can get the male children away
from the women, brand them as incomplete and themselves
turn boys into men. Women, it is true, make human beings,
but only men can make men.[20]

True, this primitive society was a "shaky structure, protected by
endless taboos and precautions"—by women's shame, fluttery fear,
indulgence of male vanity—and it survived only as long as everyone
kept the rules. "The missionary who shows the flutes to the women
has broken the culture successfully."[21] But Margaret Mead, who
might have shown American men and women "the flutes" of their
own arbitrary and shaky taboos, precautions, shames, fears, and
indulgence of male vanity, did not use her knowledge in this way.
Out of life the way it was—in Samoa, Bali, where all men envied
women—she held up an ideal for American women that gave new
reality to the shaky structure of sexual prejudice, the feminine
mystique.

The language is anthropological, the theory stated as fact is
Freudian, but the yearning is for a return to the Garden of Eden; a
garden where women need only forget the "divine discontent" born
of education to return to a world in which male achievement becomes
merely a poor substitute for child-bearing.

> The recurrent problem of civilization is to define the male role
> satisfactorily enough—whether it be to build gardens or raise
> cattle, kill game or kill enemies, build bridges or handle bank
> shares—so that the male may, in the course of his life, reach a
> solid sense of irreversible achievement of which his childhood
> knowledge of the satisfactions of child-bearing has given him a
> glimpse. In the case of women, it is only necessary that they be
> permitted by the given social arrangements to fulfill their bio-
> logical role, to attain this sense of irreversible achievement.
> If women are to be restless and questing, even in the face of
> child-bearing, they must be made so through education.[22]

What the feminine mystique took from Margaret Mead was not
her vision of woman's great untested human potential, but this glorification of the female sexual function that has indeed been tested,

in every culture, but seldom, in civilized cultures, valued as highly as the unlimited potential of human creativity, so far mainly displayed by man. The vision the mystique took from Margaret Mead was of a world where women, by merely being women and bearing children, will earn the same respect accorded men for their creative achievements—as if possession of uterus and breasts bestows on women a glory that men can never know, even though they labor all their lives to create. In such a world, all the other things that a woman can do or be are merely pale substitutes for the conception of a child. Femininity becomes more than its definition by society; it becomes a value which society must protect from the destructive onrush of civilization like the vanishing buffalo.

Margaret Mead's eloquent pages made a great many American women envy the serene femininity of a bare-breasted Samoan, and try to make themselves into languorous savages, breasts unfettered by civilization's brassieres, and brains undisturbed by pallid man-made knowledge of the goals of human progress.

> Woman's biological career-line has a natural climax structure that can be overlaid, muted, muffled and publicly denied, but which remains as an essential element in both sexes' view of themselves. . . . The young Balinese girl to whom one says, "Your name is I Tewa?" and who draws herself up and answers, "I am Men Bawa" (Mother of Bawa) is speaking absolutely. She is the mother of Bawa; Bawa may die tomorrow, but she remains the mother of Bawa; only if he had died unnamed would her neighbors have called her "Men Belasin," "Mother Bereft." Stage after stage in women's life-histories thus stand, irrevocable, indisputable, accomplished. This gives a natural basis for the little girl's emphasis on being rather than on doing. The little boy learns that he must act like a boy, do things, prove that he is a boy, and prove it over and over again, while the little girl learns that she is a girl, and all she has to do is to refrain from acting like a boy.[23]

And so it goes, on and on, until one is inclined to say—so what? You are born, you grow, you are impregnated, you have a child, it grows; this is true of all cultures, recorded or unrecorded, the one we know from life and the recondite ones which only the far-traveled anthropologist knows. But is this all there is to life for a woman today?

It is not to deny the importance of biology to question a definition of woman's nature that is based so completely on her biological difference from man. Female biology, woman's "biological career-line," may be changeless—the same in Stone Age women twenty thousand years ago, and Samoan women on remote islands, and American women in the twentieth century—but the nature of the human relationship to biology *has* changed. Our increasing knowledge, the increasing potency of human intelligence, has given us an awareness of purposes and goals beyond the simple biological needs of hunger, thirst, and sex. Even these simple needs, in men or women today, are not the same as they were in the Stone Age or in the South Sea cultures, because they are now part of a more complex pattern of human life.

As an anthropologist, of course, Margaret Mead knew this. And for all her words glorifying the female role, there are other words picturing the wonders of a world in which women would be able to realize their full capabilities. But this picture is almost invariably overlaid with the therapeutic caution, the manipulative superiority, typical of too many American social scientists. When this caution is combined with perhaps an over-evaluation of the power of social science not merely to interpret culture and personality, but to order our lives, her words acquire the aura of a righteous crusade—a crusade against change. She joins the other functional social scientists in their emphasis on adjusting to society as we find it, on living our lives within the framework of the conventional cultural definitions of the male and female roles. This attitude is explicit in the later pages of *Male and Female.*

> Giving each sex its due, a full recognition of its special vulnerabilities and needs for protection, means looking beyond the superficial resemblances during the period of later childhood when both boys and girls, each having laid many of the problems of sex adjustment aside, seem so eager to learn, and so able to learn the same things. . . . But every adjustment that minimizes a difference, a vulnerability, in one sex, a differential strength in the other, diminishes their possibility of complementing each other, and corresponds—symbolically—to sealing off the constructive receptivity of the female and the vigorous outgoing constructive activity of the male, muting them both in the end to a duller version of human life, in which each is denied the fullness of humanity that each might have had.[24]
>
> No human gift is strong enough to flower fully in a person who is threatened with loss of sex membership. . . . No matter with what good will we may embark on a program of actually rearing both men and women to make their full and special contributions in all the complex processes of civilization— medicine and law, education and religion, the arts and sciences—the task will be very difficult. . . .
>
> It is of very doubtful value to enlist the gifts of women if bringing women into fields that have been defined as male frightens the men, unsexes the women, muffles and distorts the

contribution the women could make, either because their presence excludes men from the occupation or because it changes
the quality of the men who enter it. . . . It is folly to ignore the
signs which warn us that the present terms in which women
are lured by their own curiosities and drives developed under
the same educational system as boys . . . are bad for both men
and women.[25]

The role of Margaret Mead as the professional spokesman of
femininity would have been less important if American women had
taken the example of her own life, instead of listening to what she
said in her books. Margaret Mead has lived a life of open challenge,
and lived it proudly, if sometimes self-consciously, as a woman. She
has moved on the frontiers of thought and added to the superstructure of our knowledge. She has demonstrated feminine capabilities
that go far beyond childbirth; she made her way in what was still very
much a "man's world" without denying that she was a woman; in fact,
she proclaimed in her work a unique woman's knowledge with which
no male anthropologist could compete. After so many centuries of
unquestioned masculine authority, how natural for someone to pro-
claim a feminine authority. But the great human visions of stopping
wars, curing sickness, teaching races to live together, building new
and beautiful structures for people to live in, are more than "other
ways of having children."

It is not easy to combat age-old prejudices. As a social scientist,
and as a woman, she struck certain blows against the prejudicial
image of woman that may long outlast her own life. In her insistence that women are human beings—unique human beings, not
men with something missing—she went a step beyond Freud. And
yet, because her observations were based on Freud's bodily analogies, she cut down her own vision of women by glorifying the mysterious miracle of femininity, which a woman realizes simply by
being female, letting the breasts grow and the menstrual blood
flow and the baby suck from the swollen breast. In her warning
that women who seek fulfillment beyond their biological role are
in danger of becoming desexed witches, she spelled out again an
unnecessary choice. She persuaded younger women to give up part
of their dearly won humanity rather than lose their femininity. In
the end she did the very thing that she warned against, re-creating
in her work the vicious circle that she broke in her own life:

> We may go up the scale from simple physical differences
> through complementary distinctions that overstress the role of
> sex difference and extend it inappropriately to other aspects of
> life, to stereotypes of such complex activities as those involved

in the formal use of the intellect, in the arts, in government, and in religion.

In all these complex achievements of civilization, those activities which are mankind's glory, and upon which depends our hope of survival in this world that we have built, there has been this tendency to make artificial definitions that limit an activity to one sex, and by denying the actual potentialities of human beings limit not only both men and women, but also equally the development of the activity itself. . . .

Here is a vicious circle to which it is not possible to assign either a beginning or an end, in which men's overestimation of women's roles, or women's overestimation of men's roles leads one sex or the other to arrogate, to neglect, or even to relinquish part of our so dearly won humanity. Those who would break the circle are themselves a product of it, express some of its defects in their every gesture, may be only strong enough to challenge it, not able actually to break it. Yet once identified, once analyzed, it should be possible to create a climate of opinion in which others, a little less the product of the dark past because they have been reared with a light in their hand that can shine backwards as well as forwards, may in turn take the next step.[26]

Perhaps the feminine protest was a necessary step after the masculine protest made by some of the feminists. Margaret Mead was one of the first women to emerge into prominence in American life after rights for women were won. Her mother was a social scientist, her grandmother a teacher; she had private images of women who were fully human, she had education equal to any man's. And she was able to say with conviction: it's good to be a woman, you don't need to copy man, you can respect yourself as a woman. She made a resounding feminine protest, in her life and in her work. And it was a step forward when she influenced emancipated modern women to choose, with free intelligence, to have babies, bear them with a proud awareness that denied pain, nurse them at the breast and devote mind and body to their care. It was a step forward in the passionate journey—and one made possible by it—for educated women to say "yes" to motherhood as a conscious human purpose and not a burden imposed by the flesh. For, of course, the natural childbirth-breastfeeding movement Margaret Mead helped inspire was not at all a return to primitive earth-mother maternity. It appealed to the independent, educated, spirited American woman—and to her counterparts in western Europe and Russia—because it enabled her to experience childbirth not as a mindless female animal, an object manipulated by the obstetrician, but as a whole person, able to control her own body with her aware mind. Perhaps less important than birth control and the other rights which made woman more equal to man, the work of Margaret Mead helped humanize sex. It took a scientific super-saleswoman to re-create in modern American life even a semblance of the conditions under which primitive tribesmen jealously imitated maternity and bled themselves. (The modern husband goes through the breathing exercises with his wife as she prepares for natural childbirth.) But did she oversell women?

It was, perhaps, not her fault that she was taken so literally that procreation became a cult, a career, to the exclusion of every other kind of creative endeavor, until women kept on having babies because they knew no other way to create. She was often quoted out of context by the lesser functionalists and the women's magazines. Those who found in her work confirmation of their own unadmitted prejudices and fears ignored not only the complexity of her total work, but the example of her complex life. With all the difficulties she must have encountered, pioneering as a woman in the realm of abstract thought that was the domain of man (a one-sentence review of *Sex and Temperament* indicates the resentment she often met: "Margaret, have you found a culture yet where the men had the babies?"), she has never retreated from the hard road to self-realization so few women have traveled since. She told women often enough to stay on that road. If they only heard her other words of warning, and conformed to her glorification of femininity, perhaps it was because they were not as sure of themselves and their human abilities as she was.

Margaret Mead and the lesser functionalists knew the pains, the risks, of breaking through age-old social strictures.[27] This awareness was their justification for qualifying their statements of women's potentiality with the advice that women not compete with men, but seek respect for their uniqueness as women. It was hardly revolutionary advice; it did not upset the traditional image of woman any more than Freudian thought upset it. Perhaps it was their intention to subvert the old image; but instead they gave the new mystique its scientific authority.

Ironically, Margaret Mead, in the 1960's, began to voice alarm at the "return of the cavewoman"—the retreat of American women to narrow domesticity, while the world trembled on the brink of technological holocaust. In an excerpt from a book titled *American Women: The Changing Image*, which appeared in the *Saturday Evening Post* (March 3, 1962), she asked:

> Why have we returned, despite our advances in technology, to the Stone Age picture? . . . Woman has gone back, each to her separate cave, waiting anxiously for her mate and children to

return, guarding her mate jealously against other women, almost totally unaware of any life outside her door. . . . In this retreat into fecundity, it is not the individual woman who is to blame. It is the climate of opinion that has developed in this country . . .

Apparently Margaret Mead does not acknowledge, or perhaps recognize her own role as a major architect of that "climate of opinion." Apparently she has overlooked much of her own work, which helped persuade several generations of able modern American women "in desperate cavewoman style, to devote their whole lives to narrow domesticity—first in schoolgirl dreaming and a search for roles which make them appealingly ignorant, then as mothers and then as grandmothers . . . restricting their activities to the preservation of their own private, and often boring existences."

Even though it would seem that Margaret Mead is now trying to get women out of the home, she still ascribes a sexual specialness to everything a woman does. Trying to seduce them into the modern world of science as "the teacher-mothers of infant scientists," she is still translating the new possibilities open to women and the new problems facing them as members of the human race into sexual terms. But now "those roles which have historically belonged to women" are stretched to include political responsibility for nuclear disarmament—"to cherish not just their own but the children of the enemy." Since, beginning with the same premise and examining the same body of anthropological evidence, she now arrives at a slightly different sexual role for women, one might seriously question the basis upon which she decides the roles a woman should play—and finds it so easy to change the rules of the game from one decade to the next.

Other social scientists have arrived at the astonishing conclusion that "being a woman was no more and no less than being human."[28] But a cultural lag is built into the feminine mystique. By the time a few social scientists were discovering the flaws in "woman's role," American educators had seized upon it as a magic sesame. Instead of educating women for the greater maturity required to participate in modern society—with all the problems, conflicts, and hard work involved, for educators as well as women— they began educating them to "play the role of woman."

7

The Sex-Directed Educators

It must have been going on for ten or fifteen years before the educators even suspected it—the old-fashioned educators, that is. The new sex-directed educators were surprised that anyone should be surprised, shocked that anyone should be shocked.

The shock, the mystery, to the naive who had great hopes for the higher education of women was that more American women than ever before were going to college—but fewer of them were going on from college to become physicists, philosophers, poets, doctors, lawyers, stateswomen, social pioneers, even college professors. Fewer women in recent college graduating classes have gone on to distinguish themselves in a career or profession than those in the classes graduated before World War II, the Great Divide. Fewer and fewer college women were preparing for any career or profession requiring more than the most casual commitment. Two out of three girls who entered college were dropping out before they even finished. In the 1950's, those who stayed, even the most able, showed no signs of wanting to be anything more than suburban housewives and mothers. In fact, to professors at Vassar and Smith and Barnard, resorting to desperate means to arouse students' interest in *anything* college could teach them, the girls seemed suddenly incapable of any ambition, any vision, any passion, except the pursuit of a wedding ring. In this pursuit they seemed almost desperate, as early as freshman year.

Out of loyalty to that more and more futile illusion—the importance of higher education for women—the purist professors kept quiet at first. But the disuse of, the resistance to, higher education by American women finally began to show in the statistics:[1] in the departure of the male presidents, scholars, and educators from women's colleges; in the disillusionment, the mystified frustration or cool cynicism of the ones who stayed; and in the skepticism, finally, in colleges and universities, about the value of a professorial investment in any girl or woman, no matter how apparently able and ambitious. Some women's colleges went out of business; some professors, at coeducational universities, said one out of three college places should no longer be wasted on women; the president of Sarah Lawrence, a women's college with high intellectual values, spoke of opening the place to men; the president of Vassar predicted the end of all the great American women's colleges which pioneered higher education for women.

When I read the first cautious hints of what was happening, in the preliminary report of the psychological-sociological-anthropological Mellon Foundation study of Vassar girls in 1956, I thought, "My, how Vassar must have deteriorated."

> Strong commitment to an activity or career other than that of housewife is rare. Many students, perhaps a third, are interested in graduate schooling and in careers, for example, teaching. Few, however, plan to continue with a career if it should conflict with family needs. . . . As compared to previous periods, however, e.g., the "feminist era," few students are interested in the pursuit of demanding careers, such as law or medicine, regardless of personal or social pressures. Similarly, one finds few instances of people like Edna St. Vincent Millay, individuals completely committed to their art by the time of adolescence and resistant to any attempts to tamper with it . . . [2]

A later report elaborated:

> Vassar students . . . are further convinced that the wrongs of society will gradually right themselves with little or no direct intervention on the part of women college students. . . . Vassar girls, by and large, do not expect to achieve fame, make an enduring contribution to society, pioneer any frontiers, or otherwise create ripples in the placid order of things. . . . Not only is spinsterhood viewed as a personal tragedy but offspring are considered essential to the full life and the Vassar student believes that she would willingly adopt children, if it were necessary, to create a family. In short, her future identity is largely encompassed by the projected role of wife-mother. . . . In describing the qualities to be found in an ideal husband, the majority of Vassar girls are quite explicit in their preference for the man who will assume the most important role, that is, handle his own career and make the majority of decisions affecting matters outside the home. . . . That the female should attempt, in their thinking, to usurp the prerogatives of the male is a distasteful notion which would seriously disrupt their own projected role of helpmate and faithful complement to the man of the house.[3]

I saw the change, a very real one, when I went back to my own college in 1959, to live for a week with the students in a campus house at Smith, and then went on to interview girls from colleges and universities all over the United States.

A beloved psychology professor, on the eve of his retirement, complained:

They're bright enough. They have to be, to get here at all now. But they just won't let themselves get interested. They seem to feel it will get in their way when they marry the young executive and raise all those children in the suburbs. I couldn't schedule the final seminar for my senior honor students. Too many kitchen showers interfered. None of them considered the seminar sufficiently important to postpone their kitchen showers.

He's exaggerating, I thought.

I picked up a copy of the college newspaper I had once edited. The current student editor described a government class in which fifteen of the twenty girls were knitting "with the stony-faced concentration of Madame Defarge. The instructor, more in challenge than in seriousness, announced that Western civilization is coming to an end. The students turned to their notebooks and wrote 'Western civ—coming to an end,' all without dropping a stitch."

Why do they need such baiting, I wondered, remembering how we used to stand around after class, arguing about what the professor had said—Economic Theory, Political Philosophy, the History of Western Civilization, Sociology 21, Science and the Imagination, even Chaucer. "What courses are people excited about now?" I asked a blonde senior in cap and gown. Nuclear physics, maybe? Modern art? The civilizations of Africa? Looking at me as if I were some prehistoric dinosaur, she said:

> Girls don't get excited about things like that anymore. We don't want careers. Our parents expect us to go to college. Everybody goes. You're a social outcast at home if you don't. But a girl who got serious about anything she studied—like wanting to go on and do research—would be peculiar, unfeminine. I guess everybody wants to graduate with a diamond ring on her finger. That's the important thing.

I discovered an unwritten rule barring "shop talk" about courses, intellectual talk, in some college houses. On the campus, the girls looked as if they were in such a hurry, rushing, rushing. Nobody, except a few faculty members, sat around talking in the coffee dives or the corner drugstore. We used to sit for hours arguing what-is-truth, art-for-art's-sake, religion, sex, war and peace, Freud and Marx, and all the things that were wrong with the world. A cool junior told me:

> We never waste time like that. We don't have bull sessions about abstract things. Mostly, we talk about our dates. Anyhow, I spend three days a week off campus. There's a boy I'm interested in. I want to be with him.

A dark-eyed senior in a raincoat admitted, as a kind of secret addiction, that she liked to wander around the stacks in the library and "pick up books that interest me."

> You learn freshman year to turn up your nose at the library. Lately though—well, it hits you, that you won't be at college next year. Suddenly you wish you'd read more, talked more, taken hard courses you skipped. So you'd know what you're interested in. But I guess those things don't matter when you're married. You're interested in your home and teaching your children how to swim and skate, and at night you talk to your husband. I think we'll be happier than college women used to be.

These girls behaved as if college were an interval to be gotten through impatiently, efficiently, bored but businesslike, so "real" life could begin. And real life was when you married and lived in a suburban house with your husband and children. Was it quite natural, this boredom, this businesslike haste? Was it real, this preoccupation with marriage? The girls who glibly disclaimed any serious interest in their education with talk of "when I'm married" often were not seriously interested in any particular man, I discovered. The ones who were rushing to get their college work done, to spend three days a week off campus, sometimes had no real date they wanted to keep.

In my time, popular girls who spent many weekends at Yale were often just as serious about their work as the "brains." Even if you were temporarily, or quite seriously, in love, during the week at college you lived the life of the mind—and found it absorbing, demanding, sometimes exciting, always real. Could these girls who now must work so much harder, have so much more ability to get into such a college against the growing competition, really be so bored with the life of the mind?

Gradually, I sensed the tension, the almost sullen protest, the deliberate effort—or effort deliberately avoided—behind their cool façades. Their boredom was not quite what it seemed. It was a defense, a refusal to become involved. As a woman who unconsciously thinks sex a sin is not there, is somewhere else, as she goes through the motions of sex, so these girls are somewhere else. They go through the motions, but they defend themselves against the impersonal passions of mind and spirit that college might instill in them—the dangerous nonsexual passions of the intellect.

A pretty sophomore explained to me:

> The idea is to be casual, very sophisticated. Don't be too enthusiastic about your work or anything. People who take things too seriously are more or less pitied or laughed at. Like wanting to

sing, being so intent about it you make other people uncomfortable. An oddball.

Another girl elaborated:

> They might feel sorry for you. I think you can be serious about
> your work and not be looked down upon as a total intellectual,
> if you stop now and then and think isn't this too hysterical.
> Because you do it with tongue in cheek, it's O.K.

A girl with a fraternity pin on her pink sweater said:

> Maybe we should take it more seriously. But nobody wants to
> graduate and get into something where they can't use it. If your
> husband is going to be an organization man, you can't be too
> educated. The wife is awfully important for the husband's
> career. You can't be too interested in art, or something like that.

A girl who had dropped out of honors in history told me:

> I loved it. I got so excited about my work I would sometimes go
> into the library at eight in the morning and not come out till ten
> at night. I even thought I might want to go on to graduate school
> or law school and really use my mind. Suddenly, I was afraid of
> what would happen. I wanted to lead a rich full life. I want to
> marry, have children, have a nice house. Suddenly I felt, what
> am I beating my brains out for. So this year I'm trying to lead a
> well-rounded life. I take courses, but I don't read eight books
> and still feel like reading the ninth. I stop and go to the mov-
> ies. The other way was harder, and more exciting. I don't know
> why I stopped. Maybe I just lost courage.

The phenomenon does not seem confined to any particular college; one finds it among the girls in any college, or department of a
college, which still exposes students to the life of the mind. A junior
from a Southern university said:

> Ever since I was a little girl, science has had a fascination for
> me. I was going to major in bacteriology and go into cancer
> research. Now I've switched to home economics. I realized I
> don't want to go into something that deep. If I went on, I'd have
> been one of those dedicated people. I got so caught up in the
> first two years, I never got out of the laboratory. I loved it, but
> I was missing so many things. If the girls were off swimming in
> the afternoon, I'd be working on my smears and slides. There
> aren't any girls in bacteriology here, sixty boys and me in the
> lab. I couldn't get on with the girls anymore who don't under-
> stand science. I'm not so intensely interested in home econom-
> ics as I was in bacteriology, but I realize it was better for me to
> change, and get out with people. I realized I shouldn't be that

serious. I'll go home and work in a department store until I get married.

The mystery to me is not that these girls defend themselves against an involvement with the life of the mind, but that educators should be mystified by their defense, or blame it on the "student culture," as certain educators do. The one lesson a girl could hardly avoid learning, if she went to college between 1945 and 1960, was *not* to get interested, seriously interested, in anything besides getting married and having children, if she wanted to be normal, happy, adjusted, feminine, have a successful husband, successful children, and a normal, feminine, adjusted, successful sex life. She might have learned some of this lesson at home, and some of it from the other girls in college, but she also learned it, incontrovertibly, from those entrusted with developing her critical, creative intelligence: her college professors.

A subtle and almost unnoticed change had taken place in the academic culture for American women in the last fifteen years: the new sex-direction of their educators. Under the influence of the feminine mystique, some college presidents and professors charged with the education of women had become more concerned with their students' future capacity for sexual orgasm than with their future use of trained intelligence. In fact, some leading educators of women began to concern themselves, conscientiously, with protecting students from the temptation to use their critical, creative intelligence—by the ingenious method of educating it *not* to be critical or creative. Thus higher education added its weight to the process by which American women during this period were shaped increasingly to their biological function, decreasingly to the fulfillment of their individual abilities. Girls who went to college could hardly escape those bits and pieces of Freud and Margaret Mead, or avoid a course in "Marriage and Family Life" with its functional indoctrination on "how to play the role of woman."

The new sex-direction of women's education was not, however, confined to any specific course or academic department. It was implicit in all the social sciences; but more than that, it became a part of education itself, not only because the English professor, or the guidance counselor, or the college president read Freud and Mead, but because education was the prime target of the new mystique—the education of American girls with, or like, boys. If the Freudians and the functionalists were right, educators were guilty of defeminizing American women, of dooming them to frustration as housewives and mothers, or to celibate careers, to life without orgasm. It was a damning indictment; many college presidents and educational theorists confessed their guilt without a murmur and fell into the sex-directed line. There were a few cries of outrage, of course, from the old-fashioned educators who still believed the mind was more important than the marriage bed, but they were often near retirement and soon to be replaced by younger, more thoroughly sex-indoctrinated teachers, or they were so wrapped up in their special subjects that they had little say in over-all school policies.

The general educational climate was ripe for the new sex-directed line, with its emphasis on adjustment. The old aim of education, the development of intelligence through vigorous mastery of the major intellectual disciplines, was already in disfavor among the child-centered educators. Teachers College at Columbia was the natural breeding ground for educational functionalism. As psychology and anthropology and sociology permeated the total scholarly atmosphere, education for femininity also spread from Mills, Stephens and the finishing schools (where its basis was more traditional than theoretical) to the proudest bastions of the women's Ivy League, the colleges which pioneered higher education for women in America, and were noted for their uncompromising intellectual standards.

Instead of opening new horizons and wider worlds to able women, the sex-directed educator moved in to teach them adjustment within the world of home and children. Instead of teaching truths to counter the popular prejudices of the past, or critical ways of thinking against which prejudice cannot survive, the sex-directed educator handed girls a sophisticated soup of uncritical prescriptions and presentiments, far more binding on the mind and prejudicial to the future than all the traditional do's and don'ts. Most of it was done consciously and for the best of helpful reasons by educators who really believed the mystique as the social scientists handed it to them. If a male professor or college president did not find this mystique a positive comfort, a confirmation of his own prejudices, he still had no reason *not* to believe it.

The few college presidents and professors who were women either fell into line or had their authority—as teachers and as women—questioned. If they were spinsters, if they had not had babies, they were forbidden by the mystique to speak as women. (*Modern Woman: The Lost Sex* would forbid them even to teach.) The brilliant scholar, who did not marry but inspired many generations of college women to the pursuit of truth, was sullied as an educator of women. She was not named president of the women's college whose intellectual tradition she carried to its highest point; the girls' education was put in the hands of a handsome, husbandly man, more suitable to indoctrinating girls for their proper feminine role. The scholar often left the women's college to head a department in a great university, where the potential Ph.D.'s were safely men, for whom the lure of scholarship, the pursuit of truth, was not deemed a deterrent to sexual fulfillment.

In terms of the new mystique, the woman scholar was suspect, simply by virtue of being one. She was not just working to support her home; she must have been guilty of an unfeminine commitment, to have kept working in her field all those hard, grinding, ill-paid years to the Ph.D. In self-defense she sometimes adopted frilly blouses or another innocuous version of the feminine protest. (At psychoanalytic conventions, an observer once noticed, the lady analysts camouflage themselves with pretty, flowery, smartly feminine hats that would make the casual suburban housewife look positively masculine.) M.D. or Ph.D., those hats and frilly blouses say, *let nobody question our femininity.* But the fact is, their femininity was questioned. One famous women's college adopted in defense the slogan, "We are not educating women to be scholars; we are educating them to be wives and mothers." (The girls themselves finally got so tired of repeating this slogan in full that they abbreviated it to "WAM.")

In building the sex-directed curriculum, not everyone went as far as Lynn White, former president of Mills College, but if you started with the premise that women should no longer be educated like men, but for their role as women, you almost had to end with his curriculum—which amounted to replacing college chemistry with a course in advanced cooking.

The sex-directed educator begins by accepting education's responsibility for the frustration, general and sexual, of American women.

On my desk lies a letter from a young mother, a few years out of college:

> "I have come to realize that I was educated to be a successful man and must now learn by myself to be a successful woman." The basic irrelevance of much of what passes as women's education in America could not be more compactly phrased. . . . The failure of our educational system to take into account these simple and basic differences between the life patterns of average men and women is at least in part responsible for the deep discontent and restlessness which affects millions of women. . . .
>
> It would seem that if women are to restore their self-respect they must reverse the tactics of the older feminism which indignantly denied inherent differences in the intellectual and emotional tendencies of men and women. Only by recognizing and insisting upon the importance of such differences can women save themselves, in their own eyes, of conviction as inferiors.[4]

The sex-directed educator equates as masculine our "vastly over-rated cultural creativity," "our uncritical acceptance of 'progress' as good in itself," "egotistic individualism," "innovation," "abstract construction," "quantitative thinking"—of which, of course, the dread symbol is either communism or the atom bomb. Against these, equated as feminine, are "the sense of persons, of the immediate, of intangible qualitative relationships, an aversion for statistics and quantities," "the intuitive," "the emotional," and all the forces that "cherish" and "conserve" what is "good, true, beautiful, useful, and holy."

A feminized higher education might include sociology, anthropology, psychology. ("These are studies little concerned with the laurel-crowned genius of the strong man," praises the educational protector of femininity. "They are devoted to exploring the quiet and unspectacular forces of society and of the mind. . . . They embrace the feminine preoccupation with conserving and cherishing.") It would hardly include either pure science (since abstract theory and quantitative thinking are unfeminine) or fine art, which is masculine, "flamboyant and abstract." The applied or minor arts, however, are feminine: ceramics, textiles, work shaped more by the hand than the brain. "Women love beauty as much as men do but they want a beauty connected with the processes of living . . . the hand is as remarkable and as worthy of respect as the brain."

The sex-directed educator cites approvingly Cardinal Tisserant's saying, "Women should be educated so that they can argue with their husbands." Let us stop altogether professional training for women, he insists: all women must be educated to be housewives. Even home economics and domestic science, as they are now taught at college, are masculine because "they have been pitched at the level of professional training."[5]

Here is a truly feminine education:

> One may prophesy with confidence that as women begin to make their distinctive wishes felt in curricular terms, not merely will every women's college and coeducational institution offer a firm nuclear course in the Family, but from it will radiate curricular series dealing with food and nutrition, textiles and clothing, health and nursing, house planning and interior decoration, garden design and applied botany, and child-development. . . . Would it be impossible to present a beginning course in foods as exciting and as difficult to work up after college, as a course in post-Kantian philosophy would be? . . . Let's abandon talk of proteins, carbohydrates and the like, save inadvertently, as for example, when we point out that a British hyper-boiled Brussel sprout is not merely inferior in flavor and texture, but in vitamine content. Why not study the

theory and preparation of a Basque paella, of a well-marinated shish kebob, lamb kidneys sauteed in sherry, an authoritative curry, the use of herbs, even such simple sophistications as serving cold artichokes with fresh milk.[6]

The sex-directed educator is hardly impressed by the argument that a college curriculum should not be contaminated or diluted with subjects like cooking or manual training, which can be taught successfully at the high-school level. Teach them to the girls in high school, and "with greater intensity and imagination" again in college. Boys, also, should get some "family-minded" education, but not in their valuable college time; early high-school manual training is enough to "enable them, in future years to work happily at a bench in the garage or in the garden, surrounded by an admiring circle of children . . . or at the barbecue."[7]

This kind of education, in the name of life-adjustment, became a fact on many campuses, high-school as well as college. It was not dreamed up to turn back the growth of women, but it surely helped. When American educators finally began to investigate the waste of our national resources of creative intelligence, they found that the lost Einsteins, Schweitzers, Roosevelts, Edisons, Fords, Fermis, Frosts were feminine. Of the brightest forty per cent of U.S. high-school graduates, only half went on to college: of the half who stopped, *two out of three were girls*.[8] When Dr. James B. Conant* went across the nation to find out what was wrong with the American high school, he discovered too many students were taking easy how-to courses which didn't really stretch their minds. Again, most of those who should have been studying physics, advanced algebra, analytic geometry, four years of language—and were not—were girls. They had the intelligence, the special gift which was not sex-directed, but they also had the sex-directed attitude that such studies were "unfeminine."

Sometimes a girl wanted to take a hard subject, but was advised by a guidance counselor or teacher that it was a waste of time—as, for instance, the girl in a good Eastern high school who wanted to be an architect. Her counselor strongly advised her against applying for admission anywhere in architecture, on the grounds that women are rare in that profession, and she would never get in anyhow. She stubbornly applied to two universities who give degrees

---

* James Bryant Conant (1893–1978), chemist, professor, president of Harvard University, valued scientific advisor to the United States during World War II, is important to Friedan for the study he did of U.S. high schools called "The American High School Today," published in 1959. During the Cold War there was a concern that the United States was not providing adequate scientific training to its youth. Conant's study confirmed this concern and offered solutions to schools (see entry on the Cold War, p. 11).

in architecture; both, to her amazement, accepted her. Then her counselor told her that even though she had been accepted, there was really no future for women in architecture; she would spend her life in a drafting room. She was advised to go to a junior college where the work would be much easier than in architecture and where she would learn all she needed to know when she married.[9]

The influence of sex-directed education was perhaps even more insidious on the high-school level than it was in the colleges, for many girls who were subjected to it never got to college. I picked up a lesson plan for one of these life-adjustment courses now taught in junior high in the suburban county where I live. Entitled "The Slick Chick," it gives functional "do's and don'ts for dating" to girls of eleven, twelve, thirteen—a kind of early or forced recognition of their sexual function. Though many have nothing yet with which to fill a brassiere, they are told archly not to wear a sweater without one, and to be sure to wear slips so boys can't see through their skirts. It is hardly surprising that by the sophomore year, many bright girls in this high school are more than conscious of their sexual function, bored with all the subjects in school, and have no ambition other than to marry and have babies. One cannot help wondering (especially when some of these girls get pregnant as high-school sophomores and marry at fifteen or sixteen) if they have not been educated for their sexual function too soon, while their other abilities go unrecognized.

This stunting of able girls from nonsexual growth is nationwide. Of the top ten per cent of graduates of Indiana high schools in 1955, only fifteen per cent of the boys did not continue their education: thirty-six per cent of the girls did not go on.[10] In the very years in which higher education has become a necessity for almost everyone who wants a real function in our exploding society, *the proportion of women among college students has declined, year by year*. In the fifties, women also dropped out of college at a faster rate than the men: only thirty-seven per cent of the women graduated, in contrast to fifty-five per cent of the men.[11] By the sixties, an equal proportion of boys was dropping out of college.[12] But, in this era of keen competition for college seats, the one girl who enters college for every two boys is "more highly selected," and less likely to be dropped from college for academic failure. Women drop out, as David Riesman* says, either to marry or because they fear too much education is a "marriage bar." The average age of first marriage, in the last fifteen years, has dropped to the youngest in

---

* David Riesman (1909–2002), sociologist famous for the best-selling book *The Lonely Crowd* (1950). It argued that modern institutions, such as the corporation, had helped to shape a new outer-directed character type who took cues from what other people expected of him, rather than relying on internalized values.

the history of this country, the youngest in any of the countries of the Western world, almost as young as it used to be in the so-called underdeveloped countries. In the new nations of Asia and Africa, with the advent of science and education, the marriage age of women is now rising. Today, thanks in part to the functional sex-direction of women's education, the annual rate of population increase in the United States is among the highest in the world— nearly three times that of the Western European nations, nearly double Japan's, and close on the heels of Africa and India.[13]

The sex-directed educators have played a dual role in this trend: by actively educating girls to their sexual function (which perhaps they would fulfill without such education, in a way less likely to prevent their growth in other directions); and by abdicating their responsibility for the education of women, in the strict intellectual sense. With or without education, women are likely to fulfill their biological role, and experience sexual love and motherhood. But without education, women or men are not likely to develop deep interests that go beyond biology.

Education should, and can, make a person "broad in outlook, and open to new experience, independent and disciplined in his thinking, deeply committed to some productive activity, possessed of convictions based on understanding of the world and on his own integration of personality."[14] The main barrier to such growth in girls is their own rigid preconception of woman's role, which sex-directed educators reinforce, either explicitly or by not facing their own ability, and responsibility, to break through it.

Such a sex-directed impasse is revealed in the massive depths of that thousand-page study, *The American College*, when "motivational factors in college entrance" are analyzed from research among 1,045 boys and 1,925 girls. The study recognizes that it is the need to be independent, and find identity in society not primarily through the sex role but through work, which makes boys grow in college. The girl's evasion of growth in college is explained by the fact that for a girl, identity is exclusively sexual; for the girl, college itself is seen even by these scholars not as the key to larger identity but as a disguised "outlet for sexual impulses."

> The identity issue for the boy is primarily an occupational-vocational question, while self-definition for the girl depends more directly on marriage. A number of differences follow from this distinction. The girl's identity centers more exclusively on her sex-role—whose wife will I be, what kind of a family will we have; while the boy's self-definition forms about two nuclei; he will be a husband and father (his sex-role identity) but he will also and centrally be a worker. A related difference follows and has particular importance at adolescence: the

occupational identity is by and large an issue of personal choice that can begin early and to which all of the resources of rational and thoughtful planning can be directed. The boy can begin to think and plan for this aspect of identity early. . . . The sexual identity, so critical for feminine development, permits no such conscious or orderly effort. It is a mysterious and romantic issue, freighted with fiction, mystique, illusion. A girl may learn certain surface skills and activities of the feminine role, but she will be thought ungraceful and unfeminine if her efforts toward femininity are too clearly conscious. The real core of feminine settlement—living in intimacy with a beloved man—is a future prospect, for which there is no rehearsal. We find that boys and girls in adolescence have different approaches to the future; boys are actively planning and testing for future work identities, apparently sifting alternatives in an effort to find the role that will fit most comfortably their particular skills and interests, temperamental characteristics and needs. Girls, in contrast, are absorbed much more in phantasy, particularly phantasy about boys and popularity, marriage and love.

The dream of college apparently serves as a substitute for more direct preoccupation with marriage: girls who do not plan to go to college are more explicit in their desire to marry, and have a more developed sense of their own sex role. They are more aware of and more frankly concerned with sexuality. . . . The view of phantasy as an outlet for sexual impulses follows the general psychoanalytic conception that impulses denied direct expression will seek some disguised mode of gratification.[15]

Thus, it did not surprise them that seventy per cent of freshmen women at a Midwestern university answered the question, "What do you hope to get out of college?" with, among other things, "the man for me." They also interpreted answers indicating a wish to "leave home," "travel," and answers relating to potential occupations which were given by half the girls as symbolizing "curiosity about the sexual mysteries."

College and travel are alternatives to a more open interest in sexuality. Girls who complete their schooling with high school are closer to assuming an adult sex role in early marriages, and they have more developed conceptions of their sexual impulses and sex roles. Girls who will enter college, on the other hand, will delay direct realization and settlement of sexual identity, at least for a while. During the interim, sexual energy is converted and gratified through a phantasy system that focuses on college, the glamour of college life, and a sublimation to general sensuous experience.[16]

Why do the educators view girls, and only girls, in such completely sexual terms? Adolescent boys also have sexual urges whose fulfillment may be delayed by college. But for boys, the educators are not concerned with sexual "phantasy"; they are concerned with "reality," and boys are expected to achieve personal autonomy and identity by "committing themselves in the sphere of our culture that is most morally worthwhile—the world of work—in which they will be acknowledged as persons with recognized achievements and potentials." Even if the boys' own vocational images and goals are not realistic in the beginning—and this study showed that they were not—the sex-directed educators recognize, for boys, that motives, goals, interests, childish preconceptions, can change. They also recognize that, for most, the crucial last chance for change is in college. But apparently girls are not expected to change, nor are they given the opportunity. Even at coeducational colleges, very few girls get the same education as boys. Instead of stimulating what psychologists have suggested might be a "latent" desire for autonomy in the girls, the sex-directed educators stimulated their sexual fantasy of fulfilling all desire for achievement, status, and identity vicariously through a man. Instead of challenging the girls' childish, rigid, parochial preconception of woman's role, they cater to it by offering them a potpourri of liberal-arts courses, suitable only for a wifely veneer, or narrow programs such as "institutional dietetics," well beneath their abilities and suitable only for a "stopgap" job between college and marriage.

As educators themselves admit, women's college training does not often equip them to enter the business or professional world at a meaningful level, either at graduation or afterward; it is not geared to career possibilities that would justify the planning and work required for higher professional training. For women, the sex-directed educators say with approval, college is the place to find a man. Presumably, if the campus is "the world's best marriage mart," as one educator remarked, both sexes are affected. On college campuses today, professor and student agree, the girls are the aggressors in the marriage hunt. The boys, married or not, are there to stretch their minds, to find their own identity, to fill out their life plan; the girls are there only to fulfill their sexual function.

Research reveals that ninety per cent or more of the rising number of campus wives who were motivated for marriage by "phantasy and the need to conform" are literally working their husbands' way through college.[17] The girl who quits high school or college to marry and have a baby, or to take a job to work her husband's way through, is stunted from the kind of mental growth and understanding that higher education is supposed to give, as surely as child labor used to stunt the physical growth of children. She is also prevented from realistic preparation and planning for a career or a commitment that will utilize her abilities and will be of some importance to society and herself.

During the period when the sex-directed educators were devoting themselves to women's sexual adjustment and femininity, economists charted a new and revolutionary change in American employment: beneath the ebb and flow of boom and recession, they found an absolute, spiraling decline in employment possibilities for the uneducated and the unskilled. But when the government economists on the "Womanpower" study visited college campuses, they found the girls unaffected by the statistical probability that they will spend twenty-five years or more of their adult lives in jobs outside the home. Even when it is virtually certain that most women will no longer spend their lives as full-time housewives, the sex-directed educators have told them not to plan for a career for fear of hampering their sexual adjustment.

A few years ago, sex-directed education finally infiltrated a famous women's college, which had been proud in the past of its large share of graduates who went on to play leading roles in education and law and medicine, the arts and sciences, government and social welfare. This college had an ex-feminist woman president, who was perhaps beginning to suffer a slight guilt at the thought of all those women educated like men. A questionnaire, sent to alumnae of all ages, indicated that the great majority were satisfied with their non-sex-directed education; but a minority complained that their education had made them overly conscious of women's rights and equality with men, too interested in careers, possessed of a nagging feeling that they should do something in the community, that they should at least keep on reading, studying, developing their own abilities and interests. Why hadn't they been educated to be happy housewives and mothers?

The guilty woman college president—guilty personally of being a college president, besides having a large number of children and a successful husband; guilty also of having been an ardent feminist in her time and of having advanced a good way in her career before she married; barraged by the therapeutic social scientists who accused her of trying to mold these young girls in her own impossible, unrealistic, outmoded, energetic, self-demanding, visionary, unfeminine image—introduced a functional course in marriage and the family, compulsory for all sophomores.

The circumstances which led to the college's decision, two years later, to *drop* that functional course are shrouded in secrecy. Nobody officially connected with the college will talk. But a neighboring educator, a functionalist crusader himself, said with a certain contempt for naive wrong-thinking that they were evidently shocked over there that the girls who took the functional course got married so quickly. (The class of 1959 at that college included a record number of 75 wives, nearly a quarter of the girls who still remained in the class.) He told me calmly:

> Why should it upset them, over there, that the girls got married a little early? There's nothing wrong with early marriage, with the proper preparation. I guess they can't get over the old notion that women should be educated to develop their minds. They deny it, but one can't help suspecting that they still believe in careers for women. Unfortunately, the idea that women go to college to get a husband is anathema to some educators.

At the college in question, "Marriage and the Family" is taught once again as a course in sociology, geared to critical analysis of these changing social institutions, and not to functional action, or group therapy. But in the neighboring institution, my professor-informant is second in command of a booming department of "family-life education," which is currently readying a hundred graduate students to teach functional marriage courses in colleges, state teachers' colleges, junior colleges, community colleges, and high schools across America. One senses that these new sex-directed educators do indeed think of themselves as crusaders—crusaders against the old nontherapeutic, nonfunctional values of the intellect, against the old, demanding, sexless education, which confined itself to the life of the mind and the pursuit of truth, and never even tried to help girls pursue a man, have orgasms, or adjust. As my informant elaborated:

> These kids are concerned about dating and sex, how to get along with boys, is it all right to have premarital relations. Maybe a girl is trying to decide about her major; she's thinking about a career, and she's also thinking about marriage. You set up a role-playing situation to help her work it out—so she sees the effect on the children. She sees she need not feel guilty about being just a housewife.

There often is an air of defensiveness, when a sex-directed educator is asked to define, for the uninitiated, the "functional approach." One told a reporter:

> It's all very well to talk big talk—intellectual generalizations, abstract concepts, the United Nations—but somewhere we have to start facing these problems of interpersonal relations on a more modest scale. We have to stop being so teacher-centered, and become student-centered. It's not what you think they need, but what they think they need. That's the functional

approach. You walk into a class, and your aim is no longer to cover a certain content, but to set up an atmosphere that makes your students feel comfortable and talk freely about interpersonal relations, in basic terms, not highfalutin generalizations.

Kids tend in adolescence to be very idealistic. They think they can acquire a different set of values, marry a boy from a different background, and that it won't matter later on. We make them aware it will matter, so they won't walk so lightly into mixed marriages, and other traps.[18]

The reporter asked why "Mate Selection," "Adjustment to Marriage" and "Education for Family Living" are taught in colleges at all, if the teacher is committed not to teach, if no material is to be learned or covered, and if the only aim is to help the student understand personal problems and emotions. After surveying a number of marriage courses for *Mademoiselle*, she concluded: "Only in America would you overhear one undergraduate say to another with total ingenuousness, 'You should have been in class today. We talked about male role-playing and a couple of people really opened up and got personal.'"

The point of role-playing, a technique adapted from group therapy, is to get students to understand problems "on a feeling level." Emotions more heady than those of the usual college classroom are undoubtedly stirred up when the professor invites them to "role-play" the feelings of "a boy and a girl on their wedding night."

There is a pseudotherapeutic air, as the professor listens patiently to endless self-conscious student speeches about personal feelings ("verbalizing") in the hopes of sparking a "group insight." But though the functional course is not group therapy, it is certainly an indoctrination of opinions and values through manipulation of the students' emotions; and in this manipulative disguise, it is no longer subject to the critical thinking demanded in other academic disciplines.

The students take as gospel the bits and pieces assigned in text books that explain Freud or quote Margaret Mead; they do not have the frame of reference that comes from the actual study of psychology or anthropology. In fact, by explicitly banning the usual critical attitudes of college study, these pseudoscientific marriage courses give what is often no more than popular opinion, the fiat of scientific law. The opinion may be currently fashionable, or already outdated, in psychiatric circles, but it is often merely a prejudice, buttressed by psychological or sociological jargon and well-chosen statistics to give the appearance of unquestionable scientific truth.

The discussion on premarital intercourse usually leads to the scientific conclusion that it is wrong. One professor builds up his case against sexual intercourse before marriage with statistics chosen to demonstrate that premarital sexual experience tends to make marital adjustment more difficult. The student will not know of the other statistics which refute this point; if the professor knows of them, he can in the functional marriage course feel free to disregard them as unfunctional. ("Ours is a sick society. The students need some accurate definitive kind of knowledge.") It is functional "knowledge" that "only the exceptional woman can make a go of a commitment to a career." Of course, since most women in the past have not had careers, the few who did were all "exceptional"—as a mixed marriage is "exceptional," and premarital intercourse for a girl is exceptional. All are phenomena of less than 51 per cent. The whole point of functional education often seems to be: what 51 per cent of the population does today, 100 per cent should do tomorrow.

So the sex-directed educator promotes a girl's adjustment by dissuading her from any but the "normal" commitment to marriage and the family. One such educator goes farther than imaginary role-playing; she brings real ex-working mothers to class to talk about their guilt at leaving their children in the morning. Somehow, the students seldom hear about a woman who has successfully broken convention—the young woman doctor whose sister handled her practice when her babies were born, the mother who adjusted her babies' sleeping hours to her work schedule without problems, the happy Protestant girl who married a Catholic, the sexually serene wife whose premarital experience did not seem to hurt her marriage. "Exceptional" cases are of no practical concern to the functionalist, though he often acknowledges scrupulously that there *are* exceptions. (The "exceptional child," in educational jargon, bears a connotation of handicap; the blind, the crippled, the retarded, the genius, the defier of convention—anyone who is different from the crowd, in any way unique—bears a common shame; he is "exceptional.") Somehow, the student gets the point that she does not want to be the "exceptional woman."

Conformity* is built into life-adjustment education in many ways. There is little or no intellectual challenge or discipline involved in merely learning to adjust. The marriage course is the easiest course on almost every campus, no matter how anxiously professors try to toughen it by assigning heavy reading and weekly reports. No one expects that case histories (which when read for no serious use are not much more than psychiatric soap operas),

---

* One of the central intellectual and political dilemmas of the 1950s. Increasing rationalization and bureaucratization in the economy, as well as the exponential growth of suburbs, sparked significant intellectual concerns about conformity, as displayed in books like William Whyte's *The Organization Man* and David Riesman's *The Lonely Crowd* (see entries on *The Organization Man*, p. 307, and David Riesman, p. 136). Friedan's analysis of the feminine mystique was shaped by this postwar concern with conformity.

role-playing, talking about sex in class, or writing personal papers will lead to critical thinking; that's not the point of functional preparation for marriage.

This is not to say that the study of a social science, as such, produces conformity in woman or man. This is hardly the effect when it is studied critically and motivated by the usual aims of intellectual discipline, or when it is mastered for professional use. But for girls forbidden both professional and intellectual commitment by the new mystique, the study of sociology, anthropology, psychology is often merely "functional." And in the functional course itself, the girls take those bits and pieces from Freud and Mead, the sexual statistics, the role-playing insights, not only literally and out of context, but personally—to be acted upon in their own lives. That, after all, is the whole point of life-adjustment education. It can happen among adolescents in almost any course that involves basic emotional material. It will certainly happen when the material is deliberately used not to build critical knowledge but to stir up personal emotions. Therapy, in the orthodox psychoanalytic tradition, requires the suppression of critical thinking (intellectual resistance) for the proper emotions to come out and be worked through. In therapy, this may work. But does education work, mixed up with therapy? One course could hardly be crucial, in any man or woman's life, but when it is decided that the very aim of woman's education should not be intellectual growth, but sexual adjustment, certain questions could be very crucial.

One might ask: if an education geared to the growth of the human mind weakens femininity, will an education geared to femininity weaken the growth of the mind? What is femininity, if it can be destroyed by an education which makes the mind grow, or induced by not letting the mind grow?

One might even ask a question in Freudian terms: what happens when sex becomes not only id* for women, but ego and superego as well; when education, instead of developing the self, is concentrated on developing the sexual functions? What happens when education gives new authority to the feminine "shoulds"—which already have the authority of tradition, convention, prejudice, popular opinion— instead of giving women the power of critical thought, the independence and autonomy to question blind authority, new or old? At Pembroke, the women's college at Brown University in Providence, R.I., a guest psychoanalyst was recently invited to lead a buzz session on "what it means to be a woman." The students seemed disconcerted when the guest analyst, Dr. Margaret Lawrence, said, in simple, un-Freudian English, that it was rather silly to tell women today

---

* See entry on superego, p. 86.

that their main place is in the home, when most of the work women used to do is now done outside the home, and everyone else in the family spends most of his time outside the house. Hadn't they better be educated to join the rest of the family, out there in the world?

This, somehow, was not what the girls expected to hear from a lady psychoanalyst. Unlike the usual functional, sex-directed lesson, it upset a conventional feminine "should." It also implied that they should begin to make certain decisions of their own, about their education and their future.

The functional lesson is much more soothing to the unsure sophomore who has not yet quite made the break from childhood. It does not defy the comfortable, safe conventions; it gives her sophisticated words for accepting her parents' view, the popular view, without having to figure out views of her own. It also reassures her that she doesn't have to work in college; that she can be lazy, follow impulse. She doesn't have to postpone present pleasure for future goals; she doesn't have to read eight books for a history paper, take the tough physics course. It might give her a masculinity complex. After all, didn't the book say:

> Woman's intellectuality is to a large extent paid for by the loss of valuable feminine qualities. . . . All observations point to the fact that the intellectual woman is masculinized; in her warm, intuitive knowledge has yielded to cold unproductive thinking.[19]

A girl doesn't have to be very lazy, very unsure, to take the hint. Thinking, after all, is hard work. In fact, she would have to do some very cold hard thinking about her own warm, intuitive knowledge to challenge this authoritative statement.

It is no wonder that several generations of American college girls of fine mind and fiery spirit took the message of the sex-directed educators, and fled college and career to marry and have babies before they became so "intellectual" that, heaven forbid, they wouldn't be able to enjoy sex "in a feminine way."

Even without the help of sex-directed educators, the girl growing up with brains and spirit in America learns soon enough to watch her step, "to be like all the others," not to be herself. She learns not to work too hard, think too often, ask too many questions. In high schools, in coeducational colleges, girls are reluctant to speak out in class for fear of being typed as "brains." This phenomenon has been borne out by many studies;[20] any bright girl or woman can document it from personal experience. Bryn Mawr girls have a special term for the way they talk when boys are around, compared to the real talk they can permit themselves when they are not afraid to let their intelligence show. In the coeducational colleges, girls are regarded by others—and think of themselves—primarily in terms of their sexual function as dates, future wives. They "seek my security in him" instead of finding themselves, and each act of self-betrayal tips the scale further away from identity to passive self-contempt.

There are exceptions, of course. The Mellon study found that some Vassar seniors, as compared with freshmen, showed an enormous growth in four years—the kind of growth toward identity and self-realization which scientists now know takes place in people in their twenties and even thirties, forties, and fifties, long after the period of physical growth is over. But many girls showed no signs of growth. These were the ones who resisted, successfully, involvement with ideas, the academic work of the college, the intellectual disciplines, the larger values. They resisted intellectual development, self-development, in favor of being "feminine," not too brainy, not too interested, not too different from the other girls. It was not that their actual sexual interests interfered; in fact, the psychologists got the impression that with many of these girls, "interest in men and marriage is a kind of defense against intellectual development." For such girls, even sex is not real, merely a kind of conformity. The sex-directed educator would find no fault in this kind of adjustment. But in view of other evidence, one might ask: could such an adjustment mask a failure to grow that becomes finally a human deformity?

Several years ago a team of California psychologists who had been following the development of 140 bright youngsters noticed a sudden sharp drop in IQ curves in some of the teenage records. When they investigated this, they found that while most of the youngsters' curves remained at the same high level, year after year, those whose curves dropped were all girls. The drop had nothing to do with the physiological changes of adolescence; it was not found in all girls. But in the records of those girls whose intelligence dropped were found repeated statements to the effect that "it isn't too smart for a girl to be smart." In a very real sense, these girls were arrested in their mental growth, at age fourteen or fifteen, by conformity to the feminine image.[21]

The fact is, girls today and those responsible for their education do face a choice. They must decide between adjustment, conformity, avoidance of conflict, therapy—or individuality, human identity, education in the truest sense, with all its pains of growth. But they do not have to face the mistaken choice painted by the sex-directed educators, with their dire warnings against loss of femininity and sexual frustration. For the perceptive psychologist who studied the Vassar girls uncovered some startling new evidence about the students who chose to become truly involved with their education. It seems that those seniors who showed the greatest signs of growth were more "masculine" in the sense of being less passive and conventional; but they were more "feminine" in inner emotional life, and the ability to gratify it. They also scored higher, far higher than as freshmen, on certain scales commonly supposed to measure neuroses. The psychologist commented: "We have come to regard elevations on such scales as evidence that education is taking place."[22] He found girls with conflicts showed more growth than the adjusted ones, who had no wish to become independent. The least adjusted were also the more developed—"already prepared for even further changes and more independence." In summing up the Vassar study, its director could not avoid the psychological paradox: education for women does make them less feminine, less adjusted—but it makes them grow.

> Being less "feminine" is closely related to being more educated and more mature. . . . It is interesting to note, however, that Feminine Sensitivity, which may well have sources in physiology and in early identifications, does not decrease during the four years; "feminine" interests and feminine role behavior, i.e., conventionality and passivity, can be understood as later and more superficial acquisitions, and, hence, more susceptible to decrease as the individual becomes more mature and more educated. . . .
>
> One might say that if we were interested in stability alone, we would do well to plan a program to keep freshmen as they are, rather than to try to increase their education, their maturity and their flexibility with regard to sex-role behavior. Seniors are more unstable because there is more to be stabilized, less certain of their identities because more possibilities are open to them.[23]

At graduation, such women were, however, only at a "halfway point" in their growth to autonomy. Their fate depended on "whether they now enter a situation in which they can continue to grow or whether they find some quick but regressive means for relieving the stress." The flight into marriage is the easiest, quickest way to relieve that stress. To the educator, bent on women's growth to autonomy, such a marriage is "regressive." To the sex-directed educator, it is femininity fulfilled.

A therapist at another college told me of girls who had never committed themselves, either to their work or any other activity of the college and who felt that they would "go to pieces" when their parents refused to let them leave college to marry the boys in whom they found "security." When these girls, with help, finally applied themselves to work—or even began to feel a sense of self by taking part in an activity such as student government or the school newspaper—they lost their desperate need for "security." They finished college, worked, went out with more mature young men, and are now marrying on quite a different emotional basis.

Unlike the sex-directed educator, this professional therapist felt that the girl who suffers almost to the point of breakdown in the senior year, and who faces a personal decision about her own future—faces even an irreconcilable conflict between the values and interests and abilities her education has given her, and the conventional role of housewife—is still "healthier" than the adjusted, calm, stable girl in whom education did not "take" at all and who steps smoothly from her role as parents' child to husband's wife, conventionally feminine, without ever waking up to painful individual identity.

And yet the fact is, today most girls do not let their education "take"; they stop themselves before getting this close to identity. I could see this in the girls at Smith, and the girls I interviewed from other colleges. It was clear in the Vassar research. The Vassar study showed that just as girls begin to feel the conflicts, the growing pains of identity, they stop growing. They more or less consciously stop their own growth to play the feminine role. Or, to put it in another way, they evade further experiences conducive to growth. Until now this stunting or evasion of growth has been considered normal feminine adjustment. But when the Vassar study followed women past the senior year—where they were on the verge of this painful crucial step in personal growth—out into life, where most of them were playing the conventional feminine role, these facts emerged:

1. Twenty or twenty-five years out of college, these women measured lower than seniors on the "Development Scale" which covered the whole gamut of mental, emotional, and personal growth. They did not lose all the growth achieved in college (alumnae scored higher than freshmen) but—in spite of the psychological readiness for further growth at twenty-one—they did not keep growing.

2. These women were, for the most part, adjusted as suburban housewives, conscientious mothers, active in their communities. But, except for the professional career women, they had not continued to pursue deep interests of their own. There seemed some reason to believe that the cessation of growth was related to the lack of deep personal interests, the lack of an individual commitment.

3. The women who, twenty years later, were most troubling to the psychologist were the most conventionally feminine—the ones who were not interested, even in college, in anything except finding a husband.[24]

In the Vassar study there was one group of students who in senior year neither suffered conflict to the point of near-breakdown nor stopped their own growth to flee into marriage. These were students who were preparing for a profession; they had gained, in college, interests deep enough to commit themselves to a career. The study revealed that virtually all such students with professional ambitions plan to marry, but marriage is for them an activity in which they will voluntarily choose to participate rather than something that is necessary for any sense of personal identity. Such students have a clear sense of direction, a greater degree of independence and self-confidence than most. They may be engaged or deeply in love, but they do not feel they must sacrifice their own individualities or their career ambitions if they wish to marry. With these girls, the psychologists did not get the impression, as they did with so many, that interest in men and in marriage was a kind of defense against intellectual development. Their interest in some particular man was real. At the same time, it did not interfere with their education.

But the degree to which the feminine mystique has brainwashed American educators was shown when the director of the Vassar study described to a panel of his colleagues such a girl, who "not only makes top grades, but in whose case there is high probability that a scholarly or professional career will be followed."

> Julie B's mother is a teacher and scholar and the driving force in the family. . . . Mother gets after father for being too easy-going. Father doesn't mind if his wife and daughter have high-brow tastes and ideas, only such are not for him. Julie becomes out-door girl, nonconformist, dominates her older brother, but is conscience-stricken if she doesn't do required reading or if grade average slips. Sticks to her intention to do graduate work and become teacher. Older brother now college teacher and Julie, herself a graduate student now, is married to a graduate student in natural science.
>
> When she was a freshman we presented her interview data, without interpretation, to a group of psychiatrists, psychologists, social scientists. Our idea of a really promising girl. Common question: "What's wrong with her?" Common opinion: she would need psychotherapy. Actually she got engaged to her budding scientist in her sophomore year, became increasingly conscious of herself as an intellectual and outsider, but still couldn't neglect her work. "If only I could flunk something," she said.

It takes a very daring educator today to attack the sex-directed line, for he must challenge, in essence, the conventional image of femininity. The image says that women are passive, dependent, conformist, incapable of critical thought or original contribution to society; and in the best traditions of the self-fulfilling prophecy, sex-directed education continues to make them so, as in an earlier era, lack of education made them so. No one asks whether a passively feminine, uncomplicated, dependent woman—in a primitive village or in a suburb—actually enjoys greater happiness, greater sexual fulfillment than a woman who commits herself in college to serious interests beyond the home. No one, until very recently when Russians orbited moons and men in space, asked whether adjustment should be education's aim. In fact, the sex-directed educators, so bent on women's feminine adjustment, could gaily cite the most ominous facts about American housewives—their emptiness, idleness, boredom, alcoholism, drug addiction, disintegration to fat, disease, and despair after forty, when their sexual function has been filled—without deviating a bit from their crusade to educate all women to this sole end.

So the sex-directed educator disposes of the thirty years women are likely to live after forty with three blithe proposals:

1. A course in "Law and Order for the Housewife" to enable her to deal, as a widow, with insurances, taxes, wills, investments.
2. Men might retire earlier to help keep their wives company.
3. A brief fling in "volunteer community services, politics, the arts or the like"—though, since the woman will be untrained the main value will be personal therapy. "To choose only one example, a woman who wants some really novel experience may start a campaign to rid her city or country of that nauseous eczema of our modern world, the billboard.

> "The billboards will remain and multiply like bacteria infesting the landscape, but at least she will have had a vigorous adult education course in local politics. Then she can relax and devote herself to the alumnae activities of the institution from which she graduated. Many a woman approaching middle years has found new vigor and enthusiasm in identifying herself with the on-going life of her college and in expanding her maternal instincts, now that her own children are grown, to encompass the new generations of students which inhabit its campus."[25]

She could also take a part-time job, he said, but she shouldn't take work away from men who must feed their families, and, in fact, she won't have the skills or experience for a very "exciting" job.

. . . there is great demand for experienced and reliable women who can relieve younger women of family responsibilities on regular days or afternoons, so that they may either develop community interests or hold part-time jobs of their own. . . . There is no reason why women of culture and breeding, who in any case for years have probably done most of their own housework, should recoil from such arrangements.[26]

If the feminine mystique has not destroyed her sense of humor, a woman might laugh at such a candid description of the life her expensive sex-directed education fits her for: an occasional alumnae reunion and someone else's housework. The sad fact is, in the era of Freud and functionalism and the feminine mystique, few educators escaped such a sex-distortion of their own values. Max Lerner,[27]* even Riesman in *The Lonely Crowd*, suggested that women need not seek their own autonomy through productive contribution to society—they might better help their husbands hold on to theirs, through play. And so sex-directed education segregated recent generations of able American women as surely as separate-but-equal education segregated able American Negroes from the opportunity to realize their full abilities in the mainstream of American life.

It does not explain anything to say that in this era of conformity colleges did not really educate anybody. The Jacob report,[28] which leveled this indictment against American colleges generally, and even the more sophisticated indictment by Sanford[†] and his group, does not recognize that the colleges' failure to educate women for an identity beyond their sexual role was undoubtedly a crucial factor in perpetuating, if not creating, that conformity which educators now

---

* Max Lerner (1902–1992), writer, journalist, and academic who was an influential voice for liberalism in the middle of the twentieth century. Lerner worked as an editor for the liberal journal, *The Nation* from 1936 to 1938; he was editorial director of the leftwing newspaper *PM* from 1943 to 1948, and he taught at Brandeis University from 1949 to 1973. The author of many scholarly and popular books, including *America as a Civilization* (1957), Lerner was perhaps best known, however, for his syndicated column for the *New York Post* from 1949 through the 1970s.

† Nevitt Sanford (1909–1995), psychologist famous for his work on *The Authoritarian Personality* (1950), an influential analysis of racial and religious hatred. Friedan studied with Sanford during her year of graduate study at the University of California, Berkeley, from 1942 to 1943. At the height of the Cold War, in 1950, Berkeley dismissed Sanford (along with eleven other professors) for refusing to take a loyalty oath (see entries on Cold War, p. 11, and McCarthy, p. 103). By 1961, Sanford had become a professor at Stanford University and had turned his attention to higher education. With a group of collaborators, he published the groundbreaking *The American College* in 1962, a criticism of higher education's emphasis on "publish or perish" for faculty, and its failure to address students' developmental growth. *The Jacob report*: Philip E. Jacob (1914–1985) was a political scientist at the University of Pennsylvania when he wrote *Changing Values in College: An Exploratory Study of the Impact of College Teaching* in 1957. The conclusions of the study did not directly address gender issues in higher education, but did conclude that general education in the social sciences was not entirely successful in challenging the pre-existing values of college students.

so fashionably rail against. For it is impossible to educate women to devote themselves so early and completely to their sexual role— women who, as Freud said, can be very active indeed in achieving a passive end—without pulling men into the same comfortable trap. In effect, sex-directed education led to a lack of identity in women most easily solved by early marriage. And a premature commitment to any role—marriage or vocation—closes off the experiences, the testing, the failures and successes in various spheres of activity that are necessary for a person to achieve full maturity, individual identity.

The danger of stunting of boys' growth by early domesticity was recognized by the sex-directed educators. As Margaret Mead put it recently:

> Early domesticity has always been characteristic of most savages, of most peasants and of the urban poor. . . . If there are babies, it means, you know, the father's term paper gets all mixed up with the babies' bottle. . . . Early student marriage is domesticating boys so early they don't have a chance for full intellectual development. They don't have a chance to give their entire time, not necessarily to study in the sense of staying in the library—but in the sense that the married students don't have time to experience, to think, to sit up all night in bull sessions, to develop as individuals. This is not only important for the intellectuals, but also the boys who are going to be the future statesmen of the country and lawyers and doctors and all sorts of professional men.[29]

But what of the girls who will never even write the term papers because of the baby's bottle? Because of the feminine mystique, few have seen it as a tragedy that they thereby trap themselves in that one passion, one occupation, one role for life. Advanced educators in the early 1960's have their own cheerful fantasies about postponing women's education until after they have had their babies; they thereby acknowledge that they have resigned themselves almost unanimously to the early marriages, which continue unabated.

But by choosing femininity over the painful growth to full identity, by never achieving the hard core of self that comes not from fantasy but from mastering reality, these girls are doomed to suffer ultimately that bored, diffuse feeling of purposelessness, non-existence, non-involvement with the world that can be called *anomie*, or lack of identity, or merely felt as the problem that has no name.

Still, it is too easy to make education the scapegoat. Whatever the mistakes of the sex-directed educators, other educators have fought a futile, frustrating rear-guard battle trying to make able women "envision new goals and grow by reaching for them." In the last analysis, millions of able women in this free land chose, themselves, not to use the door education could have opened for them. The choice—and the responsibility—for the race back home was finally their own.

8

The Mistaken Choice

A mystique does not compel its own acceptance. For the feminine mystique to have "brainwashed" American women of nonsexual human purposes for more than fifteen years, it must have filled real needs in those who seized on it for others and those who accepted it for themselves. Those needs may not have been the same in all the women or in all the purveyors of the mystique. But there were many needs, at this particular time in America, that made us push-overs for the mystique; needs so compelling that we suspended critical thought, as one does in the face of an intuitive truth. The trouble is, when need is strong enough, intuition can also lie.

There was, just before the feminine mystique took hold in America, a war, which followed a depression and ended with the explosion of an atom bomb. After the loneliness of war and the unspeakableness of the bomb, against the frightening uncertainty, the cold immensity of the changing world, women as well as men sought the comforting reality of home and children. In the foxholes, the GI's had pinned up pictures of Betty Grable,* but the songs they asked to hear were lullabies. And when they got out of the Army they were too old to go home to their mothers. The needs of sex and love are undeniably real in men and women, boys and girls, but why at this time did they seem to so many the *only* needs?

We were all vulnerable, homesick, lonely, frightened. A pent-up hunger for marriage, home, and children was felt simultaneously by several different generations; a hunger which, in the prosperity of postwar America, everyone could suddenly satisfy. The young GI, made older than his years by the war, could meet his lonely need for love and mother by re-creating his childhood home. Instead of dating many girls until college and profession were achieved, he could marry on the GI bill,† and give his own babies the tender mother love

---

* Betty Grable (1916–1973), film actress and the most popular "pinup girl" among the soldiers during World War II. Her picture in a bathing suit, the back of her body facing the camera with her head looking over her shoulder, represented what the G.I.'s were fighting for back home—the pretty, blond, girl next door. Grable also performed for the troops overseas.

† The Serviceman's Readjustment Act, otherwise known as the GI Bill of Rights, passed in 1944 to provide returning soldiers with federally funded tuition help, unemployment benefits, and opportunities for low-interest mortgages. Even though the social and economic impact of this program was significant, these benefits were not always equally available to women and African Americans.

he was no longer baby enough to seek for himself. Then there were the slightly older men: men of twenty-five whose marriages had been postponed by the war and who now felt they must make up for lost time; men in their thirties, kept first by depression and then by war from marrying, or if married, from enjoying the comforts of home.

For the girls, these lonely years added an extra urgency to their search for love. Those who married in the thirties saw their husbands off to war; those who grew up in the forties were afraid, with reason, that they might never have the love, the homes and children which few women would willingly miss. When the men came back, there was a headlong rush into marriage. The lonely years when husbands or husbands-to-be were away at war—or could be sent away at a bomb's fall—made women particularly vulnerable to the feminine mystique. They were told that the cold dimension of loneliness which the war had added to their lives was the necessary price they had to pay for a career, for any interest outside the home. The mystique spelled out a choice—love, home, children, or other goals and purposes in life. Given such a choice, was it any wonder that so many American women chose love as their whole purpose?

The baby boom of the immediate postwar years took place in every country. But it was not permeated, in most other countries, with the mystique of feminine fulfillment. It did not in other countries lead to the even greater baby boom of the fifties, with the rise in teenage marriages and pregnancies, and the increase in family size. The number of American women with three or more children doubled in twenty years. And educated women, after the war, led all the others in the race to have more babies.[1] (The generation before mine, the women born between 1910 and 1919, showed the change most sharply. During their twenties, their low pregnancy rate led to warnings that education was going to wipe out the human race; in their thirties, they suddenly showed a sharp *increase* in pregnancies, despite the lowered biological capacity that makes the pregnancy rate decline with age.)

More babies are always born after wars. But today the American population explosion comes in large part from teenage marriages. The number of children born to teenagers rose 165 per cent between 1940 and 1957, according to Metropolitan Life Insurance figures. The girls who would normally go to college but leave or forgo it to marry (eighteen and nineteen are the most frequent ages of marriage of American girls today; half of all American women are married by twenty) are products of the mystique. They give up education without a qualm, truly believing that they will find "fulfillment" as wives and mothers. I suppose a girl today, who knows from statistics or merely from observation that if she waits to marry until she finishes college, or trains for a profession, most of the men will be married to someone else, has as much reason to fear she may miss feminine fulfillment as the war gave the girls in the forties. But this does not explain why they drop out of college to support their husbands, while the boys continue with their education.

It has not happened in other countries. Even in countries where, during the war, many more men were killed and more women were forced forever to miss the fulfillment of marriage, women did not run home again in panic. And in the other countries today, girls are as hungry as boys for the education that is the road to the future.

War made women particularly vulnerable to the mystique, but the war, with all its frustrations, was not the only reason they went home again. Nor can it be explained by "the servant problem," which is an excuse the educated woman often gives to herself. During the war, when the cooks and maids went to work in the war plants, the servant problem was even more severe than in recent years. But at that time, women of spirit often worked out unconventional domestic arrangements to keep their professional commitments. (I knew two young wartime mothers who pooled forces while their husbands were overseas. One, an actress, took both babies in the morning, while the other did graduate work; the second took over in the afternoon, when the other had a rehearsal or matinee. I also knew a woman who switched her baby's night-and-day so he would sleep at a neighbor's house during the hours she was at medical school.) And in the cities, then, the need for nurseries and day-care centers for the children of working mothers was seen, and met.

But in the years of postwar femininity, even women who could afford, and find, a full-time nurse or housekeeper chose to take care of house and children themselves. And in the cities, during the fifties, the nursery and day-care centers for the children of working mothers all but disappeared; the very suggestion of their need brought hysterical outcries from educated housewives as well as the purveyors of the mystique.[2]

When the war ended, of course, GI's came back to take the jobs and fill the seats in colleges and universities that for a while had been occupied largely by girls. For a short time, competition was keen and the resurgence of the old anti-feminine prejudices in business and the professions made it difficult for a girl to keep or advance in a job. This undoubtedly sent many women scurrying for the cover of marriage and home. Subtle discrimination against women, to say nothing of the sex wage differential, is still an unwritten law today, and its effects are almost as devastating and as hard to fight as the flagrant opposition faced by the feminists. A woman researcher on *Time* magazine, for instance, cannot, no matter what her ability, aspire to be a writer; the unwritten law makes the men writers and editors, the women researchers. She doesn't get mad; she likes her job, she likes her boss. She is not a crusader for women's rights; it isn't a case for the Newspaper Guild.* But it is discouraging nevertheless. If she is never going to get anywhere, why keep on?

Women were often driven embittered from their chosen fields when, ready and able to handle a better job, they were passed over for a man. In some jobs a woman had to be content to do the work while the man got the credit. Or if she got the better job, she had to face the bitterness and hostility of the man. Because the race to get ahead, in the big organization, in every profession in America, is so terribly competitive for men, competition from women is somehow the last straw—and much easier to fight by simply evoking that unwritten law. During the war, women's abilities, and the inevitable competition, were welcome; after the war they were confronted with that polite but inpenetrable curtain of hostility. It was easier for a woman to love and be loved, and have an excuse not to compete with men.

Still, during the depression, able, spirited girls sacrificed, fought prejudice, and braved competition in order to pursue their careers, even though there were fewer places to compete for. Nor did many see any conflict between career and love. In the prosperous postwar years, there were plenty of jobs, plenty of places in all the professions; there was no real need to give up everything for love and marriage. The less-educated girls, after all, did not leave the factories and go back to being maids. The proportion of women in industry has steadily increased since the war—but not of women in careers or professions requiring training, effort, personal commitment.[3] "I live through my husband and children," a frank member of my own generation told me. "It's easier that way. In this world now, it's easier to be a woman, if you take advantage of it."

In this sense, what happened to women is part of what happened to all of us in the years after the war. We found excuses for not facing the problems we once had the courage to face. The American spirit fell into a strange sleep; men as well as women, scared liberals, disillusioned radicals, conservatives bewildered and frustrated by change—the whole nation stopped growing up. All of us went back into the warm brightness of home, the way it was when we were children and slept peacefully upstairs while our parents read, or played bridge in the living room, or rocked on the front porch in the summer evening in our home towns.

---

* A labor union founded in 1933, the American Newspaper Guild organized reporters and editorial workers.

Women went home again just as men shrugged off the bomb, forgot the concentration camps, condoned corruption, and fell into helpless conformity; just as the thinkers avoided the complex larger problems of the postwar world. It was easier, safer, to think about love and sex than about communism, McCarthy, and the uncontrolled bomb. It was easier to look for Freudian sexual roots in man's behavior, his ideas, and his wars than to look critically at his society and act constructively to right its wrongs. There was a kind of personal retreat, even on the part of the most far-sighted, the most spirited; we lowered our eyes from the horizon, and steadily contemplated our own navels.

We can see all this now, in retrospect. Then, it was easier to build the need for love and sex into the end-all purpose of life, avoiding personal commitment to truth in a catch-all commitment to "home" and "family." For the social worker, the psychologist and the numerous "family" counselors, analytically oriented therapy for private patients on personal problems of sex, personality, and interpersonal relations was safer and more lucrative than probing too deeply for the common causes of man's suffering. If you no longer wanted to think about the whole of mankind, at least you could "help" individuals without getting into trouble. Irwin Shaw, who once goaded the American conscience on the great issues of war and peace and racial prejudice now wrote about sex and adultery; Norman Mailer* and the young beatnik writers confined their revolutionary spirit to sex and kicks and drugs and advertising themselves in four-letter words. It was easier and more fashionable for writers to think about psychology than politics, about private motives than public purposes. Painters retreated into an abstract expressionism that flaunted discipline and glorified the evasion of meaning. Dramatists reduced human purpose to bitter, pretentious nonsense: "the theater of the absurd." Freudian thought gave this whole process of escape its dimension of endless, tantalizing, intellectual mystery: process within process, meaning hidden within

---

* Norman Mailer (1923–2007), controversial writer famous for his bestselling war novel, *The Naked and the Dead* (1948) as well as his influential non-fiction, including *The Armies of the Night* (1968) and *Miami and the Siege of Chicago* (1968). In 1957, Mailer published in *Dissent* magazine, "The White Negro," a provocative, influential, and disturbing disquisition on the violence and sexuality that he associated with both African Americans and white hipsters. Friedan is almost certainly referring to this Mailer essay here, although Mailer himself was not associated with the Beat movement (see the entry on beatniks, p. 59). *Irwin Shaw* (1913–1984), novelist, playwright, and scriptwriter most famous for his early short stories and for his World War II novel about anti-Semitism in the U.S. Army, *The Young Lions* (1948). He also dramatized McCarthyism in the novel, *The Troubled Air* (1951) (see entry on McCarthyism, p. 103) His later books were not as politically charged, nor were they as respected in the literary world as his earlier short stories, novels, and plays.

meaning, until meaning itself disappeared and the hopeless, dull outside world hardly existed at all. As a drama critic said, in a rare note of revulsion at the stage world of Tennessee Williams,* it was as if no reality remained for man except his sexual perversions, and the fact that he loved and hated his mother.

The Freudian mania in the American culture, apart from the practice of psychotherapy itself, also filled a real need in the forties and fifties: the need for an ideology, a national purpose, an application of the mind to the problems of people. Analysts themselves have recently suggested that the lack of an ideology or national purpose may be partially responsible for the personal emptiness which sends many men and women into psychotherapy; they are actually looking for an identity which therapy alone can never give. The religious revival in America coincided with the rush to psychoanalysis, and perhaps came about for the same reason—behind the search for identity, or for shelter, a vacuum of larger purpose. It is significant that many ministers now spend much of their time in giving psychotherapy—pastoral counseling—to members of their congregations. Do they thereby also evade the larger questions, the real search?

When I was interviewing on college campuses in the late fifties, chaplains and sociologists alike testified to the younger generation's "privatism." A major reason for the early marriage movement, they felt, was that the young saw no other true value in contemporary society. It's easy for the professional social critic to blame the younger generation for cynical preoccupation with private pleasure and material security—or for the empty negativism of beatnikery. But if their parents, teachers, preachers, have abdicated purposes larger than personal emotional adjustment, material success, security, what larger purpose can the young learn?

The five babies, the movement to suburbia, do-it-yourself and even beatnikery filled homely needs; they also took the place of those larger needs and purposes with which the most spirited in this nation were once concerned. "I'm bored with politics . . . there's nothing you can do about it anyhow." When a dollar was too cheap, and too expensive, to live a life for, and your whole society seemed concerned with little else, the family and its loves and problems—this, at least, was good and true. And the literal swallowing of

---

* Tennessee Williams (1911–1983), one of the most important playwrights of mid-twentieth century American theater. Among his plays were *A Streetcar Named Desire* (1949) and *Cat on a Hot Tin Roof* (1955)—both of which won him the Pulitzer Prize. Williams's work centered on themes of sexual repression and loneliness. He was extremely popular with both critics and mainstream audiences in the 1940s and 1950s, even as he focused on difficult subjects like rape and domestic violence and featured homosexual characters at the center of some of his plays.

Freud gave the illusion that it was more important than it really was for the whole of suffering society, as the literal parroting of Freudian phrases deluded suffering individuals into believing that they were cured, when underneath they had not yet even faced their real troubles.

Under the Freudian microscope, however, a very different concept of family began to emerge. Oedipus conflict and sibling rivalry became household words. Frustration was as great a peril to childhood as scarlet fever. And singled out for special attention was the "mother." It was suddenly discovered that the mother could be blamed for almost everything. In every case history of troubled child; alcoholic, suicidal, schizophrenic, psychopathic, neurotic adult; impotent, homosexual male; frigid, promiscuous female; ulcerous, asthmatic, and otherwise disturbed American, could be found a mother. A frustrated, repressed, disturbed, martyred, never satisfied, unhappy woman. A demanding, nagging, shrewish wife. A rejecting, overprotecting, dominating mother. World War II revealed that millions of American men were psychologically incapable of facing the shock of war, of facing life away from their "moms,"* Clearly something was "wrong" with American women.

By unfortunate coincidence, this attack against mothers came about at the same time that American women were beginning to use the rights of their emancipation, to go in increasing numbers to college and professional schools, to rise in industry and the professions in inevitable competition with men. Women were just beginning to play a part in American society that depended not on their sex, but on their individual abilities. It was apparent to the naked eye, obvious to the returning GI, that these American women were indeed more independent, strong-minded, assertive of will and opinion, less passive and feminine than, for instance, the German and Japanese girls who, the GI's boasted, "even washed our backs for us." It was less apparent, however, that these girls were different from their mothers. Perhaps that is why, by some strange distortion of logic, all the neuroses of children past and present were blamed on the independence and individuality of this new generation of American girls—independence and individuality which the housewife-mothers of the previous generation had never had.

The evidence seemed inescapable: the figures on the psychiatric discharges in the war and the mothers in their case histories; the early Kinsey figures on the incapacity of American women to enjoy

* "Momism" was popularized by Philip Wylie in his *Generation of Vipers* (1942) in which he wrote, "Our society is too much an institution built to appease the rapacity of loving mothers." See pp. 344–51 for articles on momism in the 1950s and early 1960s and pp. 467–73 for a discussion of the impact of momism on Betty Friedan.

sexual orgasm, especially educated women; the fact that so many women *were* frustrated, and took it out on their husbands and children. More and more men in America did feel inadequate, impotent. Many of those first generations of career women did miss love and children, resented and were resented by the men they competed with. More and more American men, women, children were going to mental hospitals, clinics, psychiatrists. All this was laid at the doorstep of the frustrated American mother, "masculinized" by her education, prevented by her insistence on equality and independence from finding sexual fulfillment as a woman.

It all fitted so neatly with the Freudian rationale that no one stopped to investigate what these pre-war mothers were really like. They were indeed frustrated. But the mothers of the maladjusted soldiers, the insecure and impotent postwar males, were not independent educated career women, but self-sacrificing, dependent, martyred-housewife "moms."

In 1940, less than a fourth of American women worked outside the home; those who did were for the most part unmarried. A minuscule 2.5 per cent of mothers were "career women." The mothers of the GI's who were 18 to 30 in 1940 were born in the nineteenth century, or the early 1900's, and were grown up before American women won the right to vote, or enjoyed the independence, the sexual freedom, the educational or the career opportunities of the twenties. By and large, these "moms" were neither feminists, nor products of feminism, but American women leading the traditional feminine life of housewife and mother. Was it really education, career dreams, independence, which made the "moms" frustrated, and take it out on their children? Even a book that helped build the new mystique—Edward Strecker's *Their Mothers' Sons**—confirms the fact that the "moms" were neither career women, nor feminists, nor used their education, if they had it; they lived for their children, they had no interests beyond home, children, family, or their own beauty. In fact, they fit the very image of the feminine mystique.

Here is the "mom" whom Dr. Strecker, as consultant to the Surgeon General of the Army and Navy, found guilty in the case histories of the vast majority of the 1,825,000 men rejected for military service because of psychiatric disorders, the 600,000 discharged from the Army for neuropsychiatric reasons, and the 500,000 more who tried to evade the draft—almost 3,000,000 men, out of

---

*   When the esteemed professor of psychiatry from the University of Pennsylvania, Edward Strecker (1886–1959), served as a consultant to the armed forces during World War II, he was disturbed by how many young men presented with psychological disorders making them unfit for service. In *Their Mothers' Sons* (1946) he identified the problem: doting and clinging moms who focused all of their attention on their sons and thereby stifled their growth and independence. This diagnosis was a part of the "momism" of the Cold War period.

15,000,000 in the service, who retreated into psychoneurosis, often only a few days after induction, because they lacked maturity, "the ability to face life, live with others, think for themselves and stand on their own two feet."

A mom is a woman whose maternal behavior is motivated by the seeking of emotional recompense for the buffets which life has dealt her own ego. In her relationship with her children, every deed and almost every breath are designed unconsciously but exclusively to absorb her children emotionally and to bind them to her securely. In order to achieve this purpose, she must stamp a pattern of immature behavior on her children. . . . The mothers of men and women capable of facing life maturely are not apt to be the traditional mom type. More likely mom is sweet, doting, self-sacrificing. . . . takes no end of trouble and spares herself no pains in selecting clothes for her grown-up children. She supervises the curl of their hair, the selection of their friends and companions, their sports, and their social attitudes and opinions. By and large she does all their thinking for them. . . . [This domination] is sometimes hard and arbitrary, more often soft, persuasive and somewhat devious. . . . Most frequent is the method of indirection in which in some way the child is made to feel that mom's hurt and trying ever so hard to conceal that hurt. The soft method is infinitely more successful in blocking manifestations of youthful thought and action. . . .

The "self-sacrificing" mom when hard-pressed may admit hesitatingly that perhaps she does look "played out" and is actually a bit tired, but she chirps brightly "What of it?" . . . The implication is that she does not care how she looks or feels, for in her heart there is the unselfish joy of service. From dawn until late at night she finds her happiness in doing for her children. The house belongs to them. It must be "just so"; the meals on the minute, hot and tempting. Food is available at all hours. . . . No buttons missing from garments in this orderly house. Everything is in its proper place. Mom knows where it is. Uncomplainingly, gladly, she puts things where they belong after the children have strewn them about, here, there, and everywhere. . . . Anything the children need or want, mom will cheerfully get for them. It is the perfect home. . . . Failing to find a comparable peaceful haven in the outside world, it is quite likely that one or more of the brood will remain in or return to the happy home, forever enwombed.[4]

The "mom" may also be "the pretty addlepate" with her cult of beauty, clothing, cosmetics, perfumes, hairdos, diet and exercise, or "the pseudo-intellectual who is forever taking courses and attending lectures, not seriously studying one subject and informing herself thoroughly about it, but one month mental hygiene, the next economics, Greek architecture, nursery schools." These were the "moms" of the sons who could not be men at the front or at home, in bed or out, because they really wanted to be babies. All these moms had one thing in common:

> ... the emotional satisfaction, almost repletion, she derives from keeping her children paddling about in a kind of psychological amniotic fluid rather than letting them swim away with the bold and decisive strokes of maturity from the emotional maternal womb. . . . Being immature herself, she breeds immaturity in her children and, by and large, they are doomed to lives of personal and social insufficiency and unhappiness . . . [5]

I quote Dr. Strecker at length because he was, oddly enough, one of the psychiatric authorities most frequently cited in the spate of postwar articles and speeches condemning American women for their lost femininity—and bidding them rush back home again and devote their lives to their children. Actually, the moral of Strecker's cases was just the opposite; those immature sons had mothers who devoted *too* much of their lives to their children, mothers who had to keep their children babies or they themselves would have no lives at all, mothers who never themselves reached or were encouraged to reach maturity: "the state or quality of being mature; ripeness, full development . . . independence of thought and action"—the quality of being fully human. Which is not quite the same as femininity.

Facts are swallowed by a mystique in much the same way, I guess, as the strange phenomenon by which hamburger eaten by a dog becomes dog, and hamburger eaten by a human becomes human. The facts of the GI's neurosis became, in the 1940's, "proof" that American women had been seduced from feminine fulfillment by an education geared to career, independence, equality with men, "self-realization at any cost"—even though most of these frustrated women were simply housewives. By some fascinating paradox, the massive evidence of psychological damage done to boys and girls by frustrated mothers who devoted all their days to filling children's needs was twisted by the feminine mystique to a summons to the new generation of girls to go back home and devote *their* days to filling children's needs.

Nothing made that hamburger more palatable than the early Kinsey figures which showed that sexual frustration in women was related to their education. Chewed and rechewed was the horrendous fact that between 50 and 85 per cent of the college women polled had never experienced sexual orgasm, while less than one-

fifth of high-school educated women reported the same problem. As
Modern Woman: The Lost Sex interpreted these early Kinsey returns:

> Among women with a grade school education or less, complete
> failure to achieve orgasm diminished toward the vanishing
> point. Dr. Kinsey and his colleagues reported that practically
> 100% full orgastic reaction had been found among uneducated
> Negro women. . . . The psychosexual rule that begins to take
> form, then, is this: the more educated the woman is, the greater
> chance there is of sexual disorder, more or less severe . . . [6]

Nearly a decade went by before publication of the full Kinsey
report on women, which completely contradicted those earlier findings. How many women realize, even now, that Kinsey's 5,940 case
histories of American women showed that the number of females
reaching orgasm in marriage, and the number of females reaching
orgasm nearly 100 per cent of the time, *was* related to education, but
the more educated the woman, the greater chance of sexual fulfillment. The woman with only a grade-school education was more
likely never to experience orgasm, while the woman who finished
college, and who went on to graduate or professional school, was far
more likely to achieve full orgasm nearly 100 per cent of the time. In
Kinsey's words:

> We found that the number of females reaching orgasm within
> any five-year period was rather distinctly higher among those
> with upper educational backgrounds. . . . In every period of
> marriage, from the first until at least the fifteenth year, a larger
> number of the females in the sample who had more limited
> educational backgrounds had completely failed to respond to
> orgasm in their marital coitus, and a small number of the bet-
> ter educated females had so completely failed. . . .
>
> These data are not in accord with a preliminary, unpublished
> calculation which we made some years ago. On the basis of a
> smaller sample, and on the basis of a less adequate method of
> calculation, we seemed to find a larger number of the females
> of the lower educational levels responding to orgasm in the
> marital coitus. These data now need correction . . . [7]

But the mystique nourished by the early incorrect figures was not
so easily corrected.

And then there were the frightening figures and case histories of
children abandoned and rejected because their mothers worked.
How many women realize, even now, that the babies in those publicized cases, who withered away from lack of maternal affection, were
not the children of educated, middle-class mothers who left them
in others' care certain hours of the day to practice a profession or

write a poem, or fight a political battle—but truly abandoned children: foundlings often deserted at birth by unwed mothers and drunken fathers, children who never had a home or tender loving care. Headlines were made by any study which implied that working mothers were responsible for juvenile delinquency, school difficulties or emotional disturbance in their children. Recently a psychologist, Dr. Lois Meek Stolz, of Stanford University, analyzed all the evidence from such studies. She discovered that at the present time, one can say *anything*—good or bad—about children of employed mothers and support the statement by *some* research findings. But there is no definitive evidence that children are less happy, healthy, adjusted, *because* their mothers work.[8]

The studies that show working women to be happier, better, more mature mothers do not get much publicity. Since juvenile delinquency is increasing, and more women work or "are educated for some kind of intellectual work," there is surely a direct cause-and-effect relationship, one says. Except that evidence indicates there is not. Several years ago, much publicity was given to a study comparing matched groups of delinquent and non-delinquent boys. It was found, among other things, that there was no more delinquency, or school truancy, when the mothers worked regularly than when they were housewives. But, spectacular headlines warned, significantly more delinquents had mothers who worked irregularly. This finding brought guilt and gloom to the educated mothers who had given up full-fledged careers, but managed to keep on in their fields by working part-time, by free-lancing, or by taking temporary jobs with periods at home in between. "Here for years I've been purposely taking temporary jobs and part-time jobs, trying to arrange my working life in the boys' best interests," one such mother was quoted by the *New York Times*, "and now it looks as though I've been doing the worst possible thing!"[9]

Actually, this mother, a woman with professional training who lived in a comfortable middle-class neighborhood, was equating herself with mothers in that study who, it turned out, not only lived in poor socio-economic circumstances, but had in many cases been juvenile delinquents themselves. And they often had husbands who were emotionally disturbed.

The researchers who did that study suggested that the sons of these women had emotional conflicts because the mother was motivated to her sporadic work "not so much to supplement family income as to escape household and maternal responsibilities." But another specialist, analyzing the same findings, thought the basic cause both of the mother's sporadic employment and the son's delinquency was the emotional instability of both parents. Whatever the reason, the situation was in no way comparable to that of most educated women who read themselves into it. In fact, as Dr. Stolz shows, many studies misinterpreted as "proof" that women cannot combine careers and motherhood actually indicate that, where other conditions are equal, the children of mothers who work because they want to are less likely to be disturbed, have problems in school, or to "lack a sense of personal worth" than housewives' children.

The early studies of children of working mothers were done in an era when few married women worked, at day nurseries which served working mothers who were without husbands due to death, divorce or desertion. These studies were done by social workers and economists in order to press for such reforms as mothers' pensions. The disturbances and higher death rate in such children were not found in studies done in this recent decade, when of the millions of married women working, only 1 out of 8 was not living with her husband.

In one such recent study, based on 2,000 mothers, the only significant differences were that more housewife-mothers stated "the children make me nervous" than working mothers; and the housewives seemed to have "more children." A famous study in Chicago which had seemed to show more mothers of delinquents were working outside the home, turned out to show only that more delinquents come from broken homes. Another study of 400 seriously disturbed children (of a school population of 16,000) showed that where no broken home was involved, three times as many of the disturbed children's mothers were housewives as working mothers.

Other studies showed that children of working mothers were less likely to be either extremely aggressive or extremely inhibited, less likely to do poorly in school, or to "lack a sense of personal worth" than children of housewives, and that mothers who worked were more likely to be "delighted" at becoming pregnant, and less likely to suffer conflict over the "role of mother" than housewives.

There also seemed to be a closer and more positive relationship to children among working mothers who liked their work, than among housewife-mothers or mothers who did not like their work. And a study during the thirties of college-educated mothers, who are more able to choose work they like, showed no adverse effect of their employment on their marital and emotional adjustment, or on number or seriousness of children's problems. In general, women who work shared only two attributes; they were more likely to have higher education and to live in cities.[10]

In our own era, however, as droves of educated women have become suburban housewives, who among them did not worry that their child's bedwetting, thumbsucking, overeating, refusal to eat, withdrawal, lack of friends, inability to be alone, aggressiveness, timidity, slow reading, too much reading, lack of discipline, rigidity, inhibition, exhibitionism, sexual precociousness, or sexual lack of interest was a sign of incipient neurosis. If not actual abnormality or actual delinquency, they must be at least signs of parental failure, portents of future neurosis. Sometimes they were. Parenthood, and especially motherhood, under the Freudian spotlight, had to become a full-time job and career if not a religious cult. One false step could mean disaster. Without careers, without any commitment other than their homes, mothers could devote every moment to their children; their full attention could be given to finding signs of incipient neurosis—and perhaps to producing it.

In every case history, of course, you can always find significant facts about the mother, especially if you are looking for facts, or memories, of those supposedly crucial first five years. In America, after all, the mother is always there; she is *supposed* to be there. Is the fact that they are always there, and there only as mothers, somehow linked to the neuroses of their children? Many cultures pass on their conflicts to children through the mothers, but in the modern cultures of the civilized world, not many educate their strongest, ablest women to make a career of their own children.

Not long ago Dr. Spock confessed, a bit uneasily, that Russian children, whose mothers usually have some purpose in their lives besides motherhood—they work in medicine, science, education, industry, government, art—seemed somehow more stable, adjusted, mature, than American children, whose full-time mothers do nothing but worry about them. Could it be that Russian women are somehow better mothers because they have a serious purpose in their own lives? At least, said the good Dr. Spock, these mothers are more sure of themselves as mothers. They are not, like American mothers, dependent on the latest word from the experts, the newest child-care fad.[11] It is clearly a terrible burden on Dr. Spock to have 13,500,000 mothers so unsure of themselves that they bring up their children literally according to his book—and call piteously to him for help when the book does not work.

No headlines marked the growing concern of psychiatrists with the problem of "dependence" in American children and grownup children. The psychiatrist David Levy, in a very famous study of "maternal overprotection," studied in exhaustive detail twenty mothers who had damaged their children to a pathological extent by "maternal infantilization, indulgence and overprotection."[12] A typical case was a twelve-year-old boy who had "infantile temper tantrums in his eleventh year when his mother refused to butter his bread for him. He still demanded her help in dressing. . . . He summed up his requirements in life very neatly by saying that his mother would butter his bread for him until he married, after which his wife would do so . . ."

All these mothers—according to physiological indexes such as menstrual flow, breast milk, and early indications of a "maternal type of behavior"—were unusually strong in their feminine or maternal instinctual base, if it can be described that way. All but two of the twenty, as Dr. Levy himself described it, were responsible, stable and aggressive: "the active or aggressive feature of the responsible behavior was regarded as a distinctly maternal type of behavior; it characterized the lives of 18 of the 20 overprotecting mothers since childhood." In none was there any tinge of unconscious rejection of the child or of motherhood.

What made these twenty strongly maternal women (evidently strength, even aggression, is not masculine when a psychiatrist considers it part of the maternal instinct) produce such pathologically infantile sons? For one thing, the "child was utilized as a means of satisfying an abnormal craving for love." These mothers freshened up, put lipstick on when the son was due home from school, as a wife for a husband or a girl for her date, because they had no other life besides the child. Most, Levy said, had thwarted career ambitions. The "maternal overprotection" was actually caused by these mothers' strength, by their basic feminine energy— responsible, stable, active and aggressive—producing pathology in the child when the mother was blocked from "other channels of expression."

Most of these mothers also had dominating mothers and submissive fathers of their own, and their husbands had also been obedient sons of dominating mothers; in Freudian terms, the castrativeness all around was rather extreme. The sons and mothers were given intensive psychoanalytical therapy for years, which, it was hoped, would break the pathological cycle. But when, some years after the original study, research workers checked on these women and the children they had pathologically overprotected, the results were not quite what was expected. In most cases psychotherapy had not been effective. Yet some of the children, miraculously, did not become pathological adults; not because of therapy, but because by circumstance the mother had acquired an interest or activity in her own life and had simply stopped living the child's life for him. In a few other cases, the child survived because, through his own ability, he had staked out an area of independence of which his mother was not a part.

Other clues to the real problem of the mother-child relationship in America have been seen by social scientists without ever penetrating the mystique. A sociologist named Arnold Green almost by accident discovered another dimension to the relationship between nurturing mother love, or its lack, and neurosis.

It seems that in the Massachusetts industrial town where Green grew up an entire generation was raised under psychological conditions which should have been traumatic: conditions of irrational, vengeful, even brutal parental authority, and a complete lack of "love" between parent and child. The parents, Polish immigrants, tried to enforce rigid old-world rules which their American children did not respect. The children's ridicule, anger, contempt made the bewildered parents resort to a "vengeful, personal, irrational authority which no longer finds support in the future hopes and ambitions of the children."

> In exasperation and fear of losing all control over their Americanized youngsters, parents apply the fist and whip rather indiscriminately. The sound of blows, screams, howls, vexations, wails of torment and hatred are so commonplace along the rows of dilapidated millhouses that the passersby pay them scant attention.[13]

Surely, here were the seeds of future neuroses, as all good post-Freudian parents in America understand them. But to Green's amazement, when he went back and checked as a sociologist on the neuroses which according to the book must surely be flourishing, he found no known case of Army rejection because of psychoneurosis in the local Polish community, and in the overt behavior of an entire generation in the village "no expression of anxiety, guilty feelings, rigidity of response, repressed hostility—the various symptoms described as characteristic of the basic neurotic character." Green wondered. Why didn't those children become neurotic, why weren't they destroyed by that brutal, irrational parental authority?

They had none of that constant and watchful nurturing love that is urged on middle-class mothers by the child psychologizers; their mothers, like their fathers, worked all day in the factory; they had been left in the care of older sisters or brothers, had run free in fields and woods, had avoided their parents wherever possible. In these families, stress was placed upon work, rather than personal sentiment: "respect, not love is the tie that binds." Demonstrations of affection were not altogether lacking, Green said, "but they had little in common with the definitions of parent-child love found in the middle-class women's magazines."

It occurred to the sociologist that perhaps the very absence of this omnipresent nurturing mother love might explain why these children did not suffer the neurotic symptoms so commonly found in the sons of middle-class parents. The Polish parents' authority, however brutal and irrational, was "external to the core of the self," as Green put it. The Polish parents did not have the technique or opportunity to "absorb the personality of the child." Perhaps, Green suggested, "lack of love" and "irrational authority" do not in themselves cause neurosis, but only within a certain context of "personality absorption"—the physical and emotional blanketing of the child which brings about that slavish dependence upon the parents found among children of the native white American urban college-educated middle class.

Is "lack of love" the cause of neurosis, or the middle-class parental nurturing which "absorbs" the child's independent self, and creates in him an excessive need for love? Psychoanalysts had always concentrated on the seeds of neuroses; Green wanted to "find out what there is to being a modern middle-class parent that fertilizes the soil of the child's neurosis, however the individual seed is planted."

As usual, the arrow pointed unerringly to the mother. But Green was not concerned with helping the modern American mother adjust to her role; on the contrary, he found that she lacked any real "role" as a woman in modern society.

> She enters marriage and perhaps bears a child with no definite role and series of functions, as formerly. . . . She feels inferior to man because comparatively she has been and is more restricted. The extent of the actual emancipation of women has been commonly exaggerated. . . .
>
> Through a "good" marriage the middle-class girl attains far more status than is possible through a career of her own. But the period of phantom dalliance with a career, or an embarkation upon one, leave her ill-fitted for the drudgery of housecleaning, diapers, and the preparation of meals. . . . The mother has little to do, in or out of the home; she is her single child's sole companion. Modern "scientific child care" enforces a constant supervision and diffused worrying over the child's health, eating spinach, and ego development; this is complicated by the fact that much energy is spent forcing early walking, toilet-training, talking, because in an intensively competitive milieu middle-class parents from the day of birth are constantly comparing their own child's development with that of the neighbors' children.

Perhaps, Green speculates, middle-class mothers

> . . . have made "love" of supreme importance in their relation to the child, theirs for him and his for them, partly because of the love-complex of our time, which is particularly ramified within the middle class, and partly as a compensation for the many sacrifices they have made for the child. The child's need for love is experienced precisely because he has been conditioned to need it . . . conditioned to a slavish emotional dependence. . . . Not the need for parental love, but the constant

threat of its withdrawal after the child has been conditioned to the need, lies at the root of the most characteristic modern neuroses; Mamma won't like you if you don't eat your spinach, or stop dribbling your milk, or get down from that davenport. To the extent that a child's personality has been absorbed, he will be thrown into a panic by this sort of treatment. . . . In such a child, a disapproving glance may produce more terror— than a twenty-minute lashing in little Stanislaus Wojcik.

Green was only concerned with mothers in terms of their effect on their sons. But it occurred to him that "personality absorption" alone cannot, after all, explain neurosis. Because otherwise, he says, middle-class women of the previous generation would all have suffered such neuroses—and nobody recorded such suffering in those women. Certainly the personality of the middle-class girl of the late nineteenth century was "absorbed" by her parents, by the demands of "love" and unquestioning obedience. However, "the rate of neurosis under those conditions was probably not too high," the sociologist concludes, because even though the woman's own personality was "absorbed," it was consistently absorbed "within a role which changed relatively slightly from childhood into adolescence, courtship, and finally into marriage"; she never could be her own person.

The modern middle-class boy, on the other hand, is forced to compete with others, to achieve—which demands a certain degree of independence, firmness of purpose, aggressiveness, self-assertion. Thus, in the boy, the mother-nourished need for everyone to love him, the inability to erect his own values and purposes is neurotic, but not in the girl.

It is provocative, this speculation made by a sociologist in 1946, but it never penetrated far beyond the inner circles of social theory, never permeated the bulwarks of the feminine mystique, despite increasing national awareness that something was wrong with American mothers. Even this sociologist, who managed to get behind the mystique and see children in terms other than their need for more mother love, was concerned only with the problem of the sons. But was not the real implication that the role of the middle-class American housewife forces many a mother to smother, absorb, the personality of both her sons and daughters? Many saw the tragic waste of American sons who were made incapable of achievement, individual values, independent action; but they did not see as tragic the waste of the daughters, or of the mothers to whom it happened generations earlier. If a culture does not expect human maturity from its women, it does not see its lack as a waste, or as a possible cause of neurosis or conflict. The insult, the real reflection on our culture's definition of the role of women, is that as a nation we only noticed that something was wrong with women when we saw its effects on their sons.

Is it surprising that we misunderstood what was really wrong? How could we understand it, in the static terms of functionalism and adjustment? Educators and sociologists applauded when the personality of the middle-class girl was "consistently" absorbed from childhood through adulthood by her "role as woman." Long live the role, if adjustment is served. The waste of a human self was not considered a phenomenon to be studied in women—only the frustration caused by "cultural inconsistencies in role-conditioning," as the great social scientist Ruth Benedict* described the plight of American women. Even women themselves, who felt the misery, the helplessness of their lack of self, did not understand the feeling; it became the problem that has no name. And in their shame and guilt they turned again to their children to escape the problem. So the circle completes itself, from mother to sons and daughters, generation after generation.

The unremitting attack on women which has become an American preoccupation in recent years might also stem from the same escapist motives that sent men and women back to the security of the home. Mother love is said to be sacred in America, but with all the reverence and lip service she is paid, mom is a pretty safe target, no matter how correctly or incorrectly her failures are interpreted. No one has ever been blacklisted or fired for an attack on "the American woman." Apart from the psychological pressures from mothers or wives, there have been plenty of nonsexual pressures in the America of the last decade—the compromising, never-ceasing competition, the anonymous and often purposeless work in the big organization—that also kept a man from feeling like a man. Safer to take it out on his wife and his mother than to recognize a failure in himself or in the sacred American way of life. The men were not always kidding when they said their wives were lucky to be able to stay home all day. It was also soothing to rationalize the rat race by telling themselves that they were in it "for the wife and kids."And so men re-created their own childhood in suburbia, and made mothers of their wives. Men fell for the mystique without a murmur of dissent. It promised them mothers for the rest of their lives, both as a reason for their being and as an excuse for their failures. Is it so strange that boys who grow up with too much mother love become men who can never get enough?

---

* Ruth Benedict (1887–1948), path-blazing cultural anthropologist who worked at Columbia University and for the U.S. government during World War II. She is best known for asserting the plasticity of cultural forms and practices as well as for challenging barriers to women in anthropology.

But why did women sit still for this barrage of blame? When a culture has erected barrier after barrier against women as separate selves; when a culture has erected legal, political, social, economic and educational barriers to women's own acceptance of maturity— even after most of those barriers are down it is still easier for a woman to seek the sanctuary of the home. It is easier to live through her husband and children than to make a road of her own in the world. For she is the daughter of that same mom who made it so hard for girl as well as boy to grow up. And freedom is a frightening thing. It is frightening to grow up finally and be free of passive dependence. Why should a woman bother to be anything more than a wife and mother if all the forces of her culture tell her she doesn't have to, will be better off not to, grow up?

And so the American woman made her mistaken choice. She ran back home again to live by sex alone, trading in her individuality for security. Her husband was drawn in after her, and the door was shut against the outside world. They began to live the pretty lie of the feminine mystique, but could either of them really believe it? She was, after all, an American woman, an irreversible product of a culture that stops just short of giving her a separate identity. He was, after all, an American man whose respect for individuality and freedom of choice are his nation's pride. They went to school together; he knows who she is. Does his meek willingness to wax the floor and wash the dishes when he comes home tired on the 6:55 hide from both their guilty awareness of the reality behind the pretty lie? What keeps them believing it, in spite of the warning signs that have cropped up all over the suburban lot? What keeps the women home? What force in our culture is strong enough to write "Occupation: housewife" so large that all the other possibilities for women have been almost obscured?

Powerful forces in this nation must be served by those pretty domestic pictures that stare at us everywhere, forbidding a woman to use her own abilities in the world. The preservation of the feminine mystique in this sense could have implications that are not sexual at all. When one begins to think about it, America depends rather heavily on women's passive dependence, their femininity. Femininity, if one still wants to call it that, makes American women a target and a victim of the sexual sell.

9

The Sexual Sell

Some months ago, as I began to fit together the puzzle of women's retreat to home, I had the feeling I was missing something. I could

trace the routes by which sophisticated thought circled back on itself
to perpetuate an obsolete image of femininity; I could see how that
image meshed with prejudice and misinterpreted frustrations to hide
the emptiness of "Occupation: housewife" from women themselves.

But what powers it all? If, despite the nameless desperation of so
many American housewives, despite the opportunities open to all
women now, so few have any purpose in life other than to be a wife
and mother, somebody, something pretty powerful must be at work.
The energy behind the feminist movement was too dynamic merely
to have trickled dry; it must have been turned off, diverted, by something more powerful than that underestimated power of women.

There are certain facts of life so obvious and mundane that one
never talks about them. Only the child blurts out: "Why do people in
books never go to the toilet?" Why is it never said that the really
crucial function, the really important role that women serve as
housewives is *to buy more things for the house.* In all the talk of femininity and woman's role, one forgets that the real business of America is business. But the perpetuation of housewifery, the growth of
the feminine mystique, makes sense (and dollars) when one realizes
that women are the chief customers of American business. Somehow, somewhere, someone must have figured out that women will
buy more things if they are kept in the underused, nameless-
yearning, energy-to-get-rid-of state of being housewives.

I have no idea how it happened. Decision-making in industry is
not as simple, as rational, as those who believe the conspiratorial
theories of history would have it. I am sure the heads of General
Foods, and General Electric, and General Motors, and Macy's and
Gimbel's and the assorted directors of all the companies that make
detergents and electric mixers, and red stoves with rounded corners, and synthetic furs, and waxes, and hair coloring, and patterns
for home sewing and home carpentry, and lotions for detergent
hands, and bleaches to keep the towels pure white, never sat down
around a mahogany conference table in a board room on Madison
Avenue or Wall Street and voted on a motion: "Gentlemen, I move,
in the interests of all, that we begin a concerted fifty-billion-dollar
campaign to stop this dangerous movement of American women
out of the home. We've got to keep them housewives, and let's not
forget it."

A thinking vice-president says: "Too many women getting educated. Don't want to stay home. Unhealthy. If they all get to be scientists and such, they won't have time to shop. But how can we
keep them home? They want careers now."

"We'll liberate them to have careers at home," the new executive
with horn-rimmed glasses and the Ph.D. in psychology suggests.
"We'll make home-making creative."

Of course, it didn't happen quite like that. It was not an economic conspiracy directed against women. It was a byproduct of our general confusion lately of means with ends; just something that happened to women when the business of producing and selling and investing in business for profit—which is merely the way our economy is organized to serve man's needs efficiently—began to be confused with the purpose of our nation, the end of life itself. No more surprising, the subversion of women's lives in America to the ends of business, than the subversion of the sciences of human behavior to the business of deluding women about their real needs. It would take a clever economist to figure out what would keep our affluent economy going if the housewife market began to fall off, just as an economist would have to figure out what to do if there were no threat of war.

It is easy to see why it happened. I learned *how* it happened when I went to see a man who is paid approximately a million dollars a year for his professional services in manipulating the emotions of American women to serve the needs of business. This particular man got in on the ground floor of the hidden-persuasion business in 1945 and kept going. The headquarters of his institute for motivational manipulation is a baronial mansion in upper Westchester. The walls of a ballroom two stories high are filled with steel shelves holding a thousand-odd studies for business and industry, 300,000 individual "depth interviews," mostly with American housewives.[1]

He let me see what I wanted, said I could use anything that was not confidential to a specific company. Nothing there for anyone to hide, to feel guilty about—only, in page after page of those depth studies, a shrewd cheerful awareness of the empty, purposeless, uncreative, even sexually joyless lives that most American housewives lead. In his own unabashed terms, this most helpful of hidden persuaders showed me the function served by keeping American women housewives—the reservoir that their lack of identity, lack of purpose, creates, to be manipulated into dollars at the point of purchase.

Properly manipulated ("if you are not afraid of that word," he said), American housewives can be given the sense of identity, purpose, creativity, the self-realization, even the sexual joy they lack—by the buying of things. I suddenly realized the significance of the boast that women wield seventy-five per cent of the purchasing power in America. I suddenly saw American women as *victims* of that ghastly gift, that power at the point of purchase. The insights he shared with me so liberally revealed many things. . . .

The dilemma of business was spelled out in a survey made in 1945 for the publisher of a leading women's magazine on the attitudes of women toward electrical appliances. The message was considered of interest to all the companies that, with the war about to end, were going to have to make consumer sales take the place of war contracts. It was a study of "the psychology of housekeeping"; "a woman's attitude toward housekeeping appliances cannot be separated from her attitude toward homemaking in general," it warned.

On the basis of a national sample of 4,500 wives (middle-class, high-school or college-educated), American women were divided into three categories: "The True Housewife Type," "The Career Woman," and "The Balanced Homemaker." While 51 per cent of the women then fitted "The True Housewife Type" ("From the psychological point of view, housekeeping is this woman's dominating interest. She takes the utmost pride and satisfaction in maintaining a comfortable and well-run home for her family. Consciously or subconsciously, she feels that she is indispensable and that no one else can take over her job. She has little, if any, desire for a position outside the home, and if she has one it is through force or circumstances or necessity"), it was apparent that this group was diminishing, and probably would continue to do so as new fields, interests, education were now open to women.

The largest market for appliances, however, was this "True Housewife"—though she had a certain "reluctance" to accept new devices that had to be recognized and overcome. ("She may even fear that they [appliances] will render unnecessary the old-fashioned way of doing things that has always suited her.") After all, housework was the justification for her whole existence. ("I don't think there is any way to make housework easier for myself," one True Housewife said, "because I don't believe that a machine can take the place of hard work.")

The second type—The Career Woman or Would-Be Career Woman—was a minority, but an extremely "unhealthy" one from the sellers' standpoint; advertisers were warned that it would be to their advantage not to let this group get any larger. For such women, though not necessarily job-holders, "do not believe that a woman's place is primarily in the home." ("Many in this group have never actually worked, but their attitude is: 'I think housekeeping is a horrible waste of time. If my youngsters were old enough and I were free to leave the house, I would use my time to better advantage. If my family's meals and laundry could be taken care of, I would be delighted to go out and get a job.'") The point to bear in mind regarding career women, the study said, is that, while they buy modern appliances, they are not the ideal type of customer. *They are too critical.*

The third type—"The Balanced Homemaker"—is "from the market standpoint, the ideal type." She has some outside interests, or has held a job before turning exclusively to homemaking; she "readily accepts" the help mechanical appliances can give—but "does not expect them to do the impossible" because she needs to use her own executive ability "in managing a well-run household."

The moral of the study was explicit: "Since the Balanced Home-maker represents the market with the greatest future potential, it would be to the advantage of the appliance manufacturer to make more and more women aware of the desirability of belonging to this group. Educate them through advertising that it is possible to have outside interests and become alert to wider intellectual influences (without becoming a Career Woman). The art of good homemaking should be the goal of every normal woman."

The problem—which, if recognized at that time by one hidden persuader for the home-appliance industry, was surely recognized by others with products for the home—was that "a whole new generation of women is being educated to do work outside the home. Furthermore, an increased desire for emancipation is evident." The solution, quite simply, was to encourage them to be "modern" housewives. The Career or Would-Be Career Woman who frankly dislikes cleaning, dusting, ironing, washing clothes, is less interested in a new wax, a new soap powder. Unlike "The True Housewife" and "The Balanced Homemaker" who prefer to have sufficient appliances and do the housework themselves, the Career Woman would "prefer servants—housework takes too much time and energy." She buys appliances, however, whether or not she has servants, but she is "more likely to complain about the service they give," and to be "harder to sell."

It was too late—impossible—to turn these modern could-or-would-be career women back into True Housewives, but the study pointed out, in 1945, the potential for Balanced Housewifery—the home career. Let them "want to have their cake and eat it too . . . save time, have more comfort, avoid dirt and disorder, have mechanized supervision, yet not want to give up the feeling of personal achievement and pride in a well-run household, which comes from 'doing it yourself.' As one young housewife said: 'It's nice to be modern—it's like running a factory in which you have all the latest machinery.'"

But it was not an easy job, either for business or advertisers. New gadgets that were able to do almost all the housework crowded the market; increased ingenuity was needed to give American women that "feeling of achievement," and yet keep housework their main purpose in life. Education, independence, growing individuality, everything that made them ready for other purposes had constantly to be countered, channeled back to the home.

The manipulator's services became increasingly valuable. In later surveys, he no longer interviewed professional women; they were not at home during the day. The women in his samples were deliberately True or Balanced Housewives, the new suburban housewives. Household and consumer products are, after all, geared to women; seventy-five per cent of all consumer advertising budgets is spent to appeal to women; that is, to housewives, the women who are available during the day to be interviewed, the women with the time for shopping. Naturally, his depth interviews, projective tests, "living laboratories," were designed to impress his clients, but more often than not they contained the shrewd insights of a skilled social scientist, insights that could be used with profit.

His clients were told they had to do something about this growing need of American women to do creative work—"the major unfulfilled need of the modern housewife." He wrote in one report, for example:

> Every effort must be made to sell X Mix, as a base upon which the woman's creative effort is used.
>
> The appeal should emphasize the fact that X Mix aids the woman in expressing her creativity because it takes the drudgery away. At the same time, stress should be laid upon the cooking manipulations, the fun that goes with them, permitting you to feel that X Mix baking is real baking.

But the dilemma again: how to make her spend money on the mix that takes some of the drudgery out of baking by telling her "she can utilize her energy where it really counts"—and yet keep her from being "too busy to bake"? ("I don't use the mix because I don't do any baking at all. It's too much trouble. I live in a sprawled-out apartment and what with keeping it clean and looking after my child and my part-time job, I don't have time for baking.") What to do about their "feeling of disappointment" when the biscuits come out of the oven, and they're really only bread and there is no feeling of creative achievement? ("Why should I bake my own biscuits when there are so many good things on the market that just need to be heated up? It just doesn't make any sense at all to go through all the trouble of mixing your own and then greasing the tin and baking them.") What to do when the woman doesn't get the feeling her mother got, when the cake *had* to be made from scratch? ("The way my mother made them, you had to sift the flour yourself and add the eggs and the butter and you knew you'd really made something you could be proud of.")

The problem can be handled, the report assured:

> By using X Mix the woman can prove herself as a wife and mother, not only by baking, but by spending more time with her family. . . . Of course, it must also be made clear that home-baked foods are in every way preferable to bakery-shop foods . . .

Above all, give X Mix "a therapeutic value" by downplaying the easy recipes, emphasizing instead "the stimulating effort of baking." From an advertising viewpoint, this means stressing that "with X Mix in the home, you will be a different woman . . . a happier woman."

Further, the client was told that a phrase in his ad "and you make that cake the easiest, laziest way there is" evoked a "negative response" in American housewives—it hit too close to their "underlying guilt." ("Since they never feel that they are really exerting sufficient effort, it is certainly wrong to tell them that baking with X Mix is the lazy way.") Supposing, he suggested, that this devoted wife and mother behind the kitchen stove, anxiously preparing a cake or pie for her husband or children "is simply indulging her own hunger for sweets." The very fact that baking is work for the housewife helps her dispel any doubts that she might have about her real motivations.

But there are even ways to manipulate the housewives' guilt, the report said:

> It might be possible to suggest through advertising that not to take advantage of all 12 uses of X Mix is to limit your efforts to give pleasure to your family. A transfer of guilt might be achieved. Rather than feeling guilty about using X Mix for dessert food, the woman would be made to feel guilty if she doesn't take advantage of this opportunity to give her family 12 different and delicious treats. "Don't waste your skill; don't limit yourself."

By the mid-fifties, the surveys reported with pleasure that the Career Woman ("the woman who clamored for equality—almost for identity in every sphere of life, the woman who reacted to 'domestic slavery' with indignation and vehemence") was gone, replaced by the "less worldly, less sophisticated" woman whose activity in PTA gives her "broad contacts with the world outside her home," but who "finds in housework a medium of expression for her femininity and individuality." She's not like the old-fashioned self-sacrificing housewife; she considers herself the equal of man. But she still feels "lazy, neglectful, haunted by guilt feelings" because she doesn't have enough work to do. The advertiser must manipulate her need for a "feeling of creativeness" into the buying of his product.

> After an initial resistance, she now tends to accept instant coffee, frozen foods, precooked foods, and labor-saving items as part of her routine. But she needs a justification and she finds it in the thought that "by using frozen foods I'm freeing myself to accomplish other important tasks as a modern mother and wife."

Creativeness is the modern woman's dialectical answer to the problem of her changed position in the household. Thesis: I'm a housewife. Antithesis: I hate drudgery. Synthesis: I'm creative!

This means essentially that even though the housewife may buy canned food, for instance, and thus save time and effort, she doesn't let it go at that. She has a great need for "doctoring up" the can and thus prove her personal participation and her concern with giving satisfaction to her family.

The feeling of creativeness also serves another purpose: it is an outlet for the liberated talents, the better taste, the freer imagination, the greater initiative of the modern woman. It permits her to use at home *all the faculties that she would display in an outside career.*

The yearning for creative opportunities and moments is a major aspect of buying motivations.

The only trouble, the surveys warned, is that she "tries to use her own mind and her own judgment. She is fast getting away from judging by collective or majority standards. She is developing independent standards." ("Never mind the neighbors. I don't want to 'live up' to them or compare myself to them at every turn.") She can't always be reached now with "keep up with the Joneses"—the advertiser must appeal to her *own* need to live.

Appeal to this thirst. . . . Tell her that you are adding more zest, more enjoyment to her life, that it is within her reach now to taste new experiences and that she is entitled to taste these experiences. Even more positively, you should convey that you are giving her "lessons in living."

"House cleaning should be fun," the manufacturer of a certain cleaning device was advised. Even though his product was, perhaps, less efficient than the vacuum cleaner, it let the housewife use more of her own energy in the work. Further, it let the housewife have the illusion that she has become "a professional, an expert in determining which cleaning tools to use for specific jobs."

This professionalization is a psychological defense of the housewife against being a general "cleaner-upper" and menial servant for her family in a day and age of general work emancipation.

The role of expert serves a two-fold emotional function: (1) it helps the housewife achieve status, and (2) she moves beyond the orbit of her home, into the world of modern science in her search for new and better ways of doing things.

As a result, there has never been a more favorable psychological climate for household appliances and products. The modern housewife . . . is actually aggressive in her efforts to find those household products which, in her expert opinion, really meet her need. This trend accounts for the popularity of different waxes and polishes for different materials in the home, for the growing use of floor polishers, and for the variety of mops and cleaning implements for floors and walls.

The difficulty is to give her the "sense of achievement" of "ego enhancement" she has been persuaded to seek in the housewife "profession," when, in actuality, "her time-consuming task, housekeeping, is not only endless, it is a task for which society hires the lowliest, least-trained, most trod-upon individuals and groups. . . . Anyone with a strong enough back (and a small enough brain) can do these menial chores." But even this difficulty can be manipulated to sell her more things:

> One of the ways that the housewife raises her own prestige as a cleaner of her home is through the use of specialized products for specialized tasks. . . .
> When she uses one product for washing clothes, a second for dishes, a third for walls, a fourth for floors, a fifth for venetian blinds, etc., rather than an all-purpose cleaner, she feels less like an unskilled laborer, more like an engineer, an expert.
> A second way of raising her own stature is to "do things my way"—to establish an expert's role for herself by creating her own "tricks of the trade." For example, she may "always put a bit of bleach in all my washing—even colored, to make them *really* clean!"

Help her to "justify her menial task by building up her role as the protector of her family—the killer of millions of microbes and germs," this report advised. "Emphasize her kingpin role in the family . . . help her be an expert rather than a menial worker . . . make housework a matter of knowledge and skill, rather than a matter of brawn and dull, unremitting effort." An effective way of doing this is to bring out a *new* product. For, it seems, there's a growing wave of housewives "who look forward to new products which not only decrease their daily work load, but actually engage their emotional and intellectual interest in the world of scientific development outside the home."

One gasps in admiration at the ingenuity of it all—the housewife can participate in science itself just by buying something new—or something old that has been given a brand new personality.

> Besides increasing her professional status, a *new* cleaning appliance or product increases a woman's feeling of economic security and luxury, just as a new automobile does for a man. This was reported by 28 per cent of the respondents, who agreed

with this particular sentiment: "I like to try out new things. I've just started to use a new liquid detergent—and somehow it makes me feel like a queen."

The question of letting the woman use her mind and even participate in science through housework is, however, not without its drawbacks. Science should not relieve housewives of too much drudgery; it must concentrate instead on creating the *illusion* of that sense of achievement that housewives seem to need.

To prove this point, 250 housewives were given a depth test: they were asked to choose among four imaginary methods of cleaning. The first was a completely automatic dust- and dirt-removal system which operated continuously like a home-heating system. The second, the housewife had to press a button to start. The third was portable; she had to carry it around and point it at an area to remove the dirt. The fourth was a brand new, modern object with which she could sweep the dirt away herself. The housewives spoke up in favor of this last appliance. If it "appears new, modern" she would rather have the one that lets her work herself, this report said. "One compelling reason is her desire to be a participant, not just a button-pusher." As one housewife remarked, "As for some magical push-button cleaning system, well, what would happen to my exercise, my feeling of accomplishment, and what would I do with my mornings?"

This fascinating study incidentally revealed that a certain electronic cleaning appliance—long considered one of our great labor-savers—actually made "housekeeping more difficult than it need be." From the response of eighty per cent of those housewives, it seemed that once a woman got this appliance going, she "felt compelled to do cleaning that wasn't really necessary." The electronic appliance actually dictated the extent and type of cleaning to be done.

Should the housewife then be encouraged to go back to that simple cheap sweeper that let her clean only as much as she felt necessary? No, said the report, of course not. Simply give that old-fashioned sweeper the "status" of the electronic appliance as a "labor-saving necessity" for the modern housewife "and then indicate that the modern homemaker would, naturally, own both."

No one, not even the depth researchers, denied that housework was endless, and its boring repetition just did not give that much satisfaction, did not require that much vaunted expert knowledge. But the endlessness of it all was an advantage from the seller's point of view. The problem was to keep at bay the underlying realization which was lurking dangerously in "thousands of depth interviews which we have conducted for dozens of different kinds of house-cleaning products"—the realization that, as one housewife said, "It stinks! I have to do it, so I do it. It's a necessary evil, that's all." What to do? For one thing, put out more and more products, make the directions more complicated, make it really necessary for the housewife to "be an expert." (Washing clothes, the report advised, must become more than a matter of throwing clothes into a machine and pouring in soap. Garments must be carefully sorted, one load given treatment A, a second load treatment B, some washed by hand. The housewife can then "take great pride in knowing just which of the arsenal of products to use on each occasion.")

Capitalize, the report continued, on housewives' "guilt over the hidden dirt" so she will rip her house to shreds in a "deep cleaning" operation, which will give her a "sense of completeness" for a few weeks. ("The times of thorough cleaning are the points at which she is most willing to try new products and 'deep clean' advertising holds out the promise of completion.")

The seller must also stress the joys of completing each separate task, remembering that "nearly all housekeepers, even those who thoroughly detest their job, paradoxically find escape from their endless fate by accepting it—by 'throwing myself into it,' as she says."

> Losing herself in her work—surrounded by all the implements, creams, powders, soaps, she forgets for a time how soon she will have to redo the task. In other words, a housewife permits herself to forget for a moment how rapidly the sink will again fill with dishes, how quickly the floor will again be dirty, and she seizes the moment of completion of a task as a moment of pleasure as pure as if she had just finished a masterpiece of art which would stand as a monument to her credit forever.

This is the kind of creative experience the seller of things can give the housewife. In one housewife's own words:

> I don't like housework at all. I'm a lousy houseworker. But once in a while I get pepped up and I'll really go to town . . . When I have some new kind of cleaning material—like when Glass Wax first came out or those silicone furniture polishes—I got a real kick out of it, and I went through the house shining everything. I like to see the things shine. I feel so good when I see the bathroom just glistening.

And so the manipulator advised:

> Identify your product with the physical and spiritual rewards she derives from the almost religious feeling of basic security provided by her home. Talk about her "light, happy, peaceful feelings"; her "deep sense of achievement." . . . But remember she doesn't really want praise for the sake of praise . . . also remember that her mood is not simply "gay." She is tired and a

bit solemn. Superficially cheerful adjectives or colors will not reflect her feelings. She will react much more favorably to simple, warm and sincere messages.

In the fifties came the revolutionary discovery of the teenage market. Teenagers and young marrieds began to figure prominently in the surveys. It was discovered that young wives, who had only been to high school and had never worked, were more "insecure," less independent, easier to sell. These young people could be told that, by buying the right things, they could achieve middle-class status, without work or study. The keep-up-with-the-Joneses sell would work again; the individuality and independence which American women had been getting from education and work outside the home was not such a problem with the teenage brides. In fact, the surveys said, if the pattern of "happiness through things" could be established when these women were young enough, they could be safely encouraged to go out and get a part-time job to help their husbands pay for all the things they buy. The main point now was to convince the teenagers that "happiness through things" is no longer the prerogative of the rich or the talented; it can be enjoyed by all, if they learn "the right way," the way the others do it, if they learn the embarrassment of being different.

In the words of one of these reports:

> 49 per cent of the new brides were teenagers, and more girls marry at the age of 18 than at any other age. This early family formation yields a larger number of young people who are on the threshold of their own responsibilities and decision-making in purchases . . .
>
> But the most important fact is of a psychological nature: Marriage today is not only the culmination of a romantic attachment; more consciously and more clear-headedly than in the past, it is also a decision to create a partnership in establishing a comfortable home, equipped with a great number of desirable products.
>
> In talking to scores of young couples and brides-to-be, we found that, as a rule, their conversations and dreams centered to a very large degree around their future homes and their furnishings, around shopping "to get an idea," around discussing the advantages and disadvantages of various products. . . .
>
> The modern bride is deeply convinced of the unique value of married love, of the possibilities of finding real happiness in marriage and of fulfilling her personal destiny in it and through it.
>
> But the engagement period today is a romantic, dreamy and heady period only to a limited extent. It is probably safe to say that the period of engagement tends to be a rehearsal of the material duties and responsibilities of marriage. While waiting

for the nuptials, couples work hard, put aside money for definite purchases, or even begin buying on an installment plan.

What is the deeper meaning of this new combination of an
almost religious belief in the importance and beauty of married life on the one hand, and the product-centered outlook, on
the other? . . .

The modern bride seeks as a conscious goal that which in
many cases her grandmother saw as a blind fate and her mother
as slavery: to belong to a man, to have a home and children of
her own, to choose among all possible careers the career of
wife-mother-homemaker.

The fact that the young bride now seeks in her marriage complete "fulfillment," that she now expects to "prove her own worth"
and find all the "fundamental meanings" of life in her home, and to
participate through her home in "the interesting ideas of the modern era, the future," has enormous "practical applications," advertisers were told. For all these meanings she seeks in her marriage,
even her fear that she will be "left behind," can be channeled into
the purchase of products. For example, a manufacturer of sterling
silver, a product that is very difficult to sell, was told:

> Reassure her that only with sterling can she be fully secure in
> her new role . . . it symbolizes her success as a modern woman.
> Above all, dramatize the fun and pride that derive from the job
> of cleaning silver. Stimulate the pride of achievement. "How
> much pride you get from the brief task that's so much fun . . ."

Concentrate on the very young teenage girls, this report further
advised. The young ones will want what "the others" want, even if
their mothers don't. ("As one of our teenagers said: 'All the gang has
started their own sets of sterling. We're real keen about it—compare
patterns and go through the ads together. My own family never had
any sterling and they think I'm showing off when I spend my money
on it—they think plated's just as good. But the kids think they're
way off base.'") Get them in schools, churches, sororities, social
clubs; get them through home-economics teachers, group leaders,
teenage TV programs and teenage advertising. "This is the big market of the future and word-of-mouth advertising, along with group
pressure, is not only the most potent influence but in the absence of
tradition, a most necessary one."

As for the more independent older wife, that unfortunate tendency to use materials that require little care—stainless steel, plas-
tic dishes, paper napkins—can be met by making her feel guilty
about the effects on the children. ("As one young wife told us: 'I'm
out of the house all day long, so I can't prepare and serve meals the
way I want to. I don't like it that way—my husband and the children

deserve a better break. Sometimes I think it'd be better if we tried to get along on one salary and have a real home life but there are always so many things we need.'") Such guilt, the report maintained, can be used to make her see the product, silver, as a means of holding the family together; it gives "added psychological value." What's more, the product can even fill the housewife's need for identity: "Suggest that it becomes truly a part of *you*, reflecting *you*. Do not be afraid to suggest mystically that sterling will adapt itself to any house and any person."

The fur industry is in trouble, another survey reported, because young high school and college girls equate fur coats with "uselessness" and "a kept woman." Again the advice was to get to the very young before these unfortunate connotations have formed. ("By introducing youngsters to positive fur experiences, the probabilities of easing their way into garment purchasing in their teens is enhanced.") Point out that "the wearing of a fur garment actually establishes femininity and sexuality for a woman." ("It's the kind of thing a girl looks forward to. It means something. It's feminine." "I'm bringing my daughter up right. She always wants to put on 'mommy's coat.' She'll want them. She's a real girl.") But keep in mind that "mink has contributed a negative feminine symbolism to the whole fur market." Unfortunately, two out of three women felt mink-wearers were "predatory . . . exploitative . . . dependent . . . socially nonproductive . . ."

Femininity today cannot be so explicitly predatory, exploitative, the report said; nor can it have the old high-fashion "connotations of stand-out-from-the-crowd, self-centeredness." And so fur's "ego-orientation" must be reduced and replaced with the new femininity of the housewife, for whom ego-orientation must be translated into togetherness, family-orientation.

> Begin to create the feeling that fur is a necessity—a delightful necessity . . . thus providing the consumer with moral permission to purchase something she now feels is ego-oriented. . . . Give fur femininity a broader character, developing some of the following status and prestige symbols . . . an emotionally happy woman . . . wife and mother who wins the affection and respect of her husband and her children because of the kind of person she is, and the kind of role she performs. . . .
>
> Place furs in a family setting; show the pleasure and admiration of a fur garment derived by family members, husband and children; their pride in their mother's appearance, in her ownership of a fur garment. Develop fur garments as "family" gifts—enable the whole family to enjoy that garment at Christmas, etc., thus reducing its ego-orientation for the owner and eliminating her guilt over her alleged self-indulgence.

Thus, the only way that the young housewife was supposed to express herself, and not feel guilty about it, was in buying products for the home-and-family. Any creative urges she may have should also be home-and-family oriented, as still another survey reported to the home sewing industry.

> Such activities as sewing achieve a new meaning and a new status. Sewing is no longer associated with absolute need. . . . Moreover, with the moral elevation of home-oriented activities, sewing, along with cooking, gardening, and home decorating—is recognized as a means of expressing creativity and individuality and also as a means of achieving the "quality" which a new taste level dictates.

The women who sew, this survey discovered, are the active, energetic, intelligent modern housewives, the new home-oriented modern American women, who have a great unfulfilled need to create, and achieve, and realize their own individuality—which must be filled by some home activity. The big problem for the home-sewing industry was that the "image" of sewing was too "dull"; somehow it didn't achieve the feeling of creating something important. In selling their products, the industry must emphasize the "lasting creativeness" of sewing.

But even sewing can't be too creative, too individual, according to the advice offered to one pattern manufacturer. His patterns required some intelligence to follow, left quite a lot of room for individual expression, and the manufacturer was in trouble for that very reason, his patterns implied that a woman "would know what she likes and would probably have definite ideas." He was advised to widen this "far too limited fashion personality" and get one with "fashion conformity"—appeal to the "fashion-insecure woman," "the conformist element in fashion," who feels "it is not smart to be dressed too differently." For, of course, the manufacturer's problem was not to satisfy woman's need for individuality, for expression or creativity, but to sell more patterns—which is better done by building conformity.

Time and time again, the surveys shrewdly analyzed the needs, and even the secret frustrations of the American housewife; and each time if these needs were properly manipulated, she could be induced to buy more "things." In 1957, a survey told the department stores that their role in this new world was not only to "sell" the housewife but to satisfy her need for "education"—to satisfy the yearning she has, alone in her house, to feel herself a part of the changing world. The store will sell her more, the report said, if it will understand that the real need she is trying to fill by shopping is not anything she can buy there.

Most women have not only a material need, but a psychological compulsion to visit department stores. They live in comparative isolation. Their vista and experiences are limited. They know that there is a vaster life beyond their horizon and they fear that life will pass them by.

Department stores break down that isolation. The woman entering a department store suddenly has the feeling she knows what is going on in the world. Department stores, more than magazines, TV, or any other medium of mass communication, are most women's main source of information about the various aspects of life . . .

There are many needs that the department store must fill, this report continued. For one, the housewife's "need to learn and to advance in life."

We symbolize our social position by the objects with which we surround ourselves. A woman whose husband was making $6,000 a few years ago and is making $10,000 now needs to learn a whole new set of symbols. Department stores are her best teachers of this subject.

For another, there is the need for achievement, which for the new modern housewife, is primarily filled by a "bargain."

We have found that in our economy of abundance, preoccupation with prices is not so much a financial as a psychological need for the majority of women. . . . Increasingly a "bargain" means not that "I can now buy something which I could not afford at a higher price"; it mainly means "I'm doing a good job as a housewife; I'm contributing to the welfare of the family just as my husband does when he works and brings home the paycheck."

The price itself hardly matters, the report said:

Since buying is only the climax of a complicated relationship, based to a large extent on the woman's yearning to know how to be a more attractive woman, a better housewife, a superior mother, etc., use this motivation in all your promotion and advertising. Take every opportunity to explain how your store will help her fulfill her most cherished roles in life . . .

If the stores are women's school of life, ads are the textbooks. They have an inexhaustible avidity for these ads which give them the illusion that they are in contact with what is going on in the world of inanimate objects, objects through which they express so much of so many of their drives . . .

Again, in 1957, a survey very correctly reported that despite the "many positive aspects" of the "new home-centered era,"

unfortunately too many needs were now centered on the home—
that home was not able to fill. A cause for alarm? No indeed; even
these needs are grist for manipulation.

> The family is not always the psychological pot of gold at
> the end of the rainbow of promise of modern life as it has
> sometimes been represented. In fact, psychological demands
> are being made upon the family today which it cannot
> fulfill. . . .
>   Fortunately for the producers and advertisers of America
> (and also for the family and the psychological well-being of our
> citizens) much of this gap may be filled, and is being filled, by
> the acquisition of consumer goods.
>   Hundreds of products fulfill a whole set of psychological
> functions that producers and advertisers should know of and
> use in the development of more effective sales approaches. Just
> as producing once served as an outlet for social tension, now
> consumption serves the same purpose.

The buying of things drains away those needs which cannot
really be satisfied by home and family—the housewives' need for
"something beyond themselves with which to identify," "a sense of
movement with others toward aims that give meaning and purpose
to life," "an unquestioned social aim to which each individual can
devote his efforts."

> Deeply set in human nature is the need to have a meaningful
> place in a group that strives for meaningful social goals. When-
> ever this is lacking, the individual becomes restless. Which
> explains why, as we talk to people across the nation, over and
> over again, we hear questions like these: "What does it all
> mean?" "Where am I going?" "Why don't things seem more
> worth while and when we all work so hard and have so darn
> many things to play with?"
>   The question is: Can your product fill this gap?

"The frustrated need for privacy in the family life," in this era of
"togetherness" was another secret wish uncovered in a depth survey. This need, however, might be used to sell a second car. . . .

> In addition to the car the whole family enjoys together, the car
> for the husband and wife separately—"Alone in the car, one
> may get the breathing spell one needs so badly and may come
> to consider the car as one's castle, or the instrument of one's
> reconquered privacy." Or "individual" "personal" toothpaste,
> soap, shampoo.

Another survey reported that there was a puzzling "desexualiza-
tion of married life" despite the great emphasis on marriage and fam-

ily and sex. The problem: what can supply what the report diagnosed as a "missing sexual spark"? The solution: the report advised sellers to "put the libido back into advertising." Despite the feeling that our manufacturers are trying to sell everything through sex, sex as found on TV commercials and ads in national magazines is too tame, the report said, too narrow. "Consumerism," is desexing the American libido because it "has failed to reflect the powerful life forces in every individual which range far beyond the relationship between the sexes." The sellers, it seemed, have sexed the sex out of sex.

> Most modern advertising reflects and grossly exaggerates our present national tendency to downgrade, simplify and water down the passionate turbulent and electrifying aspects of the life urges of mankind. . . . No one suggests that advertising can or should become obscene or salacious. The trouble lies with the fact that through its timidity and lack of imagination, it faces the danger of becoming libido-poor and consequently unreal, inhuman and tedious.

How to put the libido back, restore the lost spontaneity, drive, love of life, the individuality, that sex in America seems to lack? In an absent-minded moment, the report concludes that "love of life, as of the other sex, should remain unsoiled by exterior motives . . . let the wife be more than a housewife . . . a woman . . ."

One day, having immersed myself in the varied insights these reports have been giving American advertisers for the last fifteen years, I was invited to have lunch with the man who runs this motivational research operation. He had been so helpful in showing me the commercial forces behind the feminine mystique, perhaps I could be helpful to him. Naively I asked why, since he found it so difficult to give women a true feeling of creativeness and achievement in housework, and tried to assuage their guilt and disillusion and frustrations by getting them to buy more "things"—why didn't he encourage them to buy things for all they were worth, so they would have time to get out of the home and pursue truly creative goals in the outside world.

"But we have helped her rediscover the home as the expression of her creativeness," he said. "We help her think of the modern home as the artist's studio, the scientist's laboratory. Besides," he shrugged, "most of the manufacturers we deal with are producing things which have to do with homemaking."

"In a free enterprise economy," he went on, "we have to develop the need for new products. And to do that we have to liberate women to desire these new products. We help them rediscover that homemaking is more creative than to compete with men. This can be manipulated. We sell them what they ought to want, speed up the unconscious, move it along. The big problem is to liberate the woman not to be afraid of what is going to happen to her, if she doesn't have to spend so much time cooking, cleaning."

"That's what I mean," I said. "Why doesn't the pie-mix ad tell the woman she could use the time saved to be an astronomer?"

"It wouldn't be too difficult," he replied. "A few images—the astronomer gets her man, the astronomer as the heroine, make it glamorous for a woman to be an astronomer . . . but no," he shrugged again. "The client would be too frightened. He wants to sell pie mix. The woman has to want to stay in the kitchen. The manufacturer wants to intrigue her back into the kitchen—and we show him how to do it the right way. If he tells her that all she can be is a wife and mother, she will spit in his face. But we show him how to tell her that it's creative to be in the kitchen. We liberate her need to be creative in the kitchen. If we tell her to be an astronomer, she might go too far from the kitchen. Besides," he added, "if you wanted to have a campaign to liberate women to be astronomers, you'd have to find somebody like the National Education Association to pay for it."

The motivational researchers must be given credit for their insights into the reality of the housewife's life and needs—a reality that often escaped their colleagues in academic sociology and therapeutic psychology, who saw women through the Freudian-functional veil. To their own profit, and that of their clients, the manipulators discovered that millions of supposedly happy American housewives have complex needs which home-and-family, love-and-children, cannot fill. But by a morality that goes beyond the dollar, the manipulators are guilty of using their insights to sell women things which, no matter how ingenious, will never satisfy those increasingly desperate needs. They are guilty of persuading housewives to stay at home, mesmerized in front of a television set, their nonsexual human needs unnamed, unsatisfied, drained by the sexual sell into the buying of things.

The manipulators and their clients in American business can hardly be accused of creating the feminine mystique. But they are the most powerful of its perpetuators; it is their millions which blanket the land with persuasive images, flattering the American housewife, diverting her guilt and disguising her growing sense of emptiness. They have done this so successfully, employing the techniques and concepts of modern social science, and transposing them into those deceptively simple, clever, outrageous ads and commercials, that an observer of the American scene today accepts as fact that the great majority of American women have no ambition

other than to be housewives. If they are not solely responsible for
sending women home, they are surely responsible for keeping them
there. Their unremitting harangue is hard to escape in this day of
mass communications; they have seared the feminine mystique
deep into every woman's mind, and into the minds of her husband,
her children, her neighbors. They have made it part of the fabric of
her everyday life, taunting her because she is not a better housewife,
does not love her family enough, is growing old.

> Can a woman ever feel right cooking on a dirty range? Until
> today, no range could ever be kept really clean. Now new RCA
> Whirlpool ranges have oven doors that lift off, broiler drawers
> that can be cleaned at the sink, drip pans that slide out eas-
> ily. . . . The first range that any woman can keep completely
> clean easily . . . and make everything cooked taste better.

> Love is said in many ways. It's giving and accepting. It's pro-
> tecting and selecting . . . knowing what's safest for those you
> love. Their bathroom tissue is Scott tissue always. . . . Now in
> four colors and white.

How skillfully they divert her need for achievement into sexual
phantasies which promise her eternal youth, dulling her sense of
passing time. They even tell her that she can make time stand still:

> Does she . . . or doesn't she? She's as full of fun as her kids—
> and just as fresh looking! Her naturalness, the way her hair
> sparkles and catches the light—as though she's found the
> secret of making time stand still. And in a way she has . . .

With increasing skill, the ads glorify her "role" as an American
housewife—knowing that her very lack of identity in that role will
make her fall for whatever they are selling.

> Who is she? She gets as excited as her six-year-old about the
> opening of school. She reckons her days in trains met, lunches
> packed, fingers bandaged, and 1,001 details. She could be you,
> needing a special kind of clothes for your busy, rewarding life.

> Are you this woman? Giving your kids the fun and advan-
> tages you want for them? Taking them places and helping them
> do things? Taking the part that's expected of you in church and
> community affairs . . . developing your talents so you'll be more
> interesting? You can be the woman you yearn to be with a
> Plymouth all your own. . . . Go where you want, when you
> want in a beautiful Plymouth that's yours and nobody else's . . .

But a new stove or a softer toilet paper do not make a woman a
better wife or mother, even if she thinks that's what she needs to be.
Dyeing her hair cannot stop time; buying a Plymouth will not give

her a new identity; smoking a Marlboro will not get her an invitation to bed, even if that's what she thinks she wants. But those unfulfilled promises can keep her endlessly hungry for things, keep her from ever knowing what she really needs or wants.

A full-page ad in the *New York Times*, June 10, 1962, was "Dedicated to the woman who spends a lifetime living up to her potential!" Under the picture of a beautiful woman, adorned by evening dress and jewels and two handsome children, it said: "The only totally integrated program of nutrient make-up and skin care—designed to lift a woman's good looks to their absolute peak. The woman who uses 'Ultima' feels a deep sense of fulfillment. A new kind of pride. For this luxurious Cosmetic Collection is the *ultimate* . . . beyond it there is nothing."

It all seems so ludicrous when you understand what they are up to. Perhaps the housewife has no one but herself to blame if she lets the manipulators flatter or threaten her into buying things that neither fill her family's needs nor her own. But if the ads and commercials are a clear case of caveat emptor,* the same sexual sell disguised in the editorial content of a magazine or a television program is both less ridiculous and more insidious. Here the housewife is often an unaware victim. I have written for some of the magazines in which the sexual sell is inextricably linked with the editorial content. Consciously or unconsciously, the editors know what the advertiser wants.

> The heart of X magazine is service—complete service to the whole woman who is the American homemaker; service in all the areas of greatest interest to advertisers, who are also business men. It delivers to the advertiser a strong concentration of serious, conscientious, dedicated homemakers. Women more interested in the home and products for the home. Women more willing and able to pay . . .

A memo need never be written, a sentence need never be spoken at an editorial conference; the men and women who make the editorial decisions often compromise their own very high standards in the interests of the advertising dollar. Often, as a former editor of *McCall's* recently revealed,[2] the advertiser's influence is less than subtle. The kind of home pictured in the "service" pages is dictated in no uncertain terms by the boys over in advertising.

And yet, a company has to make a profit on its products; a magazine, a network needs advertising to survive. But even if profit is the only motive, and the only standard of success, I wonder if the media are not making a mistake when they give the client what they think

---

* "Let the buyer beware" (Latin).

he wants. I wonder if the challenge and the opportunities for the American economy and for business itself might not in the long run lie in letting women grow up, instead of blanketing them with the youth-serum that keeps them mindless and thing-hungry.

The real crime, no matter how profitable for the American economy, is the callous and growing acceptance of the manipulator's advice "to get them young"—the television commercials that children sing or recite even before they learn to read, the big beautiful ads almost as easy as "Look, Sally, Look," the magazines deliberately designed to turn teenage girls into housewife buyers of things before they grow up to be women:

> She reads X Magazine from beginning to end . . . She learns how to market, to cook and to sew and everything else a young woman should know. She plans her wardrobe 'round X Magazine's clothes, heeds X Magazine's counsel on beauty and beaus . . . consults X Magazine for the latest teen fads . . . and oh, how she buys from those X Magazine ads! Buying habits start in X Magazine. It's easier to START a habit than to STOP one! (Learn how X Magazine's unique publication, X Magazine-at-school, carries your advertising into high school home economics classrooms.)

Like a primitive culture which sacrificed little girls to its tribal gods, we sacrifice our girls to the feminine mystique, grooming them ever more efficiently through the sexual sell to become consumers of the things to whose profitable sale our nation is dedicated. Two ads recently appeared in a national news magazine, geared not to teenage girls but to executives who produce and sell things. One of them showed the picture of a boy:

> I am *so* going to the moon . . . and you can't go, 'cause you're a girl! Children are growing faster today, their interests can cover such a wide range—from roller skates to rockets. X company too has grown, with a broad spectrum of electronic products for worldwide governmental, industrial and space application.

The other showed the face of a girl:

> Should a gifted child grow up to be a housewife? Educational experts estimate that the gift of high intelligence is bestowed upon only one out of every 50 children in our nation. When that gifted child is a girl, one question is inevitably asked: "Will this rare gift be wasted if she becomes a housewife?" Let these gifted girls answer that question themselves. Over 90 per cent of them marry, and the majority find the job of being a housewife challenging and rewarding enough to make full use of all their intelligence, time and energy. . . . In her daily roles

of nurse, educator, economist and just plain housewife, she is constantly seeking ways to improve her family's life. . . . Millions of women—shopping for half the families in America—do so by saving X Stamps.

If that gifted girl-child grows up to be a housewife, can even the manipulator make supermarket stamps use all of her human intelligence, her human energy, in the century she may live while that boy goes to the moon?

Never underestimate the power of a woman, says another ad. But that power was and is underestimated in America. Or rather, it is only estimated in terms that can be manipulated at the point of purchase. Woman's human intelligence and energy do not really figure in. And yet, they exist, to be used for some higher purpose than housework and thing-buying—or wasted. Perhaps it is only a sick society, unwilling to face its own problems and unable to conceive of goals and purposes equal to the ability and knowledge of its members, that chooses to ignore the strength of women. Perhaps it is only a sick or immature society that chooses to make women "housewives," not people. Perhaps it is only sick or immature men and women, unwilling to face the great challenges of society, who can retreat for long, without unbearable distress, into that thing-ridden house and make it the end of life itself.

10

Housewifery Expands to Fill the Time Available

With a vision of the happy modern housewife as she is described by the magazines and television, by the functional sociologists, the sex-directed educators, and the manipulators dancing before my eyes, I went in search of one of those mystical creatures. Like Diogenes* with his lamp, I went as a reporter from suburb to suburb, searching for a woman of ability and education who was fulfilled as a housewife. I went first to the suburban mental health centers and guidance clinics, to reputable local analysts, to knowledgeable local residents, and, stating my purpose, asked them to steer me not to the neurotic, frustrated housewives, but to the able, intelligent, educated women who were adjusted full-time housewives and mothers.

"I know many such housewives who have found fulfillment as women," one psychoanalyst said. I asked him to name four, and went to see them.

---

* Diogenes of Sinope (fourth century B.C.E.), Greek philosopher known for living rather than writing or teaching his principles. An anecdote recounts that he is believed to have taken his lamp in broad daylight to search for an honest man.

One, after five years of therapy, was no longer a driven woman, but neither was she a full-time housewife; she had become a computer programmer. The second was a gloriously exuberant woman, with a fine successful husband and three able, exuberant children. Throughout her married life she had been a professional psychoanalyst. The third, between pregnancies, continued seriously her career as a dancer. And the fourth, after psychotherapy, was moving with an increasingly serious commitment into politics.

I reported back to my guide and said that while all four seemed "fulfilled" women, none were full-time housewives and one, after all, was a member of his own profession. "That's a coincidence with those four," he said. But I wondered if it *was* a coincidence.

In another community, I was directed to a woman who, my informant said, was truly fulfilled as a housewife ("she even bakes her own bread"). I discovered that during the years when her four children were under six and she wrote on the census blank "Occupation: housewife," she had learned a new language (with certification to teach) and had used her previous training in music first as volunteer church organist and then as a paid professional. Shortly after I interviewed her, she took a teaching position.

In many instances, however, the women I interviewed truly fitted the new image of feminine fulfillment—four, five, or six children, baked their own bread, helped build the house with their own hands, sewed all their children's clothes. These women had had no dreams of career, no visions of a world larger than the home; all energy was centered on their lives as housewives and mothers; their only ambition, their only dream already realized. But were they fulfilled women?

In one upper-income development where I interviewed, there were twenty-eight wives. Some were college graduates in their thirties or early forties; the younger wives had usually quit college to marry. Their husbands were, to a rather high degree, engrossed in challenging professional work. Only one of these wives worked professionally; most had made a career of motherhood with a dash of community activity. Nineteen out of the twenty-eight had had natural childbirth (at dinner parties there, a few years ago, wives and husbands often got down on the floor to practice the proper relaxing exercises together). Twenty of the twenty-eight breastfed their babies. At or near forty, many of these women were pregnant. The mystique of feminine fulfillment was so literally followed in this community that if a little girl said: "When I grow up, I'm going to be a doctor," her mother would correct her: "No, dear, you're a girl. You're going to be a wife and mother, like mummy."

But what was mummy really like? Sixteen out of the twenty-eight were in analysis or analytical psychotherapy. Eighteen were taking tranquilizers; several had tried suicide; and some had been hospitalized for varying periods, for depression or vaguely diagnosed psychotic states. ("You'd be surprised at the number of these happy suburban wives who simply go berserk one night, and run shrieking through the street without any clothes on," said the local doctor, not a psychiatrist, who had been called in, in such emergencies.) Of the women who breastfed their babies, one had continued, desperately, until the child was so undernourished that her doctor intervened by force. Twelve were engaged in extramarital affairs in fact or in fantasy.

These were fine, intelligent American women, to be envied for their homes, husbands, children, and for their personal gifts of mind and spirit. Why were so many of them driven women? Later, when I saw this same pattern repeated over and over again in similar suburbs, I knew it could hardly be coincidence. These women were alike mainly in one regard: they had uncommon gifts of intelligence and ability nourished by at least the beginnings of higher education—and the life they were leading as suburban housewives denied them the full use of their gifts.

It was in these women that I first began to notice the tell-tale signs of the problem that has no name; their voices were dull and flat, or nervous and jittery; they were listless and bored, or frantically "busy" around the house or community. They talked about "fulfillment" in the wife-and-mother terms of the mystique, but they were desperately eager to talk about this other "problem," with which they seemed very familiar indeed.

One woman had pioneered the search for good teachers in her community's backward school system; she had served her term on the school board. When her children had all started school, she had thought seriously at thirty-nine about her own future: should she go back to college, get an M.A., and become a professional teacher herself? But then, suddenly, she had decided not to go on—she had a late baby instead, her fifth. I heard that flat tone in her voice when she told me she had now retired from community leadership to "major again in the home."

I heard the same sad, flat tone in an older woman's voice as she told me:

> I'm looking for something to satisfy me. I think it would be the most wonderful thing in the world to work, to be useful. But I don't know how to do anything. My husband doesn't believe in wives working. I'd cut off both my arms if I could have my children little, and at home again. My husband says, find something to occupy yourself that you'll enjoy, why should you work? So now I play golf, nearly every day, just myself.

When you walk three, four hours a day, at least you can sleep at night.

I interviewed another woman in the huge kitchen of a house she had helped build herself. She was busily kneading the dough for her famous homemade bread; a dress she was making for a daughter was half-finished on the sewing machine; a handloom stood in one corner. Children's art materials and toys were strewn all over the floor of the house, from front door to stove: in this expensive modern house, like many of the open-plan houses in this era, there was no door at all between kitchen and living room. Nor did this mother have any dream or wish or thought or frustration of her own to separate her from her children. She was pregnant now with her seventh; her happiness was complete, she said, spending her days with her children. Perhaps here was a happy housewife.

But just before I left, I said, as an afterthought, that I guessed she was joking when she mentioned that she envied her neighbor, who was a professional designer as well as the mother of three children. "No, I wasn't joking," she said; and this serene housewife, kneading the dough for the bread she always made herself, started to cry. "I envy her terribly," she said. "She knows what she wants to do. I don't know. I never have. When I'm pregnant and the babies are little, I'm *somebody*, finally, a mother. But then, they get older. I can't just keep on having babies."

While I never found a woman who actually fitted that "happy housewife" image, I noticed something else about these able women who were leading their lives in the protective shade of the feminine mystique. They were so *busy*—busy shopping, chauffeuring, using their dishwashers and dryers and electric mixers, busy gardening, waxing, polishing, helping with the children's homework, collecting for mental health, and doing thousands of little chores. In the course of my interviews with these women, I began to see that there was something peculiar about the *time* housework takes today.

On one suburban road there were two colonial houses, each with a big, comfortable living room, a small library, a formal dining room, a big cheerful kitchen, four bedrooms, an acre of garden and lawn, and, in each family, one commuting husband and three school-age children. Both houses were well-kept, with a cleaning woman two days a week; but the cooking and the other housework was done by the wife, who in each case was in her late thirties, intelligent, healthy, attractive, and well-educated.

In the first house, Mrs. W., a full-time housewife, was busy most of every day with cooking, cleaning, shopping, chauffeuring, taking care of the children. Next door Mrs. D., a microbiologist, got most of these chores done before she left for her laboratory at nine, or after she got home at five-thirty. In neither family were the children neglected, though Mrs. D.'s were slightly more self-reliant. Both women entertained a fair amount. Mrs. W., the housewife, did a lot of routine community work, but she did not "have time" to take a policy-making office—which she was often offered as an intelligent capable woman. At most, she headed a committee to run a dance, or a PTA fair. Mrs. D., the scientist, did no routine community work, but, in addition to her job and home, played in a dedicated string quintet (music was her main interest outside of science), and held a policy-making post in the world-affairs organization which had been an interest since college.

How could the same size house and the same size family, under almost identical conditions of income, outside help, style of life, take so much more of Mrs. W.'s time than of Mrs. D.'s? And Mrs. W. was never idle, really. She never had time in the evening to "just read," as Mrs. D. often did.

In a large, modern apartment building in a big eastern city, there were two six-room apartments, both a little untidy, except when the cleaning woman had just left, or before a party. Both the G.'s and the R.'s had three children under ten, one still a baby. Both husbands were in their early thirties, and both were in demanding professional work. But Mr. G., whose wife is a full-time housewife, was expected to do, and did, much more housework when he got home at night or on Saturday than Mr. R., whose wife was a free-lance illustrator and evidently had to get the same amount of housework done in between the hours she spent at her drawing table. Mrs. G. somehow couldn't get her housework done before her husband came home at night and was so tired then that he had to do it. Why did Mrs. R., who did not count the housework as her main job, get it done in so much less time?

I noticed this pattern again and again, as I interviewed women who defined themselves as "housewives," and compared them to the few who pursued professions, part or full time. The same pattern held even where both housewife and professional had full-time domestic help, though more often the "housewives" chose to do their own housework, full time, even when they could well afford two servants. But I also discovered that many frantically busy full-time housewives were amazed to find that they could polish off in one hour the housework that used to take them six—or was still undone at dinnertime—as soon as they started studying, or working, or had some other serious interest outside the home.

Toying with the question, how can one hour of housework expand to fill six hours (same house, same work, same wife), I came back again to the basic paradox of the feminine mystique: that it emerged to glorify woman's role as housewife at the very moment when the barriers to her full participation in society were lowered, at the very moment when science and education and her own ingenuity made it possible for a woman to be both wife and mother and to take an active part in the world outside the home. The glorification of "woman's role," then, seems to be in proportion to society's reluctance to treat women as complete human beings; for the less real function that role has, the more it is decorated with meaningless details to conceal its emptiness. This phenomenon has been noted, in general terms, in the annals of social science and in history—the chivalry of the Middle Ages, for example, and the artificial pedestal of the Victorian woman—but it may come as somewhat of a shock to the emancipated American woman to discover that it applies in a concrete and extreme degree to the housewife's situation in America today.

Did the new mystique of separate-but-equal femininity arise because the growth of women in America could no longer be repressed by the old mystique of feminine inferiority? Could women be prevented from realizing their full capabilities by making their role in the home *equal* to man's role in society? "Woman's place is in the home" could no longer be said in tones of contempt. Housework, washing dishes, diaper-changing had to be dressed up by the new mystique to become equal to splitting atoms, penetrating outer space, creating art that illuminates human destiny, pioneering on the frontiers of society. It had to become the very end of life itself to conceal the obvious fact that it is barely the beginning.

When you look at it this way, the double deception of the feminine mystique becomes quite apparent:

1. The more a woman is deprived of function in society at the level of her own ability, the more her housework, mother-work, wife-work, will expand—and the more she will resist finishing her housework or mother-work, and being without any function at all. (Evidently human nature also abhors a vacuum, even in women.)

2. The time required to do the housework for any given woman varies inversely with the challenge of the other work to which she is committed. Without any outside interests, a woman is virtually forced to devote her every moment to the trivia of keeping house.

The simple principle that "Work Expands to Fill the Time Available" was first formulated by the Englishman C. Northcote Parkinson on the basis of his experience with administrative bureaucracy in World War II. Parkinson's Law* can easily be reformulated for

---

* Satirical laws devised by C. Northcote Parkinson (1909–1993) to explain the inefficiency of bureaucratic organizations. The phenomenon of improved household tech-

the American housewife: Housewifery Expands to Fill the Time Available, or Motherhood Expands to Fill the Time Available, or even Sex Expands to Fill the Time Available. This is, without question, the true explanation for the fact that even with all the new labor-saving appliances, the modern American housewife probably spends more time on housework than her grandmother. It is also part of the explanation for our national preoccupation with sex and love, and for the continued baby boom.

Tabling for the moment the sexual implications, which are vast, let's consider some of the dynamics of the law itself, as an explanation for the disposal of feminine energy in America. To go back several generations: I have suggested that the real cause both of feminism and of women's frustration was the emptiness of the housewife's role. The major work and decisions of society were taking place outside the home, and women felt the need, or fought for the right, to participate in this work. If women had gone on to use their newly-won education and find new identity in this work outside the home, the mechanics of housewifery would have taken the same subsidiary place in their lives as car and garden and workbench in man's life. Motherhood, wifehood, sexual love, family responsibility, would merely have acquired a new emotional importance, as they have for men. (Many observers have noticed the new joy American men have been taking in their children—as their own work week is shortened—without that edge of anger women whose children *are* their work seem to feel.)

But when the mystique of feminine fulfillment sent women back home again, housewifery had to expand into a full-time career. Sexual love and motherhood had to become all of life, had to use up, to dispose of women's creative energies. The very nature of family responsibility had to expand to take the place of responsibility to society. As this began to happen, each labor-saving appliance brought a labor-demanding elaboration of housework. Each scientific advance that might have freed women from the drudgery of cooking, cleaning, and washing, thereby giving her more time for other purposes, instead imposed new drudgery, until housework not only expanded to fill the time available, but could hardly be done in the available time.

The automatic clothes dryer does not save a woman the four or five hours a week she used to spend at the clothesline, if, for instance, she runs her washing machine and dryer every day. After all, she still has to load and unload the machine herself, sort the

nologies sometimes increasing the amount of housework for women has been supported by historians such as Ruth Schwartz Cowan in *More Work for Mother: The Ironies of Household Technology from the Open Hearth to the Microwave* (New York: 1983).

clothes and put them away. As a young mother said, "Clean sheets twice a week are now possible. Last week, when my dryer broke down, the sheets didn't get changed for eight days. Everyone complained. We all felt dirty. I felt guilty. Isn't that silly?"[1]

The modern American housewife spends far more time washing, drying, and ironing than her mother. If she has an electric freezer or mixer, she spends more time cooking than a woman who does not have these labor-saving appliances. The home freezer, simply by existing, takes up time: beans, raised in the garden, must be prepared for freezing. If you have an electric mixer, you have to use it: those elaborate recipes with the puréed chestnuts, watercress, and almonds take longer than broiling lamb chops.

According to a Bryn Mawr survey made just after the war, in a typical United States farm family, housework took 60.55 hours a week; 78.35 hours in cities under 100,000; 80.57 in cities of over 100,000.[2] With all their appliances, the suburban and city housewives spend more time on housework than the busy farmer's wife. That farmer's wife, of course, has quite a lot of other work to do.

In the 1950's, sociologists and home economists reported puzzlement, and baffling inconsistencies, as to the amount of time American women were still spending on housework. Study after study revealed that American housewives were spending almost as many, or even more, hours a day on housekeeping as women thirty years earlier, despite the smaller, easier-to-care-for homes, and despite the fact that they had seven times as much capital equipment in housekeeping appliances. There were, however, some exceptions. Women who worked many hours a week outside the home—either in paid jobs or community work—did the housekeeping, on which the full-time housewife still spent sixty hours a week, in half the time. They still seemed to do all the homemaking activities of the housewife—meals, shopping, cleaning, the children—but even with a thirty-five-hour work week on the job, their work week was only an hour and a half a day longer than the housewife's. That this strange phenomenon caused so little comment was due to the relative scarcity of such women. For the even stranger phenomenon, the real significance of which the mystique hid, was the fact that, despite the growth of the American population and the movement of that population from farm to city with the parallel growth of American industry and professions, in the first fifty years of the twentieth century the proportion of American women working outside the home increased very little indeed, while the proportion of American women in the professions actually declined.[3] From nearly half the nation's professional force in 1930, women had dropped to only 35 per cent in 1960, despite the fact that the number of women college graduates had nearly tripled. The phenomenon was the great increase in the numbers of educated women choosing to be just housewives.

And yet, for the suburban and city housewife, the fact remains that more and more of the jobs that used to be performed in the home have been taken away: canning, baking bread, weaving cloth and making clothes, educating the young, nursing the sick, taking care of the aged. It is possible for women to reverse history—or kid themselves that they can reverse it—by baking their own bread, but the law does not permit them to teach their own children at home, and few housewives would match their so-called generalist's skill with the professional expertise of doctor and hospital to nurse a child through tonsillitis or pneumonia at home.

There is a real basis, then, for the complaint that so many housewives have: "I feel so empty somehow, useless, as if I don't exist." "At times I feel as though the world is going past my door while I just sit and watch." This very sense of emptiness, this uneasy denial of the world outside the home, often drives the housewife to even more effort, more frantic housework to keep the future out of sight. And the choices the housewife makes to fill that emptiness—though she seems to make them for logical and necessary reasons—trap her further in trivial domestic routine.

The woman with two children, for example, bored and restive in her city apartment, is driven by her sense of futility and emptiness to move, "for the children's sake," to a spacious house in the suburbs. The house takes longer to clean, the shopping and gardening and chauffeuring, and do-it-yourself routines are so time-consuming that, for a while, the emptiness seems solved. But when the house is furnished, and the children are in school and the family's place in the community has jelled, there is "nothing to look forward to," as one woman I interviewed put it. The empty feeling returns, and so she must redecorate the living room, or wax the kitchen floor more often than necessary—or have another baby. Diapering that baby, along with all the other housework, may keep her running so fast that she will indeed need her husband's help in the kitchen at night. Yet none of it is quite as real, quite as necessary, as it seems.

One of the great changes in America, since World War II, has been the explosive movement to the suburbs, those ugly and endless sprawls which are becoming a national problem. Sociologists point out that a distinguishing feature of these suburbs is the fact that the women who live there are better educated than city women, and that the great majority are full-time housewives.[4]

At first glance, one might suspect that the very growth and existence of the suburbs causes educated modern American women to become and remain full-time housewives. Or did the postwar suburban explosion come, at least in part, as a result of the coincidental choice of millions of American women to "seek fulfillment in the home?" Among the women I interviewed, the decision to move to the suburbs "for the children's sake" followed the decision to give up job or profession and become a full-time housewife, usually after the birth of the first baby, or the second, depending on the age of the woman when the mystique hit. With the youngest wives, of course, the mystique hit so early that the choice of marriage and motherhood as a full-time career ruled out education for any profession, and the move to the suburbs came with marriage or as soon as the wife no longer had to work to support her husband through college or law school.

Families where the wife intends to pursue a definite professional goal are less likely to move to the suburbs. In the city, of course, there are more and better jobs for educated women; more universities, sometimes free, with evening courses, geared to men who work during the day, and often more convenient than the conventional daytime program for a young mother who wants to finish college or work toward a graduate degree. There is also a better supply of full- or part-time nurses and cleaning help, nursery schools, day-care centers, after-school play programs. But these considerations are only important to the woman who has commitments outside the home.

There is also less room for housewifery to expand to fill the time available, in the city. That sense of restless "marking time" comes early to the educated, able city housewife, even though, when her babies are little, the time is more than filled with busyness—wheeling the carriage back and forth in the park, sitting on the playground bench because the children can't play outside alone. Still, there's no room in the city apartment for a home freezer, no garden to grow beans in. And all the organizations in the city are so big; the libraries are already built; professionals run the nursery schools and recreation programs.

It is not surprising, then, that many young wives vote for a move to the suburbs as soon as possible. Like the empty plains of Kansas that tempted the restless immigrant, the suburbs in their very newness and lack of structured service, offered, at least at first, a limitless challenge to the energy of educated American women. The women who were strong enough, independent enough, seized the opportunity and were leaders and innovators in these new communities. But, in most cases, these were women educated before the era of feminine fulfillment. The ability of suburban life to fulfill, or truly use the potential of the able, educated American woman seems to depend on her own previous autonomy or self-realization— that is, on her strength to resist the pressures to conform, resist the time-filling busywork of suburban house and community, and find, or make, the same kind of serious commitment outside the home that she would have made in the city. Such a commitment in the suburbs, in the beginning at least, was likely to be on a volunteer basis, but it was challenging, and necessary.

When the mystique took over, however, a new breed of women came to the suburbs. They were looking for sanctuary; they were perfectly willing to accept the suburban community as they found it (their only problem was "how to fit in"); they were perfectly willing to fill their days with the trivia of housewifery. Women of this kind, and most of those that I interviewed were of the post-1950 college generation, refuse to take policy-making positions in community organizations; they will only collect for Red Cross or March of Dimes or Scouts or be den mothers or take the lesser PTA jobs. Their resistance to serious community responsibility is usually explained by "I can't take the time from my family." But much of their time is spent in meaningless busywork. The kind of community work they choose does not challenge their intelligence—or even, sometimes, fill a real function. Nor do they derive much personal satisfaction from it—but it does fill time.

So, increasingly, in the new bedroom suburbs, the really interesting volunteer jobs—the leadership of the cooperative nurseries, the free libraries, the school board posts, the selectmenships and, in some suburbs, even the PTA presidencies—are filled by men.[5] The housewife who doesn't "have time" to take serious responsibility in the community, like the woman who doesn't "have time" to pursue a professional career, evades a serious commitment through which she might finally realize herself; she evades it by stepping up her domestic routine until she is truly trapped.

The dimensions of the trap seem physically unalterable, as the busyness that fills the housewife's day seems inescapably necessary. But is that domestic trap an illusion, despite its all-too-solid reality, an illusion created by the feminine mystique? Take, for instance, the open plan of the contemporary "ranch" or split-level house, $14,990 to $54,990, which has been built in the millions from Roslyn Heights to the Pacific Palisades. They give the illusion of more space for less money. But the women to whom they are sold almost *have* to live the feminine mystique. There are no true walls or doors; the woman in the beautiful electronic kitchen is never separated from her children. She need never feel alone for a minute, need never be by herself. She can forget her own identity in those noisy open-plan houses. The open plan also helps expand the housework to fill the time available. In what is basically one free-flowing room, instead of many rooms separated by walls and stairs, continual messes continually need picking up. A man, of course, leaves the house for most of the day. But the feminine mystique forbids the woman this.

A friend of mine, an able writer turned full-time housewife, had her suburban dream house designed by an architect to her own specifications, during the period when she defined herself as housewife and no longer wrote. The house, which cost approximately $50,000, was almost literally one big kitchen. There was a separate studio for her husband, who was a photographer, and cubbyholes for sleeping, but there wasn't any place where she could get out of the kitchen, away from her children, during the working hours. The gorgeous mahogany and stainless steel of her custom-built kitchen cabinets and electric appliances were indeed a dream, but when I saw that house, I wondered where, if she ever wanted to write again, she would put her typewriter.

It's strange how few places there are in those spacious houses and those sprawling suburbs where you can go to be alone. A sociologist's study of upper-income suburban wives who married young and woke, after fifteen years of child-living, PTA, do-it-yourself, garden-and-barbecue, to the realization that they wanted to do some real work themselves, found that the ones who did something about this often moved back to the city.[6] But among the women I talked to, this moment of personal truth was more likely to be marked by adding a room with a door to their open-plan house, or simply by putting a door on one room in the house, "so I can have someplace to myself, just a door to shut between me and the children when I want to think"—or work, study, be alone.

Most American housewives, however, do not shut that door. Perhaps they are afraid, finally, to be alone in that room. As another social scientist said, the American housewife's dilemma is that she does not have the privacy to follow real interests of her own, but even if she had more time and space to herself, she would not know what to do with it.[7] If she makes a career of marriage and motherhood, as the mystique tells her, if she becomes the executive of the house—and has enough children to give her quite a business to run—if she exerts the human strength, which she is forbidden by the mystique to exert elsewhere, on running a perfect house and supervising her children and sharing her husband's career in such omnipresent detail that she has only a few minutes to spare for community work, and no time for serious larger interests, who is to say that this is not as important, as good a way to spend a life, as mastering the secrets of the atoms or the stars, composing symphonies, pioneering a new concept in government or society?

For the very able woman, who has the ability to create culturally as well as biologically, the only possible rationalization is to convince herself—as the new mystique tries so hard to convince her—that the minute physical details of child care are indeed mystically creative; that her children will be tragically deprived if she is not there every minute; that the dinner she gives the boss's wife is as crucial to her husband's career as the case he fights in court or the problem he solves in the laboratory. And because husband and children are soon out of the house most of the day, she must keep on having new babies, or somehow make the minutiae of housework itself important enough, necessary enough, hard enough, creative enough to justify her very existence.

If a woman's whole existence is to be justified in this way, if the housewife's work is really so important, so necessary, why should anyone raise an eyebrow because a latter-day Einstein's wife expects her husband to put aside that lifeless theory of relativity and help her with the work that is supposed to be the essence of life itself: diaper the baby and don't forget to rinse the soiled diaper in the toilet before putting it in the diaper pail, and then wax the kitchen floor.

The most glaring proof that, no matter how elaborate, "Occupation: housewife" is not an adequate substitute for truly challenging work, important enough to society to be paid for in its coin, arose from the comedy of "togetherness." The women acting in this little morality play were told that they had the starring roles, that their parts were just as important, perhaps even more important than the parts their husbands played in the world outside the home. Was it unnatural that, since they were doing such a vital job, women insisted that their husbands share in the housework? Surely it was an unspoken guilt, an unspoken realization of their wives' entrapment, that made so many men comply, with varying degrees of grace, to their wives' demands. But having their husbands share the housework didn't really compensate women for being shut out of the larger world. If anything, by removing still more of their functions, it increased their sense of individual emptiness. They needed to share vicariously more and more of their children's and husbands' lives. Togetherness was a poor substitute for equality; the glorification of women's role was a poor substitute for free participation in the world as an individual.

The true emptiness beneath the American housewife's routine has been revealed in many ways. In Minneapolis recently a schoolteacher named Maurice K. Enghausen read a story in the local newspaper about the long work week of today's housewife. Declaring in a letter to the editor that "any woman who puts in that many hours is awfully slow, a poor budgeter of time, or just plain inefficient," this thirty-six-year-old bachelor offered to take over any household and show how it could be done.

Scores of irate housewives dared him to prove it. He took over the household of Mr. and Mrs. Robert Dalton, with four children, aged two to seven, for three days. In a single day, he cleaned the first floor, washed three loads of clothes and hung them out to dry, ironed all the laundry including underwear and sheets, fixed a soup-and-sandwich lunch and a big backyard supper, baked two cakes, prepared two salads for the next day, dressed, undressed, and bathed the children, washed wood work and scrubbed the kitchen floor. Mrs. Dalton said he was even a better cook than she was. "As for cleaning," she said, "I am more thorough, but perhaps that is unnecessary."

Pointing out that he had kept house for himself for seven years and had earned money at college by housework, Enghausen said, "I still wish that teaching 115 students were as easy as handling four children and a house . . . I still maintain that housework is not the interminable chore that women claim it is."[8]

This claim, periodically expressed by men privately and publicly, has been borne out by a recent time-motion study. Recording and analyzing every movement made by a group of housewives, this study concluded that most of the energy expended in housework is superfluous. A series of intensive studies sponsored by the Michigan Heart Association at Wayne University disclosed that "women were working more than twice as hard as they should," squandering energy through habit and tradition in wasted motion and unneeded steps.

The puzzling question of "housewife's fatigue" sheds additional light. Doctors in many recent medical conventions report failure to cure it or get to its cause. At a meeting of the American College of Obstetricians and Gynecologists, a Cleveland doctor stated that mothers, who cannot get over "that tired feeling" and complain that their doctors are no help, are neither sick nor maladjusted, but actually tired. "No psychoanalysis or deep probing is necessary," said Dr. Leonard Lovshin, of the Cleveland Clinic. "She has a work day of sixteen hours, a workweek of seven days. . . . Being conscientious, she gets involved in Cubs, Brownies, PTA's, heart drives, church work, hauling children to music and dancing." But strangely enough, he remarked, neither the housewife's workload nor her fatigue seemed affected by how many children she had. Most of these patients had only one or two. "A woman with one child just worries four times as much about the one as the woman with four children, and it all comes out even," Dr. Lovshin said.

Some doctors, finding nothing organically wrong with these chronically tired mothers, told them, "It's all in your mind"; others gave them pills, vitamins, or injections for anemia, low blood pressure, low metabolism, or put them on diets (the average housewife is twelve to fifteen pounds overweight), deprived them of drinking (there are approximately a million known alcoholic housewives in America), or gave them tranquilizers. All such treatments were futile, Dr. Lovshin said, because these mothers were truly tired.[9]

Other doctors, finding that such mothers get as much or more sleep than they need, claimed the basic cause was not fatigue but boredom. This problem became so severe that the women's magazines treated it fulsomely—in the Pollyanna terms of the feminine mystique. In a spate of articles that appeared in the late 1950's, the "cures" suggested were usually of the more-praise-and-appreciation-from-husband variety, even though the doctors interviewed in these articles indicated clearly enough that the cause was in the "housewife-mother" role. But the magazines drew their usual conclusion: that is, and always will be woman's lot, and she just has to make the best of it. Thus, *Redbook* ("Why Young Mothers Are Always Tired," September, 1959) reports the findings of the Baruch study of chronic-fatigue patients:

> . . . Fatigue of any kind is a signal that something is wrong. Physical fatigue protects the organism from injury through too great activity of any part of the body. Nervous fatigue, on the other hand, is usually a warning of danger to the personality. This comes out very clearly in the woman patient who complains bitterly that she is "just a housewife," that she is wasting her talents and education on household drudgery and losing her attractiveness, her intelligence, and indeed her very identity as a person, explains Dr. Harley C. Sands, one of the co-heads of the Baruch project. In industry the most fatiguing jobs are those which only partially occupy the worker's attention, but at the same time prevent him from concentrating on anything else. Many young wives say that this mental gray-out is what bothers them most in caring for home and children. "After a while your mind becomes a blank," they say. "You can't concentrate on anything. It's like sleep-walking."

The magazine also quotes a Johns Hopkins psychiatrist to the effect that the major factor which produces chronic fatigue in patients was "monotony unpunctuated by any major triumph or disaster," noting that this "sums up the predicament of many a young mother." It even cites the results of the University of Michigan study in which of 524 women asked "what are some of the things which make you feel 'useful and important,'" almost none answered "housework"; among the women who had jobs, "the overwhelming majority, married and single, felt that the job was more satisfying than the housework." At this point the magazine interjects editorially: "This, of course, does not mean that a career is the alternative to fatigue for a young mother. If anything, the working mother may have more troubles than the housebound young matron." The magazine's happy conclusion: "Since the demands of housework and child-rearing are not very flexible, there is no complete solution to chronic-fatigue problems. Many women, however, can cut down fatigue if they stop asking too much of themselves. By trying to understand realistically what she can—and, more important, what she cannot—do, a woman may, in the long run, be a better wife and mother, albeit a tired one."

Another such article ("Is Boredom Bad for You?" *McCall's*, April 1957) asked, "Is the housewife's chronic fatigue really boredom?" and answers: "Yes. The chronic fatigue of many housewives is brought on by the repetition of their jobs, the monotony of the setting, the isolation and the lack of stimulation. The heavy household chores, it's been found, aren't enough to explain the fatigue. . . . The more your intelligence exceeds your job requirements, the greater your boredom. This is so to such an extent that experienced employers never hire above-average brains for routine jobs. . . . It is this boredom plus, of course, the day-to-day frustrations which makes the average housewife's job more emotionally fatiguing than her husband's." The cure: "honest enjoyment in some part of the job such as cooking or an incentive such as a party in the offing and, above all, male praise are good antidotes for domestic boredom."

For the women I interviewed, the problem seemed to be not that too much was asked of them, but too little. "A kind of torpor comes over me when I get home from the errands," one woman told me. "It's as if there's nothing I really have to do, though there's plenty to do around the house. So I keep a bottle of martinis in the refrigerator, and I pour myself some so I'll feel more like doing something. Or just to get through till Don comes home."

Other women eat, as they stretch out the housework, just to fill the time available. Obesity and alcoholism, as neuroses, have often been related to personality patterns that stem from childhood. But does this explain why so many American housewives around forty have the same dull and lifeless look; does it explain their lack of vitality, the deadly sameness of their lives, the furtive between-meal snacks, drinks, tranquilizers, sleeping pills? Even given the various personalities of these women, there must be something in the nature of their work, of the lives they lead, that drives them to these escapes.

This is no less true of the American housewife's work than it is of the work of most American men, on the assembly lines or in corporation offices: work that does not fully use a man's capacities leaves in him a vacant, empty need for escape—television, tranquilizers, alcohol, sex. But the husbands of the women I interviewed were often engaged in work that demanded ability, responsibility, and decision. I noticed that when these men were saddled with a domestic chore, they polished it off in much less time than it seemed to take their wives. But, of course, for them this was never the work that justified their lives. Whether they put more energy into it for this reason, just to get it over with, or whether housework did not have to take so much of their energy, they did it more quickly and sometimes even seemed to enjoy it more.

Social critics, during the togetherness era, often complained that men's careers suffered because of all this housework. But most husbands of the women I interviewed didn't seem to let housework interfere with their careers. When husbands did that bit of housework evenings and weekends because their wives had careers, or because their wives had made such a career of housework they could not get it done themselves, or because their wives were too passive, dependent, helpless to get it done, or even because the wives left housework for their husbands, for revenge—it did not expand.

But I noticed that housework did tend to expand to fill the time available with a few husbands who seemed to be using domestic chores as an excuse for not meeting the challenge of their own careers. "I wish he wouldn't insist on vacuuming the whole house on Tuesday evenings. It doesn't need it and he could be working on his book," the wife of a college professor told me. A capable social worker herself, she had managed all her professional life to work out ways of caring for her house and children without hiring servants. With her daughter's help, she did her own thorough housecleaning on Saturday; it didn't need vacuuming on Tuesday.

To do the work that you are capable of doing is the mark of maturity. It is not the demands of housework and children, or the absence of servants, that keep most American women from growing up to do the work of which they are capable. In an earlier era when servants were plentiful, most of the middle-class women who hired them did not use their freedom to take a more active part in society; they were confined by "woman's role" to leisure. In countries like Israel and Russia, where women are expected to be more than just housewives, servants scarcely exist, and yet home and children and love are evidently not neglected.

It is the mystique of feminine fulfillment, and the immaturity it breeds, that prevents women from doing the work of which they are capable. It is not strange that women who have lived for ten or twenty years within the mystique, or who adjusted to it so young that they have never experienced being on their own, should be afraid to face the test of real work in the world and cling to their identity as housewives—even if, thereby, they doom themselves to feeling "empty, useless, as if I do not exist." That housewifery can, must, expand to fill the time available when there is no other purpose in life seems fairly evident. After all, with no other purpose in her life, if the housework were done in an hour, and the children off to school, the bright, energetic housewife would find the emptiness of her days unbearable.

So a Scarsdale woman fired her maid, and even doing her own housework and the usual community work, could not use up all her energy. "We solved the problem," she said, speaking of herself and a friend who had tried to commit suicide. "We go bowling three mornings a week. Otherwise, we'd go out of our minds. At least, now we can sleep at night." "There's always some way you can get rid of it," I heard one woman saying to another over lunch at Schrafft's, debating somewhat listlessly what to do with the "afternoon off" from housewifery that their doctors had ordered. Diet foods and exercise salons have become a lucrative business in that futile battle to take off the fat that cannot be turned into human energy by the American housewife. It is slightly shocking to think that intelligent, educated American women are forced to "get rid of" their creative human energy by eating a chalky powder and wrestling with a machine. But no one is shocked to realize that getting rid of women's creative energy, rather than using it for some larger purpose in society, is the very essence of being a housewife.

To live according to the feminine mystique depends on a reversal of history, a devaluation of human progress. To get women back into the home again, not like the Nazis, by ordering them there, but by "propaganda with a view to restoring woman's sense of prestige and self-esteem as women, actual or potential mothers . . . women who live as women," meant that women had to resist their own "technological unemployment." The canning plants and bakeries did not close down, but even the mystique makers felt the need to defend themselves against the question, "are we, in suggesting that women might, of their own volition, recapture some of their functions around the home, such as cooking, preserving and decorating, trying to turn back the clock of progress?"[10]

Progress is not progress, they argued; in theory, the freeing of women from household drudgery liberates them for the cultivation of higher aims, but "as such aims are understood, many are called and few are chosen, among men no less than among women." Therefore, let all women recapture that work in the home which all women can do easily—and let society stage-manage it so that prestige for women "be shifted emphatically to those women recognized as serving society most fully as women."

For fifteen years and longer, there has been a propaganda campaign, as unanimous in this democratic nation as in the most efficient of dictatorships, to give women "prestige" as housewives. But can the sense of self in woman, which once rested on necessary work and achievement in the home, be re-created by housework that is no longer really necessary or really uses much ability—in a country and at a time when women can be free, finally, to move on to something more. It is wrong for a woman, for whatever reason, to spend her days in work that is not moving as the world around her is moving, in work that does not truly use her creative energy. Women themselves are discovering that though there is always "some way you can get rid of it," they can have no peace until they begin to *use* their abilities.

Surely there are many women in America who are happy at the moment as housewives, and some whose abilities are fully used in the housewife role. But happiness is not the same thing as the aliveness of being fully used. Nor is human intelligence, human ability, a static thing. Housework, no matter how it is expanded to fill the time available, can hardly use the abilities of a woman of average or normal human intelligence, much less the fifty per cent of the female population whose intelligence, in childhood, was above average.

Some decades ago, certain institutions concerned with the mentally retarded discovered that housework was peculiarly suited to the capacities of feeble-minded girls. In many towns, inmates of institutions for the mentally retarded were in great demand as houseworkers, and housework was much more difficult then than it is now.

Basic decisions as to the upbringing of children, interior decoration, menu-planning, budget, education, and recreation do involve intelligence, of course. But as it was put by one of the few home-and-family experts who saw the real absurdity of the feminine mystique, most housework, the part that still takes the most time, "can be capably handled by an eight-year-old child."

> The role of the housewife is, therefore, analogous to that of the president of a corporation who would not only determine policies and make over-all plans but also spend the major part of his time and energy in such activities as sweeping the plant and oiling machines. Industry, of course, is too thrifty of the capacities of its personnel to waste them in such fashion.
>
> The true satisfaction of "creating a home," the personal relationship with husband and children, the atmosphere of hospitality, serenity, culture, warmth, or security a woman gives to the home comes by way of her personality, not her broom, stove, or dishpan. For a woman to get a rewarding sense of total creation by way of the multiple monotonous chores that are her daily lot would be as irrational as for an assembly line worker to rejoice that he had created an automobile because he tightened a bolt. It is difficult to see how clearing up after meals three times a day and making out marketing lists (3 lemons, 2 packages of soap powder, a can of soup), get-

ting at the fuzz in the radiators with the hard rubber appliance of the vacuum cleaner, emptying wastebaskets and
washing bathroom floors day after day, week after week, year
after year, add up to a sum total of anything except minutiae
that laid end to end reach nowhere.[11]

A number of the more disagreeable sexual phenomena of this era
can be seen now as the inevitable result of that ludicrous consign-
ment of millions of women to spend their days at work an eight-year-
old could do. For no matter how much the "home-and-family career"
is rationalized to justify such appalling waste of able womanpower;
no matter how ingeniously the manipulators coin new scientific
sounding words, "lubrilator" and the like, to give the illusion that
dumping the clothes in the washing machines is an act akin to deci-
phering the genetic code; no matter how much housework is
expanded to fill the time available, it still presents little challenge
to the adult mind. Into this mental vacuum have flooded an endless
line of books on gourmet cooking, scientific treatises on child care,
and above all, advice on the techniques of "married love," sexual
intercourse. These, too, offer little challenge to the adult mind. The
results could almost have been predicted. To the great dismay of
men, their wives suddenly became "experts," know-it-alls, whose
unshakable superiority at home, a domain they both occupied, was
impossible to compete with, and very hard to live with. As Russell
Lynes* put it, wives began to treat their husbands as part-time
servants—or the latest new appliance.[12] With a snap course in home
economics or marriage and family under her belt and copies of Dr.
Spock and Dr. Van de Velde† side by side on the shelf; with all that
time, energy and intelligence directed on husband, children, and
house, the young American wife—easily, inevitably, disastrously—
began to dominate the family even more completely than her "mom."

11

The Sex-Seekers

I did not do a Kinsey study. But when I was on the trail of the problem that has no name, the suburban housewives I interviewed would
often give me an explicitly sexual answer to a question that was not

---

*   Russell Lynes (1910–1991), a New Yorker, was the managing editor of *Harper's* maga-
    zine between 1947 and 1967, and author of many books of popular cultural criticism.
†   Theodoor Hendrik van de Velde (1873–1937), Dutch gynecologist best known for the
    popular sex and marriage manual, *Ideal Marriage* (1926). Translated into English in
    1930, *Ideal Marriage* sold widely and became a standard advice book on sexuality in
    the middle of the twentieth century. Among other recommendations, van de Velde
    insisted that married women should experience equal pleasure with men in sex.

sexual at all. I would ask about their personal interests, ambitions, what they did, or would like to do, not necessarily as wives or mothers, but when they were not occupied with their husbands or their children or their housework. The question might even be what they were doing with their education. But some of these women simply assumed that I was asking about sex. Was the problem that has no name a sexual problem, after all? I might have thought so, except that when these women spoke of sex, there was a false note, a strange unreal quality about their words. They made mysterious allusions or broad hints; they were eager to be asked about sex; even if I did not ask, they often took pride in recounting the explicit details of some sexual adventure. They were not making them up; these adventures were real enough. But what made them sound unsexual, so unreal?

A thirty-eight-year-old mother of four told me sex was the only thing that made her "feel alive." But something had gone wrong; her husband did not give her that feeling anymore. They went through the motions, but he was not really interested. She was beginning to feel contemptuous of him in bed. "I need sex to feel alive, but I never really feel him," she said.

In a flat, matter-of-fact tone that added to the unreality, a thirty-year-old mother of five, calmly knitting a sweater, said she was thinking of going away, to Mexico perhaps, to live with a man with whom she was having an affair. She did not love him, but she thought if she gave herself to him "completely" she might find the feeling that she knew now was "the only important thing in life." What about the children? Vaguely, she guessed she would take them along—he wouldn't mind. What was the feeling she was looking for? She had found it at first with her husband, she supposed. At least she remembered that when she *married* him—she was eighteen—she had "felt so happy I wanted to die." But he did not "give himself completely" to her; he gave so much of himself to his work. So she found that feeling for a while, she thought, with her children. Shortly after she weaned her fifth baby from the breast, at three, she had her first affair. She discovered "it gave me that wonderful feeling again, to give my whole self to someone else." But that affair could not last; he had too many children, so did she. He said when they broke up, "You've given me such a feeling of identity." And she wondered, "what about my own identity?" So she went off by herself for a month that summer, leaving the children with her husband. "I was looking for something, I'm not sure what, but the only way I get that feeling is when I'm in love with someone." She had another affair, but that time the feeling did not appear. So with this new one, she wanted to go away completely. "Now that I know how to get that feeling," she said, knitting calmly, "I will simply keep trying until I find it again."

She did take off for Mexico with that shadowy, faceless man, taking her five children with her; but six months later, she was back, children and all. Evidently she did not find her phantom "feeling." And whatever happened, it was not real enough to affect her marriage, which went on as before. Just what was the feeling she expected to get from sex? And why was it, somehow, always out of reach? Does sex become unreal, a phantasy, when a person needs it to feel "alive," to feel "my own identity"?

In another suburb, I spoke to an attractive woman in her late thirties who had "cultural" interests, though they were rather vague and unfocused. She started paintings which she did not finish, raised money for concerts she did not listen to, said she had not "found her medium yet." I discovered that she engaged in a sort of sexual status-seeking which had the same vague, unfocused pretentions as her cultural dabblings, and in fact, was part of it. She boasted of the intellectual prowess, the professional distinction, of the man who, she hinted, wanted to sleep with her. "It makes you feel proud, like an achievement. You don't want to hide it. You want everyone to know, when it's a man of his stature," she told me. How much she really wanted to sleep with this man, professional stature or no, was another question. I later learned from her neighbors that she was a community joke. Everyone did indeed "know," but her sexual offerings were so impersonal and predictable that only a newcomer husband would take them seriously enough to respond.

But the evidently insatiable sexual need of a slightly younger mother of four in that same suburb was hardly a joke. Her sex-seeking, somehow never satisfied despite affair after affair, mixed with much indiscriminate "extramarital petting," as Kinsey would have put it, had real and disastrous consequences on at least two other marriages. These women and others like them, the suburban sex-seekers, lived literally within the narrow boundaries of the feminine mystique. They were intelligent, but strangely "incomplete." They had given up attempts to make housework or community work expand to fill the time available; they turned instead to sex. But still they were unfulfilled. Their husbands did not satisfy them, they said, extramarital affairs were no better. In terms of the feminine mystique, if a woman feels a sense of personal "emptiness," if she is unfulfilled, the cause must be sexual. But why, then, doesn't sex ever satisfy her?

Just as college girls used the sexual phantasy of married life to protect them from the conflicts and growing pains and work of a personal commitment to science, or art, or society, are these married women putting into their insatiable sexual search the aggressive energies which the feminine mystique forbids them to use for larger human purposes? Are they using sex or sexual phantasy to fill needs that are not sexual? Is that why their sex, even when it is real, seems like phantasy? Is that why, even when they experience orgasm, they feel "unfulfilled"? Are they driven to this never-satisfied sexual seeking because, in their marriages, they have not found the sexual fulfillment which the feminine mystique promises? Or is that feeling of personal identity, of fulfillment, they seek in sex something that sex alone cannot give?

Sex is the only frontier open to women who have always lived within the confines of the feminine mystique. In the past fifteen years, the sexual frontier has been forced to expand perhaps beyond the limits of possibility, to fill the time available, to fill the vacuum created by denial of larger goals and purposes for American women. The mounting sex-hunger of American women has been documented ad nauseam—by Kinsey, by the sociologists and novelists of suburbia, by the mass media, ads, television, movies, and women's magazines that pander to the voracious female appetite for sex phantasy. It is not an exaggeration to say that several generations of able American women have been successfully reduced to sex creatures, sex-seekers. But something has evidently gone wrong.

Instead of fulfilling the promise of infinite orgastic bliss, sex in the America of the feminine mystique is becoming a strangely joyless national compulsion, if not a contemptuous mockery. The sex-glutted novels become increasingly explicit and increasingly dull; the sex kick of the women's magazines has a sickly sadness; the endless flow of manuals describing new sex techniques hint at an endless lack of excitement. This sexual boredom is betrayed by the ever-growing size of the Hollywood starlet's breasts, by the sudden emergence of the male phallus as an advertising "gimmick." Sex has become depersonalized, seen in terms of these exaggerated symbols. But of all the strange sexual phenomena that have appeared in the era of the feminine mystique, the most ironic are these—the frustrated sexual hunger of American women has increased, and their conflicts over femininity have intensified, as they have reverted from independent activity to search for their sole fulfillment through their sexual role in the home. And as American women have turned their attention to the exclusive, explicit, and aggressive pursuit of sexual fulfillment, or the acting-out of sexual phantasy, the sexual disinterest of American men and their hostility toward women, have also increased.

I found evidence of these phenomena everywhere. There is, as I have said, an air of exaggerated unreality about sex today, whether it is pictured in the frankly lascivious pages of a popular novel or in the curious, almost asexual bodies of the women who pose for fashion photographs. According to Kinsey, there has been no increase in sexual "outlet" in recent decades. But in the past decade there has been an enormous increase in the American preoccupation with sex and sexual phantasy.[1]

In January, 1950, and again in January, 1960, a psychologist studied every reference to sex in American newspapers, magazines, television and radio programs, plays, popular songs, best-selling novels and nonfiction books. He found an enormous increase in explicit references to sexual desires and expressions (including "nudity, sex organs, scatology, 'obscenity,' lasciviousness and sexual intercourse"). These constituted over fifty per cent of the observed references to human sexuality, with "extramarital coitus" (including "fornication, adultery, sexual promiscuity, prostitution and venereal disease") in second place. In American media there were more than 2 ½ times as many references to sex in 1960 as in 1950, an increase from 509 to 1,341 "permissive" sex references in the 200 media studied. The so-called "men's magazines" not only reached new excesses in their preoccupation with specific female sex organs, but a rash of magazines blossomed frankly geared to homosexuality. The most striking new sexual phenomenon, however, was the increased and evidently "insatiable" lasciviousness of best-selling novels and periodical fiction, whose audience is primarily women.

Despite his professional approval of the "permissive" attitude to sex compared to its previous hypocritical denial, the psychologist was moved to speculate:

> Descriptions of sex organs . . . are so frequent in modern novels that one wonders whether they have become requisite for sending a work of fiction into the best-selling lists. Since the old, mild depictions of intercourse have seemingly lost their ability to excite, and even sex deviations have now become commonplace in modern fiction, the current logical step seems to be detailed descriptions of the sex organs themselves. It is difficult to imagine what the next step in salaciousness will be.[2]

From 1950 to 1960 the interest of men in the details of intercourse paled before the avidity of women—both as depicted in these media, and as its audience. Already by 1950 the salacious details of the sex act to be found in men's magazines were outnumbered by those in fiction best-sellers sold mainly to women.

During this same period, the women's magazines displayed an increased preoccupation with sex in a rather sickly disguise.[3] Such "health" features as "Making Marriage Work," "Can This Marriage Be Saved," "Tell Me, Doctor," described the most intimate sexual details in moralistic guise as "problems," and women read about them in much the same spirit as they had read the case histories in their psychology texts. Movies and the theater betrayed a growing preoccupation with diseased or perverted sex, each new film and each new play a little more sensational than the last in its attempt to shock or titillate.

At the same time one could see, almost in parallel step, human sexuality reduced to its narrowest physiological limits in the numberless sociological studies of sex in the suburbs and in the Kinsey investigations. The two Kinsey reports, in 1948 and 1953, treated human sexuality as a status-seeking game in which the goal was the greatest number of "outlets," orgasms achieved equally by masturbation, nocturnal emissions during dreams, intercourse with animals, and in various postures with the other sex, pre- extra- or post-marital. What the Kinsey investigators reported and the way they reported it, no less than the sex-glutted novels, magazines, plays, and novels, were all symptoms of the increasing depersonalization, immaturity, joylessness, and spurious senselessness of our sexual overpreoccupation.

That this spiral of sexual "lust, luridness and lasciviousness" was not exactly a sign of healthy affirmation of human intercourse became apparent as the image of males lusting after women gave way to the new image of women lusting after males. Exaggerated, perverted extremes of the sex situations seemed to be necessary to excite hero and audience alike. Perhaps the best example of this perverse reversal was the Italian movie *La Dolce Vita*,* which with all its artistic and symbolic pretentions, was a hit in America because of its much-advertised sexual titillation. Though a comment on Italian sex and society, this particular movie was in the chief characteristics of its sexual preoccupation devastatingly pertinent to the American scene.

As is increasingly the case in American novels, plays and movies, the sex-seekers were mainly the women, who were shown as mindless over- or under-dressed sex creatures (the Hollywood star) and hysterical parasites (the journalist's girl friend). In addition, there was the promiscuous rich girl who needed the perverse stimulation of the borrowed prostitute's bed, the aggressively sex-hungry women in the candlelit "hide and seek" castle orgy, and finally the divorcée who performed her writhing strip tease to a lonely, bored and indifferent audience.

All the men, in fact, were too bored or too busy to be bothered. The indifferent, passive hero drifted from one sex-seeking woman to another—a Don Juan,† an implied homosexual, drawn in phan-

---

*   Italian director Federico Fellini's (1920–1993) best-known and most popular film, released in 1960. It shows a journey through the upper class of Rome, a soulless, sterile, and degraded universe, through the eyes of a journalist played by film star Marcello Mastroianni.

†   Archetypical character that has appeared in literature since the seventeenth century. Based upon a legendary Spanish nobleman, a Don Juan is a modern, cultured man who brazenly seduces women and quickly moves between conquests. Some assume

tasy to the asexual little girl, just out of reach across the water. The exaggerated extremes of the sex situations end finally in a depersonalization that creates a bloated boredom—in hero and audience alike. (The very tedium of depersonalized sex may also explain the declining audience of Broadway theaters, Hollywood movies and the American novel.) Long before the final scenes of *La Dolce Vita*—when they all go out to stare at that huge bloated dead fish—the message of the movie was made quite clear: "the sweet life" is dull.

The image of the aggressive female sex-seeker also comes across in novels like *Peyton Place* and *The Chapman Report**—which consciously cater to the female hunger for sexual phantasy. Whether or not this fictional picture of the over-lusting female means that American women have become avid sex-seekers in real life, at least they have an insatiable appetite for books dealing with the sexual act—an appetite that, in fiction and real life, does not always seem to be shared by the men. This discrepancy between the sexual preoccupation of American men and women—in fiction or reality—may have a simple explanation. Suburban housewives, in particular, are more often sex-seekers than sex-finders, not only because of the problems posed by children coming home from school, cars parked overtime in driveways, and gossiping servants, but because, quite simply, men are not all that available. Men in general spend most of their hours in pursuits and passions that are not sexual, and have less need to make sex expand to fill the time available. So, from teen age to late middle age, American women are doomed to spend most of their lives in sexual phantasy. Even when the sexual affair—or the "extramarital petting" which Kinsey found on the increase—is real, it never is as real as the mystique has led the woman to believe.

As the male author of *The Exurbanites*† puts it:

> While her partner may be, and probably is, engaged in something quite casual to him, accompanied, of course, by verbal

---

that the relentless pursuit of women masks latent homosexuality and call this behavior the Don Juan syndrome.

* Novel (1960) by Irving Wallace that fictionalized the Kinsey report (see entry on Alfred Kinsey, p. 21) by focusing on the lives of a group of women who agree to talk about their sexual experiences with a researcher. The novel became a movie in 1962. *Peyton Place:* Novel (1956) written by New Hampshire housewife Grace Metalious. It was an exposé of sexuality, violence, class divisions, and hypocrisy in a small New England town, and it became a sensation. By 1965 *Peyton Place* had become one of the best-selling books in American history. It was adapted as a film in 1957 and as an ABC television show from 1964 to 1969.

† In 1955, magazine and TV editor A. C. Spectorsky wrote *The Exurbanites* to describe the new phenomenon of wealthy families choosing to live beyond the existing suburban subdivisions, in towns and villages surrounded by countryside. The book examined the effects of this phenomenon on a husband who continued to commute into the urban areas for work, as well as the families who remained and participated in exurban communities.

blandishments designed to persuade her of just the opposite, she is often quite genuinely caught up in what she conceives to be the real love of her life. Dismayed by the inadequacies of her marriage, confused and unhappy, angry and often humiliated by the behavior of her husband, she is psychologically prepared for the man who will skillfully and judiciously apply charm, wit and seductive behavior. . . . So, at the beach parties, at the Saturday night parties, on the long car rides from place to place—on all of which occasions the couples naturally split up—the first words can be spoken, the ground first prepared, the first fantasies conjured up, the first meaningful glance exchanged, the first desperate kiss snatched. And often, later, when the woman realizes that what was important to her was casual to him, she can cry and then she can dry her tears and look around again.[4]

But what happens when a woman bases her whole identity on her sexual role; when sex is necessary to make her "feel alive"? To state it quite simply, she puts impossible demands on her own body, her "femaleness," as well as on her husband and his "maleness." A marriage counselor told me that many of the young suburban wives he dealt with make "such heavy demands on love and marriage, but there is no excitement, no mystery, sometimes almost literally nothing happens."

It's something she has been trained and educated for, all this sexual information and preoccupation, this clearly laid out pattern that she must devote herself to becoming a wife and mother. There is no wonder of two strangers, man and woman, separate beings, finding each other. It's all laid out ahead of time, a script that's being followed without the struggle, the beauty, the mysterious awe of life. And so she says to him, do something, make me feel something, but there is no power within herself to evoke this.

A psychiatrist states that he has often seen sex "die a slow, withering death" when women, or men, use the family "to make up in closeness and affection for failure to achieve goals and satisfactions in the wider community."[5] Sometimes, he told me, "there is so little real life that finally even the sex deteriorates, and gradually dies, and months go by without any desire, though they are young people." The sexual act "tends to become mechanized and depersonalized, a physical release that leaves the partners even lonelier after the act than before. The expression of tender sentiment shrivels. Sex becomes the arena for the struggle for dominance and control. Or it becomes a drab, hollow routine, carried out on schedule."

Even though they find no satisfaction in sex, these women continue their endless search. For the woman who lives according to the feminine mystique, there is no road to achievement, or status, or identity, except the sexual one: the achievement of sexual conquest, status as a desirable sex object, identity as a sexually successful wife and mother. And yet because sex does not really satisfy these needs, she seeks to buttress her nothingness with things, until often even sex itself, and the husband and the children on whom the sexual identity rests, become possessions, things. A woman who is herself only a sexual object, lives finally in a world of objects, unable to touch in others the individual identity she lacks herself.

Is it the need for some kind of identity or achievement that drives suburban housewives to offer themselves so eagerly to strangers and neighbors—and that makes husbands "furniture" in their own homes? In a recent novel about suburban adultery, the male author says through a butcher who takes advantage of the lonely housewives in the neighborhood:

> "Do you know what America is? It's a big, soapy dishpan of boredom . . . and no husband can understand that soapy dishpan. And a woman can't explain it to another woman because they've all got their hands in that same soapy boredom. So all a man has to be is understanding. Yes, baby, I know, I know, you've got a miserable life, here're some flowers, here's some perfume, here's 'I love you,' take off your pants. . . . You, me, we're furniture in our own homes. But if we go next door, ahh! Next door, we're heroes! They're all looking for romance because they've learned it from books and movies. And what can be more romantic than a man who's willing to risk your husband's shotgun to have you. . . . And the only exciting thing about this guy is that he is a stranger . . . she doesn't own him. She tells herself she's in love, and she's willing to risk her home, her happiness, her pride, everything, just to be with this stranger who fills her once a week. . . . Anyplace you've got a housewife, you've also got a potential mistress for a stranger."[6]

Kinsey, from his interviews of 5,940 women, found that American wives, especially of the middle class, after ten or fifteen years of marriage, reported greater sexual desire than their husbands seemed to satisfy. One out of four, by the age of forty, had engaged in some extramarital activity—usually quite sporadic. Some seemed insatiably capable of "multiple orgasms." A growing number engaged in the "extramarital petting" more characteristic of adolescence. Kinsey also found that the sexual desire of American husbands, especially in the middle-class educated groups, seemed to wane as their wives' increased.[7]

But even more disturbing than the signs of increased sexual hunger, unfulfilled, among American housewives in this era of the feminine mystique are the signs of increased conflict over their own femaleness. There is evidence that the signs of feminine sexual conflict, often referred to by the euphemism of "female troubles," occur earlier than ever, and in intensified form, in this era when women have sought to fulfill themselves so early and exclusively in sexual terms.

The chief of the gynecological service of a famous hospital told me that he sees with increasing frequency in young mothers the same impairment of the ovarian cycle—vaginal discharge, delayed periods, irregularities in menstrual flow and duration of flow, sleeplessness, fatigue syndrome, physical disability—that he used to see only in women during menopause. He said:

> The question is whether these young mothers will be pathologically blown apart when they lose their reproductive function. I see plenty of women with these menopausal difficulties which are activated, I'm sure, by the emptiness of their lives. And by simply having spent the last 28 years hanging on to the last child until there's nothing left to hang on to. In contrast, women who've had children, sexual relations but who somehow have much more whole-hearted personalities, without continually having to rationalize themselves as female by having one more baby and holding on to it, have very few hot flashes, insomnia, nervousness, jitteriness.
>
> The ones with female troubles are the ones who have denied their femininity, or are pathologically female. But we see these symptoms now in more and more young wives, in their 20's, young women who are fatally invested in their children, who have not developed resources, other than their children— coming in with the same impairments of the ovarian cycle, menstrual difficulties, characteristic of the menopause. A woman 22 years old, who's had three children, with symptoms more frequently seen with menopause . . . I say to her, "the only trouble with you is that you've had too many babies too fast" and reserve to myself the opinion "your personality has not developed far enough."

At this same hospital, studies have been made of women recovering from hysterectomy, women with menstrual complaints, and women with difficult pregnancies. The ones who suffered the most pain, nausea, vomiting, physical and emotional distress, depression, apathy, anxiety, were women "whose lives revolved almost exclusively around the reproductive function and its gratification in motherhood. A prototype of this attitude was expressed by one woman who said, 'In order to be a woman, I have to be able to have children.'"[8] The ones who suffered least had "well-integrated egos," had resources of the intellect and were directed outward in their interests, even in the hospital, rather than preoccupied with themselves and their sufferings.

Obstetricians have seen this too. One told me:

> It's a funny thing. The women who have the backaches, the bleeding, the difficult pregnancy and delivery, are the ones who think their whole purpose in life is to have babies. Women who have other interests than just being reproductive machines have less trouble having babies. Don't ask me to explain it. I'm no psychiatrist. But we've all noticed it.

Another gynecologist spoke of many patients in this era of "femaleness-fulfilled" to whom neither having babies nor sexual intercourse brought "fulfillment." They were, in his words:

> Women who feel very unsure about their sex and need to have children again and again to prove that they are feminine; women who have the fourth or fifth child because they can't think of anything else to do; women who are dominant and this is something else to dominate; and then I have hundreds of patients who are college girls who don't know what to do with themselves, their mothers bring them in for diaphragms. Because they are immature, going to bed means nothing—it is like taking medicine, no orgasm, nothing. For them getting married is an evasion.

The high incidence of cramps with menstruation, nausea and vomiting during pregnancy, depression with childbirth, and severe physiological and psychological distress at menopause have come to be accepted as a "normal" part of feminine biology.[9] Are these stigmata that mark the stages of the female sexual cycle—menstruation, pregnancy, menopause—part of the fixed and eternal nature of women as they are popularly assumed to be, or are they somehow related to that unnecessary choice between "femininity" and human growth, sex and self? When a woman is a "sex creature," does she see unconsciously in each step of her feminine sexual cycle a giving up, a kind of death, of her very reason for existence? These women who crowd the clinics are personifications of the feminine mystique. The lack of orgasm, the increasing "female troubles," the promiscuous and insatiable sex-seeking, the depression at the moment of becoming a mother, the strange eagerness of women to have their female sex organs removed by hysterectomies without medical cause—all these betray the big lie of the mystique. Like the self-fulfilling prophecy of death in Samarra,* the feminine mystique, with its outcry against loss of femininity, is making it increasingly difficult for women to affirm their femininity, and for men to be truly masculine, and for either to enjoy human sexual love.

The air of unreality that hovered over my interviews with suburban housewife sex-seekers, the unreality that pervades the sex-preoccupied novels, plays, and movies—as it pervades the ritualistic sex talk at suburban parties—I suddenly saw for what it was, on an island ostensibly far removed from suburbia, where sex-seeking is omnipresent, in pure phantasy. During the week, this island is an exaggeration of a suburb, for it is utterly removed from outside stimuli, from the world of work and politics; the men do not even come home at night. The women who were spending the summer there were extremely attractive young housewives. They had married early; they lived through their husbands and children; they had no interest in the world outside the home. Here on this island, unlike the suburb, these women had no way to make committees or housework expand to fill the time available. But they found a new diversion that killed two birds with one stone, a diversion that gave them a spurious sense of sexual status, but relieved them of the frightening necessity to prove it. On this island, there was a colony of "boys" right out of the world of Tennessee Williams. During the week when their husbands were working in the city, the young housewives had "wild" orgies, all-night parties, with these sexless boys. In a sort of humorous puzzlement, a husband who took the boat over unexpectedly one midweek to console his bored and lonely wife, speculated: "Why do they do it? Maybe it has something to do with this place being a matriarchy."

Perhaps, too, it had something to do with boredom—there just was not anything else to do. But it looked like sex; that's what made it so exciting, even though there was, of course, no sexual contact. Perhaps, these housewives and their boyfriends recognized themselves in each other. For like the call girl in Truman Capote's *Breakfast at Tiffany's*† who spends the sexless night with the passive homosexual, they were equally childlike in their retreat from life. And in each other, they sought the same nonsexual reassurance.

---

*   In the play *Sheppey* (1933) by Somerset Maugham, a man flees death by traveling from Baghdad to Samarra where death had intended to take him all along. The moral of this story is that trying to escape one's fate only brings you closer to it.

†   Truman Capote (1924–1984), writer known for his celebrity status as well as for his literary talent. One of his most celebrated works was the 1958 novella *Breakfast at Tiffany's*, about Holly Golightly, a New York society girl who dates wealthy men in the hope of finding a husband. In interviews, Capote explicitly denied that her character was a prostitute.

But in the suburbs where most hours of the day there are virtually no men at all—to give even the appearance of sex—women
who have no identity other than sex creatures must ultimately seek
their reassurance through the possession of "things." One suddenly
sees why manipulators cater to sexual hunger in their attempt to
sell products which are not even remotely sexual. As long as woman's needs for achievement and identity can be channeled into this
search for sexual status, she is easy prey for any product which presumably promises her that status—a status that cannot be achieved
by effort or achievement of her own. And since that endless search
for status as a desirable sexual object is seldom satisfied in reality
for most American housewives (who at best can only try to *look* like
Elizabeth Taylor), it is very easily translated into a search for status
through the possession of objects.

Thus women are aggressors in suburban status-seeking and their
search has the same falseness and unreality as their sex-seeking.
Status, after all, is what men seek and acquire through their work
in society. A woman's work—housework—cannot give her status; it
has the lowliest status of almost any work in society. A woman must
acquire her status vicariously through her husband's work. The
husband himself, and even the children, become symbols of status,
for when a woman defines herself as a housewife, the house and
the things in it are, in a sense, her identity; she needs these external trappings to buttress her emptiness of self, to make her feel like
somebody. She becomes a parasite, not only because the things she
needs for status come ultimately from her husband's work, but
because she must dominate, own him, for the lack of an identity of
her own. If her husband is unable to provide the things she needs
for status, he becomes an object of contempt, just as she is contemptuous of him if he cannot fill her sexual needs. Her very dissatisfaction with herself she feels as dissatisfaction with her husband
and their sexual relations. As a psychiatrist put it: "She demands too
much satisfaction from her marital relations. Her husband resents it
and becomes unable to function sexually with her at all."

Could this be the reason for the rising tide of resentment among
the new young husbands at the girls whose only ambition was to
be their wives? The old hostility against domineering "moms" and
aggressive career girls may, in the long run, pale before the new
male hostility for the girls whose active pursuit of the "home career"
has resulted in a new kind of domination and aggression. To be the
tool, the sex-instrument, the "man around the house," is evidently
no dream-come-true for a man.

In March, 1962, a reporter noted in *Redbook* a new phenomenon
on the suburban scene: that "young fathers feel trapped":

Many husbands feel that their wives, firmly quoting authorities on home management, child rearing and married love, have set up a tightly scheduled, narrowly conceived scheme of family living that leaves little room for a husband's authority or point of view. (A husband said "Since I've been married, I feel I've lost all my guts. I don't feel like a man anymore. I'm still young, yet I don't get much out of life. I don't want advice, but I sometimes feel like something is bursting loose inside.") The husbands named their wives as their chief source of frustration, superseding children, employers, finances, relatives, community and friends. . . . The young father is no longer free to make his own mistakes or to swing his own weight in a family crisis. His wife, having just read Chapter VII, knows exactly what should be done.

The article goes on to quote a social worker:

The modern wife's insistence on achieving sexual satisfaction for herself may pose a major problem for her husband. A husband can be teased, flattered and cajoled into performing as an expert lover. But if his wife scorns and upbraids him as though he had proved unable to carry a trunk up the attic stairs, she is in for trouble. . . . It's alarming to note that five years after marriage, a sizable number of American husbands have committed adultery and a much larger proportion are seriously tempted to do so. Often, infidelity is less a search for pleasure than a means of self-assertion.

Four years ago, I interviewed a number of wives on a certain pseudo-rural road in a fashionable suburb. They had everything they wanted: lovely houses, a number of children, attentive husbands. Today, on that same road, there are a growing spate of dream-houses in which, for various and sometimes unaccountable reasons, the wives now live alone with the children, while the husbands—doctors, lawyers, account chiefs—have moved to the city. Divorce, in America, according to the sociologists, is in almost every instance sought by the husband, even if the wife ostensibly gets it.[10] There are, of course, many reasons for divorce, but chief among them seems to be the growing aversion and hostility that men have for the feminine millstones hanging around their necks, a hostility that is not always directed at their wives, but at their mothers, the women they work with—in fact, women in general.

According to Kinsey, the majority of the American middle-class males' sexual outlets are not in relations with their wives after the fifteenth year of marriage; at fifty-five, one out of two American men is engaging in extramarital sex.[11] This male sex-seeking—the office romance, the casual or intense affair, even the depersonalized sex-for-sex's-sake satirized in the recent movie *The Apartment**—is, as often as not, motivated simply by the need to escape from the devouring wife. Sometimes the man seeks the human relationship that got lost when he became merely an appendage to his wife's aggressive "home career." Sometimes his aversion to his wife finally makes him seek in sex an object totally divorced from any human relationship. Sometimes, in phantasy more often than in fact, he seeks a girl-child, a Lolita,† as sexual object—to escape that grownup woman who is devoting all her aggressive energies, as well as her sexual energies, to living through him. There is no doubt that male outrage against women—and inevitably, against sex—has increased enormously in the era of the feminine mystique.[12] As a man wrote in a letter to the *Village Voice*, New York's Greenwich Village‡ newspaper, in February, 1962: "It isn't a problem anymore of whether White is too good to marry Black, or vice versa, but whether women are good enough to marry men, since women are on the way out."

The public symbol of this male hostility is the retreat of American playwrights and novelists from the problems of the world to an obsession with images of the predatory female, the passive martyred male hero (in homo- or heterosexual clothes), the promiscuous childlike heroine, and the physical details of arrested sexual development. It is a special world, but not so special that millions of men and women, boys and girls cannot identify with it. Tennessee Williams' "Suddenly Last Summer" is a flagrant example of this world.

The aging homosexual hero from an old Southern family, haunted by the monstrous birds that devour baby sea turtles, has wasted his life in pursuit of his lost golden youth. He himself has been "eaten" by his seductively feminine mother, just as, in the end, he is literally eaten by a band of young boys. It is significant that the hero of this play never appears; he is without a face, without a body. The only undeniably "real" character is the man-eating mother. She appears again and again in Williams' plays and in the plays and novels of his contemporaries, along with the homosexual sons, the nymphomaniacal daughters, and the revengeful male Don Juans. All of these

---

* The Academy Award–winning film, *The Apartment* (1960), directed by Billy Wilder, satirized contemporary office bureaucracy and attitudes towards sexuality with its portrait of Bud Baxter, a clerk at an insurance company who tries to rise professionally by loaning his apartment to his bosses for their sexual trysts.

† Title character of Vladimir Nabokov's controversial novel *Lolita* published in the United States in 1958. The book tells the story of a man's obsession and love affair with a twelve-year-old girl, whom he calls Lolita.

‡ *The Village Voice* was founded in 1955 in Greenwich Village, long known as the bohemian neighborhood of New York City. The *Voice* was intended to be a weekly newspaper for the artists, writers, hipsters, and other outsiders who inhabited the neighborhood. By the early 1960s, the newspaper had become recognized nationally as a voice of alternative culture.

plays are an agonized shout of obsessed love-hate against women. Significantly, a great many of these plays are written by Southern writers, where the "femininity" which the mystique enshrines remains most intact.

This male outrage is the result, surely, of an implacable hatred for the parasitic women who keep their husbands and sons from growing up, who keep them immersed at that sickly level of sexual phantasy. For the fact is that men, too, are now being drawn away from the large world of reality into the stunted world of sexual phantasy in which their daughters, wives, mothers have been forced to look for "fulfillment." And, for men too, sex itself is taking on the unreal character of phantasy—depersonalized, dissatisfying, and finally inhuman.

Is there, after all, a link between what is happening to the women in America and increasingly overt male homosexuality?* According to the feminine mystique, the "masculinization" of American women which was caused by emancipation, education, equal rights, careers, is producing a breed of increasingly "feminine" men. But is this the real explanation? As a matter of fact, the Kinsey figures showed no increase in homosexuality in the generations which saw the emancipation of women. The Kinsey report revealed in 1948 that 37 per cent of American men had had at least some homosexual experience, that 13 per cent were predominantly homosexual (for at least three years between 16 and 55), and 4 per cent exclusively homosexual—some 2,000,000 men. But there was "no evidence that the homosexual group involved more males or fewer males today than it did among older generations."[13]

Whether or not there has been an increase in homosexuality in America, there has certainly been in recent years an increase in its overt manifestations.[14] I do not think that this is unrelated to the national embrace of the feminine mystique. For the feminine mystique has glorified and perpetuated in the name of femininity a passive, childlike immaturity, which is passed on from mothers to sons, as well as to daughters. Male homosexuals—and the male Don Juans, whose compulsion to test their potency is often caused by

---

*   Over the next few pages, Friedan represents homosexuality as a pathology and homosexuals as neurotic and psychotic, hypersexed individuals whose appearance in the cultural world was related to the values of the feminine mystique and also signaled a problem in U.S. society. This negative portrait of homosexuality was typical of the era. The psychiatric profession considered homosexuality a mental illness until the early 1970s, and in the 1950s, the federal government expelled homosexuals from civil and military service because their so-called passivity and weakness allegedly made them security threats, and even potential communists (see entries on the Cold War, p. 11, and McCarthy, p. 103). Many feminists have criticized Friedan's attack on homosexuals in *The Feminine Mystique* and used it as evidence of homophobia that continued to pervade her feminist activism. See pp. 391–95 for Friedan's relationship with the politics of sexual liberation in the 1970s.

unconscious homosexuality—are, no less than the female sex-seekers, Peter Pans, forever childlike, afraid of age, grasping at youth in their continual search for reassurance in some sexual magic.

The role of the mother in homosexuality was pinpointed by Freud and the psychoanalysts. But the mother whose son becomes homosexual is usually not the "emancipated" woman who competes with men in the world, but the very paradigm of the feminine mystique—a woman who lives through her son, whose femininity is used in virtual seduction of her son, who attaches her son to her with such dependence that he can never mature to love a woman, nor can he, often, cope as an adult with life on his own. The love of men masks his forbidden excessive love for his mother; his hatred and revulsion for all women is a reaction to the one woman who kept him from becoming a man. The conditions of this excessive mother-son love are complex. Freud wrote:

> In all the cases examined we have ascertained that the later inverts go through in their childhood a phase of very intense but short-lived fixation on the woman (usually the mother) and after overcoming it, they identify themselves with the woman and take themselves as the sexual object; that is, proceeding on a narcissistic basis, they look for young men resembling themselves in persons whom they wish to love as their mother loved them.[15]

Extrapolating from Freud's insights, one could say that such an excess of love-hate is almost implicit in the relationship of mother and son—when her exclusive role as wife and mother, her relegation to the home, force her to live through her son. Male homosexuality was and is far more common than female homosexuality. The father is not as often tempted or forced by society to live through or seduce his daughter. Not many men become overt homosexuals, but a great many have suppressed enough of this love-hate to feel not only a deep repugnance for homosexuality, but a general and sublimated revulsion for women.

Today, when not only career, but any serious commitment outside the home, are out of bounds for truly "feminine" housewife-mothers, the kind of mother-son devotion which can produce latent or overt homosexuality has plenty of room to expand to fill the time available. The boy smothered by such parasitical mother-love is kept from growing up, not only sexually, but in all ways. Homosexuals often lack the maturity to finish school and make sustained professional commitments. (Kinsey found homosexuality most common among men who do not go beyond high school, and least common among college graduates.)[16] The shallow unreality, immaturity, promiscuity, lack of lasting human satisfaction that characterize the homosexual's sex life usually characterize all his life and interests. This lack of personal commitment in work, in education, in life outside of sex, is hauntingly "feminine." Like the daughters of the feminine mystique, the sons spend most of their lives in sexual phantasy; the sad "gay" homosexuals may well feel an affinity with the young housewife sex-seekers.

But the homosexuality that is spreading like a murky smog over the American scene is no less ominous than the restless, immature sex-seeking of the young women who are the aggressors in the early marriages that have become the rule rather than the exception. Nor is it any less frightening than the passivity of the young males who acquiesce to early marriage rather than face the world alone. These victims of the feminine mystique start their search for the solace of sex at an earlier and earlier age. In recent years, I have interviewed a number of sexually promiscuous girls from comfortable suburban families, including a number—and this number is growing[17]—of girls who marry in their early teens because they are pregnant. Talking to these girls, and to the professional workers who are trying to help them, one quickly sees that sex, for them, is not sex at all. They have not even begun to experience a sexual response, much less "fulfillment." They use sex—pseudo-sex—to erase their lack of identity; it seldom matters who the boy is; the girl almost literally does not "see" him when she has as yet no sense of herself. Nor will she ever have a sense of herself if she uses the easy rationalizations of the feminine mystique to evade in sex-seeking the efforts that lead to identity.

Early sex, early marriage, has always been a characteristic of underdeveloped civilizations and, in America, of rural and city slums. One of the most striking of Kinsey's findings, however, was that a delay in sexual activity was less a characteristic of socioeconomic origin than of the ultimate destination—as measured, for instance, by education. A boy from a slum background, who put himself through college and became a scientist or judge, showed the same postponement of sexual activity in adolescence as others who later became scientists or judges, not as others from the same slum background. Boys from the right side of the tracks, however, who did not finish college or become scientists or judges showed more of that earlier sexual activity that was characteristic of the slum.[18] Whatever this indicates about the relationship between sex and the intellect, a certain postponement of sexual activity seemed to accompany the growth in mental activity required and resulting from higher education, and the achievement of the professions of highest value to society.

Among the girls in the Kinsey survey, there even seemed to be a relationship between the ultimate level of mental or intellectual growth as measured by education, and sexual satisfaction. Girls who married in their teens—who, in Kinsey's cases, usually stopped education with high school—started having sexual intercourse five or six years earlier than girls who continued their education through college or into professional training. This earlier sexual activity did not, however, usually lead to orgasm; these girls were still experiencing less sexual fulfillment, in terms of orgasm, five, ten and fifteen years after marriage than those who had continued their education.[19] As with the promiscuous girls in the suburbs, early sexual preoccupation seemed to indicate a weak core of self which even marriage did not strengthen.

Is this the real reason for the kind of compulsive sex-seeking seen today in promiscuity, early and late, heterosexual or homosexual? Is it a coincidence that the many phenomena of depersonalized sex—sex without self, sex for lack of self—are becoming so rampant in the era when American women are told to live by sex alone? Is it a coincidence that their sons and daughters have selves so weak that they resort at an increasingly early age to a dehumanized, faceless sex-seeking? Psychiatrists have explained that the key problem in promiscuity is usually "low self-esteem," which often seems to stem from an excessive mother-child attachment; the type of sex-seeking is relatively irrelevant. As Clara Thompson,* speaking of homosexuality, says:

> Overt homosexuality may express fear of the opposite sex, fear of adult responsibility . . . it may represent a flight from reality into absorption in bodily stimulation very similar to the auto-erotic activities of the schizophrenic, or it may be a symptom of destructiveness of oneself or others. . . . People who have a low self-esteem . . . have a tendency to cling to their own sex because it is less frightening. . . . However, the above considerations do not invariably produce homosexuality, for the fear of disapproval from the culture and the need to conform often drive these very people into marriage. The fact that one is married by no means proves that one is a mature person. . . . The mother-child attachment is sometimes found to be the important part of the picture. . . . Promiscuity is possibly more frequent among homosexuals than heterosexuals, but its significance in the personality structure is very similar in the two. In both, the chief interest is in genitals and body stimulation. The person chosen to share the experience is not important. The sexual activity is compulsive and is the sole interest.[20]

---

* Clara Thompson (1893–1958), psychoanalyst and executive director of the William Alanson White Institute of Psychiatry. She worked with Erich Fromm (see entry on Erich Fromm, p. 232) and Harry Stack Sullivan to develop a school of psychoanalysis divergent from orthodox Freudianism, based on the importance of interpersonal relationships.

Compulsive sexual activity, homosexual or heterosexual, usually veils a lack of potency in other spheres of life. Contrary to the feminine mystique, sexual satisfaction is not necessarily a mark of fulfillment, in woman or man. According to Erich Fromm:*

> Often psychoanalysts see patients whose ability to love and so be close to others is damaged and yet who function very well sexually and indeed make sexual satisfaction a substitute for love because their sexual potency is their only power in which they have confidence. Their inability to be productive in all other spheres of life and the resulting unhappiness is counterbalanced and veiled by their sexual activities.[21]

There is a similar undertone to the sex-seeking in colleges, even though the potential ability to be "productive in all other spheres of life" is high. A psychiatrist consultant for Harvard-Radcliffe students recently pointed out that college girls often seek "security" in these intense sexual relationships because of their own feelings of inadequacy, when, probably for the first time in their lives, they have to work hard, face real competition, think actively instead of passively—which is "not only a strange experience, but almost akin to physical pain."

> The significant facts are the lowered self-esteem and the diminution in zest, energy, and capacity to function in a creative way. The depression seems to be a kind of declaration of dependence, of helplessness, and a muted cry for help as well. And it occurs at some time and in varying intensity in practically every girl during her career at college.[22]

All this may simply represent "the first response of a sensitive, naive adolescent to a new, frighteningly complicated and sophisticated environment," the psychiatrist said. But if the adolescent is a girl, she evidently should not, like the boy, be expected to face the challenge, master the painful work, meet the competition. The psychiatrist considers it "normal" that the girl seeks her "security" in "love," even though the boy himself may be "strikingly immature, adolescent, and dependent"—"a slender reed, at least from the point of view of the girl's needs." The feminine mystique hides the fact that this early sex-seeking, harmless enough for the boy or girl who looks for no more than it offers, cannot give these young women that

---

* Erich Fromm (1900–1980), psychoanalyst who became a public intellectual known for his book, *Escape from Freedom* (1941), which paradoxically attributed the rise of fascism to the freedoms produced by individualism and capitalism. Fromm was attracted to Marxist values, and his efforts to unite Marx's ideas with those of Freud led him to rebel from orthodox circles of psychoanalysis. In his prolific writing, as well as in his political activism, Fromm criticized contemporary capitalism and called for humanistic and democratic socialist alternatives.

"clearer image of themselves"—the self-esteem they need and "the vigor to lead satisfying and creative lives." But the mystique does not always hide from the boy the fact that the girl's dependence on him is not really sexual, and that it may stifle his growth. Hence the boy's hostility—even as he helplessly succumbs to the sexual invitation.

A Radcliffe student recently wrote a sensitive account of a boy's growing bitterness at the girl who cannot study without him—a bitterness not even stilled by the sex with which they nightly evade study together.

> She was bending down the corner of a page and he wanted to tell her to stop; the little mechanical action irritated him out of all proportion, and he wondered if he was so tense because they hadn't made love for four days . . . I bet she needs it now, he thought, that's why she's so quivery, close to tears, and maybe that's why I loused up the exam. But he knew it was not an excuse; he felt his resentment heating as he wondered why he had not really reviewed. . . . The clock would never let him forget the amount of time he was wasting . . . he slammed his books closed and began to stack them together. Eleanor looked up and he saw the terror in her eyes . . .
>
> "Look, I'm going to walk you back now," he said . . . "I've got to get something done tonight" . . . He remembered that he had a long walk back, but as he bent hurriedly to kiss her she slipped her arms around him and he had to pull back hard in order to get away. She let go at last, and no longer smiling, she whispered: "Hal, don't go." He hesitated. "Please, don't go, please . . ." She strained up to kiss him and when she opened her mouth he felt tricked, for if he put his tongue between her lips, he would not be able to leave. He kissed her, beginning half-consciously to forget that he should go . . . he pulled her against him, hearing her moan with pain and excitation. Then he drew back and said, his voice already labored: "Isn't there anywhere we can go?" . . . She was looking around eagerly and hopefully and he wondered again, how much of her desire was passion and how much grasping: girls used sex to get a hold on you, he knew—it was so easy for them to pretend to be excited.[23]

These are, of course, the first of the children who grew up under the feminine mystique, these youngsters who use sex as such a suspiciously easy solace when they face the first hard hurdles in the race. Why is it so difficult for these youngsters to endure discomfort, to make an effort, to postpone present pleasure for future long-term goals? Sex and early marriage are the easiest way out; playing house at nineteen evades the responsibility of growing up alone. And even if a father tried to get his son to be "masculine," to be independent, active, strong, both mother and father encouraged their daughter in that passive, weak, grasping dependence known as "femininity," expecting her, of course, to find "security" in a boy, never expecting her to live her own life.

And so the circle tightens. Sex without self, enshrined by the feminine mystique, casts an ever-darkening shadow over man's image of woman and woman's image of herself. It becomes harder for both son and daughter to escape, to find themselves in the world, to love another in human intercourse. The million married before the age of nineteen, in earlier and earlier travesty of sex-seeking, betray an increased immaturity, emotional dependence, and passivity on the part of the newest victims of the feminine mystique. The shadow of sex without self may be dispelled momentarily in a sunny suburban dream house. But what will these childlike mothers and immature fathers do to their children, in that phantasy paradise where the pursuit of pleasure and things hides the loosening links to complex modern reality? What kind of sons and daughters are raised by girls who became mothers before they have ever faced that reality, or sever their links to it by becoming mothers?

There are frightening implications for the future of our nation in the parasitical softening that is being passed on to the new generation of children as a result of our stubborn embrace of the feminine mystique. The tragedy of children acting out the sexual phantasies of their housewife-mothers is only one sign of the progressive dehumanization that is taking place. And in this "acting out" by the children, the feminine mystique can finally be seen in all its sick and dangerous obsolescence.

12

Progressive Dehumanization: The Comfortable Concentration Camp

The voices now deploring American women's retreat to home reassure us that the pendulum has begun to swing in the opposite direction. But has it? There are already signs that the daughters of the able and energetic women who went back home to live in the housewife image find it more difficult than their mothers to move forward in the world. Over the past fifteen years a subtle and devastating change seems to have taken place in the character of American children. Evidence of something similar to the housewife's problem that has no name in a more pathological form has been seen in her sons and daughters by many clinicians, analysts, and social scientists. They have noted, with increasing concern, a new and frightening passivity, softness, boredom in American children. The danger sign is not the competitiveness engendered by the Little League or the race to get into college, but a kind of infantilism that makes the children of the housewife-mothers incapable of the effort, the endurance of pain and frustration, the discipline needed to compete on the baseball field, or get into college. There is also a new vacant sleepwalking, playing-a-part quality of youngsters who do what they are supposed to do, what the other kids do, but do not seem to feel alive or real in doing it.

In an eastern suburb in 1960, I heard a high-school sophomore stop a psychiatrist who had just given an assembly talk and ask him for "the name of that pill that you can take to hypnotize yourself so you'll wake up knowing everything you need for the test without studying." That same winter two college girls on a train to New York during the middle of midyear exam week told me they were going to some parties to "clear their minds" instead of studying for the exams. "Psychology has proved that when you're really motivated, you learn instantly," one explained. "If the professor can't make it interesting enough so that you know it without working, that's his fault, not yours." A bright boy who had dropped out of college told me it was a waste of his time; "intuition" was what counted, and they didn't teach that at college. He worked a few weeks at a gas station, a month at a bookstore. Then he stopped work and spent his time literally doing nothing—getting up, eating, going to bed, not even reading.

I saw this same vacant sleepwalking quality in a thirteen-year-old girl I interviewed in a Westchester suburb in an investigation of teenage sexual promiscuity. She was barely passing in her school work even though she was intelligent; she "couldn't apply herself," as the guidance counselor put it. She seemed always bored, not interested, off in a daze. She also seemed not quite awake, like a puppet with someone else pulling the strings, when every afternoon she got into a car with a group of older boys who had all "dropped out" of school in their search for "kicks."

The sense that these new kids are, for some reason, not growing up "real" has been seen by many observers. A Texas educator, who was troubled because college boys were not really interested in the courses they were taking as an automatic passport to the right job, discovered they also were not really interested in anything they did outside of school either. Mostly, they just "killed time." A questionnaire revealed that there was literally nothing these kids felt strongly enough about to die for, as there was nothing they actually did in which they felt really alive. Ideas, the conceptual thought which is uniquely human, were completely absent from their minds or lives.[1]

A social critic, one or two perceptive psychoanalysts, tried to pinpoint this change in the younger generation as a basic change in the American character. Whether for better or worse, whether it was a question of sickness or health, they saw that the human personality, recognizable by a strong and stable core of self, was being replaced by a vague, amorphous "other-directed personality."[2] In the 1950's, David Riesman found no boy or girl with that emerging sense of his own self which used to mark human adolescence, "though I searched for autonomous youngsters in several public schools and several private schools."[3]

At Sarah Lawrence College, where students had taken a large responsibility for their own education and for the organization of their own affairs, it was discovered that the new generation of students was helpless, apathetic, incapable of handling such freedom. If left to organize their own activities, no activities were organized; a curriculum geared to the students' own interests no longer worked because the students did not have strong interests of their own. Harold Taylor, then president of Sarah Lawrence, described the change as follows:

> Whereas in earlier years it had been possible to count on the strong motivation and initiative of students to conduct their own affairs, to form new organizations, to invent new projects either in social welfare, or in intellectual fields, it now became clear that for many students the responsibility for self-government was often a burden to bear rather than a right to be maintained. . . . Students who were given complete freedom to manage their own lives and to make their own decisions often did not wish to do so. . . . Students in college seem to find it increasingly difficult to entertain themselves, having become accustomed to depend upon arranged entertainment in which their role is simply to participate in the arrangements already made. . . . The students were unable to plan anything for themselves which they found interesting enough to engage in.[4]

The educators, at first, blamed this on the caution and conservatism of the McCarthy era, the helplessness engendered by the atom bomb; later, in the face of Soviet advances in the space race, the politicians and public opinion blamed the general "softness" of the educators. But, whatever their own weaknesses, the best of the educators knew only too well that they were dealing with a passivity which the children brought with them to school, a frightening "basic passivity which . . . makes heroic demands on those who must daily cope with them in or out of school."[5] The physical passivity of the younger generation showed itself in a muscular deterioration, finally alarming the White House. Their emotional passivity was visible in bearded, undisciplined beatnikery—a singularly passionless and purposeless form of adolescent rebellion. Juvenile delinquency ratios just as high as those in the city slums began to show up in the pleasant bedroom suburbs among the children of successful, educated, respected and self-respecting members of society, middle-class children who had all the "advantages," all the "opportunities." A movie called "I Was a Teenage Frankenstein" may not have seemed funny to parents in Westchester and Connecticut who were visited by the vice squad in 1960 because their kids were taking drugs at parties in each others' pine-paneled playrooms. Or the Bergen County parents whose kids were arrested in 1962 for mass violation of the graves in a suburban cemetery; or the parents in a Long Island suburb whose daughters at thirteen were operating a virtual "call girl" service. Behind the senseless vandalism, the riots in Florida at spring vacation, the promiscuity, the rise in teenage venereal disease and illegitimate pregnancies, the alarming dropouts from high school and college, was this new passivity. For these bored, lazy, "gimme" kids, "kicks" was the only way to kill the monotony of vacant time.

That this passivity was more than a question of boredom—that it signaled a deterioration of the human character—was felt by those who studied the behavior of the American GI's who were prisoners of war in Korea in the 1950's. An Army doctor, Major Clarence Anderson, who was allowed to move freely among the prison camps to treat the prisoners, observed:

> On the march, in the temporary camps, and in the permanent ones, the strong regularly took food from the weak. There was no discipline to prevent it. Many men were sick, and these men, instead of being helped and nursed by the others, were ignored, or worse. Dysentery was common, and it made some men too weak to walk. On winter nights, helpless men with dysentery were rolled outside the huts by their comrades and left to die in the cold.[6]

Some thirty-eight per cent of the prisoners died, a higher prisoner death rate than in any previous American war, including the Revolution. Most prisoners became inert, inactive, withdrawing into little shells they had erected against reality. They did nothing to get food, firewood, keep themselves clean, or communicate with each other. The Major was struck by the fact that these new American GI's almost universally "lacked the old Yankee resourcefulness," an ability to cope with a new and primitive situation. He concluded: "This was partly—but only partly, I believe—the result of the psychic shock of being captured. It was also, I think, the result of some new failure in the childhood and adolescent training of our young men—a new softness." Discounting the Army's propaganda point, an educational psychologist commented: "There was certainly something terribly wrong with these young men; not softness, but hardness, slickness, and brittleness. I would call it ego-failure—a collapse of identity. . . . Adolescent growth can and should lead to a completely human adulthood, defined as the development of a stable sense of self . . ."[7]

The Korean prisoners, in this sense, were models of a new kind of American, evidently nurtured in ways "inimical to clarity and growth" at the hands of individuals themselves "insufficiently characterized" to develop "the kind of character and mind that conceives itself too clearly to consent to its own betrayal."

The shocked recognition that this passive non-identity was "something new in history" came, and only came, when it began to show up in the boys. But the apathetic, dependent, infantile, purposeless being, who seems so shockingly nonhuman when remarked as the emerging character of the new American man, is strangely reminiscent of the familiar "feminine" personality as defined by the mystique. Aren't the chief characteristics of femininity—which Freud mistakenly related to sexual biology—passivity; a weak ego or sense of self; a weak superego or human conscience; renunciation of active aims, ambitions, interests of one's own to live through others; incapacity for abstract thought; retreat from activity directed outward to the world, in favor of activity directed inward or phantasy?

What does it mean, this emergence now in American boys as well as girls, of a personality arrested at the level of infantile phantasy and passivity? The boys and girls in whom I saw it were children of mothers who lived within the limits of the feminine mystique. They were fulfilling their roles as women in the accepted, normal way. Some had more than normal ability, and some had more than normal education, but they were alike in the intensity of their preoccupation with their children, who seemed to be their main and only interest.

One mother, who was terribly disturbed that her son could not learn to read, told me that when he came home with his first report card from kindergarten, she was as "excited as a kid myself, waiting for someone to ask me out on a date Saturday night." She was convinced that the teachers were wrong when they said he wandered around the room in a dream, could not pay attention long enough to do the reading-readiness test. Another mother said that she could not bear it when her sons suffered any trouble or distress at all. It was as if they were herself. She told me:

> I used to let them turn over all the furniture and build houses in the living room that would stay up for days, so there was no place for me even to sit and read. I couldn't bear to make them do what they didn't want to do, even take medicine when they

were sick. I couldn't bear for them to be unhappy, or fight, or be angry at me. I couldn't separate them from myself somehow. I was always understanding, patient. I felt guilty leaving them even for an afternoon. I worried over every page of their homework; I was always concentrating on being a good mother. I was proud that Steve didn't get in fights with other kids in the neighborhood. I didn't even realize anything was wrong until he started doing so badly in school, and having nightmares about death, and didn't want to go to school because he was afraid of the other boys.

Another woman said:

I thought I had to be there every afternoon when they got home from school. I read all the books they were assigned so I could help them with their schoolwork. I haven't been as happy and excited for years as the weeks I was helping Mary get her clothes ready for college. But I was so upset when she wouldn't take art. That had been my dream, before I got married, of course. Maybe it's better to live your own dreams.

I do not think it is a coincidence that the increasing passivity—and dreamlike unreality—of today's children has become so widespread in the same years that the feminine mystique encouraged the great majority of American women—including the most able, and the growing numbers of the educated—to give up their own dreams, and even their own education, to live through their children. The "absorption" of the child's personality by the middle-class mother—already apparent to a perceptive sociologist in the 1940's—has inevitably increased during these years. Without serious interests outside the home, and with housework routinized by appliances, women could devote themselves almost exclusively to the cult of the child from cradle to kindergarten. Even when the children went off to school their mothers could share their lives, vicariously and sometimes literally. To many, their relationship with their children became a love affair, or a kind of symbiosis.

"Symbiosis" is a biological term; it refers to the process by which, to put it simply, two organisms live as one. With human beings, when the fetus is in the womb, the mother's blood supports its life; the food she eats makes it grow, its oxygen comes from the air she breathes, and she discharges its wastes. There is a biological oneness in the beginning between mother and child, a wonderful and intricate process. But this relationship ends with the severing of the umbilical cord and the birth of the baby into the world as a separate human being.

At this point, child psychologists construe a psychological or emotional "symbiosis" between mother and child in which mother love takes the place of the amniotic fluid which perpetually bathed and fed the fetus in the womb. This emotional symbiosis feeds the psyche of the child until he is ready to be psychologically born, as it were. Thus the psychological writers—like the literary and religious eulogists of mother-love before the psychological era—depict a state in which mother and baby still retain a mystical oneness; they are not really separate beings. "Symbiosis," in the hands of the psychological popularizers, strongly implied that the constant loving care of the mother was absolutely necessary for the child's growth, for an indeterminate number of years.

But in recent years the "symbiosis" concept has crept with increasing frequency into the case histories of disturbed children. More and more of the new child pathologies seem to stem from that very symbiotic relationship with the mother, which has somehow kept children from becoming separate selves. These disturbed children seem to be "acting out" the mother's unconscious wishes or conflicts—infantile dreams she had not outgrown or given up, but was still trying to gratify for herself in the person of her child.

The term "acting out" is used in psychotherapy to describe the behavior of a patient which is not in accord with the reality of a given situation, but is the expression of unconscious infantile wishes or phantasy. It sounds mystical to say that the unconscious infantile wishes the disturbed child is "acting out" are not his own but his mother's. But therapists can trace the actual steps whereby the mother, who is using the child to gratify her own infantile dreams, unconsciously pushes him into the behavior which is destructive to his growth. The Westchester executive's wife who had pushed her daughter at thirteen into sexual promiscuity had not only been grooming her in the development of her sexual charms—in a way that completely ignored the child's own personality—but, even before her breasts began to develop, had implanted, by warnings and by a certain intensity of questioning, her expectation that the child would act out in real life her mother's phantasies of prostitution.

It has never been considered pathological for mothers or fathers to act out their dreams through their children, except when the dream ignores and distorts the reality of the child. Novels, as well as case histories, have been written about the boy who became a bad businessman because that was his father's dream for him, when he might have been a good violinist; or the boy who ends up in the mental hospital to frustrate his mother's dream of him as a great violinist. If in recent years the process has begun to seem pathological, it is because the mothers' dreams which the children are acting out have become increasingly infantile. These mothers have themselves become more infantile, and because they are forced to seek more and more gratification through the child, they are incapable of finally separating themselves from the child. Thus, it would seem, it is the child who supports life in the mother in that "symbiotic" relationship, and the child is virtually destroyed in the process.

This destructive symbiosis is literally built into the feminine mystique. And the process is progressive. It begins in one generation, and continues into the next, roughly as follows:

1. By permitting girls to evade tests of reality, and real commitments, in school and the world, by the promise of magical fulfillment through marriage, the feminine mystique arrests their development at an infantile level, short of personal identity, with an inevitably weak core of self.

2. The greater her own infantilism, and the weaker her core of self, the earlier the girl will seek "fulfillment" as a wife and mother and the more exclusively will she live through her husband and children. Thus, her links to the world of reality, and her own sense of herself, will become progressively weaker.

3. Since the human organism has an intrinsic urge to grow, a woman who evades her own growth by clinging to the childlike protection of the housewife role will—insofar as that role does not permit her own growth—suffer increasingly severe pathology, both physiological and emotional. Her motherhood will be increasingly pathological, both for her and for her children. The greater the infantilization of the mother, the less likely the child will be able to achieve human selfhood in the real world. Mothers with infantile selves will have even more infantile children, who will retreat even earlier into phantasy from the tests of reality.

4. The signs of this pathological retreat will be more apparent in boys, since even in childhood boys are expected to commit themselves to tests of reality which the feminine mystique permits the girls to evade in sexual phantasy. But these very expectations ultimately make the boys grow further toward a strong self and make the girls the worst victims, as well as the "typhoid Marys"* of the progressive dehumanization of their own children.

From psychiatrists and suburban clinicians, I learned how this process works. One psychiatrist, Andras Angyal,† describes it, not necessarily in relation to women, as "neurotic evasion of growth." There are two key methods of evading growth. One is "noncommitment": a man lives his life—school, job, marriage—"going through

---

* Phrase based on the historical events surrounding Mary Mallon (1870–1938), an Irish immigrant cook who was immune to typhoid but spread the disease to those with whom she came into contact. The phrase now refers to those who unwittingly spread disease without contracting it themselves.

† Andras Angyal (1902–1960), Hungarian psychologist and psychiatrist who emigrated to the United States in 1932. He was one of the major proponents of a holistic perspective in psychology, a perspective that interpreted life as an interplay between the entire person and his or her environment.

the motions without ever being wholeheartedly committed to any actions." He vaguely experiences himself as "playing a role." On the surface, he may appear to be moving normally through life, but what he is actually doing is "going through the motions."

The other method of evading growth Angyal called the method of "vicarious living." It consists in a systematic denial and repression of one's own personality, and an attempt to substitute some other personality, an "idealized conception, a standard of absolute goodness by which one tries to live, suppressing all those genuine impulses that are incompatible with the exaggerated and unrealistic standard," or simply taking the personality that is "the popular cliché of the time."

> The most frequent manifestation of vicarious living is a particularly structured dependence on another person, which is often mistaken for love. Such extremely intense and tenacious attachments, however, lack all the essentials of genuine love—devotion, intuitive understanding, and delight in the being of the other person in his own right and in his own way. On the contrary, these attachments are extremely possessive and tend to deprive the partner of a "life of his own." . . . The other person is needed not as someone to relate oneself to; he is needed for filling out one's inner emptiness, one's nothingness. This nothingness originally was only a phantasy, but with the persistent self-repression it approaches the state of being actual.
>
> All these attempts at gaining a substitute personality by vicarious living fail to free the person from a vague feeling of emptiness. The repression of genuine, spontaneous impulses leaves the person with a painful emotional vacuousness, almost with a sense of nonexistence . . . [8]

"Noncommitment" and "vicarious living," Angyal concludes, "can be understood as attempted solutions of the conflict between the impulse to grow and the fear of facing new situations"—but, though they may temporarily lessen the pressure, they do not actually resolve the problem; "their result, even if not their intent, is always an evasion of personal growth."

Noncommitment and vicarious living are, however, at the very heart of our conventional definition of femininity. This is the way the feminine mystique teaches girls to seek "fulfillment as women"; this is the way most American women live today. But if the human organism has an innate urge to grow, to expand and become all it can be, it is not surprising that the bodies and the minds of healthy women begin to rebel as they try to adjust to a role that does not permit this growth. Their symptoms which so puzzle the doctors and the analysts are a warning sign that they cannot forfeit their own existence, evade their own growth, without a battle.

I have seen this battle being fought by women I interviewed and by women of my own community, and unfortunately, it is often a losing battle. One young girl, first in high school and later in college, gave up all her serious interests and ambitions in order to be "popular." Married early, she played the role of the conventional housewife, in much the same way as she played the part of a popular college girl. I don't know at what point she lost track of what was real and what was façade, but when she became a mother, she would sometimes lie down on the floor and kick her feet in the kind of tantrum she was not able to handle in her three-year-old daughter. At the age of thirty-eight, she slashed her wrists in attempted suicide.

Another extremely intelligent woman, who gave up a challenging career as a cancer researcher to become a housewife, suffered a severe depression just before her baby was born. After she recovered she was so "close" to him that she had to stay with him at nursery school every morning for four months, or else he went into a violent frenzy of tears and tantrums. In first grade, he often vomited in the morning when he had to leave her. His violence on the playground approached danger to himself and others. When a neighbor took away from him a baseball bat with which he was about to hit a child on the head, his mother objected violently to the "frustration" of her child. She found it extremely difficult to discipline him herself.

Over a ten-year period, as she went correctly through all the motions of motherhood in suburbia, except for this inability to deal firmly with her children, she seemed visibly less and less alive, less and less sure of her own worth. The day before she hung herself in the basement of her spotless split-level house, she took her three children for a checkup by the pediatrician, and made arrangements for her daughter's birthday party.

Few suburban housewives resort to suicide, and yet there is other evidence that women pay a high emotional and physical price for evading their own growth. They are not, as we now know, the biologically weaker of the species. In every age group, fewer women die than men. But in America, from the time when women assume their feminine sexual role as housewives, they no longer live with the zest, the enjoyment, the sense of purpose that is characteristic of true human health.

During the 1950's, psychiatrists, analysts, and doctors in all fields noted that the housewife's syndrome seemed to become increasingly pathological. The mild undiagnosable symptoms—bleeding blisters, malaise, nervousness, and fatigue of young housewives—became heart attacks, bleeding ulcers, hypertension, bronchopneumonia; the nameless emotional distress became a psychotic breakdown. Among the new housewife-mothers, in certain sunlit suburbs, this single decade saw a fantastic increase in "maternal psychoses," mild-to-suicidal depressions or hallucinations over childbirth. According to medical records compiled by Dr. Richard Gordon and his wife, Katherine (psychiatrist and social psychologist, respectively), in the suburbs of Bergen County, N.J., during the 1950's, approximately one out of three young mothers suffered depression or psychotic breakdown over childbirth. This compared to previous medical estimates of psychotic breakdown in one out of 400 pregnancies, and less severe depressions in one out of 80.

> In Bergen County during 1953–57 one out of 10 of the 746 adult psychiatric patients were young wives who broke down over childbirth. In fact, young housewives (18 to 44) suffering not only childbirth depression, but all psychiatric and psychosomatic disorders with increasing severity, became during the fifties by far the predominant group of adult psychiatric patients. The number of disturbed young wives was more than half again as big as the number of young husbands, and three times as big as any other group. (Other surveys of both private and public patients in the suburbs have turned up similar findings.) From the beginning to the end of the fifties, the young housewives also increasingly displaced men as the main sufferers of coronary attack, ulcers, hypertension and bronchial pneumonia. In the hospital serving this suburban county, women now make up 40 per cent of the ulcer patients.[9]

I went to see the Gordons, who had attributed the increased pathologies of these new young housewives—not found among women in comparable rural areas, or older suburbs and cities—to the "mobility" of the new suburban population. But the "mobile" husbands were not breaking down as were their wives and their children. Previous studies of childbirth depression had indicated that successful professional or career women sometimes suffered "role-conflict" when they became housewife-mothers. But these new victims, whose rate of childbirth depression or breakdown was so much greater than all previous estimates, had never wanted to be anything more than housewife-mothers; that was all that was expected of them. The Gordons pointed out that their findings do not indicate that the young housewives are necessarily subjected to more stress than their husbands; for some reason the women simply show an increased tendency to succumb to stress. Could that mean that the role of housewife-mother was too much for them; or could it mean that it was not enough?

These women did not share the same childhood seeds of neurosis; some, in fact, showed none. But a striking similarity that emerged in their case histories was the fact that they had abandoned their education below the level of their ability. The sufferers were the ones who quit high school or college; more often than comparable women their age, they had started college—and left, usually after a year.[10] Many also had come from "the more restrictive ethnic groups" (Italian or Jewish) or from small towns in the South where "women were protected and kept dependent." Most had not pursued either education or job, nor moved in the world on their own in any capacity. A few who broke down had held relatively unskilled jobs, or had the beginnings of interests which they gave up when they became suburban housewife-mothers. But most had had no ambition other than that of marrying an up-and-coming man; many were fulfilling not only their own dreams but also the frustrated status dreams of their mothers, in marrying ambitious, capable men. As Dr. Gordon described them to me: "They were not capable women. They had never done anything. They couldn't even organize the committees which needed to be organized in these places. They had never been required to apply themselves, learn how to do a job and then do it. Many of them quit school. It's easier to have a baby than get an A. They never learned to take stresses, pain, hard work. As soon as the going was tough, they broke down."

Perhaps because these girls were more passive, more dependent than other women, walled up in the suburbs, they sometimes seemed to become as infantile as their children. And their children showed a passivity and infantilism that seemed pathological—very early in the sons. One finds in the suburban mental-health clinics today, the overwhelming majority of the child patients are boys, in dramatic and otherwise inexplicable reversal of the fact that most of the adult patients in all clinics and doctors' offices today are women—that is, housewives. Putting aside the theoretical terms of his profession a Boston analyst who has many women patients told me:

> It is true, there are too many more women patients than men. Their complaints are varied, but if you look underneath, you find this underlying feeling of emptiness. It is not inferiority. It is almost like nothingness. The situation is that they are not pursuing any goals of their own.

Another doctor, in a suburban mental-health clinic, told me of the young mother of a sixteen-year-old girl who, since their move to the suburb seven years ago, has been completely preoccupied with her children except for a little "do good" work in the community. Despite this mother's constant anxiety about her daughter ("I think about her all day—she doesn't have any friends and will she get into college?"), she *forgot* the day her daughter was to take her college entrance exams.

Her anxiousness about her daughter and what she was doing was her own anxiety about herself, and what she wasn't doing. When these women suffer with the preoccupation of what they aren't doing with themselves, the children actually get very little real contact with them. I think of another child, 2 years old, with very severe symptoms because he has almost no actual contact with his mother. She is very much in the home, all day, every day. I have to teach her to have even physical contact with the child. But it won't be solved until the mother faces her own need for self-fulfillment. Being available to one's children has nothing to do with the amount of time—being able to be there for each child in terms of what he needs can happen in a split second. And a mother can be there all day, and not be there for the child, because of her preoccupation with herself. So he holds his breath in temper tantrums; he fights in anger; he refuses to let her leave him at nursery school; even at 9 a boy still requires his mother to go to the bathroom with him, lie down with him or he can't go to sleep. Or he becomes withdrawn to the point of schizophrenia. And she is frantically trying to answer the child's needs and demands. But if she was really able to fulfill herself, she would be able to be there for her child. She has to be complete herself, and there herself, to help the child to grow, and learn to handle reality, even to know what his own real feelings are.

In another clinic, a therapist spoke of a mother who was panicky because her child could not learn to read at school, though his intelligence tested high. The mother had left college, thrown herself into the role of housewife, and had lived for the time when her son would go to school, and she would fulfill herself in his achievement. Until therapy made the mother "separate" herself from the child, he had no sense of himself as a separate being at all. He could, would, do nothing, even in play, unless someone told him to. He could not even learn to read, which took a self of his own.

The strange thing was, the therapist said, like so many other women of this era of the "feminine role," in her endeavor to be a "real woman," a good wife and mother, "she was really playing a very masculine role. . . . She was pushing everyone around—dominating the children's lives, ruling the house with an iron hand, managing the carpentry, nagging her husband to do odd jobs he never finished, managing the finances, supervising the recreation and the education—and her husband was just the man who paid the bills."

In a Westchester community whose school system is world famous, it was recently discovered that graduates with excellent high-school records did very poorly in college and did not make much of themselves afterwards. An investigation revealed a simple psychological cause. All during high school, the mothers literally had been doing their children's homework and term papers. They had been cheating their sons and daughters out of their own mental growth.

Another analyst illuminates how juvenile delinquency is caused by the child's acting out of the mother's needs, when the mother's growth has been stunted.

> Regularly the more important parent—usually the mother, although the father is always in some way involved—has been seen unconsciously to encourage the amoral or antisocial behavior of the child. The neurotic needs of the parent . . . are vicariously gratified by the behavior of the child. Such neurotic needs of the parent exist either because of some current inability to satisfy them in the world of adults, or because of the stunting experiences in the parent's own childhood—or more commonly, because of a combination of both of these factors.[11]

Those who have observed and tried to help young delinquents have seen this progressive dehumanization process in action, and have discovered that love is not enough to counteract it. The symbiotic love or permissiveness which has been the translation of mother-love during the years of the feminine mystique is not enough to create a social conscience and strength of character in a child. For this it takes a mature mother with a firm core of self, whose own sexual, instinctual needs are integrated with social conscience. "Firmness bespeaks a parent who has learned . . . how all of his major goals may be reached in some creative course of action . . ."[12]

A therapist reported the case of a nine-year-old girl who stole. She will outgrow it, said her protective mother—with a "permissiveness born of her own need for vicarious satisfaction." At one point, the nine-year-old asked the therapist, "When is my mother going to do her own stealing?"

At its most extreme, this pattern of progressive dehumanization can be seen in the cases of schizophrenic children: "autistic" or "atypical" children, as they are sometimes called. I visited a famous clinic which has been studying these children for almost twenty years. During this period, cases of these children, arrested at a very primitive, sub-infantile level, have seemed to some to be on the increase. The authorities differ as to the cause of this strange condition, and whether it is actually on the increase or only seems to be because it is now more often diagnosed. Until quite recently, most of these children were thought to be mentally retarded. But the condition is being seen more frequently now, in hospitals and clinics, by doctors and psychiatrists. And it is not the same as the irreversible, organic types of mental retardation. It can be treated, and sometimes cured.

These children often identify themselves with things, inanimate objects—cars, radios, etc., or with animals—pigs, dogs, cats. The crux of the problem seems to be that these children have not organized or developed strong enough selves to cope even with the child's reality; they cannot distinguish themselves as separate from the outside world; they live on the level of things or of instinctual biological impulse that has not been organized into a human framework at all. As for the causes, the authorities felt they "must examine the personality of the mother, who is the medium through which the primitive infant transforms himself into a socialized human being."[13]

At the clinic I visited (The James Jackson Putnam Children's Center in Boston) the workers were cautious about drawing conclusions about these profoundly disturbed children. But one of the doctors said, a bit impatiently, about the increasing stream of "missing egos, fragile egos, poorly developed selves" that he has encountered—"It's just the thing we've always known, if the parent has a fragile ego, the child will."

Most of the mothers of the children who never developed a core of human self were "extremely immature individuals" themselves, though on the surface they "give the impression of being well-adjusted." They were very dependent on their own mothers, fled this dependency into early marriage, and "have struggled heroically to build and maintain the image they have created of a fine woman, wife and mother."

> The need to be a mother, the hope and expectation that through this experience she may become a real person, capable of true emotions, is so desperate that of itself it may create anxiety, ambivalence, fear of failure. Because she is so barren of spontaneous manifestations of maternal feelings, she studies vigilantly all the new methods of upbringing and reads treatises about physical and mental hygiene.[14]

Her omnipresent care of her child is based not on spontaneity but on following the "picture of what a good mother should be," in the hope that "through identification with the child, her own flesh and blood, she may experience vicariously the joys of real living, of genuine feeling."

And thus, the child is reduced from "passive inertia" to "screaming in the night" to non-humanness. "The passive child is less of a threat because he does not make exaggerated demands on the mother, who feels constantly in danger of revealing that emotionally she has little or nothing to offer, that she is a fraud." When she discovers that she cannot really find her own fulfillment through the child:

> . . . she fights desperately for control, no longer of herself per-
> haps, but of the child. The struggles over toilet training and
> weaning are generally battles in which she tries to redeem
> herself. The child becomes the real victim—victim of the
> mother's helplessness which, in turn, creates an aggression in
> her that mounts to destruction. The only way for the child to
> survive is to retreat, to withdraw, not only from the dangerous
> mother, but from the whole world as well."[15]

And so he becomes a "thing," or an animal, or "a restless wan-
derer in search of no one and no place, weaving about the room,
swaying back and forth, circling the walls as if they were bars he
would break through."

In this clinic, the doctors were often able to trace a similar pattern back several generations. The dehumanization was indeed
progressive.

> In view of these clinical observations, we may assume that the
> conflict we have discovered in two generations may well have
> existed for generations before and will continue in those to
> come, unless the pattern is interrupted by therapeutic inter-
> vention or the child rescued by a masculine father-figure, a
> hope which our experience would not lead us to expect.[16]

But neither therapy nor love was enough to help these children,
if the mother continued to live vicariously through the child. I noticed
this same pattern in many of the women I interviewed, women who
dominated their daughters, or bred them into passive dependence and
conformity or unconsciously pushed them into sexual activities. One
of the most tragic women I interviewed was the mother of that "sleepwalking" thirteen-year-old girl. A wealthy executive's wife whose life
was filled with all the trappings, she lived the very image of suburban
"togetherness," except that it was only a shell. Her husband's real life
was centered in his business; a life that he could not, or would not,
share with his wife. She had sought to recapture her sense of life by
unconsciously pushing her thirteen-year-old daughter into promiscuity. She lived in her daughter's pseudo-sex life, which for the girl was
so devoid of actual feeling that she became in it merely a "thing."

Quite a few therapists and counselors were trying to "help" the
mother and the father, on the premise, I suppose, that if the mother's sexual-emotional needs were filled in her marriage by her husband, she would not need to solve them through her daughter—and
her daughter could grow out of the "thingness" to womanhood herself. It was because the husband had so many problems of his own
and the prospects of the mother ever getting enough love from him
looked dim, that the counselors were trying to get the mother to
develop some real interests in her own life.

But with other women I have encountered who have evaded their own growth in vicarious living and lack of personal purposes, not even the most loving of husbands have managed to stop the progressive damage to their own lives and the lives of their children. I have seen what happens when women unconsciously push their daughters into too early sexuality, because the sexual adventure was the only real adventure—or means of achieving status or identity—in their own lives. Today these daughters, who acted out their mothers' dreams or frustrated ambitions in the "normal" feminine way and hitched their wagons to the rising stars of ambitious, able men, are, in too many cases, as frustrated and unfulfilled as their mothers. They do not all rush barefoot to the police station for fear they will murder the husband and baby who, they think, trap them in that house. All their sons do not become violent menaces in the neighborhood and at school; all their daughters do not act out their mothers' sexual phantasies and become pregnant at fourteen. Nor do all such housewives begin drinking at 11 A.M. to hide the clunking whir of the dishwasher, the washing machine, the dryer, that are finally the only sounds of life in that empty house, as the children, one by one, go off to school.

But in suburbs like Bergen County, the rate of "separations" increased a wild 100% during the 1950's, as the able, ambitious men kept on growing in the city while their wives evaded growth in vicarious living or noncommitment, fulfilling their feminine role at home. As long as the children were home, as long as the husband was there, the wives suffered increasingly severe illnesses, but recovered. But in Bergen County, during this decade, there was a drastic increase in suicides of women over forty-five, and of hospitalized women psychiatric patients whose children had grown up and left home.[17] The housewives who had to be hospitalized and who did not recover quickly were, above all, those who had never developed their own abilities in work outside the home.[18]

The massive breakdown that may take place as more and more of these new young housewife-mothers who are the products of the feminine mystique reach their forties is still a matter of speculation. But the progressive infantilization of their sons and daughters, as it is mirrored in the rash of early marriages, has become an alarming fact. In March, 1962, at the national conference of the Child Study Association, the new early marriages and parenthood, which had formerly been considered an indication of "improved emotional maturity" in the younger generation were at last recognized as a sign of increasing "infantilization." The millions of American youngsters who, in the 1960's, were marrying before they were twenty, betrayed an immaturity and emotional dependence which seeks marriage as a magic short-cut to adult status, a magic solution to problems they cannot face themselves, professionals in the child-and-family field agreed. These infantile brides and grooms were diagnosed as the victims of this generation's "sick, sad love affair with their own children."

> Many girls will admit that they want to get married because they do not want to work any longer. They harbor dreams of being taken care of for the rest of their lives without worry, with just enough furnishing, to do little housework, interesting downtown shopping trips, happy children, and nice neighbors. The dream of a husband seems somehow less important but in the fantasies of girls about marriage, it usually concerns a man who has the strength of an indestructible, reliable, powerful father, and the gentleness, givingness, and self-sacrificing love of a good mother. Young men give as their reason for wanting to marry very often the desire to have a motherly woman in the house, and regular sex just for the asking without trouble and bother. . . . In fact, what is supposed to secure maturity and independence is in reality a concealed hope to secure dependency, to prolong the child-parent relationship with the privileges of being a child, and with as little as possible of its limitations.[19]

And there were other ominous signs across the nation of mounting uncontrollable violence among young parents and their children trapped in that passive dependence. A psychiatrist reported that such wives were reacting to hostility from their husbands by becoming even more dependent and passive, until they sometimes became literally unable to move, to take a step, by themselves. This did not make their husbands treat them with more love, but more rage. And what was happening to the rage the wives did not dare to use against their husbands? Consider this recent news item (*Time*, July 20, 1962) about the "Battered-Child Syndrome."

> To many doctors, the incident is becoming distressingly familiar. A child, usually under three, is brought to the office with multiple fractures—often including a fractured skull. The parents express appropriate concern, report that the child fell out of bed, or tumbled down the stairs, or was injured by a playmate. But x-rays and experience lead the doctor to a different conclusion: the child has been beaten by his parents.

Gathering documentation from 71 hospitals, a University of Colorado team found 302 battered-child cases in a single year; 33 died, 85 suffered permanent brain damage. The parents, who were driven "to kick and punch their children, twist their arms, beat them with hammers or the buckle end of belts, burn them with cigarettes or electric irons," were as likely to live in those suburban split-levels as in tenements. The A.M.A. predicted that when statistics on the battered-child syndrome are complete, "it is likely that it will be found to be a more frequent cause of death than such well-recognized and thoroughly studied diseases as leukemia, cystic fibrosis and muscular dystrophy."

The "parent" with most opportunity to beat that battered child was, of course, the mother. As one young mother of four said to the doctor, as she confessed to the wish to kill herself:

> There doesn't seem any reason for me to go on living. I don't have anything to look forward to. Jim and I don't even talk to each other any more except about the bills and things that need to be fixed in the house. I know he resents being so old and tied down when he's still young, and he blames it on me because it was I that wanted us to get married then. But the worst thing is, I feel so envious of my own children. I almost hate them, because they have their lives ahead, and mine is over.

It may or may not be a symbolic coincidence but the same week the child-and-family profession recognized the real significance of the early marriages, the *New York Times Book Review* (Sunday, March 18, 1962) recorded a new and unprecedented popularity among American adults of books about "love" affairs between human beings and animals. In half a century, there have not been as many books about animals on the American best-seller lists as in the last three years (1959–62). While animals have always dominated the literature for small children, with maturity human beings become more interested in other human beings. (It is only a symbol, but in the Rorschach test,* a preponderance of animal over human images is a sign of infantilism). And so progressive dehumanization has carried the American mind in the last fifteen years from youth worship to that "sick love affair" with our own children; from preoccupation with the physical details of sex, divorced from a human framework, to a love affair between man and animal. Where will it end?

I think it will not end, as long as the feminine mystique masks the emptiness of the housewife role, encouraging girls to evade their own growth by vicarious living, by noncommitment. We have gone on too long blaming or pitying the mothers who devour their children, who sow the seeds of progressive dehumanization, because they have never grown to full humanity themselves. If the mother is at fault, why isn't it time to break the pattern by urging all

---

* Personality test introduced in 1921 by Swiss psychiatrist Hermann Rorschach. The test asks a subject to describe what he or she sees in a series of inkblots. Answers are supposed to indicate the subject's personality type, as well as to allow a psychiatrist to diagnose any clinical disorders.

these Sleeping Beauties to grow up and live their own lives? There never will be enough Prince Charmings, or enough therapists to break that pattern now. It is society's job, and finally that of each woman alone. For it is not the strength of the mothers that is at fault but their weakness, their passive childlike dependency and immaturity that is mistaken for "femininity." Our society forces boys, insofar as it can, to grow up, to endure the pains of growth, to educate themselves to work, to move on. Why aren't girls forced to grow up—to achieve somehow the core of self that will end the unnecessary dilemma, the mistaken choice between femaleness and humanness that is implied in the feminine mystique?

It is time to stop exhorting mothers to "love" their children more, and face the paradox between the mystique's demand that women devote themselves completely to their home and their children, and the fact that most of the problems now being treated in child-guidance clinics are solved only when the mothers are helped to develop autonomous interests of their own, and no longer need to fill their emotional needs through their children. It is time to stop exhorting women to be more "feminine" when it breeds a passivity and dependence that depersonalizes sex and imposes an impossible burden on their husbands, a growing passivity in their sons.

It is not an exaggeration to call the stagnating state of millions of American housewives a sickness, a disease in the shape of a progressively weaker core of human self that is being handed down to their sons and daughters at a time when the dehumanizing aspects of modern mass culture make it necessary for men and women to have a strong core of self, strong enough to retain human individuality through the frightening, unpredictable pressures of our changing environment. The strength of women is not the cause, but the cure for this sickness. Only when women are permitted to use their full strength, to grow to their full capacities, can the feminine mystique be shattered and the progressive dehumanization of their children be stopped. And most women can no longer use their full strength, grow to their full human capacity, as housewives.

It is urgent to understand how the very condition of being a housewife can create a sense of emptiness, non-existence, nothingness, in women. There are aspects of the housewife role that make it almost impossible for a woman of adult intelligence to retain a sense of human identity, the firm core of self or "I" without which a human being, man or woman, is not truly alive. For women of ability, in America today, I am convinced there is something about the housewife state itself that is dangerous. In a sense that is not as far-fetched as it sounds, the women who "adjust" as housewives, who grow up wanting to be "just a housewife," are in as much danger as the millions who walked to their own death in the concentration camps—and the millions more who refused to believe that the concentration camps existed.

In fact, there is an uncanny, uncomfortable insight into why a woman can so easily lose her sense of self as a housewife in certain psychological observations made of the behavior of prisoners in Nazi concentration camps. In these settings, purposely contrived for the dehumanization of man, the prisoners literally became "walking corpses." Those who "adjusted" to the conditions of the camps surrendered their human identity and went almost indifferently to their deaths. Strangely enough, the conditions which destroyed the human identity of so many prisoners were not the torture and the brutality, but conditions similar to those which destroy the identity of the American housewife.

In the concentration camps the prisoners were forced to adopt childlike behavior, forced to give up their individuality and merge themselves into an amorphous mass. Their capacity for self-determination, their ability to predict the future and to prepare for it, was systematically destroyed. It was a gradual process which occurred in virtually imperceptible stages—but at the end, with the destruction of adult self-respect, of an adult frame of reference, the dehumanizing process was complete. This was the process as observed by Bruno Bettelheim, psychoanalyst and educational psychologist, when he was a prisoner at Dachau and Buchenwald* in 1939.[20]

When they entered the concentration camp, prisoners were almost traumatically cut off from their past adult interests. This in itself was a major blow to their identity over and above their physical confinement. A few, though only a few, were able to work privately in some way that had interested them in the past. But to do this alone was difficult; even to talk about these larger adult interests, or to show some initiative in pursuing them, aroused the hostility of other prisoners. New prisoners tried to keep their old interests alive, but "old prisoners seemed mainly concerned with the problem of how to live as well as possible inside the camp."

---

*   Concentration camps built in Germany in the 1930s. They were used to incarcerate, torture, and murder opponents of the Nazi regime, who included trade unionists, socialists and communists, professional criminals, Poles and Russians, homosexuals, and Jews. *Bruno Bettelheim* (1903–1990), survivor of Dachau and Buchenwald concentration camps, and an American psychoanalyst who directed the Sonia Shankman Orthogenic School in Chicago, a school for emotionally troubled children. He became well known for his interpretation of the Nazi camp experience, and for his application of that experience to the study of autism. The "extreme situation" of the Nazi camps, he argued, led camp inmates to embrace Nazi dogma, while the "extreme situation" created by inadequate mothering led children to develop autism. Bettelheim was revered as a theorist and practitioner in the 1950s and 1960s, but his reputation declined after the 1970s, as Holocaust survivors and families of autistic children, as well as scholars, criticized his work. See a selection from *The Informed Heart*, on pp. 377–78.

To old prisoners, the world of the camp was the only reality.[21] They were reduced to childlike preoccupation with food, elimination, the satisfaction of primitive bodily needs; they had no privacy, and no stimulation from the outside world. But, above all, they were forced to spend their days in work which produced great fatigue—not because it was physically killing, but because it was monotonous, endless, required no mental concentration, gave no hope of advancement or recognition, was sometimes senseless and was controlled by the needs of others or the tempo of machines. It was work that did not emanate from the prisoner's own personality; it permitted no real initiative, no expression of the self, not even a real demarcation of time.

And the more the prisoners gave up their adult human identity, the more they were preoccupied with the fear that they were losing their sexual potency, and the more preoccupied they became with the simplest animal needs. It brought them comfort, at first, to surrender their individuality, and lose themselves in the anonymity of the mass—to feel that "everyone was in the same boat." But strangely enough, under these conditions, real friendships did not grow.[22] Even conversation, which was the prisoners' favorite pastime and did much to make life bearable, soon ceased to have any real meaning.[23] So rage mounted in them. But the rage of the millions that could have knocked down the barbed-wire fences and the SS guns was turned instead against themselves, and against the prisoners even weaker than they. Then they felt even more powerless than they were, and saw the SS* and the fences as even more impregnable than they were.

It was said, finally, that not the SS but the prisoners themselves became their own worst enemy. Because they could not bear to see their situation as it really was—because they denied the very reality of their problem, and finally "adjusted" to the camp itself as if it were the only reality—they were caught in the prison of their own minds. The guns of the SS were not powerful enough to keep all those prisoners subdued. They were manipulated to trap themselves; they imprisoned themselves by making the concentration camp the whole world, by blinding themselves to the larger world of the past, their responsibility for the present, and their possibilities for the future. The ones who survived, who neither died nor were exterminated, were the ones who retained in some essential degree the adult values and interests which had been the essence of their past identity.

* The SS, or Schustaffel, was the elite ideological and military unit of Nazi Germany. SS officers were responsible for carrying out racial genocide in Nazi-occupied Europe. SS men engineered the deportation of Jews to their deaths, conducted mass executions of Jews in villages throughout Eastern Europe, and staffed the concentration and death camps in which millions perished.

All this seems terribly remote from the easy life of the American suburban housewife. But is her house in reality a comfortable concentration camp? Have not women who live in the image of the feminine mystique trapped themselves within the narrow walls of their homes? They have learned to "adjust" to their biological role. They have become dependent, passive, childlike; they have given up their adult frame of reference to live at the lower human level of food and things. The work they do does not require adult capabilities; it is endless, monotonous, unrewarding. American women are not, of course, being readied for mass extermination, but they are suffering a slow death of mind and spirit. Just as with the prisoners in the concentration camps, there are American women who have resisted that death, who have managed to retain a core of self, who have not lost touch with the outside world, who use their abilities to some creative purpose. They are women of spirit and intelligence who have refused to "adjust" as housewives.

It has been said time and time again that education has kept American women from "adjusting" to their role as housewives. But if education, which serves human growth, which distills what the human mind has discovered and created in the past, and gives man the ability to create his own future—if education has made more and more American women feel trapped, frustrated, guilty as housewives, surely this should be seen as a clear signal that *women have outgrown the housewife role.*

It is not possible to preserve one's identity by adjusting for any length of time to a frame of reference that is in itself destructive to it. It is very hard indeed for a human being to sustain such an "inner" split—conforming outwardly to one reality, while trying to maintain inwardly the values it denies. The comfortable concentration camp that American women have walked into, or have been talked into by others, is just such a reality, a frame of reference that denies woman's adult human identity. By adjusting to it, a woman stunts her intelligence to become childlike, turns away from individual identity to become an anonymous biological robot in a docile mass. She becomes less than human, preyed upon by outside pressures, and herself preying upon her husband and children. And the longer she conforms, the less she feels as if she really exists. She looks for her security in things, she hides the fear of losing her human potency by testing her sexual potency, she lives a vicarious life through mass daydreams or through her husband and children. She does not want to be reminded of the outside world; she becomes convinced there is nothing she can do about her own life or the world that would make a difference. But no matter how often she tries to tell herself that this giving up of personal identity is a necessary sacrifice for her children and husband, it serves no real purpose. So the aggressive energy she should be using in the world becomes instead the terrible anger that she dare not turn against her husband, is ashamed of turning against her children, and finally turns against herself, until she feels as if she does not exist. And yet in the comfortable concentration camp as in the real one, something very strong in a woman resists the death of herself.

Describing an unforgettable experience in a real concentration camp, Bettelheim tells of a group of naked prisoners—no longer human, merely docile robots—who were lined up to enter the gas chamber. The SS commanding officer, learning that one of the women prisoners had been a dancer, ordered her to dance for him. She did, and as she danced, she approached him, seized his gun and shot him down. She was immediately shot to death, but Bettelheim is moved to ask:

> Isn't it probable that despite the grotesque setting in which she danced, dancing made her once again a person. Dancing, she was singled out as an individual, asked to perform in what had once been her chosen vocation. No longer was she a number, a nameless depersonalized prisoner, but the dancer she used to be. Transformed however momentarily, she responded like her old self, destroying the enemy bent on her destruction even if she had to die in the process.
>
> Despite the hundreds of thousands of living dead men who moved quietly to their graves, this one example shows that in an instant, the old personality can be regained, its destruction undone, once we decide on our own that we wish to cease being units in a system. Exercising the lost freedom that not even the concentration camp could take away—to decide how one wishes to think and feel about the conditions of one's life—this dancer threw off her real prison. This she could do because she was willing to risk her life to achieve autonomy once more.[24]

The suburban house is not a German concentration camp, nor are American housewives on their way to the gas chamber. But they are in a trap, and to escape they must, like the dancer, finally exercise their human freedom, and recapture their sense of self. They must refuse to be nameless, depersonalized, manipulated and live their own lives again according to a self-chosen purpose. They must begin to grow.

13

The Forfeited Self

Scientists of human behavior have become increasingly interested in the basic human need to grow, man's will to be all that is in him to be. Thinkers in many fields—from Bergson to Kurt Goldstein, Heinz Hartmann, Allport, Rogers, Jung, Adler, Rank, Horney, Angyal, Fromm, May, Maslow, Bettelheim, Riesman, Tillich and the existentialists*—all postulate some positive growth tendency within the organism, which, from within, drives it to fuller development, to self-realization. This "will to power," "self-assertion" "dominance," or "autonomy," as it is variously called, does not imply aggression or competitive striving in the usual sense; it is the individual affirming his existence and his potentialities as a being in his own right; it is

---

* Those associated with the philosophical school of existentialism arising from the conditions of Western modernity. It was most popular in the 1950s and 1960s because of the work of scholars like Jean-Paul Sartre, Albert Camus, and Simone de Beauvoir. See the excerpt from Simone de Beauvoir's *The Second Sex* on pp. 355–57. *Henri Bergson* (1859–1941), French philosopher who championed intuition as the height of human cognition. His ideas were applauded by philosophers, writers, and artists, and he became an international celebrity during his time. *Kurt Goldstein* (1878–1965), psychiatrist who specialized in treating patients with brain injuries. Born in Poland, Goldstein trained and worked originally in Germany, but was forced to emigrate to the United States because of persecution by the Nazis. *Heinz Hartmann* (1894–1970), psychoanalyst and student of Sigmund Freud. He pioneered ego psychology, a school of thought that emphasized the significance of the ego as much as the id, and the ability of humans to adapt to their environment (see entry for ego, p. 86). *Gordon Allport* (1897–1967), leading social psychologist in the middle of the twentieth century. He helped to establish the study of personality as a legitimate field in psychology, and he is perhaps best known for his groundbreaking and still significant work on intergroup relations, *The Nature of Prejudice* (1954). *Carl Rogers* (1902–1987), one of the founders of humanistic, person-centered, or client-centered psychotherapy, along with Abraham Maslow and Rollo May. This approach highlighted the needs of the individual seeking therapy. According to Rogers, a successful therapeutic experience required a therapist who was fully available, accepting, and warm, and who listened empathically. *Otto Rank* (1884–1939), twentieth-century psychologist and intellectual. Born in Vienna, he studied with and was mentored by Freud. He practiced his own version of psychoanalysis in both Paris and the United States during the 1920s and 1930s. *Karen Horney* (1885–1952), German-born-and-trained psychologist, who worked at the Berlin Psychoanalytical Clinic and Institute and later the New York Psychoanalytic Institute and the New School for Social Research. Horney challenged Freud's theory of psychosexual development and male-centered perspective. She was a champion for women's ability to have lives both in and outside of the home. *Rollo May* (1909–1994), twentieth-century psychologist associated with humanistic psychology. His psychological theories and practice owed more to European existentialism than to Freud. May is best known for his opinion that modern human beings' feelings of anxiety and alienation are the issues to address in analysis. *Abraham Maslow* (1908–1970) played a leading role in founding humanistic psychology. Critical of both behavioral and psychoanalytic theory, he pioneered a "third force," a school of thought that focused on self-expression and individual needs. Maslow's concept of self-actualization was borrowed by many activists in the 1960s, including Friedan, because it emphasized an individual's need to challenge traditional wisdom and rely upon the inner self. See pp. 465–67 for Ellen Herman's selection on Maslow's importance. *Paul Tillich* (1886–1965), German academic theologian who taught in the United States after World War II. His work interrogated the relationship between the Christian faith and modernity.

"the courage to be an individual."[1] Moreover, many of these thinkers have advanced a new concept of the psychologically healthy man— and of normality and pathology. Normality is considered to be the "highest excellence of which we are capable." The premise is that man is happy, self-accepting, healthy, without guilt, only when he is fulfilling himself and becoming what he can be.

In this new psychological thinking, which seeks to understand what makes men human, and defines neurosis in terms of that which destroys man's capacity to fulfill his own being, the significant tense is the future. It is not enough for an individual to be loved and accepted by others, to be "adjusted" to his culture. He must take his existence seriously enough to make his own commitment to life, and to the future; he forfeits his existence by failing to fulfill his entire being.

For years, psychiatrists have tried to "cure" their patients' conflicts by fitting them to the culture. But adjustment to a culture which does not permit the realization of one's entire being is not a cure at all, according to the new psychological thinkers.

> Then the patient accepts a confined world without conflict, for now his world is identical with the culture. And since anxiety comes only with freedom, the patient naturally gets over his anxiety: he is relieved from his symptoms because he surrenders the possibilities which caused his anxiety. . . . There is certainly a question how far this gaining of release from conflict by giving up being can proceed without generating in individuals and groups a submerged despair, a resentment which will later burst out in self-destructiveness, for history proclaims again and again that sooner or later man's need to be free will out.[2]

These thinkers may not know how accurately they are describing the kind of adjustment that has been inflicted on American housewives. What they are describing as unseen self-destruction in man, is, I think, no less destructive in women who adjust to the feminine mystique, who expect to live through their husbands and children, who want only to be loved and secure, to be accepted by others, who never make a commitment of their own to society or to the future, who never realize their human potential. The adjusted, or cured ones who live without conflict or anxiety in the confined world of home have forfeited their own being; the others, the miserable, frustrated ones, still have some hope. For the problem that has no name, from which so many women in America suffer today, is caused by adjustment to an image that does not permit them to become what they now can be. It is the growing despair of women who have forfeited their own existence, although by so doing they may also have evaded that lonely, frightened feeling that always comes with freedom.

> Anxiety occurs at the point where some emerging potentiality or possibility faces the individual, some possibility of fulfilling his existence; but this very possibility involves the destroying of present security, which thereupon gives rise to the tendency to deny the new potentiality.[3]

The new thinking, which is by no means confined to existentialists, would not analyze "away" a person's guilt over refusing to accept the intellectual and spiritual possibilities of his existence. Not all feelings of human guilt are unfounded; guilt over the murder of another is not to be analyzed away, nor is guilt over the murder of oneself. As was said of a man: "The patient was guilty because he had locked up some essential potentialities in himself."[4]

The failure to realize the full possibilities of their existence has not been studied as a pathology in women. For it is considered normal feminine adjustment, in America and in most countries of the world. But one could apply to millions of women, adjusted to the housewife's role, the insights of neurologists and psychiatrists who have studied male patients with portions of their brain shot away and schizophrenics who have for other reasons forfeited their ability to relate to the real world. Such patients are seen now to have lost the unique mark of the human being: the capacity to transcend the present and to act in the light of the possible, the mysterious capacity to shape the future.[5]

It is precisely this unique human capacity to transcend the present, to live one's life by purposes stretching into the future—to live not at the mercy of the world, but as a builder and designer of that world—that is the distinction between animal and human behavior, or between the human being and the machine. In his study of soldiers who had sustained brain injuries, Dr. Kurt Goldstein found that what they lost was no more nor less than the ability of abstract human thought: to think in terms of "the possible," to order the chaos of concrete detail with an idea, to move according to a purpose. These men were tied to the immediate situation in which they found themselves; their sense of time and space was drastically curtailed; they had lost their human freedom.[6]

A similar dailyness shrinks the world of a depressed schizophrenic, to whom "each day was a separate island with no past and no future." When such a patient has a terrifying delusion that his execution is imminent, it is "the result, not the cause, of his own distorted attitude toward the future."

There was no action or desire which, emanating from the present, reached out to the future, spanning the dull, similar days. As a result, each day kept an unusual independence; failing to be immersed in the perception of any life continuity, each day life began anew, like a solitary island in a gray sea of passing time. . . . There seemed to be no wish to go further; every day was an exasperating monotony of the same words, the same complaints, until one felt that this being had lost all sense of necessary continuity. . . . His attention was short-lived and he seemed unable to go beyond the most banal questions.[7]

Recent experimental work by various psychologists reveals that sheep can bind past and future into the present for a span of about fifteen minutes, and dogs for half an hour. But a human being can bring the past of thousands of years ago into the present as guide to his personal actions, and can project himself in imagination into the future, not only for half an hour, but for weeks and years. This capacity to "transcend the immediate boundaries of time," to act and react, and see one's experience in the dimensions of both past and future, is the unique characteristic of human existence.[8] The brain-injured soldiers thus were doomed to the inhuman hell of eternal "dailyness."

The housewives who suffer the terror of the problem that has no name are victims of this same deadly "dailyness." As one of them told me, "I can take the real problems; it's the endless boring days that make me desperate." Housewives who live according to the feminine mystique do not have a personal purpose stretching into the future. But without such a purpose to evoke their full abilities, they cannot grow to self-realization. Without such a purpose, they lose the sense of who they are, for it is purpose which gives the human pattern to one's days.[9]

American housewives have not had their brains shot away, nor are they schizophrenic in the clinical sense. But if this new thinking is right, and the fundamental human drive is not the urge for pleasure or the satisfaction of biological needs, but the need to grow and to realize one's full potential, their comfortable, empty, purposeless days are indeed cause for a nameless terror. In the name of femininity, they have evaded the choices that would have given them a personal purpose, a sense of their own being. For, as the existentialists say, the values of human life never come about automatically. "The human being can lose his own being by his own choices, as a tree or stone cannot."[10]

It is surely as true of women's whole human potential what earlier psychological theorists have only deemed true of her sexual potential—that if she is barred from realizing her true nature, she will be sick. The frustration not only of needs like sex, but of individual abilities could result in neurosis. Her anxiety can be soothed by therapy, or tranquilized by pills or evaded temporarily by busy-work. But her unease, her desperation, is nonetheless a warning that her human existence is in danger, even though she has found fulfillment, according to the tenets of the feminine mystique, as a wife and mother.

Only recently have we come to accept the fact that there is an evolutionary scale or hierarchy of needs in man (and thus in woman), ranging from the needs usually called instincts because they are shared with animals, to needs that come later in human development. These later needs, the needs for knowledge, for self-realization, are as instinctive, in a human sense, as the needs shared with other animals of food, sex, survival. The clear emergence of the later needs seems to rest upon prior satisfaction of the physiological needs. The man who is extremely and dangerously hungry has no other interest but food. Capacities not useful for the satisfying of hunger are pushed into the background. "But what happens to man's desires when there is plenty of food and his belly is chronically filled? At once, other (and higher) needs emerge and these, rather than the physiological hungers, dominate the organism."[11]

In a sense, this evolving hierarchy of needs moves further and further away from the physiological level which depends on the material environment, and tends toward a level relatively independent of the environment, more and more self-determined. But a man can be fixated on a lower need level; higher needs can be confused or channeled into the old avenues and may never emerge. The progress leading finally to the highest human level is easily blocked—blocked by deprivation of a lower need, as the need for food or sex; blocked also by channeling all existence into these lower needs and refusing to recognize that higher needs exist.

In our culture, the development of women has been blocked at the physiological level with, in many cases, no need recognized higher than the need for love or sexual satisfaction. Even the need for self-respect, for self-esteem and for the esteem of others—"the desire for strength, for achievement, for adequacy, for mastery and competence, for confidence in the face of the world, and for independence and freedom"—is not clearly recognized for women. But certainly the thwarting of the need for self-esteem, which produces feelings of inferiority, of weakness, and of helplessness in man, can have the same effect on woman. Self-esteem in woman, as well as in man, can only be based on real capacity, competence, and achievement; on deserved respect from others rather than unwarranted adulation. Despite the glorification of "Occupation: housewife," if that occupation does not demand, or permit, realization of woman's full abilities, it cannot provide adequate self-esteem, much less pave the way to a higher level of self-realization.

We are living through a period in which a great many of the higher human needs are reduced to, or are seen as, symbolic workings-out of the sexual need. A number of advanced thinkers now seriously question such "explanations by reduction." While every kind of sexual symbolism and emotional pathology can be found by those who explore, with this aim, the works and early life of a Shakespeare, a da Vinci, a Lincoln, an Einstein, a Freud, or a Tolstoi, these "reductions" do not explain the work that lived beyond the man, the unique creation that was his, and not that of a man suffering a similar pathology. But the sexual symbol is easier to see than sex itself as a symbol. If women's needs for identity, for self-esteem, for achievement, and finally for expression of her unique human individuality are not recognized by herself or others in our culture, she is forced to seek identity and self-esteem in the only channels open to her: the pursuit of sexual fulfillment, motherhood, and the possession of material things. And, chained to these pursuits, she is stunted at a lower level of living, blocked from the realization of her higher human needs.

Of course, little is known about the pathology or the dynamics of these higher human needs—the desire to know and understand the search for knowledge, truth, and wisdom, the urge to solve the cosmic mysteries—because they are not important in the clinic in the medical tradition of curing disease. Compared to the symptoms of the classical neuroses, such as the ones Freud saw as emanating from the repression of the sexual need, this kind of psychopathology would be pale, subtle, and easily overlooked—or defined as normal.

But it is a fact, documented by history, if not in the clinic or laboratory, that man has always searched for knowledge and truth, even in the face of the greatest danger. Further, recent studies of psychologically healthy people have shown that this search, this concern with great questions, is one of the defining characteristics of human health. There is something less than fully human in those who have never known a commitment to an idea, who have never risked an exploration of the unknown, who have never attempted the kind of creativity of which men and women are potentially capable. As A. H. Maslow puts it:

> Capacities clamor to be used, and cease their clamor only when they are well used. That is, capacities are also needs. Not only is it fun to use our capacities, but it is also necessary. The unused capacity or organ can become a disease center or else atrophy, thus diminishing the person.[12]

But women in America are not encouraged, or expected, to use their full capacities. In the name of femininity, they are encouraged to evade human growth.

> Growth has not only rewards and pleasure, but also many intrinsic pains and always will have. Each step forward is a step into the unfamiliar and is thought of as possibly dangerous. It also frequently means giving up something familiar and good and satisfying. It frequently means a parting and a separation with consequent nostalgia, loneliness and mourning. It also often means giving up a simpler and easier and less effortful life in exchange for a more demanding, more difficult life. Growth forward is in spite of these losses and therefore requires courage, strength in the individual, as well as protection, permission and encouragement from the environment, especially for the child.[13]

What happens if the environment frowns on that courage and strength—sometimes virtually forbids, and seldom actually encourages that growth in the child who is a girl? What happens if human growth is considered antagonistic to femininity, to fulfillment as a woman, to woman's sexuality? The feminine mystique implies a choice between "being a woman" or risking the pains of human growth. Thousands of women, reduced to biological living by their environment, lulled into a false sense of anonymous security in their comfortable concentration camps, have made a wrong choice. The irony of their mistaken choice is this: the mystique holds out "feminine fulfillment" as the prize for being only a wife and mother. But it is no accident that thousands of suburban housewives have not found that prize. The simple truth would seem to be that women will never know sexual fulfillment and the peak experience of human love until they are allowed and encouraged to grow to their full strength as human beings. For according to the new psychological theorists, self-realization, far from preventing the highest sexual fulfillment, is inextricably linked to it. And there is more than theoretical reason to believe that this is as true for women as for men.

In the late thirties, Professor Maslow began to study the relationship between sexuality and what he called "dominance feeling" or "self-esteem" or "ego level" in women—130 women, of college education or of comparable intelligence, between twenty and twenty-eight, most of whom were married, of Protestant middle-class city background.[14] He found, contrary to what one might expect from the psychoanalytical theories and the conventional images of femininity, that the more "dominant" the woman, the greater her enjoyment of sexuality—and the greater her ability to "submit" in a psychological sense, to give herself freely in love, to have orgasm. It was not that these women higher in "dominance" were more "highly sexed," but they were, above all, more completely themselves, more free to be themselves—and this seemed inextricably linked with a greater freedom to give themselves in love. These women were not, in the usual sense, "feminine," but they enjoyed sexual fulfillment to a much higher degree than the conventionally feminine women in the same study.

I have never seen the implications of this research discussed in popular psychological literature about femininity or women's sexuality. It was, perhaps, not noticed at the time, even by the theorists, as a major landmark. But its findings are thought-provoking for American women today, who lead their lives according to the dictates of the feminine mystique. Remember that this study was done in the late 1930's, before the mystique became all-powerful. For these strong, spirited, educated women, evidently there was no conflict between the driving force to be themselves and to love. Here is the way Professor Maslow contrasted these women with their more "feminine" sisters—in terms of themselves, and in terms of their sexuality:

> High dominance feeling involves good self-confidence, self-assurance, high evaluation of the self, feelings of general capability or superiority, and lack of shyness, timidity, self-consciousness or embarrassment. Low dominance feeling involves lack of self-confidence, self-assurance and self-esteem; instead there are extensive feelings of general and specific inferiority, shyness, timidity, fearfulness, self-consciousness. . . . The person who describes herself as completely lacking in what she may call "self-confidence in general" will describe herself as self confident in her home, cooking, sewing or being a mother . . . but almost always underestimates to a greater or lesser degree her specific abilities and endowments; the high dominance person usually gauges her abilities accurately and realistically.[15]

These high-dominance women were not "feminine" in the conventional sense, partly because they felt free to choose rather than be bound by convention, and partly because they were stronger as individuals than most women.

> Such women prefer to be treated "Like a person, not like a woman." They prefer to be independent, stand on their own two feet, and generally do not care for concessions that imply they are inferior, weak or that they need special attention and cannot take care of themselves. This is not to imply that they cannot behave conventionally. They do when it is necessary or desirable for any reason, but they do not take the ordinary conventions seriously. A common phrase is "I can be nice and

sweet and clinging-vine as anyone else, but my tongue is in my cheek." . . . Rules per se generally mean nothing to these women. It is only when they approve of the rules and can see and approve of the purpose behind them that they will obey them. . . . They are strong, purposeful and do live by rules, but these rules are autonomous and personally arrived at. . . .

Low dominance women are very different. They . . . usually do not dare to break rules, even when they (rarely) disapprove of them. . . . Their morality and ethics are usually entirely conventional. That is, they do what they have been taught to do by their parents, their teachers, or their religion. The dictum of authority is usually not questioned openly, and they are more apt to approve of the status quo in every field of life, religious, economic, educational and political.[16]

Professor Maslow found that the higher the dominance, or strength of self in a woman, the less she was self-centered and the more her concern was directed outward to other people and to problems of the world. On the other hand, the main preoccupation of the more conventionally feminine low-dominance women was themselves and their own inferiorities. From a psychological point of view, a high-dominance woman was more like a high-dominance man than she was like a low-dominance woman. Thus Professor Maslow suggested that either you have to describe as "masculine" both high-dominance men and women or drop the terms "masculine" and "feminine" altogether because they are so "misleading."

Our high dominance women feel more akin to men than to women in tastes, attitudes, prejudices, aptitudes, philosophy, and inner personality in general. . . . Many of the qualities that are considered in our culture to be "manly" are seen in them in high degree, e.g., leadership, strength of character, strong social purpose, emancipation from trivialities, lack of fear, shyness, etc. They do not ordinarily care to be housewives or cooks alone, but wish to combine marriage with a career. . . . Their salary may come to no more than the salary of a housekeeper, but they feel other work to be more important than sewing, cooking, etc.[17]

Above all, the high-dominance woman was more psychologically free—more autonomous. The low-dominance woman was not free to be herself, she was other-directed. The more her self-depreciation, self-distrust, the more likely she was to feel another's opinion more valid than her own, and to wish she were more like someone else. Such women "usually admire and respect others more than they do themselves"; and along with this "tremendous respect for authority," with idolization and imitation of others, with the complete "voluntary subordination to others" and the great respect for others, went "hatred, and resentment, envy, jealousy, suspicion, distrust."

Where the high-dominance women were freely angry, the low-dominance women did not "have 'nerve' enough to say what they think and courage enough to show anger when it is necessary." Thus, their "feminine" quietness was a concomitant of "shyness, inferiority feelings, and a general feeling that anything they could say would be stupid and would be laughed at." Such a woman "does not want to be a leader except in her fantasies, for she is afraid of being in the forefront, she is afraid of responsibility, and she feels that she would be incompetent."

And again Professor Maslow found an evident link between strength of self and sexuality, the freedom to be oneself and the freedom to "submit." He found that the women who were "timid, shy, modest, neat, tactful, quiet, introverted, retiring, more feminine, more conventional," were not capable of enjoying the kind of sexual fulfillment which was freely enjoyed by women high in dominance and self-esteem.

> It would seem as if every sexual impulse or desire that has ever been spoken of may emerge freely and without inhibition in these women. . . . Generally the sexual act is apt to be taken not as a serious rite with fearful aspects, and differing in fundamental quality from all other acts, but as a game, as fun, as a highly pleasurable animal act.[18]

Moreover, Maslow found that, even in dreams and fantasies, women of above-average dominance enjoyed sexuality, while in low-dominance women the sexual dreams are always "of the romantic sort, or else are anxious, distorted, symbolized and concealed."

Did the makers of the mystique overlook such strong and sexually joyous women when they defined passivity and renunciation of personal achievement and activity in the world as the price of feminine sexual fulfillment? Perhaps Freud and his followers did not see such women in their clinics when they created that image of passive femininity. Perhaps the strength of self which Maslow found in the cases he studied was a new phenomenon in women.

The mystique kept even the behavioral scientists from exploring the relationship between sex and self in women in the ensuing era. But, quite aside from questions of women, in recent years behavioral scientists have become increasingly uneasy about basing their image of human nature on a study of its diseased or stunted specimens—patients in the clinic. In this context, Professor Maslow later set about to study people, dead and alive, who showed no evidence of neurosis, psychosis, or psychopathic personality; people who, in his view, showed positive evidence of self-realization, or "self-actualization," which he defined as "the full use and exploitation of talents, capacities, potentialities. Such people seem to be fulfilling themselves and to be doing the best that they are capable of doing. . . . They are people who have developed or are developing to the full stature of which they are capable."[19]

There are many things that emerged from this study which bear directly on the problem of women in America today. For one thing, among the public figures included in his study, Professor Maslow was able to find only two women who had actually fulfilled themselves—Eleanor Roosevelt and Jane Addams. (The men included Lincoln, Jefferson, Einstein, Freud, G. W. Carver, Debs, Schweitzer, Kreisler, Goethe, Thoreau, William James, Spinoza, Whitman, Franklin Roosevelt, Beethoven.) Apart from public and historical figures, he studied at close range a small number of unnamed subjects who met his criteria—all in their 50's and 60's— and he screened 3,000 college students, finding only twenty who seemed to be developing in the direction of self-actualization; here also, there were very few women. As a matter of fact, his findings implied that self-actualization, or the full realization of human potential, was hardly possible at all for women in our society.

Professor Maslow found in his study that self-actualizing people invariably have a commitment, a sense of mission in life that makes them live in a very large human world, a frame of reference beyond privatism and preoccupation with the petty details of daily life.

> These individuals customarily have some mission in life, some task to fulfill, some problem outside themselves which enlists much of their energies. . . . In general, these tasks are nonpersonal or unselfish, concerned rather with the good of mankind in general, or of a nation in general. . . . Ordinarily concerned with basic issues and eternal questions, such people live customarily in the widest possible frame of reference. . . . They work within a framework of values that are broad and not petty, universal and not local, and in terms of a century rather than a moment. . . . [20]

Further, Professor Maslow saw that self-actualizing people, who live in a larger world, somehow thereby never stale in their enjoyment of the day-to-day living, the trivialities which can become unbearably chafing to those for whom they are the only world. They ". . . have the wonderful capacity to appreciate again and again, freshly and naively, the basic goods of life with awe, pleasure, wonder, and even ecstasy, however stale these experiences may have become to others."[21]

He also reported "the very strong impression that the sexual pleasures are found in their most intense and ecstatic perfection in
self-actualizing people." It seemed as if fulfillment of personal
capacity in this larger world opened new vistas of sexual ecstasy.
And yet sex, or even love, was not the driving purpose in their lives.

> In self-actualizing people, the orgasm is simultaneously more
> important and less important than in average people. It is often
> a profound and almost mystical experience, and yet the absence
> of sexuality is more easily tolerated by these people. . . . Loving
> at a higher need level makes the lower needs and their frustra-
> tions and satisfactions less important, less central, more easily
> neglected. But it also makes them more wholeheartedly enjoyed
> when gratified. . . . Food is simultaneously enjoyed and yet
> regarded as relatively unimportant in the total scheme of
> life. . . . Sex can be wholeheartedly enjoyed, enjoyed far beyond
> the possibility of the average person, even at the same time that
> it does not play a central role in the philosophy of life. It is
> something to be enjoyed, something to be taken for granted,
> something to build upon, something that is very basically
> important like water or food, and that can be enjoyed as much
> as these; but gratification should be taken for granted.[22]

With such people, the sexual orgasm is not always a "mystical
experience"; it may also be taken rather lightly, bringing "fun, mer-
riment, elation, feeling of well-being, gaiety. . . . It is cheerful,
humorous, and playful—and not primarily a striving, it is basically
an enjoyment and a delight." He also found, in contradiction both
to the conventional view and to esoteric theorists of sex, that in
self-actualizing people the quality of both love and sexual satisfaction improves with the age of the relationship. ("It is a very common
report from these individuals that sex is better than it used to be and
seems to be improving all the time.") For, as such a person, with the
years, becomes more and more himself, and truer to himself, he
seems also to have deeper and more profound relations with others,
to be capable of more fusion, greater love, more perfect identification with others, more transcendence of the boundaries of the self,
without ever giving up his own individuality.

> What we see is a fusion of great ability to love and at the same
> time great respect for the other and great respect for oneself. . . .
> Throughout the most intense and ecstatic love affairs, these
> people remain themselves and remain ultimately masters of
> themselves as well, living by their own standards, even though
> enjoying each other intensely.[23]

In our society, love has customarily been defined, at least for
women, as a complete merging of egos and a loss of separateness—

"togetherness," a giving up of individuality rather than a strengthening of it. But in the love of self-actualizing people, Maslow found
that the individuality is strengthened, that "the ego is in one sense
merged with another, but yet in another sense remains separate and
strong as always. The two tendencies, to transcend individuality and
to sharpen and strengthen it, must be seen as partners and not as
contradictory."

He also found in the love of self-actualizing people the tendency to
more and more complete spontaneity, the dropping of defenses,
growing intimacy, honesty, and self-expression. These people found
it possible to be themselves, to feel natural; they could be psychologically (as well as physically) naked and still feel loved and wanted and
secure; they could let their faults, weaknesses, physical and psychological shortcomings be freely seen. They did not always have to put
their best foot forward, to hide false teeth, gray hairs, signs of age;
they did not have to "work" continually at their relationships; there
was much less mystery and glamour, much less reserve and conceal-
ment and secrecy. In such people, there did not seem to be hostility
between the sexes. In fact, he found that such people "made no really
sharp differentiation between the roles and personalities of the two
sexes."

> That is, they did not assume that the female was passive and
> the male active, whether in sex or love or anything else. These
> people were all so certain of their maleness or femaleness that
> they did not mind taking on some of the cultural aspects of
> the opposite sex role. It was especially noteworthy that they
> could be both active and passive lovers, and this was the clear-
> est in the sexual act and in physical lovemaking. Kissing and
> being kissed, being above or below in the sexual act, taking
> the initiative, being quiet and receiving love, teasing and
> being teased—these were all found in both sexes.[24]

And thus, while in the conventional and even in the sophisticated
view, masculine and feminine love, active and passive, seem to be
at opposite poles, in self-actualizing people "the dichotomies are
resolved and the individual becomes both active and passive, both
selfish and unselfish, both masculine and feminine, both self-
interested and self-effacing."

Love for self-actualizing people differed from the conventional
definition of love in yet another way; it was not motivated by need,
to make up a deficiency in the self; it was more purely "gift" love, a
kind of "spontaneous admiration."[25]

Such disinterested admiration and love used to be considered a
superhuman ability, not a natural human one. But as Maslow says,

"human beings at their best, fully grown, show many characteristics one thought, in an earlier era, to be supernatural prerogatives."

And there, in the words "fully grown," is the clue to the mystery of the problem that has no name. The transcendence of self, in sexual orgasm, as in creative experience, can only be attained by one who is himself, or herself, complete, by one who has realized his or her own identity. The theorists know this is true for man, though they have never thought through the implications for women. The suburban doctors, gynecologists, obstetricians, child-guidance clinicians, pediatricians, marriage counselors, and ministers who treat women's problems have all seen it, without putting a name to it, or even reporting it as a phenomenon. What they have seen confirms that for woman, as for man, the need for self-fulfillment—autonomy, self-realization, independence, individuality, self-actualization—is as important as the sexual need, with as serious consequences when it is thwarted. Woman's sexual problems are, in this sense, by-products of the suppression of her basic need to grow and fulfill her potentialities as a human being, potentialities which the mystique of feminine fulfillment ignores.

Psychoanalysts have long suspected that woman's intelligence does not fully flower when she denies her sexual nature; but by the same token can her sexual nature fully flower when she must deny her intelligence, her highest human potential? All the words that have been written criticizing American women for castrating their husbands and sons, for dominating their children, for their material greediness, for their sexual frigidity or denial of femininity may simply mask this one underlying fact: that woman, no more than man, can live by sex alone; that her struggle for identity, autonomy—that "personally productive orientation based on the human need for active participation in a creative task"—is inextricably linked with her sexual fulfillment, as a condition of her maturity. In the attempt to live by sex alone, in the image of the feminine mystique, ultimately she must "castrate" the husband and sons who can never give her enough satisfaction to make up for lack of a self, and pass on to her daughters her own unspoken disappointment, self-denigration, and discontent.

Professor Maslow told me that he thought self-actualization is only possible for women today in America if one person can grow through another—that is, if the woman can realize her own potential through her husband and children. "We do not know if this is possible or not," he said.

The new theorists of the self, who are men, have usually evaded the question of self-realization for a woman. Bemused themselves by the feminine mystique, they assume that there must be some strange "difference" which permits a woman to find self-realization by living through her husband and children, while men must grow to theirs. It is still very difficult, even for the most advanced psychological theorist, to see woman as a separate self, a human being who, in that respect, is no different in her need to grow than is a man. Most of the conventional theories about women, as well as the feminine mystique, are based on this "difference." But the actual basis for this "difference" is the fact that the possibility for true self-realization has not existed for women until now.

Many psychologists, including Freud, have made the mistake of assuming from observations of women who did not have the education and the freedom to play their full part in the world, that it was woman's essential nature to be passive, conformist, dependent, fearful, childlike—just as Aristotle, basing his picture of human nature on his own culture and particular period of time, made the mistake of assuming that just because a man was a slave, this was his essential nature and therefore "it was good for him to be a slave."

Now that education, freedom, the right to work on the great human frontiers—all the roads by which men have realized themselves—are open to women, only the shadow of the past enshrined in the mystique of feminine fulfillment keeps women from finding their road. The mystique promises women sexual fulfillment through abdication of self. But there is massive statistical evidence that the very opening to American women of those roads to their own identity in society brought a real and dramatic increase in woman's capacity for sexual fulfillment: the orgasm. In the years between the "emancipation" of women won by the feminists and the sexual counterrevolution of the feminine mystique, American women enjoyed a decade-by-decade increase in sexual orgasm. And the women who enjoyed this the most fully were, above all, the women who went furthest on the road to self-realization, women who were educated for active participation in the world outside the home.

This evidence is found in two famous studies, generally not cited for this purpose. The first of these, the Kinsey report, was based on interviews with 5,940 women who grew up in the various decades of the twentieth century during which the emancipation of women was won, and before the era of the feminine mystique. Even according to Kinsey's measure of sexual fulfillment, the orgasm (which many psychologists, sociologists, and analysts have criticized for its narrow, mechanistic, over-physiological emphasis, and its disregard of basic psychological nuances), his study shows a dramatic increase in sexual fulfillment during these decades. The increase began with the generation born between 1900 and 1909, who were maturing and marrying in the 1920's—the era of feminism, the winning of the vote and the great emphasis on women's rights, independence, careers, and equality with men, including the right to sexual fulfillment. The increase in wives reaching orgasm and the decrease in frigid women continued in each succeeding generation down to the youngest generation in the Kinsey sample which was marrying in the 1940's.[26]

And the most "emancipated" women, women educated beyond college for professional careers, showed a far greater capacity for complete sexual enjoyment, full orgasm, than the rest. Contrary to the feminine mystique, the Kinsey figures showed that the more educated the woman, the more likely she was to enjoy full sexual orgasm more often, and the less likely to be frigid. The greater sexual enjoyment of women who had completed college, compared to those who had not gone beyond grade school or high school, and the even greater sexual enjoyment of women who had gone beyond college into higher professional training showed up from the first year of marriage, and continued to show up in the fifth, tenth, and fifteenth years of marriage. While Kinsey found only one American woman in ten who had never experienced sexual orgasm, the majority of women he interviewed did not experience it completely, all or almost all of the time—except for those women who were educated beyond college. The Kinsey figures also showed that women who married before twenty were least likely to experience sexual orgasm, and were likely to enjoy it less frequently in or out of marriage, though they started sexual intercourse five or six years earlier than women who finished college or graduate school.

While the Kinsey data showed that over the years "a distinctly higher proportion of the better educated females, in contrast to the grade school and high school females, had actually reached orgasm in a higher percentage of their marital coitus," the increased enjoyment of sex did not, for the most part, mean an increased incidence of it, in the woman's life. On the whole, there was a slight trend in the opposite direction. And that increase in extramarital sex was less marked with professionally trained women.[27]

Perhaps something about the supposedly "unfeminine" strength, or self-realization achieved by women educated for professional careers enabled them to enjoy greater sexual fulfillment in their marriages than other women—as measured by the orgasm—and thus less likely to seek it outside of marriage. Or perhaps they simply had less need to seek status, achievement, or identity in sex. The relationship between woman's sexual fulfillment and self-realization indicated by Kinsey's findings is underlined by the fact that, as many critics have pointed out, Kinsey's sample was over-representative of professional women, college graduates, women with unusually high "dominance" or strength of self. Kinsey's sample underrepresented the "typical" American housewife who devotes her life to husband,

home, and children; it underrepresented women with little education; because of its use of volunteers, it underrepresented the kind of
passive, submissive, conformist women whom Maslow found to be
incapable of sexual enjoyment.[28] The increase in sexual fulfillment
and decrease in frigidity which Kinsey found during the decades
after women's emancipation may not have been felt by the "average"
American housewife as much as by this minority of women who
directly experienced emancipation through education and participation in the professions. Nevertheless, the decrease in frigidity was so
dramatic in that large, if unrepresentative, sample of nearly 6,000
women, that even Kinsey's critics found it significant.

It was hardly an accident that this increase in woman's sexual
fulfillment accompanied her progress to equal participation in the
rights, education, work, and decisions of American society. The
coincidental sexual emancipation of American men—the lifting of
the veil of contempt and degradation from sexual intercourse—was
surely related to the American male's new regard for the American
woman as an equal, a person like himself, and not just a sexual
object. Evidently, the further women progressed from that state, the
more sex became an act of human intercourse rather than a dirty
joke to men; and the more women were able to love men, rather than
submit, in passive distaste, to their sexual desire. In fact, the feminine mystique itself—with its acknowledgment of woman as subject
and not just object of the sexual act, and its assumption that her
active, willing participation was essential to man's pleasure—could
not have come without the emancipation of women to human equality. As the early feminists foresaw, women's rights did indeed promote greater sexual fulfillment, for men and women.

Other studies also showed that education and independence
increased the American woman's ability to enjoy a sexual relationship with a man, and thus to affirm more fully her own sexual nature
as a woman. Repeated reports, before and after Kinsey, showed
college-educated women to have a much lower than average divorce
rate. More specifically, a massive and famous sociological study by
Ernest W. Burgess and Leonard S. Cottrell indicated that women's
chances of happiness in marriage increased as their career preparation increased—with teachers, professional nurses, women doctors,
and lawyers showing fewer unhappy marriages than any other group
of women. These women were more likely to enjoy happiness in marriage than women who held skilled office positions, who in turn, had
happier marriages than women who had not worked before marriage,
or who had no vocational ambition, or who worked at a job that was
not in accordance with their own ambitions, or whose only work
training or experience was domestic or unskilled. In fact, the higher

the woman's income at the time of her marriage, the more probable her married happiness. As the sociologists put it:

> Apparently in the case of wives, the traits that make for success in the business world as measured by monthly income are the traits that make for success in marriage. The point, of course, may be made that income indirectly measures education since the amount of educational training influences income.[29]

Among 526 couples, less than 10 per cent showed "low" marital adjustment where the wife had been employed seven or more years, had completed college or professional training, and had not married before twenty-two. Where wives had been educated *beyond college*, less than 5 per cent of marriages scored "low" in happiness. The following table shows the relationship between the marriage and the educational achievement of the wife.

Marriage Adjustment Scores
at Different Educational Levels

Wife's Educational Level	MARITAL ADJUSTMENT SCORE			
	Very low	*Low*	*High*	*Very high*
Graduate work	0.0	4.6	38.7	56.5
College	9.2	18.9	22.9	48.9
High School	14.4	16.3	32.2	37.1
Grades Only	33.3	25.9	25.9	14.8

One might have predicted from such evidence a relatively poor chance of married happiness, or of sexual fulfillment, or even of orgasm, for the women whom the mystique encouraged to marry before twenty, to forgo higher education, careers, independence, and equality with men in favor of femininity. And, as a matter of fact, the youngest group of wives studied by Kinsey—the generation born between 1920 and 1929 who met the feminine mystique head-on in the 1940's when the race back home began—showed, by the fifth year of marriage, a sharp reversal of that trend toward increased sexual fulfillment in marriage which had been manifest in every decade since women's emancipation in the 1920's.

> The percentage of women enjoying orgasm in all or nearly all of their married sex life in the fifth year of marriage had risen from 37% of women in the generation born before 1900 to 42% in the generations born in the next two decades. The youngest group, whose fifth year of marriage was in the late 1940's, enjoyed full orgasm in even less cases (36%) than women born before 1900.[30]

Would a new Kinsey study find the young wives who are products of the feminine mystique enjoying even less sexual fulfillment than their more emancipated, more independent, more educated, more grownup-when-married forebears? Only fourteen per cent of Kinsey's women had married by twenty; a bare majority—fifty-three per cent—had married by twenty-five, though most did marry. This is quite a difference from the America of the 1960's, when fifty per cent of women marry in their teens.

Recently, Helene Deutsch, the eminent psychoanalyst who went even further than Freud in equating femininity with masochistic passivity and, in warning women that "outward-directed activity" and "masculinizing" intellectuality might interfere with a fully feminine orgasm, threw a psychoanalytic conference into an uproar by suggesting that perhaps too much emphasis had been put on "the orgasm" for women. In the 1960's, she was suddenly not so sure that women had to have, or could have, a real orgasm. Perhaps a more "diffuse" fulfillment was all that could be expected. After all, she had women patients who were absolutely psychotic who seemed to have orgasms; but most women she saw now did not seem to have them at all.

What did it mean? Could women, then, not experience orgasm? Or had something happened, during this time when so much emphasis has been placed on sexual fulfillment, to keep women from experiencing orgasm? The experts did not all agree. But in other contexts, not concerned with women, analysts reported that passive people who "psychologically feel empty"—who fail to "develop adequate egos," have "little sense of their own identity"— cannot submit to the experience of sexual orgasm for fear of their own non-existence.[31] Fanned into an all-consuming sexual search by the popularizers of Freudian "femininity," many women had, in effect, renounced everything for the orgasm that was supposed to be at the end of the rainbow. To say the least, they directed quite a lot of their emotional energies and needs toward the sexual act. As somebody said about a truly beautiful woman in America, her image has been so overexposed in the ads, television, movies, that when you see the real thing, you're disappointed. Without even delving into the murky depths of the unconscious, one might assume it was asking a lot of the beautiful orgasm, not only to live up to its overadvertised claims, but to constitute the equivalent of an A in sex, a salary raise, a good review on opening night, promotion to senior editor or associate professor, much less the basic "experience of oneself," the sense of identity.[32] As one psychotherapist reported:

> One of the major reasons, ironically, why so many women are not achieving full-flowering sexuality today is because they are

so over determined to achieve it. They are so ashamed if they do not reach the heights of expressive sensuality that they tragically sabotage their own desires. That is to say, instead of focusing clearly on the real problem at hand, these women are focusing on quite a different problem, namely, "Oh, what an idiot and an incompetent person I am for not being able to achieve satisfaction without difficulty." Today's women are often obsessed with the notion of *how*, rather than *what*, they are doing when they are having marital relations. That is fatal.

If sex itself, as another psychoanalyst put it, is beginning to have a "depressive" quality in America, it is perhaps because too many Americans—especially the women sex-seekers—are putting into the sexual search all their frustrated needs for self-realization. American women are suffering, quite simply, a massive sickness of sex without self. No one has warned them that sex can never be a substitute for personal identity; that sex itself cannot give identity to a woman, any more than to a man; that there may be no sexual fulfillment at all for the woman who seeks her self in sex.

The question of how a person can most fully realize his own capacities and thus achieve identity has become an important concern of the philosophers and the social and psychological thinkers of our time—and for good reason. Thinkers of other times put forth the idea that people were, to a great extent, defined by the work they did. The work that a man had to do to eat, to stay alive, to meet the physical necessities of his environment, dictated his identity. And in this sense, when work is seen merely as a means of survival, human identity was dictated by biology.

But today the problem of human identity has changed. For the work that defined man's place in society and his sense of himself has also changed man's world. Work, and the advance of knowledge, has lessened man's dependence on his environment; his biology and the work he must do for biological survival are no longer sufficient to define his identity. This can be most clearly seen in our own abundant society; men no longer need to work all day to eat. They have an unprecedented freedom to choose the kind of work they will do; they also have an unprecedented amount of time apart from the hours and days that must actually be spent in making a living. And suddenly one realizes the significance of today's identity crisis—for women, and increasingly, for men. One sees the human significance of work—not merely as the means of biological survival, but as the giver of self and the transcender of self, as the creator of human identity and human evolution.

For "self-realization" or "self-fulfillment" or "identity" does not come from looking into a mirror in rapt contemplation of one's own image. Those who have most fully realized themselves, in a sense that can be recognized by the human mind even though it cannot be clearly defined, have done so in the service of a human purpose larger than themselves. Men from varying disciplines have used different words for this mysterious process from which comes the sense of self. The religious mystics, the philosophers, Marx, Freud— all had different names for it: man finds himself by losing himself; man is defined by his relation to the means of production; the ego, the self, grows through understanding and mastering reality— through work and love.

The identity crisis, which has been noted by Erik Erikson and others in recent years in the American man, seems to occur for lack of, and be cured by finding, the work, or cause, or purpose that evokes his own creativity.[33] Some never find it, for it does not come from busy-work or punching a time clock. It does not come from just making a living, working by formula, finding a secure spot as an organization man. The very argument, by Riesman and others, that man no longer finds identity in the work defined as a paycheck job, assumes that identity for man comes through creative work of his own that contributes to the human community: the core of the self becomes aware, becomes real, and grows through work that carries forward human society.

Work, the shopworn staple of the economists, has become the new frontier of psychology. Psychiatrists have long used "occupational therapy" with patients in mental hospitals; they have recently discovered that to be of real psychological value, it must be not just "therapy," but real work, serving a real purpose in the community. And work can now be seen as the key to the problem that has no name. The identity crisis of American women began a century ago, as more and more of the work important to the world, more and more of the work that used their human abilities and through which they were able to find self-realization, was taken from them.

Until, and even into, the last century, strong, capable women were needed to pioneer our new land; with their husbands, they ran the farms and plantations and Western homesteads. These women were respected and self-respecting members of a society whose pioneering purpose centered in the home. Strength and independence, responsibility and self-confidence, self-discipline and courage, freedom and equality were part of the American character for both men and women, in all the first generations. The women who came by steerage from Ireland, Italy, Russia, and Poland worked beside their husbands in the sweatshops and the laundries, learned the new language, and saved to send their sons and daughters to college. Women were never quite as "feminine," or held in as much contempt, in America as they were in Europe. American women seemed to European travelers, long before our time, less passive, childlike, and feminine than their own wives in France or Germany or England. By an accident of history, American women shared in the work of society longer, and grew with the men. Grade- and high-school education for boys and girls alike was almost always the rule; and in the West, where women shared the pioneering work the longest, even the universities were coeducational from the beginning.

The identity crisis for women did not begin in America until the fire and strength and ability of the pioneer women were no longer needed, no longer used, in the middle-class homes of the Eastern and Midwestern cities, when the pioneering was done and men began to build the new society in industries and professions outside the home. But the daughters of the pioneer women had grown too used to freedom and work to be content with leisure and passive femininity.[34]

It was not an American, but a South African woman, Mrs. Olive Schreiner,* who warned at the turn of the century that the quality and quantity of women's functions in the social universe were decreasing as fast as civilization was advancing; that if women did not win back their right to a full share of honored and useful work, woman's mind and muscle would weaken in a parasitic state; her offspring, male and female, would weaken progressively, and civilization itself would deteriorate.[35]

The feminists saw clearly that education and the right to participate in the more advanced work of society were women's greatest needs. They fought for and won the rights to new, fully human identity for women. But how very few of their daughters and granddaughters have chosen to use their education and their abilities for any large creative purpose, for responsible work in society? How many of them have been deceived, or have deceived themselves, into clinging to the outgrown, childlike femininity of "Occupation: housewife"?

It was not a minor matter, their mistaken choice. We now know that the same range of potential ability exists for women as for men. Women, as well as men, can only find their identity in work that uses their full capacities. A woman cannot find her identity through others—her husband, her children. She cannot find it in the dull routine of housework. As thinkers of every age have said, it is only when a human being faces squarely the fact that he can forfeit his own life, that he becomes truly aware of himself, and begins to take his existence seriously. Sometimes this awareness comes only at the moment of death. Sometimes it comes from a more subtle facing of

---

* Olive Schreiner (1855–1920), South African feminist and socialist writer who addressed many topics related to women's position in society as it relates to capitalism, racism, and imperialism. Her works include the acclaimed novel *The Story of an African Farm* (1883), published under the pseudonym "Ralph Iron," as well as *Women and Labour* (1911).

death: the death of self in passive conformity, in meaningless work. The feminine mystique prescribes just such a living death for women. Faced with the slow death of self, the American woman must begin to take her life seriously.

"We measure ourselves by many standards," said the great American psychologist William James,* nearly a century ago. "Our strength and our intelligence, our wealth and even our good luck, are things which warm our heart and make us feel ourselves a match for life. But deeper than all such things, and able to suffice unto itself without them, is the sense of the amount of effort which we can put forth."[36]

If women do not put forth, finally, that effort to become all that they have it in them to become, they will forfeit their own humanity. A woman today who has no goal, no purpose, no ambition patterning her days into the future, making her stretch and grow beyond that small score of years in which her body can fill its biological function, is committing a kind of suicide. For that future half a century after the child-bearing years are over is a fact that an American woman cannot deny. Nor can she deny that as a housewife, the world is indeed rushing past her door while she just sits and watches. The terror she feels is real, if she has no place in that world.

The feminine mystique has succeeded in burying millions of American women alive. There is no way for these women to break out of their comfortable concentration camps except by finally putting forth an effort—that human effort which reaches beyond biology, beyond the narrow walls of home, to help shape the future. Only by such a personal commitment to the future can American women break out of the housewife trap and truly find fulfillment as wives and mothers—by fulfilling their own unique possibilities as separate human beings.

14

A New Life Plan for Women

"Easy enough to say," the woman inside the housewife's trap remarks, "but what can I do, alone in the house, with the children yelling and the laundry to sort and no grandmother to babysit?" It is easier to live through someone else than to become complete yourself. The freedom to lead and plan your own life is frightening if you have

---

* William James (1842–1910), psychologist and philosopher who helped to develop the modern science of psychology in the United States, as well as the American school of philosophy known as pragmatism.

never faced it before. It is frightening when a woman finally realizes that there is no answer to the question "who am I" except the voice inside herself. She may spend years on the analyst's couch, working out her "adjustment to the feminine role," her blocks to "fulfillment as a wife and mother." And still the voice inside her may say, "That's not it." Even the best psychoanalyst can only give her the courage to listen to her own voice. When society asks so little of women, every woman has to listen to her own inner voice to find her identity in the changing world. She must create, out of her own needs and abilities, a new life plan, fitting in the love and children and home that have defined femininity in the past with the work toward a greater purpose that shapes the future.

To face the problem is not to solve it. But once a woman faces it, as women are doing today all over America without much help from the experts, once she asks herself "What do I want to do?" she begins to find her own answers. Once she begins to see through the delusions of the feminine mystique—and realizes that neither her husband nor her children, nor the things in her house, nor sex, nor being like all the other women, can give her a self—she often finds the solution much easier than she anticipated.

Of the many women I talked to in the suburbs and cities, some were just beginning to face the problem, others were well on their way to solving it, and for still others it was no longer a problem. In the stillness of an April afternoon with all her children in school, a woman told me:

> I put all my energies into the children, carting them around, worrying about them, teaching them things. Suddenly, there was this terrible feeling of emptiness. All that volunteer work I'd taken on—Scouts, PTA, the League, just didn't seem worth doing all of a sudden. As a girl, I wanted to be an actress. It was too late to go back to that. I stayed in the house all day, cleaning things I hadn't cleaned in years. I spent a lot of time just crying. My husband and I talked about its being an American woman's problem, how you give up a career for the children, and then you reach a point where you can't go back. I felt so envious of the few women I know who had a definite skill and kept working at it. My dream of being an actress wasn't real—I didn't work at it. Did I have to throw my whole self into the children? I've spent my whole life just immersed in other people, and never even knew what kind of a person I was myself. Now I think even having another baby wouldn't solve that emptiness long. You can't go back—you have to go on. There must be some real way I can go on myself.

This woman was just beginning her search for identity. Another woman had made it to the other side, and could look back now and

see the problem clearly. Her home was colorful, casual, but techni-
cally she was no longer "just a housewife." She was paid for her work
as a professional painter. She told me that when she stopped conforming to the conventional picture of femininity she finally began to
enjoy being a woman. She said:

> I used to work so hard to maintain this beautiful picture of
> myself as a wife and mother. I had all of my children by natural
> childbirth. I breastfed them all. I got mad once at an older
> woman at a party when I said childbirth is the most important
> thing in life, the basic animal, and she said, "Don't you want to
> be more than an animal?"
>
> You do want something more, only you don't know what it is.
> So you put even more into housekeeping. It's not challenging
> enough, just ironing dresses for your little girls, so you go in for
> ruffly dresses that need more ironing, and bake your own
> bread, and refuse to get a dishwasher. You think if you make a
> big enough challenge out of it, then somehow it will be satisfy-
> ing. And still it wasn't.
>
> I almost had an affair. I used to feel so discontented with my
> husband. I used to feel outraged if he didn't help with the
> housework. I insisted that he do dishes, scrub floors, everything.
> We wouldn't quarrel, but you can't deceive yourself sometimes
> in the middle of the night.
>
> I couldn't seem to control this feeling that I wanted some-
> thing more from life. So I went to a psychiatrist. He kept trying
> to make me enjoy being feminine, but it didn't help. And then I
> went to one who seemed to make me find out who I was, and
> forget about this beautiful feminine picture. I realized I was
> furious at myself, furious at my husband, because I'd left school.
>
> I used to put the kids in the car and just drive because I
> couldn't bear to be alone in the house. I kept wanting to do
> something, but I was afraid to try. One day on a back road I saw
> an artist painting, and it was like a voice I couldn't control say-
> ing "Do you give lessons?"
>
> I'd take care of the house and kids all day, and after I fin-
> ished the dishes at night, I'd paint. Then I took the bedroom
> we were going to use for another baby—five children was part
> of my beautiful picture—and used it for a studio for myself. I
> remember one night working and working and suddenly it was
> 2 A.M. and I was finished. I looked at the picture, and it was
> like finding myself.
>
> I can't think what I was trying to do with my life before, trying
> to fit some picture of an oldtime woman pioneer. I don't have to
> prove I'm a woman by sewing my own clothes. I am a woman,
> and I am myself, and I buy clothes and love them. I'm not such a
> darned patient, loving, perfect mother anymore. I don't change

the kids' clothes top to bottom every day, and no more ruffles. But I seem to have more time to enjoy them. I don't spend much time on housework now, but it's done before my husband gets home. We bought a dishwasher.

The longer it takes to wash dishes, the less time you have for anything else. It's not creative, doing the same thing over and over. Why should a woman feel guilty at getting rid of this repetitive work. There's no virtue in dishwashing, scrubbing floors. Dacron, dishwashers, drip dry—this is fine, this is the direction physical life should take. This is our time, our only time on earth. We can't keep throwing it away. My time is all I've got, and this is what I want to do with it.

I don't need to make such a production of my marriage now because it's real. Somehow, once I began to have the sense of myself, I became aware of my husband. Before, it was like he was part of me, not a separate human being. I guess it wasn't till I stopped trying to be feminine that I began to enjoy being a woman.

And then, there were others, teetering back and forth, aware of the problem but not yet quite sure what to do about it. The chairman of a suburban fund-raising committee said:

I envy Jean who stays at home and does the work she wants to do. I haven't opened my easel in two months. I keep getting so involved in committees I don't care about. It's the thing to do to get in with the crowd here. But it doesn't make me feel quiet inside, the way I feel when I paint. An artist in the city told me, "You should take yourself more seriously. You can be an artist and a housewife and a mother—all three." I guess the only thing that stops me is that it's hard work.

A young Ohio woman told me:

Lately, I've felt this need. I felt we simply had to have a bigger house, put on an addition, or move to a better neighborhood. I went on a frantic round of entertaining but that was like living for the interruptions of your life.

My husband thinks that being a good mother is the most important career there is. I think it's even more important than a career. But I don't think most women are all mother. I enjoy my kids, but I don't like spending all my time with them. I'm just not their age. I could make housework take up more of my time. But the floors don't need vacuuming more than twice a week. My mother swept them every day.

I always wanted to play the violin. When I went to college, girls who took music seriously were peculiar. Suddenly, it was as if some voice inside me said, now is the time, you'll never get another chance. I felt embarrassed, practicing at forty. It exhausts me and hurts my shoulder, but it makes me feel at one with something larger than myself. The universe suddenly becomes real, and you're part of it. You feel as if you really exist.

It would be quite wrong for me to offer any woman easy how-to answers to this problem. There are no easy answers, in America today; it is difficult, painful, and takes perhaps a long time for each woman to find her own answer. First, she must unequivocally say "no" to the housewife image. This does not mean, of course, that she must divorce her husband, abandon her children, give up her home. She does not have to choose between marriage and career; that was the mistaken choice of the feminine mystique. In actual fact, it is not as difficult as the feminine mystique implies, to combine marriage and motherhood and even the kind of lifelong personal purpose that once was called "career." It merely takes a new life plan—in terms of one's whole life as a woman.

The first step in that plan is to see housework for what it is—not a career, but something that must be done as quickly and efficiently as possible. Once a woman stops trying to make cooking, cleaning, washing, ironing, "something more," she can say "no, I don't want a stove with rounded corners, I don't want four different kinds of soap." She can say "no" to those mass daydreams of the women's magazines and television, "no" to the depth researchers and manipulators who are trying to run her life. Then, she can use the vacuum cleaner and the dishwasher and all the automatic appliances, and even the instant mashed potatoes for what they are truly worth—to save time that can be used in more creative ways.

The second step, and perhaps the most difficult for the products of sex-directed education, is to see marriage as it really is, brushing aside the veil of over-glorification imposed by the feminine mystique. Many women I talked to felt strangely discontented with their husbands, continually irritated with their children, when they saw marriage and motherhood as the final fulfillment of their lives. But when they began to use their various abilities with a purpose of their own in society, they not only spoke of a new feeling of "aliveness" or "completeness" in themselves, but of a new, though hard to define, difference in the way they felt about their husbands and children. Many echoed this woman's words:

> The funny thing is, I enjoy my children more now that I've made room for myself. Before, when I was putting my whole self into the children, it was as if I was always looking for something through them. I couldn't just enjoy them as I do now, as though they were a sunset, something outside me, separate. Before, I

felt so tied down by them, I'd try to get away in my mind. Maybe a woman has to be *by herself* to be really *with* her children.

A New England lawyer's wife told me:

> I thought I had finished. I had come to the end of childhood, had married, had a baby, and I was happy with my marriage. But somehow I was disconsolate, because I assumed this was the end. I would take up upholstery one week, Sunday painting the next. My house was spotless. I devoted entirely too much time to entertaining my child. He didn't need all that adult companionship. A grown woman playing with a child all day, disintegrating herself in a hundred directions to fill the time, cooking fancy food when no one needs it, and then furious if they don't eat it— you lose your adult common sense, your whole sense of yourself as a human being.
>
> Now I'm studying history, one course a year. It's work, but I haven't missed a night in 2 1/2 years. Soon I'll be teaching. I love being a wife and mother, but I know now that when marriage is the end of your life, because you have no other mission, it becomes a miserable, tawdry thing. Who said women have to be happy, to be amused, to be entertained? You have to work. You don't have to have a job. But you have to tackle something yourself, and see it through, to feel alive.

An hour a day, a weekend, or even a week off from motherhood is not the answer to the problem that has no name. That "mother's hour off,"[1] as advised by child-and-family experts or puzzled doctors as the antidote for the housewife's fatigue or trapped feeling, assumes automatically that a woman is "just a housewife," now and forever a mother. A person fully used by his work can enjoy "time off." But the mothers I talked to did not find any magical relief in an "hour off"; in fact, they often gave it up on the slightest pretext, either from guilt or from boredom. A woman who has no purpose of her own in society, a woman who cannot let herself think about the future because she is doing nothing to give herself a real identity in it, will continue to feel a desperation in the present—no matter how many "hours off" she takes. Even a very young woman today must think of herself as a human being first, not as a mother with time on her hands, and make a life plan in terms of her own abilities, a commitment of her own to society, with which her commitments as wife and mother can be integrated.

A woman I interviewed, a mental-health educator who was for many years "just a housewife" in her suburban community, sums it up: "I remember my own feeling that life wasn't full enough for me. I wasn't using myself in terms of my capacities. It wasn't enough making a home. You can't put the genie back in the bottle. You can't just deny your intelligent mind; you need to be part of the social scheme."

And looking over the trees of her garden to the quiet, empty suburban street, she said:

> If you knock on any of these doors, how many women would you find whose abilities are being used? You'd find them drinking, or sitting around talking to other women and watching children play because they can't bear to be alone, or watching TV or reading a book. Society hasn't caught up with women yet, hasn't found a way yet to use the skills and energies of women except to bear children. Over the last fifteen years, I think women have been running away from themselves. The reason the young ones have swallowed this feminine business is because they think if they go back and look for all their satisfaction in the home, it will be easier. But it won't be. Somewhere along the line a woman, if she is going to come to terms with herself, has to find herself as a person.

The only way for a woman, as for a man, to find herself, to know herself as a person, is by creative work of her own. There is no other way. But a job, any job, is not the answer—in fact, it can be part of the trap. Women who do not look for jobs equal to their actual capacity, who do not let themselves develop the lifetime interests and goals which require serious education and training, who take a job at twenty or forty to "help out at home" or just to kill extra time, are walking, almost as surely as the ones who stay inside the housewife trap, to a nonexistent future.

If a job is to be the way out of the trap for a woman, it must be a job that she can take seriously as part of a life plan, work in which she can grow as part of society. Suburban communities, particularly the new communities where social, cultural, educational, political, and recreational patterns are not as yet firmly established, offer numerous opportunities for the able, intelligent woman. But such work is not necessarily a "job." In Westchester, on Long Island, in the Philadelphia suburbs, women have started mental-health clinics, art centers, day camps. In big cities and small towns, women all the way from New England to California have pioneered new movements in politics and education. Even if this work was not thought of as "job" or "career," it was often so important to the various communities that professionals are now being paid for doing it.

In some suburbs and communities there is now little work left for the nonprofessional that requires intelligence—except for the few positions of leadership which most women, these days, lack the independence, the strength, the self-confidence to take. If the com-

munity has a high proportion of educated women, there simply are
not enough such posts to go around. As a result, community work
often expands in a kind of self-serving structure of committees and
red tape, in the purest sense of Parkinson's law, until its real purpose seems to be just to keep women busy. Such busywork is not
satisfying to mature women, nor does it help the immature to grow.
This is not to say that being a den mother, or serving on a PTA committee, or organizing a covered-dish supper is not useful work; for a
woman of intelligence and ability, it is simply not enough.

One woman I interviewed had involved herself in an endless whirl
of worthwhile community activities. But they led in no direction for
her own future, nor did they truly utilize her exceptional intelligence.
Indeed, her intelligence seemed to deteriorate; she suffered the problem that has no name with increasing severity until she took the first
step toward a serious commitment. Today she is a "master teacher," a
serene wife and mother.

> At first, I took on the hospital fund-raising committee, the cleri-
> cal volunteers committee for the clinic. I was class mother for
> the children's field trips. I was taking piano lessons to the tune
> of $30 a week, paying baby sitters so I could play for my own
> amusement. I did the Dewey decimal system for the library we
> started, and the usual den mother and PTA. The financial out-
> lay for all these things which were only needed to fill up my life
> was taking a good slice out of my husband's income. And it still
> didn't fill up my life. I was cranky and moody. I would burst into
> tears for no reason. I couldn't even concentrate to finish a detec-
> tive story.
>
> I was so busy, running from morning till night, and yet I never
> had any real feeling of satisfaction. You raise your kids, sure, but
> how can that justify your life? You have to have some ultimate
> objective, some long-term goal to keep you going. Community
> activities are short-term goals; you do a project; it's done; then
> you have to hunt for another one. In community work, they say
> you mustn't bother the young mothers with little children. This
> is the job of the middle-aged ones whose kids are grown. But it's
> just the ones who are tied down with the kids who need to do
> this. When you're not tied down by kids, drop that stuff—you
> need real work.

Because of the feminine mystique (and perhaps because of the
simple human fear of failure, when one does compete, without sexual privilege or excuse), it is the jump from amateur to professional
that is often hardest for a woman on her way out of the trap. But even
if a woman does not have to work to eat, she can find identity only in
work that is of real value to society[2]—work for which, usually, our

society pays. Being paid is, of course, more than a reward—it implies a definite commitment. For fear of that commitment, hundreds of able, educated suburban housewives today fool themselves about the writer or actress they might have been, or dabble at art or music in the dilettante's limbo of "self-enrichment," or apply for jobs as receptionists or saleswomen, jobs well below their actual abilities. These are also ways of evading growth.

The growing boredom of American women with volunteer work, and their preference for paid jobs, no matter how low-level, has been attributed to the fact that professionals have taken over most of the posts in the community requiring intelligence. But the fact that women did not become professionals themselves, the reluctance of women in the last twenty years to commit themselves to work, paid or unpaid, requiring initiative, leadership and responsibility is due to the feminine mystique. This attitude of noncommitment among young housewives was confirmed by a recent study done in Westchester County.[3] In an upper-income suburb, more than 50% of a group of housewives between 25 and 35, with husbands in the over-$25,000-a-year income group, wanted to go to work: 13% immediately, the rest in 5 to 15 years. Of those who planned to go to work, 3 out of 4 felt inadequately prepared. (All of these women had some college education but only one a graduate degree; a third had married at twenty or before.) These women were not driven to go to work by economic need but by what the anthropologist who made the survey called "the psychological need to be economically productive." Evidently, volunteer work did not meet this need; though 62% of these women were doing volunteer work, it was of the "one-day and under" variety. And though they wanted jobs and felt inadequately prepared, of the 45% taking courses, very few were working toward a degree. The element of phantasy in their work plans was witnessed by "the small businesses that open and close with sad regularity." When an alumnae association sponsored a two-session forum in the suburb on "How Women in the Middle Years Can Return to Work," twenty-five women attended. As a beginning step, each woman was asked to come to the second meeting with a résumé. The résumé took some thought, and, as the researcher put it, "sincerity of purpose." Only one woman was serious enough to write the résumé.

In another suburb, there is a guidance center which in the early years of the mental-health movement gave real scope to the intelligence of college-educated women of the community. They never did therapy, of course, but in the early years they administered the center and led the educational parent-discussion groups. Now that "education for family living" has become professionalized, the center is administered and the discussion groups led by professionals, often brought in from the city, who have M.A.'s or doctorates in the field. In only a very few cases did the women who "found themselves" in the work of the guidance center go on in the new profession, and get their own M.A.'s and Ph.D.'s. Most backed off when to continue would have meant breaking away from the housewife role, and becoming seriously committed to a profession.

Ironically, the only kind of work which permits an able woman to realize her abilities fully, to achieve identity in society in a life plan that can encompass marriage and motherhood, is the kind that was forbidden by the feminine mystique; the lifelong commitment to an art or science, to politics or profession. Such a commitment is not tied to a specific job or locality. It permits year-to-year variation—a full-time paid job in one community, part-time in another, exercise of the professional skill in serious volunteer work or a period of study during pregnancy or early motherhood when a full-time job is not feasible. It is a continuous thread, kept alive by work and study and contacts in the field, in any part of the country.

The women I found who had made and kept alive such long-term commitments did not suffer the problem that has no name. Nor did they live in the housewife image. But music or art or politics offered no magic solution for the women who did not, or could not, commit themselves seriously. The "arts" seem, at first glance, to be the ideal answer for a woman. They can, after all, be practiced in the home. They do not necessarily imply that dreaded professionalism, they are suitably feminine, and seem to offer endless room for personal growth and identity, with no need to compete in society for pay. But I have noticed that when women do not take up painting or ceramics seriously enough to become professionals—to be paid for their work, or for teaching it to others, and to be recognized as a peer by other professionals—sooner or later, they cease dabbling; the Sunday painting, the idle ceramics do not bring that needed sense of self when they are of no value to anyone else. The amateur or dilettante whose own work is not good enough for anyone to want to pay to hear or see or read does not gain real status by it in society, or real personal identity. These are reserved for those who have made the effort, acquired the knowledge and expertise to become professionals.

There are, of course, a number of practical problems involved in making a serious professional commitment. But somehow those problems only seem insurmountable when a woman is still half-submerged in the false dilemmas and guilts of the feminine mystique—or when her desire for "something more" is only phantasy, and she is unwilling to make the necessary effort. Over and over, women told me that the crucial step for them was simply to take the first trip to the alumnae employment agency, or to send for the application for teacher certification, or to make appointments with former job contacts in the city. It is amazing how many obstacles and rationalizations the feminine mystique can throw up to keep a woman from making that trip or writing that letter.

One suburban housewife I knew had once been a newspaper woman, but she was sure she could never get that kind of job again; she had been away too long. And, of course, she couldn't really leave her children (who, by then, were all in school during the day). As it turned out, when she finally decided to do something about it, she found an excellent job in her old field after only two trips into the city. Another woman, a psychiatric social worker, said that she could not take a regular agency job, only volunteer jobs without deadlines that she could put down when she felt like it, because she could not count on a cleaning woman. Actually, if she had hired a cleaning woman, which many of her neighbors were doing for much less reason, she would have had to commit herself to the kind of assignments that would have been a real test of her ability. Obviously she was afraid of such a test.

A great many suburban housewives today step back from, or give up, volunteer activity, art, or job at the very point when all that is needed is a more serious commitment. The PTA leader won't run for the school board. The League of Women Voters' leader is afraid to move on into the rough mainstream of her political party. "Women can't get a policy-making role," she says. "I'm not going to lick stamps." Of course, it would require more effort for her to win a policy-making role in her party against the prejudices and the competition of the men.

Some women take the jobs but do not make the necessary new life plan. I interviewed two women of ability, both of whom were bored as housewives and both of whom got jobs in the same research institute. They loved the increasingly challenging work, and were quickly promoted. But, in their thirties, after ten years as housewives, they earned very little money. The first woman, clearly recognizing the future this work held for her, spent virtually her entire salary on a three-day-a-week cleaning woman. The second woman, who felt her work was justified only if it "helped out with family expenses," would not spend any money for cleaning help. Nor did she consider asking her husband and children to help out with household chores, or save time by ordering groceries by phone and sending the laundry out. She quit her job after a year from sheer exhaustion. The first woman, who made the necessary household changes and sacrifices, today, at thirty-eight, has one of the leading jobs at the institute and makes a substantial contribution to her family's income, over and above what she pays for her part-time household help. The second, after two weeks of "rest," began to suffer the old desperation. But she persuaded herself that she will "cheat" her husband and children less by finding work she can do at home.

The picture of the happy housewife doing creative work at home—painting, sculpting, writing—is one of the semi-delusions of the feminine mystique. There are men and women who can do it; but when a man works at home, his wife keeps the children strictly out of the way, or else. It is not so easy for a woman; if she is serious about her work she often must find some place away from home to do it, or risk becoming an ogre to her children in her impatient demands for privacy. Her attention is divided and her concentration interrupted, on the job and as a mother. A no-nonsense nine-to-five job, with a clear division between professional work and housework, requires much less discipline and is usually less lonely. Some of the stimulation and the new friendships that come from being part of the professional world can be lost by the woman who tries to fit her career into the physical confines of her housewife life.

A woman must say "no" to the feminine mystique very clearly indeed to sustain the discipline and effort that any professional commitment requires. For the mystique is no mere intellectual construct. A great many people have, or think they have, a vested interest in "Occupation: housewife." However long it may take for women's magazines, sociologists, educators, and psychoanalysts to correct the mistakes that perpetuate the feminine mystique, a woman must deal with them now, in the prejudices, mistaken fears, and unnecessary dilemmas voiced by her husband; her friends and neighbors; perhaps her minister, priest, or rabbi; or her child's kindergarten teacher; or the well-meaning social worker at the guidance clinic; or her own innocent little children. But resistance, from whatever source, is better seen for what it is.

Even the traditional resistance of religious orthodoxy is masked today with the manipulative techniques of psychotherapy. Women of orthodox Catholic or Jewish origin do not easily break through the housewife image; it is enshrined in the canons of their religion, in the assumptions of their own and their husbands' childhoods, and in their church's dogmatic definitions of marriage and motherhood. The ease with which dogma can be dressed in the psychological tenets of the mystique can be seen in this "Suggested Outline for Married Couples' Discussions" from the Family Life Bureau of the Archdiocese of New York. A panel of three or four married couples, after rehearsal by a "priest-moderator," are instructed to raise the question: "Can a working wife be a challenge to the authority of the husband?"

> Most of the engaged couples are convinced that there is nothing unusual or wrong in the wife working. . . . Don't antagonize.

Be suggestive, rather than dogmatic. . . . The panel couples
should point out that the bride who is happy at a 9-to-5 o'clock
job has this to think about:

a. She may be subtly undermining her husband's sense of vocation as the bread-winner and head of the house. The competitive business world can inculcate in the working bride
attitudes and habits which may make it difficult for her to
adjust to her husband's leadership. . . .

c. At the end of a working day, she presents her husband
with a tired mind and body at a time when he looks forward to the cheerful encouragement and fresh enthusiasm
of his spouse. . . .

d. For some brides, the tension of doubling as business woman
and part-time housewife may be one of several factors contributing to sterility . . .

One Catholic woman I interviewed withdrew from the state board
of the League of Women Voters, when, in addition to the displeasure of the priest and her own husband, the school psychologist
claimed that her daughter's difficulties at school were due to her
political activity. "It is more difficult for a Catholic woman to stay
emancipated," she told me. "I have retired. It will be better for everyone concerned if I am just a housewife." At this point the telephone
rang, and I eavesdropped with interest on a half-hour of high political strategy, evidently not of the League but of the local Democratic
Party. The "retired" politician came back into the kitchen to finish
preparing dinner, and confessed that she now hid her political activity at home "like an alcoholic or a drug addict, but I don't seem to be
able to give it up."

Another woman, of Jewish tradition, gave up her profession as a
doctor when she became a doctor's wife, devoting herself to bringing up their four children. Her husband was not overjoyed when
she began brushing up to retake her medical exams after her youngest reached school age. An unassertive, quiet woman, she exerted
almost unbelievable effort to obtain her license after fifteen years
of inactivity. She told me apologetically: "You just can't stop being
interested. I tried to make myself, but I couldn't." And she confessed that when she gets a night call, she sneaks out as guiltily as
if she were meeting a lover.

Even to a woman of less orthodox tradition, the most powerful
weapon of the feminine mystique is the argument that she rejects
her husband and her children by working outside the home. If, for
any reason, her child becomes ill or her husband has troubles of his
own, the feminine mystique, insidious voices in the community,
and even the woman's own inner voice will blame her "rejection" of

the housewife role. It is then that many a woman's commitment to herself and society dies aborning or takes a serious detour.

One woman told me that she gave up her job in television to become "just a housewife" because her husband suddenly decided his troubles in his own profession were caused by her failure to "play the feminine role"; she was trying to "compete" with him; she wanted "to wear the pants." She, like most women today, was vulnerable to such charges—one psychiatrist calls it the "career woman's guilt syndrome." And so she began to devote all the energies she had once put into her work to running her family—and to a nagging critical interest in her husband's career.

In her spare time in the suburbs, however, she rather absent-mindedly achieved flamboyant local success as the director of a little-theater group. This, on top of her critical attention to her husband's career, was far more destructive to his ego and a much more constant irritation to him and to her children than her professional work in which she had competed impersonally with other professionals in a world far away from home. One day, when she was directing a little-theater rehearsal, her son was hit by an automobile. She blamed herself for the accident, and so she gave up the little-theater group, resolving this time, cross her heart, that she would be "just a housewife."

She suffered, almost immediately, a severe case of the problem that has no name; her depression and dependence made her husband's life hell. She sought analytic help, and in a departure from the nondirective approach of orthodox analysts, her therapist virtually ordered her to get back to work. She started writing a serious novel with finally the kind of commitment she had evaded, even when she had a job. In her absorption, she stopped worrying about her husband's career; imperceptibly, she stopped phantasying another accident every time her son was out of her sight. And still, though she was too far along to retreat, she sometimes wondered if she were putting her marriage on the chopping block.

Contrary to the mystique, her husband—reacting either to the contagious example of her commitment, or to the breathing space afforded by the cessation of her hysterical dependence, or for independent reasons of his own—buckled down to the equivalent of that novel in his own career. There were still problems, of course, but not the old ones; when they broke out of their own traps, somehow their relationship with each other began growing again.

Still, with every kind of growth, there are risks. I encountered one woman in my interviews whose husband divorced her shortly after she went to work. Their marriage had become extremely destructive. The sense of identity that the woman achieved from her work may have made her less willing to accept the destructiveness, and perhaps precipitated the divorce, but it also made her more able to survive it.

In other instances, however, women told me that the violent objections of their husbands disappeared when they finally made up their own minds and went to work. Had they magnified their husband's objections to evade decision themselves? Husbands I have interviewed in this same context were sometimes surprised to find it "a relief" to be no longer the only sun and moon in their wives' world; they were the object of less nagging and fewer insatiable demands and they no longer had to feel guilt over their wives' discontent. As one man put it: "Not only is the financial burden lighter—and frankly, that is a relief—but the whole burden of living seems easier since Margaret went to work."

There are husbands, however, whose resistance is not so easily dispelled. The husband who is unable to bear his wife's saying "no" to the feminine mystique often has been seduced himself by the infantile phantasy of having an ever-present mother, or is trying to relive that phantasy through his children. It is difficult for a woman to tell such a husband that she is not his mother and that their children will be better off without her constant attention. Perhaps if she becomes more truly herself and refuses to act out his phantasy any longer, he will suddenly wake up and see *her* again. And then again, perhaps he will look for another mother.

Another hazard a woman faces on her way out of the housewife trap is the hostility of other housewives. Just as the man evading growth in his own work resents his wife's growth, so women who are living vicariously through their husbands and children resent the woman who has a life of her own. At dinner parties, the nursery school affair, the PTA open house, a woman who is more than just a housewife can expect a few barbs from her suburban neighbors. She no longer has the time for idle gossip over endless cups of coffee in the breakfast nook; she can no longer share with other wives that cozy "we're all in the same boat" illusion; her very presence rocks that boat. And she can expect her home, her husband, and her children to be scrutinized with more than the usual curiosity for the slightest sign of a "problem." This kind of hostility, however, sometimes masks a secret envy. The most hostile of the "happy housewives" may be the first to ask her neighbor with the new career for advice about moving on herself.

For the woman who moves on, there is always the sense of loss that accompanies change: old friends, familiar and reassuring routines lost, the new ones not yet clear. It is so much easier for a woman to say "yes" to the feminine mystique, and not risk the pains of moving on, that the will to make the effort—"ambition"—is as necessary as ability itself, if she is going to move out of the housewife trap. "Ambition," like "career," has been made a dirty word by the feminine mystique. When Polly Weaver, "College and Careers" editor of *Mademoiselle*, surveyed 400 women in 1956 on the subject of "ambition" and "competition,"[4] most of them had "guilty feelings" about being ambitious. They tried, in Miss Weaver's words, to "make it uplifting, not worldly and selfish like eating. We were surprised . . . at the number of women who drive themselves from morning to night for a job or the community or church, for example, but don't want a nickel's worth out of it for themselves. They don't want money, social position, power, influence, recognition. . . . Are these women fooling themselves?"

The mystique would have women renounce ambition for themselves. Marriage and motherhood is the end; after that, women are supposed to be ambitious only for their husbands and their children. Many women who indeed "fool themselves" push husband and children to fulfill that unadmitted ambition of their own. There were, however, many frankly ambitious women among those who responded to the *Mademoiselle* survey—and they did not seem to suffer from it.

> The ambitious women who answered our questionnaire had few regrets over sacrifices of sweet old friends, family picnics, and time for reading books no one talks about. They got more than they gave up, they said, and cited new friends, the larger world they move in, the great spurts of growth they had when they worked with the brilliant and talented—and most of all the satisfaction of working at full steam, putt-putting along like a pressure cooker. In fact, some happy ambitious women make the people around them happy—their husbands, children, their colleagues. . . . A very ambitious woman is not happy, either, leaving her prestige entirely to her husband's success. . . . To the active, ambitious woman, ambition is the thread that runs through her life from beginning to end, holding it together and enabling her to think of her life as a work of art instead of a collection of fragments . . .

For the women I interviewed who had suffered and solved the problem that has no name, to fulfill an ambition of their own, long buried or brand new, to work at top capacity, to have a sense of achievement, was like finding a missing piece in the puzzle of their lives. The money they earned often made life easier for the whole family, but none of them pretended this was the only reason they worked, or the main thing they got out of it. That sense of being complete and fully a part of the world—"no longer an island, part of the mainland"—had come back. They knew that it did not come from the work alone, but from the whole—their marriage, homes, children, work, their changing, growing links with the community. They were once again human beings, not "just housewives." Such women are the lucky ones. Some may have been driven to that ambition by childhood rejection, by an ugly-duckling adolescence, by unhappiness in marriage, by divorce or widowhood. It is both an irony and an indictment of the feminine mystique that it often forced the unhappy ones, the ugly ducklings, to find themselves, while girls who fitted the image became adjusted "happy" housewives and have never found out who they are. But to say that "frustration" can be good for a girl would be to miss the point; such frustration should not have to be the price of identity for a woman, nor is it in itself the key. The mystique has kept both pretty girls and ugly ones, who might have written poems like Edith Sitwell,* from discovering their own gifts; kept happy wives and unhappy ones who might have found themselves as Ruth Benedict did in anthropology, from even discovering their own field. And suddenly the final piece of the puzzle fits into place.

There was one thing without which even the most frustrated seldom found their way out of the trap. And, regardless of childhood experience, regardless of luck in marriage, there was one thing that produced frustration in all women of this time who tried to adjust to the housewife image. There was one thing shared by all I encountered who finally found their own way.

The key to the trap is, of course, education. The feminine mystique has made higher education for women seem suspect, unnecessary and even dangerous. But I think that education, and only education, has saved, and can continue to save, American women from the greater dangers of the feminine mystique.

In 1957 when I was asked to do an alumnae questionnaire of my own college classmates fifteen years after their graduation from Smith, I seized on the chance, thinking that I could disprove the growing belief that education made women "masculine," hampered their sexual fulfillment, caused unnecessary conflicts and frustrations. I discovered that the critics were half-right; education was dangerous and frustrating—but only when women did not use it.

Of the 200 women who answered that questionnaire in 1957, 89 per cent were housewives. They had lived through all the possible frustrations that education can cause in housewives. But when they were asked, "What difficulties have you found in working out your role as a woman? . . . What are the chief satisfactions and frustrations of your life today? . . . How have you changed inside? . . . How

---

* Edith Sitwell (1887–1964), born into a family of British nobility, went on to become a well-known and prolific English modernist poet. Her poems touched on both feminism and women's position in contemporary society.

do you feel about getting older? . . . What do you wish you had done differently? . . . "it was discovered that their real problems, as women, were not caused by their education. In general, they regretted only one thing—that they had not taken their education seriously enough, that they had not planned to put it to serious use.

Of the 97 per cent of these women who married—usually about three years after college—only 3 per cent had been divorced; of 20 per cent who had been interested in another man since marriage, most "did nothing about it." As mothers, 86 per cent planned their children's births and enjoyed their pregnancies; 70 per cent breast-fed their babies from one to nine months. They had more children than their mothers (average: 2.94), but only 10 per cent had ever felt "martyred" as mothers. Though 99 per cent reported that sex was only "one factor among many" in their lives, they neither felt over and done with sexually, nor were they just beginning to feel the sexual satisfaction of being a woman. Some 85 per cent reported that sex "gets better with the years," but they also found it "less important than it used to be." They shared life with their husbands "as fully as one can with another human being," but 75 per cent admitted readily that they could not share all of it.

Most of them (60 per cent) could not honestly say, in reporting their main occupation as homemaker, that they found it "totally ful-filling." They only spent an average of four hours a day on housework and they did not "enjoy" it. It was perhaps true that their education made them frustrated in their role as housewives. Educated before the era of the feminine mystique, many of them had faced a sharp break from their emerging identity in that housewife role. And yet most of these women continued to grow within the framework of suburban housewifery—perhaps because of the autonomy, the sense of purpose, the commitment to larger values which their education had given them.

Some 79 per cent had found some way to pursue the goals that education had given them, for the most part within the physical con-fines of their communities. The old Helen Hokinson* caricatures notwithstanding, their assumption of community responsibility was, in general, an act of maturity, a commitment that used and renewed strength of self. For these women, community activity almost always had the stamp of innovation and individuality, rather than the stamp of conformity, status-seeking, or escape. They set up cooperative nursery schools in suburbs where none existed; they started teenage

---

* Helen Hokinson (1893–1949), popular and pioneering female cartoonist best known for her work in the *New Yorker* magazine. The stock character in many of her cartoons was a middle aged, overweight, economically comfortable urban dowager with too much time on her hands. The adventures of this satirized character are what Friedan is referring to as the Hokinson caricatures.

canteens and libraries in schools where Johnny wasn't reading
because, quite simply, there were no good books. They innovated
new educational programs that finally became a part of the curriculum. One was personally instrumental in getting 13,000 signatures
for a popular referendum to get politics out of the school system. One
publicly spoke out for desegregation of schools in the South. One got
white children to attend a *de facto** segregated school in the North.
One pushed an appropriation for mental-health clinics through
a Western state legislature. One set up museum art programs for
school children in each of three cities she had lived in since marriage. Others started or led suburban choral groups, civic theaters,
foreign-policy study groups. Thirty per cent were active in local party
politics, from the committee level to the state assembly. Over 90 per
cent reported that they read the newspaper thoroughly every day and
voted regularly. They evidently never watched a daytime television
program and seemed almost never to play bridge, or read women's
magazines. Of the fifteen to three hundred books apiece they had
read in that one year, half were not best sellers.

Facing forty, most of these women could report quite frankly that
their hair was graying, and their "skin looks faded and tired," and
yet say, with not much regret for lost youth, "I have a growing sense
of self-realization, inner serenity and strength." "I have become
more my real self."

"How do you visualize your life after your children are grown?"
they were asked on the questionnaire. Most of them (60 per cent)
had concrete plans for work or study. They planned to finish their
education finally, for many who had no career ambitions in college
had them now. A few had reached "the depths of bitterness," "the
verge of disillusion and despair," trying to live just as housewives. A
few confessed longingly that "running my house and raising four
children does not really use my education or the ability I once seemed
to have. If only it were possible to combine motherhood and a career."
And the most bitter were those who said: "Never have found out what
kind of a person I am. I wasted college trying to find myself in social
life. I wish now that I had gone into something deeply enough to
have a creative life of my own." But most did know, now, who they
were and what they wanted to do; and 80 per cent regretted not having planned, seriously, to *use* their education in professional work.
Passive appreciation and even active participation in community
affairs would no longer be enough when their children were a little
older. Many women reported that they were planning to teach; fortunately for them, the great need for teachers gave them a chance to

---

* Segregation that exists in fact, but is not directly produced or supported by government
legislation. *De facto* segregation is usually related to housing and economic inequalities.

get back in the stream. Others anticipated years of further study before they would be qualified in their chosen fields.

These 200 Smith graduates have their counterparts in women all over the country, women of intelligence and ability, fighting their way out of the housewife trap, or never really trapped at all because of their education. But these graduates of 1942 were among the last American women educated before the feminine mystique.

In another questionnaire answered by almost 10,000 graduates of Mount Holyoke in 1962—its 125th anniversary year—one sees the effect of the mystique on women educated in the last two decades. The Mount Holyoke alumnae showed a similar high marriage and low divorce rate (2 per cent over-all). But before 1942, most were married at twenty-five or older; after 1942, the marriage age showed a dramatic drop, and the percentage having four or more children showed a dramatic rise. Before 1942, two-thirds or more of the graduates went on to further study; that proportion has steadily declined. Few, in recent classes, have won advanced degrees in the arts, sciences, law, medicine, education, compared to the 40 per cent in 1937. A drastically decreasing number also seem to share the larger vistas of national or international commitment; participation in local political clubs had dropped to 12 per cent by the class of 1952. From 1942 on, few graduates had any professional affiliation. Half of all the Mount Holyoke alumnae had worked at one time but were no longer working, primarily because they had chosen "the role of housewife." Some had returned to work—both to supplement income and because they liked to work. But in the classes from 1942 on, where most of the women were now housewives, nearly half did not intend to return to work.

The declining area of commitment to the world outside the home from 1942 on is a clear indication of the effect of the feminine mystique on educated women. Having seen the desperate emptiness, the "trapped" feeling of many young women who were educated under the mystique to be "just a housewife," I realize the significance of my classmates' experience. Because of their education many of them were able to combine serious commitments of their own with marriage and family. They could participate in community activities that required intelligence and responsibility, and move on, with a few years' preparation, into professional social work or teaching. They could get jobs as substitute teachers or part-time social workers to finance the courses needed for certification. They had often grown to the point where they did not want to return to the fields they had worked in after college, and they could even get into a new field with the core of autonomy that their education had given them.

But what of the young women today who have never had a taste of higher education, who quit college to marry or marked time in their classrooms waiting for the "right man?" What will they be at forty? Housewives in every suburb and city are seeking more education today, as if a course, any course, will give them the identity they are groping toward. But the courses they take, and the courses they are offered, are seldom intended for real use in society. Even more than the education she evaded at eighteen in sexual phantasy, the education a woman can get at forty is permeated, contaminated, diluted by the feminine mystique.

Courses in golf, bridge, rug-hooking, gourmet cooking, sewing are intended, I suppose, for real use, by women who stay in the housewife trap. The so-called intellectual courses offered in the usual adult education centers—art appreciation, ceramics, short-story writing, conversational French, Great Books, astronomy in the Space Age— are intended only as "self-enrichment." The study, the effort, even the homework that imply a long-term commitment are not expected of the housewife.

Actually, many women who take these courses desperately need serious education; but if they have never had a taste of it, they do not know how and where to look for it, nor do they even understand that so many adult education courses are unsatisfactory simply because they are not serious. The dimension of reality essential even to "self-enrichment" is barred, almost by definition, in a course specifically designed for "housewives." This is true, even where the institution giving the course has the highest standards. Recently, Radcliffe announced an "Institute for Executives' Wives" (to be followed presumably by an "Institute for Scientists' Wives," or an "Institute for Artists' Wives," or an "Institute for College Professors' Wives"). The executive's wife or the scientist's wife, at thirty-five or forty, whose children are all at school is hardly going to be helped to the new identity she needs by learning to take a more detailed, vicarious share of her husband's world. What she needs is training for creative work of her own.

Among the women I interviewed, education was the key to the problem that has no name only when it was part of a new life plan, and meant for serious use in society—amateur or professional. They were able to find such education only in the regular colleges and universities. Despite the wishful thinking engendered by the feminine mystique in girls and in their educators, an education evaded at eighteen or twenty-one is insuperably harder to obtain at thirty-one or thirty-eight or forty-one, by a woman who has a husband and three or four children and a home. She faces, in the college or university, the prejudices created by the feminine mystique. No matter how brief her absence from the academic proving ground, she will have to demonstrate her seriousness of purpose over and over again to be readmitted. She must then compete with the teeming hordes of children she and others like her have over-produced in this era. It is not easy for a grown woman to sit through courses geared to teenagers, to be treated as a teenager again, to have to prove that she deserves to be taken as seriously as a teenager. A woman has to exercise great ingenuity, endure many rebuffs and disappointments, to find an education that fits her need, and also make it fit her other commitments as wife and mother.

One woman I interviewed who had never gone to college, decided, after psychotherapy, to take two courses a year at a nearby univer-sity which, fortunately, had an evening school. At first, she had no idea where it was leading her, but after two years, she decided to major in history and prepare to teach it in high school. She main-tained a good record, even though she was often impatient with the slow pace and the busywork. But, at least, studying with some pur-pose made her feel better than when she used to read mystery sto-ries or magazines at the playground. Above all, it was leading to something real for the future. But at the rate of two courses a year (which then cost $420, and two evenings a week in class), it would have taken her ten years to get a B.A. The second year, money was scarce, and she could only take one course. She could not apply for a student loan unless she went full time, which she could not do until her youngest was in first grade. In spite of it all, she stuck it out that way for four years—noticing that more and more of the other housewives in her classes dropped out because of money, or because "the whole thing was going to take too long."

Then, with her youngest in first grade, she became a full-time stu-dent in the regular college, where the pace was even slower because the students were "less serious." She couldn't endure the thought of all the years ahead to get an M.A. (which she would need to teach high-school history in that state), so she switched to an education major. She certainly would not have continued this expensive, tortu-ous education if, by now, she had not had a clear life plan to use it, a plan that required it. Committed to elementary teaching, she was able to get a government loan for part of her full-time tuition (now exceeding $1,000 a year), and in another two years she will be finished.

Even against such enormous obstacles, more and more women with virtually no help from society and with belated and begrudg-ing encouragement from educators themselves, are going back to school to get the education they need. Their determination betrays women's underestimated human strength and their urgent need to use it. But only the strongest, after nearly twenty years of the femi-nine mystique, can move on by themselves. For this is not just the private problem of each individual woman. There are implications of the feminine mystique that must be faced on a national scale.

The problem that has no name—which is simply the fact that American women are kept from growing to their full human capacities—is taking a far greater toll on the physical and mental health of our country than any known disease. Consider the high incidence of emotional breakdown of women in the "role crises" of their twenties and thirties; the alcoholism and suicides in their forties and fifties; the housewives' monopolization of all doctors' time. Consider the prevalence of teenage marriages, the growing rate of illegitimate pregnancies, and even more seriously, the pathology of mother-child symbiosis. Consider the alarming passivity of American teenagers. If we continue to produce millions of young mothers who stop their growth and education short of identity, without a strong core of human values to pass on to their children, we are committing, quite simply, genocide, starting with the mass burial of American women and ending with the progressive dehumanization of their sons and daughters.

These problems cannot be solved by medicine, or even by psychotherapy. We need a drastic reshaping of the cultural image of femininity that will permit women to reach maturity, identity, completeness of self, without conflict with sexual fulfillment. A massive attempt must be made by educators and parents—and ministers, magazine editors, manipulators, guidance counselors—to stop the early-marriage movement, stop girls from growing up wanting to be "just a housewife," stop it by insisting, with the same attention from childhood on that parents and educators give to boys, that girls develop the resources of self, goals that will permit them to find their own identity.

It is, of course, no easier for an educator to say "no" to the feminine mystique than for an individual girl or woman. Even the most advanced of educators, seriously concerned with the desperate need of housewives with leftover lives on their hands, hesitate to buck the tide of early marriage. They have been browbeaten by the oracles of popularized psychoanalysis and still tremble with guilt at the thought of interfering with a woman's sexual fulfillment. The rearguard argument offered by the oracles who are, in some cases, right on college campuses themselves, is that since the primary road to identity for a woman is marriage and motherhood, serious educational interests or commitments which may cause conflicts in her role as wife and mother should be postponed until the childbearing years are over. Such a warning was made in 1962 by a psychiatric consultant to Yale University—which had been considering admitting women as undergraduates for the same serious education it gives men.

> Many young women—if not the majority—seem to be incapable of dealing with future long-range intellectual interests

until they have proceeded through the more basic phases of their own healthy growth as women. . . . To be well done, the mother's job in training children and shaping the life of her family should draw on all a woman's resources, emotional and intellectual, and upon all her skills. The better her training, the better chance she will have to do the job well, provided that emotional roadblocks do not stand in her way: provided, that is, that she has established a good basis for the development of adult femininity, and that during the course of her higher education, she is not subjected to pressures which adversely affect that development. . . . To urge upon her conflicting goals, to stress that a career and a profession in the man's world should be the first consideration in planning her life, can adversely affect the full development of her identity. . . . Of all the social freedoms won by her grandmothers, she prizes first the freedom to be a healthy, fulfilled woman, and she wants to be free of guilt and conflict about it. . . . This means that though jobs are often possible within the framework of marriage, "careers" rarely are . . . [5]

The fact remains that the girl who wastes—as waste she does— her college years without acquiring serious interests, and wastes her early job years marking time until she finds a man, gambles with the possibilities for an identity of her own, as well as the possibilities for sexual fulfillment and wholly affirmed motherhood. The educators who encourage a woman to postpone larger interests until her children are grown make it virtually impossible for her ever to acquire them. It is not that easy for a woman who has defined herself wholly as wife and mother for ten or fifteen or twenty years to find new identity at thirty-five or forty or fifty. The ones who are able to do it are, quite frankly, the ones who made serious commitments to their earlier education, the ones who wanted and once worked at careers, the ones who bring to marriage and motherhood a sense of their own identity—not those who somehow hope to acquire it later on. A recent study of fifty women college graduates in an eastern suburb and city, the year after the oldest child had left home, showed that, with very few exceptions, the only women who had any interests to pursue—in work, in community activities, or in the arts— had acquired them in college. The ones who lacked such interests were not acquiring them now; they slept late, in their "empty nests," and looked forward only to death.[6]

Educators at every women's college, at every university, junior college, and community college, must see to it that women make a lifetime commitment (call it a "life plan," a "vocation," a "life purpose" if that dirty word *career* has too many celibate connotations) to a field of thought, to work of serious importance to society. They must expect the girl as well as the boy to take some field seriously enough to want to pursue it for life. This does not mean abandoning liberal education for women in favor of "how to" vocational courses. Liberal education, as it is given at the best of colleges and universities, not only trains the mind but provides an ineradicable core of human values. But liberal education must be planned for serious use, not merely dilettantism or passive appreciation. As boys at Harvard or Yale or Columbia or Chicago go on from the liberal arts core to study architecture, medicine, law, science, girls must be encouraged to go on, to make a life plan. It has been shown that girls with this kind of a commitment are less eager to rush into early marriage, less panicky about finding a man, more responsible for their sexual behavior.[7] Most of them marry, of course, but on a much more mature basis. Their marriages then are not an escape but a commitment shared by two people that becomes part of their commitment to themselves and society. If, in fact, girls are educated to make such commitments, the question of sex and when they marry will lose its overwhelming importance.[8] It is the fact that women have no identity of their own that makes sex, love, marriage, and children seem the only and essential facts of women's life.

In the face of the feminine mystique with its powerful hidden deterrents, educators must realize that they cannot inspire young women to commit themselves seriously to their education without taking some extraordinary measures. The few so far attempted barely come to grips with the problem. Mary Bunting's new Institute for Independent Study at Radcliffe is fine for women who already know what they want to do, who have pursued their studies to the Ph.D. or are already active in the arts, and merely need some respite from motherhood to get back in the mainstream. Even more important, the presence of these women on the campus, women who have babies and husbands and who are still deeply committed to their own work, will undoubtedly help dispel the image of the celibate career woman and fire some of those Radcliffe sophomores out of the "climate of unexpectation" that permits them to meet the nation's highest standard of educational excellence to use it later only in marriage and motherhood. This is what Mary Bunting had in mind. And it can be done elsewhere, in even simpler ways.

It would pay every college and university that wants to encourage women to take education seriously to recruit for their faculties all the women they can find who have combined marriage and motherhood with the life of the mind—even if it means concessions for pregnancies or breaking the old rule about hiring the wife of the male associate professor who has her own perfectly respectable M.A. or Ph.D. As for the unmarried woman scholars, they must no longer be treated like lepers. The simple truth is that they have taken their existence seriously, and have fulfilled their human potential. They might well be, and often are, envied by women who live the very image of opulent togetherness, but have forfeited themselves. Women, as well as men, who are rooted in human work are rooted in life.

It is essential, above all, for educators themselves to say "no" to the feminine mystique and face the fact that the only point in educating women is to educate them to the limit of their ability. Women do not need courses in "marriage and the family" to marry and raise families; they do not need courses in homemaking to make homes. But they must study science—to discover in science; study the thought of the past—to create new thought; study society—to pioneer in society. Educators must also give up these "one thing at a time" compromises. That separate layering of "education," "sex," "marriage," "motherhood," "interests for the last third of life," will not solve the role crisis. Women must be educated to a new integration of roles. The more they are encouraged to make that new life plan— integrating a serious, lifelong commitment to society with marriage and motherhood—the less conflicts and unnecessary frustrations they will feel as wives and mothers, and the less their daughters will make mistaken choices for lack of a full image of woman's identity.

I could see this in investigating college girls' rush to early marriage. The few who were not in such a desperate hurry to "get a man" and who committed themselves to serious long-range interests—evidently not worried that they would thereby lose their "femininity"—almost all had mothers, or other private images of women, who were committed to some serious purpose. ("My mother happens to be a teacher." "My best friend's mother is a doctor; she always seems so busy and happy.")

Education itself can help provide that new image—and the spark in girls to create their own—as soon as it stops compromising and temporizing with the old image of "woman's role." For women as well as men, education is and must be the matrix of human evolution. If today American women are finally breaking out of the housewife trap in search of new identity, it is quite simply because so many women have had a taste of higher education—unfinished, unfocused, but still powerful enough to force them on.

For that last and most important battle *can* be fought in the mind and spirit of woman herself. Even without a private image, many girls in America who have been educated simply as people were given a strong enough sense of their human possibility to carry them past the old femininity, past that search for security in man's love, to find a new self. A Swarthmore graduate, entering her internship, told me that at first, as she felt herself getting more and more "independent" in college, she worried a lot about having dates and getting married, wanted to "latch on to a boy." "I tried to beat myself down to be feminine. Then I got interested in what I was doing and stopped worrying," she said.

> It's as if you've made some kind of shift. You begin to feel your competence in doing things. Like a baby learning to walk. Your mind begins to expand. You find your own field. And that's a wonderful thing. The love of doing the work and the feeling there's something there and you can trust it. It's worth the unhappiness. They say a man has to suffer to grow, maybe something like that has to happen to women too. You begin not to be afraid to be yourself.

Drastic steps must now be taken to re-educate the women who were deluded or cheated by the feminine mystique. Many of the women I interviewed who felt "trapped" as housewives have in the last few years started to move out of the trap. But there are as many others who are sinking back again, because they did not find out in time what they wanted to do, or because they were not able to find a way to do it. In almost every case, it took too much time, too much money, using existing educational facilities. Few housewives can afford full-time study. Even if colleges admit them on a part-time basis—and many will not—few women can endure the slow-motion pace of usual undergraduate college education stretched over ten or more years. Some institutions are now willing to gamble on housewives, but will they be as willing when the flood of their college-bound offspring reaches its full height? The pilot programs that have been started at Sarah Lawrence and the University of Minnesota begin to show the way, but they do not face the time-money problem which is, for so many women, the insurmountable one.

What is needed now is a national educational program, similar to the GI bill, for women who seriously want to continue or resume their education—and who are willing to commit themselves to its use in a profession. The bill would provide properly qualified women with tuition fees, plus an additional subsidy to defray other expenses—books, travel, even, if necessary, some household help. Such a measure would cost far less than the GI bill. It would permit mothers to use existing educational facilities on a part-time basis and carry on individual study and research projects at home during the years when regular classroom attendance is impossible. The whole concept of women's education would be regeared from four-year college to a life plan under which a woman could continue her education, without conflict with her marriage, her husband and her children.

The GI's, matured by war, needed education to find their identity in society. In no mood for time-wasting, they astonished their teachers and themselves by their scholastic performance. Women who have matured during the housewife moratorium can be counted on for similar performance. Their desperate need for education and the desperate need of this nation for the untapped reserves of women's intelligence in all the professions justify these emergency measures.[9]

For those women who did not go to college, or quit too soon, for those who are no longer interested in their former field, or who never took their education seriously, I would suggest first of all an intensive concentrated re-immersion in, quite simply, the humanities—not abridgments and selections like the usual freshman or sophomore survey, but an intensive study like the educational experiments attempted by the Bell Telephone Company or the Ford Foundation for young executives who had conformed so completely to the role of organization man* that they were not capable of the initiative and vision required in top executive ranks. For women, this could be done by a national program, along the lines of the Danish Folk-High-School movement,† which would first bring the housewife back into the mainstream of thought with a concentrated six-week summer course, a sort of intellectual "shock therapy."‡ She would be subsidized so that she could leave home and go to a resident college, which is not otherwise used during the summer. Or she could go to a metropolitan center on an equally intensive basis, five days a week for six or eight weeks during the summer, with a day camp provided for the children.

Assume that this educational shock treatment awakens able women to purposes requiring the equivalent of a four-year college program for further professional training. That college program could be completed in four years or less, without full-time classroom attendance, by a combination of these summer institutes, plus prescribed reading, papers, and projects that could be done during the winter at home. Courses taken on television or at local community colleges and universities on an extension basis, could be combined

---

* In 1956, William H. Whyte published the best-selling *The Organization Man*, a portrait of middle-class suburbanites. The book described these suburbanites as conformists who sought stability and security above all else.

† Developed in Denmark in the 1860s, this method of schooling brought young rural adults to live together briefly and cooperatively, with a curriculum that centered upon cultural nationalism. The best-known American institution inspired by the Danish folk high school was the Highlander Folk School, established in Monteagle, Tennessee, in 1932. Highlander sought to teach organizing skills to poor whites and blacks, and the school became an important training ground for the labor and civil rights movements. Friedan attended the Highlander school in 1941.

‡ Electroconvulsive Shock Therapy, devised in the 1930s and popular during the 1940s and 1950s, was a treatment for a variety for mental illnesses before more modern therapies became available. The treatment involved administering an anaesthetic and a muscle relaxant before passing an electric current through the brain to induce either convulsions or coma. Sylvia Plath famously described shock treatments in her novel, *The Bell Jar*, published in 1963.

with tutorial conferences at midyear or every month. The courses would be taken for credit, and the customary degrees would be earned. Some system of "equivalents" would have to be worked out, not to give a woman credit for work that does not meet requirements, but to give her credit for truly serious work, even if it is done at times, places, and in ways that violate conventional academic standards.

A number of universities automatically bar housewives by barring part-time undergraduate or graduate work. Perhaps they have been burned by dilettantes. But part-time college work, graduate or undergraduate, geared to a serious plan, is the only kind of education that can prevent a housewife from becoming a dilettante; it is the only way a woman with husband and children can get, or continue, an education. It could also be the most practical arrangement from the university's point of view. With their facilities already overtaxed by population pressures, universities and women alike would benefit from a study program that does not require regular classroom attendance. While it makes a great deal of sense for the University of Minnesota to work out its excellent Plan for Women's Continuing Education[10] in terms of the regular university facilities, such a plan will not help the woman who must begin her education all over again to find out what she wants to do. But existing facilities, in any institution, can be used to fill in the gaps once a woman is under way on her life plan.

Colleges and universities also need a new life plan—to become lifetime institutions for their students; offer them guidance, take care of their records, and keep track of their advanced work or refresher courses, no matter where they are taken. How much greater that allegiance and financial support from their alumnae if, instead of the teaparties to raise funds and a sentimental reunion every fifth June, a woman could look to her college for continuing education and guidance. Barnard alumnae can, and do, come back and take, free, any course at any time, if they meet the qualifications for it. All colleges could conduct summer institutes to keep alumnae abreast of developments in their fields during the years of young motherhood. They could accept part-time students and offer extension courses for the housewife who could not attend classes regularly. They could advise her on reading programs, papers, or projects that could be done at home. They could also work out a system whereby projects done by their alumnae in education, mental health, sociology, political science in their own communities could be counted as equivalent credits toward a degree. Instead of collecting dimes, let women volunteers serve supervised professional apprenticeships and collect the credits that are recognized in lieu of pay for medical internes. Similarly, when a woman has taken courses at a number of different institutions, perhaps due to her husband's geographical itinerary, and has earned her community credits from agency, hospital, library or laboratory, her college of origin, or some national center set up by several colleges, could give her the orals, the comprehensives, and the appropriate examinations for a degree. The concept of "continuing education" is already a reality for men in many fields. Why not for women? Not education for careers instead of motherhood, not education for temporary careers before motherhood, not education to make them "better wives and mothers," but an education they will use as full members of society.

"But how many American women really want to do more with their lives?" the cynic asks. A fantastic number of New Jersey housewives responded to an offer of intensive retraining in mathematics for former college women willing to commit themselves to becoming mathematics teachers. In January, 1962, a simple news story in the *New York Times* announced that Sarah Lawrence's Esther Raushenbush had obtained a grant to help mature women finish their education or work for graduate degrees on a part-time basis that could be fitted in with their obligations as mothers. The response literally put the small Sarah Lawrence switchboard out of commission. Within twenty-four hours, Mrs. Raushenbush had taken over 100 telephone calls. "It was like bank night," the operator said. "As if they had to get in there right away, or they might miss the chance." Interviewing the women who applied for the program, Mrs. Raushenbush, like Virginia Senders at Minnesota, was convinced of the reality of their need. They were not "neurotically rejecting" their husbands and children; they did not need psychotherapy, but they did need more education—in a hurry—and in a form they could get without neglecting their husbands and families.

Education and re-education of American women for a serious purpose cannot be effected by one or two far-sighted institutions; it must be accomplished on a much wider scale. And no one serves this end who repeats, even for expedience or tact, the clichés of the feminine mystique. It is quite wrong to say, as some of the leading women educators are saying today, that women must of course use their education, but not, heaven forbid, in careers that will compete with men.[11] When women take their education and their abilities seriously and put them to use, ultimately they have to compete with men. It is better for a woman to compete impersonally in society, as men do, than to compete for dominance in her own home with her husband, compete with her neighbors for empty status, and so smother her son that he cannot compete at all. Consider this recent news item about

America's latest occupational therapy for the pent-up feminine need to compete:

> It is a typical weekday in Dallas. Daddy is at work. Baby is having his morning nap. In an adjoining room, Brother (age 3) is riding a new rocking horse and Sis (5) is watching TV cartoons. And Mommy? Mommy is just a few feet away, crouching over the foul line on Lane 53, her hip twisted sharply to the left to steer the blue-white-marbled ball into the strike pocket between the one and three pins. Mommy is bowling. Whether in Dallas or Cleveland or Albuquerque or Spokane, energetic housewives have dropped dustcloth and vacuum and hauled the children off to the new alleys, where fulltime nurses stand ready to babysit in the fully equipped nurseries.
>
> Said the manager of Albuquerque's Bowl-a-Drome: "Where else can a woman compete after she gets married? They need competition just like men do. . . . It sure beats going home to do the dishes!"[12]

It is perhaps beside the point to remark that bowling alleys and supermarkets have nursery facilities, while schools and colleges and scientific laboratories and government offices do not. But it is very much to the point to say that if an able American woman does not use her human energy and ability in some meaningful pursuit (which necessarily means competition, for there is competition in every serious pursuit of our society), she will fritter away her energy in neurotic symptoms, or unproductive exercise, or destructive "love."

It also is time to stop giving lip service to the idea that there are no battles left to be fought for women in America, that women's rights have already been won. It is ridiculous to tell girls to keep quiet when they enter a new field, or an old one, so the men will not notice they are there. In almost every professional field, in business and in the arts and sciences, women are still treated as second-class citizens. It would be a great service to tell girls who plan to work in society to expect this subtle, uncomfortable discrimination—tell them not to be quiet, and hope it will go away, but fight it. A girl should not expect special privileges because of her sex, but neither should she "adjust" to prejudice and discrimination.

She must learn to compete then, not as a woman, but as a human being. Not until a great many women move out of the fringes into the mainstream will society itself provide the arrangements for their new life plan. But every girl who manages to stick it out through law school or medical school, who finishes her M.A. or Ph.D. and goes on to use it, helps others move on. Every woman who fights the remaining barriers to full equality which are masked by the feminine mystique makes it easier for the next woman. The very existence of the

President's Commission on the Status of Women,* under Eleanor Roosevelt's leadership, creates a climate where it is possible to recognize and do something about discrimination against women, in terms not only of pay but of the subtle barriers to opportunity. Even in politics, women must make their contribution not as "housewives" but as citizens. It is, perhaps, a step in the right direction when a woman protests nuclear testing under the banner of "Women Strike for Peace."† But why does the professional illustrator who heads the movement say she is "just a housewife," and her followers insist that once the testing stops, they will stay happily at home with their children? Even in the city strongholds of the big political party machines, women can—and are beginning to—change the insidious unwritten rules which let them do the political housework while the men make the decisions.[13]

When enough women make life plans geared to their real abilities, and speak out for maternity leaves or even maternity sabbaticals, professionally run nurseries, and the other changes in the rules that may be necessary, they will not have to sacrifice the right to honorable competition and contribution anymore than they will have to sacrifice marriage and motherhood. It is wrong to keep spelling out unnecessary choices that make women unconsciously resist either commitment or motherhood[14]—and that hold back recognition of the needed social changes. It is not a question of women having their cake and eating it, too. A woman is handicapped by her sex, and handicaps society, either by slavishly copying the pattern of man's advance in the professions, or by refusing to compete with man at all. But with the vision to make a new life plan of her own, she can fulfill a commitment to profession and politics, and to marriage and motherhood with equal seriousness.

Women who have done this, in spite of the dire warnings of the feminine mystique, are in a sense "mutations," the image of what the American woman can be. When they did not or could not work full time for a living, they spent part-time hours on work which truly

---

* President John F. Kennedy established this commission under the directorship of Eleanor Roosevelt in 1961 to investigate women's position in education, the workplace, and under the law. The work of the commission identified significant employment discrimination against women and sparked the creation of state commissions on the status of women throughout the nation. The state commissions that persisted were key in creating networks of women that would later give rise to the National Organization for Women (NOW). See entry on Eleanor Roosevelt, p. 26; see also pp. 364–65 for a selection by Eleanor Roosevelt on her participation in the commission.

† During the early 1960s, a group of housewives began to organize against the open-air testing of nuclear weapons in both the United States and the Soviet Union. They were concerned about the fallout of nuclear materials entering the food chain, and staged strikes, pickets, and rallies to increase awareness and push for a test-ban treaty. Despite considerable red-baiting in the hostile Cold War climate, they did succeed in getting President John F. Kennedy to sign a limited test-ban treaty in 1963. See pp. 369–70 for a document related to this organization.

interested them. Because time was of the essence, they often skipped the time-wasting, self-serving details of both housewifery and professional busywork.

Whether they knew it or not, they were following a life plan. They had their babies before or after internship, between fellowships. If good full-time help was not available in the children's early years, they gave up their jobs and took a part-time post that may not have paid handsomely, but kept them moving ahead in their profession. The teachers innovated in PTA, and substituted; the doctors took clinical or research jobs close to home; the editors and writers started free-lancing. Even if the money they made was not needed for groceries or household help (and usually it was), they earned tangible proof of their ability to contribute. They did not consider themselves "lucky" to be housewives; they competed in society. They knew that marriage and motherhood are an essential part of life, but not the whole of it.

These "mutations" suffered—and surmounted—the "cultural discontinuity in role conditioning," the "role crisis" and the identity crisis. They had problems, of course, tough ones—juggling their pregnancies, finding nurses and housekeepers, having to give up good assignments when their husbands were transferred. They also had to take a lot of hostility from other women—and many had to live with the active resentment of their husbands. And, because of the mystique, many suffered unnecessary pains of guilt. It took, and still takes, extraordinary strength of purpose for women to pursue their own life plans when society does not expect it of them. However, unlike the trapped housewives whose problems multiply with the years, these women solved their problems and moved on. They resisted the mass persuasions and manipulations, and did not give up their own, often painful, values for the comforts of conformity. They did not retreat into privatism, but met the challenges of the real world. And they know quite surely now who they are.

They were doing, perhaps without seeing it clearly, what every man and woman must do now to keep up with the increasingly explosive pace of history, and find or keep individual identity in our mass society. The identity crisis in men and women cannot be solved by one generation for the next; in our rapidly changing society, it must be faced continually, solved only to be faced again in the span of a single lifetime. A life plan must be open to change, as new possibilities open, in society and in oneself. No woman in America today who starts her search for identity can be sure where it will take her. No woman starts that search today without struggle, conflict, and taking her courage in her hands. But the women I met, who were moving on that unknown road, did not regret the pains, the efforts, the risks.

In the light of woman's long battle for emancipation, the recent sexual counterrevolution in America has been perhaps a final crisis, a strange breath-holding interval before the larva breaks out of the shell into maturity—a moratorium during which many millions of women put themselves on ice and stopped growing. They say that one day science will be able to make the human body live longer by freezing its growth. American women lately have been living much longer than men—walking through their leftover lives like living dead women. Perhaps men may live longer in America when women carry more of the burden of the battle with the world, instead of being a burden themselves. I think their wasted energy will continue to be destructive to their husbands, to their children, and to themselves until it is used in their own battle with the world. But when women as well as men emerge from biological living to realize their human selves, those leftover halves of life may become their years of greatest fulfillment.[15]

Then the split in the image will be healed, and daughters will not face that jumping-off point at twenty-one or forty-one. When their mothers' fulfillment makes girls sure they want to be women, they will not have to "beat themselves down" to be feminine; they can stretch and stretch until their own efforts will tell them who they are. They will not need the regard of boy or man to feel alive. And when women do not need to live through their husbands and children, men will not fear the love and strength of women, nor need another's weakness to prove their own masculinity. They can finally see each other as they are. And this may be the next step in human evolution.

Who knows what women can be when they are finally free to become themselves? Who knows what women's intelligence will contribute when it can be nourished without denying love? Who knows of the possibilities of love when men and women share not only children, home, and garden, not only the fulfillment of their biological roles, but the responsibilities and passions of the work that creates the human future and the full human knowledge of who they are? It has barely begun, the search of women for themselves. But the time is at hand when the voices of the feminine mystique can no longer drown out the inner voice that is driving women on to become complete.

Notes

CHAPTER 1. THE PROBLEM THAT HAS NO NAME

1. See the Seventy-fifth Anniversary Issue of *Good Housekeeping*, May, 1960, "The Gift of Self," a symposium by Margaret Mead, Jessamyn West, *et al.*
2. Lee Rainwater, Richard P. Coleman, and Gerald Handel, *Workingman's Wife*, New York, 1959.
3. Betty Friedan, "If One Generation Can Ever Tell Another," *Smith Alumnae Quarterly*, Northampton, Mass., Winter, 1961. I first became aware of "the problem that has no name" and its possible relationship to what I finally called "the feminine mystique" in 1957, when I prepared an intensive questionnaire and conducted a survey of my own Smith College classmates fifteen years after graduation. This questionnaire was later used by alumnae classes of Radcliffe and other women's colleges with similar results.
4. Jhan and June Robbins, "Why Young Mothers Feel Trapped," *Redbook*, September, 1960.
5. Marian Freda Poverman, "Alumnae on Parade," *Barnard Alumnae Magazine*, July, 1957.

CHAPTER 2. THE HAPPY HOUSEWIFE HEROINE

1. Betty Friedan, "Women Are People Too!" *Good Housekeeping*, September, 1960. The letters received from women all over the United States in response to this article were of such emotional intensity that I was convinced that "the problem that has no name" is by no means confined to the graduates of the women's Ivy League colleges.
2. In the 1960's, an occasional heroine who was not a "happy housewife" began to appear in the women's magazines. An editor of *McCall's* explained it: "Sometimes we run an offbeat story for pure entertainment value." One such novelette, which was written to order by Noel Clad for *Good Housekeeping* (January, 1960), is called "Men Against Women." The heroine—a happy career woman—nearly loses child as well as husband.

CHAPTER 3. THE CRISIS IN WOMAN'S IDENTITY

1. Erik H. Erikson, *Young Man Luther, A Study in Psychoanalysis and History*, New York, 1958, pp. 15 ff. See also Erikson, *Childhood and Society*, New York, 1950, and Erikson, "The Problem of Ego Identity," *Journal of the American Psychoanalytical Association*, Vol. 4, 1956, pp. 56–121.

CHAPTER 4. THE PASSIONATE JOURNEY

1. See Eleanor Flexner, *Century of Struggle: The Woman's Rights Movement in the United States*, Cambridge, Mass., 1959. This definitive history of the woman's rights movement in the United States, published in 1959 at the height of the era of the feminine mystique, did not receive the attention it deserves, from either the intelligent reader or the scholar. In my opinion, it should be required reading for every girl admitted to a U.S. college. One reason the mystique prevails is that very few women under the age of forty know the facts of the woman's rights movement. I am much indebted to Miss Flexner for many factual clues I might otherwise have missed in my attempt to get at the truth behind the feminine mystique and its monstrous image of the feminists.
2. See Sidney Ditzion, *Marriage, Morals and Sex in America—A History of Ideas*, New York, 1953. This extensive bibliographical essay by the librarian of New York University documents the continuous interrelationship between movements for social and sexual reform in America, and, specifically, between man's movement for greater self-realization and sexual fulfillment and the woman's rights movement. The speeches and tracts assembled reveal that the movement to emancipate women was often seen by the men as well as the women who led it in terms of "creating an equitable balance of power between the sexes" for "a more satisfying expression of sexuality for both sexes."
3. *Ibid.*, p. 107.
4. Yuri Suhl, *Ernestine L. Rose and the Battle for Human Rights*, New York, 1959, p. 158. A vivid account of the battle for a married woman's right to her own property and earnings.
5. Flexner, *op. cit.*, p. 30.
6. Elinor Rice Hays, *Morning Star, A Biography of Lucy Stone*, New York, 1961, p. 83.
7. Flexner, *op. cit.*, p. 64.
8. Hays, *op. cit.*, p. 136.

9. *Ibid.*, p. 285.
10. Flexner, *op. cit.*, p. 46.
11. *Ibid.*, p. 73.
12. Hays, *op. cit.*, p. 221.
13. Flexner, *op. cit.*, p. 117.
14. *Ibid.*, p. 235.
15. *Ibid.*, p. 299.
16. *Ibid.*, p. 173.
17. Ida Alexis Ross Wylie, "The Little Woman," *Harper's*, November, 1945.

CHAPTER 5. THE SEXUAL SOLIPSISM OF SIGMUND FREUD

1. Clara Thompson, *Psychoanalysis: Evolution and Development*, New York, 1950, pp. 131 ff:

    > Freud not only emphasized the biological more than the cultural, but he also developed a cultural theory of his own based on his biological theory. There were two obstacles in the way of understanding the importance of the cultural phenomena he saw and recorded. He was too deeply involved in developing his biological theories to give much thought to other aspects of the data he collected. Thus he was interested chiefly in applying to human society his theory of instincts. Starting with the assumption of a death instinct, for example, he then developed an explanation of the cultural phenomena he observed in terms of the death instinct. Since he did not have the perspective to be gained from knowledge of comparative cultures, he could not evaluate cultural processes as such. . . . Much which Freud believed to be biological has been shown by modern research to be a reaction to a certain type of culture and not characteristic of universal human nature.

2. Richard La Piere, *The Freudian Ethic*, New York, 1959, p. 62.
3. Ernest Jones, *The Life and Work of Sigmund Freud*, New York, 1953, Vol. I, p. 384.
4. *Ibid.*, Vol. II (1955), p. 432.
5. *Ibid.*, Vol. I, pp. 7–14, 294; Vol. II, p. 483.
6. Bruno Bettelheim, *Love Is Not Enough: The Treatment of Emotionally Disturbed Children*, Glencoe Ill. 1950, pp. 7 ff.
7. Ernest L. Freud, *Letters of Sigmund Freud*, New York, 1960, Letter 10, p. 27; Letter 26, p. 71; Letter 65, p. 145.
8. *Ibid.*, Letter 74, p. 60; Letter 76, pp. 161 ff.
9. Jones, *op. cit.*, Vol. I, pp. 176 ff.
10. *Ibid.*, Vol. II, p. 422.
11. *Ibid.*, Vol. I, p. 271:

    > His descriptions of sexual activities are so matter-of-fact that many readers have found them almost dry and totally lacking in warmth. From all I know of him, I should say that he displayed less than the average personal interest in what is often an absorbing topic. There was never any gusto or even savor in mentioning a sexual topic. . . . He always gave the impression of being an unusually chaste person—the word "puritanical" would not be out of place—and all we know of his early development confirms this conception.

12. *Ibid.*, Vol. I, p. 102.
13. *Ibid.*, Vol. I, pp. 110 ff.
14. *Ibid.*, Vol. I, p. 124.
15. *Ibid.*, Vol. I, p. 127.
16. *Ibid.*, Vol. I, p. 138.
17. *Ibid.*, Vol. I, p. 151.
18. Helen Walker Puner, *Freud, His Life and His Mind*, New York, 1947, p. 152.
19. Jones, *op. cit.*, Vol. II, p. 121.
20. *Ibid.*, Vol. I, pp. 301 ff. During the years Freud was germinating his sexual theory, before his own heroic self-analysis freed him from a passionate dependence on a series of men, his emotions were focused on a flamboyant nose-and-throat doctor named Fliess. This is one coincidence of history that was quite fateful for women. For Fliess had proposed, and obtained Freud's lifelong allegiance to, a fantastic "scientific theory" which reduced all phenomena of life and death to "bisexuality," expressed in mathematical terms through a periodic table based on the number 28, the female menstrual cycle. Freud looked forward to meetings with Fliess "as for the satisfying of hunger and thirst." He wrote him: "No one can replace the intercourse with a friend that a particular, perhaps feminine side of me, demands." Even after his own self-analysis, Freud still expected to die on the day predicted by Fliess' periodic table, in which everything

could be figured out in terms of the female number 28, or the male 23, which was derived from the end of one female menstrual period to the beginning of the next.

21. *Ibid.*, Vol. I, p. 320.
22. Sigmund Freud, "Degradation in Erotic Life," in *The Collected Papers of Sigmund Freud*, Vol. IV.
23. Thompson, *op. cit.*, p. 133.
24. Sigmund Freud, "The Psychology of Women," in *New Introductory Lectures on Psychoanalysis*, tr. by W. J. H. Sprott, New York, 1933, pp. 170 ff.
25. *Ibid.*, p. 182.
26. *Ibid.*, p. 184.
27. Thompson, *op. cit.*, pp. 12 ff:

> The war of 1914–18 further focussed attention on ego drives. . . . Another idea came into analysis around this period . . . and that was that aggression as well as sex might be an important repressed impulse. . . . The puzzling problem was how to include it in the theory of instincts. . . . Eventually Freud solved this by his second instinct theory. Aggression found its place as part of the death instinct. It is interesting that normal self-assertion, i.e., the impulse to master, control or come to self-fulfilling terms with the environment, was not especially emphasized by Freud.

28. Sigmund Freud, "Anxiety and Instinctual Life," in *New Introductory Lectures on Psychoanalysis*, p. 149.
29. Marynia Farnham and Ferdinand Lundberg, *Modern Woman: The Lost Sex*, New York and London, 1947, pp. 142 ff.
30. Ernest Jones, *op. cit.*, Vol. II, p. 446.
31. Helene Deutsch, *The Psychology of Woman—A Psychoanalytical Interpretation*, New York, 1944, Vol. I, pp. 224 ff.
32. *Ibid.*, Vol. I, pp. 251 ff.
33. Sigmund Freud, "The Anatomy of the Mental Personality," in *New Introductory Lectures on Psychoanalysis*, p. 96.

CHAPTER 6. THE FUNCTIONAL FREEZE,
THE FEMININE PROTEST, AND MARGARET MEAD

1. Henry A. Bowman, *Marriage for Moderns*, New York, 1942, p. 21.
2. *Ibid.*, pp. 22 ff.
3. *Ibid.*, pp. 62 ff.
4. *Ibid.*, pp. 74–76.
5. *Ibid.*, pp. 66 ff.
6. Talcott Parsons, "Age and Sex in the Social Structure of the United States," in *Essays in Sociological Theory*, Glencoe, Ill., 1949, pp. 223 ff.
7. Talcott Parsons, "An Analytical Approach to the Theory of Social Stratification," *op. cit.*, pp. 174 ff.
8. Mirra Komarovsky, *Women in the Modern World, Their Education and Their Dilemmas*, Boston, 1953, pp. 52–61.
9. *Ibid.*, p. 66.
10. *Ibid.*, pp. 72–74.
11. Mirra Komarovsky, "Functional Analysis of Sex Roles," *American Sociological Review*, August, 1950. See also "Cultural Contradictions and Sex Roles," *American Journal of Sociology*, November, 1946.
12. Kingsley Davis, "The Myth of Functional Analysis as a Special Method in Sociology and Anthropology," *American Sociological Review*, Vol. 24, No. 6, December, 1959, pp. 757–772. Davis points out that functionalism became more or less identical with sociology itself. There is provocative evidence that the very study of sociology, in recent years, has persuaded college women to limit themselves to their "functional" traditional sexual role. A report on "The Status of Women in Professional Sociology" (Sylvia Fleis Fava, *American Sociological Review*, Vol. 25, No. 2, April, 1960) shows that while most of the students in sociology undergraduate classes are women, from 1949 to 1958 there was a sharp decline in both the number and proportion of degrees in sociology awarded to women. (4,143 B.A.'s in 1949 down to a low of 3,200 in 1955, 3,606 in 1958). And while one-half to two-thirds of the undergraduate degrees in sociology were awarded to women, women received only 25 to 43 per cent of the master's degrees, and only 8 to 19 per cent of the Ph.D.'s. While the number of women earning graduate degrees in all fields has declined sharply during the era of the feminine mystique, the field of sociology showed, in comparison to other fields, an unusually high "mortality" rate.

13. Margaret Mead, *Sex and Temperament in Three Primitive Societies*, New York, 1935, pp. 279 ff.
14. Margaret Mead, *From the South Seas*, New York, 1939, p. 321.
15. Margaret Mead, *Male and Female*, New York, 1955, pp. 16–18.
16. *Ibid.*, p. 26.
17. *Ibid.*, footnotes, pp. 289 ff:

> I did not begin to work seriously with the zones of the body until I went to the Arapesh in 1931. While I was generally familiar with Freud's basic work on the subject, I had not seen how it might be applied in the field until I read Geza Roheim's first field report, "Psychoanalysis of Primitive Culture Types" . . . I then sent home for abstracts of K. Abraham's work. After I became acquainted with Erik Homburger Erikson's systematic handling of these ideas, they became an integral part of my theoretical equipment.

18. *Ibid.*, pp. 50 ff.
19. *Ibid.*, pp. 72 ff.
20. *Ibid.*, pp. 84 ff.
21. *Ibid.*, p. 85.
22. *Ibid.*, pp. 125 ff.
23. *Ibid.*, pp. 135 ff.
24. *Ibid.*, pp. 274 ff.
25. *Ibid.*, pp. 278 ff.
26. *Ibid.*, pp. 276–285.
27. Margaret Mead, Introduction to *From the South Seas*, New York, 1939, p. xiii. "It was no use permitting children to develop values different from those of their society . . ."
28. Marie Jahoda and Joan Havel, "Psychological Problems of Women in Different Social Roles—A Case History of Problem Formulation in Research," *Educational Record*, Vol. 36, 1955, pp. 325–333.

CHAPTER 7. THE SEX-DIRECTED EDUCATORS

1. Mabel Newcomer, *A Century of Higher Education for Women*, New York, 1959, pp. 45 ff. The proportion of women among college students in the U.S. increased from 21 per cent in 1870 to 47 per cent in 1920; it had declined to 35.2 per cent in 1958. Five women's colleges had closed; 21 had become coeducational; 2 had become junior colleges. In 1956, 3 out of 5 women in the coeducational colleges were taking secretarial, nursing, home economics, or education courses. Less than 1 out of 10 doctorates were granted to women, compared to 1 in 6 in 1920, 13 per cent in 1940. Not since before World War I have the percentages of American women receiving professional degrees been as consistently low as in this period. The extent of the retrogression of American women can also be measured in terms of their failure to develop to their own potential. According to *Womanpower*, of all the young women *capable* of doing college work, only one out of four goes to college, compared to one out of two men; only one out of 300 women capable of earning a Ph.D. actually does so, compared to one out of 30 men. If the present situation continues, American women may soon rank among the most "backward" women in the world. The U.S. is probably the only nation where the proportion of women gaining higher education has decreased in the past 20 years; it has steadily increased in Sweden, Britain, and France, as well as in the emerging nations of Asia and the communist countries. By the 1950's, a larger proportion of French women were obtaining higher education than American women; the proportion of French women in the professions had more than doubled in fifty years. The proportion of French women in the medical profession alone is five times that of American women; 70 per cent of the doctors in the Soviet Union are women, compared to 5 per cent in America. See Alva Myrdal and Viola Klein, *Women's Two Roles—Home and Work*, London, 1956, pp. 33–64.
2. Mervin B. Freedman, "The Passage through College," in *Personality Development During the College Years*, ed. by Nevitt Sanford, *Journal of Social Issues*, Vol. XII, No. 4, 1956, pp. 15 ff.
3. John Bushnel, "Student Culture at Vassar," in *The American College*, ed. by Nevitt Sanford, New York and London, 1962, pp. 509 ff.
4. Lynn White, *Educating Our Daughters*, New York, 1950, pp. 18–48.
5. *Ibid.*, p. 76.
6. *Ibid.*, pp. 77 ff.
7. *Ibid.*, p. 79.
8. See Dael Wolfle, *America's Resources of Specialized Talent*, New York, 1954.

9. Cited in an address by Judge Mary H. Donlon in proceedings of "Conference on the Present Status and Prospective Trends of Research on the Education of Women," 1957, American Council on Education, Washington, D.C.

10. See "The Bright Girl: A Major Source of Untapped Talent," *Guidance Newsletter*, Science Research Associates Inc., Chicago, Ill., May, 1959.

11. See Dael Wolfle, *op. cit.*

12. John Summerskill, "Dropouts from College," in *The American College*, p. 631.

13. Joseph M. Jones, "Does Overpopulation Mean Poverty?" Center for International Economic Growth, Washington, 1962. See also *United Nations Demographic Yearbook*, New York, 1960, pp. 580 ff. By 1958, in the United States, more girls were marrying from 15 to 19 years of age than from any other age group. In all of the other advanced nations, and many of the emerging underdeveloped nations, most girls married from 20 to 24 or after 25. The U.S. pattern of teenage marriage could only be found in countries like Paraguay, Venezuela, Honduras, Guatemala, Mexico, Egypt, Iraq and the Fiji Islands.

14. Nevitt Sanford, "Higher Education as a Social Problem" in *The American College*, p. 23.

15. Elizabeth Douvan and Carol Kaye, "Motivational Factors in College Entrance," in *The American College*, pp. 202–206.

16. *Ibid.*, pp. 208 ff.

17. Esther Lloyd-Jones, "Women Today and Their Education," *Teacher's College Record*, Vol. 57, No. 1, October, 1955; and No. 7, April, 1956. See also Opal David, *The Education of Women—Signs for the Future*, American Council on Education, Washington, D.C., 1957.

18. Mary Ann Guitar, "College Marriage Courses—Fun or Fraud?" *Mademoiselle*, February, 1961.

19. Helene Deutsch, *op. cit.*, Vol. 1, p. 290.

20. Mirra Komarovsky, *op. cit.*, p. 70. Research studies indicate that 40 per cent of college girls "play dumb" with men. Since the ones who do not include those not excessively overburdened with intelligence, the great majority of American girls who are gifted with high intelligence evidently learn to hide it.

21. Jean Macfarlane and Lester Sontag, Research reported to the Commission on the Education of Women, Washington, D.C., 1954, (mimeo ms.).

22. Harold Webster, "Some Quantitative Results," in *Personality Development During the College Years*, ed. by Nevitt Sanford, *Journal of Social Issues*, 1956, Vol. 12, No. 4, p. 36.

23. Nevitt Sanford, *Personality Development During the College Years, Journal of Social Issues*, 1956, Vol. 12, No. 4.

24. Mervin B. Freedman, "Studies of College Alumni," in *The American College*, p. 878.

25. Lynn White, *op. cit.*, p. 117.

26. *Ibid.*, pp. 119 ff.

27. Max Lerner, *America As a Civilization*, New York, 1957, pp. 608–611:

> The crux of it lies neither in the biological nor economic disabilities of women but in their sense of being caught between a man's world in which they have no real will to achieve and a world of their own in which they find it hard to be fulfilled. . . . When Walt Whitman exhorted women "to give up toys and fictions and launch forth, as men do, amid real, independent, stormy life," he was thinking—as were many of his contemporaries—of the wrong kind of equalitarianism. . . . If she is to discover her identity, she must start by basing her belief in herself on her womanliness rather than on the movement for feminism. Margaret Mead has pointed out that the biological life cycle of the woman has certain well-marked phases from menarche through the birth of her children to her menopause; that in these stages of her life cycle, as in her basic bodily rhythms, she can feel secure in her womanhood and does not have to assert her potency as the male does. Similarly, while the multiple roles that she must play in life are bewildering, she can fulfill them without distraction if she knows that her central role is that of a woman. . . . Her central function, however, remains that of creating a life style for herself and for the home in which she is life creator and life sustainer.

28. See Philip E. Jacob, *Changing Values in College*, New York, 1957.

29. Margaret Mead, "New Look at Early Marriages," interview in *U.S. News and World Report*, June 6, 1960.

CHAPTER 8. THE MISTAKEN CHOICE

1. See the *United Nations Demographic Yearbook*, New York, 1960, pp. 99–118 and pp. 476–490; p. 580. The annual rate of population increase in the U.S. in the years 1955–

59 was far higher than that of other Western nations, and higher than that of India, Japan, Burma, and Pakistan. In fact, the increase for North America (1.8) exceeded the world rate (1.7). The rate for Europe was .8; for the USSR 1.7; Asia 1.8; Africa 1.9; and South America 2.3. The increase in the underdeveloped nations was, of course, largely due to medical advances and the drop in death rate; in America it was almost completely due to increased birth rate, earlier marriage, and larger families. For the birth rate continued to rise in the U.S. from 1950 to 1959, while it was falling in countries like France, Norway, Sweden, the USSR, India and Japan. The U.S. was the only so-called "advanced" nation, and one of the few nations in the world where, in 1958, more girls married at ages 15 to 19 than at any other age. Even the other countries which showed a rise in the birth rate—Germany, Canada, the United Kingdom, Chile, New Zealand, Peru—did not show this phenomenon of teenage marriage.

2. See "The Woman with Brains (continued)," *New York Times Magazine*, January 17, 1960, for the outraged letters in response to an article by Marya Mannes, "Female Intelligence—Who Wants It?" *New York Times Magazine*, January 3, 1960.

3. See National Manpower Council, *Womanpower*, New York, 1957. In 1940, more than half of all employed women in the U.S. were under 25, and one-fifth were over 45. In the 1950's peak participation in paid employment occurs among young women of 18 and 19—and women over 45, the great majority of whom hold jobs for which little training is required. The new preponderance of older married women in the working force is partly due to the fact that so few women in their twenties and thirties now work in the U.S. Two out of five of all employed women are now over 45, most of them wives and mothers, working part time at unskilled work. Those reports of millions of American wives working outside the home are misleading in more ways than one: of all employed women, only one-third hold full-time jobs, one-third work full time only part of the year—for instance, extra saleswomen in the department stores at Christmas—and one-third work part time, part of the year. The women in the professions are, for the most part, that dwindling minority of single women; the older untrained wives and mothers, like the untrained 18-year-olds, are concentrated at the lower end of the skill ladder and the pay scales, in factory, service, sales and office work. Considering the growth in the population, and the increasing professionalization of work in America, the startling phenomenon is not the much-advertised, relatively insignificant increase in the numbers of American women who now work outside the home, but the fact that two out of three adult American women do *not* work outside the home, and the increasing millions of young women who are not skilled or educated for work in any profession. See also Theodore Caplow, *The Sociology of Work*, 1954, and Alva Myrdal and Viola Klein, *Women's Two Roles—Home and Work*, London, 1956.

4. Edward Strecker, *Their Mother's Sons*, Philadelphia and New York, 1946, pp. 52–59.

5. *Ibid.*, pp. 31 ff.

6. Farnham and Lundberg, *Modern Woman: The Lost Sex*, p. 271. See also Lynn White, *Educating Our Daughters*, p. 90.
   Preliminary results of the careful study of American sex habits being conducted at the University of Indiana by Dr. A. C. Kinsey indicate that there is an inverse correlation between education and the ability of a woman to achieve habitual orgastic experience in marriage. According to the present evidence, admittedly tentative, nearly 65 per cent of the marital intercourse had by women with college backgrounds is had without orgasm for them, as compared to about 15 per cent for married women who have gone no further than grade school.

7. Alfred C. Kinsey, *et al.*, Staff of the Institute for Sex Research, Indiana University, *Sexual Behavior in the Human Female*, Philadelphia and London, 1953, pp. 378 ff.

8. Lois Meek Stolz, "Effects of Maternal Employment on Children: Evidence from Research," *Child Development*, Vol. 31, No. 4, 1960, pp. 749–782.

9. H. F. Southard, "Mothers' Dilemma: To Work or Not?" *New York Times Magazine*, July 17, 1960.

10. Stolz, *op. cit.* See also Myrdal and Klein, *op. cit.*, pp. 125 ff.

11. Benjamin Spock, "Russian Children Don't Whine, Squabble or Break Things—Why?" *Ladies' Home Journal*, October, 1960.

12. David Levy, *Maternal Overprotection*, New York, 1943.

13. Arnold W. Green, "The Middle-Class Male Child and Neurosis," *American Sociological Review*, Vol. II, No. 1, 1946.

CHAPTER 9. THE SEXUAL SELL

1. The studies upon which this chapter is based were done by the Staff of the Institute for Motivational Research, directed by Dr. Ernest Dichter. They were made available

to me through the courtesy of Dr. Dichter and his colleagues, and are on file at the Institute, in Croton-on-Hudson, New York.

2. Harrison Kinney, *Has Anybody Seen My Father?*, New York, 1960.

CHAPTER 10. HOUSEWIFERY EXPANDS TO FILL THE TIME AVAILABLE

1. Jhan and June Robbins, "Why Young Mothers Feel Trapped," *Redbook*, September, 1960.
2. Carola Woerishoffer Graduate Department of Social Economy and Social Research, "Women During the War and After," Bryn Mawr College, 1945.
3. Theodore Caplow points out in *The Sociology of Work*, p. 234, that with the rapidly expanding economy since 1900, and the extremely rapid urbanization of the United States, the increase in the employment of women from 20.4 per cent in 1900 to 28.5 per cent in 1950 was exceedingly modest. Recent studies of time spent by American housewives on housework, which confirm my description of the Parkinson effect, are summarized by Jean Warren, "Time: Resource or Utility," *Journal of Home Economics*, Vol. 49, January, 1957, pp. 21 ff. Alva Myrdal and Viola Klein in *Women's Two Roles—Home and Work* cite a French study which showed that working mothers reduced time spent on housework by 30 hours a week, compared to a full-time housewife. The work week of a working mother with three children broke down to 35.2 hours on the job, 48.3 hours on housework; the full-time housewife spent 77.7 hours on housework. The mother with a full-time job or profession, as well as the housekeeping and children, worked only one hour a day longer than the full-time housewife.
4. Robert Wood, *Suburbia, Its People and Their Politics*, Boston, 1959.
5. See "Papa's Taking Over the PTA Mama Started," *New York Herald Tribune*, February 10, 1962. At the 1962 national convention of Parent-Teacher Associations, it was revealed that 32 per cent of the 46,457 PTA presidents are now men. In certain states the percentage of male PTA heads is even higher, including New York (33 per cent), Connecticut (45 per cent) and Delaware (80 per cent).
6. Nanette E. Scofield, "Some Changing Roles of Women in Suburbia: A Social Anthropological Case Study," transactions of the New York Academy of Sciences, Vol. 22, No. 6, April, 1960.
7. Mervin B. Freedman, "Studies of College Alumni," in *The American College*, pp. 872 ff.
8. Murray T. Pringle, "Women Are Wretched Housekeepers," *Science Digest*, June, 1960.
9. See *Time*, April 20, 1959.
10. Farnham and Lundberg, *Modern Women: The Lost Sex*, p. 369.
11. Edith M. Stern, "Women Are Household Slaves," *American Mercury*, January, 1949.
12. Russell Lynes, "The New Servant Class," in *A Surfeit of Honey*, New York, 1957, pp. 49–64.

CHAPTER 11. THE SEX-SEEKERS

1. Several social historians have commented on America's sexual preoccupation from the male point of view. "America has come to stress sex as much as any civilization since the Roman," says Max Lerner (*America as A Civilization*, p. 678). David Riesman in *The Lonely Crowd* (New Haven, 1950, p. 172 ff.) calls sex "the Last Frontier."

> More than before, as job-mindedness declines, sex permeates the daytime as well as the playtime consciousness. It is viewed as a consumption good not only by the old leisure classes but by the modern leisure masses. . . .
> One reason for the change is that women are no longer objects for the acquisitive consumer but are peer-groupers themselves. . . . Today, millions of women, freed by technology from many household tasks, given by technology many aids to romance, have become pioneers with men on the frontiers of sex. As they become knowing consumers, the anxiety of men lest they fail to satisfy the women also grows . . .

It is mainly the clinicians who have noted that the men are often less eager now than their wives as sexual "consumers." The late Dr. Abraham Stone, whom I interviewed shortly before his death, said that the wives complain more and more of sexually "inadequate" husbands. Dr. Karl Menninger reports that for every wife who complains of her husband's excessive sexuality, a dozen wives complain that their husbands are apathetic or impotent. These "problems" are cited in the mass media as additional evidence that American women are losing their "femininity"—and thus provide new ammunition for the mystique. See John Kord Lagemann, "The Male Sex," *Redbook*, December, 1956.

2. Albert Ellis, *The Folklore of Sex*, New York, 1961, p. 123.

3. See the amusing parody, "The Pious Pornographers," by Ray Russell, in *The Permanent Playboy*, New York, 1959.

4. A. C. Spectorsky, *The Exurbanites*, New York, 1955, p. 223.

5. Nathan Ackerman, *The Psychodynamics of Family Life*, New York, 1958, pp. 112–127.

6. Evan Hunter, *Strangers When We Meet*, New York, 1958, pp. 231–235.

7. Kinsey, *et al.*, *Sexual Behavior in the Human Female*, pp. 353 ff., p. 426.

8. Doris Menzer-Benaron M.D., *et al.*, "Patterns of Emotional Recovery from Hysterectomy," *Psychosomatic Medicine*, XIX, No. 5, September, 1957, pp. 378–388.

9. The fact that 75 per cent to 85 per cent of young mothers in America today feel negative emotions—resentment, grief, disappointment, outright rejection—when they become pregnant for the first time has been established in many studies. In fact, the perpetrators of the feminine mystique report findings to reassure young mothers that they are only "normal" in feeling this strange rejection of pregnancy—and that the only real problem is their "guilt" over feeling it. Thus *Redbook* magazine, in "How Women Really Feel about Pregnancy" (November, 1958), reports that the Harvard School of Public Health found 80 to 85 per cent of "normal women reject the pregnancy when they become pregnant"; Long Island College Clinic found that less than a fourth of women are "happy" about their pregnancy; a New Haven study finds only 17 of 100 women "pleased" about having a baby. Comments the voice of editorial authority:

> The real danger that arises when a pregnancy is unwelcome and filled with troubled feelings is that a woman may become guilty and panic-stricken because she believes her reactions are unnatural or abnormal. Both marital and mother-child relations can be damaged as a result. . . . Sometimes a mental-health specialist is needed to allay guilt feelings. . . . Nor is there any time when a normal woman does not have feelings of depression and doubt when she learns that she is pregnant.

Such articles never mention the various studies which indicate that women in other countries, both more and less advanced than the United States, and even American "career" women, are less likely to experience this emotional rejection of pregnancy. Depression at pregnancy may be "normal" for the housewife-mother in the era of the feminine mystique, but it is not normal to motherhood. As Ruth Benedict said, it is not biological necessity, but our culture which creates the discomforts, physical and psychological, of the female cycle. See her *Continuities and Discontinuities in Cultural Conditioning*.

10. See William J. Goode, *After Divorce*, Glencoe, Ill., 1956.

11. A. C. Kinsey, *et al.*, *Sexual Behavior in the Human Male*, Philadelphia and London, 1948, p. 259, pp. 585–588.

12. The male contempt for the American woman, as she has molded herself according to the feminine mystique, is depressingly explicit in the July, 1962 issue of *Esquire*, "The American Woman, A New Point of View." See especially "The Word to Women—'No'" by Robert Alan Aurthur, p. 32. The sexlessness of the American female sex-seekers is eulogized by Malcolm Muggeridge ("Bedding Down in the Colonies," p. 84): "How they mortify the flesh in order to make it appetizing! Their beauty is a vast industry, their enduring allure a discipline which nuns or athletes might find excessive. With too much sex to be sensual, and too ravishing to ravish, age cannot wither them nor custom stale their infinite monotony."

13. Kinsey, *et al.*, *Sexual Behavior in the Human Male*, p. 631.

14. See Donald Webster Cory, *The Homosexual in America*, New York, 1960, preface to second edition, pp. xxii ff. Also Albert Ellis, *op. cit.*, pp. 186–190. Also Seward Hiltner, "Stability and Change in American Sexual Patterns," in *Sexual Behavior in American Society*, Jerome Himelhoch and Sylvia Fleis Fava, eds., New York, 1955, p. 321.

15. Sigmund Freud, *Three Contributions to the Theory of Sex*, New York, 1948, p. 10.

16. Kinsey, *et al.*, *Sexual Behavior in the Human Male*, pp. 610 ff. See also Donald Webster Cory, *op. cit.*, pp. 97 ff.

17. Birth out of wedlock increased 194 per cent from 1956 to 1962; venereal disease among young people increased 132 per cent. (*Time*, March 16, 1962).

18. Kinsey, *et al.*, *Sexual Behavior in the Human Male*, pp. 348 ff., 427–433.

19. Kinsey, *et al.*, *Sexual Behavior in the Human Male*, pp. 293, 378, 382.

20. Clara Thompson, "Changing Concepts of Homosexuality in Psychoanalysis" in *A Study of Interpersonal Relations, New Contributions to Psychiatry*, Patrick Mullahy, ed., New York, 1949, pp. 218 ff.

21. Erich Fromm, "Sex and Character: the Kinsey Report Viewed from the Standpoint of Psychoanalysis," in *Sexual Behavior in American Society*, p. 307.

22. Carl Binger, "The Pressures on College Girls Today," *Atlantic Monthly*, February, 1961.

23. Sallie Bingham, "Winter Term," *Mademoiselle*, July, 1958.

CHAPTER 12. PROGRESSIVE DEHUMANIZATION:
THE COMFORTABLE CONCENTRATION CAMP

1. Marjorie K. McCorquodale, "What They Will Die for in Houston," *Harper's*, October, 1961.
2. See David Riesman, *The Lonely Crowd*; also Erich Fromm, *Escape from Freedom*, New York and Toronto, 1941, pp. 185–206. Also Erik H. Erikson, *Childhood and Society*, p. 239.
3. David Riesman, introduction to Edgar Friedenberg's *The Vanishing Adolescent*, Boston, 1959.
4. Harold Taylor, "Freedom and Authority on the Campus," in *The American College*, pp. 780 ff.
5. David Riesman, introduction to Edgar Friedenberg's *The Vanishing Adolescent*.
6. See Eugene Kinkead, *In Every War but One*, New York, 1959. There has been an attempt in recent years to discredit or soft-pedal these findings. But a taped record of a talk given before the American Psychiatric Association in 1958 by Dr. William Mayer, who had been on one of the Army teams of psychiatrists and intelligence officers who interviewed the returning prisoners in 1953 and analyzed the data, caused many pediatricians and child specialists to ask, in the words of Dr. Spock: "Are unusually permissive, indulgent parents more numerous today—and are they weakening the character of our children?" (Benjamin Spock, "Are We Bringing Up Our Children Too 'Soft' for the Stern Realities They Must Face?" *Ladies' Home Journal*, September, 1960.) However unpleasantly injurious to American pride, there must be some explanation for the collapse of the American GI prisoners in Korea, as it differed not only from the behavior of American soldiers in previous wars, but from the behavior of soldiers of other nations in Korea. No American soldier managed to escape from the enemy prison camps, as they had in every other war. The shocking 38 per cent death rate was not explainable, even according to military authorities, on the basis of the climate, food, or inadequate medical facilities in the camps, nor was it caused by brutality or torture. "Give-up-itis" is how one doctor described the disease the Americans died from; they simply spent the days curled up under blankets, cutting down their diet to water alone, until they were dead, usually within three weeks. This seemed to be an American phenomenon. Turkish prisoners, who were also part of the UN force in Korea, lost no men by disease or starvation; they stuck together, obeyed their officers, adhered to health regulations, cooperated in the care of their sick, and refused to inform on one another.
7. Edgar Friedenberg, *The Vanishing Adolescent*, pp. 212 ff.
8. Andras Angyal, M.D., "Evasion of Growth," *American Journal of Psychiatry*, Vol. 110, No. 5, November, 1953, pp. 358–361. See also Erich Fromm, *Escape from Freedom*, pp. 138–206.
9. See Richard E. Gordon and Katherine K. Gordon, "Social Factors in the Prediction and Treatment of Emotional Disorders of Pregnancy," *American Journal of Obstetrics and Gynecology*, 1959, 77:5, pp. 1074–1083; also Richard E. Gordon and Katherine K. Gordon, "Psychiatric Problems of a Rapidly Growing Suburb," *American Medical Association Archives of Neurology and Psychiatry*, 1958, Vol. 79; "Psychosomatic Problems of a Rapidly Growing Suburb," *Journal of the American Medical Association*, 1959, 170:15; and "Social Psychiatry of a Mobile Suburb," *International Journal of Social Psychiatry*, 1960, 6:1, 2, pp. 89–99. Some of these findings were popularized in the composite case histories of *The Split Level Trap*, written by the Gordons in collaboration with Max Gunther (New York, 1960).
10. Richard E. Gordon, "Sociodynamics and Psychotherapy," *A.M.A. Archives of Neurology and Psychiatry*, April, 1959, Vol. 81, pp. 486–503.
11. Adelaide M. Johnson and S. A. Szurels, "The Genesis of Antisocial Acting Out in Children and Adults," *Psychoanalytic Quarterly*, 1952, 21:323–343.
12. *Ibid.*
13. Beata Rank, "Adaptation of the Psychoanalytical Technique for the Treatment of Young Children with Atypical Development," *American Journal of Orthopsychiatry*, XIX, 1, January, 1949.
14. *Ibid.*
15. *Ibid.*
16. Beata Rank, Marian C. Putnam, and Gregory Rochlin, M.D., "The Significance of the 'Emotional Climate' in Early Feeding Difficulties," *Psychosomatic Medicine*, X, 5, October, 1948.
17. Richard E. Gordon and Katherine K. Gordon, "Social Psychiatry of a Mobile Suburb," *op. cit.*, pp. 89–100.

18. *Ibid.*
19. Oscar Sternbach, "Sex Without Love and Marriage Without Responsibility," an address presented at the 38th Annual Conference of The Child Study Association of America, March 12, 1962, New York City (mimeo ms.).
20. Bruno Bettelheim, *The Informed Heart—Autonomy in a Mass Age*, Glencoe, Ill., 1960.
21. *Ibid.*, pp. 162–169.
22. *Ibid.*, p. 231.
23. *Ibid.*, pp. 233 ff.
24. *Ibid.*, p. 265.

CHAPTER 13. THE FORFEITED SELF

1. Rollo May, "The Origins and Significance of the Existential Movement in Psychology," in *Existence, A New Dimension in Psychiatry and Psychology*, Rollo May, Ernest Angel and Henri F. Ellenberger, eds., New York, 1958, pp. 30 ff. (See also Erich Fromm, *Escape from Freedom*, pp. 269 ff.; A. H. Maslow, *Motivation and Personality*, New York, 1954; David Riesman, *The Lonely Crowd*.)
2. Rollo May, "Contributions of Existential Psychotherapy," in *Existence, A New Dimension in Psychiatry and Psychology*, p. 87.
3. *Ibid.*, p. 52.
4. *Ibid.*, p. 53.
5. *Ibid.*, pp. 59 ff.
6. See Kurt Goldstein, *The Organism, A Holistic Approach to Biology Derived From Pathological Data on Man*, New York and Cincinnati, 1939; also *Abstract and Concrete Behavior*, Evanston, Ill., 1950; *Case of Idiot Savant* (with Martin Scheerer), Evanston, 1945; *Human Nature in the Light of Psychopathology*, Cambridge, 1947; *After-Effects of Brain Injuries in War*, New York, 1942.
7. Eugene Minkowski, "Findings in a Case of Schizophrenic Depression," in *Existence, A New Dimension in Psychiatry and Psychology*, pp. 132 ff.
8. O. Hobart Mowrer, "Time as a Determinant in Integrative Learning," in *Learning Theory and Personality Dynamics*, New York, 1950.
9. Eugene Minkowski, *op. cit.*, pp. 133–138:

   We think and act and desire beyond that death which, even so, we could not escape. The very existence of such phenomena as the desire to do something for future generations clearly indicates our attitude in this regard. In our patient, it was this propulsion toward the future which seemed to be totally lacking. . . . In this personal impetus, there is an element of expansion; we go beyond the limits of our own ego and leave a personal imprint on the world about us, creating works which sever themselves from us to live their own lives. This accompanies a specific, positive feeling which we call contentment—that pleasure which accompanies every finished action or firm decision. As a feeling, it is unique. . . . Our entire individual evolution consists in trying to surpass that which has already been done. When our mental life dims, the future closes in front of us . . .

10. Rollo May, "Contributions of Existential Psychotherapy," pp. 31 ff. In Nietzsche's philosophy, human individuality and dignity are "given or assigned to us as a task which we ourselves must solve"; in Tillich's philosophy, if you do not have the "courage to be," you lose your own being; in Sartre's, you *are* your choices.
11. A. H. Maslow, *Motivation and Personality*, p. 83.
12. A. H. Maslow, "Some Basic Propositions of Holistic-Dynamic Psychology," an unpublished paper, Brandeis University.
13. *Ibid.*
14. A. H. Maslow, "Dominance, Personality and Social Behavior in Women," *Journal of Social Psychology*, 1939, Vol. 10, pp. 3–39; and "Self Esteem (Dominance-Feeling) and Sexuality in Women," *Journal of Social Psychology*, 1942, Vol. 16, pp. 259–294.
15. A. H. Maslow, "Dominance, Personality and Social Behavior in Women," *op. cit.*, pp. 3–11.
16. *Ibid.*, pp. 13 ff.
17. *Ibid.*, p. 180.
18. A. H. Maslow, "Self-Esteem (Dominance-Feeling) and Sexuality in Women," p. 288. Maslow points out, however, that women with "ego insecurity" pretended a "self-esteem" they did not actually have. Such women had to "dominate," in the ordinary sense, in their sexual relations, to compensate for their "ego insecurity"; thus, they were either castrative or masochistic. As I have pointed out, such women must have been very common in a society which gives women little chance for true self-esteem;

this was undoubtedly the basis of the man-eating myth, and of Freud's equation of femininity with castrative penis envy and/or masochistic passivity.

19. A. H. Maslow, *Motivation and Personality*, pp. 200 ff.
20. *Ibid.*, pp. 211 ff.
21. *Ibid.*, p. 214.
22. *Ibid.*, pp. 242 ff.
23. *Ibid.*, pp. 257 ff. Maslow found that his self-actualizing people "have in unusual measure the rare ability to be pleased rather than threatened by the partner's triumphs. . . . A most impressive example of this respect is the ungrudging pride of such a man in his wife's achievements even where they outshine his" (*Ibid.*, p. 252).
24. *Ibid.*, p. 245.
25. *Ibid.*, p. 255.
26. A. C. Kinsey, *et al.*, *Sexual Behavior in the Human Female*, pp. 356 ff.; Table 97, p. 397; Table 104, p. 403.

Decade of Birth vs. Percentage of
Marital Coitus Leading to Orgasm

In First yr. of Marriage, per cent of females
Decade of Birth

% of Marital Coitus with Orgasm	Before 1900	1900–1909	1910–1919	1920–1929
None	33	27	23	22
1–29	9	13	12	8
30–59	10	22	15	12
60–89	11	11	12	15
90–100	37	37	38	43
Number of cases	331	589	834	484

In Fifth yr. of Marriage, per cent of females
Decade of Birth

% of Marital Coitus with Orgasm	Before 1900	1900–1909	1910–1919	1920–1929
None	23	17	12	12
1–29	14	15	13	14
30–59	14	13	16	19
60–89	12	13	17	19
90–100	37	42	42	36
Number of cases	302	489	528	130

27. *Ibid.*, p. 355.
28. See Judson T. Landis, "The Women Kinsey Studied," George Simpson, "Nonsense about Women," and A. H. Maslow and James M. Sakoda, "Volunteer Error in the Kinsey Study," in *Sexual Behavior in American Society*.
29. Ernest W. Burgess and Leonard S. Cottrell, Jr., *Predicting Success or Failure in Marriage*, New York, 1939, p. 271.
30. A. C. Kinsey, *et al.*, *Sexual Behavior in the Human Female*, p. 403.
31. Sylvan Keiser, "Body Ego During Orgasm," *Psychoanalytic Quarterly*, 1952, Vol. XXI, pp. 153–166:

Individuals of this group are characterized by failure to develop adequate egos. . . . Their anxious devotion to, and lavish care of, their bodies belies the inner feelings of hollowness and inadequacy. . . . These patients have little sense of their own identity and are always ready to take on the personality of someone else. They have few personal convictions, and yield readily to the opinions of others. . . . It is chiefly among such patients that coitus can be enjoyed only up to the point of orgasm. . . . They dared not allow themselves uninhibited progression to orgasm with its concomitant loss of control, loss of awareness of the body, or death. . . . In instances of uncertainty about the structure and boundaries of the body image, one might say that the skin does not serve as an envelope which sharply defines the transition from the self to the environment; the one gradually merges into the other; there is no assurance of being a distinct entity endowed with the strength to give of itself without endangering one's own integrity.

32. Lawrence Kubie, "Psychiatric Implications of the Kinsey Report," in *Sexual Behavior in American Society*, pp. 270 ff:

> This simple biologic aim is overlaid by many subtle goals of which the individual himself is usually unaware. Some of these are attainable; some are not. Where the majority are attainable, then the end result of sexual activity is an afterglow of peaceful completion and satisfaction. Where, however, the unconscious goals are unattainable, then whether orgasm has occurred or not, there remains a post-coital state of unsated need, and sometimes of fear, rage or depression.

33. Erik H. Erikson, *Childhood and Society*, pp. 239–283, 367–380. See also Erich Fromm, *Escape from Freedom* and *Man for Himself*; and David Riesman, *The Lonely Crowd*.

34. See Alva Myrdal and Viola Klein (*Women's Two Roles*), who point out that the number of American women now working outside the home seems greater than it is because the base from which the comparison is usually made was unusually small: a century ago the proportion of American women working outside the home was far smaller than in the European countries. In other words, the woman problem in America was probably unusually severe because the displacement of American women from essential work and identity in society was far more drastic—primarily because of the extremely rapid growth and industrialization of the American economy. The women who had grown with the men in the frontier days were banished almost overnight to *anomie*—which is a very expressive sociological name for that sense of non-existence or non-identity suffered by one who has no real place in society—when the important work left the home, where they stayed. In contrast, in France where industrialization was slower, and farms and small family-size shops are still fairly important in the economy, women a century ago still worked in large numbers—in field and shop—and today the majority of French women are not full-time housewives in the American sense of the mystique, for an enormous number still work in the fields, in addition to that one out of three who, as in America, work in industry, sales, offices, and professions. The growth of women in France has much more closely paralleled the growth of the society, since the proportion of French women in the professions has doubled in fifty years. It is interesting to note that the feminine mystique does not prevail in France, to the extent that it does here; there is a legitimate image in France of a feminine career woman and feminine intellectual, and French men seem responsive to women sexually, without equating femininity either with glorified emptiness or that man-eating castrative mom. Nor has the family been weakened—in actuality or mystique—by women's work in industry and profession. Myrdal and Klein show that the French career women continue to have children—but not the great number the new educated American housewives produce.

35. Sidney Ditzion, *Marriage, Morals and Sex in America, A History of Ideas*, New York, 1953, p. 277.

36. William James, *Psychology*, New York, 1892, p. 458.

CHAPTER 14. A NEW LIFE PLAN FOR WOMEN

1. See "Mother's Choice: Manager or Martyr," and "For a Mother's Hour," *New York Times Magazine*, January 14, 1962, and March 18, 1962.

2. The sense that work has to be "real," and not just "therapy" or busywork, to provide a basis for identity becomes increasingly explicit in the theories of the self, even when there is no specific reference to women. Thus, in defining the beginnings of "identity" in the child, Erikson says in *Childhood and Society* (p. 208):

> The growing child must, at every step, derive a vitalizing sense of reality from the awareness that his individual way of mastering experience (his ego synthesis) is a successful variant of a group identity and is in accord with its space-time and life plan.
> In this children cannot be fooled by empty praise and condescending encouragement. They may have to accept artificial bolstering of their self-esteem in lieu of something better, but their ego identity gains real strength only from wholehearted and consistent recognition of real accomplishment—i.e., of achievement that has meaning in the culture.

3. Nanette E. Scofield, "Some Changing Roles of Women in Suburbia: A Social Anthropological Case Study," transactions of the New York Academy of Sciences, Vol. 22, 6, April, 1960.

4. Polly Weaver, "What's Wrong with Ambition?" *Mademoiselle*, September, 1956.
5. Edna G. Rostow, "The Best of Both Worlds," *Yale Review*, March, 1962.
6. Ida Fisher Davidoff and May Elish Markewich, "The Postparental Phase in the Life Cycle of Fifty College-Educated Women," unpublished doctoral study, Teachers College, Columbia University, 1961. These fifty educated women had been full-time housewives and mothers throughout the years their children were in school. With the last child's departure, the women suffering severe distress because they had no deep interest beyond the home included a few whose actual ability and achievement were high; these women had been leaders in community work, but they felt like "phonies," "frauds," earning respect for "work a ten-year-old could do." The authors' own orientation in the functional-adjustment school makes them deplore the fact that education gave these women "unrealistic" goals (a surprising number, now in their fifties and sixties, still wished they had been doctors). However, those women who had pursued interests—which in every case had begun in college—and were working now in jobs or politics or art, did not feel like "phonies," or even suffer the expected distress at menopause. Despite the distress of those who lacked such interests, none of them, after the child-bearing years were over, wanted to go back to school; there were simply too few years left to justify the effort. So they continued "woman's role" by acting as mothers to their own aged parents or by finding pets, plants, or simply "people as my hobby" to take the place of their children.

The interpretation of the two family-life educators—who themselves became professional marriage counselors in middle age—is interesting:

> For those women in our group who had high aspirations or high intellectual endowment or both, the discrepancy between some of the values stressed in our success-and-achievement oriented society and the actual opportunities open to the older, untrained women was especially disturbing. . . . The door open to the woman with a skill was closed to the one without training, even if she was tempted to try to find a place for herself among the gainfully employed. The reality hazards of the work situation seemed to be recognized by most, however. They felt neither prepared for the kind of job which might appeal to them, nor willing to take the time and expend the energy which would be required for training, in view of the limited number of active years ahead. . . . The lack of pressure resulting from reduced responsibility had to be handled. . . . As the primary task of motherhood was finished, the satisfactions of volunteer work, formerly a secondary outlet, seemed to be diminishing. . . . The cultural activities of the suburbs were limited. . . . Even in the city, adult education . . . seemed to be "busy work," leading nowhere. . . .
>
> Thus, some women expressed certain regrets: "It is too late to develop a new skill leading to a career." "If I had pursued a single line, it would have utilized my potential to the full."

But the authors note with approval that "the vast majority have somehow adjusted themselves to their place in society."

> Because our culture demands of women certain renunciations of activity and limits her scope of participation in the stream of life, at this point being a woman would seem to be an advantage rather than a handicap. All her life, as a female, she had been encouraged to be sensitive to the feelings and needs of others. Her life, at strategic points, had required denials of self. She had had ample opportunities for "dress rehearsals" for this latest renunciation . . . of a long series of renunciations begun early in life. Her whole life as a woman had been giving her a skill which she was now free to use to the full without further preparation . . .

7. Nevitt Sanford, "Personality Development During the College Years," *Journal of Social Issues*, 1956, Vol. 12, No. 4, p. 36.
8. The public flurry in the spring of 1962 over the sexual virginity of Vassar girls is a case in point. The real question, for the educator, would seem to me to be whether these girls were getting from their education the serious lifetime goals only education can give them. If they are, they can be trusted to be responsible for their sexual behavior. President Blanding indeed defied the mystique to say boldly that if girls are not in college for education, they should not be there at all. That her statement caused such an uproar is evidence of the extent of sex-directed education.
9. The impossibility of part-time study of medicine, science, and law, and of part-time graduate work in the top universities has kept many women of high ability from attempting it. But in 1962, the Harvard Graduate School of Education let down this

barrier to encourage more able housewives to become teachers. A plan was also announced in New York to permit women doctors to do their psychiatric residencies and postgraduate work on a part-time basis, taking into account their maternal responsibilities.

10. Virginia L. Senders, "The Minnesota Plan for Women's Continuing Education," in "Unfinished Business—Continuing Education for Women," *The Educational Record*, American Council on Education, October, 1961, pp. 10 ff.

11. Mary Bunting, "The Radcliffe Institute for Independent Study," *Ibid.*, pp. 19 ff. Radcliffe's president reflects the feminine mystique when she deplores "the use the first college graduates made of their advanced educations. Too often and understandably, they became crusaders and reformers, passionate, fearless, articulate, but also, at times, loud. A stereotype of the educated women grew up in the popular mind and concurrently, a prejudice against both the stereotype and the education." Similarly she states:

> That we have not made any respectable attempt to meet the special educational needs of women in the past is the clearest possible evidence of the fact that our educational objectives have been geared exclusively to the vocational patterns of men. In changing that emphasis, however, our goal should not be to equip and encourage women to compete with men. . . . Women, because they are not generally the principal breadwinners, can be perhaps most useful as the trail blazers, working along the bypaths, doing the unusual job that men cannot afford to gamble on. There is always room on the fringes even when competition in the intellectual market places is keen.

That women use their education today primarily "on the fringes" is a result of the feminine mystique, and of the prejudices against women it masks; it is doubtful whether these remaining barriers will ever be overcome if even educators are going to discourage able women from becoming "crusaders and reformers, passionate, fearless, articulate,"—and loud enough to be heard.

12. *Time*, November, 1961. See also "Housewives at the $2 Window," *New York Times Magazine*, April 1, 1962, which describes how babysitting services and "clinics" for suburban housewives are now being offered at the race tracks.

13. See remarks of State Assemblywoman Dorothy Bell Lawrence, Republican, of Manhattan, reported in the *New York Times*, May 8, 1962. The first woman to be elected a Republican district leader in New York City, she explained: "I was doing all the work, so I told the county chairman that I wanted to be chairman. He told me it was against the rules for a woman to hold the post, but then he changed the rules." In the Democratic "reform" movement in New York, women are also beginning to assume leadership posts commensurate with their work, and the old segregated "ladies' auxiliaries" and "women's committees" are beginning to go.

14. Among more than a few women I interviewed who had, as the mystique advises, completely renounced their own ambitions to become wives and mothers, I noticed a repeated history of miscarriages. In several cases, only after the woman finally resumed the work she had given up, or went back to graduate school, was she able to carry to term the long-desired second or third child.

15. American women's life expectancy—75 years—is the longest of women anywhere in the world. But as Myrdal and Klein point out in *Women's Two Roles*, there is increasing recognition that, in human beings, chronological age differs from biological age: "at the chronological age of 70, the divergencies in biological age may be as wide as between the chronological ages of 50 and 90." The new studies of aging in humans indicate that those who have the most education and who live the most complex and active lives, with deep interests and readiness for new experience and learning, do not get "old" in the sense that others do. A close study of 300 biographies (See Charlotte Buhler, "The Curve of Life as Studied in Biographies," *Journal of Applied Psychology*, XIX, August, 1935, pp. 405 ff.) reveals that in the latter half of life, the person's productivity becomes independent of his biological equipment, and, in fact, is often at a higher level than his biological efficiency—*that is, if the person has emerged from biological living.* Where "spiritual factors" dominated activity, the highest point of productivity came in the latter part of life; where "physical facts" were decisive in the life of an individual, the high point was reached earlier and the psychological curve was then more closely comparable to the biological. The study of educated women cited above revealed much less suffering at menopause than is considered "normal" in America today. Most of these women whose horizons had not been confined to physical housekeeping and their biological role, did not, in their

fifties and sixties feel "old." Many reported in surprise that they suffered much less discomfort at menopause than their mothers' experience had led them to expect. Therese Benedek suggests (in "Climacterium: A Developmental Phase," *Psychoana-lytical Quarterly*, XIX, 1950, p. 1) that the lessened discomfort, and burst of creative energy many women now experience at menopause, is at least in part due to the "emancipation" of women. Kinsey's figures seem to indicate that women who have by education been emancipated from purely biological living, experience the full peak of sexual fulfillment much later in life than had been expected, and in fact, continue to experience it through the forties and past menopause. Perhaps the best example of this phenomenon is Colette—that truly human, emancipated French woman who lived and loved and wrote with so little deference to her chronological age that she said on her eightieth birthday: "If only one were 58, because at that time one is still desired and full of hope for the future."

CONTEXTS

Origins and Influences

CHILDHOOD WORLD

Bettye Naomi Goldstein was born in Peoria, Illinois, in 1921 to middle-class Jewish parents. Her father owned a jewelry store and she grew up in moderate comfort. As a Jewish girl in a mid-sized midwestern town, she felt excluded from many features of social life in school and in the community. This type of small-town midwestern life in the 1920s was captured perfectly in Robert and Helen Lynd's classic *Middletown,* a sociological study of Muncie, Indiana, during that decade.

ROBERT S. LYND
AND HELEN MERRELL LYND

From Middletown: A Study in Modern American Culture[†]

* * *

In the main, as has been suggested, the cleavages which break up Middletown into its myriad sub-groups appear to have become somewhat more rigid in the last generation. When one of the grand old men of the city returned from Europe in 1890, "the whole town" was invited through a newspaper notice to meet him at the train and attend an "informal reception" at his home afterward; such an invitation would not be given even nominally to the larger, more self-conscious city today. Racial lines, according to old residents, were less felt in the days before the Jews had come so largely to dominate the retail life of the city and before the latest incarnation of the Klan. Jewish merchants mingle freely with other business men in the

† From Robert S. Lynd and Helen Merrell Lynd, *Middletown: A Study in Modern American Culture* (New York: Harcourt Brace Jovanovich, 1959), chapter XXVIII, "Things Making and Unmaking Group Solidarity," p. 479. Originally published 1929. Copyright 1929 by Harcourt, Inc., and renewed 1957 by Robert S. and Helen M. Lynd. Reprinted by permission of Houghton Mifflin Harcourt Publishing Company. All rights reserved.

smaller civic clubs, but there are no Jews in Rotary; Jews are accepted socially with just enough qualification to make them aware that they do not entirely "belong." The small group of foreign-born mingle little with the rest of the community. Negroes are allowed under protest in the schools but not in the larger motion picture houses or in Y.M.C.A. or Y.W.C.A.; they are not to be found in "white" churches; Negro children must play in their own restricted corner of the Park.

INTELLECTUAL INFLUENCES

While still in high school during the 1930s, Bettye Goldstein was aware of larger national and international events—the New Deal, the Popular Front, labor activism, and the rising tide of fascism in Europe. At Smith College in Northampton, Massachusetts, she studied literature, psychology, and political economy and worked on the school newspaper. Through her courses and her extracurricular activities, she became aware of the intellectual currents of the time. Goldstein spent the summer of 1940 studying with psychologist Kurt Lewin at the Child Welfare Research Station at the State University of Iowa. Lewin, a Jewish immigrant to the United States, was an important figure in social psychology, particularly concerned with group dynamics. Some of his work concerned anti-Semitism from outside and inside the Jewish community. Goldstein engaged this issue in a short story, "The Scapegoat," that she wrote while at Smith. During the summer of 1941, she attended the Highlander Folk School in Tennessee, where she learned about progressive labor movements in the South and honed her writing skills. She returned to Smith and engaged in a variety of campus political activities, particularly around organizing the workers who cleaned the dormitories. She received a prestigious fellowship and attended graduate school in psychology at the University of California at Berkeley for one year. Like many progressive intellectuals of the time, Goldstein was engaged in a reconciliation between the psychological insights of Sigmund Freud and the political economy of Marx and Engels. Friedrich Engels' *The Origins of the Family, Private Property and the State* had an impact on Goldstein's thinking about women and the family in the modern world.

KURT LEWIN

From When Facing Danger[†]

* * *

What makes the Jews a group and what makes an individual a member of the Jewish group? I know that many Jews are deeply concerned and puzzled by this problem. They have no clear answer and their whole life is in danger of becoming meaningless, as it has become meaningless for thousands of German half-Jews and quarter-Jews who must face fate without knowing why. Historically this problem is relatively new to the Jew. There has been a time, only one hundred and fifty years ago, when even in Germany belonging to the Jewish group was an accepted and unquestioned fact. During the time of the Ghetto Jews might have been under pressure as a group; the individual Jew, however, had a social unit to which he clearly belonged. The Jews in Poland, Lithuania and other Eastern European countries have maintained what might be termed a national life which gave to the individual a "social home." When coming to America, the Eastern Jews brought much of this group life with them. They have kept alive the inner cohesive forces of the group.

It is well to realize that every underprivileged minority group is kept together not only by cohesive forces among its members but also by the boundary which the majority erects against the crossing of an individual from the minority to the majority group. It is in the interest of the majority to keep the minority in its underprivileged status. There are minorities which are kept together almost entirely by such a wall around them. The members of these minorities show certain typical characteristics resulting from this situation. Every individual likes to gain in social status. Therefore the member of an underprivileged group will try to leave it for the more privileged majority. In other words, he will try to do what in the case of Negroes is called "passing," in the case of Jews, "assimilation." It would be an easy solution of the minority problem if it could be done away with through individual assimilation. Actually, however, such a solution is impossible for any underprivileged group. Equal rights for women could not be attained by one after the other being granted the right to vote; the Negro problem cannot be solved by individual "passing." A few Jews might be fully accepted by non-Jews. This chance, how-

---

[†] From Kurt Lewin, "When Facing Danger" (1939), in *Resolving Social Conflicts: Selected Papers on Group Dynamics* (New York: Harper and Brothers, 1948), chapter 10, "When Facing Danger," section II, pp. 163–66. Copyright © 1997 by the American Psychological Association. Reprinted by permission.

ever, is today more meager than ever and certainly it is absurd to
believe that fifteen million Jews can sneak over the boundary one
by one.

What then is the situation of a member of a minority group kept
together merely by the repulsion of the majority? The basic factor in
his life is his wish to cross this insuperable boundary. Therefore, he
lives almost perpetually in a state of conflict and tension. He dislikes or even hates his own group because it is nothing but a burden
to him. Like an adolescent who does not wish to be a child any longer but who knows that he is not accepted as an adult, such a person
stands at the border-line of his group, being neither here nor there.
He is unhappy and shows the typical characteristics of a marginal
man who does not know where he belongs. A Jew of this type will
dislike everything specifically Jewish, for he will see in it that which
keeps him away from the majority for which he is longing. He will
show dislike for those Jews who are outspokenly so and will frequently indulge in self-hatred.

There is one more characteristic peculiar to minority groups kept
together merely by outside pressure as contrasted with the members
of a minority who have a positive attitude towards their own group.
The latter group will have an organic life of its own. It will show
organization and inner strength. A minority kept together only from
outside is in itself chaotic. It is composed of a mass of individuals
without inner relations with each other, a group unorganized and
weak.

Historically, the Jews living in the Diaspora were kept together
partly by the inner cohesive forces of the group and partly by the
pressure of hostile majorities. The importance of these two factors
has varied at different times and in different countries. In some parts
of Eastern Europe the positive attitude has been strengthened by
cultural superiority to the environment. In this country the positive
attitude is also strong as yet. We should not, however, be blind to the
fact that for quite a number of Jews "being forced together" has
become the dominant, or at least an important, aspect of their inner
relation to Judaism.

I have heard Jewish students in the Middle West say that they feel
more like non-Jewish Midwesterners than like Jews from New York.
Since the religious issue has lost importance for Jews and Gentiles
alike, there does not exist an easily tangible difference between both
groups. To preach Jewish religion or nationalism to such Jews is not
likely to have any deep effect. To speak about the glorious history
and culture of the Jewish people will not convince them either. They
would not want to sacrifice their lives and happiness to things past.
In places with a limited Jewish population, and particularly among
the adolescents, one finds many who are utterly bewildered about

why and in what respect they belong to the Jewish group. One might be able to help some of them by explaining that it is not similarity or dissimilarity of individuals that constitutes a group, but interdependence of fate. Any normal group, and certainly any developed and organized one contains and should contain individuals of very different character. Two members of one family might be less alike than two members of different families; but in spite of differences in character and interest, two individuals will belong to the same group if their fates are interdependent. Similarly in spite of divergent opinions about religious or political ideas, two persons might still belong to the same group.

It is easy enough to see that the common fate of all Jews makes them a group in reality. One who has grasped this simple idea will not feel that he has to break away from Judaism altogether whenever he changes his attitude toward a fundamental Jewish issue, and he will become more tolerant of differences of opinion among Jews. What is more, a person who has learned to see how much his own fate depends upon the fate of his entire group will be ready and even eager to take over a fair share of responsibility for its welfare. This realistic understanding of the sociological facts is very important for establishing a firm social ground, especially for those who have not grown up in a Jewish environment.

* * *

BETTYE GOLDSTEIN

The Scapegoat[†]

"But the goat, on which the lot fell to be the scapegoat, shall be presented alive before the Lord, to make an atonement with him, and to let him go for a scapegoat into the wilderness." Lev. 16:10.

I don't think I noticed Shirley much during the first few weeks of college. We were all trying to get adjusted and feeling very strange and uneasy; none of us knew each other very well then; she was just one of the fourteen freshmen in the house. I remember that she came in and helped me unpack because her trunk hadn't come so she didn't have much to do. She was nice enough, I guess; I mean, fundamentally there was nothing wrong with her. I had a blind date with a Harvard man that fall who asked me if I knew her. He

---

[†] From Bettye Goldstein, "The Scapegoat," *Smith College Monthly*, October 1941, pp. 4–5, 26–30.

thought she was a swell kid and a lot of fun. But she didn't seem to fit in at Ransom House. After the first month it was obvious that no one liked her. There was something objectionable about her, I don't know what it was. I don't think the fact that she was Jewish had anything to do with it. There were several other Jewish girls in the house, and we all got along quite well. Certainly that would have nothing to do with *my* feeling for her. And when I asked Phyl and Katy about it, they said, "Absolutely not. We wouldn't like her, regardless. And after all, you're Jewish, and Alice, and we like you, silly." They are always very frank. So I don't think you could call it race prejudice.

Naturally, we were all nice enough to her. But we didn't want her hanging around with us. I don't know why, but she got on our nerves. We couldn't help feeling that way. We began to notice the way she talked, and the way she swung her hips when she walked, and the moist messy way she smoked cigarettes, and the way she bit her fingernails so low that it nauseated you to look at them. She had a pretty face, but she was short and plump and always wore her hair in the sort of tight sausage curls that were obviously rolled on curlers the night before. And she wore too much makeup for college—rouge, mascara, eye-shadow. She had an affected little giggle, and she stuck out her little finger when she drank, and there was something about the way she chewed gum . . .

She was very friendly though, and affectionate in an eager sort of way. I remember not long after college opened her mother sent her some food. She asked Alice and me to come up that night. We didn't want to go very much, but we couldn't be rude. There was a chicken. It was very greasy. She showed us a large still-life her father had painted. It wasn't very good. She said she was crazy about Smith, but it was awfully large, and didn't we think it was hard to get to know people. Maybe it was New England, but she'd never known people who were so stand-offish before. It was just at first, of course; she was sure they'd be swell as soon as you got to know them. And we three would be very good friends, naturally.

Alice said, "I don't think one should be in too much of a hurry to become good friends with anyone at a place like this. It takes time to know with whom you really want to be friends. I don't believe in rushing into things. One has to be careful." She didn't look at Shirley when she said this. Shirley didn't say anything. Then I glanced at my watch and said, "I think I'd better go. I have an English theme to do. Thank you very much, Shirley."

Shirley said, "But it's so early. We haven't really gotten acquainted or talked or anything. Why don't you stay and do your theme in here?"

I said, "No, I really have to go." Then Alice remembered that she had some math to do. So we both left. Shirley seemed a little hurt; we had stayed only twenty minutes.

Al and I were walking down the hall and Al said, "I'm glad the rest weren't there. All that greasy food." She wrinkled up her nose, and then she looked at me as if she wanted to say something but didn't know whether to or not. Finally just as we got to my door she blurted out, "You don't suppose the others think we're like her, do you? Just because we're all three . . ."

"Well, they certainly see that we're different from her," I said, "At least, I hope they do. And I don't see how they could help it. But I don't like the idea of her having just you and me up there tonight. As if we naturally belonged with her. It's people like her that cause segregation, really. They ask for it."

Alice said, "I know. And I guess for our own good we ought to make it clear that we don't intend to be a little threesome with her." Then she looked embarrassed, and said goodnight.

After that we were both careful not to sit at the same table with Shirley at dinner, and the next time she asked us into her room, we said we had to study. She offered to get us blind dates several times; she seemed to have plenty of men. We always found some excuse.

Pretty soon Al and I got to be good friends with Phyl and Katy and Liz and Janice and Marty and Jill. We all went around together, went out for coffee every night after the library closed, sat together at meals. Shirley was always following us around and trying to push into things. She didn't seem to be able to take a hint. For instance, one night we were all going to the movies. We had decided about it when Shirley wasn't around. She had a habit of assuming that she was included whenever she knew we were going to do something, so this was the only way to prevent her from coming. But she must have guessed or something, because at dinner she asked, very casually, "Has anyone seen the Calvin? It's supposed to be swell."

Katy said no in an impatient tone of voice, and the rest of us started talking about something else very fast. Then Shirley said, "Let's all go tonight."

We all looked at each other and raised our eyebrows. Phyl muttered something about not having decided yet what we were going to do that evening. No one else said anything. Then Shirley said in a stilted, self-conscious way, "Well, let me know if you decide to go."

We said we would, and then we went into the living room to play bridge. Shirley said she was dying for a good game of bridge and did anyone need a fourth? No one did. So she giggled and said, "I guess I'll kibitz. Who wants the honor of my excellent advice?"

No one paid any attention. So she said she had some studying to do and went upstairs. But she walked into Marty's room just as she was putting on her coat and asked where she was going. Marty said, "Oh, to the corner or some place. Can I get you something, Shirley?"

Shirley said, "No, I don't think so." And then, as if it had just occurred to her, "Maybe I'll go with you. I haven't been out yet tonight, and I could use some coffee."

Marty became very polite and insisted that it would be no trouble at all to bring some coffee back, so she really need not bother to come along.

Shirley said, "No, I really think I'd like to go."

The rest of us were waiting for Marty downstairs, and when Shirley came down with her, we all looked at each other, and Phyl said, "Well really!"

Katy said, "Oh, I forgot to tell you, Shirley. We decided to go to the movies after all. Or did you know?" You couldn't help smiling, Katy said this with such a suave pointedness. Shirley tried to look nonchalant, but she didn't succeed very well. I should think she would have had more pride than to insist on coming when it was so obvious that we didn't want her. And she might just as well have gone alone: no one paid any attention to her. Except for Liz's imitating her walk on our way home. We howled; it was really a scream. Shirley turned around and asked what was so funny. Phyl said, "Oh, nothing much."

Once in a while we used to talk about how heavenly it would be if Shirley moved out of the house at the end of the year. But in a way it was exciting to dodge her. And it made us feel more close to each other. There was a togetherness, a warm shared feeling when we were all in someone's room griping about the way Shirley followed us around. And it was nice, whenever Shirley committed one of her characteristic faux pas, to look at someone and know she was thinking the same thing you were. I used to wonder what would happen if she weren't there. It would be ghastly to be in her place. Our group was swell: we had fun together, we were friends, we would do anything for each other. But this was on the inside. It would be horrible to be on the outside suddenly. But this would not happen to any of us. Shirley was different.

In a way I think it was rather helpful to Alice and me, having Shirley in the house. Everyone was always so disgusted with her that they almost seemed to forget that we were Jewish, too. The things they said without any self-consciousness when we two were in the room showed that. So it was nice for us . . .

We were quite surprised at the end of the year when we found out that Shirley had no intention of moving. I guess she had no friends in any of the other houses so she thought she might as well stick it out in Ransom. And maybe she was determined not to admit there was any situation to move away from.

Sophomore year we were all rather busy. We hardly noticed Shirley; she didn't annoy us any more. We were engrossed in our own affairs and didn't think much about her, one way or the other. For the most part we didn't even bother to be witty about her idiosyncrasies. We said hello when we saw her.

She must have found this absolute indifference unnerving. I think I should have found it much more frustrating than the obvious dislike of the year before. It was less warm, less tangible. What can you do if the people around you cease to recognize your existence? You cannot penetrate finality.

I think Shirley tried to. She made some pretty undisguised pleas for attention. She bought five or six symphonies and played them obtrusively for hours at a time on the living room victrola. We used to laugh at this sudden passion for culture, or whatever you want to call it. The living room would be full of people sitting at tables or on the floor, talking or playing bridge. And Shirley would sit in the big chair by the victrola and change the records, one after the other. But I guess she couldn't just sit there and do nothing, and no one ever talked to her or asked her to play bridge . . . I wonder what she thought about when she sat there after every meal and played records while the rest of us talked and laughed. It was almost as if she weren't in the room at all, except as a sort of furniture. Like the thing they discuss in philosophy—is there a noise if a book drops off a table in an empty room, is there thunder when it storms in the middle of the ocean, does a tree exist where there is no one to see it?

She was getting desperate, I guess. She began to go in for drinking and sex in a big way. I'll never forget the Saturday night Dick Freel, a man I knew at Yale Law, came up. We had come back from Toto's a little early and were sitting on the porch talking with Katy and Jack and Phyl and her man, when Shirley came up with a town boy, both of them dead drunk. Shirley was singing an extremely risqué song at the top of her voice, and when she saw us, she came over, plopped herself on Dick's lap, and slobbered, "H'lo, Dickie baby. D'you want to know a cute joke, cutie pie?" Then she started to whisper something in his ear. He looked awfully embarrassed. More and more people were coming up; it was almost twelve. I felt horribly conspicuous. Everyone was watching us. This person Shirley had picked up kept saying, "Come on, baby, kiss me good-night," and trying to pull her off Dick's lap. But she wouldn't stop whispering in Dick's ear. It was horrible. I prayed for twelve o'clock to come so we would have to go in. Finally the town boy pulled Shirley away and

Dick straightened his tie and lit a cigarette. He said, "Who the hell is she anyway? A friend of yours?" I said "No. She's an impossible girl in our house. No one likes her. I hope she didn't embarrass you too much, Dick. I'm really very sorry."

The next morning Alice and I went into her room and told her a few simple truths. We said we didn't care what kind of reputation she got for herself but that she had to stop that sort of thing in public, if not for her sake then for ours. Shirley was very sullen and said she didn't care what people thought—she'd do as she damn pleased, and we should mind our own business.

She would get sickening mushy postcards full of x's and leave them around on the mail table for days. And once she came back from a Dartmouth weekend and told everyone in the living room how she had spent the night in some hotel with a man she had just met. She said she'd had a lot to drink and so had he. She told us in graphic detail how he seduced her. I wondered if it really happened, or if she were just talking to seem glamorous or exciting or something. Alice said to me that night, "Really, one can see why people become anti-semitic."

Whenever anyone moved into the house, Shirley immediately claimed her as a bosom friend. There was a transfer named Dotty Simpson. She was nice to Shirley at first, and Shirley clung to her with a smothering sort of adoration. She came into Dotty's room every night to talk about how misunderstood and mistreated she was, how we abused her, and how bravely she was bearing it. We all wondered how long Dotty would be able to take it. No one, not even the kindest person, could endure that devotion for long: it was so desperate, so avid, it made one embarrassed, ashamed. Dotty told us about it later, when we took her into our crowd. She said that she felt very sorry for Shirley, but that there was something horrible about her over-affectionateness, her obsequiousness. It made her so uncomfortable that she finally couldn't stand it any longer. Just because she didn't mind being nice to the girl, it didn't mean that she wanted to spend every minute with her. We told her she'd have to be pretty pointed to get Shirley to see this.

Shirley should never have come back that year. I admire her determination. But I think she carried it too far. All this was doing something to her. I guess she had been fairly likeable at first, outside of the several characteristics that grated on us. But now there was something grotesque about her. Even if she aroused one's pity, by now it could only be an objective, intellectual sort of pity. One could not force oneself to be with her, listen to her talk, be her friend, even if one knew that lack of these things was making her warped and cringing, even if one had been willing to risk sharing her ostracism.

The whole affair was very depressing. Sometimes I wonder how I should have reacted if I had been in her place. Sometimes I wonder what sort of a person I should have been after several years of that treatment. It is a horrible thing to think about.

By spring Shirley had stopped making those desperate bids for attention, stopped forcing her affection on new girls, stopped whining about herself. For days at a time no one saw her. She stayed in her room, I guess. And when she was around, she didn't speak to anyone. We were all so used to ignoring her that we hardly noticed this withdrawal, or whatever you want to call it. Once Katy remarked that Shirley was much less of a nuisance now, and we all agreed. I remember Dotty's mentioning that Shirley had complained of bad headaches, from her eyes or something, and that she couldn't sleep. She didn't get those postcards any more, and all of her men seemed to have disappeared.

At dinner one night around the first of May I asked if Shirley were in the infirmary. I hadn't seen her around for ages. Dotty said that her mother had come and that she had gone away with her—several days ago. It seems queer that I hadn't known about it: she lived three doors down the hall from me. I went into her room and all her things were gone except for her trunk, which was labeled to be sent to her. We found out later that she had a nervous breakdown.

We talked about it pretty much that week. Once I said that we were fools not to have seen it coming, that no one could stand the treatment she received and not be affected violently by it. I said that in the last analysis we were to blame for her nervous breakdown, or that at least we might have prevented it. But the others didn't agree with me. In fact, they became rather angry. Phyl said, "I don't see how you can say we were to blame. We couldn't help it if we didn't like her. She was simply impossible, and you know it."

And Katy said, "She never should have come to Smith. She didn't belong here. When she found it out—and you can't tell me she didn't realize it—she should have left."

Then Liz looked at me speculatively and said, "What are you getting so worked up for? I didn't notice you going out of your way to be nice to her."

And so I didn't say any more. The others might think I was on Shirley's side because I was Jewish too. They might think I was afraid . . . afraid that the same thing might happen to me now that Shirley was gone. I think I know how Shirley must have felt.

And so I didn't say any more. I really hadn't liked her either, from the first.

FRIEDRICH ENGELS

From The Origins of the Family, Private Property and the State[†]

* * *

* * * With the patriarchal family and still more with the single monogamous family, a change came. Household management lost its public character. It no longer concerned society. It became a *private service*; the wife became the head servant, excluded from all participation in social production. Not until the coming of modern large-scale industry was the road to social production opened to her again—and then only to the proletarian wife. But it was opened in such a manner that, if she carries out her duties in the private service of her family, she remains excluded from public production and unable to earn; and if she wants to take part in public production and earn independently, she cannot carry out family duties. And the wife's position in the factory is the position of women in all branches of business, right up to medicine and the law. The modern individual family is founded on the open or concealed domestic slavery of the wife, and modern society is a mass composed of these individual families as its molecules.

In the great majority of cases today, at least in the possessing classes, the husband is obliged to earn a living and support his family, and that in itself gives him a position of supremacy without any need for special legal titles and privileges. Within the family he is the bourgeois, and the wife represents the proletariat. In the industrial world, the specific character of the economic oppression burdening the proletariat is visible in all its sharpness only when all special legal privileges of the capitalist class have been abolished and complete legal equality of both classes established. The democratic republic does not do away with the opposition of the two classes; on the contrary, it provides the clear field on which the fight can be fought out. And in the same way, the peculiar character of the supremacy of the husband over the wife in the modern family, the necessity of creating real social equality between them and the way to do it, will only be seen in the clear light of day when both possess legally complete equality of rights. Then it will be plain that the first condition for the liberation of the wife is to bring the whole female sex back into public industry, and that this in turn demands

---

[†] From Friedrich Engels, *The Origins of the Family, Private Property and the State* (1884) (New York: Penguin, 1985), pp. 104–05. Reprinted by permission.

that the characteristic of the monogamous family as the economic unit of society be abolished.

* * *

SMITH COLLEGE ASSOCIATED NEWS

From Labor Education Described by Smith Summer Workers[†]

* * *

"Highlander," Bettye Goldstein said, "is in a section of Tennessee where most of the families are on relief. The people sent to this school are representatives from different labor unions throughout the south, and they are given instruction in economics and their own labor problems. They then return to their various positions and apply what they have learned." Since many of these people occupy positions of influence, she continued, the application of what they learn at Highlander is immediate and vital.

"Here is something," she continued, "that is really trying most vitally to get at the causes of economic chaos. The great fear of poverty has made this section of the country a potential bed of Fascism and has given rise to Fascist shirt organizations, the Ku Klux Klan and 'vigilante' groups. This is not the solution we want for American economic problems and every dollar which is contributed to Highlander helps in small measure to combat this evil."

* * *

BETTYE GOLDSTEIN

From The Right to Organize[‡]

"That employees shall have the right to organize and bargain collectively through representatives of their own choosing" is guaranteed by law in this country. In almost every other nation of the world the right to organize has ceased to exist. As the Nazis rose to power in

[†] *From* "Labor Education Described by Smith Summer Workers," *The Smith College Associated News*, October 28, 1941, p. 4. Reprinted by permission.
[‡] From an editorial by Bettye Goldstein, editor-in-chief, "The Right to Organize," *The Smith College Associated News*, October 21, 1941, p. 2. Reprinted by permission.

Germany they attacked and destroyed labor unions. One of the first acts of the Vichy government in France was a decree which took away from the worker the right to organize. For fascism to survive all free and democratic institutions must be prohibited; in no fascist government is the democratic institution of a labor union permitted.

Enemies of labor denounce unions as un-American, subversive, inimical to democracy. Unions are American; their history is almost as old as the history of the nation itself; their members are American—as American as the funny papers they read, the movies they see, the beer they drink, the streets they live on; their aims are basic to the protection and expansion of democracy in America.

The Constitution of the United States rests on a conception of the freedom and equality of men. It guarantees certain rights to all men. It is apparent that under our present economic system men are neither equal nor equally free; life, liberty and the pursuit of happiness mean one thing to the employee who works for wages, another to the employer who hires him. This inequality of economic, social, and political power has to be admitted and dealt with if democracy is to have meaning for 95% of the citizens of this country, if democracy is to continue at all in this country.

*   *   *

DOMESTICITY AND "MOMISM" DURING THE COLD WAR

After leaving graduate school, Goldstein moved to New York City to begin work as a journalist for labor journals. Despite the chill of McCarthyism, she was involved with the progressive politics and intellectual currents of the period. She also met and married Carl Friedan in 1947. During the Cold War in intellectual circles, in popular culture, and in their private worlds, Americans engaged in a conversation about women's nature and women's place in modern society. The Christmas 1956 issue of *Life* magazine was devoted to "American Woman: Her Achievement and Troubles" and Betty Friedan cited it as proof of the pervasiveness of the feminine mystique in popular culture. Margaret Mead a well-known anthropologist and author of *Male and Female*, was one of three participants in a discussion of "What U.S. Woman Has Accomplished" that appeared in this issue. In *The Feminine Mystique*, Friedan identifies Mead as someone who perpetuated "the problem that has no name." Popular and academic psychologists focused on the importance of women's compliance with traditional female roles for women, their children, their marriage, and society. The most notorious expression of this preoccupation, called "momism,"—blaming the maladjustment of children on mothers who were not happy in traditional roles—was the book *Modern Woman: The Lost Sex.* Coverage of the issue appeared in many other popular places, like the *Ladies Home Journal*, which printed Amram Scheinfeld's 1945 article. See pp. 467–73 on how scholars assess the influence of momism on Betty Friedan and her time.

MARGARET MEAD

From She Has Strength Based on a Pioneer Past[†]

*   *   *

A century or two ago the American husband and wife divided up the difficult task of making a home in the wilderness, the husband protecting the wife with his strength, the wife doing a lot of things her mother had never done. In America today the husband and wife still prefer to go it alone on housekeeping, depending on gadgets and elbow grease rather than on relatives and servants. The ideal American woman today is a woman who can afford to have the number of children she and her husband want, who has as well-equipped a house as she needs, a car at her disposal to drive her children to parties and lessons and herself to volunteer or paid work, and a helpful, cooperative, successful husband engaged in challenging work.

But it is no longer simply a case of woman's place being in the home, as it was in the Old World. Today in America everybody's place is in the home. The only truly acceptable pattern in American life is marriage, and both husband and wife are supposed to share its pleasures and its burdens. Bachelors and spinsters are both disapproved of and discriminated against. There are no really acceptable alternatives either for those women who suffer from the slight, but real, shortage of husbands or for those men who dare, in the face of this shortage, not to marry. Girls are regarded as old maids at 25 and perennial bachelors are sighed over psychiatrically. The roles which once isolated women from home life—the nun (there are only 160,000 in the U.S., including Anglicans and Lutheran deaconesses), the spinster, the prostitute, the kept woman, * * * none of these is an acceptable role in the mid-Twentieth Century U.S. The American woman lives in a world where she can be satisfied with nothing but marriage.

The home is still, as it has been through the ages, woman's natural habitat, the cave in which she kept the fire burning, the tent she sewed, the house she thatched, the place she kept safe and warm.

---

† From Margaret Mead, "She Has Strength Based on a Pioneer Past," *Life*, December 24, 1956, p. 27. Reprinted by permission of the American Anthropological Association.

But the American woman has overvalued the home as the legitimate be-all and end-all of existence. The home in the new country, into whose wide-open windows the new immigrant looked and longed, where women have always been expected to be responsible, independent and hard-working, has now become the place where both men and women focus their lives.

American women have come a long way on the road toward a role for women which is as dignified and responsible as the one assigned to men. Although she has made the home and marriage even more important than they should be, to the exclusion of other values and other roles, she has also given American life a special, unrivaled flavor. All over the world, in the harem, in the hut, in the peasant cottage, other women, who have never envied their husbands' positions, now envy and desire to emulate the American woman.

✳   ✳   ✳

FERDINAND LUNDBERG AND
MARYNIA R. FARNHAM, M.D.

From Modern Woman: The Lost Sex[†]

✳   ✳   ✳

Usually, as we have already said, the first critical event peculiar to the life of the girl is the discovery, under social and cultural conditions already portrayed, of the anatomical differences between herself and her brother or whatever boy in her life serves this purpose. Parenthetically it should be said that it is very nearly universal to our culture for a girl to have this experience, irrespective of the pattern of her own family or the supervision with which she is provided. At this point she begins to face the dominant circumstance of her life as a female. The way she solves it will be decisive, crucial, in her later life as a woman. When she discovers that her brother differs from her by possessing an organ she lacks, she comes to the conclusion, for reasons we have indicated, that his entire structure and sphere of activity is superior.

The feeling is accentuated because the girl is unable to discover in herself any compensatory anatomical possession. Her reproductive structure is wholly within her body and for many years she may believe she is completely defective and undesirable because of this

---

† From Ferdinand Lundberg and Marynia R. Farnham, M.D., *Modern Woman: The Lost Sex* (New York: Grosset & Dunlap, 1947), pp. 223–24, 228–29, 232–33, 235–36. Copyright by Ferdinand Lundberg and Marynia R. Farnham. Reprinted by permission of HarperCollins Publishers.

supposed anatomical deficiency. She cannot be expected to discover her own secret and hidden reproductive organs and their great powers and many times it is years before she learns the facts. It is not uncommon in psychiatric practice to encounter adults who are grossly ignorant of female anatomy and cherish various false beliefs. For example, some women believe the urinary and reproductive apparatus have a common orifice. This is an error easily come by, since in the male—constant yardstick—this happens to be a fact.

Thus it is that the girl is faced with an entirely uncompensated sense of loss in a social setting depreciatory of women. She regards her brother's organ with considerable awe and envy because it supplies him with sources of real and imagined satisfaction she feels are denied to her. The feeling of loss and inferiority may be further exaggerated by her mother's preference for her brother, or her lament that she is a girl in a "man's world." When this happens, the little girl will be likely to ascribe it to her lack of the penis.

* * *

The girl in struggling to become an adult woman must rely upon some pattern or model from which she can derive a design for femininity. She is provided with one in her mother and she will have to believe for a long time that her mother's nature, temperament and attitudes are ideals toward which she must strive as a woman. Not until much later in her life will she be free to discover other ideals and models. Thus it is her mother's grasp on femininity on which the little girl chiefly depends.

Here is the real crux of the situation, because the mother's feelings for herself as a woman and acceptance of her feminine role dictate her attitudes toward children and husband. If the girl has the good fortune to have a mother who finds complete satisfaction, without conflict or anxiety, in living out her role as wife and mother, it is unlikely that she will experience serious difficulties. If, however, the mother is beset by distaste for her role, strives for accomplishment outside her home and can only grudgingly give attention to her children, has regrets for whatever reason at being a woman, then, no matter how much or little of it she betrays, the child cannot escape the confused impression that the mother is without love, is not a satisfactory model.

Such a woman is not only an unsatisfactory model for her daughter, but gives her no sure grasp on the solid satisfactions inherent in feminine development. She may produce a still more dangerous impression on the small girl, in that she will inject into her attitudes her own covert strivings toward masculinity.

* * *

Further complicating elements arise when the mother also absents herself at work or career. Such absences, particularly if not compensated for by true love for the children, can only blur their image of femininity. Early twisted attitudes persist into adult life, to block and thwart the drive toward self-consummation. But whatever the distortions or inhibitions, nothing can wholly destroy the final biologic drive for womanhood. Conflicts, however, often deeply underlie the achievement of desired satisfactions, and they are disregarded or bypassed at great peril to the individual and those related to her. In the light of these fundamentals we can judge how well the "liberated" woman is able to provide herself with deep and lasting satisfactions.

We may dispose of the legal and political aspects of woman's new position as being not significantly important in and of themselves. In these areas women gained a rightful privilege and ego-support, not dangerous to her fundamental peace of mind. It is rather in the aggressive and misdirected use to which these privileges are put that we see arising the difficulties into which many women have plunged themselves. The economic, educational, social and sexual facts of the woman's life, intertwined and interdependent as they are, are those which implement all others.

The woman arriving at maturity today does so with certain fixed attitudes derived from her background and training. Her home life, very often, has been distorted. She has enjoyed an education identical with that of her brother. She expects to be allowed to select any kind of work for which she has inclination and training. She also, generally, expects to marry. At any rate, she usually intends to have "a go" at it. Some women expect to stop working when they marry; many others do not. She expects to find sexual gratification and believes in her inalienable right so to do. She is legally free to live and move as she chooses. She may seek divorce if her marriage fails to gratify her. She has access to contraceptive information so that, theoretically, she may control the size and spacing of her family. In very many instances, she owns and disposes of her own property. She has, it appears, her destiny entirely in her own hands.

All of this serves less to clarify and simplify her life than to complicate it with conflict piled on conflict. These conflicts are between her basic needs as a woman and the destiny she has carved out for herself—conflicts between the head and the heart, if you will.

Her necessity is to find some kind of consummation for her specific femininity and for herself as a human being. The circumstances with which she is now surrounded, as well as those of her upbringing, tend to prevent these two consummations—instinct and ego—from being fused together. Conflict and compromise are almost inevitable. Her basic needs for satisfaction as a woman would inevitably lead her in the direction of marriage and children inside the home. However, the woman who chooses this course runs into two serious obstacles: she does not obtain under present conditions satisfaction of her need for self-esteem nor does she obtain a sense of social importance. In attempting to gain these, she is led in the direction of economic independence, which carries her outside her home, away from children and childbearing. It was, of course, the failure of society after the Industrial Revolution to provide her with needed sources of self-esteem that forced her into the battle for her economic "rights" which, as we have shown, she has at least formally won. In winning them she was forced, too, into dubious battle for all the other rights auxiliary to them.

Thus she finds herself squarely in the middle of the most serious kind of divided purpose. If she is to undertake occupation outside her home with any kind of success, it is almost certain in the present day to be time-consuming and energy-demanding. So it is also with the problems she faces in her home. Certainly the tasks of a woman in bearing and educating children as well as maintaining, as best she may, the inner integrity of her home are capable of demanding all her time and best attention. However, she cannot obtain from them, so attenuated are these tasks now, the same sort of community approval and ego-satisfaction that she can from seemingly more challenging occupations which take her outside the home. Inevitably the dilemma has led to one compromise after another which we see exemplified on every hand in the modern woman's adaptation—an uneasy patchwork.

* * *

Work that entices women out of their homes and provides them with prestige only at the price of feminine relinquishment, involves a response to masculine strivings. The more importance outside work assumes, the more are the masculine components of the woman's nature enhanced and encouraged. In her home and in her relationship to her children, it is imperative that these strivings be at a minimum and that her femininity be available both for her own satisfaction and for the satisfaction of her children and husband. She is, therefore, in the dangerous position of having to live one part of her life on the masculine level, another on the feminine. It is hardly astonishing that few can do so with success. One of these tendencies must of necessity achieve dominance over the other. The plain fact is that increasingly we are observing the masculinization of women and with it enormously dangerous consequences to the home, the children (if any) dependent on it, and to the ability of the woman, as well as her husband, to obtain sexual gratification.

The effect of this "masculinization" on women is becoming more apparent daily. Their new exertions are making demands on them for qualities wholly opposed to the experience of feminine satisfaction. As the rivals of men, women must, and insensibly do, develop the characteristics of aggression, dominance, independence and power. These are qualities which insure success as co-equals in the world of business, industry and the professions. The distortion of character under pressure of modern attitudes and upbringing is driving women steadily deeper into personal conflict soluble only by psychotherapy. * * *

* * *

AMRAM SCHEINFELD

From Are American Moms a Menace?†

* * *

American mothers are so used to getting bouquets that it may come as a shock to hear that "mom" is often a dangerous influence on her sons and a threat to our national existence. "MOM DENOUNCED AS PERIL TO NATION" was the way the New York Times headlined it.

In brief, Prof. Edward A. Strecker, University of Pennsylvania psychiatrist and consultant to the Army and Navy surgeons general, has made this accusation: that the blame for many psychoneurotics in the armed forces, and for many neurotic rejectees, rests on their "moms," who either by overattention or stern domination during the formative years kept their sons from maturing emotionally. "Mother's boys" psychoneurotics are not to be confused with men who cracked up only under terrific battle pressures or after serious injuries, he adds. Nor are all American mothers to blame, for the majority of them are sensible, well-balanced and understanding.

Doctor Strecker is indicting the type of mother generally known as "mom." Usually she is sweet, doting and self-sacrificing, or she may be just the opposite—stern, capable and domineering. "Both these moms are busily engaged finding in their children ego satisfactions for life's thwartings and frustrations," believes Doctor Strecker. "The community applauds and fondly smiles on them. They are accorded praise and adulation for giving their lives to their children. Hidden

---

† From Amram Scheinfeld, "Are American Moms a Menace?" *Ladies Home Journal*, November 1945, p. 36.

from view is the hard and tragic fact that . . . they exact in payment the emotional lives of their children."

*   *   *

POPULAR FRONT FEMINISM

Feminism and the women's movement were "in the doldrums" during the years between 1920 and 1966, but women in the labor movement and on the left pursued feminist ideals and goals.[1] Because of the economic crisis during the Depression and antipathy toward fascism in the 1930s and the 1940s, left-wing ideas became popular in a political and cultural movement called the Popular Front, which shaped Friedan's intellectual, social, and political world. While single and newly married in New York City, Friedan worked at two labor publications, the *UE News*, the newspaper of the United Electrical, Radio, and Machine Workers of America, and the Federated Press, a news service for labor publications. Both were quite progressive and concerned with women's issues. At the Federated Press, Friedan wrote a regular column called "Wartime Living" during the last years of World War II. This work experience exposed her to many progressive causes and issues including feminism among left, progressive, and union women like communist Betty Millard. Friedan's work at the *UE News* continued her education. Her passionate reporting of a series of meetings of the United Electrical Workers District 4 Fair Practices Committee on the issues of discriminatory practices against women workers demonstrates her awareness of and engagement with these issues. Friedan was also exposed to some of the first scholarly works of women's history, such as Eleanor Flexner's *A Century of Struggle: The Woman's Rights Movement in the United States* (1959), used extensively in chapter 4, "The Passionate Journey," of *The Feminine Mystique*. Friedan also knew of the important feminist work, Simone de Beauvoir's *The Second Sex*, translated and published in English during this time. Daniel Horowitz's article on pp. 454–65 makes the strong case that Friedan's exposure to the left and participation in progressive activities during this time were formative influences on *The Feminine Mystique*.

---

1. The term "doldrums" to describe the women's movement during this period comes from Leila Rupp and Verta Taylor, *Survival in the Doldrums: The American Women's Rights Movement, 1945 to the 1960s* (Oxford University Press, 1987). For recent work on popular front feminism see Kate Weigand, *Red Feminism: American Communism and the Making of Women's Liberation* (Baltimore and London: The Johns Hopkins University Press, 2001); Dorothy Sue Cobble, *The Other Women's Movement: Workplace Justice and Social Rights in Modern America* (Princeton: Princeton University Press, 2004).

BETTY GOLDSTEIN

From Wartime Living—Women, Take Over[†]

The hand that rocks the cradle rules the nation in 1944. For the first time in American history, women will outnumber men at the voting places in November, the U.S. Census says. Of a potential voting population of 88,600,000, women will account for 44,600,000.

One of the reasons is that most of the 10 million men in the armed forces will not have the chance to vote because of the phony states rights soldier vote bill congress passed. Also, many men have moved to new cities because of war jobs and will have registration difficulties.

Reactionaries know how important the woman's vote is this year and are already counting on pulling the wool over their eyes. Native fascists are organizing "mothers" groups, playing on women's fears for their sons at war with phony "peace now" moves. The Republicans brought in Clare Boothe Luce for one of the most vicious speeches at the national convention, selling the GOP's look-backward-to-breadlines program in the name of a dead GI Jim.

Union women, the wives and mothers of union men and of honest GI Joes, have an answer for this kind of talk—and it's an answer underscored with action, political action looking ahead to winning the war and winning the peace, with jobs and security and a good life for themselves and their men. And any man who still thinks woman's place is in the home should just take another look at those census figures—and shoo his wife out that door to ring doorbells and register and vote and get out all the women on the block to do the same. From now till November—woman's place is in political action.

* * *

---

† From Betty Goldstein, "Wartime Living," Federated Press, Eastern Bureau, 25 Astor Place, New York, NY, July 17, 1944, Federated Press Records, MS#0414, reel 9174, Rare Book and Manuscript Library, Columbia University, NYC.

BETTY MILLARD

From Woman Against Myth[†]

* * *

Many of the thirty-eight million American housewives are doomed to circumscribed, petty lives, in the stultification of whatever abilities and interests, outside of motherhood, they may have had. The 15,400,000 women wage-earners are discriminated against in almost every field of employment, are notoriously paid less than men for the same work, are the first to be laid off. Yet according to a survey conducted by the Women's Bureau of the Department of Labor, 84 percent of working women work because they have to in order to support themselves and their dependents. The Bureau of Census estimates that there are now from two and a half to three million unemployed; of these, according to the Congress of American Women, over two million are women.

* * *

In 1947 women are attacked by Ferdinand Lundberg and Dr. Marynia Farnham in their best-seller, *Modern Woman: The Lost Sex*, not for attempting to subvert God's will but for unconsciously seeking to deprive the male of his power, to castrate him. They reach into history to perform a psychoanalytical autopsy upon that great pioneer, Mary Wollstonecraft, whose *Vindication of the Rights of Woman* appeared in 1793. "Mary" they say, unconsciously "probably wished to . . . kill her father, but this desire, though powerful was powerfully deflected as untenable. It came out only in her round scolding of all men. The feminists have ever since symbolically slain their fathers by verbally consigning all men to perdition as monsters." Similarly, Elizabeth Cady Stanton is said to have agitated for votes for women because of her envy of the male sex organ.

This kind of use of Freudian concepts has become a political technique which is increasingly effective among people who are no longer susceptible to religious arguments for it seems to deal "scientifically" with real problems. Women *do* envy men. But they have good cultural reasons for doing so. The majority of women who try to combine running a home and a full-time job find great difficulty in doing either satisfactorily. Economics, religion, customs, taboos impose conflicting roles and wishes in women, who are unable to function fully in society as both mothers and citizens not because

---

† *From* Betty Millard, "Woman Against Myth," *New Masses* 66 (December 30, 1947): 7–8, 10. Reprinted by permission.

of their special biological natures but because every society until the advent of socialism has made it economically and socially impossible for them to do so.

There are few women who do not look forward to marriage and children. And certainly raising a family of happy, useful citizens is an accomplishment of which any woman can be proud. But it is not in any way belittling a mother's hard work and achievement to assert that time may prove that motherhood no more exhausts a woman's potentialities as a human being than fatherhood does a man's. To him fatherhood is part of a normal happy life; he does not become a "house-husband."

The day will come, I believe, when it will no longer be necessary for any woman to refer to herself as merely a "housewife." And when that day comes there will open out before women such a future of accomplishment and satisfaction as we can only dream of today.

BETTY GOLDSTEIN

From UE Drive on Wage, Job Discrimination Wins Cheers from Women Members[†]

There are those who say women won't come out to union meetings. They should have seen how women members of the UE came out last month to a series of meetings called by the UE District 4 Fair Practices Committee as part of the union's stepped-up offensive on rate differentials and job discrimination against women.

They came in twos and threes and as many as eight from a shop, some of them traveling 100 miles and back in a single night, from all over New Jersey and New York, and the next week they came back bringing more women from their shops. They'd been waiting a long time, some of these women, to talk about their problems on the job—and they were excited about the union's new program.

Out of those meetings came a Woman's Right subcommittee of the UE Fair Practices Committee of District 4 to investigate the rate and job structure of every shop in the district to find out where women were being discriminated against, and to fight the speedup which is being forced on women in almost every shop.

Out of those meetings came the realization that the women of the UE are fighters—that they refuse any longer to be paid or treated as some inferior species by their bosses, or by any male workers who

† From Betty Goldstein, "UE Drive on Wage, Job Discrimination Wins Cheers from Women Members," *UE News*, April 16, 1951, p. 6.

have swallowed the bosses' thinking—and that they will defend to
the utmost the union that fights for them.

* * *

SIMONE DE BEAUVOIR

From The Second Sex[†]

One is not born, but rather becomes, a woman. No biological, psychological, or economic fate determines the figure that the human
female presents in society; it is civilization as a whole that produces
this creature, intermediate between male and eunuch, which is
described as feminine. Only the intervention of someone else can
establish an individual as an *Other*. In so far as he exists in and for
himself, the child would hardly be able to think of himself as sexually differentiated. In girls as in boys the body is first of all the
radiation of a subjectivity, the instrument that makes possible the
comprehension of the world: it is through the eyes, the hands, that
children apprehend the universe, and not through the sexual parts.
The dramas of birth and of weaning unfold after the same fashion
for nurslings of both sexes; these have the same interests and the
same pleasures; sucking is at first the source of their most agree-
able sensations; then they go through an anal phase in which they
get their greatest satisfactions from the excretory functions, which
they have in common. Their genital development is analogous; they
explore their bodies with the same curiosity and the same indifference; from clitoris and penis they derive the same vague pleasure. As their sensibility comes to require an object, it is turned
toward the mother: the soft, smooth, resilient feminine flesh is
what arouses sexual desires, and these desires are prehensile; the
girl, like the boy, kisses, handles, and caresses her mother in an
aggressive way; they feel the same jealousy if a new child is born,
and they show it in similar behavior patterns: rage, sulkiness, urinary difficulties; and they resort to the same coquettish tricks to
gain the love of adults. Up to the age of twelve the little girl is as
strong as her brothers, and she shows the same mental powers;
there is no field where she is debarred from engaging in rivalry with

† From *The Second Sex* by Simone de Beauvoir, translated by H. M. Parshley (New York:
Alfred A. Knopf, 1964), pp. 267–68, 726–27. Copyright © 1952 and renewed 1980 by
Alfred A. Knopf, a division of Random House, Inc. Used by permission of Alfred A.
Knopf, a division of Random House, Inc. Originally published in French in 1949, *The
Second Sex* was translated into English and published in the United States in 1952.
This excerpt is from the original English translation.

them. If, well before puberty and sometimes even from early infancy, she seems to us to be already sexually determined, this is not because mysterious instincts directly doom her to passivity, coquetry, maternity; it is because the influence of others upon the child is a factor almost from the start, and thus she is indoctrinated with her vocation from her earliest years.

*   *   *

If the little girl were brought up from the first with the same demands and rewards, the same severity and the same freedom, as her brothers, taking part in the same studies, the same games, promised the same future, surrounded with women and men who seemed to her undoubted equals, the meanings of the castration complex and of the Œdipus complex would be profoundly modified. Assuming on the same basis as the father the material and moral responsibility of the couple, the mother would enjoy the same lasting prestige; the child would perceive around her an androgynous world and not a masculine world. Were she emotionally more attracted to her father—which is not even sure—her love for him would be tinged with a will to emulation and not a feeling of powerlessness; she would not be oriented toward passivity. Authorized to test her powers in work and sports, competing actively with the boys, she would not find the absence of the penis—compensated by the promise of a child—enough to give rise to an inferiority complex; correlatively, the boy would not have a superiority complex if it were not instilled into him and if he looked up to women with as much respect as to men.[1] The little girl would not seek sterile compensation in narcissism and dreaming, she would not take her fate for granted; she would be interested in what she was *doing*, she would throw herself without reserve into undertakings.

I have already pointed out how much easier the transformation of puberty would be if she looked beyond it, like the boys, toward a free adult future: menstruation horrifies her only because it is an abrupt descent into femininity. She would also take her young eroticism in much more tranquil fashion if she did not feel a frightened disgust for her destiny as a whole; coherent sexual information would do much to help her over this crisis. And thanks to coeducational schooling, the august mystery of Man would have no occasion to enter her mind: it would be eliminated by everyday familiarity and open rivalry.

---

1. I knew a little boy of eight who lived with his mother, aunt, and grandmother, all independent and active women, and his weak old half-crippled grandfather. He had a crushing inferiority complex in regard to the feminine sex, although he made efforts to combat it. At school he scorned comrades and teachers because they were miserable males.

Objections raised against this system always imply respect for sexual taboos; but the effort to inhibit all sex curiosity and pleasure in the child is quite useless; one succeeds only in creating repressions, obsessions, neuroses. The excessive sentimentality, homosexual fervors, and platonic crushes of adolescent girls, with all their train of silliness and frivolity, are much more injurious than a little childish sex play and a few definite sex experiences. It would be beneficial above all for the young girl not to be influenced against taking charge herself of her own existence, for then she would not seek a demigod in the male—merely a comrade, a friend, a partner. Eroticism and love would take on the nature of free transcendence and not that of resignation; she could experience them as a relation between equals. There is no intention, of course, to remove by a stroke of the pen all the difficulties that the child has to overcome in changing into an adult; the most intelligent, the most tolerant education could not relieve the child of experiencing things for herself; what could be asked is that obstacles should not be piled gratuitously in her path. Progress is already shown by the fact that "vicious" little girls are no longer cauterized with a red-hot iron. Psychoanalysis has given parents some instruction, but the conditions under which, at the present time, the sexual training and initiation of woman are accomplished are so deplorable that none of the objections advanced against the idea of a radical change could be considered valid. It is not a question of abolishing in woman the contingencies and miseries of the human condition, but of giving her the means for transcending them.

*   *   *

THE POWER OF THE FEMININE MYSTIQUE
ON BETTY FRIEDAN?

In 1976, with the women's movement well underway, Betty Friedan reflected that she "did not set out consciously to start a revolution when I wrote *The Feminine Mystique*." In *It Changed My Life: Writings on the Women's Movement*, Friedan describes the effect the feminine mystique had on her. Sylvie Murray's and Daniel Horowitz's articles on pp. 487–93 and 454–65, respectively, set this account in its historical context.

BETTY FRIEDAN

From The Way We Were—1949[†]

In 1949 I was concentrating on breast-feeding and wheeling Danny, my first baby, to the park, and reading Dr. Spock. I was beginning to wonder if I really wanted to go back to work, after all, when my maternity leave was up. I bought a pressure cooker and *The Joy of Cooking* and a book by George Nelson about *The Modern House*. One Saturday, though we had no money, we went out to Rockland County and looked at old barns that my husband might be able to convert into a house. And I wrote my mother that I wanted the sterling silver—which she had offered us as a wedding present and I had scorned as too bourgeois—after all.

That was the year it really hit, the feminine mystique, though at the time we didn't know what it was. It was just that our lives seemed to have shifted in dimension, in perspective. The last of our group, which had come to New York after Smith and Vassar and shared an apartment in the Village, was getting married. During the war, we'd had jobs like "researcher" or "editorial assistant," and met GIs at the Newspaper Guild Canteen, and written V-mail letters to lonesome boys we'd known at home, and had affairs with married men—hiding our diaphragms under the girdles in the dresser. And we had considered ourselves part of the vanguard of the working-class revolution, going to Marxist discussion groups and rallies at Madison Square Garden and feeling only contempt for dreary bourgeois capitalists like our fathers—though we still read *Vogue* under the hair dryer, and spent all our salaries on clothes at Bergdorf's and Bendel's, replacing our college Braemer sweaters with black cashmere and Gucci gloves, on sale.

And then the boys our age had come back from the war. I was bumped from my job on a small labor news service by a returning veteran, and it wasn't so easy to find another job I really liked. I filled out the applications for Time-Life researcher, which I'd always scorned before. All the girls I knew had jobs like that, but it was official policy that no matter how good, researchers, who were women, could never become writers or editors. They could write the whole article, but the men they were working with would always get the by-line as writer. I was certainly not a feminist then—none of us were a bit interested in women's rights. But I could never

† From Betty Friedan, "The Way We Were—1949," in *It Changed My Life: Writings on the Women's Movement* (New York: Random House, 1976), pp. 8–10, 16. Copyright © 1976 by Betty Friedan. Reprinted by permission of Curtis Brown, Ltd.

bring myself to take that kind of job. And what else was there? The wartime government agencies where some of us had worked were being dissolved. The group on Waverly Place was breaking up— Maggie, Harriet, Madelon, everyone was getting married (and Abe Rosenthal was waiting greedily to move into that apartment so that *he* could get married).

It was very hard to find an apartment right after the war. I had left the group and found a funny apartment in the basement of a townhouse on West 86th. You had to go through the furnace room to get to it, there were pipes on the ceiling, and the cold water didn't work in the bathroom so you had to run the hot an hour ahead to take a bath. It didn't even have a kitchen, but since I had no interest in cooking, I didn't mind. It had a brick wall and lots of shelves, and a terrace door, and when Carl Friedan came back from running the Soldier Show Company in Europe to start a summer theater in New Jersey, his best friend, whom I worked with, said he knew a nice girl with an apartment. He brought me an apple and told me jokes which made me laugh, and he moved in. We got married in City Hall, but went through it again with a rabbi in Boston for his mother's sake. And while I was in the hospital having Danny, he painted the pipes on the ceiling and made a kitchen out of the closet and moved our bed into the living room so Danny could have a nursery.

After the war, I had been very political, very involved, consciously radical. Not about women, for heaven's sake! If you were a radical in 1949, you were concerned about the Negroes, and the working class, and World War III, and the Un-American Activities Committee and McCarthy and loyalty oaths, and Communist splits and schisms, Russia, China and the UN, but you certainly didn't think about being a woman, politically. It was only recently that we had begun to think of ourselves as women at all. But that wasn't political—it was the opposite of politics. Eight months pregnant, I climbed up on a ladder on street corner to give a speech for Henry Wallace. But in 1949 I was suddenly not that interested in political meetings.

Some of us had begun to go to Freudian analysts. Like the lady editor in Moss Hart's *Lady in the Dark*, we were supposedly discovering that what we really wanted was a man. Whatever the biological, psychosexual reality, a woman was hardly in a mood to argue with that message if (a) she was lonesome and tired of living alone, or (b) she was about to lose her job or (c) had become disillusioned with it. In 1949, nobody really had to tell a woman that she wanted a man, but the message certainly began bombarding us from all sides: domestic bliss had suddenly become chic, sophisticated, and whatever made you want to be a lady editor, police reporter, or political activist, could prevent or destroy that bliss—bourgeois security, no longer despised.

*   *   *

Shortly after 1949, I was fired from my job because I was pregnant again. They weren't about to put up with the inconvenience of another year's maternity leave, even though I was *entitled* to it under my union contract. It was unfair, *wrong* somehow to fire me just because I was pregnant, and to hire a man instead. I even tried calling a meeting of the people in the union where I worked. It was the first personal stirring of my own feminism, I guess. But the other women were just embarrassed, and the men uncomprehending. It was my own fault, getting pregnant again, a *personal* matter, not something you should take to the union. There was no word in 1949 for "sex discrimination."

Besides, it was almost a relief; I had begun to feel so guilty working, and I really wasn't getting anywhere in that job. I was more than ready to embrace the feminine mystique. I took a cooking course and started studying the suburban real-estate ads. And the next time the census taker came around, I was living in that old Charles Addams house we were fixing up, on the Hudson River in Rockland County. And the children numbered three. When the census taker asked my occupation, I said self-consciously, virtuously, with only the faintest stirrings of protest from that part of me I'd turned my back on—"housewife."

FEMALE LABOR FORCE PARTICIPATION TRENDS IN THE TWENTIETH CENTURY

Throughout every decade of the twentieth century, white women's participation in the labor force increased. These women's jobs were in sex-segregated employment and for less pay than men's, but this gradual yet inexorable change created a profound dissonance between the image of the 1950s suburban housewife and the reality of most women's lives.

Labor Force Participation Rate, by Sex and Race: 1850–1990[†]

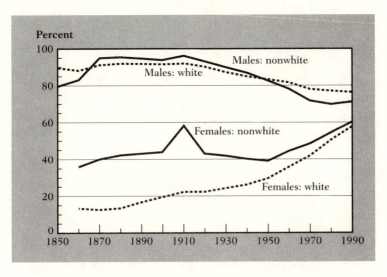

[†] Figure Ba-C, "Labor Force Participation Rate, by Sex and Race: 1850–1990," from *Historical Statistics of the United States, Earliest Times to the Present: Millennial Edition*, ed. Susan B. Carter, Scott Sigmund Gartner, Michael R. Haines, Alan L. Olmstead, Richard Sutch, and Gavin Wright. (New York: Cambridge University Press, 2006).

The Turn of the Sixties: Political, Intellectual, and Cultural Ferment

The Feminine Mystique appeared at an auspicious historical moment. The late 1950s and early 1960s witnessed the origins of many social movements of the "sixties"—civil rights, challenges to the Cold War and nuclear proliferation, student activism, and the sexual revolution and women's rights. In 2011, writing in the *New Yorker*, Louis Menand stated, "in the early nineteen-sixties, books . . . were bombs," citing Friedan's *Feminine Mystique* along with Jane Jacobs's *The Death and Life of Great American Cities* (1961), Rachel Carson's *Silent Spring* (1962), Michael Harrington's *The Other America* (1962), and Ralph Nader's *Unsafe at Any Speed* (1965) as examples.[1] In the world of literature, three female authors were expressing discontent with their lives and positions as women that echoed Friedan's "problem that has no name." Sylvia Plath's poems and best-selling novel *The Bell Jar* (1963), Doris Lessing's *The Golden Notebook* (1962) and several collections of Anne Sexton's poetry all appeared in the early 1960s. None of these authors were feminist activists, but all described the restrictions women experienced during the 1950s and early 1960s. Feminists later claimed these works as powerfully representative of women's voices of the period. One of those feminists, Gloria Steinem, a Smith College graduate and journalist, also published an important article in 1963. The future founder of *Ms.* magazine and feminist activist, who worked and sparred with Friedan, went undercover as a Playboy Bunny in New York City. Her popular and sensational article, "A Bunny's Tale" for *Show* magazine, revealed the horrible working conditions in this so-called glamorous job for women.[2]

---

1. Louis Menand, "Books as Bombs: Why the Women's Movement Needed 'The Feminine Mystique'," *The New Yorker*, January 24, 2011, p. 79. See selection on pp. 494–95.
2. Gloria Steinem, "I Was a Playboy Bunny," in *Outrageous Acts and Everyday Rebellions* (New York: Henry Holt, 1995), pp. 32–75.

WOMEN'S RIGHTS

President John F. Kennedy appointed Eleanor Roosevelt the chair of the Presidential Commission on the Status of Women when he established it in 1961. In 1963, the Equal Pay Act was passed. Neither event arose from any new movement; however, the commission set in motion the creation of networks of women in the states and in the federal bureaucracy that were dedicated to the equity issues highlighted by the act.

ELEANOR ROOSEVELT

My Day: The Presidential Commission on the Status of Women[†]

Paris—Before coming over here my last two days in the United States were spent largely in Washington, D.C., and I want to tell you about them before writing about my current month-long trip.

On last Monday morning in the White House the President opened the first meeting of the Commission on the Status of Women. . . .

We kept ourselves strictly on schedule all day and opened our afternoon meeting promptly at two o'clock at 200 Maryland Avenue, below the Capitol, where the Commission on the Status of Women will have its permanent office.

We soon began to discuss the best way to organize to achieve the maximum of work not only on the six points laid down in the President's directive to the commission but in other situations which will certainly arise. The commission will try to make its influence felt concerning women's problems not only in the Federal area but in state and local areas and in industry as well as in women's home responsibilities.

The effort, of course, is to find how we can best use the potentialities of women without impairing their first responsibilities, which are to their home, their husbands and their children. We need to use in the very best way possible all our available manpower—and that includes womanpower—and this commission, I think, can well point out some of the ways in which this can be accomplished.

[†] From Eleanor Roosevelt, "My Day: The Presidential Commission on the Status of Women," February 16, 1962, in *Courage in a Dangerous World: The Political Writings of Eleanor Roosevelt*, edited by Allida M. Black (New York: Columbia University Press, 1999), p. 299. Copyright © 1999 Columbia University Press. Reprinted with permission of the publisher.

I was glad to hear brought up the question of part-time work for women and of better training in certain areas because the possibilities available to women could be more widely publicized and education could be directed to meet and prepare for these new openings. . . .

U.S. EQUAL EMPLOYMENT OPPORTUNITY COMMISSION

From The Equal Pay Act of 1963[†]

* * *

Prohibition of sex discrimination

(1) No employer having employees subject to any provisions of this section shall discriminate, within any establishment in which such employees are employed, between employees on the basis of sex by paying wages to employees in such establishment at a rate less than the rate at which he pays wages to employees of the opposite sex in such establishment for equal work on jobs the performance of which requires equal skill, effort, and responsibility, and which are performed under similar working conditions, except where such payment is made pursuant to (i) a seniority system; (ii) a merit system; (iii) a system which measures earnings by quantity or quality of production; or (iv) a differential based on any other factor other than sex. * * *

* * *

CIVIL RIGHTS

Civil Rights activism renewed after *Brown v. Board of Education of Topeka* in 1954, sparking incidents like the Montgomery Bus Boycott in 1955; school integration struggles in Little Rock, Arkansas, in 1957; sit-ins at lunch counters throughout the South beginning in 1960; Freedom Rides on the interstate buses in 1961; and dramatic attacks on nonviolent protesters in Birmingham, Alabama, in 1963. The August 1963 March on Washington for Jobs and Freedom culminated these episodes of brave heroism and focused the civil rights work for the future.

† From U.S. Equal Employment Opportunity Commission, *Equal Pay Act of 1963*, Laws, Regulations, Guidance, and M.O.U.s. www.eeoc.gov/laws/statutes.epa.cfmn (accessed August 24, 2012).

REVEREND MARTIN LUTHER KING, JR.

I Have a Dream . . .[†]

I am happy to join with you today in what will go down in history as the greatest demonstration for freedom in the history of our nation.

Five score years ago a great American in whose symbolic shadow we stand today signed the Emancipation Proclamation. This momentous decree is a great beacon light of hope to millions of Negro slaves who had been seared in the flames of withering injustice. It came as a joyous daybreak to end the long night of their captivity. But 100 years later the Negro still is not free. One hundred years later the life of the Negro is still badly crippled by the manacles of segregation and the chains of discrimination. One hundred years later the Negro lives on a lonely island of poverty in the midst of a vast ocean of material prosperity. One hundred years later the Negro is still languished in the corners of American society and finds himself in exile in his own land. So we've come here today to dramatize a shameful condition.

In a sense we've come to our nation's capital to cash a check. When the architects of our Republic wrote the magnificent words of the Constitution and the Declaration of Independence, they were signing a promissory note to which every American was to fall heir. This note was a promise that all men—yes, black men as well as white men—would be guaranteed the unalienable rights of life, liberty and the pursuit of happiness. It is obvious today that America has defaulted on this promissory note insofar as her citizens of color are concerned. Instead of honoring this sacred obligation, America has given the Negro people a bad check, a check which has come back marked "insufficient funds."

But we refuse to believe that the bank of justice is bankrupt. We refuse to believe that there are insufficient funds in the great vaults of opportunity of this nation. So we've come to cash this check, a check that will give us upon demand the riches of freedom and the security of justice.

We have also come to this hallowed spot to remind America of the fierce urgency of now. This is no time to engage in the luxury of cooling off or to take the tranquilizing drug of gradualism. Now is the time to make real the promises of democracy. Now is the time

† From Reverend Martin Luther King, Jr., August 28, 1963, Washington, D.C., March on Washington for Jobs and Freedom, "I Have a Dream. . . ." www.archives.gov/press/exhibits/dream-speech.pdf (accessed July 22, 2011). Reprinted by arrangement with The Heirs to the Estate of Martin Luther King Jr., c/o Writers House as agent for the proprietor New York, NY. Copyright 1963 Dr. Martin Luther King Jr; copyright renewed 1991 Coretta Scott King.

to rise from the dark and desolate valley of segregation to the sunlit path of racial justice. Now is the time to lift our nation from the quicksands of racial injustice to the solid rock of brotherhood.

Now is the time to make justice a reality for all of God's children. It would be fatal for the nation to overlook the urgency of the moment. This sweltering summer of the Negro's legitimate discontent will not pass until there is an invigorating autumn of freedom and equality—1963 is not an end but a beginning. Those who hope that the Negro needed to blow off steam and will now be content will have a rude awakening if the nation returns to business as usual.

There will be neither rest nor tranquility in America until the Negro is granted his citizenship rights. The whirlwinds of revolt will continue to shake the foundations of our nation until the bright days of justice emerge. And that is something that I must say to my people who stand on the worn threshold which leads into the palace of justice. In the process of gaining our rightful place we must not be guilty of wrongful deeds. Let us not seek to satisfy our thirst for freedom by drinking from the cup of bitterness and hatred.

We must forever conduct our struggle on the high plane of dignity and discipline. We must not allow our creative protests to degenerate into physical violence. Again and again we must rise to the majestic heights of meeting physical force with soul force. The marvelous new militancy which has engulfed the Negro community must not lead us to distrust all white people, for many of our white brothers, as evidenced by their presence here today, have come to realize that their destiny is tied up with our destiny.

They have come to realize that their freedom is inextricably bound to our freedom. We cannot walk alone. And as we walk we must make the pledge that we shall always march ahead. We cannot turn back. There are those who are asking the devotees of civil rights, "When will you be satisfied!" We can never be satisfied as long as the Negro is the victim of the unspeakable horrors of police brutality.

We can never be satisfied as long as our bodies, heavy with the fatigue of travel, cannot gain lodging in the motels of the highways and the hotels of the cities.

We cannot be satisfied as long as the Negro's basic mobility is from a smaller ghetto to a larger one. We can never be satisfied as long as our children are stripped of their adulthood and robbed of their dignity by signs stating "For Whites Only."

We cannot be satisfied as long as the Negro in Mississippi cannot vote and the Negro in New York believes he has nothing for which to vote.

No, no, we are not satisfied, and we will not be satisfied until justice rolls down like waters and righteousness like a mighty stream.

I am not unmindful that some of you have come here out of great trials and tribulation. Some of you have come fresh from narrow jail cells. Some of you have come from areas where your quest for freedom left you battered by the storms of persecution and staggered by the winds of police brutality. You have been the veterans of creative suffering.

Continue to work with the faith that unearned suffering is redemptive. Go back to Mississippi, go back to Alabama, go back to South Carolina, go back to Georgia, go back to Louisiana, go back to the slums and ghettos of our Northern cities, knowing that somehow this situation can and will be changed. Let us not wallow in the valley of despair.

I say to you today, my friends, though, even though we face the difficulties of today and tomorrow, I still have a dream. It is a dream deeply rooted in the American dream. I have a dream that one day this nation will rise up, live out the true meaning of its creed: "We hold these truths to be self-evident, that all men are created equal."

I have a dream that one day on the red hills of Georgia sons of former slaves and the sons of former slave-owners will be able to sit down together at the table of brotherhood. I have a dream that one day even the state of Mississippi, a state sweltering with the heat of injustice, sweltering with the heat of oppression, will be transformed into an oasis of freedom and justice.

I have a dream that my four little children will one day live in a nation where they will not be judged by the color of their skin but by the content of their character. I have a dream . . . I have a dream that one day in Alabama, with its vicious racists, with its governor having his lips dripping with the words of interposition and nullification, one day right there in Alabama little black boys and black girls will be able to join hands with little white boys and white girls as sisters and brothers.

I have a dream today . . . I have a dream that one day every valley shall be exalted, every hill and mountain shall be made low. The rough places will be made plain, and the crooked places will be made straight. And the glory of the Lord shall be revealed, and all flesh shall see it together. This is our hope. This is the faith that I go back to the South with. With this faith we will be able to hew out of the mountain of despair a stone of hope. With this faith we will be able to transform the jangling discords of our nation into a beautiful symphony of brotherhood. With this faith we will be able to work together, to pray together, to struggle together, to go to jail together, to stand up for freedom together, knowing that we will be free one day.

This will be the day when all of God's children will be able to sing with new meaning. "My country, 'tis of thee, sweet land of liberty, of thee I sing. Land where my fathers died, land of the pilgrim's pride, from every mountain side, let freedom ring." And if America is to be a great nation, this must become true. So let freedom ring from the prodigious hilltops of New Hampshire. Let freedom ring from the mighty mountains of New York. Let freedom ring from the heightening Alleghenies of Pennsylvania. Let freedom ring from the snowcapped Rockies of Colorado. Let freedom ring from the curvaceous slopes of California.

But not only that. Let freedom ring from Stone Mountain of Georgia. Let freedom ring from Lookout Mountain of Tennessee. Let freedom ring from every hill and molehill of Mississippi, from every mountain side. Let freedom ring . . .

When we allow freedom to ring—when we let it ring from every city and every hamlet, from every state and every city, we will be able to speed up that day when all of God's children, black men and white men, Jews and Gentiles, Protestants and Catholics, will be able to join hands and sing in the words of the old Negro spiritual, "Free at last, Free at last, Great God a-mighty, We are free at last."

Peace, Environmental, and Student Movements

It was difficult to challenge U.S. foreign policy or the massive build-up of the military during the Cold War, but some did. A group of women, some of whom were known to Betty Friedan, became concerned with the open-air testing of nuclear weapons and appearance of radioactive fallout in milk. Women Strike for Peace helped to end these tests; the following poster announces one of their events in 1961 in Washington, D.C. Students for a Democratic Society, one of the most influential student groups of the 1960s, articulated a critique of Cold War society in "The Port Huron Statement," written in 1962. Later in the 1960s, both groups protested the war in Vietnam.

WOMEN STRIKE FOR PEACE

Nuclear Tests Cost Lives[†]

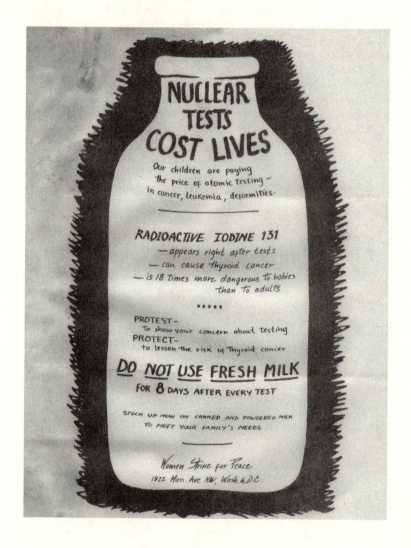

† Women Strike for Peace—Poster. Leo Goodman Papers, Archives of the Library of Congress, Washington, D.C., Box 233, folder 14. (No date, circa 1961.) Courtesy of the Library of Congress.

STUDENTS FOR A DEMOCRATIC SOCIETY

From The Port Huron Statement[†]

INTRODUCTORY NOTE: This document represents the results of several months of writing and discussion among the membership, a draft paper, and revision by the Students for a Democratic Society national convention meeting in Port Huron, Michigan, June 11–15, 1962. It is presented as a document with which SDS officially identifies, but also as a living document open to change with our times and experiences. It is a beginning: in our own debate and education, in our dialogue with society.

INTRODUCTION: AGENDA FOR A GENERATION

We are people of this generation, bred in at least modest comfort, housed now in universities, looking uncomfortably to the world we inherit.

When we were kids the United States was the wealthiest and strongest country in the world; the only one with the atom bomb, the least scarred by modern war, an initiator of the United Nations that we thought would distribute Western influence throughout the world. Freedom and equality for each individual, government of, by, and for the people—these American values we found good, principles by which we could live as men. Many of us began maturing in complacency.

As we grew, however, our comfort was penetrated by events too troubling to dismiss. First, the permeating and victimizing fact of human degradation, symbolized by the Southern struggle against racial bigotry, compelled most of us from silence to activism. Second, the enclosing fact of the Cold War, symbolized by the presence of the Bomb, brought awareness that we ourselves, and our friends, and millions of abstract "others" we knew more directly because of our common peril, might die at any time. We might deliberately ignore, or avoid, or fail to feel all other human problems, but not these two, for these were too immediate and crushing in their impact, too challenging in the demand that we as individuals take the responsibility for encounter and resolution.

While these and other problems either directly oppressed us or rankled our consciences and became our own subjective concerns, we began to see complicated and disturbing paradoxes in our surrounding America. The declaration "all men are created equal . . ."

---

† From "The Port Huron Statement," in James Miller, *Democracy is in the Streets: From Port Huron to the Siege of Chicago* (New York: Simon and Schuster, 1987), pp. 329–31. Reprinted by permission.

rang hollow before the facts of Negro life in the South and the big cities of the North. The proclaimed peaceful intentions of the United States contradicted its economic and military investments in the Cold War status quo.

We witnessed, and continue to witness, other paradoxes. With nuclear energy whole cities can easily be powered, yet the dominant nation-states seem more likely to unleash destruction greater than that incurred in all wars of human history. Although our own technology is destroying old and creating new forms of social organization, men still tolerate meaningless work and idleness. While two-thirds of mankind suffers undernourishment, our own upper classes revel amidst superfluous abundance. Although world population is expected to double in forty years, the nations still tolerate anarchy as a major principle of international conduct and uncontrolled exploitation governs the sapping of the earth's physical resources. Although mankind desperately needs revolutionary leadership, America rests in national stalemate, its goals ambiguous and tradition-bound instead of informed and clear, its democratic system apathetic and manipulated rather than "of, by, and for the people."

Not only did tarnish appear on our image of American virtue, not only did disillusion occur when the hypocrisy of American ideals was discovered, but we began to sense that what we had originally seen as the American Golden Age was actually the decline of an era. The worldwide outbreak of revolution against colonialism and imperialism, the entrenchment of totalitarian states, the menace of war, overpopulation, international disorder, supertechnology—these trends were testing the tenacity of our own commitment to democracy and freedom and our abilities to visualize their application to a world in upheaval.

Our work is guided by the sense that we may be the last generation in the experiment with living. But we are a minority—the vast majority of our people regard the temporary equilibriums of our society and world as eternally functional parts. In this is perhaps the outstanding paradox: we ourselves are imbued with urgency, yet the message of our society is that there is no viable alternative to the present. Beneath the reassuring tones of the politicians, beneath the common opinion that America will "muddle through," beneath the stagnation of those who have closed their minds to the future, is the pervading feeling that there simply are no alternatives, that our times have witnessed the exhaustion not only of Utopias, but of any new departures as well. Feeling the press of complexity upon the emptiness of life, people are fearful of the thought that at any moment things might be thrust out of control. They fear change itself, since change might smash whatever invisible framework seems to hold back chaos for them now. For most

Americans, all crusades are suspect, threatening. The fact that each individual sees apathy in his fellows perpetuates the common reluctance to organize for change. The dominant institutions are complex enough to blunt the minds of their potential critics, and entrenched enough to swiftly dissipate or entirely repel the energies of protest and reform, thus limiting human expectancies. Then, too, we are a materially improved society, and by our own improvements we seem to have weakened the case for further change.

Some would have us believe that Americans feel contentment amidst prosperity—but might it not better be called a glaze above deeply felt anxieties about their role in the new world? And if these anxieties produce a developed indifference to human affairs, do they not as well produce a yearning to believe there *is* an alternative to the present, that something *can* be done to change circumstances in the school, the workplaces, the bureaucracies, the government? It is to this latter yearning, at once the spark and engine of change, that we direct our present appeal. The search for truly democratic alternatives to the present, and a commitment to social experimentation with them, is a worthy and fulfilling human enterprise, one which moves us and, we hope, others today. On such a basis do we offer this document of our convictions and analysis: as an effort in understanding and changing the conditions of humanity in the late twentieth century, an effort rooted in the ancient, still unfulfilled conception of man attaining determining influence over his circumstances of life.

* * *

SEXUAL REVOLUTION

Philip Larkin began his poem "Annus Mirabilis" (1974) with the memorable line, "Sexual intercourse began in nineteen sixty-three . . ." The 1950s is often portrayed as a decade of sexual repression from which the sexually liberated 1960s sprang. In fact, there were stirrings, from the late 1940s through the 1950s, starting with the publication of the controversial Kinsey reports. Sex researcher Alfred Kinsey's *Sexual Behavior in the Human Male* (1948) and *Sexual Behavior in the Human Female* (1953) described a variety of sexual behaviors in a scientific and morally neutral way. In 1953 *Playboy* first appeared on the newsstands with Marilyn Monroe on the cover and as centerfold. In 1957 Grace Metalious's *Peyton Place* became a bestseller and cultural phenomenon by exposing the sexual secrets and desires of both the men and women of a small New England town. Despite serious repression, the 1950s also saw the first efforts to organize on behalf of civil rights for gays and lesbians. Helen Gurley Brown, who worked in advertising and went on to become editor-in-chief of *Cosmopolitan* magazine, proposed in her 1962 book *Sex and the Single Girl* that young, single, working girls in the city could have fun, just like married people, and that living dangerously lengthened and strengthened your life. Jennifer Scanlon, in her essay on pp. 498–503, believes that Brown's message was as important as Friedan's work in liberating women.

HELEN GURLEY BROWN

From Sex and the Single Girl[†]

Women Alone? Oh Come Now!

I married for the first time at thirty-seven. I got the man I wanted. It *could* be construed as something of a miracle considering how old *I* was and how eligible *he* was.

David is a motion picture producer, forty-four, brainy, charming and sexy. He was sought after by many a Hollywood starlet as well as some less flamboyant but more deadly types. And *I* got him! We have two Mercedes-Benzes, one hundred acres of virgin forest near San Francisco, a Mediterranean house overlooking the Pacific, a full-time maid and a good life.

I am not beautiful, or even pretty. I once had the world's worst case of acne. I am not bosomy or brilliant. I grew up in a small town. I didn't go to college. My family was, and is, desperately poor and I have always helped support them. I'm an introvert and I am sometimes mean and cranky.

But *I* don't think it's a miracle that I married my husband. I think I deserved him! For seventeen years I worked hard to become the kind of woman who might interest him. And when he finally walked into my life I was just worldly enough, relaxed enough, financially secure enough (for I also worked hard at my job) and adorned with enough glitter to attract him. He wouldn't have looked at me when I was twenty, and I wouldn't have known what to do with *him*.

There is a tidal wave of misinformation these days about how many more marriageable women there are than men (that part is true enough) and how tough is the plight of the single woman— spinster, widow, divorcee.

---

† From *Sex and the Single Girl* by Helen Gurley Brown (New York: Bernard Geiss Associates, 1962), pp. 3–7. Published by arrangement with Barricade Books Inc.

I think a single woman's biggest problem is coping with the people who are trying to marry her off! She is so driven by herself and her well-meaning but addlepated friends to become married that her whole existence seems to be an apology for *not* being married. Finding *him* is all she can think about or talk about when (a) she may not be psychologically ready for marriage; (b) there is no available husband for every girl at the time she wants one; and (c) her years as a single woman can be too rewarding to rush out of.

Although many's the time I was sure I would die alone in my spinster's bed, I could never bring myself to marry just to get married. If I had, I would have missed a great deal of misery along the way, no doubt, but also a great deal of fun.

I think marriage is insurance for the *worst* years of your life. During your best years you don't need a husband. You do need a man of course every step of the way, and they are often cheaper emotionally and a lot more fun by the dozen.

I believe that as many women over thirty marry out of fear of being alone someday—not necessarily now but *some* day—as for love of or compatibility with a particular man. The plan seems to be to get someone while the getting's good and by the time you lose your looks he'll be too securely glued to you to get away.

Isn't it silly? A man can leave a woman at fifty (though it may cost him some dough) as surely as you can leave dishes in the sink. He can leave any time *before* then too, and so may you leave *him* when you find your football hero developing into the town drunk. Then you have it all to do over again as if you hadn't gobbled him up in girlish haste.

How much saner and sweeter to marry when you have both jelled. And how much safer to marry with part of the play out of his system *and yours*. It takes guts. It can be lonely out there out of step with the rest of the folks. And you may *not* find somebody later. But since you're not finding somebody *sooner* as things stand, wouldn't it be better to stop driving . . . to stop fretting . . . to start recognizing what you have *now*?

As for marrying to have children, you can have babies until you're forty or older. And if you happen to die before *they* are forty, at least you haven't lingered into their middle age to be a doddering old bore. You also avoid those tiresome years as an unpaid baby sitter.

Frankly, the magazines and their marriage statistics give me a royal pain.

There is a more important truth that magazines never deal with, that single women are too brainwashed to figure out, that married women know but won't admit, that married men *and* single men endorse in a body, and that is that the single woman, far from being a creature to be pitied and patronized, is emerging as the newest glamour girl of our times.

She is engaging because she lives by her wits. She supports herself. She has had to sharpen her personality and mental resources to a glitter in order to survive in a competitive world and the sharpening looks good. Economically she is a dream. She is not a parasite, a dependent, a scrounger, a sponger or a bum. She is a giver, not a taker, a winner and not a loser.

Why else is she attractive? Because she isn't married, that's why! She is free to be The Girl in a man's life or at least his vision of The Girl, whether he is married or single himself.

When a man thinks of a married woman, no matter how lovely she is, he must inevitably picture her greeting her husband at the door with a martini or warmer welcome, fixing little children's lunches or scrubbing them down because they've fallen into a mudhole. She is somebody else's wife and somebody else's mother.

When a man thinks of a single woman, he pictures her alone in her apartment, smooth legs sheathed in pink silk Capri pants, lying tantalizingly among dozens of satin cushions, trying to read but not very successfully, for *he* is in that room—filling her thoughts, her dreams, her life.

Why else is a single woman attractive? She has more time and often more money to spend on herself. She has the extra twenty minutes to exercise every day, an hour to make up her face for their date. She has all day Saturday to whip up a silly, wonderful cotton brocade tea coat to entertain him in next day or hours to find it at a bargain sale.

Besides making herself physically more inviting, she has the freedom to furnish her mind. She can read Proust, learn Spanish, study *Time, Newsweek* and *The Wall Street Journal.*

Most importantly, a single woman, even if she is a file clerk, moves in the world of men. She knows their language—the language of retailing, advertising, motion pictures, exporting, shipbuilding. Her world is a far more colorful world than the one of P.T.A., Dr. Spock and the jammed clothes dryer.

A single woman never has to drudge. She can get her housework over within one good hour Saturday morning plus one other hour to iron blouses and white collars. She need never break her fingernails or her spirit waxing a playroom or cleaning out the garage.

She has more money for clothes and for trips than any but a wealthily married few.

EARLY INTELLECTUAL ENGAGEMENT WITH THE HOLOCAUST

One of the most controversial parts of *The Feminine Mystique* is chapter 12, "Progressive Dehumanization: The Comfortable Concentration Camp." Bruno Bettelheim's *The Informed Heart*, an analysis of men's psychological states within the Nazi concentration camps, influenced Friedan's argument. A survivor of Dachau and Buchenwald, Bettelheim argued that the camps' structures and practices had dehumanized many of their inmates. In this excerpt, he describes the characteristics he believed permitted some to leave the camps as whole individuals. See Kirsten Fermaglich's work on this controversial chapter on pp. 496–98.

BRUNO BETTELHEIM

From The Informed Heart: Autonomy in a Mass Age[†]

* * * But to survive as a man not a walking corpse, as a debased and degraded but still human being, one had first and foremost to remain informed and aware of what made up one's personal point of no return, the point beyond which one would never, under any circumstances, give in to the oppressor, even if it meant risking and losing one's life. It meant being aware that if one survived at the price of overreaching this point one would be holding on to a life that had lost all its meaning. It would mean surviving—not with a lowered self respect, but without any.

This point of no return was different from person to person, and changed for each person as time passed. At the beginning of their imprisonment, most inmates would have felt it beyond their point of no return to serve the SS as foreman or block chief, or to like wearing a uniform that made them look like the SS. Later, after years in the camp, such relatively external matters gave way to much more essential convictions which then became the core of their resistance. But those convictions one had to hold on to with utter tenacity. About them, one had to keep oneself informed at all times, because only then could they serve as the mainstay of a radically reduced but still present humanity. Much of the tenacity and

---

[†] Reprinted from *The Informed Heart: Autonomy in a Mass Age* by Bruno Bettelheim (New York: The Free Press, 1960), pp. 157–59. Copyright © 1960 by the Free Press. Copyright renewed © 1988 by Bruno Bettelheim. All rights reserved.

relentlessness of political prisoners in their factional warfare is thus explainable; for them, political loyalty to party was their point of no return.

Second in importance was keeping oneself informed of how one felt about complying when the ultimate decision as to where to stand firm was not called into question. While less radical, it was no less essential, because an awareness of one's attitude toward compliance was called for almost constantly. One had to comply with debasing and amoral commands if one wished to survive; but one had to remain cognizant that one's reason for complying was "to remain alive and unchanged as a person." Therefore, one had to decide, for any given action, whether it was truly necessary for one's safety or that of others, and whether committing it was good, neutral or bad. This keeping informed and aware of one's actions—though it could not alter the required act, save in extremities—this minimal distance from one's own behavior, and the freedom to feel differently about it depending on its character, this too was what permitted the prisoner to remain a human being. * * *

Those prisoners who blocked out neither heart nor reason, neither feelings nor perception, but kept informed of their inner attitudes even when they could hardly ever afford to act on them, those prisoners survived and came to understand the conditions they lived under. They also came to realize what they had not perceived before; that they still retained the last, if not the greatest, of the human freedoms; to choose their own attitude in any given circumstance. Prisoners who understood this fully, came to know that this, and only this, formed the crucial difference between retaining one's humanity (and often life itself) and accepting death as a human being (or perhaps physical death): whether one retained the freedom to choose autonomously one's attitude to extreme conditions even when they seemed totally beyond one's ability to influence them.

* * *

Impact

THE PERSONAL IS POLITICAL

The publication of *The Feminine Mystique* and the excerpts that appeared in popular women's magazines had an immediate impact on those who read Betty Friedan's work. Hundreds of women and some men wrote to her and the magazines' editors. Following is a sampling of both positive and negative responses to Friedan's argument. Over time, the impact of *The Feminine Mystique* on individuals has not waned. People still recall the importance the book had on their personal lives, as described in Stephanie Coontz's *A Strange Stirring*, excerpted on pp. 519–22.

From Betty Friedan Papers[†]

Letter to Betty Friedan, San Jose, CA, July 14, 1963[1]

I want to extend to you my appreciation of and for this perfectly wonderful piece of work. I hope you won't think me crazy or a crank of some kind. I have been a "vegetable" for about twenty-five years! You have opened my eyes, and perhaps now I can do something to become a human being, a better wife, and a better mother to my four children. Your book had such an impact, I just had to tell you.

Letter to Betty Friedan from Brooklyn, NY, June 2, 1964[2]

I can't resist the temptation to write to you since reading "The Feminine Mystique." I love you dearly for writing it—; I could hardly keep from exclaiming out loud "How true" "Oh, how true" at every page. As I look back, I wonder at myself getting into "the housewife trap" without ever meaning to. But, glory be, I got myself

---

[†] From Betty Friedan Papers, M-62, Schlesinger Library, Radcliffe Institute, Harvard University, Cambridge, MA.
1. From Betty Friedan Papers, Series III, Box 19, Folder 687.
2. From Betty Friedan Papers, Series III, Box 19, Folder 683.

out of it and can only shudder when I think of those "concentration camp" days.

Letter to Betty Friedan from Sioux City, Iowa, March 12, 1964[3]

* * * Thanks to this fascinating and delightful book I am fully confident of myself and my desire to launch the career I've always wanted for so long. The last of the cobwebs of guilt have been swept away and what a marvelous free feeling! The release of women from this subtle bondage can only be good and right . . .

Letter to Betty Friedan, March 23, 1964[4]

After re-reading your book, the Feminine Mystique, I simply have to respond to you in order to congratulate you and thank you for setting me free! Really free! I'm so sick of hearing that women should play cute little brainless tricks to get her man. That she should prove to him that he can take care of her and that he's so much more capable and intelligent than she is. And the really hysterical (and totally frustrating) thing is how the New Left women are trying to do the same thing that their mothers did: attempting to find themselves as complete *women* through a sexual experience with their husbands or lovers . . .

Letter to Editor of McCall's, March 3, 1963[5]

Having just read "The Fraud of Femininity," in your March issue of *McCall's*, I am incensed enough to write my first "letter to the editor." Mrs. Friedan should save her pity for those who really need it—the half starved, oppressed people in the world. I seem to embody most of the characteristics Mrs. Friedan deplores in the American Housewife, and I feel certain a vast number of women support my views on this subject. I am one who interrupted her College education to marry and bear five children. I have since spent the 23 years we have been married reveling in my husband's accomplishments, trying to smooth over the disappointments, chauffeuring, volunteering for the worthwhile community activities, keeping house, being part time nurse, mechanic, plumber, teacher and companion at home. In all honesty, I doubt that I am "suffering a slow deterioration of mind and spirit."

---

3. From Betty Friedan Papers, Series III, Box 19, Folder 690.
4. From Betty Friedan Papers, Series III, Box 19, Folder 701.
5. From Betty Friedan Papers, Series III, Box 21, Folder 747.

Letter to Editor of McCall's, *March 3, 1963*[6]

I never before realized how empty my life as a wife and mother has been. It positively teems with emptiness: empty mouths to feed, empty heads to put ideas in, empty hearts to pack with love, empty rooms to furnish and decorate, empty hours to practice the piano in, empty places to sew buttons on, empty washers to fill with dirty clothes. Ah, what a bunch of emptiness I have. You have certainly opened my eyes with that article.

Letter to Editor of McCall's, *February 27, 1963*[7]

Horrors! I am living the life of the "feminine mystique" . . . I ask myself: Am I "irreparably damaged" because "I have forfeited my own existence"; am I "suffering a slow deterioration of mind and spirit": am I "a biological robot preyed upon by my husband and children"; am I a "status-seeking parasite expecting my husband, my home, and my children to give me status"; is my life "non-committal and vicarious"? Heavens! Now I know! I've been suffering all these years from a sneaky sort of self-hypnosis. All this time I thought I was happy, and a nice person. Now I discover I've been miserable and some sort of a monster in disguise—now out of disguise. How awful! . . .

From Writer to Activist: NOW, NARAL, NWPC, and Women's Strike for Equality

In 1966, one of the most important organizations of second wave feminism was created, with Betty Friedan as one of its founding mothers and first president. Pauli Murray, civil rights activist and early opponent of what she called "Jane Crow," describes the birth of the National Organization for Women (NOW). NOW, whose Bill of Rights is included here, was often described as more white, middle class, and reformist in comparison to the women's liberation groups forming in the late 1960s. Robin Morgan, editor of the influential feminist anthology *Sisterhood is Powerful* (1970), provides a window into how those distinctions were understood by more radical women's liberationists. Despite divisions among feminists in the late 1960s, Friedan successfully helped to organize the unifying Women's Strike for Equality on August 26, 1970, to commemorate the fiftieth anniversary of the passage of the Nineteenth

6. From Betty Friedan Papers, Series III, Box 21, Folder 747.
7. From Betty Friedan Papers, Series III, Box 21, Folder 743.

Amendment that gave women the right to vote. While thousands of women (and men) marched down New York's Fifth Avenue carrying signs that read "Don't Iron While the Strike is Hot," and "I Am Not a Barbie Doll," among other slogans, women in Boston, Pittsburgh, Detroit, Washington, D.C., and other cities held rallies and engaged in political theater and education. In Berkeley, California, women marchers strapped pots and pans to their backs to highlight the bondage of housework; and in many cities, women demanded service in previously all-male bars and restaurants.[1] The Women's Strike for Equality was perhaps the most visible of Friedan's political work at this time. She also founded and worked in the National Association for Repeal of Abortion Laws (NARAL) and the National Women's Political Caucus (NWPC). The selection on the founding of the NWPC is by Bella Abzug, an influential New York politician and feminist who both worked and sparred with Friedan.

PAULI MURRAY

From The Autobiography of a Black Activist, Feminist, Lawyer, Priest, and Poet[†]

*   *   *

Just about the time I was packing to leave New Haven for New York, I began what was to be a productive association with Betty Friedan, then chiefly known as the author of *The Feminine Mystique.* On October 12, 1965, I spoke on Title VII at a conference held by the National Council of Women of the United States at the Biltmore Hotel in New York City.* Most of my talk was a straightforward legal analysis of issues arising from sex-based discrimination in employment. At the end I touched on some political implications, pointing out that the historical significance of the sex provision of Title VII was comparable to that of the Nineteenth Amendment because, if vigorously enforced, it would give women the opportunity of advancing in accordance with their abilities and interests. Then I added:

> But there is reason to believe that it will not be adequately enforced unless the political power of women is brought to bear. In the case of the Nineteenth Amendment, the organized resistance came in advance of the law. In the case of Title VII,

---

1. See "Nation: Women on the March," *Time,* September 7, 1970, pp. 74–76.
† From Pauli Murray, *The Autobiography of a Black Activist, Feminist, Lawyer, Priest, and Poet* (Knoxville: University of Tennessee Press, 1989), selection from, "The Birth of NOW," pp. 365–68. Used with permission of the Estate of Pauli Murray.
* Title VII of the Civil Rights Act of 1964 prohibited discrimination on the basis of sex. For more, see selection by Ruth Rosen, pp. 510–19.

the resistance is just beginning to be organized. It should not be necessary to have another March on Washington in order that there be equal job opportunities for all. But if this necessity should arise, I hope women will not flinch from the thought.

As one who had participated in the 1963 March for Jobs and Freedom, I did not think my closing statement was unusual, but apparently the fact that the audience was made up for the most part of white upper-middle-class women gave it dramatic value in the eyes of a *New York Times* reporter. In any case, the prominently placed report that appeared next day in the *Times* was headlined PROTEST PROPOSED ON WOMEN'S JOBS; YALE PROFESSOR SAYS IT MAY BE NEEDED TO OBTAIN RIGHTS. To my great embarrassment, the news story erroneously identified me as "a woman Professor of Law at Yale," but I suppose the gratuitous label gave the statement extra clout. At any rate, Betty Friedan, who had not attended the conference, read the news account and immediately tracked me down by telephone in New Haven. We arranged to get together for talks as soon as I was settled in the city.

As I recall, Betty Friedan was interviewing people for a second book, but our subsequent meetings and telephone conversations quickly moved beyond a personal interview and began to focus upon what was happening to women, particularly the shoddy treatment we were getting under Title VII, and what we should be doing about it. I put Betty in touch with Mary Eastwood, Catherine East, Marguerite Rawalt, EEOC attorney Sonia Pressman (Fuentes), and other members of the feminist network in government, and she later acknowledged the influence of this "underground network of women" who nudged her steadily on toward action. To varying degrees, each of us who had worked with government-sponsored agencies on women's issues knew their limitations, so we stressed the need for an independent national civil rights organization for women comparable to the NAACP, an organization that would have enough political power to compel government agencies to take seriously the problems of discrimination because of sex. In expressing this idea to Betty Friedan, I recall how timid I was, how modest were my expectations, and how anxious I was to avoid competing with established women's groups. I said wistfully how wonderful it would be "if we only had a network of about five hundred key women around the country who could spring into action whenever issues directly affecting women arise in Washington." Catherine East was more decisive in her approach. She said later that she saw Betty Friedan as the only woman who at that time had name recognition enough to organize a national group, and she set out to persuade Betty to take the initiative in bringing such an organization into being.

By the time the Third National Conference of State Commissions on the Status of Women convened at the Washington Hilton Hotel in June 1966, Betty Friedan was just about convinced that a new action group should be set up. Sponsored by the Interdepartmental Committee and Citizens' Advisory Council on the Status of Women and bringing together prominent women commission members from virtually every state, the conference seemed the logical setting in which to test the idea among a broad cross-section of women. As a writer-observer covering the conference, Betty was in a position to sound out leading representatives from state commissions around the country. I was to speak on the panel "Sex Discrimination—Progress in Legal Status," held on the final morning of the conference, and other members of our network were there to support Betty in exploring possibilities.

By June 29, the second day of the conference, there were enough rumblings of dissatisfaction among activists in attendance to suggest that the time was ripe. Betty was encouraged to invite a few women who might be interested in organizing a new group to join an informal discussion in her hotel room that evening, the only opportunity we would have for a meeting before the closing sessions next day.

Some fifteen women met in Betty Friedan's room at about ten o'clock. Many of us were strangers to one another; I knew only five of those present—Betty herself, Mary Eastwood, Dorothy Haener of the Women's Department of the United Automobile Workers, Catherine Conroy of the Communications Workers of America, and Kathryn Clarenbach, chair of the Wisconsin Commission on the Status of Women. Everyone present felt the general frustration over the issue of women's employment rights under Title VII. Each conference participant had been furnished with a copy of Congresswoman Martha Griffiths' angry speech of June 20, delivered on the floor of the House, in which she charged "The whole attitude of the EEOC toward discrimination based on sex is specious, negative and arrogant." Working women were outraged over a guideline issued by the EEOC in April, permitting employers to advertise jobs open to both sexes in segregated "Help Wanted, Male" or "Help Wanted, Female" newspaper columns in blatant contradiction of Title VII's prohibition of any want ad expressing a preference or limitation based on race, religion, sex, or national origin. Griffiths found the Commission's interpretation of the statute "nothing more than arbitrary arrogance, disregard of law, and a manifestation of flat hostility to the human rights of women." Conference delegates were also angry over the impending expiration of EEOC Commissioner Richard Graham's term on July 1 and the strong rumors that he would not be reappointed. Since he was the one male member of the Commission who had shown sensitivity in dealing with issues of sex bias in employment, Commissioner Graham's imminent departure was seen as calamitous. Our only differences were over strategies to meet what we all saw as an ominous situation.

But those differences were deep. The discussion quickly developed into a heated debate over the need for a new organization. Kay Clarenbach, the commissioner from Wisconsin, and Catherine Conroy of the Communications Workers union, in particular questioned the idea and argued that the issues which immediately concerned us could be handled through the existing machinery of state commissions. Kay suggested that since the theme of the conference was "Targets for Action," it would be appropriate for conference delegates to adopt strong resolutions at the closing luncheon next day, urging the enforcement of the sex provisions of Title VII and the reappointment of Commissioner Graham. Those of us who felt the time had come for action independent of government sponsorship could make little headway against the state commission approach. Tempers flared and we wrangled until after midnight without resolving the basic disagreement. The meeting finally broke up after we agreed—some of us halfheartedly—to Kay's proposal that she draft the resolutions and bring them before the entire conference the following day.

I left Betty Friedan's room that night thoroughly discouraged; it seemed to me that we had fumbled a major opportunity to begin mobilizing women nationally to press for their civil rights. I was so depressed that I seriously considered leaving for New York immediately after my panel presentation next morning, without attending the closing luncheon. But I had not reckoned with the persistent power of an idea whose time had clearly come, and I had not anticipated the radicalization of Kay Clarenbach and Catherine Conway when their plans for moderate action through existing channels were frustrated. In the morning, when Kay approached conference officials to arrange to introduce her resolutions, she was told that "government commissions cannot take action against other departments." Kay and Catherine were so outraged by this rebuff that they had an immediate change of heart. By noon, word had been passed that we were going ahead with the new organization.

During the luncheon about twenty of us gathered at two tables near the rostrum, and while conference dignitaries were making speeches just above our heads, we carried on whispered conversations and set in motion a temporary body to be called the National Organization for Women. Betty Friedan hastily scribbled its purpose on a paper napkin: "to take the actions needed to bring women into the mainstream of American society *now* . . . in fully equal partnership with men." We urged others at the luncheon to join us in a brief meeting to form the new organization.

Before the conference ended that afternoon, twenty-eight women had signed up and paid five dollars each for immediate expenses. A telegram bearing the names of the twenty-eight founding members went to the White House, urging the reappointment of Richard Graham to the Equal Employment Opportunity Commission, and night letters were sent to each EEOC commissioner, urging that the discriminatory guideline approving sex-segregated "help wanted" ads be rescinded. Kay Clarenbach was named temporary coordinator of NOW, and along with Caroline Ware, I was elected to a "temporary coordinating committee" of six to assist Kay over the summer in developing the framework for a permanent organization. The birth of NOW had happened so quickly and smoothly that most of the delegates left the conference unaware that a historic development in the women's movement had begun. Three months later, at an organizing conference held in Washington on October 29 and 30, 1966, thirty-two of us set up the permanent organization of NOW, never dreaming that within less than two decades it would have more than 200,000 members and become a potent force in American politics.

* * *

NATIONAL ORGANIZATION FOR WOMEN

Bill of Rights[†]

WE DEMAND:

I. That the U.S. Congress immediately pass the Equal Rights Amendment to the Constitution to provide that "Equality of rights under the law shall not be denied or abridged by the United States or by any State on account of sex," and that such then be immediately ratified by the several States.

II. That equal employment opportunity be guaranteed to all women, as well as men, by insisting that the Equal Employment Opportunity Commission enforces the prohibitions against racial discrimination.

III. That women be protected by law to ensure their rights to return to their jobs within a reasonable time after childbirth with-

---

[†] From National Organization for Women Bill of Rights, 1967, in *Sisterhood is Powerful: An Anthology of Writings from the Women's Liberation Movement*. Ed. Robin Morgan. (New York: Random House, 1970), pp. 513–14. Copyright © 1970 by Robin Morgan. Reprinted by permission of Edite Kroll Literary Agency Inc.

out loss of seniority or other accrued benefits, and be paid maternity leave as a form of social security and/or employee benefit.

IV. Immediate revision of tax laws to permit the deduction of home and child-care expenses for working parents.

V. That child-care facilities be established by law on the same basis as parks, libraries, and public schools, adequate to the needs of children from the pre-school years through adolescence, as a community resource to be used by all citizens from all income levels.

VI. That the right of women to be educated to their full potential equally with men be secured by Federal and State legislation, eliminating all discrimination and segregation by sex, written and unwritten, at all levels of education, including colleges, graduate and professional schools, loans and fellowships, and Federal and State training programs such as the Job Corps.

VII. The right of women in poverty to secure job training, housing, and family allowances on equal terms with men, but without prejudice to a parent's right to remain at home to care for his or her children; revision of welfare legislation and poverty programs which deny women dignity, privacy, and self-respect.

VIII. The right of women to control their own reproductive lives by removing from the penal code laws limiting access to contraceptive information and devices, and by repealing penal laws governing abortion.

ROBIN MORGAN

From Sisterhood is Powerful[†]

* * *

In 1964, Ruby Doris Smith Robinson, a young black woman who was a founder of SNCC (then the Student Non-violent Coordinating Committee) wrote a paper on the position of women in that organization. It was laughed at and dismissed. In 1965, Casey Hayden and Mary King, two white women who had been active in SNCC and other civil-rights organizations for years, wrote an article on women

---

[†] From *Sisterhood is Powerful: An Anthology of Writings from the Women's Liberation Movement*, ed. Robin Morgan (New York: Random House, 1970), "Introduction: The Women's Revolution," pp. xxi–xxiii. Copyright © 1970 by Robin Morgan. Reprinted by permission of Edite Kroll Literary Agency Inc.

in the Movement for the now-defunct journal *Studies on the Left*.
Women began to form caucuses within the Movement organizations where they worked; men's reactions ranged from fury to derision. In 1966, women who demanded that a plank on women's
liberation be inserted in the SDS (Students for a Democratic Society) resolution that year were pelted with tomatoes and thrown out
of the convention. But the caucuses went on forming, and gradually
became small groups all on their own, as women more and more
came to see the necessity of an independent women's movement,
creating its own theory, politics, tactics, and directing itself toward
goals in its own self-interest (which was also the self-interest of
more than half the world's population).

Synchronistically, the National Organization for Women (NOW)
was formed, in 1966. One of its founders was Betty Friedan, author
of *The Feminine Mystique*. A civil-rights organization pledged to
"bring women into full participation in the mainstream of American society . . . exercising all the privileges and responsibilities
thereof in truly equal partnership with men," NOW's membership
was mostly comprised of middle- and upper-middle-class women
(*and men*; it is almost the only group in the women's movement that
allows male members), professional, middle-aged, white women. The
organization, which now has members in every state of the union, as
well as about fifty chapters in twenty-four states, has been called (by
some, affectionately; by others, pejoratively) "the NAACP of the
women's movement" because it fights *within* the System, lobbying
legislators, concentrating on job discrimination, etc. NOW helped
win the airline stewardesses' fight against mandatory retirement
when a woman married or reached the age of thirty-five; the
group was also almost solely responsible for the Equal Employment Opportunities Commission ruling that segregated male-
female help-wanted ads in newspapers were discriminatory and
illegal. They have worked hard to change abortion laws and to call
attention to educational discrimination against women.

NOW is essentially an organization that wants reforms about the
second-class citizenship of women—and this is where it differs
drastically from the rest of the Women's Liberation Movement. Its
composite membership (and remember the men) determines, of
course, its politics, which are not radical. An ecumenical view
(which I hold on alternate Tuesdays and Fridays) would see that
such an organization is extremely valid and important; it reaches a
certain constituency that is never going to be reached by, say, a
group called WITCH, or The Coat Hangers, and it does valuable
work, as well. On certain Mondays and Thursdays, however, I fear
for the women's movement's falling into precisely the same trap as
did our foremothers, the suffragists: creating a bourgeois feminist

movement that never quite dared enough, never questioned enough, never really reached out beyond its own class and race. For example, with a few courageous exceptions, most of the suffragists refused to examine the family as a structure oppressive to women. Because of this type of failure, they wound up having to settle for the vote. We now see what that got us. The only hope of a new feminist movement is some kind of only now barely emerging politics of *revolutionary feminism*, which some people are trying to explore in this anthology.

* * *

BELLA ABZUG, WITH MIM KELBER

From Gender Gap: Bella Abzug's Guide to Political Power for American Women[†]

Founding the National Women's Political Caucus

The continuing evidence of the disregard for women's economic and social needs and my disgust with the type of men perpetrated on us as Presidents and political leaders made me feel the urgency of electing more women to Congress. At that time there were only twelve of us in the House and one in the Senate. True, some sympathetic male colleagues introduced or cosponsored legislation beneficial to women, but the main impetus and ideas came from the women members. We needed more of them.

In the spring of 1971 I began sounding out friends and coworkers on the notion of forming an independent women's political organization, and got a quick response of interest. I discovered that Betty Friedan, author of *The Feminine Mystique*, had been thinking along somewhat similar lines, though we disagreed on the approach to take. She seemed to feel we should support women for political office within fairly minimal guidelines, while I was not prepared to spend time getting just any woman elected. I felt our main goal should be to build a political movement of women for social change that would simultaneously help elect more women, minorities, and other underrepresented groups and build an electoral bloc strong enough to influence male politicians to support our programs.

I reserved a committee room on Capitol Hill, and on June 9 we held our first big planning session with a fairly good cross section of women. Shirley Chisholm and Patsy Takemoto Mink, a Congresswoman from Hawaii, were on hand to give the women a pep talk on the need for an independent political force, but most were already convinced. There was a large turnout of Washington women from NOW, black organizations, government agencies, religious and social action groups, and students from local colleges. Jane Galvin Lewis of the National Council of Negro Women and Edith Van Horn of the United Auto Workers were there; Republicans included several women from Governor Nelson Rockefeller's staff, and the New York contingent included Gloria Steinem, the eloquent feminist, Friedan, Ronnie Feit of NOW, Mim Kelber, my close friend and long-time associate, and other feminists. Liz Carpenter, Lady Bird Johnson's former White House press secretary, came with her young daughter, explaining that she didn't want her to face the kind of discrimination she had encountered in her own career. We gave ourselves a month to organize a national conference, and we met our deadline.

On July 10, 1971, when our founding conference of the National Women's Political Caucus (NWPC) opened at the Washington Hilton, some three hundred women from all over the country—a mix of elected officials, community activists, feminists, Democrats, Republicans, radicals, union women, homemakers, students, blacks, Hispanics, and lesbians—were on hand.

One of the putdowns that has continually plagued the women's movement is the charge that it speaks only for white middle-class women. To the contrary, there has always been an acute sensitivity to the need for representing the interests of all women. As one of the keynote speakers at that first NWPC meeting, I said the hope of building an effective women's political movement lay in "reaching out to include those who have been doubly and triply disenfranchised—reaching out to working women, to young women, to black women, to women on welfare—and joining their strength with that of millions of other American women who are on the move all over this country, demanding an end to discrimination and fighting for their rights as full and equal citizens."

There were cheers and applause when I said, "I don't think any of us intend to replace the *male* white middle-class elite that runs this country with a *female* white middle-class elite."

* * *

SEXUAL POLITICS AND THE WOMEN'S LIBERATION MOVEMENT

The Women's Liberation Movement, the radical feminist contingent of the women's movement, burst onto the public scene with a 1968 demonstration at the Miss America pageant in Atlantic City. Using guerrilla theater techniques learned from the New Left, the demonstrators challenged the conformist, exploitative, and racist versions of beauty perpetrated by the pageant. The Miss America Protest was organized by a group called New York Radical Women, but many more small, radical groups emerged within the next few years. Women in these groups participated in consciousness-raising sessions to go beyond the institutional reforms called for by the National Organization for Women. These groups, in their own ways, challenged women's oppression in the private worlds of sexuality and the family, as well as in the public cultural images and representations of women. One such group was the Furies, lesbian feminists who formed a collective in 1972. There were differences in style, philosophy, age, generation, and class between the radical and reformist wings of the women's movement. Betty Friedan was already considered a founding mother of feminism's second wave by the late 1960s and 1970s and was caught in the maelstrom of these currents. Sometimes she created the turmoil herself, particularly when she commented on the sexual politics and lesbianism in radical groups, as in this interview in *Social Policy* magazine.

BETTY FRIEDAN

Critique of Sexual Politics[†]

What do you think of the new trend in the women's movement which seems to be primarily concerned with orgasm, sexual relationships, etc.?

I'm quite disturbed by it. I think the whole trend is highly diversionary. It builds up a straw-man enemy by packaging together all the negative characteristics in man and making him the main enemy, the oppressor.

Why do you describe this as diversionary?

Because I think it diverts us from serious political action. Women fighting for the basic changes necessary in society will at once affirm themselves and produce much more positive relationships

---

† From Betty Friedan, "Critique of Sexual Politics," *Social Policy* Magazine, November 1970, in *It Changed My Life: Writings on the Women's Movement* (New York: Random House, 1976), pp. 161–64. Copyright © 1976 by Betty Friedan. Reprinted by permission of Curtis Brown, Ltd.

with men both inside and outside the bedroom. But if the main enemy is seen as the man, women will wallow around in self-pity and man-hatred and never really be moved to action.

The sexual relationship is not the issue. The concern of some women to be on top in the sexual act strikes me as quite ridiculous. The problem is that the sexual relationship is soured and dehumanized by the workaday relationships of men and women in society. Its converse is the equally obsolete image of masculinity—*machismo*—which enjoins men to dominance.

Do you feel that machismo *is characteristic of men today?*

Machismo is the extreme. It is certainly not characteristic of the younger generation. Men wearing their hair long is, in fact, a revolt against *machismo*, with all its sadism and brutality.

Why do you think that there is so much emphasis on the new bedroom politics? Why is the trend occurring?

There are two reasons: first, because it's sexy; it suits the communications media, the TV. It's more glamorous than talking about jobs and discrimination, and women in politics.

But secondly, and even more important, the extremity of the condition that needs changing is what's causing the fulmination. I predicted four years ago, when I could see nothing happening except talk, that if this country did not really begin to confront the situation and do something to change it, the most spirited of the upcoming generation would turn their backs completely on love and sex and marriage and having children, and that's what's happening.

This trend is dangerous in that it diverts women from the necessary positive action; but it is even more dangerous in that it fits in with the rise of hatred developing all over society, which a fascist movement, a fascist demagogue could easily appeal to and capture. A random hatred of men, a hatred that can lead nowhere, with no allies, will produce no significant changes; but it can serve as the soil for a fascist appeal.

What do you think about all this talk about clitoral orgasms, vaginal orgasms, and so on?

I think, to each her own, and all the fuss is very misleading. I think as women become freer and improve their own status, their sexual response will be fuller, more positive, and will not be eroticized rage or frigidity. Kinsey, Masters and many others have shown that as women have improved their status in life, their sexuality has also grown. The point is not to focus on the kinds of sexual orgasm, but on the basic human relations that need to be changed. Unfortunately, the new sexual theorists do not seem to see the possibility of sex and love combined, of joyful sex as part of a larger, meaningful relationship. And some are badly exaggerating the presumed positives of lesbian sex. We don't want a society in which there are two separate sexes, men and women, with each getting their pleasure by themselves—men with men and women with women. Such a vision is hardly the radical future. It is only pseudo-radical because it does not lead to any real institutional change of any kind. In essence, we cannot permit the image of women to be developed by the homosexual. The male homosexual omits the strength of women just as the bull dyke omits the essential tenderness of men. What is the point of reacting against one's sexual role as man or woman merely to adopt the stereotype of the opposite sex? The *machismo* image hurts men as much as it hurts women. They can't live up to it, and a good deal of the sexual war created by the new bedroom politics is simply exacerbating the difficulties between men and women, not overcoming them. The difficulties are not being transcended, they're just being expressed. As women were the scapegoats before, so now man is becoming the new scapegoat, the monster.

What action flows from orgasm politics?

No action flows from it. All that flows from it is talk and hate, and the potential manipulations of left or right demagogues. You ought to note that De Gaulle and Reagan and Nixon were all elected with the strong help of the woman vote. It is extremely important to win the women who are 53 percent of the population to their own best interests and not to permit them to go in a rightist direction. This requires allies, and men are important allies.

What do you think of the bra burning?

Sometimes it's nice not to wear a bra, but this is not the major issue of the world. And I think it's kind of silly for women to lean over backwards and want *not* to look pretty because that, presumably, is being seductive and was determined by the patriarchal society. I guess you might say that my whole approach is less titillating and less glamorous. But the other approach is a dead end. I don't want a lot of navel-gazing and consciousness-raising that doesn't go anywhere. I want people to recognize that there are tremendous positive aspects in both men and women, that both men and women have been seriously hurt by the sex roles they've been required to play in our society; and that they frequently take their anger out on each other and on their children. The new understanding that women are developing must be channeled into political action, not into a highly verbalized sexual emphasis with a lot of whining and wallowing.

Do you want to sum up?

The essence of the matter is that sexual politics is highly danger-ous and diversionary, and may even provide good soil for fascist, demagogic appeals based on hatred. No serious meaningful action emerges from a sexual emphasis. There is simply talk, anger, and wallowing. It is also based on a highly distorted, oversimplified view of our society, men and women, family relations, relations to chil-dren. The reason that I called the strike on August 26th is that I felt the movement had reached its stage of critical growth. It now must channel its energy into action that can really change political life. I feel the strike is going to help our whole movement to over-come the wallowing, navel-gazing rap sessions, the orgasm talk that leaves things unchanged, the rage that will produce a backlash—down with sex, down with love, down with childbearing. I think love and sex are real and that women and men both have real needs for love and intimacy that seems most easily structured around heterosexual relationships.

The great majority of women are not going to renounce their own need for love and shouldn't be asked to do so. My own experience tells me that family life and children can be positive experiences. And I don't want to retreat from building on those positive dimen-sions because of the distortions—rather, I want to fight against those factors in society that are producing the distortions. And although I think that childbearing shouldn't be the end-all of a woman's life, there is a real generative impulse in women. So if we define our movement in antilove, antichild terms, we are not going to have the power of the women and the help of increasing numbers of men who can identify their liberation with women's liberation. This is not just my theoretical view of the situation; this was evident beyond any-one's question on August 26th, when perhaps as many as one-third of the people who marched were men. Women in a coalition with students and blacks and intellectuals can build real change in society.

You have a vision, a hope?

Yes, it is happening, it is happening. And I know that we have the power to make it happen. The next step is human liberation!

GINNY BERSON

From The Furies[†]

We call our paper *The Furies* because we are also angry. We are angry because we are oppressed by male supremacy. We have been fucked over all our lives by a system which is based on the domination of men over women, which defines male as good and female as only as good as the man you are with. It is a system in which heterosexuality is rigidly enforced and Lesbianism rigidly suppressed. It is a system which has further divided us by class, race, and nationality.

We are working to change this system which has kept us separate and powerless for so long. We are a collective of twelve Lesbians living and working in Washington, D.C. We are rural and urban; from the Southwest, Midwest, South and Northeast. Our ages range from 18 to 28. We are high school drop-outs and Ph.D. candidates. We are lower class, middle and upper-middle class. We are white. Some of us have been Lesbians for twelve years, others for ten months. We are committed to ending all oppressions by attacking their roots—male supremacy.

* * *

The base of our ideological thought is: Sexism is the root of all other oppressions, and Lesbian and woman oppression will not end by smashing capitalism, racism, and imperialism. Lesbianism is not a matter of sexual preference, but rather one of political choice which every woman must make if she is to become woman-identified and thereby end male supremacy. Lesbians, as outcasts from every culture but their own have the most to gain by ending class, race, and national supremacy within their own ranks. Lesbians must get out of the straight women's movement and form their own movement in order to be taken seriously, to stop straight women from oppressing us, and to force straight women to deal with their own Lesbianism. Lesbians cannot develop a common politics with women who do not accept Lesbianism as a political issue.

* * *

† From Ginny Berson, "The Furies," *The Furies: Lesbian/Feminist Monthly* 1.1, (January 1972) reprinted in Nancy Myron and Charlotte Bunch, *Lesbianism and the Women's Movement* (Baltimore: Diana Press, 1975), pp. 17, 18. Reprinted by permission.

The Women's Movement Comes of Age

In the early 1970s, the ruling on *Roe v. Wade* that protected women's right to an abortion in the first trimester of pregnancy, the passage of Title IX of the Education Amendments Act ensuring equality in funding for women in educational institutions that received federal funds, the passage of the Equal Rights Amendment in both the House of the Representatives and Senate, and countless workplace-equity victories signaled growing acceptance of women's equal rights in U.S. society. A variety of women's groups, many identifying themselves as part of a Women's Liberation Movement, developed during this period. Some took on issues raised by Betty Friedan in *The Feminine Mystique*. Pat Mainardi's classic piece on housework demonstrates how this private activity truly is political. Others were the result of women's experiences and intellectual work in other movements. African American feminists started the National Black Feminist Organization in 1973; during the same period Chicana feminists organized groups around the country. As these selections suggest, these activists had their own histories and issues and organized for their own constituencies, while recognizing that they were a part of a larger movement. Feminist theorists from a variety of perspectives expanded feminism beyond Friedan's analysis. bell hooks begins her critique of the white, middle-class perspective of the feminist movement with a reading of *The Feminine Mystique*. For many, the culmination of all aspects of women's rights/ feminist activism was the first National Women's Conference held in Houston, Texas, in 1977. Friedan, along with other leaders of the women's movement, Gloria Steinem and Bella Abzug, as well as First and former First Ladies Betty Ford, Lady Bird Johnson, and Rosalynn Carter, and the wife of the slain civil rights leader Martin Luther King, Jr., Coretta Scott King, participated in this historic event. At the convention, Friedan finally relented in her opposition to including lesbian rights in the women's rights platform. Pokey Anderson, a feminist and lesbian rights activist, describes her reaction to Friedan's about-face.

Title IX, Education Amendments of 1972[†]

No person in the United States shall, on the basis of sex, be excluded from participation in, be denied the benefits of, or be subjected to discrimination under any education program or activity receiving Federal financial assistance. * * *

---

†   From United States Department of Labor, Office of the Assistant Secretary for Administration and Management, *Title IX, Education Amendments of 1972*. Section 1681, Sex (A) Prohibition against discrimination; exceptions. www.dol.gov/oasam/regs/statutes/titleIX.htm. (accessed January 4, 2012).

Equal Rights Amendment[†]

Section 1. Equality of Rights under the law shall not be denied or abridged by the United States or any state on account of sex.

Section 2. The Congress shall have the power to enforce, by appropriate legislation, the provisions of this article.

Section 3. This amendment shall take effect two years after the date of ratification.

PAT MAINARDI

The Politics of Housework[‡]

> Though women do not complain of the power of husbands, each complains of her own husband, or of the husbands of her friends. It is the same in all other cases of servitude; at least in the commencement of the emancipatory movement. The serfs did not at first complain of the power of the lords, but only of their tyranny.
> —John Stuart Mill, *On the Subjection of Women*

Liberated women—very different from women's liberation! The first signals all kinds of goodies, to warm the hearts (not to mention other parts) of the most radical men. The other signals—*housework*. The first brings sex without marriage, sex before marriage, cozy housekeeping arrangements ("You see, I'm living with this chick") and the self-content of knowing that you're not the kind of man who wants a doormat instead of a woman. That will come later. After all, who wants that old commodity anymore, the Standard American Housewife, all husband, home and kids. The New Commodity, the Liberated Woman, has sex a lot and has a Career, preferably something that can be fitted in with the household chores—like dancing, pottery, or painting.

On the other hand is women's liberation—and housework. What? You say this is all trivial? Wonderful! That's what I thought. It seemed perfectly reasonable. We both had careers, both had to work

† From *Equal Rights Amendment*, website of National Organization for Women. www. Now.org/issues/economic/eratext.html. (accessed December 27, 2011).

‡ From Pat Mainardi, "The Politics of Housework," in *Sisterhood is Powerful: An Anthology of Writings from the Women's Liberation Movement*. Ed. Robin Morgan. (New York: Random House, 1970), pp. 447–54.

a couple of days a week to earn enough to live on, so why shouldn't we share the housework? So I suggested it to my mate and he agreed—most men are too hip to turn you down flat. "You're right," he said, "It's only fair."

Then an interesting thing happened. I can only explain it by stating that we women have been brainwashed more than even we can imagine. Probably too many years of seeing television women in ecstasy over their shiny waxed floors or breaking down over their dirty shirt collars. Men have no such conditioning. They recognize the essential fact of housework right from the very beginning. Which is that it stinks. Here's my list of dirty chores: buying groceries, carting them home and putting them away; cooking meals and washing dishes and pots; doing the laundry, digging out the place when things get out of control; washing floors. The list could go on but the sheer necessities are bad enough. All of us have to do these things, or get some one else to do them for us. The longer my husband contemplated these chores, the more repulsed he became, and so proceeded the change from the normally sweet considerate Dr. Jekyll into the crafty Mr. Hyde who would stop at nothing to avoid the horrors of—*housework*. As he felt himself backed into a corner laden with dirty dishes, brooms, mops, and reeking garbage, his front teeth grew longer and pointier, his fingernails haggled and his eyes grew wild. Housework trivial? Not on your life! Just try to share the burden.

So ensued a dialogue that's been going on for several years. Here are some of the high points:

"I don't mind sharing the housework, but I don't do it very well. We should each do the things we're best at."

Meaning: Unfortunately I'm no good at things like washing dishes or cooking. What I do best is a little light carpentry, changing light bulbs, moving furniture (*how often do you move furniture?*).

Also Meaning: Historically the lower classes (black men and us) have had hundreds of years experience doing menial jobs. It would be a waste of manpower to train someone else to do them now.

Also Meaning: I don't like the dull stupid boring jobs, so you should do them.

"I don't mind sharing the work, but you'll have to show me how to do it."

Meaning: I ask a lot of questions and you'll have to show me everything everytime I do it because I don't remember so good. Also don't try to sit down and read while I'm doing my jobs because I'm going to annoy hell out of you until it's easier to do them yourself.

"We used to be so happy!" (Said whenever it was his turn to do something.)

Meaning: I used to be so happy.

Meaning: Life without housework is bliss. (*No quarrel here. Perfect agreement*.)

"We have different standards, and why should I have to work to your standards. That's unfair."

Meaning: If I begin to get bugged by the dirt and crap I will say "This place sure is a sty" or "How can anyone live like this?" and wait for your reaction. I know that all women have a sore called "Guilt over a messy house" or "Household work is ultimately my responsibility." I know that men have caused that sore—if anyone visits and the place *is* a sty, they're not going to leave and say, "He sure is a lousy housekeeper." You'll take the rap in any case. I can outwait you.

Also Meaning: I can provoke innumerable scenes over the housework issue. Eventually doing all the housework yourself will be less painful to you than trying to get me to do half. Or I'll suggest we get a maid. She will do my share of the work. You will do yours. It's women's work.

"I've got nothing against sharing the housework, but you can't make me do it on your schedule."

Meaning: Passive resistance. I'll do it when I damned well please, if at all. If my job is doing dishes, it's easier to do them once a week. If taking out laundry, once a month. If washing the floors, once a year. If you don't like it, do it yourself oftener, and then I won't do it at all.

"I *hate* it more than you. You don't mind it so much."

Meaning: Housework is garbage work. It's the worst crap I've ever done. It's degrading and humiliating for someone of *my* intelligence to do it. But for someone of *your* intelligence . . .

"Housework is too trivial to even talk about."

Meaning: It's even more trivial to do. Housework is beneath my status. My purpose in life is to deal with matters of significance. Yours is to deal with matters of insignificance. You should do the housework.

"This problem of housework is not a man-woman problem! In any relationship between two people one is going to have a stronger personality and dominate."

Meaning: That stronger personality had better be *me*.

"In animal societies, wolves, for example, the top animal is usually a male even where he is not chosen for brute strength but on the basis of cunning and intelligence. Isn't that interesting?"

Meaning: I have historical, psychological, anthropological, and biological justification for keeping you down. How can you ask the top wolf to be equal?

"Women's liberation isn't really a political movement."

Meaning: The Revolution is coming too close to home.

Also Meaning: I am only interested in how *I* am oppressed, not how I oppress others. Therefore the war, the draft, and the university are political. Women's liberation is not.

"Man's accomplishments have always depended on getting help from other people, mostly women. What great man would have accomplished what he did if he had to do his own housework?

Meaning: Oppression is built into the System and I, as the white American male receive the benefits of this System. I don't want to give them up.

Postscript

Participatory democracy begins at home. If you are planning to implement your politics, there are certain things to remember.

1. He *is* feeling it more than you. He's losing some leisure and you're gaining it. The measure of your oppression is his resistance.
2. A great many American men are not accustomed to doing monotonous repetitive work which never ushers in any lasting let alone important achievement. This is why they would rather repair a cabinet than wash dishes. If human endeavors are like a pyramid with man's highest achievements at the top, then keeping oneself alive is at the bottom. Men have always had servants (us) to take care of this bottom strata of life while they have confined their efforts to the rarefied upper regions. It is thus ironic when they ask of women—where are your great painters, statesmen, etc? Mme. Matisse ran a millinery shop so he could paint. Mrs. Martin Luther King kept his house and raised his babies.
3. It is a traumatizing experience for someone who has always thought of himself as being against any oppression or exploitation of one human being by another to realize that in his daily life he has been accepting and implementing

(and benefiting from) this exploitation; that his rationalization is little different from that of the racist who says "Black people don't feel pain" (women don't mind doing the shitwork); and that the oldest form of oppression in history has been the oppression of 50 percent of the population by the other 50 percent.

4. Arm yourself with some knowledge of the psychology of oppressed peoples everywhere, and a few facts about the animal kingdom. I admit playing top wolf or who runs the gorillas is silly but as a last resort men bring it up all the time. Talk about bees. If you feel really hostile bring up the sex life of spiders. They have sex. She bites off his head.

The psychology of oppressed people is not silly. Jews, immigrants, black men, and all women have employed the same psychological mechanisms to survive: admiring the oppressor, glorifying the oppressor, wanting to be like the oppressor, wanting the oppressor to like them, mostly because the oppressor held all the power.

5. In a sense, all men everywhere are slightly schizoid—divorced from the reality of maintaining life. This makes it easier for them to play games with it. It is almost a cliché that women feel greater grief at sending a son off to war or losing him to that war because they bore him, suckled him, and raised him. The men who foment those wars did none of those things and have a more superficial estimate of the worth of human life. One hour a day is a low estimate of the amount of time one has to spend "keeping" oneself. By foisting this off on others, man gains seven hours a week—one working day more to play with his mind and not his human needs. Over the course of generations it is easy to see whence evolved the horrifying abstractions of modern life.

6. With the death of each form of oppression, life changes and new forms evolve. English aristocrats at the turn of the century were horrified at the idea of enfranchising working men—were sure that it signaled the death of civilization and a return to barbarism. Some working men were even deceived by this line. Similarly with the minimum wage, abolition of slavery, and female suffrage. Life changes but it goes on. Don't fall for any line about the death of everything if men take a turn at the dishes. They will imply that you are holding back the Revolution (their Revolution). But you are advancing it (your Revolution).

7. Keep checking up. Periodically consider who's actually *doing* the jobs. These things have a way of backsliding so that a

year later once again the woman is doing everything. After a year make a list of jobs the man has rarely if ever done. You will find cleaning pots, toilets, refrigerators and ovens high on the list. Use time sheets if necessary. He will accuse you of being petty. He is above that sort of thing—(housework). Bear in mind what the worst jobs are, namely the ones that have to be done every day or several times a day. Also the ones that are dirty—it's more pleasant to pick up books, newspapers etc. than to wash dishes. Alternate the bad jobs. It's the daily grind that gets you down. Also make sure that you don't have the responsibility for the housework with occasional help from him. "I'll cook dinner for you tonight" implies it's really your job and isn't he a nice guy to do some of it for you.

8. Most men had a rich and rewarding bachelor life during which they did not starve or become encrusted with crud or buried under the litter. There is a taboo that says that women mustn't strain themselves in the presence of men: we haul around 50 pounds of groceries if we have to but aren't allowed to open a jar if there is someone around to do it for us. The reverse side of the coin is that men aren't supposed to be able to take care of themselves without a woman. Both are excuses for making women do the housework.

9. Beware of the double whammy. He won't do the little things he always did because you're now a "Liberated Woman," right? Of course he won't do anything else either . . .

I was just finishing this when my husband came in and asked what I was doing. Writing a paper on housework. Housework? he said, *Housework?* Oh my god how trivial can you get. A paper on housework.

Little Politics of Housework Quiz

The lowest job in the army, used as punishment is: a) working 9–5; b) kitchen duty (K.P.).

When a man lives with his family, his: a) father b) mother does his housework.

When he lives with a woman, a) he b) she does the housework.

A) his son b) his daughter learns in preschool how much fun it is to iron daddy's handkerchief.

From the *New York Times*, 9/21/69: "Former Greek Official George Mylonas pays the penalty for differing with the ruling junta in Athens by performing household chores on the island of Amorgos where he lives in forced exile" (with hilarious photo of a miserable Mylonas carrying his own water). What the *Times* means is that he ought to have a) indoor plumbing b) a maid.

Dr. Spock said (*Redbook* 3/69): "Biologically and temperamentally I believe, women were made to be concerned first and foremost with child care, husband care, and home care." Think about: a) *who* made us b) why? c) what is the effect on their lives d) what is the effect on our lives?

From *Time* 1/5/70, "Like their American counterparts, many housing project housewives are said to suffer from neurosis. And for the first time in Japanese history, many young husbands today complain of being henpecked. Their wives are beginning to demand detailed explanations when they don't come home straight from work and some Japanese males nowadays are even compelled to do housework." According to *Time*, women become neurotic: a) when they are forced to do the maintenance work for the male caste all day every day of their lives or b) when they no longer want to do the maintenance work for the male caste all day every day of their lives.

NATIONAL BLACK FEMINIST ORGANIZATION

Statement of Purpose[†]

The distorted male-dominated media image of the Women's Liberation Movement has clouded the vital and revolutionary importance of this movement to Third World women, especially Black women. The Movement has been characterized as the exclusive property of so-called "white middle-class" women, and any Black women seen involved in this movement have been seen as "selling out," "dividing the race," and an assortment of nonsensical epithets. Black Feminists resent these charges and have therefore established THE NATIONAL BLACK FEMINIST ORGANIZATION, in order to address ourselves to the particular and specific needs of the larger, but almost cast aside half of the Black race in Amerikkka, the Black woman.

Black women have suffered cruelly in this society from living the phenomenon of being Black and female, in a country that is *both* racist and sexist. There has been very little real examination of the damage it has caused on the lives and on the minds of Black women.

† From National Black Feminist Organization, "Statement of Purpose" (New York: National Black Feminist Organization, 1973), Special Collections, Michigan State University Library, East Lansing, MI. Reprinted by permission.

Because we live in a patriarchy, we have allowed a premium to be put on Black male suffering. No one of us would minimize the pain or hardship or the cruel and inhumane treatment experienced by the Black man. But history, past or present, rarely deals with the malicious abuse put upon the Black woman. We were seen as breeders by the master; despised and historically polarized from/by the master's wife; and looked upon as castrators by our lovers and husbands. The Black woman has had to be strong, yet we are perse-cuted for having survived. We have been called "matriarchs" by white racists and Black nationalists; we have virtually no positive self-images to validate our existence. Black women want to be proud, dignified and free from all those false definitions of beauty and womanhood that are unrealistic and unnatural. We, not white men or Black men, must define our own self-image as Black women and not fall into the mistake of being placed upon the pedestal which is even being rejected by white women. It has been hard for Black women to emerge from the myriad of distorted images that have portrayed us as grinning Beulahs, castrating Sapphires, and pancake box Jemimahs. As Black Feminists, we realized the need to establish ourselves as an independent Black Feminist organization. Our above ground presence will lend enormous credibility to the current Women's Liberation Movement, which unfortunately is not seen as the serious political and economic revolutionary force that it is. We will strengthen the current efforts of the Black Liberation struggle in this country by encouraging *all* of the talents and cre-ativities of Black women to emerge, strong and beautiful, not to feel guilty or devisive, and assume positions of leadership and honor in the Black community. We will encourage the Black community to stop falling into the trap of the white male Left, utilizing women only in terms of domestic or servile needs. We will continue to remind the Black Liberation Movement that there can't be libera-tion for half the race. We must together, as a people, work to elimi-nate racism from without the Black community which is trying to destroy us as an entire people, but we must remember that sexism is destroying and crippling us from within.

Standard Questions You Might be Asked and Suggested Answers That Might Work

Q. What is Feminism?

A. Feminism is the belief of the political, economic and social equality of the sexes. A Feminist is one who believes in feminism and (hopefully) works to eliminate that inequality between men and women. A Feminist believes that the society should provide the opportunity for women to develop as whole human beings . . .

that choices should be provided according to their interests and talents and not solely according to their sex.

Q. What is Sexism?

A. Sexism is prejudice or discrimination towards women on the basis of their sex.

Q. Why a Black Feminist Group?

A. Black women in this country live the phenomenon of being *both* Black and Female in a country that is *both* sexist and racist. We can't expect anyone to organize around the specific oppressions that Black women experience; not White women, because they don't experience racism; not Black men because they don't encounter sexism.

Q. Are you not separating from the Black Movement and thereby dividing the Black race?

A. No, not at all. Black women comprise over half of the Black population in this country. We see ourselves as strengthening the Black community by calling upon all the talents of an entire people to combat racism. We want *all* Black people in this country to be free, and by organizing around our needs as Black women, we are making sure that we won't be left out.

Q. Shouldn't the Black woman be behind her man, giving him support? After all, he has been discriminated against since being in America.

A. We would never deny the injustice or abuse put upon the Black man in this country. But, because we live in a patriarchy, we have allowed a premium to be placed on *male* suffering. Black women have also faced enormous hardship and pain, and rather than getting "behind" someone, we should be supportive of each other. Rather than being the day of the Black man, it is the day of the Black *people*.

Q. Wouldn't it be easier to work within the Black Liberation organizations to implement your goals?

A. Many of us come out of the Civil Rights Movement where people like Stokely Carmichael told women that our position in the Movement should be "prone." It is very difficult to get anyone to work on issues that are not close to their experience. The areas of welfare, domestic workers, reproductive freedom, the unwed mother and many other areas are things we feel are not being addressed, as well as the professional Black woman, sexuality, unemployment and a host of other issues that affect us as Black women.

Q. Are you part of the Women's Liberation Movement?

A. Very much so. Many of us come out of the Women's Movement, but we feel that the duality of being Black and Female made us want to organize around those things which affect us most. It is very important that we, as Black women, set our own priorities. We will lend support to Feminist organizations and will work in coalitions in areas that affect the 53% majority of women in this country.

Q. How can you be associated with "Women's Lib" when it is a white, middle-class bunch of women?

A. First of all, we resent the term, "Women's Lib." We realize that terminology is very important, and just as you wouldn't say Black lib because it would not be taken seriously, then we must reject that as well. Secondly, the distorted media image of the Movement has portrayed it as something that most women couldn't identify with. Those Black women who have been involved with the Movement since its inception have never received any visible recognition. The Black Civil Rights Movement was led by Black middle-class men (King, Carmichael, Newton, etc.). We didn't condemn them, rather, we applauded the fact that they were able to get up and out of their oppression and help turn this country around. But somehow, those over-educated women, with B.A. degrees standing in front of their kitchen sinks, that brought this wave of the Women's Movement around, are not given the same respect. We feel strongly that this Movement is important to all women, and Black Feminists resent the fact that the press has portrayed it as the exclusive property of white women.

Q. But, hasn't the Black woman always been liberated?

A. The Black woman has always had to be strong and survive, but we have not been liberated. The U.S. Department of Labor attests to the fact that Black women earn less annually than Black men and White men and women. While a white woman with a B.A. earns less than a Black man with a high school edu-cation, a Black woman with a B.A. earns less than a Black man with an eighth grade education. The Black woman is on welfare

in a disproportionate number and controls very little economically and politically outside and inside the Black community.

Q. Are you anti-men?

A. No. We are anti-oppression. It is ironic that just as Blacks became
pro-Black, it was seen as being anti-White. Now women are pro-
female and it is seen as anti-male. We are anti-those persons and
forces that would oppress anyone, in private or public life, because
of sex and/or race.

Q. Why can't Black men be involved in the organization?

A. Because it is important for Black women to set our priorities and
organize ourselves. We realize that some of us feel intimidated by
the presence of Black men and we don't want to fall into the trap
of letting them tell us what to do and defining goals. We welcome
the support and encouragement from brothers in terms of bodies
on picket lines for an issue, money and donations, and will assist
any group of men who are serious about forming consciousness-
raising groups.

CONSUELO NIETO

From The Chicana and the Women's Rights Movement[†]

Like the Adelitas who fought with their men in the Mexican Revolution [1910], Chicanas have joined their brothers to fight for social
justice. The Chicana cannot forget the oppression of her people,
her *raza*—male and female alike. She fights to preserve her culture
and demands the right to be unique in America. Her vision is one
of a multicultural society in which one need not surrender to a fil-
tering process and thus melt away to nothingness.

Who is the Chicana? She cannot be defined in precise terms.
Her diversity springs from the heritage of the *indio*, the *español*,
and the *mestizo*.

The heterogeneous background of her people defies the stereotyping. Her roots were planted in this land before the Pilgrims ever

---

† From Consuelo Nieto, "The Chicana and the Women's Rights Movement," *Civil Rights
Digest* 6 (Spring 1974): 36–42, in *Chicana Feminist Thought: The Basic Historical Writ-
ings.* Ed. Alma M. Garcia. (New York and London: Routledge, 1997), pp. 206–11.
Reprinted by permission of the U.S. Commission on Civil Rights.

boarded the Mayflower. As a bicultural person, she participates in two worlds, integrating her Mexican heritage with that of the majority society. The Chicana seeks to affirm her identity as a Mexican-American and a woman and to define her role within this context.

How does her definition relate to women's rights? How does the women's rights movement affect a Chicana's life? The Chicana shares with all women the universal victimhood of sexism. Yet the Chicana's struggle for personhood must be analyzed with great care and sensitivity. Hers is a struggle against sexism within the context of a racist society. Ignore this factor and it is impossible to understand the Chicana's struggle.

The task facing the Chicana is monumental. On the one hand, she struggles to maintain her identity as a Chicana. On the other hand, her demands for equity as a woman involve fundamental cultural change.

The Chicana shares with all women basic needs that cut across ethnic lines. Yet she has distinctive priorities and approaches, for the Chicana is distinct from the Anglo woman. The Chicana's world, culture, and values do not always parallel those of the Anglo woman.

Many Chicanas support the women's movement as it relates to equity in pay and job opportunities, for instance. Yet for some, particularly the non-activists, the closer the movement comes to their personal lives, the more difficult it becomes to tear themselves away from the kinds of roles they have filled.

The lifestyles of Chicanas span a broad and varied continuum. Education, geography, and socioeconomic living conditions are but a few of the variables which make a difference. The urban, educated middle-class Chicana usually has more alternatives, sophisticated skills, and greater mobility than her sisters in the barrios or the fields.

In the worlds of the barrio and *el campo* [the fields], with their limited social options, the role of the woman is often strictly defined. Fewer choices exist. Yet among all groups one finds women who are strong and who have endured.

Traditionally, the Chicana's strength has been exercised in the home where she has been the pillar of family life. It is just this role that has brought her leadership and her abilities to the larger community. The Chicano family is oftentimes an extended one, including grandparents, aunts and uncles, cousins (of all degrees), as well as relatives of spiritual affinity, such as godparents and in-laws.

Chicanas, collectively and individually, have cared for that family. It is the Chicana who goes to her children's school to ask why Juanito cannot read. It is the Chicana who makes the long trip to the social security office to obtain the support needed to keep *viejecita* Carmen going in her one-room apartment when taking in ironing will not do it.

It is *la Chicana* who fights the welfare bureaucracy for her neighbor's family. It is *la Chicana* who, by herself and with her sisters, is developing ways in which the youth of her community can be better cared for when their mothers must leave home to work.

Because life in the poorer barrios is a struggle for survival, the man cannot always participate in such community activities unless they pay a salary. He must provide the material support for his family. This is the tradition. It is in his heart, his conscience.

Chicanas owe much of their freedom to work for their communities to their men. It is the Chicana who often gains and develops those skills and attitudes that provide the basis for the transition of her culture into that of the modern United States. A transition, and yes, even a transformation—but not at the price of dissolving that culture.

Last year I taught an adult education class that included some mothers from the barrio. I'm sure they were not aware of the women's movement per se, but I was amazed at their high degree of interest and concern with the question, "How can I help my daughters so that when they get married they will be able to do things that my husband won't allow me to do?"

None of them thought of trying to change their own lives, because they knew that it was a dead end for them. They would say, "He loves me and I love him. I will accept things as they are for me, but I don't want that for my daughter."

It's not that they didn't view change as personally attractive, but that to demand it would place their family and their home in too much jeopardy. It would mean pulling away from their husbands in a manner that could not be reconciled. And they will not pay that price.

Other women who wanted to enroll in my class could not, because their husbands would not permit them to go out at night or allow them to get involved in activities outside the home during the day. This is not surprising—some Chicanas have many facets of their lives more tightly controlled by their husbands than do their Anglo sisters. For some women of the barrio, their hope is to achieve that measure of control over their own lives that many Anglo women already have.

Similarly, some Chicano men will state that they are fighting for their women, but not for that kind of status and position that would give women equal footing. They are fighting to be able to provide for their women the social and economic status and position that Anglo men have been able to give Anglo women.

The Church

The role of the Catholic Church in the history of the Chicana is an important one. Not all Chicanos are Catholic, and among those who belong to the Church, not all participate actively. But since the arrival of the Spanish, the values, traditions, and social patterns of the Church have been tightly interwoven in Chicano family life.

The respect accorded the Church by many Chicanos must not be shrugged aside. Many will support or oppose a particular issue simply on the basis of "the Church's position." For these people it is very difficult to assess a "moral" issue outside the pale of Church authority and legitimacy.

For the most part, the Church has assumed a traditional stance toward women. It has clearly defined the woman's role as that of wife and mother, requiring obedience to one's husband.

The words of the apostle Paul have been used to justify this attitude: "As Christ is head of the Church and saves the whole body, so is a husband the head of his wife, and as the Church submits to Christ, so should wives submit to their husbands in everything."

Also: "A man certainly should not cover his head, since he is the image of God and reflects God's glory; but woman is the reflection of man's glory. For man did not come from woman; no, woman came from man; and man was not created for the sake of woman, but woman was created for the sake of man."

Marianismo (veneration of the Virgin Mary) has had tremendous impact upon the development of the Chicana. Within many Chicano homes, *La Virgen*—under various titles, but especially as *La Virgen de Guadalupe*—has been the ultimate role model for the Chicano woman.

Mary draws her worth and nobility from her relationship to her son, Jesus Christ. She is extolled as mother, as nurturer. She is praised for her endurance of pain and sorrow, her willingness to serve, and her role as teacher of her son's word. She is Queen of the Church.

Some Chicanas are similarly praised as they emulate the sanctified example set by Mary. The woman par excellence is mother and wife. She is to love and support her husband and to nurture and teach her children. Thus may she gain fulfillment as a woman.

For a Chicana bent upon fulfillment of her personhood, this restricted perspective of her role as a woman is not only inadequate but crippling.

Some Chicanas further question the Church's prerogative to make basic decisions unilaterally about women's lives. When the Church speaks out on issues such as divorce, remarriage, and birth control, those Chicanas wonder, "Who can really make these decisions for me? Upon what basis should such choices be made?"

Many Chicanas still have a strong affiliation with the Church and seek its leadership and support as they attempt to work out their lives. Others try to establish their identity as women on their own, yet choose not to break with Church mandates.

Still others find this middle road too difficult. They choose not to work within Church structure and seek their independence totally outside the folds of religion. Chicanas find that to advocate feminist positions frowned upon by the Church often evokes family criticism and pressure. Thus some compromise personal values and feign conformity for the sake of peace within the family.

Concerned leaders within the Church do speak out in behalf of the Chicana's struggle for equity. But this is not the norm. While the Church supports equal pay and better working conditions, it would find it most difficult to deal with the sexism expressed in its own hierarchy or within the family model.

Brothers and Sisters

Chicanos often question the goals of the women's movement. Some see it as an "Anglo woman's trip," divisive to the cause of *el movimiento* [The Chicano movement]. These men assert the need to respect women, but women's liberation . . . ? "That deals with trivia, minutiae—we all must concentrate on the battle for social justice."

Many of our brothers see the women's movement as another force which will divert support from *la causa*. On a list of priorities, many Chicanos fail to see how the plight of *la mujer* can be of major concern within the context of la raza's problems. They see the women's movement as a vehicle to entrench and strengthen the majority of culture's dominance. They are concerned that their sister may be deceived and manipulated. They warn her never to be used as a pawn against her own people.

Yet the Chicana may sometimes ask, "Is it your real fear, my brother, that I be used against our movement? Or is it that I will assume a position, a stance, that you are neither prepared nor willing to deal with?"

Other Chicanos may be more sensitive and try to help their sisters achieve a higher status, but the fact that they, too, usually limit the aspirations of their sisters is soon evident. They would open the doors to new roles and new alternatives, but on a selective basis. Some support upward mobility for their sisters in the professions, but reneg when it comes to equality at home.

A good number of Chicanos fear that in embracing the women's movement their sisters will negate the very heritage they both seek to preserve. The Chicana would ask her brother, "To be a Chicana—proud and strong in my culture—must I be a static being? Does not the role of women change as life changes?"

Dealing with Contradictions

Participation within organizations of the women's rights movement can bring to the Chicana a painful sense of alienation from some women of the majority culture. The Chicana may often feel like a marginal figure. Her Anglo sisters assure her that their struggle unequivocally includes her within its folds.

Yet as she listens carefully, certain contradictions will soon emerge. The Anglo women will help the Chicana by providing a model, a system to emulate. The Anglo will help the Chicana erase those "differences" that separate them. Hence, "We will all be united under the banner of Woman. This will be our first and primary source of identity."

For a Chicana allied with the struggle of her people, such a simplistic approach to her identity is not acceptable. Furthermore, it is difficult for the Chicana to forget that some Anglo women have oppressed her people within this society, and are still not sensitive to minorities or their needs. With Anglo women the Chicana may share a commitment to equality, yet it is very seldom that she will find with them the camaraderie, the understanding, the sensitivity that she finds with her own people.

Anglo women sensitive to Chicanas as members of a minority must guard against a very basic conceptual mistake. All minorities are not alike. To understand the black woman is not to understand the Chicana. To espouse the cause of minority women, Anglos must recognize our distinctiveness as separate ethnic groups.

For example, in dealing with sex role stereotyping in schools, a multicultural approach should be used. Materials must encompass all groups of women. Women's studies courses should not exclude the unique history of minority women from the curriculum.

And the inclusion of one minority group is not enough. Chicanas know only too well the pain of negation that comes from omission. The affront of exclusion may not be intentional, but to the victim that doesn't matter. The result is the same.

What does it mean to be a Chicana? This question the Chicana alone must answer. Chicanas must not allow their brothers or other women to define their identity. Our brothers are often only too ready to tell us "who" we are as Chicanas.

Conversely, some Chicanas seeking fulfillment in *la causa* do not question or challenge the parameters set down for them by Chicanos—or more basically, they do not challenge the male's right to such authority.

Similarly, a woman who has never shared our culture and history cannot fully grasp the measure of our life experiences. She will be unable to set goals, priorities, and expectations for Chicanas.

Chicanas must raise their own level of awareness. Too many do not recognize their repression and the extent of it. Many have come to accept it as the norm rather than as a deviance.

Chicanas also need to deal with their men openly. Perhaps the Chicana has been overly protective of her brothers. Hers is a difficult role. She must be sensitive to his struggle, but not at the cost of her own identity. She must support him as he strives to attain the equality too long denied him, but she too must no longer be denied. To fight and provide for the fulfillment of the Chicano while denying equality to women does not serve the true aims of *la causa*, and will not liberate our people in the real sense.

What must the Chicana do? First, she must work with her own sisters to define clearly her role, her goals, and her strategies. This, I would suggest, can be done by involvement in one of the many Chicana feminist organizations that are currently emerging.

Second, she must be involved with Chicanos in the Chicano movement. Here the Chicana must sensitize the male to the fact that she, as a woman, is oppressed and that he is a part of that oppression. She must reinforce the *carnalismo* (spirit of fraternity) that is theirs, but point out that as long as his status as a man is earned at her expense, he is not truly free.

The Chicana must tell her brother, "I am not here to emasculate you; I am here to fight with you shoulder to shoulder as an equal. If you can only be free when I take second place to you, then you are not truly free—and I want freedom for you as well as for me."

A third mandate I would give the Chicana is to participate in the mainstream of the women's rights movement. She is needed here to provide the Chicana perspective as well as to provide support for the activities designed to help all women. Moreover, her unique role as a liaison person is crucial. How tragic it would be if all women did not promote and participate in a valid working coalition to advance our common cause?

Chicanas must avoid a polarization that isolates them from Chicanos as well as other women. They must carefully analyze each situation, as well as the means to reconcile differences. This is not easy—it requires a reservoir of understanding, patience, and commitment. Yet unless it is done, success will not be ours.

Finally, the Chicana must demand that dignity and respect within the women's rights movement that allows her to practice

feminism within the context of her own culture. The timing and
the choices must be hers. Her models and those of her daughters
will be an Alicia Escalante and a Dolores Huerta. Her approaches
to feminism must be drawn from her own world, and not be shadowy replicas drawn from Anglo society. The Chicana will fight for
her right to uniqueness; she will not be absorbed.

For some it is sufficient to say, "I am woman." For me it must be,
"I am Chicana."

BELL HOOKS

From Feminist Theory from Margin to Center[†]

Feminism in the United States has never emerged from the women
who are most victimized by sexist oppression; women who are daily
beaten down, mentally, physically, and spiritually—women who are
powerless to change their condition in life. They are a silent majority. A mark of their victimization is that they accept their lot in life
without visible question, without organized protest, without collective anger or rage. Betty Friedan's *The Feminine Mystique*[1] is still
heralded as having paved the way for contemporary feminist
movement—it was written as if these women did not exist. Friedan's
famous phrase, "the problem that has no name," often quoted to
describe the condition of women in this society, actually referred to
the plight of a select group of college-educated, middle and upper
class, married white women—housewives bored with leisure, with
the home, with children, with buying products, who wanted more
out of life. Friedan concludes her first chapter by stating: "We can
no longer ignore that voice within women that says: 'I want something more than my husband and my children and my house.'" That
"more" she defined as careers. She did not discuss who would be
called in to take care of the children and maintain the home if
more women like herself were freed from their house labor and
given equal access with white men to the professions. She did not
speak of the needs of women without men, without children, without homes. She ignored the existence of all non-white women and
poor white women. She did not tell readers whether it was more

---

[†] From bell hooks, *Feminist Theory From Margin to Center* (Boston: South End Press,
   1984) pp. 1–4, 165. All notes are the author's. Reprinted by permission.
1. Although *The Feminine Mystique* has been criticized and even attacked from various
   fronts, I call attention to it again because certain biased premises about the nature of
   woman's social status put forth initially in this text continue to shape the tenor and
   direction of feminist movement.

fulfilling to be a maid, a babysitter, a factory worker, a clerk, or a prostitute, than to be a leisure class housewife.

She made her plight and the plight of white women like herself synonymous with a condition affecting all American women. In so doing, she deflected attention away from her classism, her racism, her sexist attitudes towards the masses of American women. In the context of her book, Friedan makes clear that the women she saw as victimized by sexism were college-educated, white women who were compelled by sexist conditioning to remain in the home. She contends:

> It is urgent to understand how the very condition of being a housewife can create a sense of emptiness, non-existence, nothingness in women. There are aspects of the housewife role that make it almost impossible for a woman of adult intelligence to retain a sense of human identity, the firm core of self or "I" without which a human being, man or woman, is not truly alive. For women of ability, in America today, I am convinced that there is something about the housewife state itself that is dangerous.[2]

Specific problems and dilemmas of leisure class white housewives were real concerns that merited consideration and change but they were not the pressing political concerns of masses of women. Masses of women were concerned about economic survival, ethnic and racial discrimination, etc. When Friedan wrote *The Feminine Mystique*, more than one third of all women were in the work force. Although many women longed to be housewives, only women with leisure time and money could actually shape their identities on the model of the feminine mystique. They were women who, in Friedan's words, were "told by the most advanced thinkers of our time to go back and live their lives as if they were Noras, restricted to the doll's house by Victorian prejudices."[3]

From her early writing, it appears that Friedan never wondered whether or not the plight of college-educated, white housewives was an adequate reference point by which to gauge the impact of sexism or sexist oppression on the lives of women in American society. Nor did she move beyond her own life experience to acquire an expanded perspective on the lives of women in the United States. I say this not to discredit her work. It remains a useful discussion of the impact of sexist discrimination on a select group of women. Examined from a different perspective, it can also be seen as a case study of narcissism, insensitivity, sentimentality, and self-indulgence which reaches its peak when Friedan, in a chapter titled "Progressive

2. Betty Friedan, *The Feminine Mystique*, p. 15.
3. Friedan, p. 32.

Dehumanization," makes a comparison between the psychological effects of isolation on white housewives and the impact of confinement on the self-concept of prisoners in Nazi concentration camps.[4]

Friedan was a principal shaper of contemporary feminist thought. Significantly, the one-dimensional perspective on women's reality presented in her book became a marked feature of the contemporary feminist movement. Like Friedan before them, white women who dominate feminist discourse today rarely question whether or not their perspective on women's reality is true to the lived experiences of women as a collective group. Nor are they aware of the extent to which their perspectives reflect race and class biases, although there has been a greater awareness of biases in recent years. Racism abounds in the writings of white feminists, reinforcing white supremacy and negating the possibility that women will bond politically across ethnic and racial boundaries. Past feminist refusal to draw attention to and attack racial hierarchies suppressed the link between race and class. Yet class structure in American society has been shaped by the racial politic of white supremacy; it is only by analyzing racism and its function in capitalist society that a thorough understanding of class relationships can emerge. *Class struggle is inextricably bound to the struggle to end racism.* Urging women to explore the full implication of class in an early essay, "The Last Straw," Rita Mae Brown explained:

> Class is much more than Marx's definition of relationship to the means of production. Class involves your behavior, your basic assumptions about life. Your experience (determined by your class) validates those assumptions, how you are taught to behave, what you expect from yourself and from others, your concept of a future, how you understand problems and solve them, how you think, feel, act. It is these behavioral patterns that middle class women resist recognizing although they may be perfectly willing to accept class in Marxist terms, a neat trick that helps them avoid really dealing with class behavior and changing that behavior in themselves. It is these behavioral patterns which must be recognized, understood, and changed.[5]

White women who dominate feminist discourse, who for the most part make and articulate feminist theory, have little or no understanding of white supremacy as a racial politic, of the psychological impact of class, of their political status within a racist, sexist, capitalist state.

---

4. Friedan, "Progressive Dehumanization," p. 305.
5. Rita Mae Brown, "The Last Straw," in *Class and Feminism*, p. 15.

Plan of Action adopted at 1977 National Women's Conference, Houston, Texas[†]

The plan of action adopted at the 1977 National Women's Conference featured 26 resolutions, or planks, on the following topics:

Arts and humanities: Women should have equal opportunities in federal posts and equal access to arts grants.

Battered women: A national clearinghouse must be created to support local organizations helping battered women and working to prevent domestic violence.

Business: More government contracts to women-owned businesses, which numbered less than one percent in 1977.

Child abuse: More prevention, treatment and protective services.

Child care: Care must be low cost and high quality.

Credit: The Equal Credit Opportunity Act must be enforced to make sure that women are no longer denied credit on the basis of gender.

Disabled women: Equal access to education, training, employment and child custody rights.

Education: More women in leadership positions and in textbooks. Title IX must be enforced.

Elective and appointive office: More representation of women.

Employment: More job opportunities and less discrimination.

Equal Rights Amendment: The ERA must be ratified.

Health: Health insurance benefits must include family planning and other concerns relevant to women.

Homemakers: Must be covered under Social Security and have greater economic security, especially in the event of divorce or the death of a spouse.

† From "Resolution Topics" on website for the film "Sisters of '77," a film produced by Public Broadcasting Service, Independent Lens on the National Women's Conference in Houston, Texas, in 1977. http://www.pbs.org/independentlens/sistersof77/conference .html (accessed July 31, 2011). Text written by Lisa Ko. Reprinted by permission of Independent Television Services, Inc.

Insurance: Eliminate practices that deny women coverage on the basis of gender.

International affairs: Increase the number of women in the departments of state and defense, aid women in developing nations and promote nuclear disarmament.

Media: More women in media jobs, especially in leadership positions.

Minority women: Eliminate discrimination, support affirmative action, guarantee tribal rights and prevent deportation of mothers of American-born children.

Offenders: Improve health services and educational and vocational training.

Older women: Help older women live with dignity.

Rape: Expand the definition of rape to include married men who abuse their wives and reduce legal burdens on victims.

Reproductive freedom: Support *Roe v. Wade*, promote family planning and allow Medicaid payments for abortion.

Rural women: Create a federal rural education policy and expand ownership rights for farm wives.

Sexual preference: Implement legislation to eliminate discrimination on the basis of sexual preference and repeal state laws restricting private sexual behavior between consenting adults.

Statistics: Federal agencies should collect and analyze data in ways that assess the impact on women.

Women, welfare and poverty: Improve social security and retirement systems, raise minimum wage, provide child care and focus on welfare and poverty as major women's issues.

Continuing committee of the conference: Create a committee to follow up on recommendations and take steps to convene a Second National Women's Conference.

POKEY ANDERSON

From An Idiosyncratic Tour of Houston[†]

Albert Thomas Convention Center, Smith at Capitol. On November 18–21, 1977, 2,000 delegates from all over the United States gathered for the International Women's Year (IWY) conference. I was a Texas IWY delegate and a board member of the National Gay Task Force, which had worked in coalitions for a year to get progressive delegates elected at the state level, outorganizing and outmaneuvering the right wing. On the last day of the national plenary sessions, it came time for lesbian issues to be considered. Jean O'Leary, Charlotte Bunch, and Ellie Smeal were among those who spoke. Then Betty Friedan, legendary mother of modern feminism and equally legendary opponent of lesbian rights, stepped up to the mike. "I am known to be violently opposed to the lesbian issue in the women's movement, and in fact I have been," Friedan said that night. "As someone who has grown up in Peoria, Illinois, and who has loved men—perhaps too well—I have had trouble with this issue. I now see that there is nothing in the ERA that will give any protection to homosexuals. We must help women who are lesbians win their own civil rights." I was dumbfounded. She'd reversed herself! When the vote was taken, an overwhelming majority rose to confirm the lesbian rights resolution. As our 1,000 helium-filled balloons proclaiming "We Are Everywhere" floated to the ceiling, pandemonium broke out. We cried, we jumped on the chairs, we danced in the aisles. * * *

THE BACKLASH AGAINST FEMINISM AND *THE FEMININE MYSTIQUE*

The Feminine Mystique and its author have always been a touchstone for the backlash against feminism. When the book was excerpted in women's magazines, large numbers of women responded angrily, testifying to their own fulfillment as wives and mothers, and accusing Friedan of trying to destroy American families (see selections from letters on pp. 380–81, and the essay by Jessica Weiss, pp. 504–09). These readers soon found a public defender. Friedan had been critical of conservative housewife-writers in *The Feminine Mystique*, including the popular, Pulitzer Prize–winning, poet-housewife Phyllis McGinley. Friedan

---

[†] From Pokey Anderson, "An Idiosyncratic Tour of Houston," in *Good*, ed. Toni Beauchamp and Jeff Beauchamp (Houston, Texas, 2000) p. 31. Reprinted by permission.

accused them of denying the "satisfying hard work involved in their stories, poems and plays" (108). Encouraged by her publisher, McGinley
mounted a spirited rebuttal in her book, *Sixpence in My Pocket*. Her
anti-Friedan position resonated with the public. The book became a
bestseller, and on June 18, 1965, she was featured in the cover story of
Time magazine. The story subtly derided feminists like Friedan, suggesting they were "rigid and somewhat outmoded," while applauding McGinley's message that "there are still ample rewards and nourishment to be
found in woman's noblest and most venerable role as keeper of the
home."[1] This skirmish was just the start of a larger battle. In the 1970s,
Phyllis Schlafly, a Harvard-educated Republican Party activist, wife,
and mother, mounted a powerful grassroots campaign to stop the Equal
Rights Amendment (STOP ERA). She organized a counter-demonstration
at the 1977 National Women's Conference that drew thousands. Schlafly
wrote *The Power of the Positive Woman* (1977) to challenge the core
goals and values of the women's movement. The ERA did not become
law, in part because of Schlafly's successful organizing. According to
Susan Faludi, the author of *Backlash: The Undeclared War Against
American Women*, the 1980s saw a multi-front backlash against feminism. Even Betty Friedan herself was implicated in this turn to the right.

PHYLLIS SCHLAFLY

From Feminist Fantasies[†]

Choosing a Career

Marriage and motherhood have always been the number-one career
choice of the large majority of women. Do they still make a viable
career for the modern woman? Do they represent servitude or fulfillment? Are they, as the women's liberation movement would have
us believe, a relic from a bygone era, the institutionalized serfdom
from which women must be freed if they are to find their own identity and self-fulfillment?

What is it that the women's liberation movement invites women
to be liberated from? An objective reading of feminist literature
compels the conclusion that the answer must be marriage, home,
husband, family, and children—because, by definition, those are
all evidences of the "second-class status" of women. Feminist literature paints marriage as slavery, the home (in Betty Friedan's words)
as a "comfortable concentration camp," the husband as the oppres-

---

1. See "Books: The Telltale Hearth," *Time* June 18, 1965, pp. 75–76.
† From Phyllis Schlafly, *Feminist Fantasies* (Dallas, TX: Spence Publishing Co., 2003),
   "Choosing a Career" (1977) pp. 195–98. Reprinted by permission of Phyllis Schlafly
   from *Feminist Fantasies*.

sor, the family as an anachronism no longer relevant to woman's happiness, and children as the daily drudgery from which the modern woman must be freed in order to pursue more fulfilling careers.

Long before women's lib came along and made "housewife" a term of derision, it had its own unique dignity. The 1933 edition of the *Oxford English Dictionary* defined a housewife as "a woman (usually, a married woman) who manages or directs the affairs of her household; the mistress of a family; the wife of a householder. Often (with qualifying words), a woman who manages her household with skill and thrift, a domestic economist." A housewife is a home executive: planning, organizing, leading, coordinating, and controlling. She can set her own schedule and standards and have the freedom to engage in everything from children to civic work, from politics to gardening. What man on a job can do that? Marriage and motherhood are not for every woman, but before a young woman rejects it out of hand, she should give it fair consideration as one of her options.

What does a woman want out of life? If you want to love and be loved, marriage offers the best opportunity to achieve your goal. Men may want, or think they want, a cafeteria selection of lunch-counter sex. But most women continue to want what the old popular song calls "a Sunday kind of love." Marriage and motherhood give a woman new identity and the opportunity for all-round fulfillment as a woman.

Israeli premier Golda Meir was the outstanding career woman of her time. She achieved more in a man's world than any woman in any country—and she did it on ability, not on her looks or her legs: The Gallup Poll repeatedly identified her as the most admired woman in the world. Yet Golda Meir said that having a baby is the most fulfilling thing a woman can ever do, and she put down the women's liberationists as a bunch of "bra-burning nuts."

If young women think that there are greater career satisfactions in being elected to important positions, traveling to exciting far-away places, having executive authority over large numbers of people, winning a big lawsuit, or earning a financial fortune than there are in having a baby, they are wrong. None of those measures of career success can compare with the thrill, satisfaction, and fun of having and caring for babies and watching them respond and grow under a mother's loving care.

The joys of motherhood return late in life when grandchildren appear. Most feminist leaders, including Gloria Steinem, Germaine Greer, Kate Millett, and Simone de Beauvoir chose to be childless and will never know the thrill of being "born again" with grandchildren.

Amelia Earhart has been a longtime heroine of feminists because she lived such an independent and exciting life. Yet when her true story was dramatized on national television in October 1976, she was shown cuddling another woman's baby—and wishing it were her own.

One of the most successful writers of the twentieth century was Taylor Caldwell. When *Family Weekly* asked her if it didn't give her solid satisfaction to know that her novel *Captains and Kings* was to be seen as a nine-hour television production, she replied: "There is no solid satisfaction in any career for a woman like myself. There is no home, no true freedom, no hope, no joy, no expectation for tomorrow, no contentment. I would rather cook a meal for a man and bring him his slippers and feel myself in the protection of his arms than have all the citations and awards and honors I have received worldwide, including the Ribbon of the Legion of Honor and my property and my bank accounts."

Anne Morrow Lindbergh spoke for the majority of women when she described her own priorities in *Hour of Gold, Hour of Lead*: "The sheer fact of finding myself loved was unbelievable and changed my world, my feelings about life and myself. I was given confidence, strength, and almost a new character. The man I was to marry believed in me and what I could do, and consequently, I found I could do more than I realized, even in that mysterious outer world that fascinated me but seemed unattainable. He opened the door to 'real life.' . . . The first months of motherhood were totally normal, joyful, and satisfying and I would have been content to stay home and do nothing else but care for my baby. This was 'real life' at its most basic level."

Marriage and motherhood have their trials and tribulations, but what lifestyle doesn't? If you look upon your home as a cage, you will find yourself just as imprisoned in an office or a factory. The flight from the home is a flight from self, from responsibility, from the nature of woman, in pursuit of false hopes and fading fantasies.

If you complain about servitude to a husband, servitude to a boss will be more intolerable. Everyone in the world has a boss of some kind. It is easier for most women to achieve a harmonious working relationship with a husband than with a foreman, supervisor, or office manager.

That American women have always been fortunate was confirmed more than 150 years ago by the famous French commentator Alexis de Tocqueville: "Although the women of the United States are confined within the narrow circle of domestic life, and their situation is in some respects one of extreme dependence, I have nowhere seen woman occupying a loftier position; and if I were asked, now that I am drawing to the close of this work, in which I have spoken of so many important things done by the Americans, to what the singular prosperity and growing strength of that people ought mainly to be attributed, I should reply: to the superiority of their women."

SUSAN FALUDI

From Backlash: The Undeclared War Against American Women[†]

* * *

In *The Second Stage*, published in 1981, Friedan issued many * * * charges against the women's movement. Its leaders had ignored the maternal call: "Our failure was our blind spot about the family." Not only that, Friedan's book alleged, the feminist campaign often mistakenly concentrated on "direct" and "confrontational" political tactics—tactics she herself had pioneered but which she now found too "masculine"—when they should be trying volunteerism and taking up a more genteel "Beta style."

Friedan was not the only famous feminist yanking out the stitches in her own handiwork. A handful of authors whose best-selling books helped popularize the women's liberation movement in the '70s were busy issuing retractions. To the New Right, the new words of the old-line feminists were almost too good to be true. "Feminism, which once helped open windows of opportunity for women, has turned against itself," rejoiced Reagan aide Dinesh D'Souza, managing editor of the neoconservative *Policy Review*. After the *New York Times Magazine* featured an excerpt of *The Second Stage* on its cover, Phyllis Schlafly exulted in her news letter that Friedan had "just put another nail in the coffin of feminism."

By the mid-'80s, the voices of feminist recantation became a din, as the media picked up the words of a few symbolically important feminists and rebroadcast them nationwide. Many of these new books read like extended and hastily slapped together press releases. For the most part, these "leaders'" moment under the camera lights had actually long since passed; but, like the retiring male feminist Warren Farrell, they hoped to reclaim center stage.

While there were plenty of feminist thinkers—new and old, famous and obscure—who stood firm in their political beliefs, they were invisible to the media's roving eye. The one new self-proclaimed "feminist" theoretician that the press did pluck from obscurity was actually an embittered antifeminist academic. Literary scholar Camille Paglia became an overnight celebrity, landing on the cover of both *New York* and *Harper's* the same month, soon after launching a vitriolic attack on "whining" feminists in her 1990 book, *Sexual*

---

† From "Betty Friedan: Revisionism as a Marketing Tool," Copyright © 1991 by Susan Faludi, from *Backlash: The Undeclared War Against American Women* by Susan Faludi (New York: Crown Publishers, 1991), pp. 318–24. Used by permission of Crown Publishers, a division of Random House, Inc.

Personae: Art and Decadence from Nefertiti to Emily Dickinson. The press assiduously recycled her antifemale and antifeminist zingers ("If civilization had been left in female hands, we would still be living in grass huts," and, "[Feminist scholars] can't think their way out of a wet paper bag"); *Newsday* featured her dismissal of date rape as feminist nonsense; and television producers raced to option her book. And what was Paglia's motive—freely admitted—for assailing feminists? Simple spite. Rival literary scholars who were feminists, she complained, had grabbed all the "acclaim" and failed to be "respectful" of her prodigious talents, a situation that consigned her to the nontenure track at the unsung Philadelphia University of the Arts and allowed her book to be snubbed by seven publishers. It was then, as she told a *New York* writer later, that she began "preparing my revenge" against feminist academics.

In 1984, feminist Germaine Greer followed up *The Female Eunuch*, her 1970 smash-hit celebration of female independence and sexuality, with the dour and deterministic *Sex and Destiny*. Formerly the media's favorite as a flamboyant advocate of sexual emancipation—a "saucy feminist that even men like," a *Life* cover story had declared at the time—Greer now championed arranged marriages, chastity, and the chador, and named as her new role model the old-fashioned peasant wife, happily confined to kitchen and nursery and happily concealed under her chador. Greer herself billed the book an "attack upon the ideology of sexual freedom." Ironically, just as Concerned Women of America's Beverly LaHaye was endorsing birth control, sex for fun, and clitoral orgasms, Greer was signaling her opposition to all three. The best form of contraception, she asserted, was abstinence. Clitoral orgasms are too "one-dimensional" and "masculine," she wrote.

By 1986, antifeminist spokesmen were also making much of the revisionist murmurings of feminist activist Susan Brownmiller, author of the 1975 landmark work on rape, *Against Our Will*, who was now saying the women's movement may have overlooked "profound biological and psychological differences" between the sexes. The author of a meticulously documented historical analysis of sexual violence, Brownmiller now produced a footnoteless and fuzzy look at feminine behavior through the ages. *Femininity* pondered such pressing issues as whether a hair on Brownmiller's face was the result of "unholy ambition"—or, perhaps, "some dormant source of testosterone within my system"—and whether she should pluck it. The answer to that last question: yes.

As the decade progressed, these famous '70s feminists would continue to churn out increasingly retrograde fare. In her 1990 memoir about her weak-willed father, *Daddy, We Hardly Knew You*, Greer nearly outdid Philip Wylie's Momism in her demonization of mother—"the mad dog in the kitchen," as she called her, a literalized bitch who was always "foaming at the mouth" and emasculating dad. Meanwhile, Brownmiller turned her literary gun sights on a *victim* of domestic violence; on the *New York Times* op-ed page and in *Waverly Place*, a fictionalized and hurriedly issued account of the celebrated case of Lisa Steinberg (the New York City child beaten to death by her adoptive father), Brownmiller reserved her harshest words for the failings of the battered wife. (She finished the book before the court verdict even came in.) And celebrated feminist author Erica Jong quickly joined the recanters. (Her support for feminism had actually always been rather equivocal, despite a public reputation as a leading "libber," bestowed upon her by the press after *Fear of Flying* became a hit.) Not only did her liberated characters eat their words, she disavowed the cause herself—in *Ms.*, of course. Women of "my generation," she wrote, "look longingly at the marriages of our parents and grandparents. . . . Alone in our single-parent families, still searching for the one great love, we begin to smell a rat."

But of all the declarations of apostasy, *The Second Stage* had the potential to be the most damaging to the feminist cause. Betty Friedan was the household name, synonymous in the minds of millions of Americans with the women's liberation movement. She was "the mother of the modern women's movement," as hundreds of newspaper articles had called her, ever since her 1963 classic, *The Feminine Mystique*, first gave voice to "the problem that has no name" and helped catalyze a movement for social change. That book was Friedan's labor of love; she spent years researching and writing in an annex of the dusty New York Public Library. Yet, here she was, two decades later, attacking the "feminist mystique" and accusing the women's movement of "breeding a new problem that has no name'"—in a thinly documented book that often reads as if it were dictated into a tape machine. What happened?

One gets few insights directly from Friedan herself. "I don't use the term 'feminist mystique' in my book," Friedan says in an interview, sounding indignant. Reminded that she, in fact, uses that term *twice* in the first fifty pages, she responds, "Well, there was some extremism in the '70s. The radical feminists started a reactive feminism that was limited and wrong and distorted." Anyone who disagrees with her is simply dismissed as one of those radical feminists who is "still locked into first-stage thinking themselves" and "threatened by my attempt to reconceptualize the movement."

The "radical feminists" of the '70s have executed many serious strategic missteps, according to Friedan's book. Feminists, she says, were so caught up seeking access to the men's world that they failed to "affirm the differences between men and women" and celebrate the "female sensitivities to life." They shouldn't have devoted their

energies to protesting rape (a problem that 88 percent of women
cited in a 1989 Yankelovich poll as the "most important issue for
women today"); in her view, marching against sexual violence is a
"kind of wallowing in that victim-state" that "dissipates our own
well-springs of generative power." (Her words recall George Gilder's
in *Men and Marriage*; he, too, complained of feminists "palavering
endlessly" about rape.) They lost the ERA by being "co-opted by 'masculine' political power." They focused too much on issues like abortion rights, which are "surely," she sniffs, "not the main problems in
America today." In fact, the movement's continued emphasis on
women's rights itself is misguided. "I do not think," Friedan writes,
"women's rights are the most urgent business for American women."

Why was Friedan stomping on a movement that she did so much
to create and lead? Perhaps under the backlash the tendency to
turn and bite one's tail is inevitable. As feminist scholar Judith Stacey writes: "Aging, in the right-wing and 'postfeminist' climate of
the 1980s, has been a traumatic experience for many Second Wave
feminists, and we lack convenient scapegoats for our distress. . . .
Perhaps this accounts for the strident and unmodulated quality of
recantation in the new pro-family feminism." But in Friedan's case,
another possibility presents itself as well. A closer reading of *The
Second Stage* suggests that the prime mistake the "radical feminists"
made was not following her orders. Friedan may say she "easily
related" to the "Beta style" of leaderless, cooperative, and "relational"
organization that her book expounds. Yet her book is punctuated
with the tantrums of a fallen leader who is clearly distressed and
angry that she wasn't allowed to be the Alpha wolf as long as she
would have liked.

Much of the book is insistently self-referential, devoted to rehash-
ing power struggles she lost at long-forgotten feminist conferences,
reprints of her old speeches, and complaints that other feminists
kept ignoring her proposals. Friedan's penchant for imperial
decrees and self-dramatization is long-standing. In 1970, she
retired as president of NOW with the words, "I have led you into
history. I leave you now—to make new history."

Her departure was an embattled one—Friedan versus the "radical feminists" was how she cast it at the time—and ever since, her
accounts of political infighting have featured the same subtext: she
was unfairly locked out of the feminist power structure. While the
general public may have been under the impression that she was
the movement's leading "mother," she felt that she had been too
quickly relegated to the media sidelines, shoved aside in favor of
younger and more photogenic leaders. She may have been dubbed
feminism's "mother," but the media had designated Gloria Steinem

literally, the movement's "glamour girl"—and Friedan well knew which was the more prized honorific in America.

Rather than understanding the media bias as the press's typical preference for youthful blondes, she came to suspect that feminist women themselves were plotting to depose her. While philosophical differences certainly existed, sometimes sharply, within the women's liberation movement (as they do within every political movement), Friedan seemed to believe all the internal debates added to, in her words, a "scheme," a cabal that excluded her. She lashed back in the press in 1972, accusing Steinem of "ripping off the movement for private profit" and announcing "No one should mistake [Steinem] for a leader." Years later, in Marcia Cohen's *The Sisterhood*, the 1988 chronicle of the women's movement, Friedan was still fixated on this theme. "Gloria [Steinem] wanted me to disappear," she told the author. "She just wanted to *disappear* me."

The "new history" Friedan's book scripts for feminism is a "second-stage solution," a call for a murkily defined new order that is heavy on old Victorian rhetorical flourishes. In this new stage she envisions, women will rediscover the family circle "as the base of their identity and human control." Like the 19th-century proponents of separate sphere, Friedan proposes that women can exert influence from the home front: "The power of 'women's spheres' in shaping political as well as personal consciousness has clearly been underestimated by feminists today," she asserts—a strange statement from a woman who eagerly broke out of that sphere and has since chosen to live almost exclusively, and with great relish, in the public realm. This solution puts the burden on women; the need for men to change barely figures in Friedan's new plan. In fact, she blithely dismisses feminists' observations that men have been loathe to shoulder their share of household and child care responsibilities. If men haven't changed, she writes, then "why, in 1981, do three out of every four gourmet dinners suddenly seem to be cooked, soup to mousse, by men?" Where does this "statistic" come from? She invented it—based on some off-the-cuff remarks from "a number of my women colleagues."

The book also borrows some points of style and substance from the Reagan program. In the "second stage," she proposes, feminists should stop pressing corporations, legislatures, and the "tired welfare state" to expand women's rights—and get involved in volunteer and neighborhood work instead. "Individual" responsibility and "voluntary pooling of community resources," she writes, will be the second-stage's watchwords. To liberate themselves, she proposes, women should become Girl Scout leaders or join the Junior League. Friedan is convinced that the women's movement has made a big error in overlooking the potential of such institutions, which "may be as important" as political-action groups in advancing women's rights. In one of the book's more bewildering passages—the writing is often jumbled—Friedan assails NOW for encouraging women "to volunteer only for social change and feminist groups, and not in community service where their labor was exploited. . . . I myself never liked that stand on volunteerism—though we should indeed have opposed the exploitation of women in volunteer work as in office and home . . ."

The rhetoric of the New Right in refurbished form is strewn throughout the book. Connie Marshner's phrase for overambitious career women: "macho feminists." Betty Friedan's: "female machismo." Friedan sketches a grim scenario indeed of what could happen to the young liberated woman who succumbs to "the insatiable demands of female machismo":

> What if, in reaction, she strips her life clean of all these unmeasured, unvalued feminine tasks and frills—stops baking cookies altogether, cuts her hair like a monk, decides not to have children, installs a computer console in her bedroom? She suffers finally a new "crisis of confidence." She does not feel grounded in life. She shivers inside. She is depleted by female machismo.

By accepting the New Right language, Friedan has walked right into the New Right's "pro-family" semantics trap. She is reacting to the backlash rather than setting her own agenda, even referring to the women's movement now as "the feminist reaction."

In the end, the language and logic of *The Second Stage* is so muddled that it's ultimately impossible to say what Friedan really believes in today. At times in the book she seems to be retreating into a domestic haze, but at other points she seems simply to be restating fundamental feminist principles—as when she writes that the "second stage" is all about "the restructuring of our institutions on a basis of real equality for women and men." Maybe Friedan actually meant to recant many of the tenets of *The Feminine Mystique.* Or maybe she just got tangled in her own words.

In the end, sadly, Friedan's bitterness about her lost authority would alienate the very women who most admired her, the many women who still saw her as their leader. Friedan's tirades against anyone who didn't pay proper homage to her legacy are legendary. In the winter of 1988, Friedan sponsored a women's conference on the twenty-fifth anniversary of *The Feminine Mystique's* publication. At the lunch break, an older woman sat in the campus cafeteria near tears. Earlier she had seen Friedan in the ladies' room and gathered the courage to introduce herself to this longtime idol. "I just wanted to tell her how grateful I was for the book [*The Feminine Mystique*], how much it had meant to me. And I was really nervous and I said something stupid like 'I'm so glad you're at this conference,' and she nearly bit my head off. She started yelling, 'Of course I'm here; it's my conference; I organized the whole thing.' I was so embarrassed. I just feel terrible."

THIRD WAVE FEMINISM

When Rebecca Walker announced the arrival of the third wave in 1992, there was already discontent and political awareness developing among young women coming of age in the 1980s and early 1990s. In these women's efforts to come to an understanding of this new historical development and its similarities to and differences from what had come before, Betty Friedan's *The Feminine Mystique* was often a touchstone. One important text of the third wave, Naomi Wolf's *The Beauty Myth*, built upon the work Friedan had started. Jennifer Baumgardner and Amy Richards saw the roots of "girlie feminism" of the third wave in both Friedan's *The Feminine Mystique* and Helen Gurley Brown's *Sex and The Single Girl*.

REBECCA WALKER

Becoming the Third Wave[†]

I am not one of the people who sat transfixed before the television, watching the Senate hearings. I had classes to go to, papers to write, and frankly, the whole thing was too painful. A black man grilled by a panel of white men about his sexual deviance. A black woman claiming harassment and being discredited by other women. . . . I could not bring myself to watch that sensationalized assault of the human spirit.

To me, the hearings were not about determining whether or not Clarence Thomas did in fact harass Anita Hill. They were about checking and redefining the extent of women's credibility and power.

[†] From Rebecca Walker, "Becoming the Third Wave," *Ms.* January/February 1992, pp. 39–41. Reprinted by permission of *Ms.* magazine, © 1992.

Can a woman's experience undermine a man's career? Can a woman's voice, a woman's sense of self-worth and injustice, challenge a structure predicated upon the subjugation of our gender? Anita Hill's testimony threatened to do that and more. If Thomas had not been confirmed, every man in the United States would be at risk. For how many senators never told a sexist joke? How many men have not used their protected male privilege to thwart in some way the influence or ideas of a woman colleague, friend, or relative?

For those whose sense of power is so obviously connected to the health and vigor of the penis, it would have been a metaphoric castration. Of course this is too great a threat.

While some may laud the whole spectacle for the consciousness it raised around sexual harassment, its very real outcome is more informative. He was promoted. She was repudiated. Men were assured of the inviolability of their penis/power. Women were admonished to keep their experiences to themselves.

The backlash against U.S. women is real. As the misconception of equality between the sexes becomes more ubiquitous, so does the attempt to restrict the boundaries of women's personal and political power. Thomas' confirmation, the ultimate rally of support for the male paradigm of harassment, sends a clear message to women: "Shut up! Even if you speak, we will not listen."

I will not be silenced.

I acknowledge the fact that we live under siege. I intend to fight back. I have uncovered and unleashed more repressed anger than I thought possible. For the umpteenth time in my 22 years, I have been radicalized, politicized, shaken awake. I have come to voice again, and this time my voice is not conciliatory.

The night after Thomas' confirmation I ask the man I am intimate with what he thinks of the whole mess. His concern is primarily with Thomas' propensity to demolish civil rights and opportunities for people of color. I launch into a tirade. "When will progressive black men prioritize my rights and well-being? When will they stop talking so damn much about 'the race' as if it revolved exclusively around them?" He tells me I wear my emotions on my sleeve. I scream "I need to know, are you with me or are you going to help them try to destroy me?"

A week later I am on a train to New York. A beautiful mother and daughter, both wearing green outfits, sit across the aisle from me. The little girl has tightly plaited braids. Her brown skin is glowing and smooth, her eyes bright as she chatters happily while looking out the window. Two men get on the train and sit directly behind me, shaking my seat as they thud into place. I bury myself in *The Sound and the Fury*. Loudly they begin to talk about women. "Man, I fucked that bitch all night and then I never called her again." "Man, there's lots of girlies over there, you know that ho, live over there by Tyrone? Well, I snatched that shit up."

The mother moves closer to her now quiet daughter. Looking at her small back I can see that she is listening to the men. I am thinking of how I can transform the situation, of all the people in the car whose silence makes us complicit.

Another large man gets on the train. After exchanging loud greetings with the two men, he sits next to me. He tells them he is going to Philadelphia to visit his wife and child. I am suckered into thinking that he is different. Then, "Man, there's a ton of females in Philly, just waitin' for you to give 'em some." I turn my head and allow the fire in my eyes to burn into him. He takes up two seats and has hands with huge swollen knuckles. I imagine the gold rings on his fingers slamming into my face. He senses something, "What's your name, sweetheart?" The other men lean forward over the seat.

A torrent explodes: "I ain't your sweetheart, I ain't your bitch, I ain't your baby. How dare you have the nerve to sit up here and talk about women that way, and then try to speak to me." The woman/mother chimes in to the beat with claps of sisterhood. The men are momentarily stunned. Then the comeback: "Aw, bitch, don't play that woman shit over here 'cause that's bullshit." He slaps the back of one hand against the palm of the other. I refuse to back down. Words fly.

My instinct kicks in, telling me to get out. "Since I see you all are not going to move, I will." I move to the first car. I am so angry that thoughts of murder, of physically retaliating against them, of separatism, engulf me. I am almost out of body, just shy of being pure force. I am sick of the way women are negated, violated, devalued, ignored. I am livid, unrelenting in my anger at those who invade my space, who wish to take away my rights, who refuse to hear my voice. As the days pass, I push myself to figure out what it means to be a part of the Third Wave of feminism. I begin to realize that I owe it to myself, to my little sister on the train, to all of the daughters yet to be born, to push beyond my rage and articulate an agenda. After battling with ideas of separatism and militancy, I connect with my own feelings of powerlessness. I realize that I must undergo a transformation if I am truly committed to women's empowerment. My involvement must reach beyond my own voice in discussion, beyond voting, beyond reading feminist theory. My anger and awareness must translate into tangible action.

I am ready to decide, as my mother decided before me, to devote much of my energy to the history, health, and healing of women. Each of my choices will have to hold to my feminist standard of justice.

To be a feminist is to integrate an ideology of equality and female empowerment into the very fiber of my life. It is to search for personal clarity in the midst of systemic destruction, to join in sisterhood with women when often we are divided, to understand power structures with the intention of challenging them.

While this may sound simple, it is exactly the kind of stand that many of my peers are unwilling to take. So I write this as a plea to all women, especially the women of my generation: Let Thomas' confirmation serve to remind you, as it did me, that the fight is far from over. Let this dismissal of a woman's experience move you to anger. Turn that outrage into political power. Do not vote for them unless they work for us. Do not have sex with them, do not break bread with them, do not nurture them if they don't prioritize our freedom to control our bodies and our lives.

I am not a postfeminism feminist. I am the Third Wave.

NAOMI WOLF

From The Beauty Myth: How Images of Beauty Are Used Against Women[†]

At last, after a long silence, women took to the streets. In the two decades of radical action that followed the rebirth of feminism in the early 1970s, Western women gained legal and reproductive rights, pursued higher education, entered the trades and the professions, and overturned ancient and revered beliefs about their social role. A generation on, do women feel free?

The affluent, educated, liberated women of the First World, who can enjoy freedoms unavailable to any women ever before, do not feel as free as they want to. And they can no longer restrict to the subconscious their sense that this lack of freedom has something to do with—with apparently frivolous issues, things that really should not matter. Many are ashamed to admit that such trivial concerns—to do with physical appearance, bodies, faces, hair, clothes—matter so much. But in spite of shame, guilt, and denial, more and more women are wondering if it isn't that they are entirely neurotic and alone but

[†] Excerpts from pp. 9–14, 18–19 from *The Beauty Myth: How Images of Beauty Are Used Against Women* by Naomi Wolf. Copyright © 1991 by Naomi Wolf. Reprinted by permission of HarperCollins Publishers.

rather that something important is indeed at stake that has to do with the relationship between female liberation and female beauty.

The more legal and material hindrances women have broken through, the more strictly and heavily and cruelly images of female beauty have come to weigh upon us. Many women sense that women's collective progress has stalled; compared with the heady momentum of earlier days, there is a dispiriting climate of confusion, division, cynicism, and above all, exhaustion. After years of much struggle and little recognition, many older women feel burned out; after years of taking its light for granted, many younger women show little interest in touching new fire to the torch.

During the past decade, women breached the power structure; meanwhile, eating disorders rose exponentially and cosmetic surgery became the fastest-growing medical specialty. During the past five years, consumer spending doubled, pornography became the main media category, ahead of legitimate films and records combined, and thirty-three thousand American women told researchers that they would rather lose ten to fifteen pounds than achieve any other goal. More women have more money and power and scope and legal recognition than we have ever had before; but in terms of how we feel about ourselves *physically*, we may actually be worse off than our unliberated grandmothers. Recent research consistently shows that inside the majority of the West's controlled, attractive, successful working women, there is a secret "underlife" poisoning our freedom; infused with notions of beauty, it is a dark vein of self-hatred, physical obsessions, terror of aging, and dread of lost control.

It is no accident that so many potentially powerful women feel this way. We are in the midst of a violent backlash against feminism that uses images of female beauty as a political weapon against women's advancement: the beauty myth. It is the modern version of a social reflex that has been in force since the Industrial Revolution. As women released themselves from the feminine mystique of domesticity, the beauty myth took over its lost ground, expanding as it waned to carry on its work of social control.

The contemporary backlash is so violent because the ideology of beauty is the last one remaining of the old feminine ideologies that still has the power to control those women whom second wave feminism would have otherwise made relatively uncontrollable: It has grown stronger to take over the work of social coercion that myths about motherhood, domesticity, chastity, and passivity, no longer can manage. It is seeking right now to undo psychologically and covertly all the good things that feminism did for women materially and overtly.

This counterforce is operating to checkmate the inheritance of feminism on every level in the lives of Western women. Feminism gave us laws against job discrimination based on gender; immediately case law evolved in Britain and the United States that institutionalized job discrimination based on women's appearances. Patriarchal religion declined; new religious dogma, using some of the mind-altering techniques of older cults and sects, arose around age and weight to functionally supplant traditional ritual. Feminists, inspired by Friedan, broke the stranglehold on the women's popular press of advertisers for household products, who were promoting the feminine mystique; at once, the diet and skin care industries became the new cultural censors of women's intellectual space, and because of their pressure, the gaunt, youthful model supplanted the happy housewife as the arbiter of successful womanhood. The sexual revolution promoted the discovery of female sexuality; "beauty pornography"—which for the first time in women's history artificially links a commodified "beauty" directly and explicitly to sexuality—invaded the mainstream to undermine women's new and vulnerable sense of sexual self-worth. Reproductive rights gave Western women control over our own bodies; the weight of fashion models plummeted to 23 percent below that of ordinary women, eating disorders rose exponentially, and a mass neurosis was promoted that used food and weight to strip women of that sense of control. Women insisted on politicizing health; new technologies of invasive, potentially deadly "cosmetic" surgeries developed apace to re-exert old forms of medical control of women.

Every generation since about 1830 has had to fight its version of the beauty myth. "It is very little to me," said the suffragist Lucy Stone in 1855, "to have the right to vote, to own property, etcetera, if I may not keep my body, and its uses, in my absolute right." Eighty years later, after women had won the vote, and the first wave of the organized women's movement had subsided, Virginia Woolf wrote that it would still be decades before women could tell the truth about their bodies. In 1962, Betty Friedan quoted a young woman trapped in the Feminine Mystique: "Lately, I look in the mirror, and I'm so afraid I'm going to look like my mother." Eight years after that, heralding the cataclysmic second wave of feminism, Germaine Greer described "the Stereotype": "To her belongs all that is beautiful, even the very word beauty itself . . . she is a doll . . . I'm sick of the masquerade." In spite of the great revolution of the second wave, we are not exempt. Now we can look out over ruined barricades: A revolution has come upon us and changed everything in its path, enough time has passed since then for babies to have grown into women, but there still remains a final right not fully claimed.

The beauty myth tells a story: The quality called "beauty" objectively and universally exists. Women must want to embody it and men must want to possess women who embody it. This embodiment is an imperative for women and not for men, which situation is necessary and natural because it is biological, sexual, and evolutionary: Strong men battle for beautiful women, and beautiful women are more reproductively successful. Women's beauty must correlate to their fertility, and since this system is based on sexual selection, it is inevitable and changeless.

None of this is true. "Beauty" is a currency system like the gold standard. Like any economy, it is determined by politics, and in the modern age in the West it is the last, best belief system that keeps male dominance intact. In assigning value to women in a vertical hierarchy according to a culturally imposed physical standard, it is an expression of power relations in which women must unnaturally compete for resources that men have appropriated for themselves.

"Beauty" is not universal or changeless, though the West pretends that all ideals of female beauty stem from one Platonic Ideal Woman; the Maori admire a fat vulva, and the Padung, droopy breasts. Nor is "beauty" a function of evolution: Its ideals change at a pace far more rapid than that of the evolution of species, and Charles Darwin was himself unconvinced by his own explanation that "beauty" resulted from a "sexual selection" that deviated from the rule of natural selection; for women to compete with women through "beauty" is a reversal of the way in which natural selection affects all other mammals. Anthropology has overturned the notion that females must be "beautiful" to be selected to mate: Evelyn Reed, Elaine Morgan, and others have dismissed sociobiological assertions of innate male polygamy and female monogamy. Female higher primates are the sexual initiators; not only do they seek out and enjoy sex with many partners, but "every nonpregnant female takes her turn at being the most desirable of all her troop. And that cycle keeps turning as long as she lives." The inflamed pink sexual organs of primates are often cited by male sociobiologists as analogous to human arrangements relating to female "beauty," when in fact that is a universal, nonhierarchical female primate characteristic.

Nor has the beauty myth always been this way. Though the pairing of the older rich men with young, "beautiful" women is taken to be somehow inevitable, in the matriarchal Goddess religions that dominated the Mediterranean from about 25,000 B.C.E. to about 700 B.C.E., the situation was reversed: "In every culture, the Goddess has many lovers. . . . The clear pattern is of an older woman with a beautiful but expendable youth—Ishtar and Tammuz, Venus and Adonis, Cybele and Attis, Isis and Osiris . . . their only function the service of the divine 'womb.'" Nor is it something only women do and only men watch: Among the Nigerian Wodaabes, the women hold economic power and the tribe is obsessed with male beauty. Wodaabe men spend hours together in elaborate makeup sessions, and compete—provocatively painted and dressed, with swaying hips and seductive expressions—in beauty contests judged by women. There is no legitimate historical or biological justification for the beauty myth; what it is doing to women today is a result of nothing more exalted than the need of today's power structure, economy, and culture to mount a counteroffensive against women.

If the beauty myth is not based on evolution, sex, gender, aesthetics, or God, on what is it based? It claims to be about intimacy and sex and life, a celebration of women. It is actually composed of emotional distance, politics, finance, and sexual repression. The beauty myth is not about women at all. It is about men's institutions and institutional power.

The qualities that a given period calls beautiful in women are merely symbols of the female behavior that that period considers desirable: *The beauty myth is always actually prescribing behavior and not appearance.* Competition between women has been made part of the myth so that women will be divided from one another. Youth and (until recently) virginity have been "beautiful" in women since they stand for experiential and sexual ignorance. Aging in women is "unbeautiful" since women grow more powerful with time, and since the links between generations of women must always be newly broken: Older women fear young ones, young women fear old, and the beauty myth truncates for all the female life span. Most urgently, women's identity must be premised upon our "beauty" so that we will remain vulnerable to outside approval, carrying the vital sensitive organ of self-esteem exposed to the air.

* * *

The caricature of the Ugly Feminist was resurrected to dog the steps of the women's movement. The caricature is unoriginal; it was coined to ridicule the feminists of the nineteenth century. Lucy Stone herself, whom supporters saw as "a prototype of womanly grace . . . fresh and fair as the morning," was derided by detractors with "the usual report" about Victorian feminists: "a big masculine woman, wearing boots, smoking a cigar, swearing like a trooper." As Betty Friedan put it presciently in 1960, even before the savage revamping of that old caricature: "The unpleasant image of feminists today resembles less the feminists themselves than the image fostered by the interests who so bitterly opposed the vote for women in state after state." Thirty years on, her conclusion is more true than ever: That resurrected caricature, which sought to punish women for their public acts by going after their private sense of self, became the paradigm for new limits placed on aspiring women everywhere. After the success of the women's movement's second wave, the beauty myth was perfected to checkmate power at every level in individual women's lives. The modern neuroses of life in the female body spread to woman after woman at epidemic rates. The myth is undermining—slowly, imperceptibly, without our being aware of the real forces of erosion—the ground women have gained through long, hard, honorable struggle.

The beauty myth of the present is more insidious than any mystique of femininity yet: A century ago, Nora slammed the door of the doll's house; a generation ago, women turned their backs on the consumer heaven of the isolated multiapplianced home; but where women are trapped today, there is no door to slam. The contemporary ravages of the beauty backlash are destroying women physically and depleting us psychologically. If we are to free ourselves from the dead weight that has once again been made out of femaleness, it is not ballots or lobbyists or placards that women will need first; it is a new way to see.

JENNIFER BAUMGARDNER
AND AMY RICHARDS

From Manifesta: Young Women, Feminism, and the Future[†]

* * *

Girlie, like all strands of the women's movement, is hindered by a divorce from history: specifically, the history of other versions of Girlie that have existed, women who have reinvented the image of feminism and brought new life to the movement. But when the image change is complete, the inequality remains. And it is the inequality and injustice based on gender that feminism addresses. But, when we are separated from our political history, it is primarily the reinventions that continue, as if women's aesthetics were what we wanted to transform rather than women's rights. Much of the story of the Second Wave is fragmented, mythologized, or difficult to

† Excerpt from *Manifesta: Young Women, Feminism, and the Future* by Jennifer Baumgardner and Amy Richards. (New York: Farrar, Straus, and Giroux, 2000), pp. 152–54. Copyright © 2000 by Jennifer Baumgardner and Amy Richards. Reprinted by permission of Farrar, Straus and Giroux, LLC.

find. In some ways, Girlie can't be blamed for its shortsightedness; the story of women wasn't part of school when we were growing up. But it is our fault that we haven't sought out our history.

This fuzzy sense of where we've been plays out when something like *Bust* or Bikini Kill or the phrase "girl power" turns masses of females on to feminism—and then peters out after that first rush. Having no sense of how we got here condemns women to reinvent the wheel and often blocks us from creating a political strategy.

One of the ways we got here was through a groundbreaking book by an atypical woman who tapped into a typical plight: being a housewife in the postwar, boom economy of America. In 1963, Betty Friedan wrote in *The Feminine Mystique* that "for more than fifteen years there was no word of the yearning in the millions of words written about women, for women, in all the columns, books and articles by experts telling women their role was to seek fulfillment as wives and mothers." She was describing "the problem that has no name," that well-educated middle-class housewives were bored out of their minds in the suburbs with endlessly expanding, Sisyphean housework. Friedan has been credited with starting the Second Wave of feminism by naming that problem, and sparking women to demand political rights and flood the job market.

One year earlier, another atypical "typical" woman had written another earth-shattering book—this one not nearly so well respected by history. It was *Sex and the Single Girl*, by Helen Gurley Brown. Whether or not most feminists now see it as significant, with that little book, Brown, the *Cosmo* queen, resolved another clash between what we want (nookie and the bachelorette life) and what we're supposed to want (marriage and keeping house). And her philosophy sounds familiar to anyone who's conversant with Girlie.

Brown suggested that single women like sex, and don't need to be married to enjoy it, but are badgered into marriage by a conservative, misogynist culture. She championed the career girl at a time when the culture painted an ambitious woman, or a woman who simply had to work, as doomed to be lonely, and a sexually active woman as a slut. In a small, gossipy tome, Brown told it like it was for girls like her. She made visible the emerging independent and sexual working woman, and seemed almost to summon into being the urban, swinging singles scene. Liberation was key for both Friedan and Brown, but the routes differed greatly. Brown had always worked—not necessarily by choice—and she believed that a full sex life was an essential right for working stiffs. Today, women can be as serious as Friedan and as sexual (and single) as Gurley Brown is (and was). Girlie feminists, for their part, are creating an embraceable culture, one that acknowledges the realities of mostly single, mostly childless working girls' lives, with a healthy focus on sexuality. That said, a little brunette called Helen Gurley Brown seems to be at the root of platinum-blond Girlie feminism, as much as a suburban intellectual named Betty Friedan was at the root of housewives' rebellion.

* * *

The Scholarship on
THE FEMININE MYSTIQUE

Origins and Influences

Some historians' analyses of Betty Friedan have focused on the origins of and influences on her work. In many important ways, Friedan was silent about these influences, and that silence, historians have argued, has contributed to the perception of Friedan's work as simply the product of a white, middle-class housewife's narrow point of view. Probing and exposing this silence allows us to appreciate the radical and Jewish roots of her work, and also to come to terms with the social and cultural constraints that led her to obscure those roots.

By exploring the unspoken background behind *The Feminine Mystique*, scholars have been able to expose the significance of this text in multiple contexts. Sandra Dijkstra's essay directs attention to the trans-Atlantic connections between American and French feminists. Joyce Antler's essay provokes scholars to reconsider the impact of Jewish women in American feminism. Daniel Horowitz's pathbreaking work has led American historians to reconsider the relationships among American social movements in the twentieth century.

It is important to note, however, that Friedan was open about some of her intellectual influences, particularly contemporary trends in psychology. Historians Ellen Herman and Rebecca Jo Plant analyze these influences on Friedan, and use her book to help argue for the significant impact of psychological theories such as momism and humanism on twentieth-century American life.

SANDRA DIJKSTRA

From Simone de Beauvoir and Betty Friedan: The Politics of Omission†

* * *

Exactly ten years separates the English translation of *The Second Sex* from its first illegitimate offspring, *The Feminine Mystique*. And it took Friedan another twelve years to own up to the relationship. In the Preface and Acknowledgments to the first edition of 1963, Friedan acknowledged her debts to scores of individuals, but de Beauvoir's name was notably absent. The entire project, Friedan pointed out in her opening words, was born out of a "personal question mark" which led her in 1957 to survey her Smith College classmates (*FM*, p. 7).* Later, on page 345 of the book, she admitted that

---

† From Sandra Dijkstra, "Simone de Beauvoir and Betty Friedan: The Politics of Omission," *Feminist Studies* 6.2 (Summer 1980): 293, 294–95, 300–301. Reprinted by permission. Notes have been renumbered.

* Parenthetical references to *The Feminine Mystique* in this selection are from the 1963 Norton edition.

443

she was "*asked* to do an alumnae questionnaire . . ." (my emphasis). Friedan claimed to have undergone an *individual* awakening, a realization for which "a Frenchwoman named Simone de Beauvoir," as she described her predecessor, need get no credit (*FM*, p. 14). Friedan would later call de Beauvoir "an intellectual heroine of our history."[1] But in 1963, she presented her only through the words of a male American critic who charged that de Beauvoir "didn't know what life was all about," and "besides she was talking about French women" (*FM*, p. 14). Instead of acknowledging de Beauvoir's influence, Friedan left this critical presentation standing as evidence of the general problem that existed by the end of the fifties: "Words like 'emancipation' and 'career' sounded strange and embarrassing; no one had used them for years" (*FM*, p. 14).[2] Thus, her own discovery seemed all the more portentous and original, and American readers were left with a much less weighty and less subversive book, and a new mystique, "the problem that has no name" (*FM*, p. 11).

Finally, in a 1975 interview with de Beauvoir, Friedan felt compelled to pay her intellectual debt, at least partially. She admitted that she, Betty Friedan, "who had helped start women on the new road" had been herself "started on that road" by de Beauvoir.[3] When it came to specifying the nature of the influence, Friedan demurred, reluctantly avowing that she had "learned my own existentialism from her. . . . [This] led me to whatever original analysis of women's existence I have been able to contribute. . . ."[4] * * *

*   *   *

Friedan's belated and grudging admission of de Beauvoir's influence is curious: *The Feminine Mystique* achieved success on its own grounds and became the best-seller that *The Second Sex* never was, regardless of its intellectual origins. But Friedan's reticence, her conscious or unconscious attempt to obscure the pattern of influence, seems to come from an ideological source: the French book was simply too radical even for 1963, and certainly for Friedan, who adapted many of its basic premises to make them "safe" for America, reducing them from radical to reformist solutions, from

---

1. Betty Friedan, "No Gods, No Goddesses," *Saturday Review*, 14 June 1975, p. 71.
2. Friedan does make a vague, if inaccurate, allusion to *The Second Sex* earlier, on page 11: "For over fifteen years there was no work of this yearning in the millions of words written about women. . . ." More recently, in her new autobiographical book, *It Changed My Life* (New York: Random House, 1976), Friedan presents her feminist awakening in much the same way, jumping from her experience as a Spock mother in the late forties, to the Smith alumnae questionnaire of the late fifties, without mentioning the possible effect of her reading of de Beauvoir. Her intellectual debt is paid toward the end of the book, in a chapter reprinting the *Saturday Review* article cited above.
3. Friedan, "No Gods, No Goddesses," pp. 16–17.
4. Ibid., p. 16.

philosophical to popular jargon, and from European to American references.

Indeed, Friedan "Americanized" *The Second Sex* on many levels. She chose her materials from an American rather than a European context, and from popular rather than philosophical or literary sources: she catered to the American fascination for figures and provided statistics for college enrollment, for birthrate, for sexual satisfaction. In this sense, she anchored her book more concretely in time and place than had de Beauvoir, who was more concerned with presenting a sweeping panorama of the situation of women. In effect, Friedan's survey of the contemporary sources of American women's limited options was the strong point of her book. But in her analysis of the problem, Friedan rarely moved beyond sociological description.

In observing the process by which Friedan selected and transformed de Beauvoir's central insights, we witness a shrinking of conceptualization. At the very center of *The Feminine Mystique* lies one of de Beauvoir's crucial discoveries: "One is not born but rather one becomes woman" (*SS*, p. 301). Instead of analyzing the phenomenon that de Beauvoir had described ("It is civilization as a whole which produces this creature . . ." *SS*, p. 301) and instead of examining the specific institutions that oppress women (such as housework, motherhood, marriage), Friedan limited her attack to the more superficial enemies, such as the media, the social sciences, and consumerism, themselves not the *cause* but rather the *means*, the agents by which the subordinate condition of women is ideologically maintained and reinforced. Thus her solution was much more simplistic: women must reject a certain *image* of themselves, they must "say 'no' to the feminine mystique . . ." (*FM*, p. 338). It is not necessary to destroy or even remake the institutions which incarcerate women; they can simply "say 'no' to the housewife image" (*FM*, p. 330). Housewifery itself remains intact. Indeed, Friedan did not analyze the effect of domestic service on women in any concrete way. Her recommendation to women trapped therein is a shift in perception: "See housework for what it is—not a career, but something that must be done as quickly and efficiently as possible" (*FM*, p. 330). Thus, her solutions were based on the endorsement of the very consumerism she had criticized. How else could the housewife achieve efficiency except through the purchase of time-saving devices offered her by the capitalist marketplace?

De Beauvoir's examination of the problem of housework was much more devastating: "Few tasks are more like the torture of Sisyphus than housework, with its endless repetition: the clean becomes soiled, the soiled is made clean, over and over. . . . The housewife wears herself out marking time: she makes nothing, simply perpetuates the present" (*SS*, p. 504). "The worst of it all is that this labor does not even tend toward the creation of anything durable" (*SS*, p. 508). The result of this process is the deformation of women's personality, and de Beauvoir assesses the psychological toll incisively. Labor-saving devices cannot remedy the structural marginalization of women that occurs by restricting them to the private sphere. Although de Beauvoir did not take her analysis to its logical conclusion here, it is clear that she understood the meaning of women's exclusion from productive, creative work. * * *

                                    *   *   *

Friedan * * * promised American women self-fulfillment within this society, without advocating transformation of its institutions. Not only because her text was more accessible to an American audience, but also because her ideological disposition was more suitable, did *The Feminine Mystique* have such an enormous impact. Juliet Mitchell guessed that "If a single inspiration for the [American] movement is to be cited, it was the publication in 1963 of Betty Friedan's *The Feminine Mystique* (and her subsequent foundation of NOW in 1966)."[5] With its limited reformist message, this book influenced the direction of the new wave of feminism more than its European predecessor had. Its legacy, the National Organization for Women and the raising of feminist consciousness in millions of women cannot be denied, nor denigrated. Yet, to the extent that it gave women the illusion that equality within the system is possible, that education, a change in perception, a "new life plan" and legal reform are adequate, the book reinforced the status quo and preached a feminism accessible only to middle-class women.

                                    *   *   *

JOYCE ANTLER

From The Journey Home: How Jewish Women Shaped Modern America[†]

                                    *   *   *

On August 26, 1970, on the fiftieth anniversary of the passage of the amendment entitling women to the vote, 50,000 women marched

---

5. Mitchell, *Woman's Estate*, p. 52.
† From Joyce Antler, *The Journey Home: How Jewish Women Shaped Modern America* (New York: Schocken Books, 1997), pp. 259–60, 261–64, 266–67. Reprinted with the permission of Free Press, a division of Simon & Schuster, Inc. Copyright © 1997 by Joyce Antler. All rights reserved. Notes have been renumbered.

down Fifth Avenue to demand equal rights and a political voice of their own. This Women's Strike for Equality, the first nationwide women's action since the suffrage victory, had been organized by Betty Friedan, the writer whose exposé of the so-called feminine mystique had sparked a new wave of feminist activism. The size of the march considerably altered depictions of the resurgent women's rights movement. No longer could the media portray the movement as a fringe action, for it was clear that it was attracting a large and significantly mainstream following.[1]

At the defining moment of the march, as Friedan came forward to address a vast, cheering throng in Bryant Park behind New York's Public Library, she found herself speaking—and revising—the ancient Hebrew prayer that Orthodox Jewish men recited every morning. "Down through the generations in history," Friedan declared, "my ancestors prayed, 'I thank Thee, Lord, I was not created a woman,' and from this day forward I trust that women all over the world will be able to say, 'I thank Thee, Lord, I *was* created a woman.'"[2]

Unable to remember ever having heard the prayer before, Friedan was startled by her own words. But the joining together of her feminism and her Jewishness at this historic moment was not as strange as it seemed. Friedan confessed to having always had "very strong feelings" about her Jewish identity; it is not so surprising that this Orthodox prayer, emblematic of gender differences in Jewish religious roles, now emerged from the recesses of her memory. For Friedan, it had become necessary to confront "the anti-woman aspects of the Jewish tradition in order to accept both feminism and Judaism." She had the sense that "having broken through the feminine mystique to affirm my authentic full identity as a person, as a woman, brought me to confront my Jewish identity."[3] Because feminism insisted on making the personal political, her exploration would inevitably become a public one, as her oratory in Bryant Park confirmed. Assisted by a growing Jewish feminist movement, Friedan and other women's rights pioneers would slowly find their way home to a more viable Jewish identity in the 1970s and 1980s. The increasing virulence of anti-Semitism within the international feminist movement intensified their struggle and challenged many other Jewish-born American feminists to join the quest for a positive, usable, feminist Jewish identity.

1. Naomi Braun Rosenthal, "Consciousness Raising: From Revolution to Re-Evaluation," *Psychology of Women Quarterly* 8, No. 4 (Summer 1984): 318.
2. For an account of her speech at the march, see Betty Friedan, "Women and Jews: The Quest for Selfhood," *Congress Monthly* (Feb./March 1985): 7, and Francine Klagsbrun, "Marching in Front," *Hadassah Magazine* (Nov. 1993): 24.
3. Klagsbrun, "Marching in Front," 24; Friedan, "Women and Jews," 7.

Like Friedan, many of the leaders and theorists of the 1960s feminist movement had been Jews, albeit largely secular, unidentified ones. Bella Abzug, Phyllis Chesler, Letty Cottin Pogrebin, and Vivian Gornick—as well as the half-Jewish Gloria Steinem[4]—all played prominent roles in spearheading women's rights in the 1960s and early 1970s. Shulamith Firestone, Robin Morgan, Meredith Tax, Andrea Dworkin, and Naomi Weisstein were among the Jewish women active in the more radical wing of feminism—women's liberation.

Several reasons have been suggested for the prominence of Jewish women within not only the leadership but the rank and file of feminism. Friedan suggests that contemporary feminism originated in the United States because there were such large numbers of highly educated women who were expected to concentrate their energies upon the narrow sphere of the home. She speculates that the disparity between talent, ambition, and role identity was especially severe for Jewish women, who were probably the most highly educated of all American women, yet whose self-definition was based almost entirely on the family. According to writer Anne Roiphe, the "women's movement was fueled by Jewish energies" because Jewish women felt "pain and anguish" at the way they had been portrayed in the media and by Jewish men. When their anger ignited, it "exploded" into the women's movement.[5]

*   *   *

*   *   * In *The Feminine Mystique*, Betty Friedan explodes the myth of domestic contentment, which she argues had infantilized women, burying them alive in their suburban homes as if in a "concentration camp." Like the victims of the Holocaust, she suggests, they too had undergone "progressive dehumanization" and could not fight back.[6] Friedan's appropriation of Holocaust imagery did not attract much attention or criticism, nor did Friedan seem especially troubled that she had broken an implicit taboo by comparing ordinary, albeit disturbing, social ills to the moral enormities of the Jewish catastrophe.

Friedan used the language of the Holocaust not merely as a metaphor, or as a tactic to shock readers, but because she had already made the connection between the oppression of women and that of

---

4. Steinem's father, Leo, was Jewish. Her grandmother, Pauline, was a pioneer feminist who served as president of the Ohio Women's Suffrage Association. On Steinem's life, see Carolyn G. Heilbrun, *The Education of a Woman: The Life of Gloria Steinem* (New York: Dial Press, 1995).

5. "Jewish Roots: An Interview with Betty Friedan," *Tikkun* 3, No. 1 (Jan./Feb. 1988): 26. Remarks of Anne Roiphe in "Woman as Jew, Jew as Woman," *Congress Monthly* 52, No. 2 (Feb./March 1985): 13. Also see interview with Phyllis Chesler, *Lilith* 1, No. 2 (Winter 1976/1977).

6. Betty Friedan, *The Feminine Mystique* (W. W. Norton & Co., 1963), 337, 281.

Jews. Her family history provides evidence that they had long been joined in her own experience.

Born Bettye Goldstein in Peoria, Illinois, in 1921, she was the oldest of the three children of Harry Goldstein, then forty, and his wife, Miriam Horwitz Goldstein, eighteen years younger; a sister came a year and a half later and a brother five years later. Harry Goldstein had immigrated with his family from a village near Kiev when he was still a boy; leaving the rest of the family in St. Louis, where they settled, at age thirteen Harry went on to Peoria, peddling collar buttons on street corners. Eventually he owned the finest jewelry store in the community—a "Tiffany of the Midwest" according to Betty—and put his youngest brother through Harvard Law School.[7] Goldstein became a leader of Peoria's business elite and a prominent member of its Jewish community.

Despite this success, to his wife, Goldstein was a failure because he could not provide social acceptability or, especially during the Depression, sufficient material comforts. Friedan believes that her mother's scorn for her father sprang not only from these alleged deficiencies but from Miriam's dissatisfaction with her own role as a housewife and mother.

Miriam Horwitz Goldstein was the only daughter of a prominent Illinois physician and his wife. The family delighted in the apocryphal story that Miriam's father, an immigrant from Hungary, had gone through high school and college in one year; he graduated in the first class of Washington University Medical School and eventually became health commissioner of Peoria. Despite her father's status, Miriam grew up "fairly isolated as a Jew," resentful of the community's snubs. After attending the local college, she became society page editor of the Peoria newspaper, a job she loved. But, as was customary at the time, Miriam gave up her work when she married. She never recovered from the loss. Thereafter, "nothing my father did, nothing he bought her, nothing we did ever seemed to satisfy her," Betty notes.[8] Beautiful and self-possessed, Miriam nonetheless lacked fulfillment and lived vicariously through her children, especially the bright and able Betty. "She could hardly wait until I got to junior high," Friedan notes, "to put the idea into my head to try out for the school newspaper, to start a literary magazine in high school. She could hardly wait for me to go to the college she had no chance to go to, to edit the newspaper there."[9]

---

7. See "Women and Jews: The Quest for Selfhood"; "Jewish Roots"; and Friedan, *"It Changed My Life": Writings on the Women's Movement* (New York: W. W. Norton & Co., 1985), 6–19; Amy Stone, "Friedan at 55: From Feminism to Judaism," *Lilith* 1, No. 1 (1976): 11.
8. Friedan, *"It Changed My Life,"* 6.
9. *Ibid.*

Her mother's unhappiness caused her not only to live through her children, but to snipe at her husband. "It was obvious she belittled, cut down my father because she had no place to channel her terrific energies," Betty recalled.[1] Things got especially bad during the Depression when Mr. Goldstein's jewelry business suffered enormous losses. Miriam did not cope well with the downturn in the family's fortunes. Betty recalled her "hiding the bills she charged, secretly trying her hand at gambling . . . and losing more, until she had to confess." The combination of her mother's greediness and her father's ferocious temper caused "terrible battles that shook our house at night."[2]

Friedan blamed Miriam for "dominating the family," for being "hypocritical" and selfish. "Discontented, running the Sunday School one year, Hadassah the next, the Community Chest, talking about 'writing,' though she wouldn't or didn't do it, taking up . . . fads," Miriam was a terrible role model. "When I still used to say prayers, even as a child, after the 'Now I lay me down to sleep' and the Sh'ma Yisrael—I would pray for a 'boy to like me best' and a '*work* of my own to do' when I grew up. I did not want to be discontented like my mother was. . . ."[3] Years later, when asked what had motivated her to write *The Feminine Mystique,* Friedan responded that it had been "a combination of circumstances" in her own life, along with the "massive crisis of identity already brewing in my mother's generation." But the first specific cause she names is her "mother, and her discontent, which I never understood."[4]

Friedan was not unaware of the specifically Jewish dimension to her mother's discontent. Despite Harry Goldstein's prominence in Peoria, the Goldsteins were never accepted socially. People who associated with her father in business would not associate with him elsewhere, and Friedan recalls that the family was not allowed into the Peoria country club, to which all the children's friends belonged.[5]

This discrimination hit her mother hardest. But Miriam blamed her husband rather than the community for the family's isolation and ostracism, faulting Harry Goldstein's immigrant background, accent, lack of education. Recalling these years, Betty acknowledged that her mother, like many Jews in smaller cities who distanced themselves as far as possible from other Jews and Judaism, had in fact become an "anti-Semitic Jew." These were people who

1. Paul Wilkes, "Mother Superior to Women's Lib," *New York Times,* Nov. 29, 1970, cited in Stone, "Friedan at 55," 40.
2. Sondra Henry and Emily Taitz, *Betty Friedan: Fighter for Women's Rights* (Hillside, N.J.: Enslow Publishers, 1990), 14: Justine Blau, *Betty Friedan* (New York: Chelsea House, 1990), 22.
3. Betty Friedan Papers, Schlesinger Library, Radcliffe College.
4. Friedan, *"It Changed My Life,"* 5–6.
5. Stone, "Friedan at 55," 11.

"changed their names and did something to their noses, tried not to talk with their hands . . . and denied the very richness, the warmth, the specialness, the good taste of their own background as Jews."[6] Although Friedan told herself that her family "was somehow better, finer, more sensitive, smarter" than their neighbors, she too could not avoid internalizing some of Peoria's anti-Semitic prejudices. She grew up feeling "marginal," with the sense of being an "outsider," apart, special, "not like the others." She emphasized her Americanness. Once, in fact, she won an essay contest on "Why I Am Proud to Be an American." As a prize, she "recited the Declaration of Independence on July 4th at the fairgrounds, and Congressman Everett Dirksen patted my head."[7] Though she attended Sunday school and enjoyed family seders, she became disconnected from the religious elements of Judaism. A month before her confirmation, she announced to her rabbi that she no longer believed in God. The rabbi told her to keep it to herself until the ceremony was over. "Actress that I am," Friedan recalled years later, "I gave the flower offering, raising my eyes to the heavens."[8]

It was at about this time that the first "real trauma" of her life erupted. Although previously she had been popular, now Friedan—the only Jewish girl at school—was the only one not invited to join a sorority. "Terribly alone," "self-conscious and miserable," she felt herself a "social outcast" throughout her remaining high school years and "plumbed the depth of misery."[9] She blamed the rejection squarely on being Jewish—on not being "one of 'them.'" Her father agreed, explaining that "the people friendly to him in business would not speak to him after sundown."[1] In Peoria, Jews and Gentiles did not mix. These painful experiences strengthened her social conscience. "Ever since I was a little girl," Friedan muses, "I remember my father telling me that I had a passion for justice. But I think it was really a passion against injustice which originated from my feelings of the injustice of anti-Semitism."[2]

When Friedan was seventeen, she vowed to herself that "they may not *like* me but they're going to look up to me. . . ."[3] She made good on that vow at Smith College, becoming editor of the newspaper, starting a literary magazine, and graduating summa cum laude. Yet even at Smith, Friedan encountered anti-Semitism and the

6. Friedan, "Women and Jews," 8.
7. Betty Friedan, "The ERA—Does It Play in Peoria?" *New York Times Magazine,* Nov. 19, 1978, 39, 134.
8. "Jewish Roots," 25.
9. Milton Meltzer, *Betty Friedan: A Voice for Women's Rights* (New York: Viking Kestrel, 1985), 9; Blau, *Betty Friedan,* 24.
1. "The Era—Does It Play in Peoria?" 39, 134; Henry and Taitz, *Betty Friedan,* 15.
2. Stone, "Friedan at 55," 11.
3. "Jewish Roots," 25.

phenomenon of the anti-Semitic Jew. In her freshman year, just before the outbreak of World War II, she lived in a house with four wealthy Jewish girls from Cincinnati; when the president of the college initiated a petition urging President Roosevelt to relax the immigration quotas for refugees from Nazism, offering to admit some college-aged girls among them to Smith, many of Friedan's housemates argued against the proposal. But Friedan was most shocked by the fact that the four Cincinnati girls refused to sign the petition—"they were the type that spoke in whispery voices . . . because they did not want to be known as Jews."[4]

In a short story she later wrote entitled "The Scapegoat," Friedan dramatized the plight of Shirley, not Wouk's ambitious, sexy "princess" who matures into a bourgeois housewife, but an all-too-Jewish college girl who has a nervous breakdown when she is rejected by fellow Jews to curry favor with their Gentile housemates. Friedan's professor commented that although the theme was somewhat familiar, the "factor of race prejudice, and the less usual device of having it written by a Jewish girl," were "probably to the good."[5] After graduating Friedan came home to speak at Peoria's Reform Synagogue on "Affirming One's Jewishness." The talk—which acknowledged the problem of turning anti-Semitism "against oneself instead of affirming one's own identity"—was "strong meat" for the community, but it helped her come to terms with the anti-Semitism that she believed had been the "dominant menace" of her childhood.[6]

* * *

* * * Friedan's breakthrough was to acknowledge that the feminine "mystique" was not an individual—and not a Jewish—problem. She recognized her mother's "impotent rage" as a "typical female disorder" perpetuated by Freudian psychoanalysts, functionalist sociologists, advertisers, business leaders, educators, and child development experts.[7]

The Feminine Mystique, and Friedan's subsequent establishment of the National Organization for Women, assured her a leading role in the women's rights movement and eventually facilitated her return to Judaism. Having rejected religion early in life and identified with an "agnostic, atheistic, scientific, humanist" tradition, she had no feeling for the spiritual "mystery of being Jewish." Friedan's sons were given "aesthetic bar mitzvahs" appropriate to Rockland

4. Stone, "Friedan at 55," 12.
5. Bettye Goldstein, "The Scapegoat," Betty Friedan Papers, Schlesinger Library.
6. Stone, "Friedan at 55," 12.
7. Stone, "Friedan at 55," 40.

County, where most Jews were Unitarians; her daughter did not receive confirmation or a bat mitzvah. Feminism, however, by leading her to explore her gendered identity, started her on a journey to reevaluate her religious heritage. After the 1970 suffrage anniversary march at which she publicly connected the reform of patriarchal Judaism to feminist goals, Friedan took her first trip to Israel as part of an attempt to "get in touch with my Jewish roots." She was shocked, however, to find herself attacked by the Israeli press as a radical "women's libber" and generally treated as a "leper"; Golda Meir, then prime minister, refused to see her, a particularly disappointing affront since Friedan had met with the pope and many world leaders.[8] But Friedan made contact with a few women eager to confront the gender inequalities in Israel; along with other prominent American feminists, she worked with them over the next years helping to start a women's rights movement in Israel.

At home, Friedan began to explore her relationship with the American Jewish community, becoming cochair of the American Jewish Congress's National Commission on Women's Equality. Unhappily, she found that organized leaders seemed as disturbed by feminism as the Israelis. Even though Jewish women had been prominent in the women's rights movement, Jewish leaders seemed more profoundly threatened by feminism than non-Jews.[9]

Friedan's journey back to Judaism continued with her participation in a Jewish study group where she explored the "mystery of being Jewish." As a newly self-aware Jewish feminist, she remains concerned about the myriad issues facing Jewish women, including the perpetuation of "obscene" travesties of the Jewish mother. Friedan wants to "take back" the denigrating images of possessive, manipulating Jewish mothers spooning out chicken soup to control their children's lives and show Jewish women as strong, energetic, and nurturant, as they have been throughout history. "I hereby affirm my own right as a Jewish American feminist to make chicken soup," she declares, "even though I sometimes take it out of a can."[1] Thus, in later life she has joined the modern aspirations of feminism with the popular emblems of her Jewish heritage, understanding that the myth of a controlling, aggressive *Jewish* mother had been as dangerous to the self-esteem of Jewish women (including her own) as the earlier "feminine mystique" was to all women.

*　　*　　*

8. Friedan, "Women and Jews," 8.
9. *Ibid.*, 9.
1. Friedan, "Jewish Roots," 27; and "Women and Jews," 10.

DANIEL HOROWITZ

From Rethinking Betty Friedan
and The Feminine Mystique: Labor Union Radicalism
and Feminism in Cold War America[†]

✳   ✳   ✳

What the written record reveals of Friedan's life from her arrival at
Smith in the fall of 1938 until the publication of *The Feminine
Mystique* makes possible a story different from the one she has told.
To begin with, usually missing from her narrative is full and specific information about how at college she first developed a sense of
herself as a radical.[1] Courses she took, friendships she established
with peers and professors, events in the United States and abroad,
and her campus leadership all turned Friedan from a provincial
outsider into a determined advocate of trade unions as the herald of
progressive social change, a healthy skeptic about the authority and
rhetorical claims of those in power, a staunch opponent of fascism,
a defender of free speech, and a fierce questioner of social privilege
expressed by the conspicuous consumption of some of her peers.[2]

✳   ✳   ✳

In the fall of her junior year, Friedan took an economics course
taught by Dorothy W. Douglas, Theories and Movements for Social
Reconstruction. Douglas was well known at the time for her radicalism.[3] In what she wrote for Douglas, and with youthful enthusiasm
characteristic of many members of her generation, Friedan sympa-

---

[†] From Daniel Horowitz, "Rethinking Betty Friedan and The Feminine Mystique: Labor
    Union Radicalism and Feminism in Cold War America," *American Quarterly* 48.1 (March
    1996): 8, 9–10, 11–17, 29, 31. © 1996 The American Studies Association. Reprinted with
    permission of the Johns Hopkins University Press. Notes have been renumbered.
1. Marcia Cohen, *The Sisterhood: The True Story of the Women Who Changed the World*
    (New York, 1988), 63 and Paul Wilkes, "Mother Superior to Women's Lib," *New York
    Times Magazine*, 29 Nov. 1970, 140 briefly draw a picture of Friedan as a college rebel
    but to the best of my knowledge, the politics of that rebellion have remained largely
    unknown.
2. This summary relies on unsigned editorials that appeared under Friedan's editorship,
    which can be found in *SCAN* from 14 Mar. 1941 to 10 Mar. 1942, p. 2. Although mem-
    bers of the editorial board held a wide range of opinions, I am assuming that as editor-
    in-chief Friedan had a significant role in shaping editorials. Friedan placed four
    editorials in her papers: "They Believed in Peace," "Years of Change and Unrest,"
    "Behind Closed Doors," and "Answer No Answer": carton 7, folder 310, BF-SLRC.
3. In 1955 Douglas took the Fifth Amendment before HUAC as she was redbaited,
    accused of having been a member of a communist teachers union in the late 1930s.
    I am grateful to Margery Sly and Jacquelyn D. Hall for providing this information on
    Douglas. See also, Betty Friedan, "Was Their Education UnAmerican?" unpublished
    article, 1953 or 1954, carton 11, folder 415, BF-SLRC, 3. For Friedan's continued use
    of Marxist analysis, see Friedan, *It Changed My Life*, 110.

thetically responded to the Marxist critique of capitalism as a cultural, economic, and political force.[4]

Friedan also gained an education as a radical in the summer of 1941 when, following Douglas's suggestion, she participated in a writers' workshop at the Highlander Folk School in Tennessee, an institution active in helping the CIO organize in the South. The school offered a series of summer institutes for fledgling journalists which, for 1939 and 1940 (but not 1941), the communist-led League of American Writers helped sponsor. For three years beginning in the fall of 1939, opponents of Highlander had sustained a vicious redbaiting attack, but a FBI investigator found no evidence of subversive activity.[5] In good Popular Front language, Friedan praised Highlander as a truly American institution that was attempting to help America to fulfill its democratic ideals. She explored the contradictions of her social position as a Jewish girl from a well-to-do family who had grown up in a class-divided Peoria, gave evidence of her hostility to the way her parents fought over issues of debt and extravagance, and described the baneful influence of the mass media on American life. Though she also acknowledged that her Smith education did "not lead to much action," she portrayed herself as someone whose radical consciousness relied on the American labor movement as the bulwark against fascism.[6]

At Smith Friedan linked her journalism to political activism. She served as editor-in-chief of the campus newspaper for a year beginning in the spring of 1941. The campaigns she undertook and the editorials she wrote reveal a good deal of her politics. Under Friedan's leadership, the newspaper's reputation for protest was so strong that in a skit a fellow student portrayed an editor, perhaps Friedan herself, as "a strident voice haranguing from a perpetual soap-box."[7] While at Smith, a Peoria paper reported in 1943, Friedan helped organize college building and grounds workers into a union.[8] Under her leadership, the student paper took on the

4. Bettye Goldstein, "Discussion of Reading Period Material," paper for Economics 319, 18 Jan. 1941, carton 1, folder 257, BF-SLRC, 1, 2, 4, 8. See also "Questions on *Communist Manifesto*" and "Questions on Imperialism," papers for Economics 319, carton 1, folder 257, BF-SLRC.
5. John M. Glen, *Highlander: No Ordinary School, 1932–1962* (Lexington, Ky., 1988), 47–69. I am grateful to Professor Glen for a letter in which he clarified the timing of the League's sponsorship. Meltzer, *Friedan*, 20 says that Friedan's economics professor pointed her to Highlander but identifies that professor as a male; since the only economics course Friedan took was from Douglas, I am assuming that it was she who urged her student to attend the workshop. Meltzer thinks that is a reasonable assumption: Milton Meltzer, phone conversation with Daniel Horowitz, 24 Sept. 1995.
6. Bettye Goldstein, "Highlander Folk School—American Future," unpublished paper, 1941, carton 6, folder 274, BF-SLRC; Goldstein, "Learning the Score," 22–24.
7. "Epilogue of Failure," *SCAN*, 10 Mar. 1942, 2.
8. "Betty Goldstein, Local Girl, Makes Good in New York," clipping from Peoria newspaper, probably 10 Dec. 1943 issue of *Labor Temple News*, carton 1, folder 86, BF-SLRC.

student government for holding closed meetings, fought successfully to challenge the administration's right to control what the
newspaper printed, campaigned for the relaxation of restrictions on
student social life, censured social clubs for their secrecy, and published critiques of professors' teaching.[9] In response to an article
in a campus humor magazine that belittled female employees who
cleaned the students' rooms and served them food, an editorial supported the administration's censorship of the publication on the
grounds that such action upheld "the liberal democratic tradition
of the college."[1]

The editorials written on her watch reveal a young woman who
believed that what was involved with almost every issue—at Smith,
in the United States and abroad—was the struggle for democracy,
freedom, and social justice. Under Friedan's leadership the editors
supported American workers and their labor unions in their struggles to organize and improve their conditions. * * *

* * *

* * * By her senior year, Friedan and her peers conveyed a sense
that they were chafing against the isolation of Smith College from
the world of action, eager to find ways to act upon their commitments.[2] When she left Smith, she dropped the "e" from her first
name, perhaps a symbolic statement that she was no longer a girl
from Peoria.

* * *

The period which Friedan has treated most summarily in her narrative covers the years from 1943 to 1952, when she worked as a
labor journalist. Off and on from October 1943 until July 1946
she was a staff writer for the Federated Press, a left-wing news
service that provided stories for newspapers, especially union
ones, across the nation.[3] Here Friedan wrote articles that sup-

9. "Behind a Closed Door," *SCAN*, 3 Oct. 1941, 2; "Declaration of Student Independence," *SCAN*, 5 Dec. 1941, 1–2; "SCAN Protests Against Censorship," *SCAN*, 5 Dec.
   1941, 1; "A Few Hours More," *SCAN*, 10 Oct. 1941, 2; "Review of Philosophy Courses,"
   SCAN, 10 Mar. 1942, 2.
1. "The Tatler Suspension," *SCAN*, 7 Nov. 1941, 2; for the article in question see "Maids
   We Have Known and Loved," *Tatler*, Oct. 1941, 9, 21. When the administration moved
   against *SCAN*, over a different incident, the editors changed their minds about the
   earlier suspension of the *Tatler: SCAN*, 5 Dec. 1941, 1–2.
2. "We Cannot Rejoice," *SCAN*, 9 Dec. 1941, 2; "Our Duty Now," *SCAN*, 12 Dec. 1941,
   2; "Campus Cooperatives," *SCAN*, 24 Feb. 1942, 2; "No Change in Emphasis," *SCAN*,
   26 Sept. 1941, 2.
3. To date her work for the Federated Press, see Betty Friedan, job application for Time
   Inc., 1 July 1951, carton 1, folder 61, BF-SLRC. For information on the Federated
   Press, see Doug Reynolds, "Federated Press," *Encyclopedia of the American Left*, ed.
   Mari Jo Buhle, Paul Buhle, and Dan Georgakas (New York, 1990), 225–27.

ported the aspirations of African Americans and union members. She also criticized reactionary forces that, she believed, were working secretly to undermine progressive social advances.[4] As early as 1943, she pictured efforts by businesses, coordinated by the National Association of Manufacturers (NAM), to develop plans that would enhance profits, diminish the power of unions, reverse the New Deal, and allow businesses to operate as they pleased.[5]

At Federated Press, Friedan also paid attention to women's problems. Right after she began to work there, she interviewed UE official Ruth Young, one of the clearest voices in the labor movement articulating women's issues. In the resulting article, Friedan noted that the government could not solve the problem of turnover "merely by pinning up thousands of glamorous posters designed to lure more women into industry." Neither women, unions, nor management, she quoted Young as saying, could solve problems of escalating prices or inadequate child care that were made even more difficult by the fact that "women still have two jobs to do." Action of the federal government, Friedan reported, was needed to solve the problems working women faced.[6] In the immediate postwar period, she pictured the wife in a union family as more savvy than her husband in figuring out how large corporations took advantage of the consumer.[7] She paid special attention to stories about protecting the jobs and improving the situation of working women, including married ones with children.

For about six years beginning in July, 1946, precisely at the moment when the wartime Popular Front came under intense attack, Friedan was a reporter for the union's paper *UE News*.[8] At least as early as 1943, when she quoted Young, Friedan was well

4. Betty Goldstein, "Negro Pupils Segregated, Parents Strike; Issue Headed for Courts," Federated Press, 15 Sept. 1943, carton 8, folder 328, BF-SLRC; Betty Goldstein, "Peace Now: Treason in Pious Garb," Federated Press, 16 Feb. 1944, carton 8, folder 328, BF-SLRC; Betty Goldstein, "Well-Heeled 'White Collar League' Seen as Disguised Native Fascist Threat," Federated Press, 16 Mar. 1944, carton 8, folder 328, BF-SLRC.

5. Betty Goldstein, "Big Business Getting Desperate, Promising Postwar Jobs," Federated Press, 19 Nov. 1943, carton 8, folder 328, BF-SLRC; Betty Goldstein, "NAM Convention Pro-War—For War on Labor, New Deal, Roosevelt," Federated Press, 14 Dec. 1943, carton 8, folder 328, BF-SLRC; Betty Goldstein, "Details of Big Business Anti-Labor Conspiracy Uncovered," Federated Press, 11 Feb. 1946, carton 8, folder 328, BF-SLRC. For the larger story, see Elizabeth A. Fones-Wolf, *Selling Free Enterprise: The Business Assault on Labor and Liberalism, 1945–60* (Urbana, 1994).

6. Betty Goldstein, "Pretty Posters Won't Stop Turnover of Women in Industry," Federated Press, 26 Oct. 1943, and Ruth Young quoted in same, carton 8, folder 328, BF-SLRC.

7. Betty Goldstein, "Post War Living: 'Are They Putting Something Over on Us?' Mrs. Jones Wonders," Federated Press, 23 Jan. 1946, carton 8, folder 329, BF-SLRC.

8. Job application, 1951.

aware of the UE's commitments to equity for women.[9] Friedan's years on *UE News*, which made her familiar with radicalism in the 1940s and early 1950s, provided a seed bed of her feminism. Her writings in the 1940s and early 1950s reveal that although she did not focus on the Soviet Union or on American-Soviet relations, Popular Front ideology shaped the way Friedan viewed American society and politics. As Flexner said of her own work for justice for working-class and African American women from the 1930s to the 1950s, left-wing movements welcomed "an enormous latitude of opinions under a very broad umbrella."[1] Specific political affiliation was not important; what was critical was commitment to a broad range of issues within the framework of a fight for social justice. The end of the cold war makes it possible to look at the left in the 1940s without the baggage of redbaiting. Indeed, the world in which Friedan moved in the 1940s and early 1950s was varied, containing as it did Party members, pacificists, socialists, union activists, fighters for justice for African Americans—and at *UE News*, Katherine Beecher, the grandniece of the nineteenth-century feminist Catharine Beecher.[2]

In the immediate postwar period, the UE fought for justice for African Americans and women.[3] In 1949–50, union activists who followed the recommendations of the Communist Party, torn in the postwar years by bitter internal divisions, advocated the automatic granting of several years of seniority to all African Americans as compensation for their years of exclusion from the electrical industry. If the UE pioneered in articulating what we might call affirmative action for African Americans, then before and during World War II it advocated what a later generation would label comparable worth. Against considerable resistance from within its ranks, the UE also worked to improve the conditions of working-

9. For information on women in the UE see Schatz, *Electrical Workers*; Ruth Milkman, *Gender at Work: The Dynamics of Job Segregation by Sex During World War II* (Urbana, 1987); Kannenberg, "Impact"; Lisa A. Kannenberg, "From World War to Cold War: Women Electrical Workers and Their Union, 1940–1955," M.A. thesis, University of North Carolina, Charlotte, 1990. Robert H. Zieger, *The CIO, 1935–1955* (Chapel Hill, N.C., 1995), 253–93 assesses the role of communists in the CIO, including the UE and discusses the vagueness of the line between sympathy and Party membership in unions like the UE; Ronald L. Filippelli and Mark McCulloch, *Cold War in the Working Class: The Rise and Decline of the United Electrical Workers* (Albany, N.Y., 1994) charts the attack on the UE and discusses the issue of communist presence in the UE.
1. Van Voris, Flexner interview, 8 Jan. 1977, 16 Oct. 1982, and 11 May 1983, 2, 62, 67, 70–71, 81–82. Helen K. Chinoy, who shared a house with Friedan in the summer of 1944 or 1945, confirmed this judgment that in the 1940s Party membership was not the critical issue among those on the left who identified themselves with a wide range of political positions: Daniel Horowitz, interview with Helen K. Chinoy, Northampton, Mass., 7 Oct. 1995.
2. For Beecher's ancestry, I am relying on James Lerner, interview with Daniel Horowitz, Brooklyn, N.Y., 21 Aug. 1995.
3. For the positive responses of this union and other communist-led ones to problems of minority and female workers, see Zieger, *CIO*, 87 and 255–56.

class women in part by countering a seniority system which gave advantage to men.[4] After 1949, with the UE out of the CIO and many of the more conservative union members out of the UE, women's issues and women's leadership resumed the importance they had in the UE during World War II, when it had developed, Ruth Milkman has written, a "strong ideological commitment to gender equality."[5]

Beginning in 1946, Friedan witnessed the efforts by federal agencies, congressional committees, major corporations, the Roman Catholic Church, and the CIO to break the hold of what they saw as the domination of the UE by communists. The inclusion of a clause in the Taft-Hartley Act of 1947, requiring union officers to sign an anti-communist affidavit if they wished to do business with the National Labor Relations Board, helped encourage other unions to challenge the UE, whose leaders refused to sign.[6] Internecine fights took place within the UE, part of a longer term fight between radicals and anti-communists in its ranks. One anti-communist long active in the union spoke of how a communist minority "seized control of the national office, the executive board, the paid staff, the union newspaper and some district councils and locals." The division in union ranks had reverberations in national politics as well: in 1948 the anti-communists supported President Harry S. Truman, while their opponents campaigned for Henry Wallace. In the short term the attack on the UE intensified its commitment to equity for working women, something that grew out of both ideological commitments and practical considerations. Before long, however, the UE was greatly weakened: in 1949, its connection with the CIO was severed and the newly-formed and CIO-backed IUE recruited many of its members. Membership in UE, numbering more than 600,000 in 1946, fell to 203,000 in 1953 and to 71,000 four years later.[7]

Reading the pages of *UE News* in the late 1940s and early 1950s opens a world unfamiliar to those who think that in this period Americans heard only hosannas to American exceptionalism. The villains of the publication were Truman, Hubert H. Humphrey, Richard M. Nixon, Walter Reuther, HUAC, and American capitalists. The heroes included Wallace, Franklin D. Roosevelt, and

---

4. Schatz, *Electrical Workers*, 30, 89, 116–27, 129–30.
5. Milkman, *Gender at Work*, 77–78; see also Kannenberg, "Impact," esp. 311, 315. Nancy B. Palmer, "Gender, Sexuality, and Work: Women and Men in the Electrical Industry, 1940–1955," Ph.D. diss., Boston College, 1995, more skeptical of women's gains in the UE, focuses on how the construction of gender in labor unions, including the UE, limited women's advances: see esp. chap. 4.
6. Zieger, *CIO*, 251.
7. This summary relies on Schatz, *Electrical Workers*, 167–240. The 1946 quote is from Harry Block in Schatz, *Electrical Workers*, 181. For the impact of the attack on UE on women's issues, see Kannenberg, "From World War to Cold War," 95.

union leaders who fought to protect the rights and lives of working people. Above all, the paper celebrated ordinary workers, including women and African Americans, who found themselves engaged in a class struggle against greedy corporations and opportunistic politicians.

At *UE News*, from her position as a middle-class woman interested in the lives of the working class, Friedan continued to articulate a progressive position on a wide range of issues. She again pointed to concerted efforts, led by big corporations under the leadership of the NAM, to increase profits, exploit labor, and break labor unions.[8] In 1951, she contrasted the extravagant expenditures of the wealthy with the family of a worker who could afford neither fresh vegetables nor new clothes.[9] Friedan also told the story of how valiant union members helped build political coalitions to fight Congressional and corporate efforts to roll back gains workers made during the New Deal and World War II.[1] She drew parallels between the United States in the 1940s and Nazi Germany in the 1930s as she exposed the way HUAC and big business were using every tactic they could to destroy the UE. Friedan hailed the launching of the Progressive Party in 1948.[2] She exposed the existence of racism and discrimination, even when they appeared among union officials and especially when directed against Jews and African Americans. Praising heroic workers who struggled against great odds as they fought monopolies, Friedan, probably expressing her hopes for herself, extolled the skills of a writer "who is able to describe with sincerity and passion the hopes, the struggle and the romance of the working people who make up most of America."[3]

8. Betty Goldstein, "NAM Does Gleeful War Dance to Profits, Wage Cuts, Taft Law," *UE News*, 13 Dec. 1947, 4. What follows relies on the more than three dozen articles signed by Betty Goldstein in the *UE News* from the fall of 1946 until early 1952.

9. Betty Goldstein, "A Tale of 'Sacrifice': A Story of Equality in the United States, 1951," *March of Labor*, May 1951, 16–18, carton 8, folder 334, BF-SLRC. This also appeared in *UE News*, 12 Mar. 1951, 6–7.

1. Betty Goldstein, "It'll Take a Strong Union To End Winchester Tyranny," *UE News*, 7 Dec. 1946, 9; Betty Goldstein, "Fighting Together: We Will Win!" *UE News*, 31 May 1947, 5, 8; Betty Goldstein, "Labor Builds New Political Organization To Fight for a People's Congressman," *UE News*, 23 Aug. 1947, 4.

2. Betty Goldstein, "People's Needs Forgotten: Big Business Runs Govt.," *UE News*, 12 May 1947, 5; Betty Goldstein, "In Defense of Freedom! The People Vs. the UnAmerican Committee," *UE News*, 8 Nov. 1947, 6–7; Betty Goldstein, "They Can't Shove the IBEW Down Our Throats," *UE News*, 4 Sept. 1948, 6–7; Betty Goldstein, "UnAmerican Hearing Exposed as Plot By Outsiders to Keep Grip on UE Local," *UE News*, 22 Aug. 1949, 4; Betty Goldstein, "New NAM Theme Song: Labor-Management Teamwork," *UENews*, 9 Jan. 1950, 5; Betty Goldstein, "Plain People of America Organize New Political Party of Their Own," *UE News*, 31 July 1948, 6–7.

3. B. G., review of Sinclair Lewis, *Kingsblood Royal*, *UE News*, 6 Sept. 1947, 7; B. G., review of the movie "Gentleman's Agreement," *UE News*, 22 Nov. 1947, 11; B. G., review of movie "Crossfire," *UE News*, 9 Aug. 1947, 8–9; Betty Goldstein, "CIO Sold Out Fight for FEPC, T-H Repeal, Rep. Powell Reveals," *UE News*, 17 Apr. 1950, 4; B. G., review of Fielding Burke, *Sons of the Stranger*, *UE News*, 24 Jan. 1948, 7.

Throughout her years at *UE News*, Friedan participated in discussions on women's issues, including the issue of corporations' systematic discrimination against women. Going to factories to interview those whose stories she was covering, she also wrote about working women, including African Americans and Latinas.[4] In the worlds Friedan inhabited in the decade beginning in 1943, as the historian Kathleen Weigand has shown, people often discussed the cultural and economic sources of women's oppression, the nature of discrimination based on sex, the special difficulties African American women faced, and the dynamics of discrimination against women in a variety of institutions, including the family.[5] Moreover, for the people around Friedan and doubtlessly for Friedan herself, the fight for justice for women was inseparable from the more general struggle to secure rights for African Americans and workers.[6] As she had done at the Federated Press, at *UE News* in the late 1940s and early 1950s she reported on how working women struggled as producers and consumers to make sure their families had enough to live on.[7]

Friedan's focus on working women's issues resulted in her writing the pamphlet, *UE Fights for Women Workers*, published by the UE in June of 1952.[8] She began by suggesting the contradiction in industry's treatment of women as consumers and as producers. "In advertisements across the land," Friedan remarked, "industry glorifies the American woman—in her gleaming GE kitchen, at her

4. These two sentences rely on James Lerner, interview. For treatments of the relationship between communism and women's issues, see Ellen K. Trimberger, "Women in the Old and New Left: The Evolution of a Politics of Personal Life," *Feminist Studies* 5 (fall 1979): 432–61; Van Gosse, "'To Organize in Every Neighborhood, in Every Home': The Gender Politics of American Communists Between the Wars," *Radical History Review* 50 (spring 1991): 109–41; Kannenberg, "From World War to Cold War"; and Weigand, "Vanguards." For her coverage of Latinas, see Betty Goldstein, "'It's a Union That Fights for All the Workers,'" *UE News*, 3 [?] Sept. 1951, 6–7.
5. Though she does not discuss Friedan's situation, the best treatment of the prominent role of women's issues in radical circles in the 1940s and 1950s is Weigand, "Vanguards." In working on *The Feminine Mystique*, Friedan may have been influenced by writings she may have encountered in the 1940s, such as Mary Inman, *In Women's Defense* (Los Angeles, 1940) and Betty Millard, "Woman Against Myth," *New Masses*, 30 Dec. 1947, 7–10 and 6 Jan. 1948, 7–20. There is evidence that Friedan was well aware of *New Masses*. Under a pseudonym, she published two articles in *New Masses*: Lillian Stone, "Labor and the Community," *New Masses* 57 (23 Oct. 1945): 3–5; Lillian Stone, "New Day in Stamford," *New Masses* 58 (22 Jan. 1946): 3–5. In identifying Friedan as the author, I am relying on a 22 Sept. 1995 conversation with Kathy Kraft, an archivist at the Schlesinger Library and on a letter in carton 49, folder 1783, BF-SLRC.
6. Chinoy, interview.
7. Betty Goldstein, "Price Cuts Promised in Press Invisible to GE Housewives," *UE News*, 1 Feb. 1947, 7; Betty Goldstein, "Union Members Want to Know—WHO Has Too Much Money to Spend," *UE News*, 26 Mar. 1951, 8.
8. [Betty Goldstein], *UE Fights for Women Workers*, UE Publication no. 232, June 1952 (New York, 1952). To authenticate her authorship, I am relying on the following: Horowitz, interview; James Lerner, interview; Betty Friedan, postcard to author, late August, 1995; Meltzer, *Friedan*, 25. Meltzer, who knew Friedan in the 1940s, discusses her work on women's issues at the UE. Friedan may also have written *Women Fight For a Better Life!* (New York, 1953): see Friedan, postcard.

Westinghouse laundromat, before her Sylvania television set. Nothing," she announced as she insightfully explored a central contradiction women faced in the postwar world, "is too good for her—unless"
she worked for corporations, including GE, or Westinghouse, or
Sylvania.[9]

The central theme of the piece was how, in an effort to improve
the pay and conditions of working women, the UE fought valiantly
against greedy corporations that sought to increase their profits by
exploiting women. Friedan discussed a landmark 1945 National
War Labor Board decision on sex-based wage discrimination in
favor of the UE. Remarking that *fighting the exploitation of women
is men's business too*," she emphasized how discriminatory practices
corporations used against women hurt men as well by exerting
downward pressure on wages of all workers. To back up the call for
equal pay for equal work and to fight against segregation and discrimination of women, she countered stereotypes justifying lower
pay for women: they were physically weaker, entered the work force
only temporarily, had no families to support, and worked only for
pin money. She highlighted the "even more shocking" situation
African American women faced, having to deal as they did with the
"double bars" of being female and African American.[1] Friedan set
forth a program that was, Lisa Kannenberg has noted, "a prescription for a gender-blind workplace."[2]

Nor did Friedan's interest in working women end with the publication of this pamphlet. For a brief period, she worked as a free-
lance labor journalist. In the winter of 1952–53, she was probably
the author of a series of articles for *Jewish Life: A Progressive
Monthly*. These pieces were somewhat more radical in tone than
those Friedan had written for *UE News*, in part because her foil was
the International Ladies' Garment Workers' Union, whose commitment to women workers and progressive politics was no match for
the UE's. She explored the contradiction of a situation where
wealthy women dressed in clothes working-class women labored to
produce. She told a story of rising profits and declining wages in a
union that had, she argued, taken a conciliatory position with
employers.[3] Then, in May 1953, she carefully tracked and probably
participated in what a historian has said "appears to be one of the
first national women's conferences in the postwar era."[4] There

9. [Goldstein], *UE Fights*, 5.
1. [Goldstein], *UE Fights*, 9–18, 26–27, 38.
2. Kannenberg, "Impact," 318.
3. See the following articles in *Jewish Life* by Rachel Roth: "'We're Worse Off Every Year,'"
   7 (April 1953): 11–14; "A 'Sick' Industry—But the Bosses Don't Suffer," 7 (May 1953):
   10–13; "The Price of 'Collaboration,'" 7 (June 1953): 21–24. In identifying Friedan as
   the author, I am relying on the 22 Sept. 1995 conversation with Kathy Kraft.
4. Kannenberg, "Impact," 318; the conference took place in New York in early May, 1953.

Friedan followed discussions of the importance of sharing of household duties. She also heard of the efforts of profit-hungry corporations to divide the working class by emphasizing divisions between whites and African Americans as well as between men and women. She again learned of the union's advocacy of federal legislation to lower military expenditures and support programs for child care, maternity benefits, and equal pay.[5]

Friedan's association with the labor movement gave her a sustained education in issues of sexual discrimination and shaped her emergence as a feminist. However, the precise impact of the influence is not clear. If, as some historians have suggested, the UE remained committed to gender equality, then Friedan's years as a labor journalist may well have provided a positive inspiration.[6] In contrast, the historian Nancy Palmer has argued that women in the UE persistently faced difficulties when they articulated their grievances but, in the name of solidarity, were told not to rock the boat.[7] Such a situation might mean that her experience with radical organizations that could not live up to their vision of a just and egalitarian society served more as a negative spur than a positive inspiration. At both the Federated Press and *UE News*, she lost her jobs to men who had more seniority, a general policy issue that had concerned the UE at least since the early 1940s.

The conditions under which she left Federated Press and *UE News* are not entirely clear. In May of 1946, during her second stint at Federated Press, she filed a grievance with the Newspaper Guild, saying she had lost her job in June of 1945 to a man she had replaced during the war. Later she claimed she was "bumped" from her position "by a returning veteran." There is evidence, however, that Friedan had to give up her position to a man who returned to the paper after two years in prison because he refused to serve in the military during what he considered a capitalists' war.[8] Friedan later claimed that she lost her job at the UE during her second pregnancy because the labor movement failed to honor its commitment to maternity leaves. Yet a knowledgeable observer has written that when the union had to cut the staff because of the dramatic drop in its membership, something that resulted from McCarthyite

5. These issues appear in "Resolution on Job Discrimination," "Resolution on Legislative Action," and "National Conference on the Problems of Working Women," mimeographed documents in carton 8, folder 336, BF-SLRC.
6. Generally speaking, Kannenberg and Schatz emphasize the genuineness of the UE's commitments, despite opposition within the union.
7. Palmer, "Gender, Sexuality, and Work."
8. Betty Goldstein to Grievance Committee of Newspaper Guild of New York, 23 May 1946, carton 8, folder 330, BF-SLRC; Friedan, *Changed My Life*, 9; Mim Kelber, phone conversation with Daniel Horowitz, 16 Sept. 1995, identified the man as James Peck; obituary for James Peck, *New York Times* 13 July 1993, B7.

attacks, Friedan "offered to quit so another reporter," a man with more seniority, could remain at *UE News*.[9] Although her experience with unions may have provided a negative spur to her feminism, it also served as a positive inspiration. Friedan was indebted to the UE for major elements of her education about gender equity, sex discrimination, and women's issues.

The reason Friedan left out these years in her life story is now clear. Her stint at the *UE News* took place at the height of the anti-communist crusade, which she experienced at close quarters. When she emerged into the limelight in 1963, the issue of affiliation with communists was wracking SANE, SDS, and the civil rights movement. In the same years, HUAC was still holding hearings, the United States was pursuing an anti-communist war in Vietnam, and J. Edgar Hoover's FBI was wiretapping Martin Luther King, Jr., ostensibly to protect the nation against communist influence. Had Friedan revealed all in the mid-1960s, she would have undercut her book's impact, subjected herself to palpable dangers, and jeopardized the feminist movement, including the National Organization for Women (NOW), an institution she was instrumental in launching. Perhaps instead of emphasizing continuities in her life, she told the story of her conversion in order to heighten the impact of her book and appeal to white middle-class women. Or maybe, having participated in social movements that did not live up to her dreams, in *The Feminine Mystique*, whether consciously or not, she was trying to mobilize middle-class readers and thus prove something to the men on the left. When constructing a narrative, she may have adopted a convention that made it difficult to discuss anger, ambition, excitement, and power.[1] * * *

*   *   *

A reconsideration of Friedan's career deepens our understanding of the relationship of the 1930s, 1940s, and 1950s to the social protests of the 1960s.[2] Her life underscores the difficulty of separating history into neatly packaged decades. Friedan's experiences in the 1940s and 1950s show us once again that life in the years before

9. Meltzer, *Friedan*, 29. For additional perspectives on Friedan's departure from the *UE News*, see Kelber, conversation and James Lerner, interview. Lerner, who had more seniority than Friedan, worked for the UE for more than 40 years, eventually becoming managing editor of *UE News*. He shared an office with Friedan during her years at *UE News* and has noted that the union protected Friedan's position during her first pregnancy: James Lerner, interview.

1. Margery Sly pointed me toward discussions of how women write about themselves, especially Carolyn G. Heilbrun, *Writing a Woman's Life* (New York, 1988), 13, 17, 24, 25; Jill K. Conway, "Introduction," *Written by Herself: Autobiographies of American Women: An Anthology*, ed. Jill K. Conway (New York, 1992), x–xi.

2. See, for example, Todd Gitlin, *The Sixties: Years of Hope, Days of Rage* (New York, 1987), 11–71.

the 1960s was hardly calm.[3] It reminds us of how issues of Communism and anti-Communism shaped a generation. * * *

* * *

* * * Friedan's story suggests that, at least as far as she and some others are concerned, what we have seen as liberal feminism had radical origins. Consequently, it underscores the importance of a reconsideration of the nature of the breach between the proponents of women's rights in the early 1960s and the late 1960s advocates of women's liberation, especially socialist feminists. For Friedan, labor union activity in the 1940s and early 1950s provided the bridge over which she moved from the working class to women as the repository of her hopes as well as much of the material from which she would fashion her feminism in *The Feminine Mystique.*

ELLEN HERMAN

From The Romance of American Psychology: Political Culture in the Age of Experts[†]

* * *

* * * Years before a mass women's movement materialized Betty Friedan * * * blamed the "new psychological religion" of adjustment for endowing a self-destructive femininity with social and scientific authority.[1] Friedan, a Smith College graduate and middle-class housewife who had once aspired to a career in psychology herself, launched a journalistic attack on psychological experts in her bestselling *The Feminine Mystique* (1963). Freudian theories about femininity, she claimed, were "an obstacle to truth for women in America today, and a major cause of the pervasive problem that has no name."[2] Her survey of stories in women's magazines like *Redbook* and *Good Housekeeping* (publications for which she had written herself during the 1950s) convinced Friedan that after 1945, "Freudian and pseudo-Freudian theories settled everywhere, like

3. For some examples of this reinterpretation of the 1950s, see Wini Breines, *Young, White, and Miserable: Growing Up Female in the Fifties* (Boston, 1992); Brett Harvey, *The Fifties: A Women's Oral History* (New York, 1993); Lary May, ed., *Recasting America: Culture and Politics in the Age of Cold War* (Chicago, 1989).
† From Ellen Herman, *The Romance of American Psychology: Political Culture in the Age of Experts* (Berkeley: University of California Press, 1995), pp. 290–292. Copyright © 1995 by The Regents of the University of California. Reprinted by permission. Notes have been renumbered.
1. Betty Friedan, *The Feminine Mystique* (New York: Dell, 1963), 115.
2. Ibid., 96.

fine volcanic ash."[3] Because the gospel according to Freud allowed women to derive true happiness only from their relationships to husbands and children, popularizers made housewives feel neurotic for hungering after any independent self at all. Convinced that something was deeply wrong with their mental and emotional health, middle-class housewives lined up in psychotherapists' offices, seeking yet more expert help in their quest for feminine adjustment.

These were certainly harsh criticisms, coming as they did at a moment of widespread enthusiasm about psychoanalytic ideas. But Friedan was also careful to note the "basic genius of Freud's discoveries" and insisted there was no conspiracy against women among the experts.[4] Most important, she saw the liberating possibilities of harnessing psychological theory to feminist purposes. She emphasized the notion of "some positive growth tendency within the organism," advanced by Gordon Allport, Carl Rogers, Karen Horney, and Rollo May, among others.[5] Their humanistic formulations, and especially Abraham Maslow's motivational theory, could be used as ammunition to argue that the tragedy of the (middle-class) female condition was due to "the forfeited self."[6] Maslow's theory suggested that people moved progressively through a series of human motivations, from lower, material needs to higher, nonmaterial needs. When their needs for food and housing were assured, in other words, people could be expected to attend to their desires for creative experience and accomplishment. The most popular feature of his theory was Maslow's portrait of "self-actualizing" individuals, a term he used to designate those people who had climbed to the top of the motivational ladder in order to explore their humanity through exciting, "peak experiences."

Friedan was alarmed at the almost complete absence of women on Maslow's list of peakers. (The only two exceptions were historical figures Eleanor Roosevelt and Jane Addams.) She turned women's relative exclusion from the ultimate in psychological integration, at least according to Maslow, into an appeal for feminism. She treated the scarcity of female peakers as powerful evidence that cultural prescriptions requiring middle-class housewives to devote themselves exclusively to the needs of husbands and children also doomed them to a psychological hell, or at least a decidedly second-class emotional existence. The core of the feminine mystique, Friedan wrote, was that "our culture does not permit women to accept or gratify their basic need to grow and fulfill their potentialities as human beings."[7] Why, she asked, should women be expected to

3. Ibid., 115.
4. Ibid., 95.
5. Ibid., 299.
6. Ibid., chap. 13.
7. Ibid., 69.

renounce their natural tendencies toward individuality and creativity? Were they not entitled to equal psychological opportunities?

If the ideology of femininity directly contradicted the process of self-actualization, as Friedan maintained, then psychology could provide real support to feminist arguments. Women deserved rights and opportunities, not only to employment and equal pay, but to the less tangible rewards of living as whole human beings. That her commitment to the value of psychological knowledge was not an abstract exercise is evident in the National Organization for Women's 1966 statement of purpose, which explicitly incorporated the humanistic refrain: "NOW is dedicated to the proposition that women first and foremost are human beings, who, like all other people in our society, must have the chance to develop their fullest human potential."[8]

REBECCA JO PLANT

From Mom: The Transformation of Motherhood in Modern America[†]

* * *

Whatever role Friedan's connections to political radicalism played in shaping her work as a whole, the antimaternalist component of her argument must be traced to other sources.[1] Its origins lay not in the legacy of popular front radicalism but rather in the 1920s cultural rebellion against the late Victorian matriarch and the concomitant rise of a therapeutic culture. As Friedan recollected in her autobiography, "When Philip Wylie's book attacking the American 'mom' came out, and I started studying Freud in college, I would say things

---

8. The National Organization for Women, "Statement of Purpose," in Betty Friedan, *It Changed My Life: Writings on the Women's Movement* (New York: Random House, 1976), 87.

† From Rebecca Jo Plant, *Mom: The Transformation of Motherhood in Modern America* (Chicago: The University of Chicago Press, 2010), pp. 150–54. Reprinted by permission of the University of Chicago Press. Notes have been renumbered.

1. While mother-blaming often went hand-in-hand with politically progressive views on race and other social issues, as Ruth Feldstein has shown, it appealed more to liberals who embraced psychological concepts of the self than radicals who privileged class-based approaches to social problems. This was not a hard and fast division; some leading intellectuals who sought to combine psychoanalytic and Marxist approaches were influenced by the momism critique. (For instance, T. W. Adorno's *The Authoritarian Personality*, which Friedan cited as a major influence, briefly refers to "Wylie's theory of momism.") Still, antimaternalism does not appear to have figured prominently in the left-wing labor or communist movements of the 1940s and 1950s. See Dorothy Sue Cobble, *The Other Women's Movement: Workplace Justice and Social Justice in Modern America* (Princeton, NJ: Princeton University Press, 2004); and Kate Weigand, *Red Feminism: American Communism and the Making of Women's Liberation* (Baltimore: Johns Hopkins University Press, 2001).

like: All mothers should be drowned at birth."[2] In the social and cultural milieu in which she came of age, such a vehement pronouncement may not have seemed all that extraordinary. Friedan * * * graduated in 1942, the same year that *Generation of Vipers* appeared.[3] When privileged youth of her generation attacked the all-American mom, they were not simply airing their views about childrearing techniques; they felt themselves to be doing something far more subversive. Mother-blaming allowed them to signal a rejection of Victorian moral strictures and a commitment to a more secular, psychologically oriented approach to sexuality and the self. It could also be a way of mocking a middlebrow popular culture that seemed hopelessly sentimental, or a means of repudiating nativist patriotism in favor of a more democratic notion of American identity. And for an ambitious young woman like Friedan, it could be a way of conveying a fervent desire for a different kind of life than that which her mother led.

If the cultural climate of Friedan's youth sanctioned a generalized hostility toward mothers, her attraction to *Generation of Vipers* also had deeply personal origins. Friedan grew up in the 1920s and 1930s in Peoria, Illinois, the daughter of Harry Goldstein, a Jewish immigrant from Kiev, and Miriam Goldstein, an American-born Jew. During the 1920s, Harry ran a successful jewelry store that supported the lavish lifestyle of his beautiful and much younger wife. With a nursemaid to tend the three children and a maid to cook and clean, Miriam was free to spend her time shopping, playing bridge and tennis, and pursuing desultory voluntary activities. Nevertheless, to her first-born, she often seemed angry and malcontent; according to Friedan, she badgered her children, belittled her husband, and suffered from periodic bouts of colitis that left her bedridden and "screaming in pain." Familial relations grew still more strained during the Depression, when Miriam refused to curb her spending and even resorted to gambling. Eventually, Harry's heart began to fail, and Miriam assumed responsibility for running the store, at which point her physical problems abated and her incessant nagging lessened. But by then, Friedan's resentment toward her mother had hardened into implacable hostility. In 1943, after her father died, she began suffering severe asthma attacks and entered psychoanalysis (or what she called "Freudian therapy"). Reflecting on the experience many years later, what she recalled was "lying on a couch and talking endlessly about how I hated my mother and how she had killed my father."[4]

---

2. Betty Friedan, *Life So Far: A Memoir* (New York: Simon & Schuster, 2000), 31.
3. For a highly informative account of Friedan's college years, see Horowitz, *Betty Friedan and the Making of "The Feminine Mystique,"* chaps. 2–4.
4. Friedan, *Life So Far*, 121. According to biographer Judith Hennessee, Friedan told friends that Miriam was paying for the analysis because, after all, her mother was the

A socially ambitious wife who drives her husband to an early grave and her children to a psychiatrist, an economic parasite who consumes with abandon, a neurotic who conspicuously suffers from psychosomatic ailments—these are, of course, the classic images of midcentury antimaternalism. As Friedan recounted in *The Feminine Mystique*, two negative images of womanhood haunted her throughout early adulthood. While she "dreaded" becoming like the women she knew who had remained single and childless—"the old-maid high-school teachers; the librarian; the one woman doctor in our town, who cut her hair like a man; and a few of my college professors"—she also recoiled from the model presented by her own mother and her friends' mothers. "In my generation, many of us knew that we did not want to be like our mothers, even when we loved them," she explained. "Did we understand, or only resent, the sadness, the emptiness, that made them hold too fast to us, try to live our lives, run our fathers' lives, spend their days shopping or yearning for things that never seemed to satisfy them, no matter how much money they cost?"[5] To Friedan, Wylie's mom—the woman who bossed her husband, dominated her children, engaged in rampant consumption, and whiled away her time with bridge games and charity work—was not simply a misogynist caricature. She was a real, all-too-prevalent social type, and she represented a potential threat to young women who desired a life beyond the home.[6]

Still, if Friedan portrayed Miriam Goldstein as a Wyliesque mom, she also implied (inadvertently, it would seem) that her mother had played a crucial role in her success as a writer and feminist critic. In 1973, when she attempted to explain the genesis of *The Feminine Mystique*, she began with her mother:

> There was my mother, and her discontent, which I never understood. I didn't want to be like my mother. Nothing my father did, nothing he bought her, nothing we did ever seemed to satisfy her. When she married my father, she'd had to give

reason why she needed psychoanalysis in the first place. Hennessee, *Betty Friedan: Her Life*, 38–39. For a more extensive account of Friedan's childhood and college years, see Horowitz, *Betty Friedan and the Making of "The Feminine Mystique*," chaps. 1–5.

5. Friedan, *The Feminine Mystique*, 72–3.

6. Historian Joyce Antler, who has analyzed the cultural constructions of Jewish mothers, writes, "It was Friedan's negative perception of her mother . . . that provided the driving force of the liberation movement that younger feminists put in motion by the end of the 1960s. Young Jewish women's relationships with their own Jewish mothers served as one factor in the mix of causes that generated the energy of women's liberation. Alternatively resentful of their mothers' domination of their lives or disappointed in their weaknesses, these women scornfully rejected both their mothers' authority and their compromises and sought other models." Joyce Antler, *You Never Call! You Never Write! A History of the Jewish Mother* (New York: Oxford University Press, 2007), 151.

up her job editing the woman's page of the newspaper in Peoria. She could hardly wait until I got to junior high to put the idea into my head to try out for the school newspaper, to start a literary magazine in high school. She could hardly wait for me to go to the college she had no chance to go to, to edit the newspaper there.

Friedan believed that her mother had pushed her to excel as a student and a writer to compensate for her own disappointments—the missed opportunity to attend a prestigious college, the reluctantly relinquished newspaper job. If one accepts this narrative, then one must conclude that it was at least partially because of Miriam's attempts to live vicariously through her daughter that Friedan came to possess the requisite skills and drive to write such a damning indictment of domesticity. Years later, when Friedan sent her mother a copy of *The Feminine Mystique*, she seemed to acknowledge as much. "With all the troubles we have had, you gave me the power to break through the feminine mystique," she wrote in an enclosed note. "I hope you accept the book for what it is, an affirmation of the values of your life and mine."[7]

Despite the ambivalence Friedan harbored toward her own mother, she enthusiastically embraced the experience of motherhood. Her children, she would later write in her autobiography, "seemed like a *bonus* in my life, an unexpected, maybe undeserved, marvelous bonus."[8] In certain respects, Friedan was fairly typical of highly educated mothers of the late 1940s and 1950s. She bore three children (in 1948, 1952, and 1956), avidly read Dr. Spock, and chose to breastfeed, despite a lack of support from hospital personnel.[9] But unlike the vast majority of her peers, Friedan also worked outside the home, even when her children were quite young.[1] Following the birth of her first child, Daniel, she took an eleven-month leave from her job with the *UE News*, the official publication of the left-wing United Electrical, Radio, and Machine Workers of America. Three years later, when she was pregnant with her second child, Jonathan, she lost her job.[2] Friedan later claimed that she felt angry but also relieved, "because all those negative

---

7. Quoted in Susan Oliver, *Betty Friedan: The Personal Is Political* (New York: Pearson Longman, 2008), 76.
8. Friedan, *Life So Far*, 77. Emphasis in the original.
9. Ibid., 74.
1. Friedan also married somewhat later, at age twenty-six, and spaced her children less closely together than most women of her generational cohort: Daniel was born in 1948; Jonathan in 1952; and Emily in 1956. For informative accounts of postwar marital and childbearing patterns, see May, *Homeward Bound*, introduction and chap. 6; and Weiss, *To Have and to Hold*, chap. 1.
2. Daniel Horowitz discusses the complicated circumstances surrounding her departure from *UE News* in *Betty Friedan and the Making of "The Feminine Mystique,"* 141–43.

books and magazine articles about 'career women' were beginning to get to me." She had been "too indoctrinated in psychology, Freudian psychology and its derivatives sweeping America in the years after World War II," she explained, to easily dismiss the notion that professional women "were losing their femininity, undermining their husband's masculinity, and destroying or stunting their children."[3] But soon after Friedan had "dispensed with the nursemaid," she grew depressed and experienced a recurrence of severe asthma, driving her back into therapy. Before Jonathan had reached his first birthday, she had employed a maid to come three days a week, allowing her to embark on a new career as a freelance journalist.[4]

If Friedan's own life failed to fit the contours of the "feminine mystique," neither did the messages that she received about motherhood from her doctors and therapists. When she returned to work at the *UE News* in 1949, her "wonderful" pediatrician repeatedly assured her that "despite what Dr. Spock said, it did not have to hurt my baby that I went back to work."[5] Similarly, the psychoanalyst William Menaker, whom she began to see after Jonathan's birth, questioned why she tried to confine herself to "'playing the role' of suburban housewife." During one of her sessions, he interpreted a dream that centered on the journalist John Hersey not as evidence of "penis envy" but rather "as a message to take my own writing more seriously." In fact, Friedan's experience with Menaker proved so positive that she sought him out again in 1958 after signing the contract for what would become *The Feminine Mystique*. No longer a patient, she asked Menaker whether he would be interested in collaborating with her, for she believed that his expertise would lend the book "more authority."[6]

Thus, had Friedan's editor not nixed the idea, the name of an "eminent male psychoanalyst" might have graced the cover of *The Feminine Mystique*. The notion is mind-boggling, for it is so thoroughly at odds with Friedan's well-established reputation as an ardent foe of psychoanalysis.[7] In her book, she argued unequivocally

3. Friedan, *Life So Far*, 79.
4. Ibid., 81–82.
5. Ibid., 75.
6. Ibid., 121–22.
7. For example, historian Mari Jo Buhle contrasts Friedan to later writers like Nancy Chodorow, who sought to reconcile the insights of feminism with those of psychoanalysis. "While Betty Friedan and Kate Millett busied themselves lambasting Freud," she writes, "a small coterie of feminists were preparing the way for a reunion with psychoanalysis." Mari Jo Buhle, *Feminism and Its Discontents: A Century of Struggle with Psychoanalysis* (Cambridge, MA: Harvard University Press, 1998), 240. Similarly, Eva Illouz writes, "Consensus grew among feminists to the effect that psychology reinforced traditional gender roles and inequality. Nowhere was this voice more strident than in Betty Friedan's *The Feminine Mystique*." Eva Illouz, *Saving the Modern Soul: Therapy, Emotions, and the Culture of Self-Help* (Berkeley: University of California Press, 2008), 113. Such formulations, however, imply a more hostile and critical stance toward psychoanalysis than Friedan actually assumed.

that the oppressive "feminine mystique" "derived its power from Freudian thought," and she devoted an entire chapter to portraying Freud as a "prisoner of his time" when it came to women.[8] Yet Friedan always differentiated between Freudian theory and its clinical application, and her disdain for popularized Freudianism never translated into a wholesale rejection of the psychoanalytic establishment. As she explained:

> No one can question the basic genius of Freud's discoveries, nor the contribution he has made to our culture. Nor do I question the effectiveness of psychoanalysis as it is practiced today by Freudian or anti-Freudian. But I do question, from my own experience as a woman, and from my reporter's knowledge of other women, the application of the Freudian theory of femininity to women today. I question its use, not in therapy, but as it has filtered into the lives of American women through the popular magazines and the opinions and interpretations of so-called experts.[9]

This surprising defense of psychoanalytic therapy seems to have reflected Friedan's positive experiences as an analytic patient in the 1940s and 1950s. At two crucial points in her life, psychoanalysis allowed her to affirm an independent identity that felt threatened by familial ties—specifically, by the intensity of the mother-child relationship. As a young single woman struggling to make her way in the 1940s, psychoanalysis helped her separate from her own mother and renounce her mother's bourgeois values and expectations. As a depressed and newly unemployed mother in the early 1950s, psychoanalysis helped her to affirm her ambitions as a writer and thereby retain a sense of self amid the relentless demands of rearing young children. In both cases, therapy provided Friedan with a means of addressing and resolving the difficulties that motherhood posed to individualism.

Friedan's critique of suburban motherhood in *The Feminine Mystique* strongly reflected her commitment to a psychotherapeutic notion of self-realization. She argued that full-time motherhood and homemaking could not serve as the basis of a mature identity, and that women who confined their energies to the mother-housewife role ultimately harmed both themselves and their loved ones.[1] "If an

8. Friedan, *The Feminine Mystique*, 103.
9. Ibid., 104.
1. According to Friedan's biographer, Judith Hennessee, such arguments "deeply hurt" and angered women neighbors and friends who had been "a support system" for Friedan during the years that she worked on *The Feminine Mystique*. These homemakers, who had "fed and cared for her children along with their own," felt "dismissed" and "used" when they learned that she had been busily writing about how "housework was something an eight-year-old could do." Hennessee, *Betty Friedan: Her Life*, 85–86.

able American woman does not use her human energy and ability in some meaningful pursuit," she insisted, "she will fritter away her energy in neurotic symptoms, or unproductive exercise, or destructive 'love.'"[2] Until women learned to "carry more of the burden of the battle with the world, instead of being a burden themselves," she warned, their "wasted energy" would "continue to be destructive to their husbands, to their children, and to themselves."[3] Friedan's (rather cursory) proposals for combating the "feminine mystique" therefore focused on freeing women from the all-consuming demands of motherhood and homemaking: she called for maternity leaves; greater access to childcare; and a "GI Bill" for mothers and housewives so that women could further their education.[4] "The only way for a woman, as for a man, to find herself, to know herself as a person, is by creative work of her own," she asserted. "There is no other way."[5]

✻   ✻   ✻

THE FEMININE MYSTIQUE:
ANALYZING BETTY FRIEDAN AS HISTORIAN

A number of scholars, including Joanne Meyerowitz, Eva Moskowitz, and Sylvie Murray, have questioned Betty Friedan's portrait of the feminine mystique in American Cold War culture. They have doubted, in particular, whether her description of the mystique found in women's magazine fiction (see chapter 2, "The Happy Housewife Heroine") accurately reflected stringent constraints on women's roles in the 1950s, or whether there existed more diversity, ambiguity, and even resistance in women's roles than she was willing to admit.

These scholars all successfully illustrate that Friedan was not the lone critic of 1950s domestic culture that she portrays herself to be. Friedan was actually part of a broad, diverse conversation about women's roles during the Cold War era. Indeed, had the feminine mystique been truly all-encompassing, Friedan's text could not have gained the wide readership that it did. The flaws of The Feminine Mystique, as these critics all note, thus offer us a valuable window onto the complicated role of women in the United States in the post–World War II era.

---

2. Friedan, *The Feminine Mystique*, 374.
3. Ibid., 377.
4. For Friedan's practical suggestions as to how to improve women's status, see ibid., 370–78.
5. Ibid., 344. Although Friedan did not stipulate that women had to engage in remunerative labor, most of the positive models she discussed in *The Feminine Mystique* were women who pursued professional careers.

JOANNE MEYEROWITZ

From Beyond *The Feminine Mystique*
A Reassessment of Postwar Mass Culture, 1946–1958[†]

* * *

The Feminine Mystique had an indisputable impact. Hundreds of women have testified that the book changed their lives, and historical accounts often credit it with launching the recent feminist movement. But the book has also had other kinds of historical impact. For a journalistic exposé, Friedan's work has had a surprisingly strong influence on historiography. In fact, since Friedan published *The Feminine Mystique,* historians of American women have adopted wholesale her version of the postwar ideology. While many historians question Friedan's homogenized account of women's actual experience, virtually all accept her version of the dominant ideology, the conservative promotion of domesticity.[1]

According to this now-standard historical account, postwar authors urged women to return to the home, and only a handful of social scientists, trade unionists, and feminists protested. As one recent rendition states: "In the wake of World War II . . . the short-lived affirmation of women's independence gave way to a pervasive endorsement of female subordination and domesticity."[2] Much of this secondary literature relies on a handful of conservative post-

---

† Selections from "Beyond *The Feminine Mystique*: A Reassessment of Postwar Mass Culture, 1946–1958," from *Not June Cleaver: Women and Gender in Postwar America, 1945–1960,* edited by Joanne Meyerowitz. (Philadelphia: Temple University Press, 1994), pp. 230; 231; 232–34; 251–52. Used by permission of Temple University Press. © 1994 by Temple University. All rights reserved. Notes have been renumbered.

1. Testimony on the impact of the book is found in the many letters written to Friedan. See Elaine Tyler May, *Homeward Bound: American Families in the Cold War Era* (New York: Basic Books, 1988), 209–217. Friedan's discussion of American women implicitly excludes the experiences of many lesbians, women of color, and working-class, activist, employed, and unmarried women. For a different account of women's postwar experience, see Eugenia Kaledin, *Mothers and More: American Women in the 1950's* (Boston: Twayne, 1984); for an overview, see Sara M. Evans, *Born for Liberty: A History of Women in America* (New York: Free Press, 1989), 250–260.
2. May, *Homeward Bound,* 89. On the late 1940s, see especially Susan Hartmann, "Prescriptions for Penelope: Literature on Women's Obligations to Returning World War II Veterans," *Women's Studies,* no. 3 (1978): 223–239; on the 1950s, see especially May, *Homeward Bound.* This interpretation is also found in overviews of the era and in women's history textbooks: See, for example, Marty Jezer, *The Dark Ages: Life in the United States, 1945–1960* (Boston: South End Press, 1982), 226–231; John Patrick Diggins, *The Proud Decades: America in War and in Peace, 1941–1960* (New York: Norton, 1988), 211–225; Evans, *Born for Liberty,* 234–239, 246–250; Nancy Woloch, *Women and the American Experience* (New York: Knopf, 1984), 496, 499–501. For the most balanced extended account, which notes that social scientist dissenters from the domestic ideology had some impact on mass culture, see William Henry Chafe, *The American Woman: Her Changing Social, Political and Economic Roles, 1920–1970* (New York: Oxford University Press, 1972), 199–225.

war writings, the same writings cited liberally by Friedan. In particular, the work of Dr. Marynia Farnham, a viciously antifeminist
psychiatrist, and her sidekick, sociologist Ferdinand Lundberg, is
invoked repeatedly as typical of the postwar era.[3] In this standard
account, the domestic ideology prevailed until such feminists as
Friedan triumphed in the 1960s.

* * *

With a somewhat different sample and a somewhat different inter-
pretive approach, I come to different conclusions about postwar
mass culture than did Friedan and her followers. Friedan's widely
accepted version of the "feminine mystique," I suggest, is only one
piece of the postwar cultural puzzle. The popular literature I sampled did not simply glorify domesticity or demand that women
return to or stay at home. All of the magazines sampled advocated
both the domestic and the nondomestic, sometimes in the same sentence. In this literature, domestic ideals coexisted in ongoing tension
with an ethos of individual achievement that celebrated nondomestic
activity, individual striving, public service, and public success.

* * *

In popular magazines, the theme of individual achievement rang
most clearly in the numerous articles on individual women. These
articles appeared with frequency throughout the postwar era: they
constituted more than 60 percent, or 300, of the 489 nonfiction
articles sampled. These articles usually recounted a story of a woman's life or a particularly telling episode in her life. In formulaic
accounts, they often constructed what one such article labeled
"this Horatio Alger success story—feminine version."[4] Of these articles, 33 percent spotlighted women with unusual talents, jobs, or
careers, and another 29 percent focused on prominent entertain-
ers. Typically they related a rise to public success punctuated by a
lucky break, a dramatic comeback, a selfless sacrifice, or a persistent struggle to overcome adversity. Such stories appeared in all the

3. Ferdinand Lundberg and Marynia F. Farnham, *Modern Woman: The Lost Sex* (New
York: Harper & Brothers, 1947). For Friedan's view of their influence, see Friedan,
Feminine Mystique, 37, 111. Historians who use Lundberg and Farnham to illustrate
the postwar ideology include Diggins, *The Proud Decades*, 214; Jezer, *The Dark Ages*,
227; Evans, *Born for Liberty*, 238–239, 248; Woloch, *Women and the American Experience*, 499; Leila J. Rupp and Verta Taylor, *Survival in the Doldrums: The American
Women's Rights Movement, 1945 to the 1960s* (New York: Oxford University Press,
1987), 19; Cynthia Harrison, *On Account of Sex: The Politics of Women's Issues, 1945–
1968* (Berkeley: University of California Press, 1988), 24–25; Glenna Matthews, *"Just
a Housewife": The Rise and Fall of Domesticity in America"* (New York: Oxford University Press, 1987), 209; Myra Dinnerstein, *Women Between Two Worlds: Midlife Reflec-
tions on Work and Family* (Philadelphia: Temple University Press, 1992), 4–5.
4. Alfred E. Smith, "Woman Realtor," *Negro Digest*, June 1950, 69.

magazines sampled, but they appeared most frequently in the African American magazines, *Ebony* and *Negro Digest,* and the white
"middlebrow" magazines, *Coronet* and *Reader's Digest.* Journalists
reworked the formula for different readers: In *Negro Digest,* for
example, articles returned repeatedly to black performers who
defied racism; in *Reader's Digest,* they more often addressed white
leaders in community service.[5] In general, though, the articles suggested that the noteworthy woman rose above and beyond ordinary
domesticity. Or, as one story stated: "This is the real-life fairy tale of
a girl who hurtled from drab obscurity to sudden, startling fame."[6]

At the heart of many such articles lay a bifocal vision of women
both as feminine and domestic and as public achievers. In one article, "The Lady Who Licked Crime in Portland," the author, Richard
L. Neuberger, juxtaposed domestic stereotypes and newsworthy nondomestic achievement. The woman in question, Dorothy McCullough
Lee, was, the article stated, an "ethereally pale housewife" who
tipped "the scales at 110 pounds." More to the point, she was also the
mayor of Portland, Oregon, who had defeated, singlehandedly it
seems, the heavyweights of organized crime. Before winning the
mayoral election in 1948, this housewife had opened a law firm and
served in the state legislature, both House and Senate, and as Portland's commissioner of public utilities. Despite her "frail, willowy"
appearance, the fearless mayor had withstood ridicule, recall petitions, and threatening mail in her "relentless drive" against gambling and prostitution. She was, the article related without further
critique, a "violent feminist" who had "intense concern with the
status of women." And, according to all, she was "headed for
national distinction." The article concluded with an admiring quo-
tation describing Mayor Lee's fancy hats as the plumes of a crusading knight in armor. Here the feminine imagery blended with a
metaphor of masculine public service.[7]

The joint endorsement of domestic and nondomestic roles
appeared in numerous stories that offered a postwar version of

5. The other articles on individual women covered a range of topics, including women
   royalty, women who overcame illnesses or disabilities, women who had telling experiences with racism (only in African American magazines), and women criminals. (The
   magazines were highly segregated. With only a few exceptions, the white magazines—
   Coronet, Reader's Digest, Harper's, Atlantic Monthly, Ladies' Home Journal, and *Woman's Home Companion*—presented stories about white women, and the African
   American magazines—*Ebony* and *Negro Digest*—presented stories about black
   women.) Stories about individual women were least prevalent in the highbrow magazines. The percentage of individual stories among all nonfiction stories on women was:
   Negro Digest, 95 percent; *Ebony,* 75 percent; *Coronet,* 69 percent; *Reader's Digest,* 61
   percent; *Woman's Home Companion,* 57 percent; *Ladies' Home Journal,* 41 percent;
   Harpers, 36 percent; *Atlantic Monthly,* 20 percent.
6. "The Jane Russell Story," *Coronet,* March 1950, 107.
7. Richard L. Neuberger, "The Lady Who Licked Crime in Portland," *Coronet,* June
   1952, 51–54.

today's "superwoman," the woman who successfully combines motherhood and career. As Jacqueline Jones has noted, *Ebony* magazine sometimes featured this type of article. One story, for example, presented Louise Williams, the mother of two and the only black mechanic at American Airlines. As *Ebony* reported: "She is a good cook, but an even better mechanic." She was also an inventor and an active member of her union. And, according to *Ebony*, she was "never a lazy housewife." Such stories in African American magazines clearly provided lessons in surmounting racism. In *Ebony*'s female version of racial advancement, women often excelled both in the workplace and at home.[8]

Similar articles appeared regularly in magazines geared to white readers. *Coronet* magazine, for example, presented the "amazing" Dorothy Kilgallen, "star reporter," who wrote a syndicated column, ad-libbed a daily radio program, ran forty charity benefits a year, and had "a handsome and successful husband, a beautiful home, [and] two lovely children." The successful combination of home and career made her "Gotham's busiest glamour girl." Articles of this type resolved the tension between domesticity and public achievement superficially by ignoring the difficulties that women usually faced in pursuing both.[9]

While feminine stereotypes sometimes provided convenient foils that enhanced by contrast a woman's atypical public accomplishment, they also served as conservative reminders that all women, even publicly successful women, were to maintain traditional gender distinctions.[1] In their opening paragraphs, numerous authors described their successful subjects as pretty, motherly, shapely, happily married, petite, charming, or soft voiced. This emphasis on femininity and domesticity (and the two were often conflated) seems to have cloaked a submerged fear of lesbian, mannish, or man-hating women. This fear surfaced in an unusual article on the athlete Babe Didrikson Zaharias. In her early years, the article stated, the Babe's "boyish bob and freakish clothes . . . [her] dislike of femininity" had led observers to dismiss her as an "Amazon." But after her marriage, she "became a woman," a transformation signaled, according to the approving author, by lipstick, polished nails, and "loose, flowing" hair, as well as by an interest in the domestic arts of cooking, sewing, and entertaining. In this article, as in others, allusions to femininity and domesticity probably helped legitimate

---

8. Jacqueline Jones, *Labor of Love, Labor of Sorrow: Black Women, Work, and the Family from Slavery to the Present* (New York: Basic Books, 1985), 274; "Lady Plane Mechanic," *Ebony*, January 1948, 30. See also "Milwaukee's First Lady Councilman," ibid., June 1958, 40–45.
9. Carol Hughes, "Dorothy Kilgallen: Star Reporter," *Coronet*, June 1950, 53–57. For another example, see Jana Guerrier, "Wall Street Woman," ibid., January 1954, 26–29.
1. See, for example, Neuberger, "Lady Who Licked Crime."

women's public achievements. Authors attempted to reassure readers that conventional gender distinctions and heterosexuality remained intact even as women competed successfully in work, politics, or sports. It is worth noting that in *The Feminine Mystique,* Friedan adopted this approach. She attempted to legitimate the early feminists by repeated insistence that most of them were feminine, married, and not man-hating.[2]

Nonetheless, the emphasis on the domestic and feminine should not be overstated; these articles on women's achievement did not serve solely or even primarily as lessons in traditional gender roles. The theme of nondomestic success was no hidden subtext in these stories. In most articles, the rise to public achievement was the first, and sometimes the only, narrative concern. When addressing both the domestic and the nondomestic, these articles placed public success at center stage: They tended to glorify frenetic activity, with domesticity at best a sideshow in a woman's three-ring circus.

*   *   *

When *The Feminine Mystique* appeared in 1963, it won positive reviews. Reviewers appreciated Friedan's "passionate drive," "convincing" feminism, and "sensible" suggestions. They rarely dwelt on her analysis of popular magazines; they commented instead on her overall findings. They deplored the discontent of housewives and joined Friedan in welcoming reform. One reviewer stated: "Friedan has put her finger on the key problem of American women today: recognition as individuals." And another said: "The argument needed to be made; women, like Negroes, have too often given equal rights in name only."[3]

Along with the general praise, though, negative comments abounded. Reviewers complained of Friedan's "sweeping generalities" and of her occasional tendency "to discover what she sets out

2. Lawrence Lader, "The Unbeatable Babe," *Coronet,* January 1948, 158. For a similar, though more veiled, account of "maturing as a woman," see the article on pianist Dorothy Donegan: "Queen of the Keys," *Ebony,* March 1958, 86. For a strikingly blatant account (outside this sample), see Gladys Bentley, "I Am a Woman Again," ibid., August 1952, 92–98. On postwar hostility to lesbians and gender transgression, see John D'Emilio, *Sexual Politics, Sexual Communities: The Making of a Homosexual Minority in the United States, 1940–1970* (Chicago: University of Chicago Press, 1983), 40–53; Donna Penn, "The Meanings of Lesbianism in Post-War America," *Gender and History,* Summer 1991, 190–203; and Lillian Faderman, *Odd Girls and Twilight Lovers: A History of Lesbian Life in Twentieth-Century America* (New York: Columbia University Press, 1991), 139–158. Friedan, *Feminine Mystique,* 73–94. For disparagement of male homosexuality, see ibid., 264–265.

3. Lillian Smith, "Too Tame the Shrew," *Saturday Review,* February 23, 1963, 44; Maurice Richardson, "Time for Eros," *New Statesman,* May 24, 1963, 798; Marya Mannes, "Don't Sweep the Ladies under the Rug," *New York Herald Tribune Books,* April 28, 1963, 1; Sylvia Fleis Fava, review of *Feminine Mystique* by Betty Friedan, *American Sociological Review,* December 1963, 1054; "The Segregated Sex," *Economist,* August 10, 1963, 519.

to find." Several reviewers believed that the discontent Friedan uncovered had deeper roots. The women's magazines, Madison Avenue advertisers, Sigmund Freud, and individual psychology were not, various reviewers claimed, the source of the problem. The noted novelist and civil rights advocate Lillian Smith suggested that "a vast complex of world-size problems and ancient customs" created the attitudes and images that oppressed women, and other reviewers pointed to "social institutions" and women themselves. The most damning assessment came from the *Yale Review*. The anonymous reviewer claimed that Friedan's account was nothing new: "It would seem by now that it has been amply demonstrated that women are both human beings and women. . . . This is all very well—and we have heard it before." As to housewives' unhappiness, this reviewer claimed that Friedan had "discovered later than many of her readers how prevalent this discontent has been and for how long."[4]

Indeed, many readers had "heard it before." *The Feminine Mystique* was not only a visionary work, a harbinger of the new liberal feminism; it also remained remarkably rooted in postwar culture. A free-lance journalist herself, Friedan adopted the terms of the prevailing popular discourse and restated the postwar cultural contradiction between the ideals of domesticity and achievement. Like other postwar journalists, Friedan did not question women's responsibility for home and children. She encouraged marriage and femininity, disparaged homosexuality, and expressed fears that neurotic, overbearing mothers ruined their children. Also like other postwar journalists, Friedan embraced liberal individualism and validated women's public participation. She saw women's achievements outside the home as a source of both personal fulfillment and public service, and she presented domesticity as a problem.

This is not to say that Friedan's work was simply derivative. In the more liberal political climate of the early 1960s, Friedan reworked older themes in significant ways. While both achievement and domesticity were middle-class ideals, Friedan elevated nondomestic achievement to the higher status of a natural human need and demoted full-time domesticity to the lower status of a false consciousness foisted on women by mass culture and pseudo-scientific experts. She thus legitimated open protest against "the housewife trap."[5] She exposed the tension between public achievement and domesticity in ways that affirmed the undeniable anger many

---

4. Lucy Freeman, review of *Feminine Mystique* by Friedan, *New York Times Book Review*, April 7, 1963, 46; review of *Feminine Mystique* by Friedan, *Virginia Quarterly Review*, Summer 1963, cviii; Smith, "Too Tame the Shrew," 44; Fava, review of *Feminine Mystique* by Friedan, 1054; Freeman, review of *Feminine Mystique* by Friedan, 46; review of *Feminine Mystique* by Friedan, *Yale Review*, March 1963, xii.
5. Friedan, *Feminine Mystique*, 325.

middle-class women felt as they increasingly tried to pursue both domestic and nondomestic ideals.

The continuities with the postwar discourse are nonetheless important because they may help explain Friedan's (and liberal feminism's) success. Friedan's account of the "feminine mystique" may have hit such a resonant chord among middle-class women in part because it reworked themes already rooted in the mass culture. The success of an oppositional discourse, like Friedan's, relies not only on how it counters the mainstream but also on how it draws on and reshapes familiar themes.

EVA MOSKOWITZ

From "It's Good to Blow Your Top": Women's Magazines and a Discourse of Discontent, 1945–1965[†]

Americans of the Cold War years are often remembered for their zealous commitment to domesticity. One prominent source identified with this cult of domesticity is women's magazines. As such, they became targets of feminist criticism. Beginning with *The Feminine Mystique* (1963), Betty Friedan condemned women's magazines for their "happy housewife" images. She accused them of representing women as "gaily content in a world of bedroom, kitchen, sex, babies, and home," while women experienced pain, dissatisfaction, and self-loathing.[1] Building upon these complaints, radical feminists took direct action against the magazines. In the 1970s, for example, feminists occupied the offices of the *Ladies Home Journal*.[2]

* * *

This article reexamines the myths about womanhood that feminists sought to deconstruct and that Cold War era women's magazines promoted, by looking at the three with the largest circulation of the period 1945 to 1965: *Ladies Home Journal, McCall's,* and *Cosmopolitan*.[3] My research suggests that these magazines did not merely

---

† From Eva Moskowitz, "'It's Good to Blow Your Top': Women's Magazines and a Discourse of Discontent, 1945–1965," *Journal of Women's History* 8.3 (Fall 1996): 66, 67, 68–69, 77–78, 87–88, 89, 91. © 1996 *Journal of Women's History*. Reprinted with permission of The Johns Hopkins University Press. Notes have been renumbered.

1. Betty Friedan, *The Feminine Mystique* (New York: Dell Publishing Co., 1963), 30.
2. Incident described in Marcia Cohen, *The Sisterhood: The Inside Story of the Women's Movement and the Leaders Who Made It Happen* (New York: Fawcett Columbine: 1989), 185.
3. My effort to reevaluate women's magazines is part of a more general effort by scholars working in a variety of disciplines to reevaluate the Cold War era. Rejecting a reductionist portrait of the 1950s, they have portrayed the period as more complex and

promote "the happy housewife" image. Indeed, far from imagining the home as a haven, the women's magazines often rendered it as a deadly battlefield on which women lost their happiness, if not their minds. Images of unhappy, angry, and depressed women figure prominently in these magazines, and this is found to be particularly evident in marital relations. In monthly columns such as "Can This Marriage Be Saved?," "Making Marriage Work," and "Why Marriages Fail," the magazines document women's discontent.

*   *   *

Drawing upon the work of pollsters and social scientists, the magazines provided statistical as well as qualitative pictures of the precarious psychological situation of the American housewife. As one magazine announced, it had made "a scientific study of the problem within recent years" and was in the process of "uncovering the hard, cold facts of what causes happiness and unhappiness. . . ."[4] Investigations of the American woman's state of mind indicated that women were more unhappy than men. Their unhappiness apparently stemmed from their dissatisfaction with their domestic roles:

> The explanation seems to be bound up with the responsibility of marriage and rearing a family. Women are inclined to think an undue share of these responsibilities falls on the wives; the majority of women think they lead a harder life than men; and they think their happiest years end sooner. Perhaps too, they think a housewife's life is duller; an earlier *Journal* survey

---

contradictory than previously thought, often finding within the Cold War era the seeds of its own destruction. Political scientist Michael Rogin, for example, in his provocative article, "Kiss Me Deadly: Communism, Motherhood, and Cold War Movies" in *Ronald Reagan, the Movie and Other Episodes in Political Demonology* (Berkeley: University of California Press, 1987), finds that postwar popular culture simultaneously glorified and vilified motherhood. Sociologist Wini Breines, in her recent book *Young, White, and Miserable: Growing Up Female in the 1950s* (Boston: Beacon Press, 1992), argues that women's revolt "surreptitiously began in the quiet fifties." Far from being monolithic and merely constraining for women, postwar popular culture, with all its tensions and contradictions, actually provided the basis for women's construction of new identities and new means of empowerment. Historian Susan Ware in a study of League of Women Voters's local chapters entitled "American Women in the 1950s: Nonpartisan Politics and Women's Politicization" in *Women, Politics, and Change*, eds. Louise Tilly and Patricia Gurin (New York: Russell Sage Foundation, 1990), suggests that League women defied the stereotype of the unfulfilled, politically reticent Cold War woman. Challenging Friedan's characterization of women in postwar America, Ware argues that League women were "not suffering from a crisis in women's identity." I examined all of the nonfiction articles dealing with women and their state of mind during the years under consideration. I did a less systematic review of other women's magazines, including *Woman's Home Companion, Good Housekeeping, Better Homes and Gardens, Redbook, Colliers*, and *Coronet*. See endnote 8, p. 482 for the prevalence of the theme of women's dissatisfaction.

4. Dr. James F. Bender, Director of the National Institute for Human Relations, "What Sends People to Reno?," *Ladies Home Journal*, April 1948, 296.

found that the group of workers least likely to enjoy their jobs was—housewives![5]

Women's magazines also found that marriage contributed greatly to women's dissatisfaction. As one article reported, "from the testimony of more than a thousand married couples" and the "replies from the one hundred unhappiest wives," surveyors concluded that unhappy wives were dissatisfied with their marriages and, given the chance, would not marry their husband again.[6] Drawing upon surveys and in-depth interviews, the magazines kept readers up-to-date on the housewife's dissatisfactions.[7]

Articles on selected topics also indicate that women's magazines gave considerable attention to women's unhappiness. In articles such as "How Do You Beat the Blues?," "What Do You Do When Worries Get You Down?," "I Can't Stand It Anymore," "Why Do Women Cry?," "How to Recognize Suicidal Depression," "Blues and How to Chase Them," and "How to Get Over Feeling Low," women's magazines normalized their readers' feelings of discontent.[8] They reported that unhappiness was a common affliction among women. "Crying as Catharsis," for example, reminded readers that they were not alone in feeling frustrated and unhappy. As the author explained, "tears are a natural and universal release for many minor emotions. They siphon off the small frustrations that confront all of us every hour of every day. They are a way of protesting the things we can't do anything about." The article recommended crying as "a natural safety valve to dissolve away many of our tensions."[9] Recognition of acute emotional tension was not uncommon for women's magazines.

5. Barbara Benson, "Would You Marry Your Husband Again?," *Ladies Home Journal*, February 1947, 26.
6. "What Makes Wives Unhappy," *Ladies Home Journal*, January 1949, 26.
7. Before presenting the results of surveys and in-depth interviews, the magazines often instructed women to measure their own responses against those of the nation's. One article, for example, recommended that "before reading the replies of other husbands and wives, you might jot down your answer to these questions. Express your honest opinions, frankly and in detail." Benson, "Would You Marry Your Husband Again?," 31.
8. For some further examples see, "How Do You Beat the Blues?," *Women's Home Companion*, March 1948, 153–155; "What Do You Do When Worries Get You Down?," *Women's Home Companion*, December 1952, 9; "How to Live With Yourself," *McCall's*, March 1960, 116–117; "I Can't Stand It Anymore," *Good Housekeeping*, March 1961, 86–87; "Why Do Women Cry?," *Ladies Home Journal*, October 1948, 44; "How to Recognize Suicidal Depression," *Ladies Home Journal*, September 1964, 26; "Blues and How to Chase Them," *McCall's*, August 1960, 98; "How to Get Over Feeling Low," *Better Homes and Gardens*, October 1950, 66–67; "When Don't You Need a Psychiatrist?," *Coronet*, March 1956, 93–97; "Lonely Wife," *Women's Home Companion*, June 1956, 16–18; "You Can Be Happier Than You Are," *Better Homes and Gardens*, February 1956, 31; "Are You Afraid You're Going Crazy?," *Good Housekeeping*, August 1957, 118–121; "Do You Need a Psychiatrist?," *Coronet*, December 1954, 31–34; "Emotional Upsets Are Good For You," *Colliers*, September 1953, 88–93.
9. Karl Huber, "Crying as Catharsis," *McCall's*, November 1960, 46, 48.

* * *

These images of the American housewife as unhappy, frustrated, and angry presented in this and other articles reveal that women's magazines did not avoid the question of how women felt about their lives; rather they devoted considerable attention to the subject by focusing on the psychological tensions experienced by the housewife and her difficulties conforming to the domestic ideal. Applying the new standard of psychological happiness, the magazines found evidence of women's dissatisfaction. Of course, their purpose was to persuade women to overcome it. They assumed that women needed to be educated about the value of domesticity and helped with adjusting to its gendered effects. Women's magazines informed readers that their feelings of frustration, anger, and sadness were normal.[1] They also promoted a variety of therapeutic techniques to help women achieve moods of joy and purposefulness. As feminists, however, have been quick to point out, the magazines did not promote feminist solutions to the problem of discontent. Indeed, some have argued that the magazines' solutions were antifeminist. Women's magazines of the postwar era have been read in most accounts as having functioned to depoliticize discontent; they have been condemned for suggesting that women deal with their dissatisfaction by autoconditioning or crying instead of protesting.[2]

There is, however, another way to understand this chapter in women's cultural history. By focusing public attention on the plight of the American housewife, turning her into a national social problem, these magazines contributed to a discourse of discontent. They documented on an unprecedented scale the difficulty women had in

1. This normalization of discontent contrasts with the claims made by many scholars that women's magazines defined unhappy women as abnormal. Historian Glenna Matthews, for example, explains the logic she found at work in women's magazines and other forms of popular culture: "The 'normal', feminine woman would be happy staying at home. One who was unhappy was, in fact, by definition not normal." Matthews, *Just a Housewife*, 211.

2. As Elaine May explains, for example, this rhetoric and its therapeutic corollary "undermined the potential for the political activism and reinforced the chilling effects of anticommunism and the cold war consensus," May, *Homeward Bound*, 14. For examples of works not already cited that treat women's magazines as obstacles to feminist protest, see Maureen Honey, *Creating Rosie the Riveter*; Cynthia White, *Women's Magazines, 1693–1968* (London: Joseph, 1970); Janice Winship, *Inside Women's Magazines* (New York: Pandora, 1987); Ester R. Sineman, "What the Ladies Were Reading," (Ph.D. dissertation, University of Chicago, 1976); Marjorie Ferguson, "Imagery and Ideology: The Cover Photographs of Traditional Women's Magazines," in *Hearth and Home*, ed. Gaye Tuchman, Arlene Kaplan Daniels, and James Benet (New York: Oxford University Press, 1978); Joy Leman, "The Advice of a Real Friend: Codes of Intimacy and Oppression in Women's Magazines, 1937–1955," *Women's Studies International Quarterly* 3 (Fall 1980); Susan M. Hartmann, "Prescriptions for Penelope: Literature on Women's Obligations to Returning World War II Veterans," *Women's Studies* 5 (1978): 223–239; Maureen Honey, "Images of Women in the *Saturday Evening Post*, 1931–1936," *Journal of Popular Culture* 10 (1976): 352–358.

finding satisfaction in their homes and personal lives. In an admittedly oblique way, they pointed to a problem that Betty Friedan would later name, "the problem that has no name." * * *

*   *   *

Friedan's investigation of women's lives and her conclusions about domesticity were clearly innovative. Injecting an unprecedented drama into the public discussion of women's roles, Friedan turned womanhood and domesticity into matters of intense public controversy. She identified a pathological tendency in American culture to deny women a sense of identity, offering a profound indictment of domestic ideology. Friedan urged women to reject "the feminine mystique" which she believed prevented women from gratifying "their basic need to grow and fulfill their potentialities as human beings." She also insisted that only an entirely new understanding of themselves and their roles as women would enable women to develop "a new sense of identity" and to live with "the enjoyment, the sense of purpose that is characteristic of true human health." Thus, Friedan put her critique of domesticity directly in the service of women, ultimately leading to important changes in the political, cultural, intellectual, and economic landscape of America.[3]

But while Friedan's view of domesticity was innovative, her discussion of women's psychological condition was not as unprecedented as she or subsequent historians believed. Her view that "in the millions of words" written about women there was "no word" of the yearning and dissatisfaction women experienced was incorrect.[4] In fact, like Friedan, the women's magazines used personal testimony from women across the country to document unhappiness. Similarly, her discovery of "a strange discrepancy between the reality of our lives as women and the image to which we are trying to conform" was one women's magazines had been making for years. They, too, found that despite domesticity's promise of fulfillment, "the group of workers least likely to enjoy their jobs was—housewives."[5]

---

3. Friedan, *The Feminine Mystique*, 69, 281. Most accounts of recent feminism emphasize its distinctiveness. This was particularly true of those accounts that came directly out of the movement. See, for example, Robin Morgan, *Going Too Far: The Personal Chronicle of a Feminist* (New York: Vintage Books, 1978); and Ellen Willis, *Beginning to See the Light* (New York: Knopf, 1981). There were also contemporary accounts of the movement, including Jo Freeman, *The Politics of Women's Liberation: A Case Study of an Emerging Social Movement and its Relation to the Policy Process* (New York: Longman, 1975); and Edith Hole and Ellen Levine, *Rebirth of Feminism* (New York: Quadrangle Books, 1971).
4. Friedan, *The Feminine Mystique*, 11.
5. Barbara Benson, "Would You Marry Your Husband Again?," *Ladies Home Journal*, February 1947, 26.

Though Friedan claimed that this problem of dissatisfaction "lay buried, unspoken of" and that each woman "struggled with it alone," month after month millions of readers learned from their trusted women's magazines about such problems as "spiraling-down marriage interaction patterns" and depression. Indeed, there exists more discursive continuity between the women's magazines and Betty Friedan than has been acknowledged.

One other indication of discursive continuity comes, surprisingly, from contemporary readers of women's magazines, who reacted strongly to a Betty Friedan article published in 1963 by *McCall's* magazine. "Fraud of Femininity" summarizes the arguments against domesticity found in her book published that same year. * * *

Women readers accused Friedan and women's magazines of promoting a "negativistic attitude" toward domesticity in general and women's roles as housewives in particular.[6] As one housewife and devoted women's magazine reader explained, I am "a proud and fulfilled wife, mother, daughter, sister, daughter-in-law, and friend; trying to live up to my purpose of being here on this earth; no small nor ignominious task, I can assure you. And I am sick, sick, sick of reading just this type of article, as I am sure many other happily married women are."[7] Respondents objected to the portrait of women as "empty, wasted, or filled with frustration."[8]

* * *

Ironically, while Friedan saw herself in opposition to the experts who promoted the "feminine mystique," many housewives perceived her as yet another expert analyzing and complaining about the state of women's lives.[9] They wanted Friedan and the magazines to "stop knocking the homemaker."[1] Signing their letters with closures such as "from a very happy, contented, but obviously without knowing it, trapped housewife," some even insisted that they would cancel their subscriptions, if the magazines did not stop publishing "Friedan-type articles."[2] Readers did not appear to make a distinction between

6. Betty Friedan papers, Schlesinger Library, Radcliffe College (hereafter BF), Box 744.
7. BF, Box 743.
8. BF, Box 744.
9. It is important to note that Friedan's relationship to expertise even in her book is contradictory. Rhetorically, she emphasizes experts' neglect of the "problem that has no name" and the silence of professionals on the question of women's unhappiness. But in her preface she thanks a long list of experts. She does, however, qualify her acknowledgments by adding that although "experts in a great many fields have been holding pieces of the truth under their microscopes for a long time" they have often not realized it. Friedan, *The Feminine Mystique*, preface.
1. BF, Box 741.
2. BF, Box 742.

Friedan's critique of domesticity and that of the magazines; instead, they found continuity.

While readers overlooked some very real and substantial differences, they were not completely off the mark. Betty Friedan, like many of the antifeminist and afeminist writers for women's magazines that came before her, viewed women as unhappy, frustrated, and stifled. Both focused on the psychological effects of domesticity and emphasized the importance of self-fulfillment. But whereas women's magazines and the experts who wrote for them sought to help women be happy within the confines of domesticity, Friedan categorically rejected both. She did so, I suggest, not by uncovering "what lay buried and unspoken of," but by speaking in new ways about what had already been identified as a problem and taking what was a constant concern of women's magazines and putting it to new political uses. Friedan described domesticity and the effects of experts in pathological terms. She insisted that the psychological effects of domesticity were so damaging that only a wholesale rejection of it would save women from obliterating their sense of self. While Friedan firmly rejected the adjustment strategies promoted by women's magazines, her critique of domesticity and political demands relied heavily upon a psychological discourse that itself emphasized unhappiness and self-fulfillment.

* * *

* * * While feminists often imagined themselves as beginning completely anew, rejecting the categories of thought foisted upon them by experts and the mass media, and creating a politics purely out of their immediate experiences and personal feelings, their political discourse was connected to the popular culture and expertise of their era. A survey of women's magazines during the postwar period suggests that there was, indeed, a popular context and a history to the ideological work they performed. Recent feminism took as its starting point the cult of domesticity and its psychological effects upon women. Women's magazines and the experts who wrote for them, however, had already focused mass attention on the psychological difficulties women had in adjusting to domesticity. They publicized the problems women experienced in conforming to domesticity and their difficulty securing happiness. They also simultaneously emphasized the virtues of domesticity and the value of psychological happiness. While they clearly did not advocate feminist solutions or have feminist intentions, they contributed to a discourse of discontent and a new standard of psychological happiness. In addition, it can be argued that this legacy of revealed discontent and unresolved contradictions was a source of a new political discourse fashioned by Betty Friedan and subsequent feminists.

SYLVIE MURRAY

From The Progressive Housewife: Community Activism in Suburban Queens, 1945–1965[†]

* * *

* * * The early 1950s was a period of professional transition for Friedan. After leaving her job as a reporter for the labor press, she began writing for popular magazines.[1] Some of the early articles she wrote in the mid-1950s, while living at Parkway Village, are especially revealing of the political environment she then inhabited. One of these was "They Found Out 'Americans Aren't So Awful, After All!'" In this unpublished article, the author not only celebrates Parkway Village's multiculturalism, but describes a process by which politically timid housewives were gaining assurance through their involvement in community politics. Such is the gist of her discussion of the internal dynamics of the Village's numerous committees:

> Parkway Village abounds with committees. . . . (At first these committees consisted only of American and Canadian women, and men from the other countries—they considered committees not only men's business, and our men left it to the women.) The women, of course, did most of the work—getting playgrounds built, starting a nursery school, running international potluck suppers. So pretty soon the Dutch and Indian men were getting their wives to run in their place. My Dutch friend . . . had never been on a committee before. She didn't say a word the first few meetings. At the end of the year she was running the whole show. "In my country everything is done by officials, we would not think of organizing ourselves to improve matters," she told me. "But with a committee you can do anything, are they not wonderful, committees?"[2]

American and Canadian women, in this case, had shown their neighbors—first the men, then their wives—the virtues of a female-led participatory democracy.

† From Sylvie Murray, *The Progressive Housewife: Community Activism in Suburban Queens, 1945–1965* (Philadelphia: University of Pennsylvania Press, 2003), pp. 143–45, 147–50, 151, 152. Reprinted with permission of the University of Pennsylvania Press. Notes have been renumbered.
1. For the first solid treatment of Friedan's background, see Daniel Horowitz, *Betty Friedan and the Making of* The Feminine Mystique: *The American Left, the Cold War, and Modern Feminism* (Amherst: University of Massachusetts Press, 1998).
2. "They Found Out 'Americans Aren't So Awful, After All!'" folders 381–85, box 10, Betty Friedan Papers, Schlesinger Library, Radcliffe Institute, Harvard University, Cambridge, Mass. (hereafter Friedan Papers).

The women's initiative in community affairs that Friedan described above, and the assertiveness that they gained through their experience of volunteer work, figure prominently in "More than a Nose-wiper," the original draft of an article published in *Parents' Magazine* in 1957 under the title "Day Camp in the Driveways."[3] In this article, which relates the experience of housewives who organized a back-yard camp for their kids, Friedan focused her investigation on Bell Park Manor and Terrace. This garden apartment, built in Hollis Hills in 1951, represented a suburban haven for lower-middle-class families. As the author described in her original draft, the residents had "paid $1,200 down to move out here, 20 minutes beyond the end of the subway line, so their kids could play in fresh air and sunshine and green grass." They were "ex-GI salesmen and postal clerks and $100-a-week accountants who'd played in the streets of Brooklyn and the Bronx themselves."[4] Unfortunately, the pastoral life promised had turned sour:

> The trouble was—they had a thousand kids under eight among them—and no place out here for kids to play at all! . . . All the rest of Bell Park's fifty, long, low, red-brick and white-shuttered buildings had the same grassy lawns—chained to keep the kids off. The cement drying yards were always full of wash. The black asphalt driveways just led to garages most tenants couldn't afford to rent. And so many kids had already cracked their heads in the pintsize [*sic*] playgrounds, the swings had to be taken down. There wasn't even a Y or a library or a candy store out here at the end of Queens—just miles and miles of new little houses and raw developments as crowded with kids as theirs.[5]

Friedan's story, based on interviews with Alice Barsky, a thirty-two-year-old housewife and mother, describes how a group of energetic young housewives had "masterminded" the "'Bell Park Manor-Terrace Summer Day Camp'—a fabulous operation which she [Bar-

3. Folders 378–79, box 10, Friedan Papers. Another version of this story, "They Made the City into 'Country' for Their Kids," can be found in folder 478, box 13. For the pub-lished version, see *Parents' Magazine*, May 1957, 36–37, 131–34.
4. "More than a Nosewiper," 1. It is significant to note that the specific information indi-cating the socioeconomic status of the residents—"they'd paid $1,200 down" and "salesmen and postal clerks and $100-a-week accountants"—was omitted from the version published in *Parents' Magazine*. The published version referred simply to "ex-GI couples." The result of these editorial changes was to turn lower-middle-class families into generic, classless families. In "They Made the City into 'Country' for Their Kids," the author was even more specific about the residents' socioeconomic status, including information about which neighborhood of Manhattan they had moved from: "Most of them had grown up playing on the streets themselves, city kids from New York's lower east side and Hell's kitchen, Brooklyn and the Bronx. It's not a rags to riches story, because most of them are still young, still not rich, still living in the city. But their kids aren't playing in the streets."
5. "More than a Nosewiper," 1–2.

sky] and other housing project mothers have created out of the bare asphalt driveways of their own backyard." In contrast with the published "Day Camp in the Driveways"—which was printed under the rubric "Child Rearing" in *Parents' Magazine* and which presented the case as a "parental do-it-yourself story"—the original version stresses women's accomplishment and assertiveness.[6] It is the story of how the process of dealing with the various experts involved in this project—from city officials to the young, college-educated, male directors who were hired to supervise the summer activities—led to a growing politicization.

At the outset it is clear that Alice Barsky and her neighbors were eager to defer to the authority of experts. As related by Friedan, extensively quoting Barsky,

> It was "simply to get out of the house for a change" that she went to her first meeting of Bell Park mothers on "the summer problem" back four years ago [1951]. She certainly didn't expect "a bunch of ignorant housewives" (which was the way she thought of herself then) could figure it out. Like all the rest, she "ran to Spock every time the kid cried, and checked with Gesell before saying yes or no."

*   *   *

Gaining experience in dealing with "outside experts," when the time came in the spring of 1955 to hire their director for the next summer, the once self-effacing housewives adopted a different strategy:

> "We've got to be more businesslike," said ex-chairman Pat, an elder statesman now on the committee. "Maybe we should stop serving coffee."
>
> Before the applicant came in, the team would pass around his letter, noting degrees, experience—but now that was just the beginning. Mrs. Sari Berns, ex-Powers model sitting in slacks on the couch, Mrs. Dornee Robinson, ex-secretary, taking notes at the dining table, 8-months pregnant Mrs. Pat Berkowitz on the easy chair, Mrs. Alice Barsky who had just taken up knitting—would pounce on the 6-foot tweedy Ph.D. with questions that left him gasping. And if he was too suave, and didn't start asking them questions—they'd signal with their eyebrows to each other, cut the interview short, and rush to the next apartment where another team was interviewing.

6. Not included in the final printed version were the passages where Friedan described Alice Barsky's feelings of being "absolutely liberated" and the triumphant reference to "this new breed of Jill."

A man who passed the first team, had to come back and be interviewed by the full 21 camp top brass.

"Never went through such a trial in my life," said Harry Janoson, a livewire New York public school principal. . . .

He asked: "Whom will I be working for?" "Us," said the women calmly.

He's an up-and-coming big city educator, and his colleagues thought he was crazy. Despite his misgivings, he took the job—because "I was impressed, I couldn't believe such women existed." He still finds it hard to believe, working now for the second summer for his housewife bosses.[7]

In its third summer, the Bell Park Manor-Terrace Day Camp was a success. Registration was no longer done "from door to door, on foot, but in a basement room 'like registration to vote.'" The budget committee was now handling a $40,000 budget; 870 children were taking the bus every day to Alley Pond Park or to other outdoor activities, leaving "not a child in the community at loose ends, only women going about their business." Even Miss Margolin, "the once dubious social worker," was impressed by the work accomplished: "'A true pioneer,' she said when she introduced this not a bit nervous housewife from Bell Park [Alice Barsky] to speak to a national conference on children's problems. . . . Now housewives from housing projects miles away, and many experts too, follow Alice on a 'guided tour' through Bell Park's 'backyard.'" Friedan concluded her twenty-page article on a triumphant tone:

> [As the local] PTA . . . recently put on its own original musical comedy about "this new breed of Jill," Alice Barsky, and at least 200 others on Bell Park committees, recognized themselves as the heroine[,] dumped a bag of frozen food in her husband's arms as he came in the door from work, and ran out herself to "the nominating meeting."
>
> "Where's mommy going?" asks the little girl in the play. "She's going to be president," says daddy. "Of the United States?" asks her little girl. "Could be," says daddy, "could be."[8]

In this account of the Bell Park mothers' accomplishment, Friedan portrayed volunteerism as pregnant with possibilities, not only for women who use this outlet to grow personally, but for their communities as well.

---

7. "More than a Nosewiper," 11–12.
8. Ibid., 20–21.

There never was a camp like it before. But there may be many in the decade to come. For Alice Barsky and the other Bell Park mothers, sociologists say, are a new kind of pioneer—out of the social frontiers of the new suburbia where the birthrate is multiplying problems so fast only a parental 'do it yourself' can solve them. The Bell Park mothers had to solve theirs without training and experience, without funds or facilities, without ever having been to a 'real camp' themselves. And if Alice Barsky isn't quite the same frustrated housewife she used to be— well, they say our great-great-great-grandmothers thrived on pioneering, too.[9]

True pioneers they were.

More accurately than her later published work, "More than a Nose-wiper" reflects the dynamics at work in community politics. Women at Food Fair making decisions about their future endeavors while kids pulled at their skirts, or "gentle" Mrs. Robinson "besieging" the Board of Education for a permission to use the high school pool were familiar images for the observer of grassroots politics. Equally illuminating of her neighbors' experience as community activists was Friedan's characterization of the defiant relationship that these "ignorant," yet resourceful, housewives entertained with experts of all kinds. Although having encountered the incredulity of social workers at the Health Department, then the condescension of the pipe-smoking Ph.D. whom they interviewed for the position of director, they succeeded in asserting their own authority—with the help of a man at first, but eventually on their own. Significantly, the success of the Bell Park "pioneers" was marked not only by the creation of the day camp but by the metamorphosis of once-ignorant housewives into experts. In brief, in this account, Friedan draws a picture of mothers who, concerned for the well-being of their children, did not hesitate to confront bureaucratic and professional expertise head on and emerged transformed in the process.

Friedan's mid-1950s writings raise interesting questions about the political consciousness of housewives at the height of "the feminine mystique." It sheds a new light on the conclusion that the author herself reached in her 1963 influential best-seller. In *The Feminine Mystique*, Friedan was concerned with exposing the oppressive nature of the domestic ideology of the time "which defined woman only as husband's wife, children's mother, . . . and never as person defining herself by her own actions in society." A housewife's personal and individual fulfillment in that context—her cure to the "terrible feeling of emptiness" that haunted her—had to be sought

9. Ibid., 2.

outside the bounds of family and home, although this by no means
required the breaking of domestic bonds: "She does not have to
choose between marriage and career; that was the mistaken choice
of the feminine mystique." Access to the status and social respecta-
bility conferred by paid work, however, was crucial: "But even if a
woman does not have to work to eat, she can find identity only in
work that is of real value to society—work for which, usually, our
society pays." But if being "just a housewife" was not enough, neither
could "a job, any job" allow women "to grow up to their full human
capacities." The "endless whirl of worthwhile community activities"
was also inadequate in providing the type of long-term personal commitment and societal respect that was necessary to women's actual-
ization as individuals. The "new life plan for women" that she
prescribed was indeed very specific: only if women were to "let themselves develop the lifetime interests and goals which require serious
education and training," dispose of their "'guilty feelings' about being
ambitious," and "learn to compete" could they achieve self-realization.
In brief, not a job, not voluntary activities, but a career was the path
toward liberation. As reflected in her call for "a national educational
program, similar to the GI Bill, for women who seriously want to
continue or resume their education," Friedan was not totally blind to
the structural constraints that made such a solution illusory for the
majority of women. But she did uncompromisingly embrace the professional ethos as not only the best but the only way for women to
escape the traps of the feminine mystique.[1]

* * *

* * * Central to Friedan's argument was her conception of a historical process by which women's voluntary involvement had become
less rewarding and less respected. This is to be understood as part of
the larger theory of declension that framed her narrative. As Joanne
Meyerowitz reminded us, Friedan believed that the portrayal of
women's roles in mass culture had narrowed in the late 1940s and
1950s compared with the 1930s when "women's magazines encouraged women to participate in the wider world outside the home."[2] By
the late 1950s, when she researched and wrote her book, she was
convinced that the era of women's fulfilling and meaningful volunteerism was past: "In some suburbs and communities there is now
little work left for the nonprofessional that requires intelligence—
except for the few positions of leadership which most women, these
days, lack the independence, the strength, the self-confidence to
take." Her conviction that "professionals have taken over most of the

---

1. *The Feminine Mystique*, xi, 342, 344, 346, 355, 369, 370.
2. Meyerowitz, *Not June Cleaver*, 248.

posts in the community requiring intelligence" drove her negative evaluation of women's ability to fulfill themselves through volunteerism as well as her call for women's entry in the professions.[3]

* * *

Regardless of Friedan's * * * later criticism of female volunteerism, the experience of women in the 1950s was critically and, I believe, positively shaped by their participation in such activities. As she described in her 1950s writings, this was a way for housewives to gain experience as well as self-confidence. As we have also seen * * * images of women as intelligent and rational political actors were prevalent in 1950s political culture. * * *

THE MOMENT: THE TURN OF THE 1960s

As the previous discussion of women's magazines makes clear, *The Feminine Mystique* was a product of its moment. The years at the turn of the 1960s witnessed tremendous political, cultural, and intellectual ferment. The civil rights and peace movements' growing visibility sparked excitement among activists on the left, and worries among activists on the right. Major books on poverty, the environment, consumer rights, and women's lives landed on bookshelves and convinced ordinary individuals that there were major problems to be solved in American society and that their voices could make a difference. Betty Friedan's work was an important part of this ferment, described by Louis Menand in the piece below.

The next two essays, by Kirsten Fermaglich and Jennifer Scanlon, explore Friedan alongside very different public intellectuals of the moment. Although Friedan did not personally know all of these individuals, nor did she always share their political struggles, looking at her work in relationship to theirs helps to shed light on both the energy and the fears of this era.

3. *The Feminine Mystique*, 345, 346.

LOUIS MENAND

From Books as Bombs: Why the Women's Movement Needed "The Feminine Mystique"†

* * * There were plenty of laws enforcing the second-tier status of women in 1963. Why was a long and semi-scholarly study by a magazine writer the catalyst for a social change that might have got under way years before? The answer may have something to do not with the status of women but with the status of books. In the early nineteen-sixties, books, for some reason, were bombs.

Books were always an important force in the women's movement, possibly because the book was a medium that women had relatively unobstructed access to as authors and as readers. Kate Millett's "Sexual Politics," Germaine Greer's "The Female Eunuch," Sandra Gilbert and Susan Gubar's "Madwoman in the Attic," and Susan Faludi's "Backlash" all had an effect on the public conversation about gender and women's rights. And many best-selling books since the nineteen-sixties have galvanized (or polarized) opinion—from the leftish "The Greening of America," in 1970, to the rightish "The Closing of the American Mind," in 1987. But books that led directly to political change have been rare.

"The Feminine Mystique" came out around the same time as four other books that had an unusually immediate impact on public policy. Jane Jacobs's "The Death and Life of Great American Cities" was published in 1961. It has been credited with, in the long run, changing urban-renewal policies in the United States; in the short run, it helped bring an end to the career of New York City's "master builder," Robert Moses.

In 1962, Rachel Carson published "Silent Spring." It became a No. 1 best-seller, and is often said to have started the movement that led to the ban on DDT and, ultimately, the creation of the Environmental Protection Agency. Michael Harrington's "The Other America" came out the same year. It got the attention of the Kennedy Administration, and the discussions it provoked in Washington became the basis for Lyndon Johnson's War on Poverty. And, in 1965, Ralph Nader published "Unsafe at Any Speed." It helped lead to the passage, the following year, of the National Traffic and Motor Vehicle Safety Act, which for the first time made the government the regulator of auto safety.

† From Louis Menand, "Books as Bombs: Why the Women's Movement Needed 'The Feminine Mystique,'" *New Yorker,* January 24, 2011, 76–79. www.newyorker.com/arts/critics/books/2011/01/24/110124crbo_books_menand (accessed August 8, 2011). Copyright © 2011 by Louis Menand, used by permission of The Wylie Agency LLC.

In all these cases, it can be said (and in most of them it has been said) that the changes the books are associated with would have happened anyway. * * * But people like to be able to point to a book as the cause for a new frame of mind, possibly for the same reason that people prefer anecdotes to statistical evidence. A book personalizes an issue. It has an Erin Brockovich effect: it puts a face on the problem; it sets up a David-and-Goliath drama.

It's not irrelevant, therefore, that three of these books were written by women, outsiders almost by definition in the early nineteen-sixties, and the others were by men largely unknown to the general public. Harrington was a socialist, who, to his subsequent regret, and much like Friedan, chose to elide that fact when he wrote his book. He was invited to Washington to advise on the poverty program, but left in disgust. Nader was a staff consultant to the Labor Department when he wrote "Unsafe at Any Speed." But after General Motors launched a vindictive and ill-conceived investigation of him he was cast as a lone man against the System—a role that, as it turned out, suited his personality completely. People don't like the System.

It may be that in the nineteen-sixties, when television was still muzzling itself, from fear of provoking advertiser displeasure or F.C.C. reaction, books were a more accessible form for social criticism and dissent. It may also be that books were still a little radioactive then, a little dangerous. Friedan's book came out in the wake of some celebrated censorship trials—"Lady Chatterley's Lover," "Tropic of Cancer," "Fanny Hill." One of Coontz's respondents recalled "The Feminine Mystique" being treated "like a banned book."* The sense that an object is somehow forbidden gives it greater power.

* * *

* * * these books became totems. They even acquired reputations for policies and ideas they never proposed. "The Feminine Mystique" did not recommend that women pursue full-time careers, or that they demand their legal rights. It only advised women to be prepared for life after the children left home. "The Silent Spring" did not call for a ban on pesticides. It only suggested that their use be regulated. These are books whose significance exceeds anything they actually said. For many people, it doesn't even matter what they said or why they were written. What matters is that, when the world turned, they were there.

* See selection from Stephanie Coontz, A Strange Stirring, on pp. 519–22.

KIRSTEN FERMAGLICH

From "The Comfortable Concentration Camp":
The Significance of Nazi Imagery in Betty Friedan's
The Feminine Mystique (1963)†

* * *

Betty Friedan was not the only Jewish thinker at the time to develop extended analogies between Nazi Germany and American society while remaining silent on the subject of Jews. Between 1959 and 1967, a significant cohort of American-born Jewish writers, academics, and artists—at least eight men and women—used Hitler, Nazis, and concentration camps as analogues for American society in their popular and influential works, while making virtually no mention of Jews, or their own Jewish background. Historian Stanley Elkins, for example, compared Nazi concentration camps to American slave plantations in his book *Slavery* (1959), while psychiatrist Robert Jay Lifton linked the suffering of survivors of Hiroshima with those of concentration camps in *Death in Life* (1967). Psychologist Stanley Milgram's obedience experiments compared ordinary Americans in a laboratory experiment to Nazi concentration camp guards, and Mel Brooks's *The Producers* (1967) turned Broadway chorus girls into marching SS troopers and a flower child high on drugs into Hitler himself.[1]

Images of Nazi Germany or concentration camps have been pervasive throughout post-World War II American history. Americans have used metaphors of Nazi Germany fairly continuously since at least 1945, when a letter to *Newsweek* magazine called on fellow readers to "storm" the "concentration camp" of a Jersey City dominated by machine politics.[2] The vast majority of these metaphors, however, have been brief and rhetorical; few of the speakers or writers have carefully delineated the similarities between the American phenomena they described and the Nazi imagery they employed, and few have sustained the metaphor for more than one or perhaps two sentences. The comparisons constructed by people like Betty

---

† From Kirsten Lise Fermaglich, "'The Comfortable Concentration Camp': The Significance of Nazi Imagery in Betty Friedan's *The Feminine Mystique* (1963)," *American Jewish History* 91.2 (June 2003): 219–20, 222–23. © 2004 by the American Jewish Historical Society. Reprinted with permission of The Johns Hopkins University Press. Notes have been renumbered.

1. Other members of the cohort include Erving Goffman, Arthur Miller, and Lawrence Kohlberg. For more on this cohort, see Kirsten Fermaglich, "Perpetrators, Bystanders, Victims: Jewish Intellectuals and the Holocaust in Postwar America" (Ph.D. diss., New York University, 2001).

2. "Letters," *Newsweek*, April 30, 1945, 8.

Friedan, Stanley Milgram, and Robert Jay Lifton, on the other hand, were thoroughly developed and extended throughout at least one full chapter of a book. These sorts of sustained analogies have been more unusual in American writing.

Even more significant, all the members of this early 1960s cohort examined Nazi concentration camps as metaphors for individual destruction in a mass society. Although Americans now are most likely to compare the Third Reich's murderous antisemitism with America's ugly and brutal history of racism, none of the people in this cohort addressed the issue of antisemitism or Jews in Nazi Germany in their famous works during this era. None even addressed the issue of race.[3] Only one mentioned his own Jewish background. Rather than exploring questions of Jewishness or race, these American Jewish thinkers in the late 1950s and early to mid 1960s were most concerned with understanding the impact of bureaucracy, conformity, and government power upon individual personality.

* * *

The existence of a cohort of American Jewish thinkers who used Nazi Germany to explore American social problems in the 1950s and 1960s, without emphasizing the murder of European Jewry, helps contemporary historians to examine the impact of the Holocaust on American Jews in a new way. This group of men and women offers evidence that American Jews have not used the imagery of Nazi Germany only to define their ethnic or religious identity or to support Israel, as scholars like Peter Novick have suggested. Instead, Betty Friedan, Stanley Elkins, Robert Lifton, and other members of their cohort used Nazi concentration camps to criticize American society from a liberal perspective in the early 1960s.

In the early 1960s, liberals were probably best identified by their quiet dissent from the Cold War consensus. In the immediate post-World War II era, liberals participated in a national consensus that glorified American democracy in its struggle against the Soviet Union. By the late 1950s, however, this consensus began to crack. Sit-ins at segregated lunch counters and public protests against civil defense programs vividly demonstrated the possibility of political alternatives to the Cold War consensus. Liberals supported the dissent of the growing civil rights and peace movements in the early 1960s, though they generally did not engage in civil disobedience or suggest significant restructuring of the American political

3. Stanley Elkins might seem like an exception to this statement but, curiously, he is not. Elkins purposely focused on concentration camps because he believed it would allow him to avoid talking about race. See John A. Garraty, *Interpreting American History: Conversations With Historians. Part I* (New York, 1970), 1–198, cited in Fermaglich, "Perpetrators, Bystanders, Victims," 154.

system. Friedan's stance against sexism clearly fit this mold; in *The Feminine Mystique*, Friedan dissented from the Cold War consensus that glorified women's domesticity as a means of battling the Soviet Union, while she offered a quiet solution to sexism that proposed no civil disobedience, nor any fundamental restructuring of the American system.[4]

Friedan's use of Nazi imagery suggests an additional way in which she, along with other members of her cohort, quietly dissented from the dominant Cold War consensus. During the Cold War, intellectuals and politicians popularized the term "totalitarianism" as a way of linking the extreme left in the Soviet Union with the far right of Nazism, thereby delegitimizing the left.[5] By finding compelling similarities between Nazi Germany and the United States, not the Soviet Union, liberals like Lifton, Elkins, and Milgram began quietly to reject, or at least to question, the concept of totalitarianism.

Friedan's "comfortable concentration camp" thus offers a window into the ways that American Jewish thinkers in the late 1950s and early 1960s used the destruction of European Jewry in order to offer a liberal perspective on American politics, while at the same time representing themselves as American intellectuals, without any special provincial interests in Jews.

* * *

JENNIFER SCANLON

From Bad Girls Go Everywhere: The Life of Helen Gurley Brown[†]

When people think about the early years of the second wave of feminism, many believe, simply, that "Betty Friedan did it all, with maybe a little help from Gloria Steinem."[1] Until Betty Friedan wrote *The Feminine Mystique*, the story goes, no one, not even women themselves, understood that sexism existed or that women could make a variety of choices about their lives.[2] In recent years historians have

---

4. For discussion of the significance of women's domesticity in the Cold War consensus, see Elaine Tyler May, *Homeward Bound* (New York, 1988).
5. See Abbott Gleason, *Totalitarianism: The Inner History of the Cold War* (New York, 1995).
† From Jennifer Scanlon, *Bad Girls Go Everywhere: The Life of Helen Gurley Brown* (New York: Oxford University Press, 2009), pp. 94–95, 101–102, 110–11. Reprinted by permission of Oxford University Press, Inc. Notes have been renumbered.
1. Linda Kerber, "'I Was Appalled': The Invisible Antecedents of Second-Wave Feminism," *Journal of Women's History* 14, no. 2 (Summer 2002), 94.
2. Janaan Sherman, introduction to *Interviews with Betty Friedan*, ed. Janaan Sherman (Jackson: University Press of Mississippi, 2002), ix.

begun to unravel the complexities of the feminists and feminisms that circulated in the 1960s and 1970s, but few acknowledge—never mind consider—Helen Gurley Brown. Yet *Sex and the Single Girl*, like Betty Friedan's *The Feminine Mystique*, introduced feminist thinking to millions of readers, documented both women's aspirations and their discontents, and refused to apologize for its bold demands for women. On top of that, *Sex and the Single Girl*, which came out a year before *The Feminine Mystique*, shifts not only the date of popular feminism's emergence but also broadens the movement's message and its audience. Helen Gurley Brown sought to liberate not the married woman but the single woman, not the suburban but the urban dweller, not the college-educated victim but the working-class survivor. "I had no idea what I was doing," Brown remembered about the time, demonstrating the ways she could at times buy into the narrative that erased her influential and deliberate contribution. "Feminism was nowhere then. . . . And what I was saying—that single girls, nice single girls, had sex lives—really caused a great ruckus." A ruckus, yes, and in hindsight, an indisputably feminist ruckus at that.[3]

Helen Gurley Brown and Betty Friedan shared more than the experience of seeing their books reach publication in the early 1960s. They had been born almost exactly a year apart, Bettye (she dropped the "e" when she graduated from college) Goldstein on February 4, 1921, and Helen Gurley on February 18, 1922.[4] Each spoke from personal experience and with an internal confidence that millions of other women could relate to their own stories. Each responded passionately to the postwar obsession with domesticity and the resulting tension experienced by women who pursued any interests outside of marriage and family. As young girls and women, Helen and Bettye

3. Alice Steinbach, "The Cosmo Girl at 60 Fights Back the Jungle," *Sun*, November 21, 1982, 6, Helen Gurley Brown papers at Sophia Smith Collection, Smith College. Hereafter referred to as HGB-SSCSC (28). Daniel Horowitz's groundbreaking work, *Betty Friedan and the Making of* The Feminine Mystique: *The American Left, the Cold War, and Modern Feminism* (Amherst: University of Massachusetts Press, 1998), demonstrates that Friedan wrote her book within a larger context of critical social commentary. See also Eva Moskowitz, "'It's Good to Blow Your Top': Women's Magazines and a Discourse of Discontent," *Journal of Women's History* 8, no. 3 (Fall 1996), 66–98; and Joanne Meyerowitz, "Beyond the Feminine Mystique: A Reassessment of Postwar Mass Culture," in *Not June Cleaver: Women and Gender in Postwar America* (Philadelphia: Temple University Press, 1994). The first work to compare Friedan and Brown, and argue that Brown's analysis was "in some ways the more radical," was Barbara Ehrenreich, Elizabeth Hess, and Gloria Jacobs, *Remaking Love: The Feminization of Sex* (Garden City, NY: Anchor Books, 1987), 56–57. Ruth Rosen makes a similar argument in *The World Split Open: How the Modern Women's Movement Changed America* (New York: Penguin, 2000), 51. At times Brown claimed a position as second-wave pioneer. "I was there before Betty Friedan and *The Feminine Mystique*," she told one reporter. "I was there saying 'You're your own person, go out there and be somebody . . . You don't have to get your identity from being somebody's appendage.'" Quoted in Imelda Whelehan, *The Feminist Bestseller: From "Sex and the Single Girl" to "Sex and the City"* (New York: Palgrave Macmillan, 2005), 30.
4. See Horowitz, *Betty Friedan and the Making of The Feminine Mystique*, 87.

saw firsthand the damaging price of the domesticity-is-all agenda, having been raised by somewhat embittered, somewhat broken women whose husbands had demanded that they abandon meaningful work to raise their children. As adults, neither Brown nor Friedan believed that women could be satisfied by the options contemporary life afforded them, even as their generation concretely replaced that of their parents. With long work histories themselves, they held an inordinate faith in the value of work, paired with a stubborn and healthy skepticism about women's supposedly nurturing dispositions. Each believed that she, through her particular brand of self-help, could assist other women in their search for a more rewarding way of living a woman's life. Finally, contrary to what they might always have voiced publicly, Helen Gurley Brown and Betty Friedan shared another significant characteristic: the desire to achieve not only fame but fortune as popular, even populist writers.

✻   ✻   ✻

Although both Brown and Friedan extolled the virtues of work, important differences emerge in their treatment of women's employment. Friedan, in *The Feminine Mystique*, if not in other of her writings, has long been considered the spokesperson for one type of emergent 1960s feminist: the college-educated housewife who clamored for paid work to alleviate some of the burdens of her vapid suburban existence. Younger feminists who emerged from the Civil Rights and New Left political arenas, and who promoted a more radical philosophy, have been considered representative of the second significant feminist cohort, that of college- and movement-educated women coming of age angry with the costs of sexism in their lives and in the lives of their mothers. Helen Gurley Brown, who herself fits comfortably in neither category, invited in to feminism another important but often invisible group, working-class women, largely but by no means exclusively white, whose goals included financial independence, the freedom to engage in sexual activity outside of marriage, and the enjoyment of, rather than a rejection of, the fruits of capitalism. Hers was no insignificant agenda, nor was her audience insignificant in number.[5]

In *Sex and the Single Girl*, Brown encourages women to scrape away at whatever job they find themselves in and to look for opportunities to improve their positions, all the while acknowledging that the world remains unfair to the working girl. She also invites readers,

5. For histories of the second wave of feminism, see Ruth Rosen, *The World Split Open: How the Modern Women's Movement Changed America* (New York: Viking, 2000); Estelle Freedman, *No Turning Back: The History of Women and the Future of Feminism* (New York: Ballantine, 2002); and Sara M. Evans, *Tidal Wave: How Women Changed America at Century's End* (New York: Free Press, 2003).

without apology, to indulge in some of the narcissism that capitalism allows. Rather than simply avoiding what Friedan calls, in *The Feminine Mystique*, the "sex sell" of contemporary advertising, Brown's working women use their consumer dollars wisely but well, adorning their bodies and their apartments while they simultaneously put away a few dollars for the future.[6] Friedan portrays work as critical to women's sense of self, although she views it as less critical to survival. "Men no longer need to work all day to eat," she writes. Her readers face additional expectations in the service of their identity as workers: they should work not to pay the rent but to improve the lives of others, not by punching the clock but by contributing creatively to work that "carries forward human society." Friedan worries about her peers accepting unfulfilling jobs in bleak suburban environments. "Women who do not look for jobs equal to their capacity, who do not let themselves develop the lifetime interests and goals which require serious education and training," she writes, "who take a job at twenty or thirty or forty to 'help out at home' or just to kill extra time, are walking, almost as surely as the ones who stay inside the housewife trap, to a non-existent future."

This notion of domesticity's "trap," the element of *The Feminine Mystique* that has garnered Friedan the most attention, points to a significant difference between these competing forms of early second-wave feminism. Betty Friedan's exposure of the "problem that has no name" relies primarily on a juxtaposition of family life and personhood, while Brown's celebration of the single woman defines the home as a site of potential liberation rather than oppression. *The Feminine Mystique* relies heavily on Friedan's reading of women's magazines, in which marriage, motherhood, and suburban living are promoted as the only acceptable paths to adult womanhood. Friedan introduces the beleaguered middle-class housewife into the feminist lexicon, where she resides virtually unchanged for the remainder of the second wave of feminism. Having bought into the magazines' messages, Friedan argues, women increasingly become imprisoned in their homes. This second-wave employment of the lost housewife needing liberation, introduced by Friedan and refined by others, would make it exceedingly difficult to imagine the home as a site of fabulous or even fun feminist activity.[7]

In this regard, *The Feminine Mystique* played an enormously formative role in defining feminism among its fans and its critics, and in the popular imagination, as an anti-housewife phenomenon. Rhetorically, certainly, Friedan's argument aligned nicely with that

6. Friedan, *Feminine Mystique*, 206–32, 333, 334, 344.
7. Joanne Hollows provides an enormously helpful discussion in "The Feminist and the Cook: Julia Child, Betty Friedan and Domestic Femininity," in *Gender and Consumption*, ed. Emma Casey and Lydia Martens (Aldershot, UK: Ashgate, 2006), 59–84.

of many white male intellectuals of the time who similarly equated the home with women and therefore characterized women as inferior.[8] Friedan set up the opposition between feminist and housewife, arguing as vociferously as anyone that the public world, the male world, the work of paid rather than unpaid work, trumped women's work in the home to such a degree that little further discussion of domestic life's ups or downs was warranted. Housewives who claimed to get any pleasure out of their roles would simply have been operating with what Friedan, during her years of involvement in leftist politics, might have labeled false consciousness.[9]

* * *

* * * Like Friedan, Brown subscribed to male cultural values in her dismissal of women's concerns about housework and children. She repeatedly referred to her single women as "superlative" and hence superior. She repeatedly mocked married women's suburban lifestyles and their dinner-party conversations. She found housewives decidedly not sexy, easily threatened, and often disingenuous. Nevertheless, although she disapproved of what she considered the drab and tiresome women who filled the ranks of housewives, Helen Gurley Brown believed her sexy single woman could reclaim the home and liberate herself within its walls. * * *

* * *

After the publication of *The Feminine Mystique*, it was inevitable that journalists would ask Helen Gurley Brown to comment on it. In one instance, "It's very sound" formed the extent of Brown's tepid response. * * *

Brown would publicly and then privately attempt to find commonalities with Friedan, particularly around the issue of work. "Frankly, I haven't been able to convince anybody so far but Betty Friedan that women should have jobs," she wrote, "and you know every time she says roughly the same thing in her own way she gets her head chopped off."[1] Friedan would prove less desirous of seeing herself in the same category as Brown, and her denial of Brown's feminism would prove instrumental in fostering a cultural dismissal of Brown's sex-friendly, performance-friendly, capitalist-friendly philosophy for many years. Nevertheless, Brown's agenda continued to exist side by

---

8. See Philip Wylie, *Generation of Vipers* (New York: Farrar & Rinehart, 1942); William H. Whyte Jr., *The Organization Man* (New York: Simon & Schuster, 1956); David Riesman, et al., *The Lonely Crowd: A Study of the Changing American Character* (New Haven, CT: Yale University Press, 1969).
9. On the connections between Friedan's Old Left past and the popular feminism she espoused in *The Feminine Mystique*, see Horowitz, *Betty Friedan and the Making of* The Feminine Mystique.
1. Helen Gurley Brown, speech, early 1960s, HGB-SSCSC (15).

side with more radical forms of feminism, only to reemerge in full force, decades later, as something called the third wave.

Although they rarely shared a platform either physically or metaphorically, and they were constantly contrasted in the media and in interpretations of feminist history, Brown and Friedan would privately and tentatively court each other. "Dear Mrs. Friedan," Brown wrote in 1963, "I wanted you to know how much I admire you and your work." She told Friedan that she incessantly promoted *The Feminine Mystique* while on tour for her own book, saying, "I know my publisher wonders sometimes whose book I'm selling." Perhaps because Helen Gurley Brown broke the ice, or perhaps because she had already been planning to do so, Betty Friedan wrote back and attempted to further secure a relationship. She refrained from extending the same level of praise for *Sex and the Single Girl* that Brown had offered for *The Feminine Mystique*, but she thanked Brown for her kind words and then got to her point: did Brown have any suggestions for how she might interest someone in a movie dramatization of *The Feminine Mystique*? "If you have any thoughts as to someone who might be helpful to talk to about this. . . . I would certainly appreciate your dropping me a line at the Beverly Hills." Brown responded immediately, providing contact information for a literary agent in Beverly Hills who was a good friend of the Browns.[2] Like Helen Gurley Brown, Betty Friedan, feminist, hoped not only for liberation for women but also for a bit of fame and fortune for herself. And just as Friedan attempted to cast a wider net, in the aftermath of the publication of *The Feminine Mystique*, Brown, too, wasted no time, in the wake of her success with *Sex and the Single Girl*, in looking for additional opportunities to keep her own name, face, and written work in the public eye.

THE IMPACT AND LEGACY OF *THE FEMININE MYSTIQUE*

Betty Friedan's *The Feminine Mystique* lands regularly on lists of the most influential books of the twentieth century. It has become axiomatic to identify her text as one of the most important documents of the women's movement. In *The Feminine Mystique*, Friedan decided to craft her language to identify with suburban housewives. That decision won her legions of admirers, as hundreds of women wrote letters to

---

2. Letter from Helen Gurley Brown to Betty Friedan, June 6, 1963; letter from Betty Friedan to Helen Gurley Brown, July 14, 1963; letter from Helen Gurley Brown to Betty Friedan, July 16, 1963. All letters quoted above from the Schlesinger Library, Radcliffe Institute for Advanced Study, Harvard University, Betty Friedan Papers, Folder 1790.

Friedan testifying to the impact her words had on them, and countless more reevaluated their lives in the wake of reading the *Mystique*.

Friedan's plea for women to be allowed equal entry into the political, intellectual, and professional world was not unanimously embraced, however. Angry letters to *McCall's* in 1963 indicated that many women were insulted and worried by Friedan's attacks on their roles as housewives. In the midst of the Cold War, Jessica Weiss argues, these women found profound personal and political meaning in their domestic lives.

As Friedan moved into political activism in the late 1960s, the celebrity that she had won with *The Feminine Mystique* helped to make her a prominent and influential voice for the insurgent women's movement. Although young radicals, lesbians, and women of color challenged Friedan's voice as the women's movement grew, the author's work in the National Organization for Women helped to transform women's status in America, as illustrated in Ruth Rosen's piece below.

Friedan's legacy is still the subject of much controversy. Housewives' incipient anger at Friedan's feminism in 1963 expanded and grew as the New Right flourished in the 1970s and 1980s, and conservatives continue to attack Friedan and her work. Some on the left still associate Friedan with homophobia and racism. Many women, however, testify that Friedan's feminism remains relevant to their struggles with work and family today. In recent interviews, historian Stephanie Coontz found that large numbers of women remembered finding *The Feminine Mystique* revelatory, and that they linked their own political, professional, and personal liberation to their readings of the book. Fifty years after the publication of *The Feminine Mystique*, Friedan's legacy and impact on American life may be the most important contemporary question for scholars to explore.

JESSICA WEISS

From "Fraud of Femininity": Domesticity, Selflessness, and Individualism in Responses to Betty Friedan[†]

"When the home falls apart, it isn't long until the nation falls apart. Let[']s keep the wife and mother as the 'heart' of the home," wrote an angry California housewife who disagreed with an article by Betty Friedan in *McCall's* magazine published to coincide with the release of *The Feminine Mystique*. The excerpt, "The Fraud of Femininity,"

† From Jessica Weiss, "'Fraud of Femininity': Domesticity, Selflessness, and Individualism in Responses to Betty Friedan," reprinted from *Liberty and Justice for All? Rethinking Politics in Cold War America*, ed. Kathleen G. Donohue, pp. 124, 132, 134–39, 145–46. Copyright © 2012 by the University of Massachusetts Press and published by the University of Massachusetts Press. Notes have been renumbered.

introduced many Americans to Friedan and her "new life plan for women." While Betty Friedan's bestselling book generated a flood of fan mail, a torrent of critical correspondence also greeted the *McCall's* excerpt. Concern about Friedan's description of and prescription for postwar women, as presented in *McCall's*, tinged with worry over the future of American democracy, reverberated through the "Fraud of Femininity" mail. As one reader put it, "If the mothers, (or housewives as we are called) took this advice, what would become of our children? Or better yet, the future of the world?" In 1963, Friedan's call for women to grasp their individual potential raised fears about national survival.[1] * * *

* * *

Cold War Americans connected a reinvigorated family life to the strengths of capitalist democracy and the American way of life, making the baby-boom family style a buttress against Communism. The home, in particular, had long been sacrosanct in Americans' conception of their identity. In this context, the automatic connection Americans saw between feminism and Communism in the early twentieth century made discussion of gender role change during the Cold War both problematic and bold. In *McCall's* Friedan abstracted her new plan for women, emphasizing proposals for federal programs for reentry education and professional childcare agencies. She called for a "national educational program, similar to the GI Bill, for women who seriously want to continue or resume their education." To handle the practical matter of childcare, Friedan suggested "day camp provided for the children." She imagined a future in which women "speak out for maternity sabbaticals, professionally run nurseries, and other changes in the rules." * * * Her ideas promised to expand the role of government at a time when such programs symbolized socialism to many.[2]

* * *

Especially in the Cold War context, the imagery of a domestic mother rearing young children offered a more personalized, democratic alternative to Communism. Correspondents leveled criticism

1. 16 March 1963, folder 749, 20 February, March 1963, folder 741, box 21, Betty Friedan Papers, Schlesinger Library, Radcliffe Institute, Harvard University (hereafter BFP).
2. Friedan, "The Fraud of Femininity," 81, 130–32. Friedan's proposal for government-subsidized child care was certainly significant, but not as radical as it may sound, despite its negative reception. Many American women experienced federally subsidized childcare during World War II, when their labor was a wartime necessity, and if the services provided never met the needs of the female labor force, they did set important precedents. The provision of childcare for working mothers was one service that women fought to preserve on a grassroots level in the immediate postwar years. Only in

at Friedan's proposals for group childcare. Regardless of whether such care existed on the American or the Soviet side of the iron curtain, they viewed it as impersonal. A California correspondent complained, "Too many women today are out beating their brains out competing in an already overcrowded business world as it is, flooding the market of the unemployed, leaving small children at home or in day nurseries cared for by uncaring people in the business for the money when they should be home keeping their families together, raising children who are happy and secure." This reader crafted a two-pronged critique, of materialistic women in the rat race driving men out of jobs on the one hand, and money-motivated childcare workers on the other. Each stood in contrast to the homemaker. Individual mothers, correspondents wrote, raised their own children out of love, not financial interest. A New Jersey homemaker demanded, "What better thing can I do in life than bring up 5 children who can contribute good will to mankind & peace on earth?" A Pennsylvania correspondent wrote, "The home and family represent labor of love." A woman from New York claimed, "A mother's full-time care, love, guidance, and interest in her children cannot be bought at any nursery or school." The intimate, personal home, where women, in particular, provided services seemingly outside the capitalist market, held important rhetorical value and contrasted with childcare arrangements where money exchanged hands. In the home, mothers bestowed maternal service and love. These women posed the home as both retreat from and counterweight to an impersonal world of commercial transactions, competition, and personal ambition. This compelling association had important ideological value that affected Friedan's reception.[3]

McCall's readers identified what linked women's pursuit of individual ambition to Communism: institutionalized childcare. From Texas came a "fear the time will come when our children will be taken from us and placed in institutions and taught differently to our own way of thinking and principles." Mothers exiting the home and leaving their children in care outside of it thus symbolized Communist influence to many. It sounded to one reader that Friedan was proclaiming, "Down with mothers raising their own children. Let the state do it!" * * *

California and a few other states did they achieve the state's commitment to the children of working mothers when the federal government cut off funds. These successes, and the advocacy necessary to preserve them, kept childcare in the national consciousness. During his 1960 campaign for the presidency, John F. Kennedy wrote to a childcare advocate that he endorsed the concept of federal aid for childcare, for example. Harrison, *On Account of Sex: The Politics of Women's Issues, 1945–1968*, 75.

3. 19 February 1963, 21 February 1963, folder 741; 28 February 1963, folder 742, BFP.

To upset readers, Friedan's attack on the feminine mystique equaled Communist subversion because of its impact on American family life. From California, a reader responded, "I have heard many times that one of communism's tactics in defeat of a country is breaking up the structure of the family. I would hate to see that happen here, so I hope there aren't too many people who agree with this article." The home was in this vision a precarious but necessary buttress of national defense. As a homemaker in South Carolina put it, "the family is one sure bulwark against Communism and strength for our Nation." Another reader wrote, "If ever I have read an article that could do such irreparable damage to the care of our way of life, mainly the American home, I do not know what it was!" Yet another asserted that Friedan's ideas "weaken[ed] the fiber of the American home and undermin[ed] the strength of the nation."[4] Friedan's threat to the fiber of the nation? Her proposal that women pursue interests outside of the home.

Those who identified women with the home and capitalism saw them as the glue that held the family together. Their presence was essential for the well-being of men and children, and by extension, the nation. There was a particular Cold War nuance to this seemingly traditional refrain. From Texas came the opinion, "The home is the beginning, the foundation for all other interests for children as well as the adults. Take a wife and mother away and watch it all fall." According to this line of Cold War thinking, homemaking was patriotic service to the nation. Apart from anticommunist concerns, readers allayed fears of burgeoning national selfishness with proposals to keep "the mother in the home where she belongs." Women who stayed home staved off the decline of American society from within, according to *McCall's* correspondents.[5]

* * *

Friedan's correspondents connected Cold War mother love and labor to the particular quality in American life that distinguished Americans from Russians: individualism. Readers who did not explicitly reference anticommunism nonetheless expressed concern for the maintenance of this American value. Friedan's proposal for childcare received much criticism along these lines. An Oregon woman "particularly object[ed] to placing a pre-schooler in a professionally run nursery because I feel that it would lead to a lessening of

4. 20 February 1963, folder 741; 19 March 1963, folder 749, box 21, BFP.
5. 21 February 1963, folder 741; 5 March 1963, folder 746; 12 March 1963, folder 748; 29 March 1963, folder 749; n.d., folder 752; 19 February 1963, folder 743; 1 March 1963, folder 745, box 21, BFP.

individuality in the child." Another reader noted, "I should think this early collectivism could conceivably lead to an easy acceptance of group thought, of group pressures, eventually to a collectivistic society." Rejecting organized childcare, one reader from California wrote, "I want to be on hand during these years when bandages, Kool Aid, cookies and love need dispensing. Let the Russians raise their children in institutions, but why copy them?" Mothers at home kept children out of collective, impersonal childcare, preserving the next generation's individuality.[6]

In these formulations, women's political contribution to the Cold War state was "the bearing and educating of future citizens." At home, they raised patriotic, individually minded children. From readers' perspectives, American individualism was fragile and easily subject to outside influences. Even doing things outside the family in age-segregated groups might be perceived as collectivizing. Friedan's correspondents believed that full-time mothering protected and nurtured children's individuality, preserving the American tradition of individualism. In Cold War thought, individualism not only helped distinguish the United States from the Soviet Union, but was also under threat. * * * Americans in the 1950s perceived the "modern self" as "fragile" and "softened" and thus susceptible to subversion. * * *

Individual mothers nurturing their children in their homes personified the American way of life and preserved it for the future. "Don't knock motherhood or housewifery," a Michigan correspondent wrote. "It is upon these two occupations that the formulation of character and morals of our great men and women depends. To belittle these professions is to care nothing about the ultimate condition of our country in the hands of future leaders." Mothering was "one of life's deepest responsibilities, the greatest service they can do for a society—that of helping another human being develop from infancy into a worthwhile citizen." Women who lived up to their responsibilities reared a citizenry resistant to Communism and able to accept the mantle of American citizenship.[7]

* * *

* * * In proposing both female individualism and public childcare programs, Friedan, in "Fraud of Femininity," and *The Feminine Mystique*, threatened two central ingredients in American gender and political ideology in the Cold War years: female selfless-

6. 27 February 1963, 28 February 1963, folder 744; 20 February 1963, folder 741, BFP.
7. 8 March 1963, folder 747; 28 February 1963, folder 742, BFP.

ness and its emblem, stay-at-home motherhood, at a time when it was becoming increasingly apparent that middle-class American women were working in greater numbers after marriage and motherhood. Friedan's naysayers acknowledged these shifts, seeing selflessness as patriotic behavior to be enacted, rather than as an inherent female trait.[8]

The cries of "selfishness" that greeted one of the first public discussions of modern feminist ideas allow us to see the early 1960s as more hostile to feminist change than we have assumed. The angry greeting from women readers that coexisted with the warmer welcome with which we are familiar reminds us of the ideological investment many Americans, including women, had in retaining women's homemaking roles during the lengthy Cold War. Through the 1960s and beyond, even as feminism undertook its remaking of American society and the economy continued to alter women's marriage, childrearing, and employment patterns, domesticity and motherhood maintained cultural saliency. The Cold War and increasing political instability of the 1960s allowed gender conservatives, antifeminists and nonfeminists alike, to perceive a continued embrace of women's domesticity not as a backward-looking reaction to modern opportunities and a negative reassertion of male power, but instead as a positive, proactive means of countering social disintegration and incipient national decline freighted with real urgency.

Feminism grew to flourish during the Cold War, but the Cold War also nurtured the New Right. The active strain of antifeminism in contemporary American society is more understandable when we acknowledge its feisty presence in the 1960s and its usefulness to Cold War political opponents of social and gender reform. Cold War gender conservatism was a strong undercurrent that shaped and accompanied second-wave feminism as well as the response to it. While the conservative movement explicitly turned to social issues and a family values strategy in the 1970s, in the early 1960s the seeds of that successful strategy were already sown.[9]

8. Aware of the Cold War emphasis on domesticity and its cultural clout, an admiring *McCall's* reader wrote, "I should imagine that a majority of your readers will be incensed by her heresy; if so their anger offers further evidence that the 'back to the kitchen' campaign has succeeded." 20 February 1963, folder 741, BFP.

9. Ruth Feldstein identifies mid-century liberalism's celebration of traditional gender roles, along with the related notion that "good motherhood was a precondition to healthy citizens," and concludes, "As liberals began to abandon a psychosocial narrative of citizenship that wed political and psychological health to maternal behavior, conservatives increasingly adopted this narrative as their own." Ruth Feldstein, *Motherhood in Black and White: Race and Sex in American Liberalism, 1930–1965* (Ithaca:

RUTH ROSEN

From The World Split Open: How the Modern
Women's Movement Changed America[†]

* * *

The Turning Point, Title VII

Nineteen sixty-three had been a banner year. The Equal Pay Act, the
Presidential Report on American Women, and *The Feminine Mystique* all helped to publicize a growing sense of gender consciousness.
The next year was no less momentous. After President Kennedy's
assassination in November 1963, Congress began considering the
comprehensive civil rights bill. Congressman "Judge" Howard Smith,
the southern chairman of the House Rules Committee, offered an
amendment to add "sex" to Title VII, the section of the bill that prohibited discrimination in employment on the basis of race, color,
religion, or national origin by private employers. A longtime supporter of the Equal Rights Amendment, as well as an ardent segrega-
tionist, Smith saw his amendment as purely a win-win proposition.
A prohibition on sex discrimination would give northern representatives a reason to vote against the act without facing the accusation of
being racists. And if it passed, at least he wanted to be sure that
"white women" would be the beneficiaries.[1]

Cornell University Press, 2000), 168–69. William Chafe suggests that a "social atmosphere conducive to reform" was a necessary and existing precondition for the feminist
movement. I am suggesting that the political atmosphere of the Cold War was less recep-
tive to feminism than historians have depicted it and that strong oppositional undertows
greeted the second wave. William Chafe, *The Paradox of Change: American Women in
the 20th Century* (New York: Oxford University Press, 1991), 145. Feminist scholars have
begun to question the utility of the wave metaphor because it implies peaks and valleys
of activism, privileges eras of successful mass action over other eras, and masks continuity. See Nancy Hewitt, *No Permanent Waves: Recasting Histories of U.S. Feminism* (New
Brunswick, N.J.: Rutgers University Press, 2010). For a terrific discussion of how feminism was portrayed by opponents as against mothers, see Susan Douglas and Meredith
Michaels, *The Mommy Myth: The Idealization of Motherhood and How It Has Undermined All Women* (New York: Simon & Schuster, 2004), chap. 1. Friedan tackled what
she perceived to be "second-wave" feminism's neglect of the issue of family and motherhood in her 1981 book, *The Second Stage.* She wrote, "I think we must at least admit and
begin openly to discuss feminist denial of the importance of family, of women's own
needs to give and get love and nurture, tender loving care." Friedan, *Second Stage,* 2.
Donald T. Critchlow and Cynthia L. Stachecki, "The Equal Rights Amendment Recon-
sidered: Politics, Policy, and Social Mobilization in a Democracy," *Journal of Policy History* 20 (2008): 165–66.

[†] From Ruth Rosen, *The World Split Open: How the Modern Women's Movement Changed
America* (New York: Penguin, 2000), pp. 70–72, 72–75, 78–81. Copyright © 2000 by
Ruth Rosen. Used by permission of Viking Penguin, a division of Penguin Group (USA).
Notes have been renumbered.

1. See "Resolution Adopted Unanimously by the National Council of the National Woman's Party—Regarding the Proposed Civil Rights Bill (H.R. 7152)," December 16,
1963, Reel 108, National Woman's Party papers, on microfilm.

At first, Smith's colleagues did not even take the amendment seriously. In an excessive display of chivalric oratory, Smith regaled the House with a letter from a woman who complained of the paucity of men available as husbands. Playing for laughs, he asked the House to take these "real grievances" seriously. The House erupted in riotous laughter. Emmanuel Celler, the liberal New York chairman of the Judiciary Committee, added to the jocular spirit when he announced that it was he—never his wife—who always had the last two words in his houseold, and those were "Yes, dear."[2]

When the laughter subsided, coalitions began forming for and against Smith's amendment. Prodded by the Virginia members of the National Woman's Party—never known for its progressive views on race—these women now turned to Smith as a natural ally. Democratic representative Edith Green, the sponsor of the 1963 Equal Pay Act, worried that the amendment would gather opposition to the civil rights bill and risk African-Americans' chance to win their civil rights. She decided to vote against Smith's amendment. On the other hand, yes votes came from those representatives who had decided that they would not endure another "Negro's hour"—the post–Civil War moment when suffrage was granted to black men, but not to black or white women. Representative Martha Griffiths, a Republican who had long sought to include a prohibition on sex discrimination in the civil rights bill, helped forge a bizarre coalition of southern congressmen and their feminist supporters who seized the unexpected opportunity. The amendment passed.

Women activists immediately began a lobbying campaign to ensure passage of the entire bill itself. Betty Friedan, Martha Griffiths, Pauli Murray, members of the National Woman's Party, the Business and Professional Women's Clubs, and dozens of other women's organizations invaded legislators' offices, warning of the consequences if they dared vote against half of their constituency. Supported by President Lyndon Johnson's wife, Lady Bird, and various members of the administration, the Civil Rights Act of 1964—including Title VII—passed.[3]

---

2. Cynthia Harrison, *On Account of Sex: The Politics of Women's Issues, 1945–1968* (University of California Press, 1989), p. 178. Much of my discussion on the Presidential Commission on the Status of Women is grounded in Harrison's meticulous work.

3. Probably the best account of the history behind this so-called "fluke" is Jo Freeman's "How 'Sex' Got into Title VII: Persistent Opportunism as a Maker of Public Policy," *Law and Inequality: A Journal of Theory and Practice* 9 (March 1991): 163–84, reprinted on the H-Net for Women's History. Freeman demonstrates how a small group of women took advantage of a long-standing desire to legislate against sex discrimination. The debate on Smith's amendment can be found in the *Congressional Record*, 88th Congress, 2nd sess., February 8, 1964, 2577–84; EEOC, *Legislative History of Titles VII and XI of Civil Rights Act of 1964*, Washington, D.C., Government Printing Office, n.d., 3312–28; Caroline Bird, *Born Female* (New York: Pocket Books, 1971), chapter 1; Harrison, chapter 9.

* * * The legislation created a new agency, the Equal Employment Opportunity Commission (EEOC), charged with investigating complaints of racial and sexual discrimination. But women quickly discovered that its director, Herman Edelsberg, considered sex discrimination a joke, or at least a distraction from the more important work of assisting black men. Edelsberg called Title VII "a fluke . . . conceived out of wedlock," "There are people on this commission," he informed the press, "who think that no man should be required to have a male secretary and I am one of them." When it was signed into law at the White House ceremony, no women were present, and the *New York Times*'s account of the bill did not even mention that the new legislation prohibited sex discrimination in employment.[4]

When someone at a White House Conference on Equal Opportunity openly wondered if Playboy clubs would now have to employ male "bunnies," the press quickly picked up the joke and dubbed the sex amendment the "Bunny Law." A *New York Times* editorial coyly suggested that

> Federal officials . . . may find it would have been better if Congress had just abolished sex itself. Handyman must disappear from the language; he was pretty much a goner anyway, if you ever started looking for one in desperation. No more milkman, iceman, serviceman, foreman or pressman. . . . The Rockettes may become bi-sexual, and a pity, too . . . Bunny problem, indeed! This is revolution, chaos. You can't even safely advertise for a wife any more.[5]

Title VII remained a joke. In August 1965, the EEOC shocked women activists when it ruled that sex-segregated help-wanted ads were perfectly legal. The *New Republic*, a liberal journal of opinion, agreed. Why should a mischievous joke perpetrated on the floor of the House of Representatives be treated by a responsible administration body with this kind of seriousness?" The idea of banishing sex discrimination challenged deeply held ideas about gender and elicited much nervous ridicule. The *Wall Street Journal* asked its readers to imagine "a shapeless, knobby-kneed male 'bunny' serving drinks to a group of astonished businessmen or a 'matronly vice-president' lusting after her male secretary." What are we going to do now, asked a personnel officer of a large airline, "when a gal walks into our

---

4. Martha Griffiths' speech, U.S. Congress, House, 89th Congress, June 20, 1966, *Congressional Record* 112: 13689–94. *Washington Post*, November 23, 1965, in Folder "Title VII Civil Rights Act of 1963, Legislation 1964–65." National Business and Professional Women's Clubs (BPW) Archives cited in Harrison, 187. *New York Times*, July 3, 1964.
5. *New York Times* editorial, August 21, 1965, 37.

office, demands a job as an airline pilot and has the credentials to qualify?" In companies that traditionally hired only women, businessmen grew edgy. One manager of an electronics component company lamented, "I suppose we'll have to advertise for people with small, nimble fingers and hire the first male midget with unusual dexterity [who] shows up."[6]

Even if the EEOC had taken sex discrimination seriously, Congress had severely limited its powers. The agency could only investigate individual complaints, issue findings, and seek voluntary settlements. If a company refused to concede race or sex discrimination, the EEOC had to persuade the Civil Rights Division of the Justice Department to seek judicial enforcement. If the division refused, the complainant's only recourse was to file suit in federal court.[7]

Nonetheless, by 1965, working women began flooding the EEOC with their grievances. In some parts of the country, nearly half the complaints came from working women who identified acts of discrimination. Shocked by the volume of these grievances, the EEOC nevertheless remained committed to monitoring only racial discrimination. Mired in the Vietnam War and unsettled by race riots in American cities, neither President Johnson nor Congress gave women's complaints any attention. On June 20, 1966, Representative Martha Griffiths, a tireless fighter for women's rights, denounced the EEOC for its "specious, negative, and arrogant" attitude toward sex discrimination. "I would remind them," she announced on the floor of Congress, "that they took an oath to uphold the law, not just the part of it that they are interested in."[8]

No one seemed to care—except members of the state commissions who had convened for their third conference in Washington, D.C., ten days after Griffiths attacked the EEOC. Within their respective states, the commissions had supported more flexible working hours, the repeal of discriminatory laws, equal pay, and dozens of other "women's issues." The state commissions had also created a national network of women who, by gathering and sharing data about women in their respective states, had gained expert knowledge about women's subordinate status in American society. But by themselves, as delegates to the third conference on state commissions, they were almost powerless. As Betty Friedan later noted, "It is more than a

---

6. *New Republic*, September 4, 1965, 3; *Wall Street Journal*, June 22, 1965.
7. A good source for Title VII is Donald Allen Robinson, *Signs* 4 (Spring 1979) 411–34, and "Development in the Law: Employment Discrimination and Title VII of the Civil Rights Act of 1964," *Harvard Law Review* 84 (March 1971).
8. Martha Griffiths, statement on floor of Congress, June 20, 1966, *Congressional Record*, 13054.

historical fluke that the organization of the women's movement was ignited by that law, never meant to be enforced, against sex discrimination in employment."[9]

The Founding of NOW

They did have one vital resource to call on—what Betty Friedan called "an underground feminist movement" that existed in the nation's capital. Friedan was in constant contact with women who risked their government jobs to promote women's issues there. She credited women like "Catherine East of the Women's Bureau of the Labor Department for spreading the feminist underground around Washington and acting as midwife to the women's movement." The network also included Esther Peterson; Mary Eastwood, a former member of the President's Commission; EEOC commissioner Richard Graham; Sonia Pressman, an attorney in the EEOC; legal scholar Pauli Murray; and congresswoman Martha Griffiths. Frustrated by the government's unwillingness to influence the EEOC and angered by the EEOC's unwillingness to address sex discrimination—especially sex-segregated "want ads"—fifteen women finally agreed to meet one evening during the conference in Friedan's hotel room to discuss the possibility of starting a new women's organization.[1]

Some of the women wondered whether they could even trust one another. For some, surfacing in any advocacy group for women was risky. Friedan later recalled how difficult it was for "women who didn't know each other personally, who hadn't yet acquired the trust we would later earn in action together." The McCarthy period had left a legacy of fear and many activists had learned to keep their silence on political issues. The discussion continued past midnight, interrupted by "ladylike rows," and filled with suspicion and timidity. When the meeting ended, the group was still unable to agree on the nature of the new organization or whether there should even be one. Betty Friedan went to bed feeling the bitter taste of defeat. "I thought the battle was over before it had even begun, not realizing that the same fear and finally the daring necessary to act despite those fears were now under way in the others, just as in me."[2]

In fact, the struggle had just begun. At the conference the next day, a group of delegates presented a resolution insisting that the EEOC enforce Title VII of the Civil Rights Act. Conference officials, worried about pressuring the Johnson administration, refused to allow the resolution to come to a vote. The delegates, from vari-

---

9. Betty Friedan, *It Changed My Life: Writings on the Women's Movement* (New York: Random House, 1976), 80.
1. Friedan, *It Changed My Life*, 80.
2. Friedan, 80, 82.

ous state commissions, grew furious. They were tired of talk; they wanted action.

At lunch, a group hastily gathered around two tables to discuss their next move. Time was running out, because, as Friedan later explained, "most of us had plane reservations that afternoon, when the conference ended, and had to get back in time to make dinner for their families." In conspiratorial fashion, they whispered, passed around notes on paper napkins, and discussed forming a new organization. On one of those paper napkins, Friedan wrote down a name—the National Organization for Women. Its purpose, she scribbled, would be "to take the actions needed to bring women into the mainstream of American society, now" and to fight for "full equality for women, in full equal partnership with men."[3] As they left to catch their planes, the conspirators agreed to call a formal meeting to create the new organization that fall.

❊   ❊   ❊

In 1966, the radicalism of this challenge to American political culture was not yet fully grasped by Betty Friedan, by young feminists in the women's liberation movement, nor even by their opponents. Although feminists would long debate whether to emphasize women's difference from or similarity to men, neither choice fully embraced the reality of women's lives. Women were both like and unlike men. Any society that didn't honor women's ability to bear and raise children was clearly violating their rights to fully participate in society. Any society that equated equality with women living as men could not be viewed as a genuine democracy. A true "gender democracy" would have to honor the life of the family as much as it honored the life of work. Men would no longer be the frame of reference. But nor would women. The revolutionary thrust of feminism required an extensive expansion of democracy at work, in the home, in public, in private. Nothing less would do.

On October 29, 1966, NOW convened its official founding conference in Washington, D.C. Of the three hundred women who became charter members, 120 came from the Midwest, which once again highlighted the indigenous female activism in this region of the nation. Of these three hundred members, only thirty could be present to adopt the "Statement of Purpose" and new bylaws. This small convocation elected Friedan its first president and former EEOC commissioners Aileen Hernandez and Richard Graham its vice presidents. NOW's "Statement of Purpose" declared that women's demands for equality were "part of the world-wide revolution of human rights now taking place within and beyond our national borders." The writers

3. Friedan, 83.

were determined to avoid the kind of separatism just then emerging in black activist organizations, so the first sentence of the "Statement" began, "We men and women," and called for "a fully equal partnership of the sexes. . . ." It also enumerated the dramatic changes that had created the basis for a new surge of demands for women's rights: an extended life span of seventy-five years and the development of technology that reduced the importance of muscular strength.[4]

NOW's statement challenged American society to heed women's grievances. One of those issues was that despite the optimistic social programs of Kennedy's New Frontier and Johnson's Great Society, the economic status of women had actually declined. By 1966, the wages of full-time year-round women workers averaged only 60 percent of those of men, a drop of 3.6 percent in a decade. Black women, burdened by the double discrimination of sex and race, earned even less. In addition, although 46.4 percent of American adult women now worked, 75 percent of them labored in routine clerical, sales, or factory jobs or as household workers, cleaning women, and hospital attendants.[5]

In all the professions, women were also losing ground. Though they constituted 53 percent of the population, they represented less than 1 percent of federal judges, less than 4 percent of lawyers, and only 7 percent of doctors. In addition, since World War II, men had been replacing women in professions once considered "women's fields"—as administrators of secondary and elementary schools, librarians, and social workers. This hidden and "dangerous decline," NOW's "Statement" declared, had to be "recognized and reversed by 'the power of American law' [and the] protection guaranteed by the U.S. Constitution to the civil rights of all individuals." Token appointments were unacceptable; the government would have to stop discriminating against women in all areas of public life.[6]

The "Statement" pointedly criticized the United States for lagging behind other industrialized countries in providing the kinds of social welfare—health care, child care, and pregnancy leave—that supported women's domestic and work needs. Women "should not have to choose between family life and participation in industry or the

4. Friedan, *It Changed My Life*, 87, "Statement of Purpose." For much of the history of NOW, I have used the late Frances Kolb's uncompleted manuscript, "The National Organization for Women: A History of the First Ten Years," which she generously shared with me before her death. Unpublished ms., chapter 1, APA.

5. U.S. Department of the Census: "Money Income of Families and Persons in the United States," *Current Population Reports, 1957 to 1975*, U.S. Department of Labor, Bureau of Labor Statistics: *Handbook of Labor Statistics*, 1975, cited in *The Earnings Gap Between Women and Men*, U.S. Department of Labor Employment Standards Administration, Women's Bureau, 1976; and U.S. Department of Labor, Women's Bureau, "Background Facts on Women Workers in the United States," January 1962, Document VI-39, PCSW papers, Washington, D.C., cited in Harrison, 90; Women's Bureau, "Fact Sheet on the Earnings Gap" (Washington, D.C., 1970); Friedan, *It Changed My Life*, 89.

6. Friedan, 90, 89.

professions." Nor should "all normal women . . . retire from jobs or professions for ten or fifteen years, to devote their full time to raising children, only to reenter the job market at a relatively minor level." The "Statement" questioned the "assumption that these problems are the unique responsibility of each individual woman, rather than a basic social dilemma which society must solve."

Contrary to later accusations that feminists ignored the issue of child-rearing and denied women the choice of remaining full-time mothers, NOW's "Statement" called for a nationwide network of child care centers, as well as national programs to provide retraining, after their children grew up, "for women who have chosen to care for their own children full-time." The "Statement" also urged recasting traditional gender roles within marriage, proposing that "a true partnership between the sexes demands a different concept of marriage, an equitable sharing of the responsibilities of home and children and of the economic burden of their support."[7]

During NOW's first few years, the press gave the new organization only slightly more respect—and far less attention—than the sexier young women's liberation movement that sprang to life in 1967. To report NOW's first convention, the *New York Times* placed an article headlined "They Meet in Victorian Parlor to Demand 'True Equality'" right beneath exciting new recipes for turkeys and stuffing. The *Washington Post* headlined its report "Neo-Suffragettes on the March; Mrs. Friedan Is Fighting for Women's Equality NOW" and ran it next to an ad for a "fashion clearance" and below photographs of diplomatic wives greeting each another.[8]

NOW also suffered from meager resources. For three years, the organization lacked an office of its own. Nevertheless, NOW members made do, much as those in the civil rights and students' movements had, by borrowing any resources to which they had access. The new secretary-treasurer, Caroline Davis of the United Auto Workers, gave NOW a valuable "free ride" by allowing it to use the UAW's facilities—especially its precious WATS phone line,* as well as copy and mimeograph machines. Betty Friedan's apartment in New York City served as the center of policy-making and organization. Fearful of centralization, NOW quickly developed local chapters to counterbalance the power of a national headquarters. Local leadership identified their own priorities and projects, while the national leadership made policy and coordinated national actions.

---

7. Friedan, "Statement," 89ff.
8. *New York Times*, November 22, 1966, 44:1; *Washington Post*, November 23, 1966, n.p.
* WATS telephone lines allowed either free or deeply discounted calls from institutions like unions and universities. Without them, national organization was far more difficult. All social movements at the time depended upon the use of WATS lines to do what e-mail would do in the 1990s.

With these slim resources, NOW plunged into action. Predictably, its first official act was to pressure the EEOC to prohibit segregated "help wanted" advertising. Such a division of ads, NOW argued, ensured that women would not be able to enter the higher-paid and more skilled occupations reserved for men. To dramatize the issue, NOW members picketed the *New York Times* in August 1967. In December, NOW declared a National Day of Demonstration against the EEOC, mobilizing women to picket local EEOC offices. After tipping off the television networks, small groups of NOW members, in an attempt to demonstrate the worthlessness of sex-segregated want ads, dumped bundles of newspapers in front of EEOC local offices. In August 1968, after years of protracted struggles with the government and the newspaper industry, the EEOC finally barred segregated want ads.[9]

Contrary to conventional wisdom, NOW members—although mostly white and middle class—targeted the problems of ordinary working women, not those of professional women. The assault on segregated classified ads, for instance, benefited working women who wanted to enter the skilled blue collar jobs formerly designated as men's work. NOW also waged a successful campaign against airlines that forced stewardesses to resign once they married or turned thirty-two. This requirement had produced windfall profits for the airlines that fired wave after wave of stewardesses, without having to give them raises, pensions, or Social Security payments. "Sex discrimination," observed Friedan, "*was* big business."[1]

NOW next pressed the government, as well as federal contractors and subcontractors, to ban sex discrimination—again, something that did not particularly benefit professional women. In the fall of 1965, President Johnson had signed an Executive Order banning racial (but not sexual) discrimination in businesses and institutions that received funds from the government. Two years later, NOW leaders began lobbying President Johnson for similar treatment. He responded by adding "sex" to the new Executive Order. The results were far-reaching: any university or company that received federal contracts now had to ensure fair employment to women as well as to racial minorities.

During its first year, NOW also pushed for enforcement of Title VII by the EEOC, so that minority women in federal poverty programs would get equal attention and so that child care expenses would be deductible. In its first court action, for which it established its Legal Defense Fund, NOW supported southern factory women

---

9. NOW mimeographed pamphlet, *Special Edition #2: NOW vs. Segregated Help-Wanted Ads.* Unpaginated. 1965, APA. See Hole and Levine, *Rebirth*, for a full description.
1. Friedan, *It Changed My Life*, 94.

who sued Colgate-Palmolive and Southern Bell Telephone for denying women jobs—an action that had been prohibited by state laws.
All these campaigns were aimed at improving the lives of ordinary
working women.

STEPHANIE COONTZ

From A Strange Stirring: *The Feminine Mystique* and American Women at the Dawn of the 1960s[†]

The Feminine Mystique "left me breathless," recalled Glenda Schilt
Edwards, who was twenty-eight when she read the book, shortly
after it was published. "I felt as though Betty Friedan had looked into
my heart, mind, and psyche and . . . put the unexplainable distress
I was suffering into words. I was astonished that before [reading the
book] I could not express why I felt so depressed, even though my
distress drove me to see two therapists at different times. Both therapists seemed to feel that I was having trouble 'accepting my role as a
wife.'"

Janice K. was thirty-six and the mother of ten-year-old twins when
a friend sent her *The Feminine Mystique* in 1963. The year before,
she had seen a psychiatrist for eight months without ever getting to
the bottom of her "troubles." She became so indignant when she read
the book that she sent a copy to her therapist "with a note saying he
should read it before he ever again told a woman that all she needed
was to come to terms with her 'feminine nature.'"

Laura M., now a veteran journalist, read it in high school. "My
most vivid memory is that I finally realized I wasn't crazy. I was still
part of a generation expected to embrace family life as the 'end all
and be all,' to subsume my ambitions to my husband's goals. But
I didn't want to! What was wrong with me?" Reading Friedan's book
made Laura realize that having aspirations beyond being a housewife
might actually be healthy, not sick.

"I had forgotten all about *The Feminine Mystique*," wrote Mary
Lee Fulkerson, whose husband was a career military officer in the
1960s. "Reading it now, more than 45 years after it was written and
maybe 40 years after I first read it, it seems so superficial and mealy-
mouthed. It took me a few days to remember how it was for me back
then. And then the agony and despair of those times came flooding
back to my heart and mind."

For some women, the book was literally a lifesaver. When Rose Garrity read the book she was a young mother whose husband regularly beat her. She had married at age fifteen, dropped out of school after just one week in the tenth grade, had her first child at age seventeen, and then had four more in the next five and a half years. "I was trapped in what felt like hell," Rose recalls. "I had been forced to drop out of school. . . . There were no domestic violence programs and no one ever talked about the issue. . . . I thought I was the only one being beaten and there was something terribly wrong with me. I was ashamed."

Rose worked on getting her high school diploma in secret, hiding her study materials from her husband. "When I read this book it was like the curtain was thrown back on the 'wizard'! I suddenly understood what was going on, how sexism works, and was energized to begin to survive as an individual person." Today Rose runs a domestic violence program in rural New York and serves on the board of directors of the National Coalition Against Domestic Violence.

Most women had less burning reasons for their discontent, which made them even more likely to feel there was something "terribly wrong" with themselves. "I didn't think I had any 'excuse' for what I was feeling," says Sharon G. "My dad used to hit my mom, and I swore I would never put up with that. But no one was hitting me. I loved my husband and he loved me. Yet I was miserable."

Judy J. remembers crying helplessly as she tried to explain her depression to her unsympathetic mother. "What more could you want?" her mother kept asking, "Do you remember what my life was like when I was raising you and your brother, with no washing machine and a wood stove I had to feed four times a day? What's wrong with you?" Friedan's book told Judy it was okay for her to want more, and helped her figure out what that "more" might be.

Cam Stivers recalls that around the time she read *The Feminine Mystique*, "I had the feeling (at 25!) that my life was over, and that nothing interesting would ever happen to me again. . . . I told myself that the fix I was in was my own fault, that there was something wrong with me. I had everything a woman was supposed to want— marriage to a nice, dependable guy (a good provider), a wonderful little kid, a nice house in the suburbs—and I was miserable."

"I didn't know why I was so unhappy," recalls Danielle B., "until I read *The Feminine Mystique*. Then something clicked." The letters Friedan received at the time were full of similar phrases: "Like light bulbs going off again and again"; "What a sense of relief"; "Now I know I'm not alone"; "It's not just me"; "Suddenly I understand." Nearly fifty years later, women recollected the same tremendous sense of relief. "I suddenly realized maybe I wasn't an outcast"; "I wasn't a nut-case"; "I wasn't going mad"; "I recognized what was missing from my life"; "I understood what I was feeling and felt validated!!"

Cam Stivers remembers thinking, *Your unhappiness isn't just you. There's something wrong with the whole arrangement.* "I can't express how freeing it was for me to realize that my predicament was not all my own fault."

After finishing the book, Glenda Schilt Edwards, who still felt terrible after being treated by two different psychiatrists, "realized that what I thought might be wrong with me, was in fact, right with me!" "It was a real 'click' moment for me," commented Linda Smolak, who went on to become a professor of psychology and women's studies. "It literally changed (and perhaps saved) my life."

Jeri G., then a thirty-six-year-old mother of three, read *The Feminine Mystique* in 1963. She had taken an overdose of sleeping pills the year before. "Maybe it was just a 'bid for attention,' as the cliché goes, and not a serious attempt at the time," Jeri said, "but if so, no one gave me the kind of attention I needed. My doctor sent me to a psychiatrist, but he only made me more ashamed of my feelings. I truly believe that if I hadn't found that book when I did, I might really have killed myself the next time."

A look at the life of Anne Parsons reveals how tormented some women were by the pressures of the feminine mystique. Anne was the daughter of Talcott Parsons, the renowned Harvard sociologist who insisted on society's need for "normal" families consisting of male breadwinners and female homemakers. Even though Anne's parents encouraged her to develop her own intellect, she felt pressured to live the kind of life her father prescribed for most women. In an eight-page letter she wrote to Betty Friedan in 1963 after reading the book, Anne recalled that she had chosen not to take fourth-year math in high school "for fear of being called a brain," and while in college had agreed to a marriage based more on the desire for security than anything else.

When she came to grips with her motivation, Anne explained, she broke off the engagement and pursued advanced work in psychiatric theory and anthropology, but at age twenty-five she was haunted by the price she felt she had been forced to pay for her choice. The unmarried career woman, she complained, was not seen "as a person at all." Instead, she was stereotyped as "aggressive, competitive, rejecting of femininity and all the rest." It "is like being a Negro or Jew," she commented, "with the difference that the prejudices are manifest in such subtle ways that it is very hard to pin them down, and that the feminine mystique is so strong and attractive an ideology that it is very hard to find a countervailing point of view from which to fight for oneself."

Feeling increasingly marginalized in her relations with colleagues, Anne committed herself to a mental institution in September 1963, where she kept a diary recording her fears about the Cold War and the arms race and her frustration with her psychiatrist's insistence that she was "resisting insight into my feminine instincts." Page-long sentences veer back and forth between Anne's anxieties about the state of the world and the refrain, written in caps, "you CANNOT COME TO TERMS WITH YOUR BASIC FEMININE INSTINCTS." Nine months later, after writing to her father that she thought the psychiatric treatments had made her worse and trying in vain to get released from the hospital, Anne committed suicide.

Anne Parsons might have developed her mental problems even in a world where single female intellectuals were not regarded as defective women and psychiatrists did not tell patients they were resisting their feminine instincts if they held strong political opinions or harbored intellectual ambitions. But many other women insisted it was the tenets of Freudian psychiatry that had made them feel crazy, and it was Friedan's book, not talk therapy or medication, that allowed them to reclaim their sanity.

Some, like Edwards, echoed Anne Parsons's claim that seeing a psychiatrist had made things worse. Edwards recalls: "My presenting complaint was that I did not know why I had such sad and distressed feelings, as I had everything I thought I should have to feel happy; a successful husband, three wonderful children, a house in the suburbs, a station wagon and a family dog, what else could possibly be lacking? They told me I was having trouble 'accepting my role as a wife.'"

A self-described "ex–newspaper woman" with two young children wrote to Friedan in November 1963 that when she talked to a psychiatrist about the sense of emptiness she felt in being a full-time homemaker, he kept asking "if I was *sure* there wasn't 'Another Man' involved and whether I really loved my children."

Other women reported a better experience, finding psychiatrists who sympathized with their frustration or depression and made useful suggestions about how to alleviate it. But most of the women I interviewed told me that the turning point in their lives came when they started seeing their anxiety as a legitimate social grievance rather than an individual problem. This insight gave them the courage to pursue their dreams, or sometimes just the permission to *have* a dream. For that, most credit *The Feminine Mystique*.

✳   ✳   ✳

Betty Friedan:
A Chronology

1921   Born at Proctor Hospital in Peoria, IL on February 4; named Bettye Naomi Goldstein, the first child of Harry and Miriam Goldstein.

1938   Graduates from Central High School.

1938   Begins freshman year at Smith College in Northhampton, MA.

1939-1940   Revives student-sponsored magazine, *Smith College Monthly* (SCM) and changes it from monthly literary magazine to social and political journal; serves as managing editor.

1940   Works with Kurt Lewin during the summer at the Child Welfare Research Station at the State University of Iowa on early experiments on group dynamics.

1940-1941   Works on staff of the college newspaper, *Smith College Associated News* (SCAN); is promoted to news editor.

1941   Attends six-week summer workshop/internship at the Highlander Folk School near Monteagle, TN.

1941-1942   Works as editor-in-chief of *SCAN*.

1942   Graduates from Smith College as a *summa cum laude* major in psychology; thesis is published in 1944 in *Psychological Review*.

1942-1943   Begins graduate school in psychology at University of California-Berkeley with a fellowship.

1943   Harry Goldstein dies.

1943   Receives the prestigious and lucrative Abraham Rosenberg Research Fellowship at UC Berkeley, the first time it had been given to either a woman or a student in the psychology department; turns down fellowship.

1943   Moves to New York City and starts working at Federated Press (FP).

1946   Starts working at *UE News*.

1947   Meets and marries Carl Friedan.

1948   Gives birth to Daniel Friedan.

1950   Friedan family moves to Parkway Village, Queens.

1952   Gives birth to Jonathan Friedan; fired from *UE News*.

1952   Becomes editor of the community newsletter, *Parkway Villager*, and begins freelance magazine writing.

1956   Friedan family moves to Sneden's Landing, Rockland County, NY.

1956   Gives birth to Emily Friedan.

1957   Friedan family moves to Grandview-on-Hudson, Rockland County, NY.

1957   Organizes the Intellectual Resources Pool, organization that enlists local intellectuals and experts to enrich public education in Rockland County.

1958   *Harper's* magazine publishes Friedan's "The Coming Ice Age."

1959   Receives a contract and advance for *The Feminine Mystique* from W. W. Norton and Company.

1963   W. W. Norton publishes 3,000 hardcover copies of *The Feminine Mystique*.

1964   Dell Publishing Company purchases paperback rights.

1964   *The Feminine Mystique* is the best-selling nonfiction paperback in the United States.

1964   Friedan family moves to the Dakota apartment building in New York City.

1966   National Organization for Women (NOW) officially founded; Friedan is named first president.

1969   Betty and Carl Friedan divorce.

1969   Helps establish NARAL (initially National Association for the Repeal of Abortion Laws, now NARAL Pro-Choice America).

1970   Steps down as president of NOW.

1970   Co-organizes Women's Strike for Equality; tens of thousands of women participate.

1971   Co-founds National Women's Political Caucus (NWPC).

1975   Founds and acts as first director of the First Women's Bank and Trust Company in New York City.

1975   Attends United Nations–sponsored International Women's Year (IWY) conference in Mexico City.

1976   Publishes *It Changed My Life*.

1977   Helps organize National Women's Conference in Houston, TX.

1978   Purchases home in Sag Harbor, NY.

1979   Consults for the U.S. Military Academy on first class
        of women graduates.
1979   Receives Ford Foundation grant to fund research at
        Columbia University on aging.
1981   Publishes *The Second Stage.*
1988   Miriam Goldstein dies.
1993   Publishes *The Fountain of Age.*
1995   Attends UN Conference on the Status of Women in
        Beijing, China.
1997   Publishes *Beyond Gender: The Real Politics of Work
        and Family.*
1998   Receives Ford Foundation grant sponsored by Cornell
        University to continue research and support seminars
        on "new paradigm" for working families and public
        policy.
2000   Publishes *Life So Far.*
2006   Dies on 85th birthday, February 4.

Selected Bibliography

• Indicates items excerpted in this Norton Critical Edition.

PRIMARY DOCUMENTS

• Betty Friedan's voluminous collection of papers, documents, and manuscripts are called Betty Friedan Papers, Schlesinger Library, Radcliffe College, Cambridge, Massachusetts.
There are online finding aids at: http://oasis.lib.harvard.edu/oasis/deliver/findingAidDisplay?_collection=oasis&inoid=51 46
http://nrs.harvard.edu/urn-3:RAD.SCHL:sch00060
http://nrs.harvard.edu/urn-3:RAD.SCHL:sch01204
Sherman, Janann, ed. *Interviews with Betty Friedan.* Jackson, MS: University of Mississippi Press, 2002.
Interview with Betty Friedan, "The First Measured Century," at www.pbs.org/fmc/interviews/friedan.htm. Accessed August 9, 2011.
Murray, Sylvie, ed. "How Did Suburban Development and Domesticity Shape Women's Activism in Queens, New York, 1945–1968?" *Women & Social Movements in the United States, 1600–2000* 10.1 (March 2006): 1, at http://asp6new.alexanderstreet.com/wam2/wam2.index.map.aspx. Accessed August 9, 2011.

BIOGRAPHIES OF FRIEDAN

Several authors have written biographies of Friedan for children; the biographies below were written for adult readers.

Hennessee, Judith Adler. *Betty Friedan: Her Life.* New York: Random House, 1999.
Horowitz, Daniel. *Betty Friedan and the Making of* The Feminine Mystique: *The American Left, The Cold War, and Modern Feminism.* Amherst: University of Massachusetts Press, 1998.
Oliver, Susan. *Betty Friedan: The Personal is Political.* New York: Pearson Longman, 2008.

OTHER BOOKS BY BETTY FRIEDAN IN CHRONOLOGICAL ORDER

Betty Friedan wrote many articles throughout her life. Only books are included here.

• Friedan, Betty. *It Changed My Life: Writings on the Women's Movement.* New York: Random House, 1976.
———. *The Second Stage.* New York: Summit Books, 1981.
———. *The Fountain of Age.* New York; London: Simon & Schuster, 1993.
———. *Beyond Gender: The New Politics of Work and Family.* Washington, D.C.: Woodrow Wilson Center Press; 1997.
———. *Life So Far: A Memoir.* New York: Simon & Schuster, 2000.

SELECTED TEXTS THAT ADDRESS BETTY FRIEDAN AND *THE FEMININE MYSTIQUE*

Anderson, Sara F. "The View from the Outside: How Three Women's Work Contributed to Changes toward Equity and Human Rights: A Study of the Work of Rachel Carson, Jane Jacobs, and Betty Friedan." *New England Journal of History* 52 (Spring 1995): 40–53.

• Antler, Joyce. *The Journey Home: Jewish Women and the American Century.* New York: Free Press, 1997.

• Baumgardner, Jennifer, and Amy Richards. *Manifesta: Young Women, Feminism and the Future.* New York: Farrar, Straus, and Giroux, 2000.

Boucher, Joanne. "Betty Friedan and the Radical Past of Liberal Feminism." *New Politics* 9.3 (new series), whole no. 35 (Summer 2003), at ww3.wpunj.edu/newpol/issue35/boucher35.htm. Accessed August 8, 2011.

Bowlby, Rachel. "'The Problem with No Name': Rereading Friedan's *The Feminine Mystique.*" *Feminist Review* 27 (Autumn 1987): 61–75.

Bradley, Patricia. *Mass Media and the Shaping of American Feminism, 1963–1975.* Jackson: University Press of Mississippi, 2003.

Brown, Susan L. *The Politics of Individualism: Liberalism, Liberal Feminism, and Anarchism.* Montreal, New York: Black Rose Press, 2004.

Chansky, Dorothy. "Usable Performance Feminism for Our Time: Reconsidering Betty Friedan." *Theatre Journal.* 60.3 (October 2008): 341–64.

Cobble, Dorothy Sue. *The Other Women's Movement: Workplace Justice and Social Rights in Modern America.* Princeton, NJ: Princeton University Press, 2004.

Cohen, Marcia. *The Sisterhood: The True Story of the Women Who Changed the World.* New York: Ballantine, 1988.

• Coontz, Stephanie. *A Strange Stirring: The Feminine Mystique and American Women at the Dawn of the 1960s.* New York: Basic Books, 2011.

Critchlow, Donald. *Phyllis Schlafly and Grassroots Conservatism.* Princeton, NJ: Princeton University Press, 2005.

Davis, Flora. *Moving the Mountain: The Women's Movement in America since 1960.* New York: Simon and Schuster, 1991.

• Dijkstra, Sandra. "Simone de Beauvoir and Betty Friedan: The Politics of Omission." *Feminist Studies* 6 (Summer 1980): 290–303.

Eisenmann, Linda. "Thinking Feminist in 1963: Challenges from Betty Friedan and the U.S. President's Commission on the Status of Women," in Jean Spence, Sarah Jane Aiston, Maureen M. Meikle eds., *Women, Education, and Agency, 1600–2000.* New York: Routledge, 2010.

Eisenstein, Zillah R. *The Radical Future of Liberal Feminism.* New York: Longman, 1981.

Elshtain, Jean Bethke. *Public Man, Private Woman: Women in Social and Political Thought.* Princeton, NJ: Princeton University Press, 1981.

Evans, Sara. *The Personal Is Political: The Roots of Women's Liberation in the Civil Rights Movement and the New Left.* New York: Vintage Books, 1979.

• Faludi, Susan. *Backlash: The Undeclared War on American Women.* New York: Crown, 1991.

Feldstein, Ruth. *Motherhood in Black and White: Race and Sex in American Liberalism.* Ithaca, NY: Cornell University Press, 2000.

Fermaglich, Kirsten. *American Dreams and Nazi Nightmares: Early Holocaust Consciousness and Liberal America, 1957–1965.* Hanover, NH: University Press of New England for Brandeis University Press, 2006.

• ———. "'The Comfortable Concentration Camp': The Significance of Nazi Imagery in Betty Friedan's *The Feminine Mystique* (1963)." *American Jewish History* 91.2 (June 2003): 205–32.

Freeman, Jo. *The Women's Liberation Movement: Its Aims, Structures, and Ideas.* Pittsburgh: KNOW, Inc., 1971.

Gilmore, Stephanie, and Elizabeth Kaminski. "A Part and Apart: Lesbian and Straight Feminist Activists Negotiate Identity in a Second-Wave Organization." *Journal of History of Sexuality* 16.1 (2007): 95–113.

• Herman, Ellen. *The Romance of American Psychology: Political Culture in the Age of Experts.* Berkeley: University of California Press, 1995.

Hollows, Joanne. "The Feminist and the Cook: Julia Child, Betty Friedan and Domestic Femininity," in Emma Casey and Lydia Martens, eds., *Gender and Consumption.* Aldershot, UK: Ashgate, 2006.

• Horowitz, Daniel. "Rethinking Betty Friedan and *The Feminine Mystique*: Labor Union Radicalism and Feminism in Cold War America." *American Quarterly* 48.1 (March 1996): 1–42.

• hooks, bell. *Feminist Theory from Margin to Center.* Boston: South End Press, 1984.

May, Elaine Tyler. *Homeward Bound: American Families in the Cold War Era.* New York: Basic Books, 1988.

• Menand, Louis. "Books as Bombs: Why the Women's Movement Needed 'The Feminine Mystique.'" *New Yorker,* January 24, 2011, 76–79.

• Meyerowitz, Joanne. "Beyond *The Feminine Mystique*: A Reassessment of Postwar Mass Culture, 1946–1958," in Joanne Meyerowitz, ed., *Not June Cleaver: Women and Gender in Postwar America, 1945–1960.* Philadelphia: Temple University Press, 1994.

Miller, Meredith. "*The Feminine Mystique*: Sexual Excess and the Pre-political Housewife." *Women* 16.1 (April 1, 2005): 1–17.

• Moskowitz, Eva. "'It's Good to Blow Your Top': Women's Magazines and a Discourse of Discontent, 1945–1965." *Journal of Women's History* 8 (Fall 1996): 66–98.

• Murray, Pauli. *Songs in a Weary Throat: An American Pilgrimage.* New York: Harper & Row, 1987.

• Murray, Sylvie. *The Progressive Housewife: Community Activism in Suburban Queens, 1945–1965.* Philadelphia: University of Pennsylvania Press, 2003.

Neuhaus, Jessamyn. "'Is It Ridiculous for Me to Say I Want to Write?' Domestic Humor and Redefining the 1950s Housewife Writer in Fan Mail to Shirley Jackson." *Journal of Women's History* 21.2 (2009): 115–37.

Olcott, Jocelyn. "Cold War Conflicts and Cheap Cabaret: Sexual Politics at the 1975 United Nations International Women's Year Conference." *Gender & History* 22.3 (November 2010): 733–54.

Pinke, Caroline. "The Problem Sylvia Plath Has Left Unnamed: Understanding the Complexity of Female Disenchantment in the Cold War Era." *Valley Humanities Review* (Spring 2011) at www.lvc.edu/vhr/Articles/pinke.pdf. Accessed August 9, 2011.

• Plant, Rebecca Jo. *Mom: The Transformation of Motherhood in Modern America.* Chicago: The University of Chicago Press, 2010.

Pollock, Anne. "Reading Friedan toward a Feminist Articulation of Heart Disease." *Body & Society* 16.4 (December 2010): 77–97.

• Rosen, Ruth. *The World Split Open: How the Modern Women's Movement Changed America.* New York: Viking, 2000.

• Scanlon, Jennifer. *Bad Girls Go Everywhere: The Life of Helen Gurley Brown.* New York: Oxford University Press, 2009.

Stacey, Judith. "The New Conservative Feminism," *Feminist Studies* 9.3 (Fall 1983): 559–83.

• Weiss, Jessica. "'Fraud of Femininity': Domesticity, Selflessness, and Individualism in Responses to Betty Friedan," in Kathleen G. Donohue, ed., *Liberty and Justice for All? Rethinking Politics in Cold War America.* Amherst: University of Massachusetts Press, 2012.